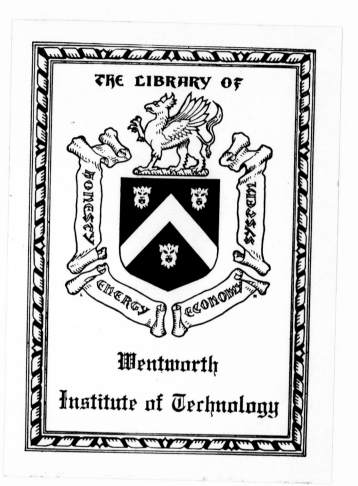

X-Rays: Health Effects of Common Exams

John W. Gofman, M.D., Ph.D.
and
Egan O'Connor

Sierra Club Books · San Francisco

Library of Congress Cataloging in Publication Data
Gofman, John W.
    X-rays, health effects of common exams.

    Bibliography: p.
    Includes index.
    1. Tumors, Radiation-induced. 2. Radiography,
Medical—Complications and sequelae. 3. X-rays—
Toxicology. I. O'Connor, Egan. II. Title. [DNLM:
1. Radiation, Ionizing—adverse effects. WN 620 G612x]
RC268.55.G64 1985   616.9'897   84-23527
ISBN 0-87156-838-1

Cover Jacket design by **Paul Bacon**
Book design by **Rodelinde Albrecht**
Illustrations by **Rodelinde Albrecht**

Printed in U.S.A.
10 9 8 7 6 5 4 3 2 1

To
Dr. Marvin Rosenstein and Dr. Kenneth W. Taylor,
two scientists whose separate,
magnificent contributions provided the inspiration
for writing this book

ACKNOWLEDGMENTS

Soon after the publication of *Radiation and Human Health* (Sierra Club Books, 1981), everyone closely involved with that project learned of the keen interest of radiologists, referring physicians, and members of the general public in obtaining risk estimates for specific diagnostic X-ray examinations. Peter Beren and Don Oppenheim of Sierra Club Books suggested that it might be a good idea to prepare a "handbook" in which everyone could simply look up the different sizes of risk associated with each of the most common exams.

However, one obstacle to the project seemed to remain in spite of *Radiation and Human Health.* It would be necessary to figure out the radiation dose absorbed by each separate organ during each diagnostic shot for patients of different sizes and ages, and for different beam directions. This handbook did not become possible until its authors had found the work of Marvin Rosenstein and his colleagues on the dosimetry problem.

Meanwhile, the authors had been thinking over the implications of *Radiation and Human Health* as they applied to the work by Kenneth Taylor and his colleagues at the University of Toronto. Taylor's team had demonstrated how readily the average surface doses of radiation could be reduced in diagnostic radiology without any loss of image quality. They had shown that a three-fold reduction is easy. We concluded that widespread achievement of such dose reduction would lead to the prevention of over one million unnecessary cancers per generation in the United States, without sacrificing any diagnostic exams or their benefits. Such ready ways to prevent massive amounts of suffering are rare indeed. Therefore we agreed that a practical handbook must include specific suggestions for those who give, recommend, and receive X-ray exams on how to avoid unnecessarily high doses.

Daniel Moses and Jon Beckmann of Sierra Club Books decided that a valuable public service could be rendered by providing such a book. We are most appreciative of the opportunity to do so.

Daniel Moses, Editorial Director of Sierra Club Books, his associate David Spinner, and their independent colleagues Mary Lou Van Deventer and Rodelinde Albrecht, have been most cooperative and helpful at all stages in the preparation of this book. It has been a privilege to benefit from their suggestions and their meticulous care.

Also with pleasure, we acknowledge the kind permission of Blackwell Scientific Publications, Ltd. (Oxford, England) to quote extensively from the elegant book *Complications in Diagnostic Radiology,* edited by G. Ansell (1976).

No book is ever free from residual lack of clarity and occasional errors. For any such defects in *X-Rays: Health Effects of Common Exams,* the authors take full responsibility.

CONTENTS

The Chapters

The Risk Tables

The Other Tables

CHAPTER 1

A Survey of the Book

Making Individual Benefit–Risk Decisions

Medical and dental X-rays provide health benefits which are just as real as the health hazards evaluated in this book. We wish to state emphatically, at the outset, that the benefits from X-ray exams can be substantial. X-rays which provide special diagnostic information—especially when effective treatments are possible for the suspected problem—can be extremely valuable. Nevertheless, the benefits from X-ray exams are not evaluated in this book, for two reasons:

- *First:* We have no new information to contribute on the subject of benefits, whereas we have new and unique contributions to offer about assessing one of the main hazards, radiation-induced later cancer.
- *Second:* The expected benefits from the exams depend on the specifics of a particular patient's condition and on the effectiveness of possible treatments under the special circumstances, whereas the hazards are estimated by other methods.

Every X-ray exam involves a benefit-risk decision about doing it or not doing it. By 1982, Americans were doing approximately 312 million medical and dental X-ray exams per year (Wolfe, 1983). This book applies directly to such exams. Physicians, dentists, patients, and parents who use it will be able to make their future decisions with much more confidence and knowledge than before.

New Information

As the user of this book will soon realize, the tables in its various chapters present information which has never before existed. This information could not have come into existence without the pioneering work of numerous earlier investigators, who deserve credit and gratitude; we will be naming as many as space reasonably permits.

The information in this book provides both reassuring news which will prevent many unnecessary worries and feelings of guilt, and stunning news which will alert users about some serious risks not previously evaluated. Indeed, it reveals a number of surprises for all who give X-rays, recommend X-rays, and receive X-rays. Among the surprises are the findings that:

- A Full-Mouth Dental Exam confers a higher risk than a full Skull Exam, for reasons explained in Chapter 9;
- Some exams confer a considerably higher risk on one sex than the other, for reasons presented in Chapter 3;
- The highest risk from a given exam most often falls on those who are about 10 years old at the time of irradiation, even though infants are *more* sensitive to radiation injury than 10-year-olds; the reasons are given in Chapters 3 and 22.

So that patients and parents can follow such explanations and every other part of this book, we have given the meaning of technical terms and abbreviations either in the Glossary or right in the text; explanations made in the text can be located with the Index. For anyone at all who would like to increase his or her comfort with numbers, there is Chapter 22.

One of the most important lessons from the new information is that it is utterly foolish ever to generalize about either the danger or the safety of diagnostic X-rays. *The risk from one situation to another varies by more than 10,000-fold.*

Just as it would be nonsense to assume that all medical drugs produce the same rate of serious side-effects, so it would be nonsense to make that kind of generalization about X-ray exams. This book does for diagnostic X-rays what is always done for pharmaceuticals: it evaluates the distinctly different risks from different ones.

For instance, the tables evaluating C.A.T. Scan "slices" (Chapter 10) show that the hazard from X-rays varies greatly according to the particular region of the body which needs examination. The risk for a 20-year-old male, for example, will be 100-fold higher from the riskiest C.A.T. Scan slice than from the least risky slice, even if the dose is held constant. The tables also make it easy to compare the magnitude of risk at a given dose from the least sensitive slice at the least sensitive age (55 years) with the risk from the most sensitive slice at a very sensitive age (5 years). The latter is 11,200 times more hazardous than the former. Consequently, it would be foolish ever to speak about "the cancer risk from C.A.T. Scans" without specifying clearly what region of whose body is being scanned.

Another illustration (Chapter 6) shows a 738-fold difference in risk from X-rays when the *same* abdominal region of two different patients is examined by fluoroscopy. Because the relative risks from various fluoroscopic X-ray exams have previously been very hard to evaluate, many people (ourselves included) have commonly assumed that they are more dangerous than the routine X-ray films. But in Chapter 7, which evaluates some common arteriographies, it turns out that the risk from the routine films exceeds the risk from the fluoroscopy in some cases.

The lesson is that generalizations are no substitute for the numbers. So the very heart of this book is its useful numbers. In the box, numerical examples demonstrate how easily some typical questions are answered by the tables in this book. The exams listed in the box, and the ages chosen, are simply illustrative; every person has a unique medical history. Some individuals will have fewer than 10 exams in a lifetime, and some will have many more than 10. For instance, among the 5% to 10% of American children who have a curvature of the spine, those whose treatment is monitored by X-rays may have 10 exams or more within just a few years.

Both Good News and Bad News

The common X-ray exams, including C.A.T Scans, fluoroscopies, and some common angiographies, are the subject of this book. This book is not about the use of radioisotopes (nuclear medicine), high-dose X-ray treatment (radiation therapies), ultra-sound, infra-red, nuclear magnetic resonance (NMR), positron emission tomography (PET), or other diagnostic techniques. Nor is it a book detailing side-effects from the chemical contrast media and catheters used in performing some X-ray exams, although Chapter 15 gives a broad overview. This is a book evaluating health effects *from X-rays* used for diagnostic purposes.

Exceedingly good news will be found in the relatively low cancer risks for older people from many of the X-ray exams associated with ulcers, other gastro-intestinal problems, kidney stones, gallbladder problems, broken hips, and dental problems. A man's risk of getting cancer, from having an Intravenous Pyelogram Exam of the kidneys at age 50, is about 1 chance in 11,000. A woman's risk from having a Hip Exam at age 50 is 1 chance in 133,000. A man's risk from having a Full-Mouth Dental Exam at age 50 is 1 chance in about 59,000.

EXAMPLES OF INFORMATION FROM THE TABLES

Question 1: What is a person's lifetime chance of getting cancer as a *result* of having one of the following 10 common X-ray exams under common conditions?

- *Newborn Infant: Chest Exam (2 shots)*
  Male: 1 chance in 3,500   Female: 1 chance in 1,800
- *Age 5: Lower Arm Exam (2 shots)*
  Male: 1 chance in 300,000   Female: 1 chance in 350,000
- *Age 5: Angiocardiography*
  (40 films plus 30 minutes fluoroscopy)
  Male: 1 chance in 120   Female: 1 chance in 80
- *Age 10: Full-Mouth Dental Exam (16 films)*
  Male: 1 chance in 600   Female: 1 chance in 1,400
- *Age 15: Full-Mouth Dental Exam (16 films)*
  Male: 1 chance in 900   Female: 1 chance in 2,400
- *Age 20: Full-Mouth Dental Exam (22 films)*
  Male: 1 chance in 650   Female: 1 chance in 1,750
- *Age 20: Thoracic Spine Exam (2 films, wide)*
  Male: 1 chance in 1,300   Female: 1 chance in 600
- *Age 35: Mammography*
  (2 shots of each breast) by Xeroradiographic method
  Male: Not Applicable   Female: 1 chance in 900
  (breast cancer)
- *Age 40: Angiocardiography*
  (40 films plus 30 minutes fluoroscopy)
  Male: 1 chance in 800   Female: 1 chance in 500
- *Age 55: Hip Exam (2 shots)*
  Male: 1 chance in 210,000   Female: 1 chance in 190,000

Question 2: What is a person's cancer risk, resulting from the exams, if he or she has *each* of the exams above, at the ages illustrated?

Male: 1 chance in 67   Female: 1 chance in 51

- If there is no angiography at age 5, the aggregate risks are lower:
  Male: 1 chance in 151   Female: 1 chance in 142

The aggregate risk from seven X-ray exams, which might be needed by a person badly injured in a car wreck, is calculated for a 50-year-old man in Chapter 4, Example 17. His risk is much lower than he imagines. On the other hand, his accumulated risk from exams taken at younger ages is calculated in Example 18 and is probably higher than he imagines.

Indeed, the bad news in this book will be found most often in the very high risks for children from numerous exams, including many of the spinal exams, all the gastrointestinal exams, and all the arteriographies. Fortunately, only a small percentage of American children have the serious problems calling for these types of exams, whose frequency is relatively low in the pediatric age groups. By far the most frequent non-dental exam for children is the simple chest film (Beck and Rosenstein, 1979, pp. 7–9).

The more serious exams are performed most often, of course, exactly where expected: among newborn infants in an intensive-care unit. In a special maternity hospital studied by Robinson (1983), about 3% of the newborns were in such a unit, naturally a higher rate than in general hospitals. The fact that a few of the infants each received some 40 X-rays, plus scans or a barium enema, illustrates an important point: in a desperate medical situation, the achievement of an infant's immediate survival prevails over considerations about the delayed consequences.

We want to emphasize that even X-ray exams which confer virtual certainty of serious but delayed side-effects can be quite worthwhile, for the individual having them, when the medical situation warrants them. No one need feel guilty about such decisions, in our opinion. What is more, such risks can usually be reduced at least 3-fold by taking the practical low-cost measures discussed in Chapter 16.

Some risks can be reduced dramatically. The frequency of spinal exams is high among the estimated 5% to 10% (Moe, 1979) of American adolescents who have the curvature of the spine called idiopathic scoliosis. Among those whose treatment is monitored by X-ray exams, females in particular have been at serious risk of radiation-induced cancer due to their special risk of breast cancer. Concerned about that hazard, two teams of researchers (Nash and co-workers at Case Western Reserve University in Ohio, 1979, and Gray and co-workers at the Mayo Clinic in Minnesota, 1983) have been pioneers in finding out exactly how to lower it. By developing practical steps which significantly reduce the dose to the breasts, they have reduced the risk of radiation-induced breast cancer by 55- to 69-fold. In Chapter 16, Section 5, we summarize this inspiring work.

When both the irreducible risk from an exam and the need for the exam are high, the quality of the necessary benefit-risk decision can only be improved by using the information in this book. In responsible medical decisions, few participants say, "Don't bother me about the probability of deadly side-effects. I prefer making uninformed decisions!"

It would be a big mistake to assume, from the comments above, that every X-ray exam produces a large risk for children. Parents can heave a sigh of relief about the very low cancer risk, even for children, from X-rays of elbows, forearms, wrists, hands, fingers, knees, lower legs, ankles, feet, and toes. For a 10-year-old, the typical risk is in the ballpark of 1 chance in 200,000 of getting a later cancer as a result of such an exam (Chapter 5).

Another source of relief for parents will be found in Chapter 13, which shows how to quantify the genetic risk from each of the common diagnostic exams (risks to a child *already* in the womb are evaluated separately in Chapter 12). We hope that Chapter 13 will contribute to two distinct and compatible benefits. First, it should help undo and prevent much of the unjustified guilt we hear, directly in our mail, from parents who have had diagnostic X-rays and have given birth years later to a handicapped infant; the odds are overwhelmingly *against* the exams as the cause. At the same time, however, the chapter should help fortify great caution about unnecessary X-ray doses to ovaries and testes, since research is just beginning to discover the full frequency of inherited medical problems. Chapter 13 describes, for instance, some of the recent evidence about *heritable* types of cancer.

We hope readers have noticed that this book contains no section on sterility or cataracts. Because sterility is associated with high doses of ionizing radiation, some people worry that the risk also exists at diagnostic doses. Likewise, because the frequency of cataracts increases due to high doses, some people simply assume the frequency is increased by low doses. No evidence supports either worry.

Not *every* effect resulting from high-dose radiation also occurs at low doses. Nausea, for instance, is a well-known effect showing a threshold, which means the effect occurs only after the cause reaches a particular level of intensity. Some biological events have a threshold, and some do not. Only valid studies can determine which are which, as we caution in Chapter 12 with respect to infant mortality from causes unrelated to malignancies. Valid studies do exist now (see Chapters 2, 11, and 12) showing in humans that no threshold separates the effects of high doses and diagnostic doses with respect to excess cancer, leukemia, congenital injury, and enduring chromosomal damage.

How to Use This Book

People who are contemplating giving or taking a particular diagnostic X-ray exam can find, in this book, the first quantitative estimates by age and sex of leukemia risk and cancer risk from a particular exam done under common conditions. "Common conditions" means the conditions which a patient is most likely to encounter, according to surveys in the United States, if he or she chooses a radiologic facility at random.

A special feature of this book is applicable to everyone who needs check-up X-rays to monitor the progress of healing or therapy, or to detect problems early, such as tooth decay or cancer. Chapter 4, Section 9, demonstrates the power to evaluate the *aggregate* risk from several X-ray exams under consideration in a person's foreseeable future. This information can be most helpful in determining the appropriate frequency, for a particular individual, of the exams.

No one need worry whether the tables in this book fit the conditions at a specific X-ray office. This book provides a base of information which can be applied universally. The data in the tables readily convert to fit any entrance dose, any hardness of X-ray beam, any combination of shots needed, any region of the torso examined by fluoroscopy with any duration or beam-size, and any amount of the head or torso examined by C.A.T. Scan. Since all these factors *do* vary and depend both on the facility and the particular patient, the easy convertibility of the tables is a key element in their usefulness.

Numerous examples are provided in Chapter 4 to demonstrate exactly how modifications are made for dose, beam quality, more or fewer shots, and also for different opinions about risk per rad of dose. When an exam calls for more than one modification, they are simply made one at a time, independently, on a pocket calculator. Chapter 4 contains a section on how to evaluate exams which are *not* in this book, too.

Examination equipment and practices differ among radiologic facilities in a great many variables: the kind of beam-generating equipment, the kind and amount of filters, the kind and amount of coning and shielding, the film sizes, the distance between radiation source and film, the kinds of grids, intensifying screens, film-speeds, freshness of film and developer, type of current control, peak kilovoltages, duration of exposure, number of films, different projections per exam, duration and beam-size of fluoroscopy, computer-assisted enhancement of images, memory devices, and more.

The reason that so many differences do not prevent an evaluation of risk is that risk depends on so few variables:

1. the beam quality and entrance dose;
2. the particular organs irradiated;
3. the risk per rad of dose, according to age and sex.

Users of this book will find out which irradiated organs generate the most cancer risk from a particular exam; in specific cases, this information will make it possible to reduce the hazard by protecting some high-risk organs from the direct beam. Also, for many exams, tables in Chapter 5 evaluate four standard shots, although some are optional or seldom used. Those who know which shot in an exam will create most of the risk can, in some cases, cut a patient's hazard in half by avoiding it, as illustrated in Chapter 4, Example 4. The expected *benefit* from a high-risk shot will play a decisive role in such decisions.

Also provided in this book are risk values with respect to genetic and congenital injury (Chapters 12 and 13) and side-effects associated with contrast agents used in some exams (Chapter 15).

Two Ways of Expressing Risk

Risks are expressed in two ways in this book, and each can be easily converted to the other. For example, the cancer risk from the Pelvis Exam for a 15-year-old male is given in Chapter 5 as 1,194 per million, or 1 in 838.

Expressing the risk as a rate "per million" makes it easy to add, subtract, compare, and adjust risks, because the denominator (one million) is always the same. On the other hand, the size of the risk is clearest to many people, perhaps most, if they can compare it to the number 1 instead of to an almost unimaginably large number like 1,000,000. That is why they yearn to convert a risk of 1,194 per million to its equivalent, 1 per 838, or 1 chance in 838.

In the box, for easy relocation, is the "recipe" for converting in either direction. Readers who wish to consider this "recipe" at a more fundamental level may enjoy Chapter 22.

The tables in this book mean that it is no longer necessary for millions of benefit-risk decisions to be made each year concerning diagnostic X-rays without the foggiest notion about the magnitude of the risk. When someone takes an automobile for repair, he or she usually finds out if the job is likely to cost approximately $100, $300, $900, or $1,400 before going

---

- To convert a risk of 1,194 per million into odds of 1 in 838, divide a million by 1,194 and say "1 in" *before* the answer.
- To convert a risk of 1 in 838 into a rate of 1,194 per million, divide a million by 838 and say "per million" *after* the answer.
- In both cases, the *first* step is simply to divide 1,000,000 by the other number. Anyone with a pocket calculator can make such conversions in a moment.

ahead with it. Similarly, physicians, dentists, patients, and parents can find out from this book whether a contemplated diagnostic X-ray exam is going to give 1 chance in 20 of a serious later side-effect, or 1 chance in a million.

Why This Book Is Late

Diagnostic X-ray exams have been used in medicine and dentistry for many decades. We were startled to read (Blatz, in Shapiro, 1981, p. 411) that some of the conscientious parents who could afford routine pediatric check-ups for their infants in the 1940s and 1950s were, in fact, delivering the infants for *monthly* fluoroscopic X-ray "check-ups." Why was there no handbook like this one evaluating the frequency of delayed but serious side-effects, long ago?

The answer is that new insights and handbooks in any field are the product of a slow, costly, and cooperative effort by many different humans with different specialties. A book like this depends on a mountain of background information and analysis, some of which became available only recently. As more data have appeared, a number of people have started work on quantifying the hazards from certain X-ray exams. Pioneers in this effort include Laws, Rosenstein, Gregg and Nash.

But no one could have performed this kind of analysis until certain sorts of evidence were firm. For instance, clear evidence now exists down to 5 rads, and even lower doses, that there is no threshold or harmless dose of ionizing radiation; it is exceedingly unlikely that one exists at any dose. Moreover, clear evidence now exists that there are more than just four or five "critical organs" which generate radiation-induced cancer; the evidence shows that virtually *every* human organ which can generate cancer "spontaneously" will respond to radiation with an excess rate of later cancer. Also essential to a proper evaluation of cancer risk are the data which now show reliably that the young are far more at risk than older people (for *leukemia,* no age differences are proven). Gathering such evidence required decades of work by numerous scientists and conscientious clerks.

The fine studies on radiation done by many different investigators were synthesized for the first time in 1981 (Gofman, 1981). From that combination of all the world's applicable data came the statistically stable risk-per-rad estimates used in this book. For some readers who may prefer to apply either lower or higher risk-per-rad estimates, a simple adjustment (demonstrated in Chapter 4) makes this book fully useful.

The recent work of another group of investigators has also contributed greatly to this book. Their expertise has been directed toward figuring out what dose of radiation is actually received during a diagnostic exam by various organs inside the body. The relationship between the entrance dose as the beam enters the body, and the dose to internal organs at various depths, can be quite complex. While such measurements and calculations have been done for high-dose radiation therapies, far less work has been done for doses in the diagnostic range. Whenever possible, we have gratefully used the values provided by the fine work of Rosenstein (1976a, b, 1979, 1980, 1982), Jones and co-workers (1973), and Webster and co-workers (1974). Whenever necessary, we have filled in the gaps by using our own method, which yields results nicely consistent with their values.

And "last but not least," the information in this book's tables owes its existence to the personal-computer industry. Anyone who examines Chapter 19, which illustrates the method required to obtain the cancer risk for just *one* shot for *one* age for *one* sex for *one* exam, will understand why.

The point is that, ten years ago, this book could not have been attempted. Not all the necessary ingredients existed. Even now, not quite all the desirable information is available. This book therefore incorporates some useful approximations and reasonable assumptions, which will be clear from the text. Little mystery concerning their nature will remain for interested readers who can go step by step through sample calculations of organ dose and cancer risk in Chapter 19.

The Aggregate Impact of Individual Risks

To the many physicians, dentists, patients, and parents who take pride in helping to prevent human suffering, we offer an important reminder: a serious side-effect, whose probability for an individual may seem low from his or her point of view, represents a "heap of misery" if that probability is multiplied by a million individuals, or by 250 million. An individual may face "only" 1 chance in 2,000 of getting a later cancer from a particular exam given under average conditions. But "only" 1 cancer induced per 2,000 exams turns into 20,000 cancers initiated every year, if exams with the equivalent "low" risk are given 40 million times each year.

The frequency of diagnostic X-ray exams per 100 people, by age groups, is provided in Table 1.

Countless radiologic professionals surely have been inspired by Karl Z. Morgan, "father" of the health physics profession, to do their individual shares toward reducing the aggregate impact of "low" individual risks. Also leaders in this effort are Kenneth Taylor, Harold Elford Johns, and their associates who develop and teach practical, low-cost measures which reduce dose but *not* image-quality.

They are no longer alone. Professional journals such as *Radiology* and *The British Journal of Radiology* now carry an impressive number of

Table 1. Annual Rate of X-Ray Examinations (U.S.A.)

Dental Examinations	
Age Group	Number of Examinations per 100 Persons
Under 15 years	28
15–24 years	46
25–34 years	44
35–44 years	37
45–54 years	32
55–64 years	27
65+ years	13

Medical Radiographic Examinations (excluding examinations of extremities)	
Under 15 years	16
15–24 years	42
25–34 years	56
35–44 years	65
45–54 years	72
55–64 years	73
65+ years	73

Fluoroscopic Examinations (with spot films and plates)	
Under 15 years	1
15–24 years	3
25–34 years	5
35–44 years	9
45–54 years	12
55–64 years	13
65–74 years	15

SOURCE: From Figure 2. Shleien and co-workers, 1977.

papers about techniques to lower the doses in mammography, C.A.T. Scans, and some other exams. We salute those who are writing such papers, those who are reading them, and all the radiologists, physicists, and radiologic technicians at many fine facilities who are using initiative and extra care to minimize risks, by keeping entrance doses and exposed areas as small as possible.

Such care is especially important when examining children. A child at the age of 5 is about five times more likely to get later radiation-induced cancer than an adult given the *same* radiation dose at age 35. Readers should note a big distinction between cancer risk and leukemia risk. Radiation-induced leukemia remains a risk for patients irradiated at older ages, whereas diagnostic doses received at older ages create such a trivial individual risk of radiation-induced cancer that this book's tables of cancer risk stop at age 55. But children are another matter. Their sensitivity to radiation injury moves us to mention, gratefully, the growing number of experts, such as the Mayo Clinic's Dr. Joel Gray, who are developing and teaching ways to reduce pediatric doses from diagnostic X-rays.

Clearing Away Some Confusion

With respect to a child's risk of leukemia or cancer from a diagnostic X-ray exam, much confusion is no doubt resulting from recent articles in three major medical journals, *Pediatrics,* the *New England Journal of Medicine,* and the *Journal of Nuclear Medicine.* All three articles report *no* excess cancer or leukemia found among patients who had received medical irradiation, and two of the three sets of patients were children. The failure to detect any provable excess of cancer or leukemia in those studies is the very same result which this book would have predicted. Readers will understand why after reading Chapters 2 and 11, where each study is analyzed. No contradiction whatsoever exists between those three studies and the risk values for cancer and leukemia in this book.

It is inevitable and unfortunate that many (perhaps most) readers of those three studies will end up with the dangerously mistaken impression that diagnostic doses of radiation confer no risk of later leukemia or cancer. Patients will pay the consequences of such confusion. That is why we have emphasized, especially in Chapters 2 and 11, the overwhelming evidence that doses in the diagnostic range *do* increase the rates of both diseases.

Readers who are eager to recognize some of the pitfalls in medical literature will probably be particularly interested in Chapters 2, 11, and 14. Together, they amount to a "mini-course" in separating truth from untruth in epidemiological reports. While Chapter 2 examines twelve of the most common myths about radiation, it is really dealing with principles and pitfalls common to epidemiological research in all fields of medicine.

Epidemiology is a branch of science which detects cause-and-effect by counting and comparing. Which kinds of people have the highest rate of lung cancer: heavy smokers, light smokers, or non-smokers? One counts, and compares, and discovers if there is a consistent dose-response (cause-effect) relationship. Which kind of patients did the best in the long run: those taking heavy doses of "Medicine A," those taking light doses, or those taking none at all? Which kind of people has the highest rate of cancer: those who have been heavily irradiated, those who have been lightly irradiated, or those who are irradiated exclusively by the planet's natural background radiation? Do obese people have a higher rate of atherosclerosis than non-obese people? Do joggers really live longer than non-joggers? Statistical comparisons are the only known way to find out about delayed effects (both good and bad) from a whole host of biological agents including medicines, surgery, poisons, and ionizing radiation.

Among irradiated groups, delayed but deadly effects from a given dose are found especially frequently among *children*, as the newest evidence from the bombings of Hiroshima and Nagasaki is confirming yet again (Chapter 2).

An Exciting Prospect

One of the outstanding and undeniable facts about diagnostic X-rays is that the dose used for the same exam commonly varies 10-fold, often 20-fold, and even up to 100-fold, from one facility to another, and even from room to room in the same facility (Tables 19 and 20, in Chapter 16). A patient can unknowingly step into a cancer risk 10 or 20 times greater than those tabulated in this book, which are based upon *average* entrance doses. Yet when proper measures are taken, the quality of the diagnostic information can be as good or better at the low doses as at the high ones.

Dr. Joel Gray of the Mayo Clinic says about offices which won't tell patients the dose:

> My feeling is that if they won't tell you, they don't know, and
> if they don't know, they could be among the facilities delivering
> a hundred times the necessary dose. (*Science Digest*, p. 96,
> March 1984.)

It turns out that even offices which are confident that they *do* know their entrance doses are often seriously mistaken. It is common to calculate a patient's entrance dose from data in manuals on kilovoltage, milliampere-seconds, and filtration. But the assumption that calculations are an adequate substitute for measurement is shattered by extensive surveys taken at both dental and medical X-ray facilities. True doses ranged from 0.1 to 4.0 times the calculated dose—a factor of 40 for the range (Chapters 9 and 16).

The good news is that simple remedies are available. It is not expensive to measure actual doses and to reduce them without any loss of diagnostic information. This assertion is not speculation. It has been achieved and demonstrated repeatedly in the field by professionals. The team at the University of Toronto, for instance, has developed a dose-reduction program which is applied to whatever equipment a facility already possesses and requires no purchase of major new items; it is described in Chapter 16. In their classic book, Johns and Cunningham say about this program:

> We have evidence (Taylor, 1979) that the dose from diagnostic radiology can be reduced by a factor of at least 3 with little work and by a factor of 10 or more if all conditions are optimized. (*The Physics of Radiology,* fourth edition, p. 557, 1983.)

What would be the impact on health for Americans if a 3-fold reduction in average dose were achieved? In Chapter 17, starting with Table 22, we present a careful estimate which in no way exaggerates the benefits. The estimate is for cancer only and excludes the simultaneous reductions in leukemia and genetic and congenital injuries, and excludes of course the whole field of diagnostic exams in nuclear medicine. For the United States, *the dose reduction would prevent more than 1.5 million cases of cancer per generation.*

Preventing this many cancer casualties for a coming generation would be at least comparable to having prevented all the American casualties of World War II for a passing generation.

It would take a heart made of stone, in our opinion, to neglect such an opportunity. And we hope it is perfectly clear, from Chapter 16, that there is no conflict whatsoever between reducing risks from diagnostic X-rays and continuing to do *all* the exams which are useful for diagnostic purposes. We emphatically oppose governmental regulation in this field, however. Coercion by government would be a dangerous and unnecessary way to achieve an enormously attractive goal which now is lying *within the easy reach of all who truly want it.*

CHAPTER 2

Twelve
Common Misconceptions
about
Ionizing Radiation

The human evidence has convinced almost everyone who has personally examined it that ionizing radiation, even at low doses, produces an excess of human cancer, leukemia, genetic injury, and birth defects. Interested readers will find the massive amount of human evidence in *Radiation and Human Health* (Gofman, 1981), a book which was ranked beside the *BEIR Report* (1980) and the *UNSCEAR Report* (1977) as one of the three major works in this field by Judge Bruce Jenkins, in his landmark May 1984 decision in the Utah fallout case (*Allen* versus *the United States,* pp. 356–57).

But physicians, dentists, patients, and parents still encounter misconceptions. A dozen of the most common are briefly discussed in this chapter. Each receives much fuller analysis, with supporting evidence, in *Radiation and and Human Health* (R&HH). This chapter provides references to additional evidence published after that book went to press.

Myth 1: Studies of Irradiated Humans
Produce Contradictory Results

It is easy to assume, mistakenly, that when a published study finds no effect at all from exposure to radiation, it contradicts the hazards reported in this book and elsewhere. Not so. Some published studies report no excess cancers and leukemias in humans exposed to the low dose-range, but they do not contradict other studies which do report excesses. Indeed, the absence of an excess in some studies is exactly what must be predicted from the studies' own designs.

If the number of people studied is small, or if the follow-up time is not as long as required to prove an excess (see Myth 11), or if the people were exposed in their older years when radiation is less likely to induce cancer, or if a study combines one or more of the preceding characteristics, then the absence of a detectable excess is no surprise—it is virtually guaranteed.

The meaning of negative studies (those which find no effect) is closely examined in R&HH. Here we call attention to three negative studies involving medical irradiation.

From the journal *Pediatrics:* Spengler and co-workers (1983) reported on an average 14-year follow-up of almost 5,000 children who had cardiac catheterization with fluoroscopy. They found no significant excess of leukemia. In Chapter 11 of this book, we show why none *should* have been found. The researchers also found no excess cancer, but the cancer story has really not even begun for irradiated children only 14 years after their exposure (see Myth 11). The excess cancer will start showing up gradually after the children pass the age of 30; it will peak about 40 years after their exposure; and it will probably continue (at a declining level) for their full lifespans. There is no contradiction whatsoever between this negative study in *Pediatrics* and the leukemia and cancer risks presented in this book.

From the *New England Journal of Medicine:* Linos and co-workers (1980) reported finding no provable excess leukemia in patients who had received "low-dose radiation" for medical purposes. The study's many flaws, which are explained in detail in R&HH (pp. 699–706), completely undermine its power to discover anything useful about induction of leukemia by diagnostic X-rays. The Linos paper's final conclusion is perfectly consistent with the magnitude of risk-per-rad used in this book, as shown in Chapter 11.

From the *Journal of Nuclear Medicine:* Freitas and co-workers (1979) reported on 51 patients who had each received a whole-body dose of 10 rads from radioiodine therapy, at an average age of 16. The average follow-up time was only 15 years. Using the same risk values now incorporated into this book, *Radiation and Human Health* (pp. 645–47) showed that only one-half of one case of excess cancer could be expected during such a short follow-up period on such a small group. Naturally, no excess was detectable. Yet the same study is completely consistent with a remarkable side-effect from that therapeutic dose: 1 out of every 20 patients so treated at age 16 will die prematurely of radiation-induced cancer somewhere in his or her body. Unfortunately, the authors of the radioiodine paper mistakenly claimed that their study showed the treatment to be *safe* with respect to cancer induction.

Recommendations

If X-ray and nuclear medical researchers plan to test for consequences with a magnitude equal to the risk values provided in R&HH and this book, they must design studies capable in size and duration of perceiving such consequences.

A first rule for readers, when confronted with seemingly contradictory studies about the effects of radiation (serious effects, such as those evaluated in this book, versus no effect at all), is to ask whether the contradiction is real. We have used three studies to illustrate apparent contradictions which were *not* real.

An important habit is to ask, "If the *serious* effects are true, then what results would have been observed (found) under the *particular conditions* of the negative study?" If, under those conditions, the findings would have been negative (no discernible effect), then no contradiction exists. Ways to do such an analysis are demonstrated in Chapter 11.

A related and useful habit is to ask, "Can these ostensibly contradictory studies validly be compared at all?" If one compares studies involving different ages and different follow-up periods without first converting their findings to a common standard or base, the "answers" about risk per rad are sure to be different. But the apparent contradictions rarely remain after data are properly converted to a comparable basis (R&HH, Chapter 5).

A second rule about contradictions is that if a contradiction appears to be real, or if one does not have the data or know-how to test its reality, then the presumption of truth in science belongs (if no bias is operating) with the great bulk of the *evidence.* The stress on evidence is important, to distinguish it from the bulk of *opinion.*

Exceptions and contradictions deserve the most careful attention in case they are real, but there is certainly no basis in *science* for discarding a huge body of evidence—the aggregate weight of numerous valid studies —the first moment someone declares one piece of data to be out of line with all the rest. When such discarding is done on a flimsy basis, wishful thinking or other anti-truth temptations are triumphing.

Myth 2: Only a Few Kinds of Cancer Can Be Induced by Ionizing Radiation

The evidence says otherwise. It already shows that radiation can induce virtually every major kind of cancer. By major kind, we mean the kinds which, combined, account for about 90% of American cancer deaths.

Again and again, one hears scientifically meaningless statements such as, "But no one found an excess of *that* kind of cancer" in a particular irradiated group. One needs to remember that cancer can be divided into more than one hundred different categories. In a group of irradiated people who show a total of 50 excess cancers, obviously many individual kinds of cancer simply cannot be found in excess. If the studied group is finely subdivided by age and sex, even more types of cancer will fail to appear in excess than if the group is considered as a unit.

What is more, the missing types of cancers will differ from study to study. Such differences are exactly what must be expected, and it would be strange indeed if they did not occur. Single studies not only show the natural fluctuations of small numbers, but they also differ in the ages of the people when irradiated and in the duration of the follow-up studies. That is why the truth about radiation can emerge most clearly from a properly done *combination* of all the worldwide studies.

The combined evidence now makes it fully reasonable, scientifically, to infer that *all* kinds of cancer can be induced by radiation. The alleged exception of chronic lymphatic leukemia may well be explained by its very low *spontaneous* rate. With respect to the more common types of cancer, when a study offers a reasonable chance of observing a radiation-induced excess, the evidence unfolds very gradually.

In 1970, experts were ridiculing the idea that breast cancer could be induced by radiation. Thyroid cancer, yes, but not *other* kinds. Now the glib assurances, still uttered only five or ten years ago, have ceased. The latest data from Hiroshima and Nagasaki, for instance, report excesses of breast, bladder, colon, esophagus, liver, lung, myeloma, pancreas, prostate, rectum, and thyroid cancers (Kato and Schull, 1982; Wakabayashi et al., 1983). There is also a wealth of earlier data, from more than 20 other studies, showing radiation induction of additional types of cancer (R&HH, Chapters 6 and 7). It would be hard, after examining the evidence, to disagree with the following opinions:

- "If, as it now appears, most forms of human cancer are produced by ionizing radiation, we may have much to learn about carcinogenesis from the few exceptions" (Beebe, 1980).
- "Irradiation to the body can cause leukemia or other malignancy. . . . There is now little doubt that neoplasia can be produced in almost any organ . . ." (Ardran and Crooks, p. 411 in Ansell, 1976).
- "The point I feel is important is the consistency with which radiation has proved to be carcinogenic in man. It is far and away the most consistent agent we know of to cause cancer of any type" (Radford, 1982).

Myth 3: Different Kinds of Cells
Respond Differently to Ionizing Radiation

The evidence suggests something quite different.

First of all, it is true that different kinds of cells show very different *spontaneous* rates of cancer. The frequencies of stomach and liver cancers provide an example: they are different. Moreover, the spontaneous rate of a single type of cancer, from a single type of cell, varies between men and women and between countries. The reasons for all these differences are still unknown.

But in spite of all the variation among organs in their spontaneous rates of cancer, the evidence is strong and growing ever stronger that they all display the *same* response to ionizing radiation; their individual spontaneous rates of cancer—whether high or low—increase by about the same percentage per rad of dose received.

The observation that the excess cancer rate from irradiating a particular organ is relative to that organ's spontaneous cancer rate was made almost 20 years ago in separate studies by Stewart and Kneale (1968) and by Court-Brown and Doll (1965), and it is the key to the "relative risk" concept or law stated in Chapter 18. The evidence, accumulating ever since the initial observations, has led steadily to their confirmation. The same evidence has shown more and more clearly that the "absolute risk" concept, which is used by the UNSCEAR Committee, produces predictions which turn out to be much too low. In a 1982 analysis of the evidence from Hiroshima and Nagasaki, Kato and Schull compare the relative risk and absolute risk models, and conclude (p. 408) that the data "support the relative risk model projection more strongly."

Inspection of the combined evidence at this time from Smith and Doll (1978), Kato and Schull (1982), and Wakabayashi et al. (1983) provides no reason whatsoever to think that one type of cancer increases, over its spontaneous rate, by a different percentage per rad than any other type. Kato and Schull (p. 404) concur:

> As shown in Fig. 1, the 90% confidence limits of the relative risks of breast, stomach, lung, and colon cancers overlap each other, and the relative risk of cancers of all sites (except leukemia) is within the confidence limit, *so, statistically it cannot be said that the relative risk differs according to target organ.* (Emphasis added.)

For diagnostic radiology, the conclusion that radiation induces different cancers in proportion to their spontaneous incidence in a population carries important implications. For example, it means that one rad of dose to the large intestine will produce a much higher lifetime risk of later cancer than one rad to the larynx, among American patients exposed at the same age. The reason is that, in the United States, the spontaneous rate of colon cancer is much higher than that of laryngeal cancer. The difference is reflected in Special Tables A and B, Chapter 21.

Myth 4: Maybe Radiation Is Just Speeding Up Cancers Which Were Going to Occur Anyway

---

Since radiation acts as a multiplier upon the age-specific spontaneous rates of human cancer, it is proper to ask: is radiation raising the cancer rates among irradiated people by accelerating the cancers which they would have gotten later "anyway"?

Of course, for the unlucky people who get cancer—one out of every four Americans—acceleration surely makes a big difference. Getting cancer at age 45 is very different from getting it "anyway" at age 65.

But also there is overwhelming evidence that radiation does indeed induce cancers which would not have otherwise occurred. For instance by 1969, only 24 years after the atom-bombings at Hiroshima and Nagasaki, the studied survivors already had more breast cancers than would be expected in the completed lifespan of a comparable unirradiated group (McGregor and co-workers, 1977). Many more have occurred since 1969, and the extra cases are bound to rise even further in future years.

Hempelmann (1975) provides additional proof that radiation induces cancers which would not have occurred "anyway" in his follow-up of children whose necks were irradiated in infancy. Studying a large group, he found that the rate of thyroid cancer was 121 times as high as the normal incidence by the fourth decade after exposure, with the excess cancers still appearing in abundance compared with controls. The lifetime incidence will exceed the spontaneous incidence by a very large factor.

We have really had unappreciated evidence on this question for about 400 years. That is how long we have known that 50% to 70% of the uranium miners of Schneeberg, Germany, and Joachimstahl, Czechoslovakia, were dying of lung cancer. We now know that this effect was caused by exposure to radon and its radioactive daughter products. Any rate of spontaneous lung cancer accounting for more than 5%, and at most 10%, of all deaths in a population would be rare indeed. The miners' death rate from radiation-induced lung cancer has been far higher than would occur "anyway."

Similarly, Stehney and co-workers (1978) reported on 58 bone sarcoma deaths in a series of 1,235 women who had been exposed to radium in the dial-painting industry. This rate is astronomically higher than the *lifetime* expectation of bone cancer in unirradiated persons.

It is overwhelmingly evident that exposure to radiation does not simply accelerate cancers which would occur "anyway." It indeed produces *extra* cancers.

Myth 5: Radiation Gets Blamed for Cancers Caused by Heredity, Etc.

This misconception arises from the fact that ionizing radiation is not the only agent firmly proven to cause cancer in the human. However, the number of cancers caused in a group by radiation is never exaggerated in a properly arranged study (like the Hiroshima-Nagasaki study, for example), because all the other proven and suspected causes of cancer operate at equal rates in both the irradiated and non-irradiated groups. Therefore, when the irradiated groups show a higher cancer rate, and the rate rises as the radiation dose rises, radiation is correctly blamed.

A less certain situation occurs whenever one seeks the correct cause of a cancer appearing in a particular individual. Then, in most cases, the answer must be found in probabilities discovered by proper studies of groups. Even when there are 9 chances out of 10 that radiation caused a particular case of cancer, the possibility (1 chance in 10) does persist that something else caused it.

Myth 6: Diagnostic Doses Are below the Level
Where Direct Evidence of Human Injury Exists

The effects of low-dose radiation are not extrapolated from high-dose data. On the contrary, there is human evidence down even to one-quarter of one rad (Stewart, 1970; MacMahon, 1962), and there are several studies of effects in the common diagnostic range between 1 and 30 rads (details in R&HH, Chapters 6, 7, and 20). Moreover, it would be a mistake to assume, as many do, that the studied survivors of Hiroshima and Nagasaki received high doses. Their average absorbed dose was below 30 rads (details in R&HH, Chapter 6). One should note that the irradiated survivors are customarily divided into several dose groups, and that the strongest evidence of excess cancer is coming from the *lowest* dose groups, which are the largest and therefore the most reliable of all.

In the bomb survivors, even the lowest-dose group (under about 5 rads absorbed bone-marrow dose) showed excess leukemia as well as cancer. At doses as low as 5 to 9 rads to the fetus, there was also unmistakable evidence of excess congenital injury in the form of small brains and mental retardation.

Lastly, there is no doubt that, in the human, enduring (unrepaired) chromosomal injuries occur at doses of just a few rads (Evans and co-workers, 1979).

Myth 7: Current Reevaluation
of the Doses at Hiroshima and Nagasaki
Will Change "Everything"

It is true that radiation physicists are recalculating the doses received by the survivors at Hiroshima and Nagasaki; indeed, such reevaluation has been an on-going process for several decades. Early comments from the current round of recalculations, which will not be complete until approximately 1988 (see *Diagnostic Imaging*, November, 1983, p. 94), suggest that, previously, the doses may have been overestimated. If true, it will mean that smaller doses account for the observed effects, and that the hazards per rad are *greater* than some people think. On the other hand, the recalculations may end up by not altering the doses appreciably. In either case, the recalculations are going to provide little comfort for people who hope that the radiation effect will go away.

The impact from possible revisions of the Japanese doses on this book will be small. We are using risk values from *Radiation and Human Health*, which synthesized all the worldwide studies and did not rely exclusively on the Japanese data. What is more, the discovery (Loewe and Mendel-sohn, 1982) that neutrons delivered virtually no special dose in Hiroshima after all, was deduced in *Radiation and Human Health,* and treated there correctly.

Myth 8: The Risk from Radiation Is Exaggerated by the Linear Model, Which Says Risk Is Directly Proportional to Dose

---

It is natural for everyone, ourselves included, to wish that radiation would be less harmful per rad at low dose-ranges than at high dose-ranges. This wish corresponds to a non-linear, or quadratic, dose-response curve. Those who cling to this wish, in spite of all the evidence, claim that the linear "hypothesis" exaggerates the risk of getting cancer from radiation at low doses. But wishful thinking is gradually yielding to evidence.

For instance, the studies from Hiroshima and Nagasaki keep yielding additional data on this issue, as follow-up time lengthens, and the data do not support this wish. Both Tokunaga (1982, p. 924) and Wakabayashi (1983) address the linearity issue explicitly. Wakabayashi and co-workers (p. 130) say: "In the dissenting section in the BEIR-III report, Rossi (19) stated that the dose response for mortality from all cancers in Nagasaki (1950–1974) fits a quadratic model best. The present analysis does not support this. Rather, the data suggest a linear model or at least a linear-quadratic model. . . ."

They add, concerning the linear-quadratic (L-Q): "The linear term is significant in the L-Q model, whereas the quadratic term is not."

In short, the new evidence completely supports the use of the linear model, on which the risk values in *Radiation and Human Health* and in this book are based. The linear model says that the risk of getting cancer is directly proportional to dose, or stated differently, the risk *per rad* of dose is constant through all levels of dose.

We must warn users of this book that this linear model may actually underestimate the risk of getting cancer and leukemia. There is, unfortunately, evidence which is accumulating and growing ever stronger that the cancer risk per rad of dose is worse in the low-dose range than in the high-dose range. The data fit a supra-linear dose-response curve. This evidence is fully presented in *Radiation and Human Health,* and when the analysis in that book is extended to cover even more recent data reported elsewhere (Wakabayashi and co-workers, 1983), the newest data also confirm supra-linearity. For leukemia, too, the Japanese evidence shows supra-linearity (R&HH, Chapter 20, p. 679).

Myth 9: There Could Well Be a Safe Threshold for Radiation Exposure— A Dose below Which the Body Repairs All Injury

The human body definitely can repair some types of injury to DNA and chromosomes. But the evidence of excess cancer and leukemia, from doses between one-quarter of one rad and 10 rads, signifies that the body is unfortunately *not* able to repair all the types of injury from radiation which lead to these serious delayed effects. Once again, wishful thinking must yield to evidence. The hope that a safe threshold will still be found is especially unreasonable as evidence accumulates that effects per rad are worse in the low-dose range than the high-dose range (supra-linearity).

Therefore, we must comment specifically about an astounding statement made by Robert Brent, a consultant to the BEIR Committee. In *Pediatrics* (February, 1983, p. 288), he said, "In order to observe an increase in cancer in an exposed population, there are two important features: (1) whole body radiation exposure; (2) exposures greater than 50 rads."

This statement, which is contrary to fact on both its points, is extremely likely to leave pediatricians with the erroneous and literally deadly impression that there is probably a safe threshold dose around 50 rads. The effect would be to deny all the evidence on excess cancer from Hiroshima and Nagasaki, where the average dose was below 30 rads, as well as to deny the evidence from numerous other studies based upon partial-body radiation.

Analysis of the real-world data indicates just how serious 50 rads of whole-body dose is. If such a dose were received by a population of mixed ages, it would double the people's lifetime incidence of cancer (R&HH, p. 294, p. 363, p. 365). And if such a dose were received by a group of children age 10 and younger, it would virtually guarantee that each child in the group would get some sort of cancer later. Since children are far more sensitive than adults to radiation-induction of cancer, it is particularly unfortunate that Brent's statement appeared in a journal widely read by pediatricians.

Myth 10: Delayed Effects Are Reduced by Dividing a Radiation Exposure into Several Smaller Doses

The fractionation myth is a variant on the non-linear and threshold myths. Dividing a *high* dose into several smaller doses definitely reduces a high dose's acute and temporary effects such as nausea, but with respect to delayed and deadly effects such as cancer, there is definite evidence that dividing a dose does *not* reduce the risk. For instance, careful follow-up studies of excess breast cancer have been conducted on tubercular women who each received more than one hundred fluoroscopic chest exams, with doses per exam between 1 and 8 rads (Myrden and Hiltz, 1969; Boice and Monson, 1977; Boice and co-workers, 1979). The rate of excess breast cancer per rad was not significantly different from the rate found in other studies in which women received single doses of 30 to 100 rads to the breasts.

Myth 11: The Youngest Are Not the Most Sensitive to Induction of Cancer by Radiation

---

It is hard to assess how far this very dangerous myth has spread. We have seen it already put forth in the *Canadian Medical Association Journal* (May 1, 1982, pp. 1076–78) and in a sworn affidavit by Dr. Jacob I. Fabrikant (October 1, 1983, p. 34), who is head of the BEIR Committee's section on cancer induction by radiation.

Because there is no matter more serious with respect to making decisions about X-ray exams than the special sensitivity of children, this subject deserves special emphasis.

The evidence that children are more sensitive than adults to cancer induction by ionizing radiation was overwhelming even as early as 1970. The first *BEIR Report* (1972, p. 184, p. 185) strongly and explicitly acknowledged the evidence, presented an age-sensitivity curve having a shape virtually identical to the ones in *Radiation and Human Health* (p. 272), and concurred specifically with the second "law" exactly as stated by Gofman and Tamplin (1969–1970); that law appears with three others in Chapter 18 of this book.

All the data which have accumulated since 1969, up to and including the newest reports on the survivors of Hiroshima and Nagasaki, simply fortify the conclusion that the younger the child, the greater the sensitivity. It is one of the firmest and most widely recognized facts in this field. Kato and Schull (1982, p. 408), discussing the excess cancer deaths in the overall Hiroshima-Nagasaki series, state, "For age-at-death specific groups, the relative risk for all cancer except leukemia (Table IV) is higher the younger the age ATB." (ATB stands for At Time of Bombing.)

We find it bizarre, and menacing to human health, that anyone would spread factually unsupported denials.

When *Radiation and Human Health* went to press in 1981, the data were still sparse, when breast cancer was singled out and considered all alone, from the youngest age group (ages 0–9) exposed at Hiroshima-

Nagasaki. A specific prediction was made in that book (p. 260): "The author of this book will readily go out on a limb and predict that the next 5 to 10 years of study of those who were 0–9 years of age at the time of bombing will demonstrate a startling number of breast cancers induced by radiation."

The very next year, in the *Lancet,* Tokunaga and co-workers (1982) reported that the rate of excess breast cancer in that youngest age group is higher than in any other exposed age-group. And this group (0–9 years ATB) has only recently reached the age-bracket where the climb occurs in breast cancer's spontaneous rate, the rate which will be raised by radiation exposure (see discussion, Myth 3).

Some readers, who may be amazed that a cancer can begin secretly stalking an irradiated child 35 years and longer before making its clinical appearance, may appreciate a reminder about the numerous *genetic* diseases which wait to express themselves clinically until decades after birth. Huntington's Disease, which caught up with composer-singer Woodie Guthrie after he had passed the age of 40, is only one of many.

Myth 12: It Is Impossible to Understand
Why Risk Estimates Vary

Actually it is a rather simple matter to understand. First, it is important to recognize three distinct categories of risk estimation:

1. Whole-body exposure of a general population, with its natural mixture of ages from newborn to 90 years and older;

2. Whole-body exposure of people at specific ages;

3. Partial-body exposure (to specific organs) of people at specific ages —for example, the exposure which individuals receive from medical and dental X-ray exams.

There is a tight, logical relationship among the three kinds of estimates. An individual's whole-body risk is the sum of the risk contributed by individual irradiated organs; a population's risk is the sum of the lifetime risks contributed by individual irradiated people. If experts disagree on one category of risk, they are bound to disagree on all three.

The disagreement examined here is limited to exposure of a mixed-age population, for a straightforward reason: only *one* set of age-specific estimates exists so far—the set developed in *Radiation and Human Health* and reflected in all the tables of this book. The quasi-official BEIR and UNSCEAR committees, and the national and international councils on radiation protection, have not yet published comparable age-specific risk estimates, nor have they provided organ-specific risk estimates by age.

The published risk estimates for whole-body exposure of populations of mixed ages come from three sources: *Radiation and Human Health* (1981); the *BEIR Report* (1980) from the National Academy of Sciences; and the *UNSCEAR Report* (1977) from the United Nations. These sources have tried to answer the question: if each of one million people of mixed ages receives one rad of whole-body exposure, how many radiation-induced cancer deaths will occur among them during their remaining lifespans? The estimates are:

R&HH, p. 314	3,771	or 1 cancer-death per 265 person-rads.
BEIR, p. 195	226	or 1 cancer-death per 4,425 person-rads.
UNSCEAR, p. 414	100	or 1 cancer-death per 10,000 person-rads.

According to BEIR (relative risk model), the risk of a radiation-induced cancer-death is about 17 times lower than stated in R&HH; according to UNSCEAR, it is 38 times lower. How to use these lower rates is demonstrated in Chapter 4, Section 7, so that this book can be fully used by readers who prefer other cancer values. But we remind the readers that the cancer values from R&HH may themselves be underestimates of the true risk, not overestimates.

The reasons for the large differences above are not mysterious. Readers will find them explained elsewhere in full detail, with the pertinent numbers and calculations (R&HH, Chapter 9, and Gofman, 1983, AAAS). We shall only summarize here.

Causes of the Disagreements

One reason the committees' estimates are so low is that they excluded a great deal of important evidence. *Radiation and Human Health* is based upon the worldwide human evidence—some 22 valid studies, validly combined. By contrast, the *BEIR Report* (1980) is based almost exclusively on the single Hiroshima-Nagasaki study—according to the BEIR chairman himself (Radford, his dissent, p. 227 BEIR, 1980).

The BEIR Committee may have ignored so much evidence because no valid method for comparing and combining different studies had yet been developed when it was preparing its report. But it also excluded some of the evidence provided *within* the Hiroshima-Nagasaki study, on the ground that certain data were too sparse to achieve enough reliability (a high level of statistical significance).

Readers should be warned that even a mountain of evidence about something can be subdivided into sections until each section contains data too sparse to show statistical significance. If, for instance, a mountain of data about radiation-induced cancer is subdivided into fine age-groups or into 130 different types of tumors, or both, then most of the categories will fail to meet the test of statistical significance. Consequently, most of the evidence can be declared "too sparse" and be discarded. When valid evidence is thrown out on such a basis, wrong answers are bound to follow.

After data are discarded, there are still many ways to mishandle the remaining data. Three deserve mention.

Ignoring a Still-Rising Excess: The newest evidence from Japan shows that the difference in cancer rates between exposed and unexposed groups is still *increasing* 33 years after irradiation (Kato and Schull, 1982; Wakabayashi and co-workers, 1983; Tokunaga and co-workers, 1982). This is what was predicted in *Radiation and Human Health* on the basis of four other studies, much smaller in scope.

The lifetime risk-estimates in that book, and this one, are made on the basis that the cancer rates of irradiated and unirradiated people peak at their maximum difference about 40 years after exposure; then the difference continues, but shrinks. If it turns out that the disparity continues to widen even after 40 years, or that it remains steady instead of diminishing, such evidence would make the estimates of cancer risk in *Radiation and Human Health* and in this book too low.

To make their estimates, the BEIR and UNSCEAR committees also had to make judgments about what the future data would show. By ignoring the fact that the rate of excess cancer is still *rising* in the Hiroshima-Nagasaki series, the committees were bound to produce underestimates of the risks.

Obliterating the Effect of Age: In addition, the lifetime consequences will be drastically underestimated if the different sensitivity of the young and old is obliterated; this occurs when data from different age-groups are combined by the wrong method. It appears that the BEIR Committee may have done this, although it is impossible to be sure, since the committee does not tell what it did in this respect. The right and wrong ways to handle the data, and the consequences of each method, are contrasted in *Radiation and Human Health* (Chapter 9).

Injecting a Non-Linear Dose-Effect Response: The BEIR Committee applied an assumption, unsupported by any human evidence from Japan or elsewhere, that the risk per rad at low doses would be less than at high doses—the quasi-quadratic model (Myth 8). In the *BEIR Report,* Dr. Radford (the BEIR chairman) wrote a vigorous dissent to this scientifically indefensible behavior, and to some other practices of his committee.

In an interview when the report was released, Radford (July, 1980) said that the quasi-quadratic model "has already been refuted by the evidence" and that most people who support it "have a strong personal stake in seeing the dose-risk estimates lowered." On that occasion and subsequently (1982), Radford has warned the public to pay attention to the possible self-interests of those who support or attack certain assertions in science.

Dr. Radford states elsewhere that, while he rejects parts of *Radiation and Human Health,* he agrees that the cancer risk from radiation has been underestimated in the BEIR and UNSCEAR reports. "I agree that the BEIR III, the Radiological Protection Commission, and the U.N. Scientific Committee cancer risk coefficients are much too low, but they are unlikely to be off by more than a factor of five to eight, unless total *incident* cancer cases are considered for risk determination" (*Bulletin of the Atomic Scientists,* June/July 1983, p. 31; emphasis in original).

The Basis for Confidence

Those are the main reasons that the estimates differ for the risk of getting cancer from low-dose radiation. We were confident that the methods and conclusions of *Radiation and Human Health* were scientifically correct, within the limits of the existing data, when the book went to press in 1981. Even greater confidence is justified now. All the newest data reported since 1981 from Hiroshima-Nagasaki and elsewhere further fortify the book's conclusions. This is the case on crucial matters such as age-sensitivity, supra-linearity, the still-increasing excess of cancer 33 years after irradiation, the inducibility of all types of cancer, and radiation's behavior as a constant multiplier of the spontaneous cancer rates.

Moreover, during nearly four years of extraordinary scrutiny and widespread peer review of the book in professional journals, scientific symposia, and in trials concerning radiation injury, no one has made a single scientifically valid refutation or modification of any of its data, methods, or conclusions. Probably no work in this field has received more review by peers.

The scrutiny continues, and quite properly so. We, too, keep examining the earlier book in the light of new information and new insights. Indeed, to the three "laws" of carcinogenesis expounded in the earlier book, a fourth law is newly added in Chapter 18 of *this* book.

CHAPTER 3

Cancer
as a Delayed Effect

Section 1: What the Tables Tell

The tables in this book make it possible to answer the question, "What is the chance that this diagnostic X-ray exam will give cancer to the person who is examined?" Specifically, the tables can tell the *lifetime* risk of the *examined* person *getting* a cancer of *any* type as a *result* of the exam. The five italicized points should be clearly understood.

Lifetime Risk: The tables tell the probability or odds that the examined person will get a radiation-induced cancer sometime during his or her remaining lifespan; they do not tell when such a cancer will appear. The chance is exceedingly low that such a cancer will appear in the first ten years after irradiation (see Chapter 18, fourth law). Moreover, since radiation acts as a multiplier upon the spontaneous rate of cancer, most radiation-induced cancers appear when exposed individuals reach the age-bracket (middle years and up) in which *spontaneous* cancer rates are high.

Examined Person: The tables of cancer risk in this book apply to the person who is examined with X-rays. They do not include the risk of radiation-induced cancer conferred upon children who are in the womb during an X-ray examination of their mother; that risk is discussed sepa-

30

rately in Chapter 12. Nor do the tables include any risk of radiation-induced cancer which a person may inherit from irradiated parents, grandparents, or even earlier ancestors. Exceedingly strong evidence now exists, however, that certain types of cancer are associated with heritable chromosomal injuries of the same types which X-rays can easily cause (R&HH, Chapter 22).

Getting a Cancer: The tables tell how probable it is that an exam will cause cancer in the examined person later. The tables refer to diagnosis, not death. Chapter 4, Section 8 demonstrates how to convert the risk of getting a cancer into the risk of getting a *fatal* cancer.

Cancer of Any Type: There is no X-ray exam which exposes only one cancer-prone organ (see Chapter 19). Every exam increases the risk of several types of cancer. To produce this book's tables, the radiation-induced cancer risks from each separate organ have been added together, so that the tables tell the aggregate risk of *some* type of radiation-induced cancer as a result of the exam. The introductions to the separate exams tell which types are most likely.

For instance, the table for an examination of the ribs shows that, in males, the risk of cancer comes primarily from the irradiated lungs (bronchi), kidneys, and stomach. In females there is an added risk; because the breasts are irradiated, it turns out that this exam is almost twice as risky for a non-smoking female as for a non-smoking male. We shall return to the smoking issue in Section 3.

Result of the Exam: Whether or not an individual ever has a diagnostic X-ray exam, every American today has a risk of about 1 in 4 (or 250,000 per million) of getting some sort of cancer during his or her lifespan. The tables in this book tell the *additional* cancer risk which results from being irradiated during various typical exams.

These tables tell *future* risk resulting from an exam; they do not reach back in time to tell what fraction of the blame for an existing cancer belongs to earlier exposure to radiation. Such fractions of causation can, indeed, be calculated with the method and extensive tables provided in *Radiation and Human Health*, Chapter 18, but not from the tables in *this* book.

One of the most important lessons from this book is that no one is entitled to make generalizations about the "hazard from diagnostic X-rays." The riskiness varies by more than 10,000-fold, from simply trivial for many exams (especially at older ages) to very worrisome for some others (especially at younger ages).

Individual attitudes about voluntary risks differ greatly (Chapter 17, Section 2). Obviously an additional cancer risk of, say, 1 in 1,250 is small compared with a 1 in 4 risk of getting cancer "anyway." In fact, even the biggest risks are small compared with the certainty of dying sometime "anyway." The individual patient who needs ten exams over time, which is not at all unusual, has accumulated a risk of 1 chance in 125 of getting cancer from the exams, if each exam confers a risk of 1 in 1,250.

From another point of view, if an exam confers a cancer rate of 1 in 1,250, it means that after 1,250 such exams have been performed, someone is going to get a cancer later as a *result,* although no one knows who it will be.

We are impressed by the growing effort in the radiological professions to reduce entrance doses and the size of areas exposed, during exams of all types, since even small individual risks per exam translate into a very large amount of cancer when they are multiplied by millions of exams. For instance, a cancer risk of 1 in 1,250 is the same as 800 per million (see box in Chapter 1). If—and we repeat *if*—a comparable risk were conferred each year by 100 million exams, the yearly "price" would be initiation of 80,000 radiation-induced cancers. The actual impact of diagnostic X-rays, in the aggregate, is evaluated with care in Chapter 17.

Table 2. Sensitivity Factors, by Ages Compared with Newborn, for Cancer-Induction by Ionizing Radiation

Entries: Each entry denotes how many times *less* sensitive is that age than the newborn age. Example: it takes 2.80 times more dose to cause later cancer in a 15-year-old male than in a newborn.

Age	Males	Females
Newborn	—	—
1	1.01	1.02
5	1.11	1.16
10	1.38	1.52
15	2.80	3.18
20	3.14	3.64
30	3.68	4.17
40	8.44	9.31
50	210.89	213.98
55	307.53	306.88

SOURCE: Values are the ratios of whole-body cancer doses from *Radiation and Human Health,* Tables 21 and 22.

Section 2: Considerations of Age

A general rule, with respect to the lifetime risk of cancer induced by X-rays, is that children are much more sensitive than adults.

How Sensitivity Changes with Age

A glance at Table 2, above, shows that about 300 times more radiation is required to produce cancer in a 55-year-old than in a newborn infant. In other words, a newly born child is about 300 times more sensitive than a 55-year-old to induction of cancer by radiation; it takes 300 times less radiation to cause a cancer in the newborn than in the 55-year-old.

Between the ages of newborn and 40, however, the difference is much less. For males, the ratio between age 40 and newborn is 8.44, which means it takes only 8.44 times more radiation to produce cancer in a 40-year-old male than in a newborn.

The difference between age 20 and newborn is far less, and between age 10 and newborn, it is relatively small. Other comparisons are discussed in Chapter 22, A Guide to Factors and Ratios.

Cancer Risk Tables, Age 20 and Younger

The table for the Cystogram Exam (Chapter 5) illustrates an important point: although sensitivity to radiation-induced cancer increases with each younger age, the risk from diagnostic X-ray exams is *not* necessarily the highest at the youngest age. The risk usually peaks at age 5 or 10. Why?

The primary reason is that the entrance dose needed to obtain good diagnostic information generally increases as body size increases. Whenever the entrance dose increases by a factor which is larger than the factor by which the cancer sensitivity is falling, the cancer risk will *increase* despite increasing age. But exceptions to this rule do occur, because several additional factors help determine the net cancer risk. These factors, and some of the surprises they produce, are discussed in Section 5 of this chapter.

The Tables above Age 20

By age 20, the cancer-prone organs have stopped increasing in size and in average (midpoint) distance from each other. If, for example, the center of the pancreas is a certain number of centimeters away from the center of a kidney at age 20, we can assume the distance remains approximately the same throughout the remaining lifespan.

Because adults are anatomically stable relative to children, a great deal is simplified with respect to determining cancer risk. The only important variable which continues to change with age is the sensitivity to induction of cancer.

Therefore, we can obtain the cancer risk to a person over 20 from any given shot or exam simply by multiplying the risk at age 20 by the lowering factor appropriate for the advanced ages. These lowering factors are provided in the tables of Chapter 5. Their use is illustrated in Chapter 4.

The Obesity Issue

After age 20, the cancer-prone organs no longer increase much in size. What increases, as adults commonly fatten, are the size of the fat cells, the connective tissue which holds them in place, and the skin area. Cancers of these organs contribute a very small share of the cancer risk from diagnostic X-rays.

Of course, whenever X-rays are taken of a person who is fatter (or thinner) than average, appropriate adjustments in dose, beam quality, or both are made in order to obtain good diagnostic images. With respect to using the tables of cancer risk, such adjustments are handled the same way for obese (and skinny) patients as for anyone else; one uses exactly the same, simple methods illustrated in Chapter 4.

It is true that obesity introduces changes in cancer risk which are not *perfectly* managed by the regular methods of Chapter 4, but the small error introduced by fat is quite tolerable for all practical purposes.

Section 3: Considerations of Exposure Area

A second general rule about X-ray exams is that the ones which expose the torso and mouth will confer much higher cancer risks than those which expose only arms or legs. The reason is that radiation acts as a multiplier upon the *spontaneous* rates of human cancer, and the organs which spontaneously generate most human cancer are in the chest, abdomen, pelvis, and mouth—not in the limbs.

Low-Risk Areas

The risks from examining the outermost limb-parts (elbow to fingers, knee to toes) are exceedingly low, even at the youngest years. This point should greatly lessen anxiety among conscientious parents whose children need X-rays to determine the best "fix" for injured arms and legs.

In the adult years, the risks from arm and leg X-rays become so low that we have provided entries in the tables at age intervals of ten years instead of five.

High-Risk Areas

For exams involving the torso, the areas of especially high cancer risk, from neck to pelvic base, can be readily noted in the tables for both C.A.T. Scans (Chapter 10) and fluoroscopy (Chapter 6).

For both males and females, the central pelvis is an area of especially high risk. And for females, any anterior-posterior (front-to-back) shot of the chest is far riskier than the same shot for males, because of the risk of breast cancer. The effect shows up, for instance, in the tables for exams of the thoracic spine and ribs. Likewise, chest shots have special implications for smokers.

The Smoking Issue

All the cancer risks presented in this book's tables are for non-smokers. No one disputes the evidence that non-smokers have a much lower rate of lung cancer than smokers, whatever the reason. There is also overwhelming evidence that non-smokers and smokers respond differently to irradiation of their lungs. Although Radford and Renard (1984) have questioned this observation, their case is far from convincing; their basis is a series which is tiny by comparison with the series analyzed by Archer and co-workers (1976) and by Saccomanno (1978). The larger, more reliable body of evidence shows that smokers have a very much higher frequency of radiation-induced lung cancer per unit of dose than do non-smokers (R&HH, pp. 449–50). Such findings are well in accord with the more general observation that radiation acts as a multiplier upon other factors (smoking, for instance) which are causing human cancer.

With respect to diagnostic radiology, the evidence means that X-ray exams which irradiate the bronchi create different cancer risks for non-smokers than for smokers. Therefore, the risk tables in Chapters 5 and 7 provide smoking factors; these tell how many times worse the risk of cancer will be from an exam if the person examined is a moderate smoker (about 20 full-strength cigarettes per day during the adult lifespan) rather than a non-smoker. No refinements have been made concerning heavier or lighter smoking, or for quitting or resuming the habit. Chapter 4, Section 6, shows how to apply the smoking factors.

Size of Field

Since radiation-induced cancer arises from the organs which also spontaneously develop the disease, the fewer such organs irradiated, the lower the risk will be of radiation-induced cancer. Therefore, the size of the "field"—the area directly in the X-ray beam—was an important consideration in arriving at the risk values in this book.

Unless stated otherwise, the risks evaluated for children, newborn through age 15, are based on adjusting the X-ray beam to body part rather than to film size. This point needs emphasis, especially with respect to the vertical dimension of the beam. If it is lined up (collimated) to film size instead of to body part, the risk for children can be enormously higher than the values in this book's tables.

An illustration, using an anterior-posterior shot of an infant's abdomen, is provided in Chapter 16, Section 3. Collimation to body part, instead of film size, reduced the dose to the infant's lungs by more than 5-fold—a direct 5-fold reduction in the infant's risk of later lung cancer from the exam.

Adults also benefit from collimation to body part. Chapter 5 illustrates a great risk reduction in the Thoracic Spine Exam. When the narrow field is used instead of the wide field, the risk of later cancer is cut in half for females, because their biggest risk from this exam is cancer of the breast.

Section 4: Considerations of Dose

A third general rule, with respect to lifetime risk of radiation-induced cancer, is that reducing the entrance dose in half will reduce the cancer risk in half, if all other conditions remain unchanged.

Roentgens and Rads: Convertibility

All the entrance doses in this book are measured in roentgens free-in-air (FIA), with no backscatter. (A capitalized R is the symbol for roentgen, a unit named after Wilhelm Roentgen, who discovered X-rays.)

The meaning of "free-in-air" is specific. Entrance doses can be measured either "at skin" with a patient (or substitute) in place, or measured free-in-air with no patient in place. In the latter case, the beam is measured where the patient's skin would be, if a patient were there.

Because the body itself causes radiation to backscatter to the skin, if the skin entrance dose is measured with the patient in place, it will be about 1.3 times higher than the entrance dose measured free-in-air with no patient present.

Diagnostic entrance doses can also be expressed in rads or millirads of "skin entrance dose" or just "skin dose." There is nothing at all wrong about the use of rads instead of roentgens. The important thing is simply for people to know which kind of measurement is meant.

Converting from one to the other is simple. One roentgen FIA corresponds (at diagnostic beam qualities) to about 0.93 rads of dose absorbed by the surface of the skin. But with a patient in place, the backscatter increases the dose received by the skin by about 1.3. The net effect is to raise the number by a factor of 1.21. The rules are as follows:

- To convert from roentgens FIA to rads of skin entrance dose, multiply roentgens by a raising factor of 1.21. *Example:* an entrance dose of 0.323 roentgen FIA × 1.21 yields 0.391 rad, or 391 millirads.
- To convert from rads of skin entrance dose to roentgens FIA, multiply rads by a lowering factor of 0.83. *Example:* a skin entrance dose of 0.391 rad × 0.83 yields 0.324 roentgen FIA. (The discrepancy between 0.323 and 0.324 results from rounding off.)

When comparing entrance doses, it is a good idea to develop the habit of asking these questions: do these doses, in their present form, really qualify for comparison? Are some in rads and others in roentgens? Are the ones in roentgens measured free-in-air, or measured with backscatter included? Are the beam qualities (see below) at least close?

But when this information is not available (which is very often), there is no reason to "throw in the towel." For many purposes, a ballpark comparison is far more helpful than none at all.

How Absorbed Dose Changes with Beam Quality

The doses which the body absorbs internally (as distinct from entrance doses) are always given in rads or millirads (mrad) in this book. The term "rem" is unneeded because there is no difference at all between rems and rads for ionizing radiation of the X-ray class.

Probably few people outside the fields of radiology have paused to realize the inevitably huge differences among entrance doses to the skin, absorbed doses to the internal organs, and exit doses to the surface of skin which is nearest the film or other image-receptor. The energy which the photons of an X-ray carry, as the beam enters the body, is almost completely absorbed within the body before any photons reach the film. Almost all the beam is "swallowed up" as it travels through the body. Very little of it is required to expose a film on the patient's exit side.

This absorption accounts for the great variation in the *rads per entrance roentgen* received by different organs. The internal organs closest to the surface where the beam enters feel, of course, a great deal more X-ray energy than those closest to the exit surface where the greatly diminished beam emerges.

For every major organ, the ratio of rads per entrance roentgen is given (for a "reference adult") in Special Table C, Chapter 21.

The ratio varies when the beam quality varies. A higher or "harder" beam quality means organs absorb higher average doses *per entrance roentgen;* a lower beam quality means lower average doses absorbed and lower cancer risk *per entrance roentgen.* The size of the effect differs for anterior-posterior, posterior-anterior, lateral, and oblique shots. Special Table D of Chapter 21 provides the factors to convert any cancer risk in this book according to the beam quality preferred at different facilities and for different diagnostic purposes. How to use Table D is illustrated in Chapter 4, Section 12.

We have emphasized "per entrance roentgen" because we want *no* reader to imagine that every increase in peak kilovoltage, which hardens the beam, necessarily means a higher absorbed dose. Whenever a hardened beam permits significant reduction in entrance dose, the *net* effect can be to reduce the absorbed dose in spite of the hardened beam.

When beam quality is hardened (or softened) by raising (or lowering) the peak kilovoltage, or by adding (or removing) filters, the milliampere-seconds of exposure are usually adjusted too. It is commonplace to calculate the altered entrance dose from tables of kilovoltage, milliampere-seconds, and amount of filtration. A survey, reported in Chapter 16, Section 1, will shatter the assumption that this is a reliable way of knowing the approximate entrance dose.

Section 5: Surprises, but Not Mysteries

We predict that most users of this book will share our initial surprise that there is a bigger risk for males than females from the Skull Exam and the Dental Exam.

The mystery disappears when one remembers that radiation exposure does not cause a *special* type of cancer; it increases the frequency of the *same* types which occur spontaneously. Males in the United States have a rate of spontaneous cancer of the mouth (buccal cavity) and pharynx which is more than double the rate for females; but rates of brain cancer in males and females are similar. So it is the males' higher rate of cancers of the buccal cavity and pharynx which accounts for their higher risk from X-rays of the skull and teeth.

In Chapter 4, Section 6, we explain another unexpected consequence from the different rates of spontaneous cancer. The rate of breast cancer is exceedingly low in American men, but high in American women. This ends up accounting for the difference between males and females in the *smoking* factor for certain exams! Because such results are not self-evident, they are surprising.

A number of other surprises occur in the tables for the routine films (Chapter 5). Sometimes, for instance:

- A cancer or leukemia risk may go up, down, and then up again (or down, up, and then down again) as age advances;
- An ovarian or unshielded testes dose may show a "wobble" as age advances;
- An exam which confers a higher risk on newborn females than males may confer the higher risk on males as age advances;
- The ratio of risk from two shots (especially the ratio between the anterior-posterior and the lateral shots) may change greatly as age advances.

We have checked such unexpected results, traced their origins, and found them not to be errors. On the contrary, it turns out they are exactly what to expect. Each is a net number resulting from a complex interplay of variables, all of which are changing at different rates with respect to each other, as age advances. Moreover, the magnitude of net effect on dose and risk necessarily varies among the different exams, according to the shots and the size of the fields.

Six of the Major Variables

Some of the major variables which interact are the following:

1. The rate of decline, as age advances, in sensitivity to cancer induction by radiation (Table 2, this chapter);
2. The difference, for males and females, in the rate at which sensitivity changes with age, and the somewhat different effects produced on the rates by separating smokers and non-smokers;
3. The rate at which the entrance dose changes during the childhood years (Table 3, Chapter 5);
4. The rate at which rads per roentgen of entrance dose change

with age, as round infants change in both thickness and shape to become elliptical adults;

5. The different rates, as children grow, at which major cancer-prone organs, such as the prostate or breasts, move away from the direct X-ray beam of certain exams;

6. The different spontaneous rates at which the same type of cancer occurs in males and females (clearly reflected in Special Tables A and B, Chapter 21).

It bears repeating that it is primarily the interaction of rising dose with declining sensitivity, as age advances, which causes cancer risk from most exams to peak at age 10, rather than to decline steadily at every age-interval following birth.

This book would be fat and forbidding if we explained exactly how all the major variables interact to produce every result which could conceivably surprise one reader or another. Therefore, we must settle for providing this list of the major variables; we hope that the curious reader can successfully use it to answer his or her particular questions.

CHAPTER 4

How to Use
the Risk Tables

Patients and parents can regard the lifetime risks of getting radiation-induced cancer, shown in Chapters 5, 7, and 9, as the values which are most likely to apply if a radiologic office is chosen at random. The tables are based on typical conditions of dose, beam quality, and number of shots, as determined by surveys of U.S. facilities (Kereiakes and Rosenstein, 1980). For exams which such surveys do not cover, we used related conditions, or conditions reported by other sources, which we identify.

No physician or dentist, of course, will be satisfied with average values. Not only does he or she deliberately adjust conditions to fit individual patients, but the odds are astronomically high against his or her average conditions exactly matching a survey's average for each of the hundreds of shots evaluated in this book. Besides, many offices can—and we hope they will—take credit for routinely using conditions which are far *better* than average.

This chapter demonstrates for both the careful professionals and for everyone else how to convert the values in this book to non-typical and special conditions. Anyone with a pocket calculator which adds, subtracts, multiplies, and divides (nothing fancier is needed) is equipped to use this book fully. But before demonstrating any conversions, we shall demonstrate how to use a table or two exactly "as is."

The key to abbreviations used throughout this chapter is located in Chapter 5, Section 1.

41

Section 1: No Changes, Age 20 and Younger

Example 1: Boy

What is the cancer risk for a 5-year-old boy from the routine Skull Exam?

ANSWER: From the table for Skull Exam, located alphabetically in Chapter 5, we see that the lifetime cancer risk resulting from this exam is 746 per million, which means that when this exam is given to a million boys of this age, 746 will get a cancer later as a result.

A risk of 746 per million is the *same* as 1 in 1,340, as we demonstrated in Chapter 1. To get 1 in 1,340, we simply divided 1,000,000 by 746 and said "1 in" before the answer.

When the risk from an exam is 1 in 1,340, it means that a small fraction (1 / 1,340) of the patients will get a cancer from the exam, and that whoever gets it will get a regular full cancer, indistinguishable from spontaneous cancer. This is very different from saying that every patient will get a small fraction (1 / 1,340) of a cancer!

Rounding Off and Significant Figures

Before proceeding to Example 2, we want to answer a natural question. In Example 1, do we mean the cancer price is *exactly* 746 per million exams? Of course not. We mean that the risk is in the neighborhood of 750 —between 700 and 800. We purposely avoided rounding off numbers in this book to their formally significant figures for an important reason: many users of this book will be "operating" on our numbers as they convert them to particular conditions. Because prematurely rounding off numbers would introduce unnecessary uncertainty and error, reports of this nature do not do it.

Example 2: Girl

What is the cancer risk for a 15-year-old girl from a routine Ribs Exam?

ANSWER: We see that the lifetime cancer risk from this exam is 1,408 per million. From the table, we can also see exactly where the number is coming from. The common exam is described at the top as one anterior-posterior (AP) shot, one posterior-anterior (PA) shot, and one oblique (OBL) shot with the beam entering the patient's back and exiting from her front, which makes it an oblique-PA shot. The value of 1,408 is simply the *sum* of the risks from the individual shots which are used in this particular common exam:

817 per million conferred by the AP shot
+169 per million conferred by the PA shot
+422 per million conferred by the OBL-PA shot

1,408 per million conferred by the common exam,
   or a lifetime cancer risk of 1 chance in 710 as a result of this exam.

Section 2: Changes in Number of Shots, Age 20 and Younger

Example 3: Adding a Shot

If a 5-year-old boy having a Skull Exam (Example 1) moves his head during the PA shot, and consequently a second PA shot is needed, what will his cancer risk be from the whole exam?

ANSWER: Obviously it will be raised by the extra shot. We have seen in Example 2 that the risk from a whole exam is simply the sum of the risks from the individual shots. In the table, we see that the risk from one PA shot in the Skull Exam is 198 per million. Adding an extra PA shot means we add 198 to 746, which is the risk per million without the extra PA shot. The adjusted risk is 944 per million, or 1 chance in 1,059 of cancer. Before the extra shot, the risk was 1 in 1,340.

Example 4: Omitting a Shot

Suppose, in the case of the 15-year-old girl needing the Ribs Exam (Example 2), the physician wonders if the benefit of the AP shot justifies its risk. How much would the cancer risk fall if the physician could omit the AP shot?

ANSWER: From the table, we see that the AP shot accounts for 817 of the 1,408 chances per million. More than half the cancer risk comes from this shot. If it could be omitted in this particular case, then we would subtract 817 from 1,408. The risk would become 591 per million, or 1 chance in 1,692 instead of 1 in 710.

Section 3: No Changes, Age 20 and Older

Example 5: Man

A man at age 40 needs a Lumbo-Sacral Spine Exam. What will be his risk of later radiation-induced cancer from the exam?

ANSWER: His risk will be 1,266 per million, or 1 chance in 790, if his exam matches the Common Exam for adults; it is always described in the age-20 section of the tables. In this case, the Common Exam consists of 3 shots: one AP, one LAT, and one OBL-PA.

Role of the Lowering Factors for Age

If we compare the risks at ages 40 and 20, we see that it is lower at age 40 because of the lower sensitivity described in Chapter 3. How much lower? The lowering factor found next to the entry for age 40 tells us the age-40 risk is 0.372 times lower than the age-20 risk. We can see that it is so, if we multiply the male's risk at age 20, which is 3,402 per million, by 0.372. We get the risk shown in the age-40 table, which is 1,266 per million.

A lowering factor is always a number smaller than 1.0; otherwise, it would not *lower* the value which it multiplies.

All the entries for ages 25 through 55 were obtained by multiplying the risk at age 20 by the appropriate lowering factor for each older age. These lowering factors appear right in the tables, because users will need them for special circumstances. Such a need is illustrated in Example 7.

When the risk at any of the older ages is *divided* by the lowering factor used to obtain it, of course the result is the risk at age 20. Division can "undo" multiplication.

Example 6: Woman

A woman at age 50 needs an Intravenous Pyelogram (I.V.P.) Exam. If she has a routine exam, what will be her risk of later cancer from it?

ANSWER: Her risk will be 82 per million, or 1 chance in 12,195.

Section 4: Changes in Number of Shots, Ages above 20

Example 7: Adding Two Shots

Suppose in the case of the 40-year-old man (Example 5), the physician needs information from a PA shot and from OBL-PA shots on *both* the right and left sides of the lumbo-sacral spine, rather than from just one side?

ANSWER: The cancer risk will, of course, increase with the addition of another OBL-PA shot and the PA shot. To find out how much, we move from the entries for age 40 back to their source: the entries for age 20.

Without the additional shots, the risk at age 20 is 3,402 per million. To this, we must now add the risk of 1,485 per million for the PA shot, and 974 per million for the additional OBL-PA shot. The new total for this exam at age 20 is therefore 5,861 per million.

The last step in converting risks to particular conditions is to end up with the right age. To go from age 20 to age 40, males, we must use the lowering factor, 0.372, which is given in the age-40 table. So we multiply 5,861 by 0.372, and end up with a cancer risk from the exam at age 40 of 2,180 per million, or 1 chance in 459.

Notice that the lowering factor is applied to the *risk per million.* It is *never* applied to the "1 chance in 294" expression.

Example 8: Adding a Borrowed Shot

It turns out that the woman who needed the I.V.P. Exam at age 50 (Example 6) needs two additional shots, which are not at all unusual. To produce the desired diagnostic information, a PA shot is needed, as well as an AP bladder shot. With these additions, what will be her risk of later cancer from the exam?

ANSWER: First, we must move from the entries at age 50 back to their source: the entries at age 20, where the female risk for the average exam is 4,828 per million.

To the risk of 4,828 at age 20, we must now add 343 per million for the PA shot. But there is no bladder AP shot listed. We simply borrow the information from the Cystogram (Bladder) Exam, where we find that the value for the AP shot is 453 per million. Adding 4,828 per million + 343 per million for the PA shot + 453 per million for the bladder AP shot, we obtain a new total of 5,624 per million, or 1 in 178. But *that* risk applies to females at age 20.

The last step for any age above 20 always is to multiply the risk per million by the proper lowering factor. So we multiply 5,624 by the lowering factor of 0.017, which is provided in the table for 50-year-old females. We obtain the revised risk of 95.6, or simply 96 per million (1 chance in 10,417).

Section 5: Low-Dose and High-Dose Offices

Example 9: A Careful Referral

A 5-year-old girl has a serious problem requiring a Thoracic Spine Exam at least once, and maybe more often. The X-ray facility, which the referring physician finds for the parents, generally gives doses 4 times lower than average. What is the child's risk of future cancer from each exam?

ANSWER: Let us assume that an office which is careful about reducing its dose is also careful about reducing the area exposed. The office uses the narrow films for this exam and also collimates the beam to body-part. So we are entitled to use the table for the Thoracic Spine—Narrow Exam.

At the average entrance doses and beam qualities, the girl's risk of future cancer from each exam would be 1,936 per million, or 1 in 516. But in this case, the dose is four times lower than average. Since cancer risk is directly proportional to dose, her risk from each exam would be four times lower than average, too. It would be 1,936 / 4, or 484 per million (1 chance in 2,066). Her risk would be lower if it were possible to use a PA shot instead of an AP shot.

Example 10: A Careless Referral

Suppose the parents of the same 5-year-old girl (Example 9) are referred to a facility which generally uses doses 4 times higher than average. What is the girl's risk of future cancer from each Thoracic Spine Exam?

ANSWER: Let us assume that the office which is careless about its doses is also careless about exposing unnecessary areas of the body. We shall use the table for the Thoracic Spine—Wide Exam.

At the average entrance doses and beam qualities, the girl's risk of future cancer from each exam would be 3,653 per million, or 1 in 274. But she has been referred to an office where the dose is 4 times higher than average. Therefore, her cancer risk from each exam also would be 4 times higher than average. It would be 3,653 × 4, or 14,612 per million (1 chance in 68). If she needs extra shots, or more than one exam, the risk would be even higher.

The risk from each careless exam (higher dose, wider area) is 30 times higher than from the careful exam (lower dose, narrower area): 14,612 versus 484 per million.

Comparison of Two Wide Exams

How big would be the difference if the careful office also had exposed the entire thorax instead of using a narrow field? Since one office is giving entrance doses four times lower than average, and the other is giving doses four times higher than average, there would be a 16-fold difference. The girl's risk would have been 3,653 per million at the average dose. It would be reduced to 913 per million in the careful office, and raised to 14,612 in the careless office—a 16-fold higher risk.

This example of the difference in risk is not an exaggerated one. Dose differences of 20-fold, 50-fold, and even 100-fold for the *same exams* have been measured among radiologic facilities (Chapter 16).

Section 6: The Raising Factors for Smokers

Example 11: Male

A man, age 45, needs a Thoracic Spine Exam. It is possible to obtain the desired information with the narrow films. This man is a lifelong smoker. What will be his risk of future cancer from the Thoracic Spine—Narrow Exam?

ANSWER: The table for age 45 tells us that the risk for a non-smoking male is 78 per million or 1 in 12,820. But because this man is a smoker, we also need to consult the table for age 20, where the smoking factors for adult males and females are provided. They tell us to multiply the male's risk by a raising factor of 2.42. Therefore, this smoker's risk becomes 189 per million, or 1 in 5,291.

Example 12: Female

A female smoker of the same age needs the same exam. What will be her risk?

ANSWER: The table for age 45 tells us that the risk for a non-smoking female is 153 per million, and the table for age 20 tells us that the raising factor for female smokers for this exam is 1.44. Therefore, her risk is 153 × 1.44 = 220 per million.

Reason for Female's Lower Smoking Factor

Notice that the female smoking factor for this exam is much lower than for the males: 1.44 instead of 2.42. The primary reason is that the female's risk of lung cancer is swamped by the even greater risk of breast cancer conferred upon her by this exam's AP shot. To see how this occurs, one can imagine that non-smoking men and women have identical risks of lung cancer from an AP shot if it delivers the same entrance dose; this is not true, as the tables in the fluoroscopy chapter show, but one can imagine it anyway. One can further imagine that a particular AP shot confers equally upon a man and a woman a lung-cancer risk of 100 per million, and that smoking raises the risk to 500 per million for each of them. The smoking factor would be 5.00 for both male and female in such a case. But if the same AP shot also confers a breast-cancer risk of 2,700 per million on *just the woman,* then the female *non-smoker* risk would be 100 (lung)

+ 2700 (breast) = 2,800 per million. The female *smoker* risk would be 500 (lung) + 2,700 (breast) = 3,200 per million. The female smoking factor would not be 500 / 100 = 5.00, like the male's. It would be much lower: 3,200 / 2,800 = 1.14.

In this imaginary example, radiation would have the same effect on the *lung-cancer* risk for both male and female. But the smoking factor does not apply exclusively to the lung-cancer risk. It applies to the non-smoker's total risk from a Common Exam—a risk which is the aggregate risk from all the exposed organs. The factor simply tells how many times worse the risk will be if the patient is a smoker. In the imaginary example, the risk for female smokers is correctly reported as 1.14 times worse than for non-smokers, as demonstrated.

Whenever the risk of breast cancer from a particular exam is reduced relative to the risk of lung cancer, the female's smoking factor rises. For instance, in the Thoracic Spine—Special Exam, the female's smoking factor (2.76) is close to the male's smoking factor (2.98) simply because that particular exam replaces the AP shot with a PA shot, and thus dramatically reduces the female's breast-cancer risk but *not* her lung-cancer risk.

Section 7: Using Other Risk-per-Rad Estimates

In Chapter 2, we indicated why the tables in this book may underestimate the risk of cancer. Nevertheless, the risk values are 17-fold and 38-fold higher, on the average, than estimates which the BEIR and UNSCEAR committees, respectively, might produce *if* they were to produce comparable tables. The reasons are summarized in Chapter 2.

We are happy to demonstrate how simple it is for people to use the tables in this book fully, regardless of what they believe about the true cancer risk per rad.

Example 13: Using Lower Estimates

A user of this book wishes to lower its cancer values to BEIR-level risks. How is this done?

ANSWER: Because the BEIR Committee has made no age-specific estimates of risk, the only thing to do is to treat risks at all ages the same way. For instance, for males at age 30, the cancer risk from the I.V.P. Exam is 4,946 per million exams. One can simply divide 4,946 by 17 to obtain a converted risk of 291 per million. Or one can do the same thing by *multiplying* 4,946 by a "BEIR factor," which would be, of course, 1 / 17 or 0.059. Anyone who wishes to simplify matters could settle for dividing cancer risks by 10.

All the aggregate risks from Common Exams and from single shots can be lowered by *any* preferred lowering factor: 0.50, 0.33, 0.077, 0.025, or whatever. But it is important to remember that conversions are always performed on *cancers per million*. They are never performed on the "1 in 202" type of expression.

Implications for the Young

The lowering of a risk value is a serious matter. The risk estimates from the BEIR and UNSCEAR committees apply to a population of mixed ages; they are not differentiated by age at irradiation. But the available human evidence leads to the conclusion, reflected in Table 2 of Chapter 3, that infants are about 300 times more sensitive to having cancer induced by radiation than are adults at age 55.

One should think at least twice, in making real-world health decisions, before applying a risk-per-rad estimate which is not adjusted for the evidence on age sensitivity. Even several attorneys, after spending days in various courtrooms trying to demolish such kinds of evidence, have unofficially approached one of us (JWG) to ask for personal advice about the consequences for their *own* children of some contemplated X-ray exams.

Example 14: Using Higher Estimates

A user of this book believes that its cancer values are probably underestimates. For instance, rumors often circulate in sections of the disarmament movement that effects from atomic fallout are more severe than already known. Suppose that a person wants to "play it safe" with his or her family's health. How to adjust the numbers?

ANSWER: He or she could easily multiply all this book's values for cancers per million by a raising factor of 2.0.

Although the tables can be adjusted easily for either higher or lower risk-per-rad beliefs, there is no reason to do so unless errors can truly be demonstrated in the risk-per-rad values from *Radiation and Human Health*.

Section 8: Converting Incidence to Mortality

The cancer rates presented in this book are rates of *getting* some sort of cancer later as a result of diagnostic X-ray shots or Common Exams. Fortunately, not everyone who gets cancer dies from it. Therefore, if one asks what the chance is that a person will die from a cancer caused by a particular X-ray exam, the risk values in the tables need lowering.

- The lowering factor for male non-smokers is approximately 0.492; this is another way of saying that, for every 2.03 non-smoking males who get cancer, 1 dies from it.
- The lowering factor for female non-smokers is approximately 0.432; this is another way of saying that their ratio of incidence to mortality from cancer is about 2.32 to 1.0. If 1.0 is divided by 2.32, of course, the value of 0.432 reappears (discussion in Chapter 22, Section 5).

Example 15: Lowering Factors for Death

A man 40 years old needs Pulmonary Arteriography (tables for some common arteriographies are in Chapter 7). What will be his risk of dying from later cancer as a result of the exam?

ANSWER: His risk of *getting* some sort of cancer from the exam is 2,059 per million (or 1 chance in 486), if his exam matches the conditions described in the table. His cancer *mortality* risk from the exam is 2,059 times the lowering factor of 0.492, or 1,013 per million (1 chance in 987).

Example 16: The Difference for Smokers

Suppose the same patient is a lifelong smoker. Then what will be his risk of dying from some sort of cancer as a result of the exam?

ANSWER: Because he is a smoker, we must also apply the raising factor for smoking. The table for age 20 shows the factor as 3.24 times the Common Exam. Therefore, his risk of getting cancer from the exam is 2,059 × 3.24 = 6,671 per million, or 1 in 150. To convert this value to his mortality risk, a *special* lowering factor for smokers is needed because lung cancer is so often fatal; the ratio of incidence to mortality is about 1.2 to 1.0.

For male smokers, the lowering factor to convert incidence to mortality is 0.611, and for female smokers, it is 0.525.

In this example, to obtain the smoker's risk of dying from cancer induced by the Pulmonary Arteriography, we must multiply 6,671 per million by 0.611. His risk is 4,076 per million, or 1 chance in 245.

Both a raising factor (for smoking) and a lowering factor (for converting incidence to mortality) were applied in this example. When a string of risk conversions involves no addition or subtraction, the *sequence* in which we use various raising and lowering factors makes no difference at all.

Section 9: Cumulative Risk from Several Exams

Because the common base of "cancers per million" permits people to add risks, a user of this book is able to evaluate the *aggregate* cancer risk from several different exams. A similar operation was illustrated in Example 3, where the risk from a Common Exam was adjusted for an extra shot. Since risks of leukemia, genetic and congenital injuries, and side-effects from the use of contrast agents are also provided with the common "per million" base, they too can be added whenever appropriate.

Example 17: Sudden Accident

A man (non-smoker) at age 50 is seriously injured in an automobile accident. He needs the Skull, Cervical Spine, Thoracic Spine, and Lumbar Spine X-ray Exams. In addition, his right upper arm (humerus) is broken in three places, and requires examination by X-ray three times to monitor its healing. Also, one insurance company wants its own set of X-rays on the man's skull and neck.

This man is beside himself with worry about radiation-induced cancer. "As if I don't have enough problems from the accident, now they're going to give me cancer too?"

ANSWER: Let's evaluate the size of his cancer risk from the combined exams:

Skull Exam	6.0 per million
Skull, additional exam for insurance company	6.0 per million
Cervical Spine Exam	3.6 per million
Cervical Spine, additional exam for insurance company	3.6 per million
Thoracic Spine—Wide Exam	12.0 per million
Lumbar Spine—Wide Exam	45.0 per million
Humerus Exam, 3 times @ 0.2 per million	0.6 per million
Total	76.8 per million

This man could be spared some anxiety if he knew his risk would be 76.8 per million (rounded off to 77), or 1 chance in 13,000 of some sort of later cancer from all the exams combined. His age is a major risk-reducer.

Example 18: Lifelong Accumulation

The same man has had a number of X-ray exams earlier in his life. How does his cancer risk from all his earlier exams compare with the risk from the set taken due to the accident?

ANSWER: He fell at age 5 from a height onto a hard surface, and he had a Skull Exam. At age 10, serious dental problems were discovered which required much dental work, many X-rays, and frequent monitoring until he got dentures at the age of 50. He estimates that he had a Full-Mouth Dental Exam about every other year from the age of 10 to about 25, and then about once every five years until the age of 50. At age 15, he hurt his knee in sports and had Knee Exams three times. He had a Chest Exam at age 19 when he did his military service. At age 40, he had an Upper Gastro-Intestinal Series when an ulcer was suspected. Let us add up his risks:

Skull Exam, Age 5	746 per million
Full-Mouth Dental Exams	
(tables in Chapter 9):	
Age 10	1,712 per million
Age 12 (Age 10 value used)	1,712 per million
Ages 14, 16 (age 15 value used), two exams @ 1,072	2,144 per million
Ages 18, 20, 22 (age 20 value used), three exams @ 1,120	3,360 per million
Age 24 (age 25 value used)	1,113 per million
Age 30	956 per million
Age 35	684 per million
Age 40	417 per million
Age 45	181 per million
Age 50	17 per million
Knee Exam, Age 15, three times @ 11	33 per million
Chest Exam, Age 19 (age 20 value used)	46 per million
Upper Gastro-Intestinal Series, Age 40:	
Routine films	688 per million
Fluoroscopy (see note below)	550 per million
Total	14,359 per million
	(or 1 in 70)

NOTE: Additional risk from fluoroscopy and spot films varies greatly with the individual case and office; the risk can be figured out as demonstrated in Chapter 6. For the purpose purely of illustration, we shall say it adds a risk 80% as great as the routine films in *this* case. Therefore, 688 per million × 0.80 = 550 per million.

This man's true risk could be higher, because X-ray doses were generally higher in past decades than the average doses used in this book's tables. On the other hand, his true risk could be lower, because he may well have assumed he was having Full-Mouth Exams when he was really having only eight or ten films per exam.

In any case, there would be no point in this man fretting over what is past. Instead of adding up risks from past exams, we favor adding up risks from *contemplated* exams, as an aid to physicians, dentists, patients, and parents in making well-informed decisions.

Section 10: Risk for Ages Not in Tables

In Examples 17 and 18, we dealt with some ages not included in this book's tables. We think that for almost every purpose, using the risk estimates for the nearest provided age is quite satisfactory. However, for people who would prefer to interpolate values between those which are provided, we shall demonstrate how to do it.

Example 19: When Risk is Rising

A boy at age 2 needs an Abdominal Exam (K.U.B.). What will be his risk of later cancer from this exam?

ANSWER: The first step is to look up the risks at the nearest ages below and above age 2, and then subtract the smaller risk from the larger risk. When we look up the K.U.B. Common Exam, however, we see that at age 5, another shot (standing up) is usually added. At age 2, only one AP shot (lying down) is contemplated, so we must extract from the table for 5-year-olds the risk from only one shot, not two.

Risk, AP shot, age 5	= 1,869 per million
Risk, AP shot, age 1	= 1,344 per million
Difference	= 525 per million

The second step is to notice the number of years in the interval between ages (4 years, in this case) and to make it the bottom of a fraction. The top of the fraction is the number of years the patient has advanced along the interval. At age 2, this patient has advanced from age 1 toward age 5 by 1 year. So the fraction is ¼, or 0.25.

The third step is to multiply the difference in risk (525) by the fraction (0.25), which produces a value of 131. This is the share of 525 which the patient has acquired in one year.

The fourth and final step, when the risk is *rising* during the age interval, is to *add* the share obtained in step three to the risk at the younger age: 1,344 + 131 = 1,475 per million, or 1 chance in 678.

Example 20: When Risk Is Falling

Suppose a woman at age 32 has a Hysterosalpingography Exam. What will be her risk of later cancer from the routine films? (The risk from the fluoroscopy and spot films will be *additional*.)

ANSWER: The cancer risk from most but not all Common Exams rises until age 10 and then starts falling, for the reasons given in Chapter 3. The procedure for interpolating when the risk is falling differs from rising (Example 19) only in the fourth step.

Step 1, The Difference:

Risk at age 30	= 1,829
Risk at age 35	= 1,305
Difference	= 524

Step 2, The Fraction: The interval (5 years) goes on the bottom of the fraction, and the number of years along the way (2 years) goes on the top: 2 / 5, or 0.4.

Step 3, The Share of the Difference: The share of the difference is the fraction times the difference. Thus, 0.4 × 524 = 210.

Step 4, Adjustment to Younger Risk: Because the risk is *falling* during this age interval, the share of the difference is *subtracted* from the risk at the younger age: 1,829 − 210 = 1,619 per million, or 1 in 618 from the routine films, fluoroscopy excluded.

Section 11: Dose Adjustments for Individual Shots

Doses for every single shot in this book will often vary from the average, according to the size and shape of the particular patient, the particular equipment and film, and the particular operator. Adjusting the cancer risk for other doses is a routine and brief matter.

Example 21: Lower Dose

A 10-year-old boy needs a Lumbar Spine Exam. The radiologic office decides that this case requires the wide field. The boy's risk of later cancer from the lateral shot would be 6,166 per million under typical conditions, or 1 chance in 162. But this facility is able to obtain the desired information with a much-reduced entrance dose. If the entrance dose is lowered from 1.974 roentgens free-in-air (FIA) to 1.110 R, how much lower will the boy's risk of future cancer be from this shot?

ANSWER: We will never go wrong if we remember two simple principles. Lower dose means lower risk. Therefore what we need is a *lowering* factor (a number less than 1.0) to adjust the cancer risk.

Since cancer risk is directly proportional to dose, we just use the ratio of the low and high doses as the lowering factor. If we divide the lower dose by the higher dose, we are guaranteed to get a ratio less than 1.0.

In this example, 1.110 R divided by 1.974 R produces a lowering factor of 0.562. The factor of 0.562, times the risk of 6,166 per million, yields the answer: 3,465 per million. It is one unbroken operation on a pocket calculator.

Example 22: Higher Dose

Suppose, for the same Lumbar Spine Exam, that the same patient requires a slightly higher dose for the OBL-PA shot than the table shows. If the entrance dose is raised from 0.685 roentgen FIA to 0.812 R, what will be the revised cancer risk from this shot?

ANSWER: Higher doses mean higher cancer risk. Therefore, we immediately know that we must adjust the cancer risk (2,160 per million) by a *raising* factor. We are guaranteed to get such a factor (greater than 1.0) if we divide the bigger dose by the smaller dose: 0.812 R divided by 0.685 R produces a raising factor of 1.185. This factor of 1.185, times the risk of 2,160 per million, yields the answer: 2,560 per million from the OBL-PA shot. This, too, is one unbroken operation on a pocket calculator.

Lastly, the radiologic office is able to obtain the desired information from the AP shot with a narrow field instead of a wide one, and the table shows the risk at 2,283 per million.

With all three shots considered (AP-NAR, LAT, and OBL-PA), what will be the boy's aggregate risk of future cancer from this exam?

AP-NAR	= 2,283 per million
LAT	= 3,465 per million
OBL-PA	= 2,560 per million
Sum	= 8,308 per million, or 1 chance in 120.

Dose adjustments for ages older than 20 years are demonstrated in Section 15 of this chapter.

Section 12: Adjustments for Beam Quality

Cancer risk from individual shots is always matched, in the tables, not only with a specific entrance dose, but also with a specific beam quality. Even though both factors often vary at the same time, each requires a separate adjustment upon the resulting cancer risk.

A higher number for the half-value layer (HVL) means a harder beam, which means a higher average dose delivered to tissue *per roentgen of entrance dose.* Therefore, for a given entrance dose, using a higher (harder) beam quality than the one in the table will increase the cancer risk and call for a raising factor (a multiplier greater than 1.0). Using a lower (softer) beam quality than the one shown in the table will reduce the cancer risk and call for a lowering factor (a multiplier less than 1.0).

However, we *cannot* obtain a lowering factor by simply dividing one HVL value by another, because the beam does not transfer its energy in direct proportion to millimeters of aluminum HVL. There is an intermediate step which takes proper account of the physics of the altered energy-per-photon and the distribution of the energy for AP, PA, LAT, and OBL shots. This step makes use of Special Table D in Chapter 21.

As the reader will soon discover, adjusting for small HVL differences of 0.1 mm aluminum will rarely alter the cancer risk from a particular shot by more than 10%. This can be a relatively small matter compared with differences of 100% and 1,000% in risk—differences caused by differences in entrance dose which sometimes occur between one X-ray facility and another. For many practical purposes, one can forget about adjusting risk for small differences in beam quality.

On the other hand, the radiologic office which knows how to adjust risk values for different beam qualities can evaluate almost any conceivable exam, whether or not it is included in this book (see Section 13). Therefore, we will demonstrate how to use Special Table D by holding entrance dose constant while making some *big* changes in beam quality.

Example 23: Harder Beam Quality

In the Cervical Spine Exam at age 20, the LAT shot confers a cancer risk for males of 42 per million when the entrance dose is 0.170 roentgen FIA and the beam quality has a half-value layer of 2.4 mm aluminum. What would be the cancer risk if the beam were hardened to an HVL of 3.3 mm Al?

ANSWER: In Special Table D, in the column for lateral shots, we look up the entries for both the lower and the higher beam qualities. We will use the ratio of *these entries* as our multiplier for the cancer risk. Since a harder beam increases cancer risk (when entrance dose is held constant), we need a multiplier greater than 1.0. Therefore, we divide the bigger entry by the smaller entry: 1.85 / 1.09 = a raising factor of 1.697. We multiply this factor by the cancer risk: 1.697 × 42 per million = 71 per million. That is the answer, and it is obtained by one unbroken operation on a pocket calculator.

Example 24: Softer Beam Quality

Suppose, for some exam, that the same view were needed as the LAT of the Cervical Spine, but the appropriate beam quality were 1.9 mm Al instead of the 2.4 mm in the table. What would be the cancer risk for the 20-year-old male?

ANSWER: In Special Table D, in the column for lateral shots, we look up the entries for both the lower and higher beam qualities. The ratio of these entries will be our multiplier for cancer risk. Since a softer beam quality decreases cancer risk (when entrance dose is held constant), we need a multiplier less than 1.0. Therefore, we divide the smaller entry by the bigger one: 0.67 / 1.09 = a lowering factor of 0.615. We apply this factor to the cancer risk: 0.615 × 42 per million = 26 per million.

Examples 23 and 24 show the risk almost tripling, from 26 per million to 71 per million. The change is due exclusively to the unusually large changes in beam quality, from 1.9 mm to 3.3 mm Al.

One needs to be cautious, however, before generalizing about risk and beam quality. If a beam for a shot is hardened enough to double the cancer risk, but the entrance dose is simultaneously cut in half, there will be no *net* change in cancer risk. Subtleties of this issue are discussed in Chapter 19, Section 2, "The Derivation of Special Table D."

Beam quality adjustments for ages older than 20 years are demonstrated in Section 15 of this chapter.

Section 13: Evaluating Exams Not in This Book

Every area of the body is covered, in this book, by some exam and generally by several. Cancer risks have been provided for AP, PA, LAT, and OBL beam directions almost literally "from head to toe."

In Example 8, we demonstrated how to borrow shots from one exam and incorporate them into another. Numerous additional exams can be evaluated by making use of the "mix-and-match" potential of the tables. Also, because risk can be easily adjusted for any entrance dose or beam quality, the risk shown from a bone shot can be converted to risk from a soft-tissue shot—and vice versa—if the exposed area and beam direction are the same. For instance, the data for the Cervical Spine Exam might be converted, in the appropriate circumstances, to evaluate the risk from examining the soft tissue of the neck.

The fluoroscopy (FLU) chapter is another resource for evaluating exams not specifically tabulated in this book. Because the FLU tables divide the torso into nine sections and provide risk evaluations for each one, from both AP and PA projections, it is hard to conceive of any AP or PA shot whose consequences could *not* be evaluated simply by adjusting a part of the FLU tables to any desired entrance dose or beam quality.

Lastly, the fluoroscopist trying to minimize cancer risk and the radiologist designing special exams will find the tables in Chapter 21 very useful. Which organs are especially important to keep out of the beam whenever possible? Which ones are the chief generators of cancer? Tables A and B tell, for both males and females. Separately, Table C shows what dose adults *absorb* in each of these cancer-prone organs *per roentgen (FIA) of entrance dose,* if each organ is fully in the field. Values are provided for each organ for five different projections: AP, PA, LAT-LR, OBL-PA, and OBL-AP.

Section 14: Fluoroscopies

The reader is reminded here that the tables for routine films do *not* include the cancer risks from fluoroscopy and spot films. Those risks can also be evaluated, as demonstrated in Chapter 6. The results must then be added to the risks from the routine films, as demonstrated in Example 18.

These evaluations are especially useful if they provide estimates *before* the exam, not afterwards. For contemplated fluoroscopies, reasonable estimates can be made in *advance* about the average size of the field, duration of exposure, and entrance dose for a particular case. Special situations will, of course, arise during some fluoroscopies and lead to doses different from those anticipated.

Section 15: Checklist for Five Common Adjustments

The checklist demonstrated below is just a suggestion; checklists with other sequences will work too. But no checklist will work for ages older than 20 unless its early steps are applied to the data provided for *age 20.* In this checklist, the risks are adjusted for the true age in Step 4.

The goal in each step is simply to find out how much a special condition modifies the *cancer risk.* The risk is the number which matters.

Example 25: A String of Adjustments Demonstrated

A woman, age 30, needs an extensive Pelvis Exam because she was injured in a car crash. She will need not only the AP shot, but also the LAT and two OBL-AP shots. What will be her risk of later cancer from this exam?

Step 1, The Shots: Make a column listing *only* the shots to be used in the contemplated exam, and be sure to note if a shot will be used more than once:

1 AP
1 LAT
2 OBL-AP

Step 2, Dose and Beam Quality: One shot at a time, adjust the cancer risk for dose and HVL changes if appropriate, and build a column of revised risks. If no revisions are necessary, enter the risk from the table. If a shot is taken twice, be careful to double the risk. Step 2 for this Pelvis Exam is demonstrated below.

The AP shot will have a lower entrance dose (0.495 roentgen FIA instead of 0.545 R) and a higher beam quality (HVL of 2.5 mm Al instead of 2.4 mm). So we multiply the given risk (381 per million) by a "string" of two factors—the lowering factor from dose (0.495 / 0.545 = 0.908) and the raising factor from beam quality, out of Special Table D (1.10 / 1.05 = 1.048). Thus: 0.908 × 1.048 × 381 per million = 363 per million. The new risk is not very different from the given risk for this shot.

The LAT shot will have a higher entrance dose (1.500 roentgen FIA instead of 1.343 R) and a higher beam quality (HVL of 2.7 mm Al instead of 2.6 mm), so the given risk of 190 per million will be modified by two raising factors. Thus: (1.500 / 1.343) × (1.37 / 1.28) × (190 per million) = a new risk of 227 per million.

The two OBL-AP shots will use the same entrance dose and beam quality shown in the table, so we multiply the given risk of 828 per million *by 2,* and enter 1,656 in the risk column.

Step 3, Summing Up: Add up all the risks. In this case, their sum is the cancer risk which applies to a 20-year-old woman.

Special Pelvis Exam:

1 AP	=	363 per million
1 LAT	=	227 per million
2 OBL@ 828	=	1,656 per million
Aggregate risk	=	2,246 per million, at age 20

Step 4, Adult Lowering Factor: Always apply a lowering factor to the result in Step 3 when the patient is older than age 20. The age factor is 0.873 for females at age 30, so this patient's risk is 2,246 × 0.873 = 1,961 per million, or 1 chance in 510.

Step 5, Smoking Factor: Multiply the result in Step 4 by the smoking factor found in the age-20 section of the table, if the patient is a smoker. Since there is no smoking factor for any pelvic exam, the analysis for Example 25 is complete at the end of Step 4.

CHAPTER 5

The Routine Films

Although there are no standard conditions of dose, beam quality, and shots per exam which prevail throughout the practice of radiology, we did *not* have to make random choices about such conditions for the risk tables which follow. Whenever possible, we used the data on *typical* American conditions reported in the NEXT surveys (Kereiakes-Rosenstein, 1980). Therefore, similar conditions are likely to be encountered by a patient if an X-ray facility is chosen at random. Such information is all that is wanted, for a great many practical purposes.

When conditions prevailing at a specific facility or designed for a specific patient are known, then the risk values in the tables can be readily adapted, as demonstrated in Chapter 4.

Sometimes a number in our tables for an entrance dose (or a dose to testes, ovaries, or embryo) is sharply different from a dose we have seen elsewhere from particular equipment, particular institutions, particular states, and other countries. Such differences have to be expected, since a 10-fold to 20-fold range in dose for the same exams is common (Table 19 in Chapter 16).

Sometimes, also, a risk value in a table appears too high or too low compared with other shots in the same exam. In such cases, readers are reminded to look at entrance doses, beam qualities, and beam directions; the large effect of beam direction on the dose absorbed by cancer-prone organs is demonstrated in Special Table C, Chapter 21. Additional reasons for some surprising risk entries are reviewed in Chapter 3, Section 5.

Section 1: Terms and Abbreviations Used in the Tables

Throughout the book, we have almost always used the colloquial term "shot" instead of "film," "projection," or "view." One reason is that film is not even used in all circumstances; see mammography in Chapter 8, for instance. And the other terms seem to cause some confusion. The term "projection" is meant to name the surface where the beam enters a patient, and "view" is meant to name the surface of the patient nearest to the film, where the beam emerges. But we have observed some inconsistency on this matter in the literature, so we can try to prevent uncertainty by avoiding both terms altogether and using the word "shot." *We describe shots by the path which the beam travels.*

CE: Common Exam; based in most cases on the NEXT surveys.

AP: Anterior-posterior; X-ray beam enters the patient's front and exits from the back.

PA: Posterior-anterior; X-ray beam travels from back to front.

LAT: Lateral; beam travels from side to side. These tables, like the data provided by Jones and co-workers, are based on the beam entering the patient's left side and exiting from the right side (LAT-LR). The cancer risk will fall somewhat whenever the beam enters the right side (LAT-RL).

OBL: Oblique; the patient is positioned with respect to the beam at an angle halfway between LAT and either AP or PA. Some exams use OBL-AP shots, others use OBL-PA shots, and different facilities sometimes make opposite choices for the same Common Exam.

Nar: Narrow; indicates a narrow rather than a wide film in three of the Common Exams (Barium Swallow, Lumbar Spine, and Thoracic Spine).

Wi: Wide; indicates a wide rather than a narrow film in three of the Common Exams.

Ent Dose: This refers in the tables to *entrance* dose measured in roentgens (R) free-in-air, at the given beam quality, without any backscatter from the patient. Multiplying these doses by 1.21 converts them into skin entrance doses, including backscatter, in the rad unit (Chapter 3, Section 4).

R: Roentgen, a unit for measuring the energy of an X-ray beam. The convertibility of roentgens with rads is demonstrated in Chapter 3, Section 4.

HVL: Half-value layer; a property of the X-ray beam; see Glossary.

mm Al: Millimeters of aluminum.

mrad: Millirad, or 0.001 rad, or one-thousandth of a rad. Rads always refer to absorbed doses, never free-in-air.

<: Less than, below.

< <: Very much less than, far below.

Age New: Newborn infant; often called age 0 in the literature.

Section 2: Rules Followed in the Tables

Shape of Field: All fields are assumed to be rectangular, not circular; exceptions are the Dental Exams, some fluoroscopy, and some spot films.

Length of Field: The vertical length of the field for torso shots is described by customary "landmarks," and such landmarks are the same for all ages unless otherwise specified. In other words, the risks have been based on collimation to body part (not to film size), with the *same* organs receiving the direct beam at *all* ages (Chapter 3, Section 3).

Width of Field: The width exposed at all ages for torso shots is assumed to extend one centimeter beyond the width of the rib-cage, abdominal walls, or pelvis. When the film is wider than the body, we have assumed collimation to body part (not to film size) because body-part collimation reduces dose from scatter. For certain exams, the center of the field (from side to side) is not at the body midplane. In such cases, the table specifies the position of field center.

Testes Dose: This is always the dose in millirads which they would absorb if *no shielding* were used.

Testes, Ovaries, and Embryo Doses: Chapters 12 and 13 show how to evaluate risks from such doses. No lowering factor for age is applied to these doses at ages above 20 years. No values for these doses are provided when the sum from all shots in a Common Exam is below 1 millirad. The embryo dose applies to early pregnancy, before the fetus is large enough to make a woman visibly pregnant.

Leukemia Risk: Above age 20, leukemia risk stays the same as it is at age 20 (details in Chapter 11). Since risk does not fall, *no* lowering factor should be applied for older ages to the leukemia risk at age 20. When the leukemia risk is smaller than 1 per 10 million, it is simply entered as < 1 per 10 million.

Table 3. Factors Used to Derive Pediatric Entrance Doses

Lateral Shots: A somewhat larger lowering factor might be applicable to entrance doses for lateral shots for young children, because they have a rounder shape than adults.

Newborn:	Entrance dose at age 20 times 0.196.
Age 1:	Entrance dose at age 20 times 0.242.
Age 5:	Entrance dose at age 20 times 0.408.
Age 10:	Entrance dose at age 20 times 0.617.
Age 15:	Entrance dose at age 20 times 0.825.

SOURCE: The factors below are composites derived from Webster and co-workers' dose data for a large variety of pediatric X-ray exams (1974).

Pediatric Entrance Doses: Except for the Chest Exam, Cardiac Series, and the Angiographies (Chapter 7), the pediatric entrance doses were obtained by applying the lowering factors in Table 3 to the adult entrance doses.

Smoking Factor: This raising factor for patients who smoke is applied to the *cancer risk per million,* at a given age, from the whole Common Exam (Chapter 4, Section 6). It is *never* applied to the "1 in 2,000" type of expression.

Lowering Factor: This factor, which is provided for ages above 20, is used *only* to convert the Common Exam to special conditions, as demonstrated in Chapter 4. In such cases, it is applied to the adjusted cancer risk per million *at age 20* from the Common Exam. Note that it is applied only to the *cancer risk.*

Shots Less Commonly Used: We include a shot in the Common Exam whenever surveys have shown that, typically, it is more likely than not to be taken. When the probability is only 45% (or even as low as 1%) that a particular shot will be taken during a particular exam, we have evaluated its risk, but that value is *not* included in the risk stated for the typical Common Exam. When the typical frequency of a shot is 1.7 per exam, we say it is most commonly done twice per exam; when its typical frequency is 1.3 per exam, we say it is most commonly done once.

Minimal Rounding Off: We purposely did not round off numbers in these tables to their formally significant figures, because many users of this book will operate on the numbers to convert them to particular conditions. Prematurely rounding off numbers introduces unnecessary uncertainty and error, so reports of this nature should not and do not do it (see BEIR, UNSCEAR, and IAEA reports, for example). All workers in this field are well aware of the true precision of the measurements.

Section 3: The Tables for the Routine Films

ANKLE INCLUDING FOOT

Contrast Medium: No.

Fluoroscopy and Spot Films: No.

Length of Field: Body part.

Organs Generating Most Cancer Risk:
> *Males:* Lymphatic tissue (producing lymphomas, multiple myeloma, and Hodgkin's Disease), skin, connective tissue, bone.
> *Females:* Same.

Special Comments:
- Cancer and leukemia risks are for examination of *one* ankle plus foot.
- Because the risk will be virtually identical regardless of the beam's direction, the table provides one entry for a "basic" shot.
- Cancer risk is based on the estimate that 4.2% of body bone is in each ankle plus foot.

AGE NEW
ANKLE INCLUDING FOOT

Testes, dose CE: $\ll$ 1 mrad
Ovaries, dose CE: $\ll$ 1 mrad

Common Exam (CE): One AP, one LAT, and one OBL (Total: 3 shots)
Rate of future *leukemia* from Common Exam:
> Males: 1 per million = 1 in one million
> Females: 0.6 per million = 1 in 1.7 million

Rate of future *cancer* from Common Exam:
> Males: 13 per million = 1 in 76,900
> Females: 13 per million = 1 in 76,900

Per Shot	Ent Dose	Beam HVL	Male Cancer Risk	Female Cancer Risk
Basic	0.051 R	2.4 mm Al	4.25 per million	4.29 per million

AGE 1   Testes, dose CE: $<<$ 1 mrad
ANKLE INCLUDING FOOT   Ovaries, dose CE: $<<$ 1 mrad

Common Exam (CE): One AP, one LAT, and
                      one OBL (Total: 3 shots)
Rate of future *leukemia* from Common Exam:
          Males: 1 per million = 1 in one million
          Females: 0.7 per million = 1 in 1.4 million
Rate of future *cancer* from Common Exam:
          Males: 14 per million = 1 in 71,400
          Females: 14 per million = 1 in 71,400

Per Shot	*Ent Dose*	*Beam HVL*	*Male Cancer Risk*	*Female Cancer Risk*
Basic	0.063 R	2.4 mm Al	4.68 per million	4.75 per million

AGE 5   Testes, dose CE: $<<$ 1 mrad
ANKLE INCLUDING FOOT   Ovaries, dose CE: $<<$ 1 mrad

Common Exam (CE): One AP, one LAT, and
                      one OBL (Total: 3 shots)
Rate of future *leukemia* from Common Exam:
          Males: 1.3 per million = 1 in 769,000
          Females: 0.8 per million = 1 in 1.25 million
Rate of future *cancer* from Common Exam:
          Males: 19 per million = 1 in 52,600
          Females: 18 per million = 1 in 55,600

Per Shot	*Ent Dose*	*Beam HVL*	*Male Cancer Risk*	*Female Cancer Risk*
Basic	0.106 R	2.4 mm Al	6.44 per million	6.16 per million

AGE 10   Testes, dose CE: $<<$ 1 mrad
ANKLE INCLUDING FOOT   Ovaries, dose CE: $<<$ 1 mrad

Common Exam (CE): One AP, one LAT, and
                      one OBL (Total: 3 shots)
Rate of future *leukemia* from Common Exam:
          Males: 1.2 per million = 1 in 833,000
          Females: 0.8 per million = 1 in 1.25 million
Rate of future *cancer* from Common Exam:
          Males: 22 per million = 1 in 45,450
          Females: 20 per million = 1 in 50,000

Per Shot	*Ent Dose*	*Beam HVL*	*Male Cancer Risk*	*Female Cancer Risk*
Basic	0.160 R	2.4 mm Al	7.46 per million	6.79 per million

AGE 15   Testes, dose CE: $\ll 1$ mrad
ANKLE INCLUDING FOOT   Ovaries, dose CE: $\ll 1$ mrad

Common Exam (CE): One AP, one LAT, and
                     one OBL (Total: 3 shots)
Rate of future *leukemia* from Common Exam:
         Males: 0.7 per million = 1 in 1.4 million
         Females: 0.4 per million = 1 in 2.5 million
Rate of future *cancer* from Common Exam:
         Males: 13 per million = 1 in 76,900
         Females: 11 per million = 1 in 90,900

Per Shot	Ent Dose	Beam HVL	Male Cancer Risk	Female Cancer Risk
Basic	0.214 R	2.4 mm Al	4.18 per million	3.69 per million

AGE 20   Testes, dose CE: $\ll 1$ mrad
ANKLE INCLUDING FOOT   Ovaries, dose CE: $\ll 1$ mrad
                                               Embryo, dose CE: $\ll 1$ mrad

Common Exam (CE): One AP, one LAT, and
                     one OBL (Total: 3 shots)
Rate of future *leukemia* from Common Exam:
         Males: < 0.1 per million = < 1 in 10 million
         Females: < 0.1 per million = < 1 in 10 million
Rate of future *cancer* from Common Exam: **(Smokers)**
         Males: 11 per million = 1 in 90,900   (CE × 1.00)
         Females: 10 per million = 1 in 100,000   (CE × 1.00)

Per Shot	Ent Dose	Beam HVL	Male Cancer Risk	Female Cancer Risk
Basic	0.260 R	2.4 mm Al	3.69 per million	3.19 per million

All values are for the Common Exam

Age 30, Ankle incl. Foot   Cancer Rate. . . . . *(Lowering Factor)*
             Males: 9.4 per million = 1 in 106,400   (Age 20 × 0.854)
             Females: 8.7 per million = 1 in 114,900   (Age 20 × 0.873)
Age 40, Ankle incl. Foot   Cancer Rate. . . . . *(Lowering Factor)*
             Males: 4.1 per million = 1 in 243,900   (Age 20 × 0.372)
             Females: 3.9 per million = 1 in 256,400   (Age 20 × 0.391)
Age 50, Ankle incl. Foot   Cancer Rate. . . . . *(Lowering Factor)*
             Males: 0.16 per million = 1 in 6.2 million   (Age 20 × 0.015)
             Females: 0.17 per million = 1 in 5.9 million   (Age 20 × 0.017)

BARIUM ENEMA

Contrast Medium: Yes. Barium sulfate suspension, administered by enema.

Fluoroscopy and Spot Films: Generally yes. Dose and risks from the FLU and spot films are additional to the values in the following table; for evaluation of risks from FLU, please see Chapter 6.

Length of Field: In the adult AP shot, the field center is at the bi-iliac crest and the body midline. The field (total length = 43.2 cm) extends vertically from the xiphoid process of the sternum down to 5 cm below the pubic symphysis. All pediatric calculations for this exam assume that the same body region (*not* the same length) is encompassed in the field.

Organs Generating Most Cancer Risk:
> *Males:* Stomach, prostate, bladder, kidney, pancreas. Large intestine plus rectum also generate comparable risk.
> *Females:* Corpus uteri, ovaries, stomach, pancreas, cervix, and large intestine plus rectum.

Special Comments:
- Dose estimates to specific organs took account of the shielding provided by the barium sulfate itself.
- In the pediatric examinations, the lateral shot makes a high contribution to cancer risk; see Table 3 in Section 2 of this chapter.
- In this exam, and several others, a particularly steep decrease in risk from the LAT shot occurs as age advances from 10 to 20 years old. The LAT beam direction is characterized by a steep decrease in rads *per entrance roentgen* received by cancer-prone organs, especially in the pelvis, as these organs become protected *in wider bodies* by greater distance and thicker bone-shielding from the incident X-ray beam. See also Chapter 3, Section 5, and Table 3 in Section 2 of this chapter.

AGE NEW	Testes, dose CE: 133 mrads
BARIUM ENEMA	Ovaries, dose CE: 1,046 mrads

Common Exam (CE): Two AP, one PA,
                                    one LAT, and one OBL-PA
Rate of future *leukemia* from Common Exam:
        Males: 84 per million = 1 in 11,900
        Females: 53 per million = 1 in 18,900
Rate of future *cancer* from Common Exam:
        Males: 11,132 per million = 1 in 90
        Females: 12,960 per million = 1 in 77

Per Shot	Ent Dose	Beam HVL	Male Cancer Risk	Female Cancer Risk
AP	0.149 R	3.0 mm Al	1,397 per million	1,376 per million
PA	0.152 R	2.9 mm Al	782 per million	984 per million
LAT	0.786 R	3.1 mm Al	5,777 per million	7,103 per million
OBL-PA	0.264 R	3.0 mm Al	1,779 per million	2,122 per million

AGE 1　　　　　　　　　　　　　　　Testes, dose CE:　140 mrads
BARIUM ENEMA　　　　　　　　　Ovaries, dose CE: 1,006 mrads

Common Exam (CE): Two AP, one PA,
　　　　　　　　one LAT, and one OBL-PA
Rate of future *leukemia* from Common Exam:
　　　　Males:　　　79 per million = 1 in 12,700
　　　　Females:　　49 per million = 1 in 20,400
Rate of future *cancer* from Common Exam:
　　　　Males:　　11,204 per million = 1 in 89
　　　　Females: 12,985 per million = 1 in 77

Per Shot	Ent Dose	Beam HVL	Male Cancer Risk	Female Cancer Risk
AP	0.184 R	3.0 mm Al	1,502 per million	1,449 per million
PA	0.187 R	2.9 mm Al	817 per million	1,005 per million
LAT	0.971 R	3.1 mm Al	5,607 per million	6,959 per million
OBL-PA	0.326 R	3.0 mm Al	1,776 per million	2,123 per million

AGE 5　　　　　　　　　　　　　　　Testes, dose CE:　155 mrads
BARIUM ENEMA　　　　　　　　　Ovaries, dose CE: 1,360 mrads

Common Exam (CE): Two AP, one PA,
　　　　　　　　one LAT, and one OBL-PA
Rate of future *leukemia* from Common Exam:
　　　　Males:　　　107 per million = 1 in 9,350
　　　　Females:　　67 per million = 1 in 14,930
Rate of future *cancer* from Common Exam:
　　　　Males:　　14,706 per million = 1 in 68
　　　　Females: 15,808 per million = 1 in 63

Per Shot	Ent Dose	Beam HVL	Male Cancer Risk	Female Cancer Risk
PA	0.310 R	3.0 mm Al	2,082 per million	1,892 per million
PA	0.315 R	2.9 mm Al	1,142 per million	1,282 per million
LAT	1.636 R	3.1 mm Al	7,044 per million	8,205 per million
OBL-PA	0.550 R	3.0 mm Al	2,356 per million	2,537 per million

AGE 10   Testes, dose CE: 160 mrads
BARIUM ENEMA   Ovaries, dose CE: 1,694 mrads

Common Exam (CE): Two AP, one PA,
                    one LAT, and one OBL-PA
Rate of future *leukemia* from Common Exam:
        Males: 126 per million = 1 in 7,400
        Females: 79 per million = 1 in 12,660
Rate of future *cancer* from Common Exam:
        Males: 15,906 per million = 1 in 63
        Females: 16,411 per million = 1 in 61

Per Shot	Ent Dose	Beam HVL	Male Cancer Risk	Female Cancer Risk
AP	0.469 R	3.0 mm Al	2,396 per million	2,019 per million
PA	0.477 R	2.9 mm Al	1,288 per million	1,359 per million
LAT	2.475 R	3.1 mm Al	7,432 per million	8,412 per million
OBL-PA	0.832 R	3.0 mm Al	2,394 per million	2,602 per million

AGE 15   Testes, dose CE: 106 mrads
BARIUM ENEMA   Ovaries, dose CE: 1,452 mrads

Common Exam (CE): Two AP, one PA,
                    one LAT, and one OBL-PA
Rate of future *leukemia* from Common Exam:
        Males: 120 per million = 1 in 8,330
        Females: 75 per million = 1 in 13,300
Rate of future *cancer* from Common Exam:
        Males: 7,135 per million = 1 in 140
        Females: 6,709 per million = 1 in 149

Per Shot	Ent Dose	Beam HVL	Male Cancer Risk	Female Cancer Risk
AP	0.627 R	3.0 mm Al	1,350 per million	1,104 per million
PA	0.638 R	2.9 mm Al	663 per million	674 per million
LAT	3.309 R	3.1 mm Al	2,666 per million	2,760 per million
OBL-PA	1.112 R	3.0 mm Al	1,106 per million	1,067 per million

AGE 20   Testes, dose CE: 74 mrads
BARIUM ENEMA   Ovaries, dose CE: 804 mrads
                                           Embryo, dose CE: 812 mrads
Common Exam (CE): Two AP, one PA,
                    one LAT, and one OBL-PA
Rate of future *leukemia* from Common Exam:
        Males: 85 per million = 1 in 11,800
        Females: 53 per million = 1 in 18,900
Rate of future *cancer* from Common Exam: **(Smokers)**
        Males: 4,942 per million = 1 in 202   (CE × 1.04)
        Females: 4,353 per million = 1 in 230   (CE × 1.03)

Per Shot	Ent Dose	Beam HVL	Male Cancer Risk	Female Cancer Risk
AP	0.760 R	3.0 mm Al	1,227 per million	983 per million
PA	0.773 R	2.9 mm Al	569 per million	529 per million
LAT	4.011 R	3.1 mm Al	1,182 per million	1,191 per million
OBL-PA	1.348 R	3.0 mm Al	737 per million	667 per million

All values are for the Common Exam

Age 25, Barium Enema	Cancer Rate...............	*(Lowering Factor)*
Males:	4,912 per million = 1 in 204	(Age 20 × 0.994)
Females:	4,301 per million = 1 in 232	(Age 20 × 0.988)
Age 30, Barium Enema	Cancer Rate...............	*(Lowering Factor)*
Males:	4,220 per million = 1 in 237	(Age 20 × 0.854)
Females:	3,800 per million = 1 in 263	(Age 20 × 0.873)
Age 35, Barium Enema	Cancer Rate...............	*(Lowering Factor)*
Males:	3,020 per million = 1 in 331	(Age 20 × 0.611)
Females:	2,712 per million = 1 in 369	(Age 20 × 0.623)
Age 40, Barium Enema	Cancer Rate...............	*(Lowering Factor)*
Males:	1,838 per million = 1 in 544	(Age 20 × 0.372)
Females:	1,702 per million = 1 in 588	(Age 20 × 0.391)
Age 45, Barium Enema	Cancer Rate...............	*(Lowering Factor)*
Males:	801 per million = 1 in 1,248	(Age 20 × 0.162)
Females:	766 per million = 1 in 1,305	(Age 20 × 0.176)
Age 50, Barium Enema	Cancer Rate...............	*(Lowering Factor)*
Males:	74 per million = 1 in 13,514	(Age 20 × 0.015)
Females:	74 per million = 1 in 13,514	(Age 20 × 0.017)
Age 55, Barium Enema	Cancer Rate...............	*(Lowering Factor)*
Males:	49 per million = 1 in 20,408	(Age 20 × 0.010)
Females:	52 per million = 1 in 19,231	(Age 20 × 0.012)

BARIUM SWALLOW—WIDE

Contrast Medium: Yes. Barium sulfate suspension, administered by mouth.

Fluoroscopy and Spot Films: Sometimes. If FLU is done, doses and risks are additional to the values in the following tables; for evaluation of risks from FLU, see Chapter 6.

Length of Field: In the adult AP shot, the field center is 9.5 cm below the sternal notch at body midline. The field (total length = 43.2 cm) extends from 2 cm below the external auditory canal to 10 cm above the bi-iliac crest. All pediatric calculations for this exam assume that the same body region (*not* the same length) is encompassed in the field.

Organs Generating Most Cancer Risk:
  Males: Bronchi, kidneys, stomach, larynx, large intestine, pancreas.
  Females: Breasts, bronchi, large intestine, kidney, pancreas, stomach.

Barium Swallow—Wide *(continued)*

The breasts contribute 55% of the cancer risk from this exam. Even though the esophagus is the organ examined, it ranks lower in cancer risk than the organs listed above, due to its lower *spontaneous* cancer rate (Chapter 2, Myth 3).

Special Comments:

- This exam is designated "wide" not to suggest that its field is any wider than normal (see Section 2 of this chapter), but rather to help distinguish it from the Barium Swallow—Narrow Exam, which follows.
- The risk from identical shots would be higher if no barium were present. The values in this table incorporate a significant reduction in stomach-cancer risk, for instance, because the barium itself shields one wall of the stomach from much of the beam.

AGE NEW   Testes, dose CE: < 1 mrad
BARIUM SWALLOW—WIDE   Ovaries, dose CE: 3 mrads

Common Exam (CE): One AP, one LAT, and
                       two OBL-PA (Total: 4 shots)
Rate of future *leukemia* from Common Exam:
        Males: 11 per million = 1 in 90,900
        Females: 7 per million = 1 in 143,000
Rate of future *cancer* from Common Exam:
        Males: 1,265 per million = 1 in 791
        Females: 2,395 per million = 1 in 418

Per Shot	*Ent Dose*	*Beam HVL*	*Male Cancer Risk*	*Female Cancer Risk*
AP	0.070 R	2.2 mm Al	219 per million	774 per million
PA	0.057 R	2.4 mm Al	189 per million	232 per million
LAT	0.036 R	3.0 mm Al	204 per million	343 per million
OBL-PA	0.123 R	2.4 mm Al	421 per million	639 per million

AGE 1   Testes, dose CE: < 1 mrad
BARIUM SWALLOW—WIDE   Ovaries, dose CE: 3 mrads

Common Exam (CE): One AP, one LAT, and
                       two OBL-PA (Total: 4 shots)
Rate of future *leukemia* from Common Exam:
        Males: 12 per million = 1 in 83,300
        Females: 7 per million = 1 in 143,000
Rate of future *cancer* from Common Exam:
        Males: 1,357 per million = 1 in 737
        Females: 2,599 per million = 1 in 385

Per Shot	Ent Dose	Beam HVL	Male Cancer Risk	Female Cancer Risk
AP	0.086 R	2.2 mm Al	259 per million	894 per million
PA	0.070 R	2.4 mm Al	206 per million	252 per million
LAT	0.045 R	3.0 mm Al	202 per million	359 per million
OBL-PA	0.152 R	2.4 mm Al	448 per million	673 per million

AGE 5   Testes, dose CE: < 1 mrad
BARIUM SWALLOW—WIDE   Ovaries, dose CE: 4 mrads

Common Exam (CE): One AP, one LAT, and
                      two OBL-PA (Total: 4 shots)
Rate of future *leukemia* from Common Exam:
        Males: 16 per million = 1 in 62,500
        Females: 10 per million = 1 in 100,000
Rate of future *cancer* from Common Exam:
        Males: 1,806 per million = 1 in 554
        Females: 3,397 per million = 1 in 294

Per Shot	Ent Dose	Beam HVL	Male Cancer Risk	Female Cancer Risk
AP	0.146 R	2.2 mm Al	338 per million	1,215 per million
PA	0.118 R	2.4 mm Al	289 per million	324 per million
LAT	0.076 R	3.0 mm Al	260 per million	452 per million
OBL-PA	0.256 R	2.4 mm Al	604 per million	865 per million

AGE 10   Testes, dose CE: < 1 mrad
BARIUM SWALLOW—WIDE   Ovaries, dose CE: 8 mrads

Common Exam (CE): One AP, one LAT, and
                      two OBL-PA (Total: 4 shots)
Rate of future *leukemia* from Common Exam:
        Males: 19 per million = 1 in 52,600
        Females: 12 per million = 1 in 83,300
Rate of future *cancer* from Common Exam:
        Males: 1,985 per million = 1 in 504
        Females: 3,631 per million = 1 in 275

Per Shot	Ent Dose	Beam HVL	Male Cancer Risk	Female Cancer Risk
AP	0.220 R	2.2 mm Al	392 per million	1,360 per million
PA	0.178 R	2.4 mm Al	326 per million	341 per million
LAT	0.115 R	3.0 mm Al	275 per million	471 per million
OBL-PA	0.387 R	2.4 mm Al	659 per million	900 per million

AGE 15   Testes, dose CE: < 1 mrad
BARIUM SWALLOW—WIDE   Ovaries, dose CE: 5 mrads

Common Exam (CE): One AP, one LAT, and
                    two OBL-PA (Total: 4 shots)
Rate of future *leukemia* from Common Exam:
          Males: 17 per million = 1 in 58,800
          Females: 11 per million = 1 in 90,900
Rate of future *cancer* from Common Exam:
          Males: 916 per million = 1 in 1,092
          Females: 1,795 per million = 1 in 557

Per Shot	Ent Dose	Beam HVL	Male Cancer Risk	Female Cancer Risk
AP	0.295 R	2.2 mm Al	219 per million	776 per million
PA	0.238 R	2.4 mm Al	172 per million	164 per million
LAT	0.153 R	3.0 mm Al	105 per million	217 per million
OBL-PA	0.517 R	2.4 mm Al	296 per million	401 per million

AGE 20   Testes, dose CE: <1 mrad
BARIUM SWALLOW—WIDE   Ovaries, dose CE: 1 mrad
                                                    Embryo, dose CE: <1 mrad

Common Exam (CE): One AP, one LAT, and
                    two OBL-PA (Total: 4 shots)
Rate of future *leukemia* from Common Exam:
          Males: 14 per million = 1 in 71,400
          Females: 9 per million = 1 in 111,000
Rate of future *cancer* from Common Exam: **(Smokers)**
          Males: 730 per million = 1 in 1,370   (CE × 2.92)
          Females: 1,487 per million = 1 in 672   (CE × 1.58)

Per Shot	Ent Dose	Beam HVL	Male Cancer Risk	Female Cancer Risk
AP	0.357 R	2.2 mm Al	218 per million	738 per million
PA	0.289 R	2.4 mm Al	155 per million	124 per million
LAT	0.186 R	3.0 mm Al	60 per million	151 per million
OBL-PA	0.627 R	2.4 mm Al	226 per million	299 per million

All values are for the Common Exam

Age 25, Barium Swal. Wide   Cancer Rate............... *(Lowering Factor)*
          Males: 726 per million = 1 in 1,377   (Age 20 × 0.994)
          Females: 1,469 per million = 1 in 681   (Age 20 × 0.988)
Age 30, Barium Swal. Wide   Cancer Rate............... *(Lowering Factor)*
          Males: 623 per million = 1 in 1,605   (Age 20 × 0.854)
          Females: 1,298 per million = 1 in 770   (Age 20 × 0.873)

Age 35, Barium Swal. Wide   Cancer Rate.............. *(Lowering Factor)*
      Males: 446 per million = 1 in 2,242   (Age 20 × 0.611)
      Females: 926 per million = 1 in 1,080   (Age 20 × 0.623)
Age 40, Barium Swal. Wide   Cancer Rate.............. *(Lowering Factor)*
      Males: 272 per million = 1 in 3,676   (Age 20 × 0.372)
      Females: 581 per million = 1 in 1,721   (Age 20 × 0.391)
Age 45, Barium Swal. Wide   Cancer Rate.............. *(Lowering Factor)*
      Males: 118 per million = 1 in 8,475   (Age 20 × 0.162)
      Females: 262 per million = 1 in 3,817   (Age 20 × 0.176)
Age 50, Barium Swal. Wide   Cancer Rate.............. *(Lowering Factor)*
      Males: 11 per million = 1 in 90,900   (Age 20 × 0.015)
      Females: 25 per million = 1 in 40,000   (Age 20 × 0.017)
Age 55, Barium Swal. Wide   Cancer Rate.............. *(Lowering Factor)*
      Males: 7.3 per million = 1 in 137,000   (Age 20 × 0.010)
      Females: 18 per million = 1 in 55,600   (Age 20 × 0.012)

BARIUM SWALLOW—NARROW

Contrast Medium: Yes. Barium sulfate suspension, administered by mouth.

Fluoroscopy and Spot Films: Sometimes. See notes for Barium Swallow—Wide.

Length of Field: Vertical dimensions are the same as for Barium Swallow—Wide Exam.

Width of Field: The field is *centered* as in the Wide Exam, but the width of the total field is half that of the wide film; it is 17.8 cm wide instead of the usual 35.6 cm.

Organs Generating Most Cancer Risk:
    Males: Bronchi, larynx, stomach, kidney, large intestine, pancreas.
    Females: Breasts, bronchi, large intestine, stomach, kidney, thyroid.

Special Comment:
- Because the risk of breast cancer is greatly reduced by using the narrow films, the risks for males and females are closer in magnitude than they are from the same exam done with wide films.

AGE NEW   Testes, dose CE: < 1 mrad
BARIUM SWALLOW—NARROW   Ovaries, dose CE: 3 mrad

Common Exam (CE): One AP, one LAT, and
                 two OBL-PA (Total: 4 shots)
Rate of future *leukemia* from Common Exam:
      Males: 7 per million = 1 in 143,000
      Females: 4 per million = 1 in 250,000
Rate of future *cancer* from Common Exam:
      Males: 799 per million = 1 in 1,252
      Females: 1,097 per million = 1 in 912

Age New, Barium Swallow—Narrow *(continued)*

Per Shot	Ent Dose	Beam HVL	Male Cancer Risk	Female Cancer Risk
AP-Nar	0.070 R	2.2 mm Al	146 per million	356 per million
LAT-Nar	0.036 R	3.0 mm Al	147 per million	141 per million
OBL-PA-Nar	0.123 R	2.4 mm Al	253 per million	300 per million

AGE 1
BARIUM SWALLOW—NARROW

Testes, dose CE: <1 mrad
Ovaries, dose CE: 1.8 mrad

Common Exam (CE): One AP, one LAT, AND
           two OBL-PA (Total: 4 shots)
Rate of future *leukemia* from Common Exam:
      Males: 8 per million = 1 in 125,000
      Females: 5 per million = 1 in 200,000
Rate of future *cancer* from Common Exam:
      Males: 857 per million = 1 in 1,167
      Females: 1,190 per million = 1 in 840

Per Shot	Ent Dose	Beam HVL	Male Cancer Risk	Female Cancer Risk
AP-Nar	0.086 R	2.2 mm Al	174 per million	411 per million
LAT-Nar	0.045 R	3.0 mm Al	145 per million	147 per million
OBL-PA-Nar	0.152 R	2.4 mm Al	269 per million	316 per million

AGE 5
BARIUM SWALLOW—NARROW

Testes, dose CE: < 1 mrad
Ovaries, dose CE: 2.4 mrads

Common Exam (CE): One AP, one LAT, and
           two OBL-PA (Total: 4 shots)
Rate of future *leukemia* from Common Exam:
      Males: 10 per million = 1 in 100,000
      Females: 6 per million = 1 in 167,000
Rate of future *cancer* from Common Exam:
      Males: 1,137 per million = 1 in 880
      Females: 1,558 per million = 1 in 642

Per Shot	Ent Dose	Beam HVL	Male Cancer Risk	Female Cancer Risk
AP-Nar	0.146 R	2.2 mm Al	226 per million	559 per million
LAT-Nar	0.076 R	3.0 mm Al	187 per million	185 per million
OBL-PA-Nar	0.256 R	2.4 mm Al	362 per million	407 per million

AGE 10   Testes, dose CE: < 1 mrad
BARIUM SWALLOW—NARROW   Ovaries, dose CE: 4.8 mrads

Common Exam (CE): One AP, one LAT, and
                    two OBL-PA (Total: 4 shots)
Rate of future *leukemia* from Common Exam:
        Males: 12 per million = 1 in 83,300
        Females: 8 per million = 1 in 125,000
Rate of future *cancer* from Common Exam:
        Males: 1,251 per million = 1 in 799
        Females: 1,665 per million = 1 in 601

Per Shot	Ent Dose	Beam HVL	Male Cancer Risk	Female Cancer Risk
AP-Nar	0.220 R	2.2 mm Al	263 per million	626 per million
LAT-Nar	0.115 R	3.0 mm Al	198 per million	193 per million
OBL-PA-Nar	0.387 R	2.4 mm Al	395 per million	423 per million

AGE 15   Testes, dose CE: < 1 mrad
BARIUM SWALLOW—NARROW   Ovaries, dose CE: 3 mrads

Common Exam (CE): One AP, one LAT, and
                    two OBL-PA (Total: 4 shots)
Rate of future *leukemia* from Common Exam:
        Males: 11 per million = 1 in 90,900
        Females: 7 per million = 1 in 143,000
Rate of future *cancer* from Common Exam:
        Males: 579 per million = 1 in 1,727
        Females: 822 per million = 1 in 1,217

Per Shot	Ent Dose	Beam HVL	Male Cancer Risk	Female Cancer Risk
AP-Nar	0.295 R	2.2 mm Al	147 per million	357 per million
LAT-Nar	0.153 R	3.0 mm Al	76 per million	89 per million
OBL-PA-Nar	0.517 R	2.4 mm Al	178 per million	188 per million

AGE 20   Testes, dose CE: < 1 mrad
BARIUM SWALLOW—NARROW   Ovaries, dose CE: < 1 mrad
                                               Embryo, dose CE: < 1 mrad

Common Exam (CE): One AP, one LAT, and
                    two OBL-PA (Total: 4 shots)
Rate of future *leukemia* from Common Exam:
        Males: 9 per million = 1 in 111,000
        Females: 5.5 per million = 1 in 182,000
Rate of future *cancer* from Common Exam: **(Smokers)**
        Males: 461 per million = 1 in 2,169   (CE × 3.40)
        Females: 685 per million = 1 in 1,460   (CE × 1.99)

Age 20, Barium Swallow—Narrow *(continued)*

Per Shot	Ent Dose	Beam HVL	Male Cancer Risk	Female Cancer Risk
AP-Nar	0.357 R	2.2 mm Al	146 per million	343 per million
LAT-Nar	0.186 R	3.0 mm Al	43 per million	62 per million
OBL-PA-Nar	0.627 R	2.4 mm Al	136 per million	140 per million

All values are for the Common Exam

Age 25, Barium Swal. Narrow Cancer Rate. . . . . *(Lowering Factor)*
        Males: 458 per million = 1 in 2,183   (Age 20 × 0.994)
        Females: 677 per million = 1 in 1,477   (Age 20 × 0.988)
Age 30, Barium Swal. Narrow Cancer Rate. . . . . *(Lowering Factor)*
        Males: 394 per million = 1 in 2,538   (Age 20 × 0.854)
        Females: 598 per million = 1 in 1,672   (Age 20 × 0.873)
Age 35, Barium Swal. Narrow Cancer Rate. . . . . *(Lowering Factor)*
        Males: 282 per million = 1 in 3,546   (Age 20 × 0.611)
        Females: 427 per million = 1 in 2,341   (Age 20 × 0.623)
Age 40, Barium Swal. Narrow Cancer Rate. . . . . *(Lowering Factor)*
        Males: 330 per million = 1 in 3,030   (Age 20 × 0.372)
        Females: 268 per million = 1 in 3,731   (Age 20 × 0.391)
Age 45, Barium Swal. Narrow Cancer Rate. . . . . *(Lowering Factor)*
        Males: 75 per million = 1 in 13,330   (Age 20 × 0.162)
        Females: 121 per million = 1 in 8,264   (Age 20 × 0.176)
Age 50, Barium Swal. Narrow Cancer Rate. . . . . *(Lowering Factor)*
        Males: 6.9 per million = 1 in 145,000   (Age 20 × 0.015)
        Females: 12 per million = 1 in 83,300   (Age 20 × 0.017)
Age 55, Barium Swal. Narrow Cancer Rate. . . . . *(Lowering Factor)*
        Males: 4.6 per million = 1 in 217,000   (Age 20 × 0.010)
        Females: 8.2 per million = 1 in 122,000   (Age 20 × 0.012)

CARDIAC SERIES—PEDIATRIC

Contrast Medium: No.

Fluoroscopy and Spot Films: No.

Length of Field: Field center is at a level approximately 3 cm above the nipples in body midline. The field extends vertically from the external auditory meatus to the bottom of the twelfth rib (Rosenstein and co-workers, 1979) for all ages.

Organs Generating Most Cancer Risk:
    Males: Bronchi, stomach, kidneys, pancreas, larynx, esophagus.
    Females: Breasts, stomach, pancreas, bronchi, kidneys, large intestine.

Special Comments:
- This exam is evaluated for ages 5, 10, and 15.
- Note that the AP and AP-OBL shots are commonly used for the 5-year-olds, whereas the PA direction is used for other ages. Whenever the PA direction can be used for the 5-year-old female, the risk of later breast cancer is much reduced.
- The Cardiac Series is one of the few exams for which pediatric entrance doses do not follow the schedule in Table 3 (this chapter, Section 2).

AGE 5   Testes, dose CE: < 1 mrad
CARDIAC SERIES—PEDIATRIC   Ovaries, dose CE: < 1 mrad

Common Exam (CE): One AP, one LAT, and
                  two OBL-AP (Total: 4 shots)
Rate of future *leukemia* from Common Exam:
        Males: 4 per million = 1 in 250,000
        Females: 2.4 per million = 1 in 426,700
Rate of future *cancer* from Common Exam:
        Males: 731 per million = 1 in 1,368
        Females: 1,553 per million = 1 in 644

Per Shot	Ent Dose	Beam HVL	Male Cancer Risk	Female Cancer Risk
AP	0.027 R	2.4 mm Al	102 per million	280 per million
PA	0.014 R	2.5 mm Al	40 per million	46 per million
LAT	0.044 R	2.8 mm Al	177 per million	271 per million
OBL-PA	0.064 R	2.5 mm Al	198 per million	275 per million
OBL-AP	0.064 R	2.5 mm Al	226 per million	501 per million

AGE 10   Testes, dose CE: < 1 mrad
CARDIAC SERIES—PEDIATRIC   Ovaries, dose CE: < 1 mrad

Common Exam (CE): One PA, one LAT, and
                  two OBL-PA (Total: 4 shots)
Rate of future *leukemia* from Common Exam:
        Males: 3 per million = 1 in 333,000
        Females: 2 per million = 1 in 500,000
Rate of future *cancer* from Common Exam:
        Males: 465 per million = 1 in 2,151
        Females: 639 per million = 1 in 1,565

Per Shot	Ent Dose	Beam HVL	Male Cancer Risk	Female Cancer Risk
AP	0.031 R	2.4 mm Al	86 per million	242 per million
PA	0.016 R	2.5 mm Al	31 per million	35 per million
LAT	0.051 R	2.8 mm Al	136 per million	204 per million
OBL-PA	0.073 R	2.5 mm Al	149 per million	200 per million

AGE 15
CARDIAC SERIES—PEDIATRIC

Testes, dose CE: < 1 mrad
Ovaries, dose CE: < 1 mrad

Common Exam (CE): One PA, one LAT, and
two OBL-PA (Total: 4 shots)
Rate of future *leukemia* from Common Exam:
Males: 3.6 per million = 1 in 278,000
Females: 2.3 per million = 1 in 435,000
Rate of future *cancer* from Common Exam:
Males: 202 per million = 1 in 4,950
Females: 278 per million = 1 in 3,597

Per Shot	Ent Dose	Beam HVL	Male Cancer Risk	Female Cancer Risk
AP	0.042 R	2.4 mm Al	54 per million	134 per million
PA	0.021 R	2.5 mm Al	16 per million	16 per million
LAT	0.068 R	2.8 mm Al	52 per million	88 per million
OBL-PA	0.098 R	2.5 mm Al	67 per million	87 per million

CERVICAL SPINE

Contrast Medium: No.

Fluoroscopy and Spot Films: No.

Length of Field: The field center is 8.5 cm below the external acoustic meatus in the adult. Total length of field is only 30.5 cm (in contrast to the 43.2 cm length of field for many exams). Field extends from vertex to approximately 6 cm below the sternal notch. Field is adjusted to encompass the same organs for the pediatric examinations.

Organs Generating Most Cancer Risk:
Males: Larynx, lips, tongue, pharynx, mouth, thyroid.
Females: Thyroid, mouth, tongue, pharynx, breasts, larynx.

Special Comments:
- In the AP shot, the field is centered at body midline. In the LAT shot, it is centered 5 cm to patient's rear.
- A smaller field size is sometimes used; its use lowers the risk.

AGE NEW
CERVICAL SPINE

Testes, dose CE: < 1 mrad
Ovaries, dose CE: < 1 mrad

Common Exam (CE): Two AP, one LAT, and
one OBL-PA (Total: 4 shots)

Rate of future *leukemia* from Common Exam:
        Males: 0.7 per million = 1 in 1,430,000
        Females: 0.5 per million = 1 in 2,000,000
Rate of future *cancer* from Common Exam:
        Males: 249 per million = 1 in 4,016
        Females: 178 per million = 1 in 5,618

Per Shot	Ent Dose	Beam HVL	Male Cancer Risk	Female Cancer Risk
AP	0.051 R	2.2 mm Al	59 per million	47 per million
PA	0.029 R	2.4 mm Al	33 per million	21 per million
LAT	0.033 R	2.4 mm Al	70 per million	45 per million
OBL-PA	0.039 R	2.4 mm Al	61 per million	39 per million

AGE 1   Testes, dose CE: < 1 mrad
CERVICAL SPINE   Ovaries, dose CE: < 1 mrad

Common Exam (CE): Two AP, one LAT, and
                        one OBL-PA (Total: 4 shots)
Rate of future *leukemia* from Common Exam:
        Males: 0.9 per million = 1 in 1,110,000
        Females: 0.5 per million = 1 in 2,000,000
Rate of future *cancer* from Common Exam:
        Males: 275 per million = 1 in 3,636
        Females: 204 per million = 1 in 4,902

Per Shot	Ent Dose	Beam HVL	Male Cancer Risk	Female Cancer Risk
AP	0.063 R	2.2 mm Al	68 per million	56 per million
PA	0.036 R	2.4 mm Al	37 per million	23 per million
LAT	0.041 R	2.4 mm Al	73 per million	49 per million
OBL-PA	0.048 R	2.4 mm Al	66 per million	43 per million

AGE 5   Testes, dose CE: < 1 mrad
CERVICAL SPINE   Ovaries, dose CE: < 1 mrad

Common Exam (CE): Two AP, one LAT, and
                        one OBL-PA (Total: 4 shots)
Rate of future *leukemia* from Common Exam:
        Males: 1.2 per million = 1 in 833,000
        Females: 0.8 per million = 1 in 1,250,000
Rate of future *cancer* from Common Exam:
        Males: 387 per million = 1 in 2,584
        Females: 265 per million = 1 in 3,774

Age 5, Cervical Spine *(continued)*

Per Shot	Ent Dose	Beam HVL	Male Cancer Risk	Female Cancer Risk
AP	0.106 R	2.2 mm Al	100 per million	79 per million
PA	0.061 R	2.4 mm Al	55 per million	30 per million
LAT	0.069 R	2.4 mm Al	98 per million	56 per million
OBL-PA	0.081 R	2.4 mm Al	89 per million	51 per million

AGE 10
CERVICAL SPINE

Testes, dose CE: < 1 mrad
Ovaries, dose CE: < 1 mrad

Common Exam (CE): Two AP, one LAT, and
one OBL-PA (Total: 4 shots)
Rate of future *leukemia* from Common Exam:
Males: 1.5 per million = 1 in 667,000
Females: 1 per million = 1 in 1,000,000
Rate of future *cancer* from Common Exam:
Males: 453 per million = 1 in 2,208
Females: 293 per million = 1 in 3,413

Per Shot	Ent Dose	Beam HVL	Male Cancer Risk	Female Cancer Risk
AP	0.160 R	2.2 mm Al	120 per million	88 per million
PA	0.092 R	2.4 mm Al	60 per million	32 per million
LAT	0.105 R	2.4 mm Al	111 per million	60 per million
OBL-PA	0.122 R	2.4 mm Al	102 per million	57 per million

AGE 15
CERVICAL SPINE

Testes, dose CE: < 1 mrad
Ovaries, dose CE: < 1 mrad

Common Exam (CE): Two AP, one LAT, and
one OBL-PA (Total: 4 shots)
Rate of future *leukemia* from Common Exam:
Males: 1.6 per million = 1 in 625,000
Females: 1 per million = 1 in 1,000,000
Rate of future *cancer* from Common Exam:
Males: 249 per million = 1 in 4,016
Females: 166 per million = 1 in 6,024

Per Shot	Ent Dose	Beam HVL	Male Cancer Risk	Female Cancer Risk
AP	0.214 R	2.2 mm Al	72 per million	54 per million
PA	0.124 R	2.4 mm Al	34 per million	18 per million
LAT	0.140 R	2.4 mm Al	53 per million	29 per million
OBL-PA	0.163 R	2.4 mm Al	52 per million	29 per million

AGE 20
CERVICAL SPINE

Testes, dose CE: < 1 mrad
Ovaries, dose CE: < 1 mrad
Embryo, dose CE: < 1 mrad

Common Exam (CE): Two AP, one LAT, and
one OBL-PA (Total: 4 shots)
Rate of future *leukemia* from Common Exam:
Males: 1.8 per million = 1 in 556,000
Females: 1.1 per million = 1 in 909,000
Rate of future *cancer* from Common Exam: **(Smokers)**
Males: 240 per million = 1 in 4,167   (CE × 1.21)
Females: 158 per million = 1 in 6,329   (CE × 1.09)

Per Shot	Ent Dose	Beam HVL	Male Cancer Risk	Female Cancer Risk
AP	0.259 R	2.2 mm Al	76 per million	53 per million
PA	0.150 R	2.4 mm Al	32 per million	16 per million
LAT	0.170 R	2.4 mm Al	42 per million	27 per million
OBL-PA	0.198 R	2.4 mm Al	46 per million	25 per million

All values are for the Common Exam

Age 25, Cervical Spine   Cancer Rate................ *(Lowering Factor)*
Males: 239 per million = 1 in 4,184   (Age 20 × 0.994)
Females: 156 per million = 1 in 6,410   (Age 20 × 0.988)
Age 30, Cervical Spine   Cancer Rate................ *(Lowering Factor)*
Males: 205 per million = 1 in 4,878   (Age 20 × 0.854)
Females: 138 per million = 1 in 7,246   (Age 20 × 0.873)
Age 35, Cervical Spine   Cancer Rate................ *(Lowering Factor)*
Males: 147 per million = 1 in 6,803   (Age 20 × 0.611)
Females: 98 per million = 1 in 10,200   (Age 20 × 0.623)
Age 40, Cervical Spine   Cancer Rate................ *(Lowering Factor)*
Males: 89 per million = 1 in 11,240   (Age 20 × 0.372)
Females: 62 per million = 1 in 16,100   (Age 20 × 0.391)
Age 45, Cervical Spine   Cancer Rate................ *(Lowering Factor)*
Males: 39 per million = 1 in 25,650   (Age 20 × 0.162)
Females: 28 per million = 1 in 35,700   (Age 20 × 0.176)
Age 50, Cervical Spine   Cancer Rate................ *(Lowering Factor)*
Males: 3.6 per million = 1 in 277,800   (Age 20 × 0.015)
Females: 2.7 per million = 1 in 370,400   (Age 20 × 0.017)
Age 55, Cervical Spine   Cancer Rate................ *(Lowering Factor)*
Males: 2.4 per million = 1 in 417,000   (Age 20 × 0.010)
Females: 1.9 per million = 1 in 526,300   (Age 20 × 0.012)

CHEST

Contrast Medium: No.

Fluoroscopy and Spot Films: No.

Length of Field: In the adult, the field center is 7.6 cm above the xiphoid process and at the body midline. The field length (adult) is 43.2 cm, so it extends from approximately 10 cm above the sternal notch to approximately 10 cm above the bi-iliac crests. Its lower edge lies halfway between the xiphoid process and the bi-iliac crests.

Organs Generating Most Cancer Risk:
>   *Males:* Bronchi, stomach, kidney, larynx, pancreas, esophagus.
>   *Females:* Breasts, stomach, bronchi, pancreas, kidneys, large intestine.

Special Comments:
- For pediatric exams, the fields are adjusted to encompass the same organs. Rosenstein reports "external auditory meatus to bottom, 12th rib."
- Chest is one of the few exams for which pediatric entrance doses fall from age-20 values less steeply than shown in Table 3 (this chapter, Section 2).
- The Common Exam changes; the newborn's AP shot commonly becomes a PA shot by age 1.

AGE NEW   Testes, dose CE: < 1 mrad
CHEST   Ovaries, dose CE: < 1 mrad

Common Exam (CE): One AP and one LAT
                    (Total: 2 shots)
Rate of future *leukemia* from Common Exam:
>   Males: 1.6 per million = 1 in 625,000
>   Females: 1 per million = 1 in 1,000,000
Rate of future *cancer* from Common Exam:
>   Males: 289 per million = 1 in 3,460
>   Females: 556 per million = 1 in 1,799

Per Shot	Ent Dose	Beam HVL	Male Cancer Risk	Female Cancer Risk
AP	0.019 R	2.4 mm Al	90 per million	260 per million
PA	0.010 R	2.5 mm Al	37 per million	49 per million
LAT	0.031 R	2.8 mm Al	199 per million	296 per million

AGE 1
CHEST

Testes, dose CE: < 1 mrad
Ovaries, dose CE: < 1 mrad

Common Exam (CE): One PA and one LAT
(Total: 2 shots)
Rate of future *leukemia* from Common Exam:
        Males: 1.5 per million = 1 in 667,000
        Females: 1 per million = 1 in 1,000,000
Rate of future *cancer* from Common Exam:
        Males: 234 per million = 1 in 4,274
        Females: 393 per million = 1 in 2,545

Per Shot	Ent Dose	Beam HVL	Male Cancer Risk	Female Cancer Risk
AP	0.023 R	2.4 mm Al	95 per million	283 per million
PA	0.012 R	2.5 mm Al	37 per million	49 per million
LAT	0.036 R	2.8 mm Al	197 per million	344 per million

AGE 5
CHEST

Testes, dose CE: < 1 mrad
Ovaries, dose CE: < 1 mrad

Common Exam (CE): One PA and one LAT
(Total: 2 shots)
Rate of future *leukemia* from Common Exam:
        Males: 1.5 per million = 1 in 667,000
        Females: 0.9 per million = 1 in 1,110,000
Rate of future *cancer* from Common Exam:
        Males: 217 per million = 1 in 4,608
        Females: 317 per million = 1 in 3,155

Per Shot	Ent Dose	Beam HVL	Male Cancer Risk	Female Cancer Risk
AP	0.027 R	2.4 mm Al	102 per million	280 per million
PA	0.014 R	2.5 mm Al	40 per million	46 per million
LAT	0.044 R	2.8 mm Al	177 per million	271 per million
OBL-PA	0.064 R	2.5 mm Al	198 per million	275 per million
OBL-AP	0.064 R	2.5 mm Al	226 per million	501 per million

AGE 10
CHEST

Testes, dose CE: < 1 mrad
Ovaries, dose CE: < 1 mrad

Common Exam (CE): One PA and one LAT
(Total: 2 shots)
Rate of future *leukemia* from Common Exam:
        Males: 1.4 per million = 1 in 714,000
        Females: 0.9 per million = 1 in 1,110,000

Age 10, Chest *(continued)*

Rate of future *cancer* from Common Exam:
        Males: 167 per million = 1 in 5,988
        Females: 239 per million = 1 in 4,184

Per Shot	Ent Dose	Beam HVL	Male Cancer Risk	Female Cancer Risk
AP	0.031 R	2.4 mm Al	86 per million	242 per million
PA	0.016 R	2.5 mm Al	31 per million	35 per million
LAT	0.051 R	2.8 mm Al	136 per million	204 per million
OBL-PA	0.073 R	2.5 mm Al	149 per million	200 per million

AGE 15
CHEST

Testes, dose CE: < 1 mrad
Ovaries, dose CE: < 1 mrad

Common Exam (CE): One PA and one LAT
                (Total: 2 shots)
Rate of future *leukemia* from Common Exam:
        Males: 1.6 per million = 1 in 625,000
        Females: 1 per million = 1 in one million
Rate of future *cancer* from Common Exam:
        Males: 68 per million = 1 in 14,710
        Females: 104 per million = 1 in 9,615

Per Shot	Ent Dose	Beam HVL	Male Cancer Risk	Female Cancer Risk
AP	0.042 R	2.4 mm Al	54 per million	134 per million
PA	0.021 R	2.5 mm Al	16 per million	16 per million
LAT	0.068 R	2.8 mm Al	52 per million	88 per million
OBL-PA	0.098 R	2.5 mm Al	67 per million	87 per million

AGE 20
CHEST

Testes, dose CE: < 1 mrad
Ovaries, dose CE: < 1 mrad
Embryo, dose CE: < 1 mrad

Common Exam (CE): One PA and one LAT
                (Total: 2 shots)
Rate of future *leukemia* from Common Exam:
        Males: 1.2 per million = 1 in 833,000
        Females: 0.7 per million = 1 in 1.4 million
Rate of future *cancer* from Common Exam: **(Smokers)**
        Males: 46 per million = 1 in 21,740   (CE × 3.11)
        Females: 93 per million = 1 in 10,750   (CE × 1.71)

Per Shot	Ent Dose	Beam HVL	Male Cancer Risk	Female Cancer Risk
AP	0.051 R	2.4 mm Al	44 per million	124 per million
PA	0.026 R	2.5 mm Al	15 per million	13 per million
LAT	0.082 R	2.8 mm Al	31 per million	80 per million
OBL-PA	0.119 R	2.5 mm Al	51 per million	76 per million

All values are for the Common Exam

Age 25, Chest   Cancer Rate................ *(Lowering Factor)*
        Males: 46 per million = 1 in 21,740   (Age 20 × 0.994)
        Females: 92 per million = 1 in 10,870   (Age 20 × 0.988)
Age 30, Chest   Cancer Rate................ *(Lowering Factor)*
        Males: 39 per million = 1 in 25,640   (Age 20 × 0.854)
        Females: 81 per million = 1 in 12,350   (Age 20 × 0.873)
Age 35, Chest   Cancer Rate................ *(Lowering Factor)*
        Males: 28 per million = 1 in 35,710   (Age 20 × 0.611)
        Females: 58 per million = 1 in 17,240   (Age 20 × 0.623)
Age 40, Chest   Cancer Rate................ *(Lowering Factor)*
        Males: 17 per million = 1 in 58,820   (Age 20 × 0.372)
        Females: 36 per million = 1 in 27,780   (Age 20 × 0.391)
Age 45, Chest   Cancer Rate................ *(Lowering Factor)*
        Males: 7.5 per million = 1 in 133,300   (Age 20 × 0.162)
        Females: 16 per million = 1 in 62,500   (Age 20 × 0.176)
Age 50, Chest   Cancer Rate................ *(Lowering Factor)*
        Males: 0.7 per million = 1 in 1.4 million   (Age 20 × 0.015)
        Females: 1.6 per million = 1 in 625,000   (Age 20 × 0.017)
Age 55, Chest   Cancer Rate................ *(Lowering Factor)*
        Males: 0.46 per million = 1 in 2.2 million   (Age 20 × 0.010)
        Females: 1.1 per million = 1 in 909,000   (Age 20 × 0.012)

CHOLECYSTOGRAM (ORAL)

Contrast Medium: Yes. An organically bound iodine compound taken by mouth.

Fluoroscopy and Spot Films: Sometimes. Dose and risks from the FLU and spot films are additional to the values in the following table; for evaluation of risks from FLU, please see Chapter 6.

Length of Field: In the adult, the field is centered 5.5 cm below the xiphoid process, and 8.5 cm to the *right* of the midline. The field length is 30.5 cm, so it extends from 10 cm above the xiphoid process to the bi-iliac crests. The field is narrower than the usual one, extending only approximately 4 cm to the left of the body's midline.

Cholecystogram, Oral *(continued)*

Organs Generating Most Cancer Risk:
   Males: Kidneys, stomach, pancreas, large intestine, liver, bronchi.
   Females: Breasts, large intestine, liver, kidneys, pancreas, stomach.

Special Comments:
   • No data are provided for newborns or 1-year-olds since the exam is so
     rarely done at these ages.
   • For pediatric exams, the fields are adjusted to cover the same organs as
     in adults.

AGE 5   Testes, dose CE: < 1 mrad
CHOLECYSTOGRAM, ORAL   Ovaries, dose CE: 5 mrads

Common Exam (CE): One AP, one PA, and
                      one OBL-PA (Total: 3 shots)
Rate of future *leukemia* from Common Exam:
         Males: 6 per million = 1 in 167,000
         Females: 4 per million = 1 in 250,000
Rate of future *cancer* from Common Exam:
         Males: 1,018 per million = 1 in 982
         Females: 1,326 per million = 1 in 754

Per Shot	Ent Dose	Beam HVL	Male Cancer Risk	Female Cancer Risk
AP	0.222 R	2.5 mm Al	308 per million	588 per million
PA	0.223 R	2.4 mm Al	246 per million	261 per million
LAT	0.307 R	2.5 mm Al	518 per million	570 per million
OBL-PA	0.304 R	2.5 mm Al	464 per million	477 per million

AGE 10   Testes, dose CE: <1 mrads
CHOLECYSTOGRAM, ORAL   Ovaries, dose CE: 5 mrads

Common Exam (CE): One AP, one PA, and
                      one OBL-PA (Total: 3 shots)
Rate of future *leukemia* from Common Exam:
         Males: 8 per million = 1 in 125,000
         Females: 5 per million = 1 in 200,000
Rate of future *cancer* from Common Exam:
         Males: 1,101 per million = 1 in 908
         Females: 1,426 per million = 1 in 701

Per Shot	Ent Dose	Beam HVL	Male Cancer Risk	Female Cancer Risk
AP	0.336 R	2.5 mm Al	325 per million	655 per million
PA	0.337 R	2.4 mm Al	281 per million	276 per million
LAT	0.465 R	2.5 mm Al	564 per million	574 per million
OBL-PA	0.459 R	2.5 mm Al	495 per million	495 per million

AGE 15
CHOLECYSTOGRAM, ORAL

Testes, dose CE: < 1 mrad
Ovaries, dose CE: 4.5 mrads

Common Exam (CE): One AP, one PA, and
one OBL-PA (Total: 3 shots)
Rate of future *leukemia* from Common Exam:
Males: 9 per million = 1 in 111,000
Females: 5 per million = 1 in 200,000
Rate of future *cancer* from Common Exam:
Males: 548 per million = 1 in 1,825
Females: 701 per million = 1 in 1,426

Per Shot	Ent Dose	Beam HVL	Male Cancer Risk	Female Cancer Risk
AP	0.449 R	2.5 mm Al	190 per million	357 per million
PA	0.450 R	2.4 mm Al	148 per million	134 per million
LAT	0.621 R	2.5 mm Al	199 per million	221 per million
OBL-PA	0.614 R	2.5 mm Al	210 per million	210 per million

AGE 20
CHOLECYSTOGRAM, ORAL

Testes, dose CE: < 1 mrad
Ovaries, dose CE: 4.7 mrads
Embryo, dose CE: 4.3 mrads

Common Exam (CE): One AP, one PA, and
one OBL-PA (Total: 3 shots)
Rate of future *leukemia* from Common Exam:
Males: 8 per million = 1 in 125,000
Females: 5 per million = 1 in 200,000
Rate of future *cancer* from Common Exam: **(Smokers)**
Males: 466 per million = 1 in 2,146   (CE × 2.1)
Females: 589 per million = 1 in 1,698   (CE × 1.4)

Per Shot	Ent Dose	Beam HVL	Male Cancer Risk	Female Cancer Risk
AP	0.544 R	2.5 mm Al	173 per million	330 per million
PA	0.546 R	2.4 mm Al	137 per million	109 per million
LAT	0.753 R	2.5 mm Al	107 per million	139 per million
OBL-PA	0.744 R	2.5 mm Al	156 per million	150 per million

All values are for the Common Exam

Age 25, Cholecystogram   Cancer Rate............... *(Lowering Factor)*
Males: 463 per million = 1 in 2,160   (Age 20 × 0.994)
Females: 582 per million = 1 in 1,718   (Age 20 × 0.988)
Age 30, Cholecystogram   Cancer Rate............... *(Lowering Factor)*
Males: 398 per million = 1 in 2,512   (Age 20 × 0.854)
Females: 514 per million = 1 in 1,946   (Age 20 × 0.873)

Cholecystogram, Oral *(continued)*

Age 35, Cholecystogram   Cancer Rate............... *(Lowering Factor)*
      Males: 285 per million = 1 in 3,509   (Age 20 × 0.611)
      Females: 367 per million = 1 in 2,725   (Age 20 × 0.623)
Age 40, Cholecystogram   Cancer Rate............... *(Lowering Factor)*
      Males: 173 per million = 1 in 5,780   (Age 20 × 0.372)
      Females: 230 per million = 1 in 4,348   (Age 20 × 0.391)
Age 45, Cholecystogram   Cancer Rate............... *(Lowering Factor)*
      Males: 75 per million = 1 in 13,330   (Age 20 × 0.162)
      Females: 104 per million = 1 in 9,615   (Age 20 × 0.176)
Age 50, Cholecystogram   Cancer Rate............... *(Lowering Factor)*
      Males: 7 per million = 1 in 142,900   (Age 20 × 0.015)
      Females: 10 per million = 1 in 100,000   (Age 20 × 0.017)
Age 55, Cholecystogram   Cancer Rate............... *(Lowering Factor)*
      Males: 5 per million = 1 in 200,000   (Age 20 × 0.010)
      Females: 7 per million = 1 in 142,900   (Age 20 × 0.012)

CYSTOGRAM—URETHROGRAM

Contrast Medium: Yes. An organically bound iodine compound administered by catheter.

Fluoroscopy and Spot Films: Sometimes. Particularly in the pediatric exams, Beck and Rosenstein (1979) comment that fluoroscopy is sometimes done. If FLU is done, its risks are additional to the values in the following table. For evaluation of risks from FLU, please see Chapter 6.

Length of Field: In the adult, the field center is 4 cm above the pubic symphysis, in the body midline (for the AP shot). The field length is 30.5 cm, so it extends from approximately the bi-iliac crests to about 11 cm below the pubic symphysis. For pediatric exams, the field is reduced to encompass the same organs as in the adult.

Organs Generating Most Cancer Risk:
    Males: Prostate, bladder, rectum, large intestine, testes.
    Females: Corpus uteri, cervix uteri, bladder, ovaries, large intestine,
      rectum.

Special Comments:
- Shielding of the testes deserves consideration.
- The Common Exam changes with age (see age 20).

AGE NEW   Testes, dose CE: 249 mrads
CYSTOGRAM—URETHROGRAM   Ovaries, dose CE: 129 mrads

Common Exam (CE): One AP and one OBL-AP
             (Total: 2 shots)

Rate of future *leukemia* from Common Exam:
        Males: 5 per million = 1 in 200,000
        Females: 3 per million = 1 in 333,000
Rate of future *cancer* from Common Exam:
        Males: 1,583 per million = 1 in 632
        Females: 1,504 per million = 1 in 665

Per Shot	Ent Dose	Beam HVL	Male Cancer Risk	Female Cancer Risk
AP	0.117 R	2.5 mm Al	680 per million	608 per million
OBL-AP	0.179 R	2.6 mm Al	903 per million	897 per million

AGE 1
CYSTOGRAM—URETHROGRAM

Testes, dose CE: 265 mrads
Ovaries, dose CE: 136 mrads

Common Exam (CE): One AP and one OBL-AP
                (Total: 2 shots)
Rate of future *leukemia* from Common Exam:
        Males: 5 per million = 1 in 200,000
        Females: 3 per million = 1 in 333,000
Rate of future *cancer* from Common Exam:
        Males: 1,676 per million = 1 in 597
        Females: 1,615 per million = 1 in 619

Per Shot	Ent Dose	Beam HVL	Male Cancer Risk	Female Cancer Risk
AP	0.144 R	2.5 mm Al	740 per million	659 per million
OBL-AP	0.221 R	2.6 mm Al	936 per million	956 per million

AGE 5
CYSTOGRAM—URETHROGRAM

Testes, dose CE: 418 mrads
Ovaries, dose CE: 197 mrads

Common Exam (CE): One AP and one OBL-AP
                (Total: 2 shots)
Rate of future *leukemia* from Common Exam:
        Males: 6 per million = 1 in 167,000
        Females: 4 per million = 1 in 250,000
Rate of future *cancer* from Common Exam:
        Males: 2,287 per million = 1 in 437
        Females: 2,113 per million = 1 in 473

Per Shot	Ent Dose	Beam HVL	Male Cancer Risk	Female Cancer Risk
AP	0.242 R	2.5 mm Al	1,050 per million	891 per million
OBL-AP	0.372 R	2.6 mm Al	1,237 per million	1,222 per million

AGE 10   Testes, dose CE: 603 mrads
CYSTOGRAM—URETHROGRAM   Ovaries, dose CE: 255 mrads

Common Exam (CE): One AP and one OBL-AP
                     (Total: 2 shots)
Rate of future *leukemia* from Common Exam:
          Males: 7 per million = 1 in 142,800
          Females: 4 per million = 1 in 250,000
Rate of future *cancer* from Common Exam:
          Males: 2,507 per million = 1 in 399
          Females: 2,265 per million = 1 in 442

Per Shot	Ent Dose	Beam HVL	Male Cancer Risk	Female Cancer Risk
AP	0.367 R	2.5 mm Al	1,128 per million	975 per million
OBL-AP	0.563 R	2.6 mm Al	1,379 per million	1,290 per million

AGE 15   Testes, dose CE: 696 mrads
CYSTOGRAM—URETHROGRAM   Ovaries, dose CE: 294 mrads

Common Exam (CE): One AP and one OBL-AP
                     (Total: 2 shots)
Rate of future *leukemia* from Common Exam:
          Males: 7 per million = 1 in 142,800
          Females: 5 per million = 1 in 200,000
Rate of future *cancer* from Common Exam:
          Males: 1,398 per million = 1 in 715
          Females: 1,171 per million = 1 in 854

Per Shot	Ent Dose	Beam HVL	Male Cancer Risk	Female Cancer Risk
AP	0.491 R	2.5 mm Al	665 per million	509 per million
OBL-AP	0.753 R	2.6 mm Al	733 per million	662 per million

AGE 20   Testes, dose CE: 1,070 mrads
CYSTOGRAM—URETHROGRAM   Ovaries, dose CE: 454 mrads
                                              Embryo, dose CE: 635 mrads

Common Exam (CE): One AP and *two* OBL-AP
                     (Total: 3 shots)
Rate of future *leukemia* from Common Exam:
          Males: 12 per million = 1 in 83,330
          Females: 8 per million = 1 in 125,000
Rate of future *cancer* from Common Exam: **(Smokers)**
          Males: 1,936 per million = 1 in 516   (CE × 1.00)
          Females: 1,639 per million = 1 in 610   (CE × 1.00)

Per Shot	Ent Dose	Beam HVL	Male Cancer Risk	Female Cancer Risk
AP	0.595 R	2.5 mm Al	620 per million	453 per million
OBL-AP	0.913 R	2.6 mm Al	658 per million	593 per million

All values are for the Common Exam

Age 25, Cysto-Urethrogram   Cancer Rate............... *(Lowering Factor)*
        Males: 1,924 per million = 1 in 518   (Age 20 × 0.994)
        Females: 1,619 per million = 1 in 618   (Age 20 × 0.988)
Age 30, Cysto-Urethrogram   Cancer Rate............... *(Lowering Factor)*
        Males: 1,653 per million = 1 in 605   (Age 20 × 0.854)
        Females: 1,431 per million = 1 in 699   (Age 20 × 0.873)
Age 35, Cysto-Urethrogram   Cancer Rate............... *(Lowering Factor)*
        Males: 1,183 per million = 1 in 845   (Age 20 × 0.611)
        Females: 1,021 per million = 1 in 979   (Age 20 × 0.623)
Age 40, Cysto-Urethrogram   Cancer Rate............... *(Lowering Factor)*
        Males: 720 per million = 1 in 1,389   (Age 20 × 0.372)
        Females: 641 per million = 1 in 1,560   (Age 20 × 0.391)
Age 45, Cysto-Urethrogram   Cancer Rate............... *(Lowering Factor)*
        Males: 314 per million = 1 in 3,185   (Age 20 × 0.162)
        Females: 288 per million = 1 in 3,472   (Age 20 × 0.176)
Age 50, Cysto-Urethrogram   Cancer Rate............... *(Lowering Factor)*
        Males: 29 per million = 1 in 34,480   (Age 20 × 0.015)
        Females: 28 per million = 1 in 35,710   (Age 20 × 0.017)
Age 55, Cysto-Urethrogram   Cancer Rate............... *(Lowering Factor)*
        Males: 19 per million = 1 in 52,630   (Age 20 × 0.010)
        Females: 20 per million = 1 in 50,000   (Age 20 × 0.012)

ELBOW

Contrast Medium: No.

Fluoroscopy and Spot Films: No.

Length of Field: Body part.

Organs Generating Most Cancer Risk:
    Males: Lymphatic tissue, skin, connective tissue, bone.
    Females: Same.

Elbow *(continued)*

Special Comments:
- Risks are from examination of *one* elbow.
- The cancer risk incorporates the approximation that 2.18% of body bone is exposed by one elbow exam. Included in the field are half the ulna, half the radius, and half the humerus.
- Because the risk will be virtually identical regardless of the beam's direction, the table provides one entry for "either" shot.

AGE NEW   Testes, dose CE: < 1 mrad
ELBOW   Ovaries, dose CE: < 1 mrad

Common Exam (CE): One AP and one LAT
                    (Total: 2 shots)
Rate of future *leukemia* from Common Exam:
          Males: 0.3 per million = 1 in 3.3 million
          Females: 0.2 per million = 1 in 5 million
Rate of future *cancer* from Common Exam:
          Males: 4.2 per million = 1 in 238,000
          Females: 4.2 per million = 1 in 238,000

Per Shot	*Ent Dose*	*Beam HVL*	*Male Cancer Risk*	*Female Cancer Risk*
Either	0.050 R	2.2 mm Al	2.1 per million	2.1 per million

AGE 1   Testes, dose CE: < 1 mrad
ELBOW   Ovaries, dose CE: < 1 mrad

Common Exam (CE): One AP and one LAT
                    (Total: 2 shots)
Rate of future *leukemia* from Common Exam:
          Males: 0.3 per million = 1 in 3.3 million
          Females: 0.2 per million = 1 in 5 million
Rate of future *cancer* from Common Exam:
          Males: 4.6 per million = 1 in 217,000
          Females: 4.7 per million = 1 in 213,000

Per Shot	*Ent Dose*	*Beam HVL*	*Male Cancer Risk*	*Female Cancer Risk*
Either	0.062 R	2.2 mm Al	2.3 per million	2.4 per million

AGE 5   Testes, dose CE: < 1 mrad
ELBOW   Ovaries, dose CE: < 1 mrad

Common Exam (CE): One AP and one LAT
                    (Total: 2 shots)

Rate of future *leukemia* from Common Exam:
          Males: 0.4 per million = 1 in 2.5 million
          Females: 0.3 per million = 1 in 3.3 million
Rate of future *cancer* from Common Exam:
          Males: 6.4 per million = 1 in 156,000
          Females: 6.1 per million = 1 in 164,000

Per Shot	*Ent Dose*	*Beam HVL*	*Male Cancer Risk*	*Female Cancer Risk*
Either	0.105 R	2.2 mm Al	3.2 per million	3.05 per million

AGE 10   Testes, dose CE: < 1 mrad
ELBOW   Ovaries, dose CE: < 1 mrad

Common Exam (CE): One AP and one LAT
                              (Total: 2 shots)
Rate of future *leukemia* from Common Exam:
          Males: 0.4 per million = 1 in 2.5 million
          Females: 0.3 per million = 1 in 3.3 million
Rate of future *cancer* from Common Exam:
          Males: 7.4 per million = 1 in 135,000
          Females: 6.7 per million = 1 in 149,000

Per Shot	*Ent Dose*	*Beam HVL*	*Male Cancer Risk*	*Female Cancer Risk*
Either	0.158 R	2.2 mm Al	3.7 per million	3.35 per million

AGE 15   Testes, dose CE: < 1 mrad
ELBOW   Ovaries, dose CE: < 1 mrad

Common Exam (CE): One AP and one LAT
                              (Total: 2 shots)
Rate of future *leukemia* from Common Exam:
          Males: 0.2 per million = 1 in 5 million
          Females: 0.1 per million = 1 in 10 million
Rate of future *cancer* from Common Exam:
          Males: 3.8 per million = 1 in 263,000
          Females: 3.3 per million = 1 in 303,000

Per Shot	*Ent Dose*	*Beam HVL*	*Male Cancer Risk*	*Female Cancer Risk*
Either	0.212 R	2.2 mm Al	1.9 per million	1.67 per million

AGE 20
ELBOW

Testes, dose CE: < 1 mrad
Ovaries, dose CE: < 1 mrad
Embryo, dose CE: < 1 mrad

Common Exam (CE): One AP and one LAT
(Total: 2 shots)
Rate of future *leukemia* from Common Exam:
      Males: < 0.1 per million = < 1 in 10 million
      Females: < 0.1 per million = < 1 in 10 million
Rate of future *cancer* from Common Exam: **(Smokers)**
      Males: 3.4 per million = 1 in 294,000   (CE × 1.00)
      Females: 2.9 per million = 1 in 345,000   (CE × 1.00)

Per Shot	Ent Dose	Beam HVL	Male Cancer Risk	Female Cancer Risk
Either	0.257 R	2.2 mm Al	1.7 per million	1.45 per million

All values are for the Common Exam

Age 30, Elbow   Cancer Rate............... *(Lowering Factor)*
      Males: 2.9 per million = 1 in 345,000   (Age 20 × 0.854)
      Females: 2.5 per million = 1 in 400,000   (Age 20 × 0.873)
Age 40, Elbow   Cancer Rate............... *(Lowering Factor)*
      Males: 1.3 per million = 1 in 769,000   (Age 20 × 0.372)
      Females: 1.1 per million = 1 in 909,000   (Age 20 × 0.391)
Age 50, Elbow   Cancer Rate............... *(Lowering Factor)*
      Males: 0.05 per million = 1 in 20 million   (Age 20 × 0.015)
      Females: 0.05 per million = 1 in 20 million   (Age 20 × 0.017)

FEMUR

Contrast Medium: No.

Fluoroscopy and Spot Films: No.

Length of Field: In the adult, the field center is 19 cm below the pubic symphysis, and 8.5 cm away from the body midline. The field length is 43.2 cm, so it extends from approximately 3 cm above the pubic symphysis to some 40 cm below it. In pediatric exams, the fields are adjusted to cover the same organ regions.

Organs Generating Most Cancer Risk:
    Males: Prostate, other genital organs, bladder, lymphatic tissues, rectum,
      skin.
    Females: Corpus uteri, cervix uteri, lymphatic tissues, bladder, skin,
      ovaries.

Special Comments:
- The risks apply to examination of *one* femur.
- In the male, well over 50% of the cancer risk comes from such shieldable organs as the testes, prostate, and bladder.
- In the female, well over 50% of the cancer risk comes from such shieldable organs as the corpus uteri, bladder, cervix uteri, and ovaries.
- Even though this is a "bone exam" (for a large bone, at that), radiation-induced bone cancer accounts for less than 1% of the hazard. This is so because the *spontaneous* rate of bone cancer is so low—a rare disease. (See Chapter 3, Section 3.)
- Although the risks from the AP and LAT shots are not really equal in this exam, so much risk would disappear with shielding that an entry for one "basic" shot seems sufficient.

AGE NEW   Testes, dose CE: 19 mrads
FEMUR   Ovaries, dose CE: 1.1 mrads

Common Exam (CE): One AP and one LAT
(Total: 2 shots)
Rate of future *leukemia* from Common Exam:
      Males: 0.4 per million = 1 in 2.5 million
      Females: 0.3 per million = 1 in 3.3 million
Rate of future *cancer* from Common Exam:
      Males: 28 per million = 1 in 35,700
      Females: 20 per million = 1 in 50,000

Per Shot	*Ent Dose*	*Beam HVL*	*Male Cancer Risk*	*Female Cancer Risk*
Basic	0.088 R	2.4 mm Al	14 per million	10 per million

AGE 1   Testes, dose CE: 22 mrads
FEMUR   Ovaries, dose CE: 1.2 mrads

Common Exam (CE): One AP and one LAT
(Total: 2 shots)
Rate of future *leukemia* from Common Exam:
      Males: 0.5 per million = 1 in 2 million
      Females: 0.3 per million = 1 in 3.3 million
Rate of future *cancer* from Common Exam:
      Males: 30 per million = 1 in 33,300
      Females: 22 per million = 1 in 45,500

Per Shot	*Ent Dose*	*Beam HVL*	*Male Cancer Risk*	*Female Cancer Risk*
Basic	0.109 R	2.4 mm Al	15 per million	11 per million

AGE 5   Testes, dose CE: 47 mrads
FEMUR   Ovaries, dose CE: 1.9 mrads
_____

Common Exam (CE): One AP and one LAT
                    (Total: 2 shots)
Rate of future *leukemia* from Common Exam:
        Males: 0.8 per million = 1 in 1.25 million
        Females: 0.5 per million = 1 in 2.0 million
Rate of future *cancer* from Common Exam:
        Males: 46 per million = 1 in 21,740
        Females: 30 per million = 1 in 33,300

Per Shot	*Ent Dose*	*Beam HVL*	*Male Cancer Risk*	*Female Cancer Risk*
Basic	0.184 R	2.4 mm Al	23 per million	15 per million

AGE 10   Testes, dose CE: 91 mrads
FEMUR   Ovaries, dose CE: 2.7 mrads
_____

Common Exam (CE): One AP and one LAT
                    (Total: 2 shots)
Rate of future *leukemia* from Common Exam:
        Males: 0.9 per million = 1 in 1.1 million
        Females: 0.6 per million = 1 in 1.7 million
Rate of future *cancer* from Common Exam:
        Males: 50 per million = 1 in 20,000
        Females: 32 per million = 1 in 31,250

Per Shot	*Ent Dose*	*Beam HVL*	*Male Cancer Risk*	*Female Cancer Risk*
Basic	0.278 R	2.4 mm Al	25 per million	16 per million

AGE 15   Testes, dose CE: 149 mrads
FEMUR   Ovaries, dose CE: 2.8 mrads
_____

Common Exam (CE): One AP and one LAT
                    (Total: 2 shots)
Rate of future *leukemia* from Common Exam:
        Males: 0.9 per million = 1 in 1.1 million
        Females: 0.6 per million = 1 in 1.7 million
Rate of future *cancer* from Common Exam:
        Males: 28 per million = 1 in 35,700
        Females: 16 per million = 1 in 62,500

Per Shot	*Ent Dose*	*Beam HVL*	*Male Cancer Risk*	*Female Cancer Risk*
Basic	0.372 R	2.4 mm Al	14 per million	8 per million

AGE 20
FEMUR

Testes, dose CE: 200 mrads
Ovaries, dose CE: 3.1 mrads
Embryo, dose CE: 3.7 mrads

Common Exam (CE): One AP and one LAT
                (Total: 2 shots)
Rate of future *leukemia* from Common Exam:
        Males: 0.7 per million = 1 in 1.4 million
        Females: 0.5 per million = 1 in 2.0 million
Rate of future *cancer* from Common Exam: **(Smokers)**
        Males: 26 per million = 1 in 38,500   (CE × 1.00)
        Females: 12 per million = 1 in 83,300   (CE × 1.00)

Per Shot	Ent Dose	Beam HVL	Male Cancer Risk	Female Cancer Risk
Basic	0.451 R	2.4 mm Al	13 per million	6 per million

All values are for the Common Exam

Age 30, Femur   Cancer Rate.............. *(Lowering Factor)*
        Males: 22 per million = 1 in 45,500   (Age 20 × 0.854)
        Females: 10 per million = 1 in 100,000   (Age 20 × 0.873)
Age 40, Femur   Cancer Rate.............. *(Lowering Factor)*
        Males: 9.7 per million = 1 in 103,000   (Age 20 × 0.372)
        Females: 4.7 per million = 1 in 213,000   (Age 20 × 0.391)
Age 50, Femur   Cancer Rate.............. *(Lowering Factor)*
        Males: 0.4 per million = 1 in 2.5 million (Age 20 × 0.015)
        Females: 0.2 per million = 1 in 5 million   (Age 20 × 0.017)

FOREARM

Contrast Medium: No.

Fluoroscopy and Spot Films: No.

Length of Field: Body part.

Organs Generating Most Cancer Risk:
    Males: Lymphatic tissue, skin, connective tissue, bone.
    Females: Same.

Special Comments:
    • The risks are for examination of *one* forearm.
    • Risks incorporate the estimate that the ulna and radius, combined,
      represent 1.36% of body bone.
    • Because the risk will be virtually identical regardless of the beam's
      direction, the table provides one entry for "either" shot.

AGE NEW   Testes, dose CE: $\ll 1$ mrad
FOREARM   Ovaries, dose CE: $\ll 1$ mrad

Common Exam (CE): One AP and one LAT
                      (Total: 2 shots)
Rate of future *leukemia* from Common Exam:
          Males: 0.2 per million = 1 in 5 million
          Females: 0.1 per million = 1 in 10 million
Rate of future *cancer* from Common Exam:
          Males: 2.6 per million = 1 in 384,000
          Females: 2.7 per million = 1 in 370,000

Per Shot	*Ent Dose*	*Beam HVL*	*Male Cancer Risk*	*Female Cancer Risk*
Either	0.050 R	2.2 mm Al	1.3 per million	1.35 per million

AGE 1   Testes, dose CE: $\ll 1$ mrad
FOREARM   Ovaries, dose CE: $\ll 1$ mrad

Common Exam (CE): One AP and one LAT
                      (Total: 2 shots)
Rate of future *leukemia* from Common Exam:
          Males: 0.2 per million = 1 in 5 million
          Females: 0.1 per million = 1 in 10 million
Rate of future *cancer* from Common Exam:
          Males: 2.9 per million = 1 in 345,000
          Females: 2.9 per million = 1 in 345,000

Per Shot	*Ent Dose*	*Beam HVL*	*Male Cancer Risk*	*Female Cancer Risk*
Either	0.062 R	2.2 mm Al	1.45 per million	1.45 per million

AGE 5   Testes, dose CE: $\ll 1$ mrad
FOREARM   Ovaries, dose CE: $\ll 1$ mrad

Common Exam (CE): One AP and one LAT
                      (Total: 2 shots)
Rate of future *leukemia* from Common Exam:
          Males: 0.3 per million = 1 in 3.3 million
          Females: 0.2 per million = 1 in 5 million
Rate of future *cancer* from Common Exam:
          Males: 3.2 per million = 1 in 312,500
          Females: 2.9 per million = 1 in 345,000

Per Shot	*Ent Dose*	*Beam HVL*	*Male Cancer Risk*	*Female Cancer Risk*
Either	0.105 R	2.2 mm Al	1.6 per million	1.45 per million

AGE 10
FOREARM

Testes, dose CE: $<<$ 1 mrad
Ovaries, dose CE: $<<$ 1 mrad

Common Exam (CE): One AP and one LAT
(Total: 2 shots)
Rate of future *leukemia* from Common Exam:
　　　Males:　0.2 per million = 1 in 5 million
　　　Females: 0.2 per million = 1 in 5 million
Rate of future *cancer* from Common Exam:
　　　Males:　4.6 per million = 1 in 217,000
　　　Females: 4.2 per million = 1 in 238,000

Per Shot	Ent Dose	Beam HVL	Male Cancer Risk	Female Cancer Risk
Either	0.158 R	2.2 mm Al	2.3 per million	2.1 per million

AGE 15
FOREARM

Testes, dose CE: $<<$ 1 mrad
Ovaries, dose CE: $<<$ 1 mrad

Common Exam (CE): One AP and one LAT
(Total: 2 shots)
Rate of future *leukemia* from Common Exam:
　　　Males:　0.1 per million = 1 in 10 million
　　　Females: 0.1 per million = 1 in 10 million
Rate of future *cancer* from Common Exam:
　　　Males:　2.4 per million = 1 in 417,000
　　　Females: 2.1 per million = 1 in 476,000

Per Shot	Ent Dose	Beam HVL	Male Cancer Risk	Female Cancer Risk
Either	0.212 R	2.2 mm Al	1.2 per million	1.05 per million

AGE 20
FOREARM

Testes, dose CE: $<<$ 1 mrad
Ovaries, dose CE: $<<$ 1 mrad
Embryo, dose CE: $<<$ 1 mrad

Common Exam (CE): One AP and one LAT
(Total: 2 shots)
Rate of future *leukemia* from Common Exam:
　　　Males:　$<$ 0.1 per million = $<$ 1 in 10 million
　　　Females: $<$ 0.1 per million = $<$ 1 in 10 million
Rate of future *cancer* from Common Exam:　　　　　　**(Smokers)**
　　　Males:　　2.1 per million = 1 in 476,000　　(CE $\times$ 1.00)
　　　Females:　1.8 per million = 1 in 556,000　　(CE $\times$ 1.00)

Per Shot	Ent Dose	Beam HVL	Male Cancer Risk	Female Cancer Risk
Either	0.257 R	2.2 mm Al	1.05 per million	0.9 per million

Forearm *(continued)*

All values are for the Common Exam

Age 30, Forearm		Cancer Rate...............	*(Lowering Factor)*
	Males:	1.8 per million = 1 in 556,000	(Age 20 × 0.854)
	Females:	1.6 per million = 1 in 625,000	(Age 20 × 0.873)
Age 40, Forearm		Cancer Rate...............	*(Lowering Factor)*
	Males:	0.8 per million = 1 in 1.3 million	(Age 20 × 0.372)
	Females:	0.7 per million = 1 in 1.4 million	(Age 20 × 0.391)
Age 50, Forearm		Cancer Rate...............	*(Lowering Factor)*
	Males:	0.03 per million = 1 in 33 million	(Age 20 × 0.015)
	Females:	0.03 per million = 1 in 33 million	(Age 20 × 0.017)

FULL SPINE—CHIROPRACTIC

Contrast Medium: No.

Fluoroscopy and Spot Films: No.

Length of Field: This examination's field has unusual dimensions. Kereiakes and Rosenstein (1980) show the length to be 92 cm; in some instances this is divided into two parts, for improved diagnostic quality. Although the field center is not provided in the cited reference, the dose data indicate the field extends from the top of spine to the pubic symphysis.

Organs Generating Most Cancer Risk:
   Males: Prostate, bladder, large intestine, stomach, bronchi, pancreas.
   Females: Breasts, corpus uteri, large intestine, cervix uteri, stomach, bladder.

Special Comments:
- It is unclear how frequently such an exam is used for the very young; we made no estimates for newborns, but we made them even for 1-year-olds because this exam provides a useful illustration of full-torso exposure with the AP beam direction, and of the cancer risks which go with such exposure.
- The risks in this table are for the appropriate beam quality of 3.5 mm Al HVL, which is very different from the beam quality used for most exams in this book. *Always check beam qualities* before attempting to compare results of one exam with another.
- The risks from this exam can be easily adjusted for all other beam qualities by the simple method demonstrated in Chapter 4, Section 12.
- This "bone exam" is another example of one whose leading cancer consequences all arise from organs other than bone.

AGE 1
FULL SPINE—CHIROPRACTIC

Testes, dose CE: 29 mrads
Ovaries, dose CE: 44 mrads

Common Exam (CE): One AP
                (Total: 1 shot)
Rate of future *leukemia* from Common Exam:
        Males: 3 per million = 1 in 333,000
        Females: 2 per million = 1 in 500,000
Rate of future *cancer* from Common Exam:
        Males: 1,219 per million = 1 in 820
        Females: 2,024 per million = 1 in 494

Per Shot	Ent Dose	Beam HVL	Male Cancer Risk	Female Cancer Risk
AP	0.068 R	3.5 mm Al	1,219 per million	2,024 per million

AGE 5
FULL SPINE—CHIROPRACTIC

Testes, dose CE: 43 mrads
Ovaries, dose CE: 65 mrads

Common Exam (CE): One AP
                (Total: 1 shot)
Rate of future *leukemia* from Common Exam:
        Males: 4 per million = 1 in 250,000
        Females: 2.5 per million = 1 in 400,000
Rate of future *cancer* from Common Exam:
        Males: 1,752 per million = 1 in 571
        Females: 2,754 per million = 1 in 363

Per Shot	Ent Dose	Beam HVL	Male Cancer Risk	Female Cancer Risk
AP	0.114 R	3.5 mm Al	1,752 per million	2,754 per million

AGE 10
FULL SPINE—CHIROPRACTIC

Testes, dose CE: 21 mrads
Ovaries, dose CE: 83 mrads

Common Exam (CE): One AP
                (Total: 1 shot)
Rate of future *leukemia* from Common Exam:
        Males: 6 per million = 1 in 167,000
        Females: 3.5 per million = 1 in 286,000
Rate of future *cancer* from Common Exam:
        Males: 2,048 per million = 1 in 488
        Females: 3,070 per million = 1 in 326

Per Shot	Ent Dose	Beam HVL	Male Cancer Risk	Female Cancer Risk
AP	0.173 R	3.5 mm Al	2,048 per million	3,070 per million

AGE 15   Testes, dose CE: 13 mrads
FULL SPINE—CHIROPRACTIC   Ovaries, dose CE: 96 mrads

Common Exam (CE): One AP
                     (Total: 1 shot)
Rate of future *leukemia* from Common Exam:
        Males: 7 per million = 1 in 143,000
        Females: 4 per million = 1 in 250,000
Rate of future *cancer* from Common Exam:
        Males: 1,144 per million = 1 in 874
        Females: 1,721 per million = 1 in 581

Per Shot	Ent Dose	Beam HVL	Male Cancer Risk	Female Cancer Risk
AP	0.231 R	3.5 mm Al	1,144 per million	1,721 per million

AGE 20   Testes, dose CE: 10 mrads
FULL SPINE—CHIROPRACTIC   Ovaries, dose CE: 101 mrads
                                                    Embryo dose CE: 136 mrads

Common Exam (CE): One AP
                     (Total: 1 shot)
Rate of future *leukemia* from Common Exam:
        Males: 7 per million = 1 in 143,000
        Females: 4 per million = 1 in 250,000
Rate of future *cancer* from Common Exam: **(Smokers)**
        Males: 1,056 per million = 1 in 947   (CE × 1.56)
        Females: 1,590 per million = 1 in 629   (CE × 1.17)

Per Shot	Ent Dose	Beam HVL	Male Cancer Risk	Female Cancer Risk
AP	0.280 R	3.5 mm Al	1,056 per million	1,590 per million

All values are for the Common Exam

Age 25, Full Spine-Chiro.   Cancer Rate............... *(Lowering Factor)*
            Males: 1,050 per million = 1 in 952   (Age 20 × 0.994)
            Females: 1,571 per million = 1 in 637   (Age 20 × 0.988)
Age 30, Full Spine—Chiro.   Cancer Rate............... *(Lowering Factor)*
            Males: 902 per million = 1 in 1,109   (Age 20 × 0.854)
            Females: 1,388 per million = 1 in 720   (Age 20 × 0.873)
Age 35, Full Spine—Chiro.   Cancer Rate............... *(Lowering Factor)*
            Males: 645 per million = 1 in 1,550   (Age 20 × 0.611)
            Females: 991 per million = 1 in 1,009   (Age 20 × 0.623)

Age 40, Full Spine—Chiro.   Cancer Rate............... *(Lowering Factor)*
    Males: 393 per million = 1 in 2,545   (Age 20 × 0.372)
    Females: 622 per million = 1 in 1,608   (Age 20 × 0.391)
Age 45, Full Spine—Chiro.   Cancer Rate............... *(Lowering Factor)*
    Males: 171 per million = 1 in 5,848   (Age 20 × 0.162)
    Females: 280 per million = 1 in 3,571   (Age 20 × 0.176)
Age 50, Full Spine—Chiro.   Cancer Rate............... *(Lowering Factor)*
    Males: 16 per million = 1 in 62,500   (Age 20 × 0.015)
    Females: 27 per million = 1 in 37,000   (Age 20 × 0.017)
Age 55, Full Spine—Chiro.   Cancer Rate............... *(Lowering Factor)*
    Males: 11 per million = 1 in 90,900   (Age 20 × 0.010)
    Females: 19 per million = 1 in 52,630   (Age 20 × 0.012)

HIP

Contrast Medium: No.

Fluoroscopy and Spot Films: No.

Length of Field: In the adult, the field center is at the pubic symphysis. In the AP exam, the center is 8.5 cm from the midline of the body. In the LAT exam, the field center is at body midline (viewed from side). The field length is 30.5 cm for an adult, so it extends from the bi-iliac crests to 15 cm below the pubic symphysis. Fields are correspondingly adjusted for pediatric exams.

Organs Generating Most Cancer Risk:
    Males: Prostate, bladder, rectum, large intestine, other genital organs.
    Females: Corpus uteri, cervix uteri, ovaries, bladder, rectum, large
        intestine.

Special Comments:
- Risks apply to the examination of *one* hip.
- Genetic risk from this exam will be reduced by shielding the testes.
- Shielding of the testes cannot lower the male cancer risk from the exam by much, because the other organs listed above are each bigger contributors to that risk.
- The Common Exam changes with age (see age 5).

AGE NEW,   Testes, dose CE: 111 mrads
HIP   Ovaries, dose CE: 33 mrads

Common Exam (CE): Two AP
               (Total: 2 shots)
Rate of future *leukemia* from Common Exam:
        Males: 2 per million = 1 in 500,000
        Females: 1.2 per million = 1 in 833,000

Age New, Hip *(continued)*

Rate of future *cancer* from Common Exam:
        Males: 736 per million = 1 in 1,359
        Females: 589 per million = 1 in 1,698

Per Shot	*Ent Dose*	*Beam HVL*	*Male Cancer Risk*	*Female Cancer Risk*
AP	0.088 R	2.4 mm Al	368 per million	294 per million
PA	0.085 R	1.8 mm Al	117 per million	121 per million
LAT	0.178 R	2.4 mm Al	378 per million	585 per million
OBL-AP	0.182 R	2.3 mm Al	540 per million	558 per million

AGE 1   Testes, dose CE: 135 mrads
HIP   Ovaries, dose CE: 35 mrads

Common Exam (CE): Two AP
                (Total: 2 shots)
Rate of future *leukemia* from Common Exam:
        Males: 2 per million = 1 in 500,000
        Females: 1.2 per million = 1 in 833,000
Rate of future *cancer* from Common Exam:
        Males: 810 per million = 1 in 1,235
        Females: 646 per million = 1 in 1,548

Per Shot	*Ent Dose*	*Beam HVL*	*Male Cancer Risk*	*Female Cancer Risk*
AP	0.109 R	2.4 mm Al	405 per million	323 per million
PA	0.104 R	1.8 mm Al	121 per million	128 per million
LAT	0.219 R	2.4 mm Al	367 per million	574 per million
OBL-AP	0.225 R	2.3 mm Al	571 per million	582 per million

AGE 5   Testes, dose CE: 185 mrads
HIP   Ovaries, dose CE: 108 mrads

Common Exam (CE): One AP and one LAT
                (Total: 2 shots)
Rate of future *leukemia* from Common Exam:
        Males: 4 per million = 1 in 250,000
        Females: 2.5 per million = 1 in 400,000
Rate of future *cancer* from Common Exam:
        Males: 1,028 per million = 1 in 973
        Females: 1,071 per million = 1 in 934

Per Shot	*Ent Dose*	*Beam HVL*	*Male Cancer Risk*	*Female Cancer Risk*
AP	0.184 R	2.4 mm Al	573 per million	424 per million
PA	0.176 R	1.8 mm Al	163 per million	160 per million
LAT	0.370 R	2.4 mm Al	455 per million	647 per million
OBL-AP	0.379 R	2.3 mm Al	777 per million	716 per million

AGE 10
HIP

Testes, dose CE: 284 mrads
Ovaries, dose CE: 149 mrads

Common Exam (CE): One AP and one LAT
(Total: 2 shots)
Rate of future *leukemia* from Common Exam:
      Males: 5 per million = 1 in 200,000
      Females: 3 per million = 1 in 333,000
Rate of future *cancer* from Common Exam:
      Males: 1,137 per million = 1 in 880
      Females: 1,140 per million = 1 in 877

Per Shot	*Ent Dose*	*Beam HVL*	*Male Cancer Risk*	*Female Cancer Risk*
AP	0.278 R	2.4 mm Al	659 per million	463 per million
PA	0.267 R	1.8 mm Al	180 per million	171 per million
LAT	0.560 R	2.4 mm Al	478 per million	677 per million
OBL-AP	0.572 R	2.3 mm Al	851 per million	768 per million

AGE 15
HIP

Testes, dose CE: 327 mrads
Ovaries, dose CE: 168 mrads

Common Exam (CE): One AP and one LAT
(Total: 2 shots)
Rate of future *leukemia* from Common Exam:
      Males: 5 per million = 1 in 200,000
      Females: 3 per million = 1 in 333,333
Rate of future *cancer* from Common Exam:
      Males: 546 per million = 1 in 1,832
      Females: 555 per million = 1 in 1,802

Per Shot	*Ent Dose*	*Beam HVL*	*Male Cancer Risk*	*Female Cancer Risk*
AP	0.372 R	2.4 mm Al	364 per million	243 per million
PA	0.356 R	1.8 mm Al	85 per million	78 per million
LAT	0.748 R	2.4 mm Al	182 per million	312 per million
OBL-AP	0.766 R	2.3 mm Al	446 per million	383 per million

AGE 20
HIP

Testes, dose CE: 368 mrads
Ovaries, dose CE: 168 mrads
Embryo, dose CE: 186 mrads

Common Exam (CE): One AP and one LAT
(Total: 2 shots)
Rate of future *leukemia* from Common Exam:
      Males: 4 per million = 1 in 250,000
      Females: 2.5 per million = 1 in 400,000

Age 20, Hip *(continued)*

Rates of future *cancer* from Common Exam: **Smokers)**
      Males: 469 per million = 1 in 2,132   (CE × 1.00)
      Females: 444 per million = 1 in 2,252   (CE × 1.00)

Per Shot	*Ent Dose*	*Beam HVL*	*Male Cancer Risk*	*Female Cancer Risk*
AP	0.451 R	2.4 mm Al	338 per million	220 per million
PA	0.432 R	1.8 mm Al	66 per million	60 per million
LAT	0.907 R	2.4 mm Al	131 per million	224 per million
OBL-AP	0.928 R	2.3 mm Al	398 per million	327 per million

All values are for the Common Exam

Age 25, Hip   Cancer Rate............... *(Lowering Factor)*
      Males: 466 per million = 1 in 2,146   (Age 20 × 0.994)
      Females: 439 per million = 1 in 2,278   (Age 20 × 0.988)
Age 30, Hip   Cancer Rate............... *(Lowering Factor)*
      Males: 401 per million = 1 in 2,494   (Age 20 × 0.854)
      Females: 388 per million = 1 in 2,577   (Age 20 × 0.873)
Age 35, Hip   Cancer Rate............... *(Lowering Factor)*
      Males: 287 per million = 1 in 3,484   (Age 20 × 0.611)
      Females: 277 per million = 1 in 3,610   (Age 20 × 0.623)
Age 40, Hip   Cancer Rate............... *(Lowering Factor)*
      Males: 174 per million = 1 in 5,747   (Age 20 × 0.372)
      Females: 174 per million = 1 in 5,747   (Age 20 × 0.391)
Age 45, Hip   Cancer Rate............... *(Lowering Factor)*
      Males: 76 per million = 1 in 13,160   (Age 20 × 0.162)
      Females: 78 per million = 1 in 12,820   (Age 20 × 0.176)
Age 50, Hip   Cancer Rate............... *(Lowering Factor)*
      Males: 7.0 per million = 1 in 143,000   (Age 20 × 0.015)
      Females: 7.5 per million = 1 in 133,300   (Age 20 × 0.017)
Age 55, Hip   Cancer Rate............... *(Lowering Factor)*
      Males: 4.7 per million = 1 in 213,000   (Age 20 × 0.010)
      Females: 5.3 per million = 1 in 189,000   (Age 20 × 0.012)

HUMERUS

Contrast Medium: No.

Fluoroscopy and Spot Films: No.

Length of Field: In the adult, the field center (AP exam) is 4.8 cm below the sternal notch, and positioned 16.8 cm to one side of the body midline. The field width is only 17.8 cm, so the medial edge of the field is still some 8 cm from the body midline in the AP exam. The field extends vertically from the external auditory meatus to approximately xiphoid level.

Organs Generating Most Cancer Risk:
  Males: Bronchi, lymphatic tissues, skin, kidney, male breasts.
  Females: Breasts, bronchi, lymphatic tissues, kidney.

Special Comments:
  • The risks apply to examination of *one* humerus.
  • The risk of breast cancer accounts for some 85%–90% of the exam's total cancer risk for females. Shielding would appear to offer real advantages. In this "bone exam," the bone itself accounts for only about 1% of the resulting cancer risk.
  • Because the risk will be virtually identical from the AP and LAT shots in this exam, the table provides one entry for "either" shot.

AGE NEW Testes, dose CE: < 1 mrad
HUMERUS Ovaries, dose CE: < 1 mrad

Common Exam (CE): One AP and one LAT (by twist)
                  (Total: 2 shots)
Rate of future *leukemia* from Common Exam:
        Males: 0.4 per million = 1 in 250,000
        Females: 0.25 per million = 1 in 400,000
Rate of future *cancer* from Common Exam:
        Males: 14 per million = 1 in 71,400
        Females: 92 per million = 1 in 10,900

Per Shot	Ent Dose	Beam HVL	Male Cancer Risk	Female Cancer Risk
Either	0.050 R	2.2 mm Al	7 per million	46 per million

AGE 1 Testes, dose CE: < 1 mrad
HUMERUS Ovaries, dose CE: < 1 mrad

Common Exam (CE): One AP and one LAT (by twist)
                  (Total: 2 shots)
Rate of future *leukemia* from Common Exam:
        Males: 0.4 per million = 1 in 250,000
        Females: 0.25 per million = 1 in 400,000
Rate of future *cancer* from Common Exam:
        Males: 14 per million = 1 in 71,400
        Females: 106 per million = 1 in 9,430

Per Shot	Ent Dose	Beam HVL	Male Cancer Risk	Female Cancer Risk
Either	0.062 R	2.2 mm Al	7 per million	53 per million

AGE 5
HUMERUS

Testes, dose CE: < 1 mrad
Ovaries, dose CE: < 1 mrad

Common Exam (CE): One AP and one LAT (by twist)
(Total: 2 shots)
Rate of future *leukemia* from Common Exam:
  Males: 0.6 per million = 1 in 1.7 million
  Females: 0.4 per million = 1 in 2.5 million
Rate of future *cancer* from Common Exam:
  Males: 20 per million = 1 in 50,000
  Females: 144 per million = 1 in 6,944

Per Shot	*Ent Dose*	*Beam HVL*	*Male Cancer Risk*	*Female Cancer Risk*
Either	0.105 R	2.2 mm Al	10 per million	72 per million

AGE 10
HUMERUS

Testes, dose CE: < 1 mrad
Ovaries, dose CE: < 1 mrad

Common Exam (CE): One AP and one LAT (by twist)
(Total: 2 shots)
Rate of future *leukemia* from Common Exam:
  Males: 0.7 per million = 1 in 1.4 million
  Females: 0.4 per million = 1 in 2.5 million
Rate of future *cancer* from Common Exam:
  Males: 24 per million = 1 in 41,700
  Females: 164 per million = 1 in 6,098

Per Shot	*Ent Dose*	*Beam HVL*	*Male Cancer Risk*	*Female Cancer Risk*
Either	0.158 R	2.2 mm Al	12 per million	82 per million

AGE 15
HUMERUS

Testes, dose CE: < 1 mrad
Ovaries, dose CE: < 1 mrad

Common Exam (CE): One AP and one LAT (by twist)
(Total: 2 shots)
Rate of future *leukemia* from Common Exam:
  Males: 0.7 per million = 1 in 1.4 million
  Females: 0.4 per million = 1 in 2.5 million
Rate of future *cancer* from Common Exam:
  Males: 13 per million = 1 in 76,900
  Females: 92 per million = 1 in 10,900

Per Shot	*Ent Dose*	*Beam HVL*	*Male Cancer Risk*	*Female Cancer Risk*
Either	0.212 R	2.2 mm Al	6.5 per million	46 per million

AGE 20
HUMERUS

Testes, dose CE: < 1 mrad
Ovaries, dose CE: < 1 mrad
Embryo, dose CE: < 1 mrad

Common Exam (CE): One AP and one LAT (by twist)
(Total: 2 shots)
Rate of future *leukemia* from Common Exam:
Males: 0.6 per million = 1 in 1.7 million
Females: 0.4 per million = 1 in 2.5 million
Rate of future *cancer* from Common Exam:　　　　　　　(Smokers)
Males: 12 per million = 1 in 83,300　　　　(CE × 5.79)
Females: 86 per million = 1 in 11,630　　　　(CE × 1.39)

Per Shot	*Ent Dose*	*Beam HVL*	*Male Cancer Risk*	*Female Cancer Risk*
Either	0.257 R	2.2 mm Al	6 per million	43 per million

All values are for the Common Exam

Age 30, Humerus　　　　　　Cancer Rate............... *(Lowering Factor)*
　　　Males: 10 per million = 1 in 100,000　　　(Age 20 × 0.854)
　　　Females: 75 per million = 1 in 13,300　　　(Age 20 × 0.873)
Age 40, Humerus　　　　　　Cancer Rate............... *(Lowering Factor)*
　　　Males: 4.5 per million = 1 in 222,000　　　(Age 20 × 0.372)
　　　Females: 34 per million = 1 in 29,400　　　(Age 20 × 0.391)
Age 50, Humerus　　　　　　Cancer Rate............... *(Lowering Factor)*
　　　Males: 0.2 per million = 1 in 5.6 million　　　(Age 20 × 0.015)
　　　Females: 1.5 per million = 1 in 667,000　　　(Age 20 × 0.017)

HYSTEROSALPINGOGRAPHY

Contrast Medium: Yes. An organically bound iodine compound administered by catheter in cervix.

Fluoroscopy and Spot Films: Yes, fluoroscopy with or without spot films is done. The dose and risks from the FLU and spot films are additional to the values in the following table; for evaluation of risks from FLU, please see Chapter 6.

Length of Field: Field dimensions are essentially those of the Pelvis Exam.

Organs Generating Most Cancer Risk:
　　Female only: Corpus uteri, bladder, cervix uteri, ovaries, rectum, large intestine.

Hysterosalpingography *(continued)*

Special Comments:
- This table begins at age 15.
- This exam usually involves 3 to 5 injections (via catheter inserted into the cervical canal) of an organically-bound iodine contrast compound, with FLU and spot films taken at various points during these injections. Films are also taken at various intervals after the injections. We have used the data of Meschan (1975) for the number of films and the beam directions. If additional shots are taken, risk values would need adjustment upwards, by the simple method demonstrated in Chapter 4, Sections 2 and 4.
- In this exam, a steep decrease in risk from the LAT shot occurs as age advances from 15 to 20 years old. See the last "Special Comment," Barium Enema Exam.

AGE 15   Ovaries, dose CE: 701 mrads
HYSTEROSALPINGOGRAPHY

Common Exam (CE): Five AP and one LAT
                     (Also FLU and spot films)
Rate of future *leukemia* from Common Exam:
         Females: 21 per million = 1 in 47,600
Rate of future *cancer* from Common Exam:
         Females: 2,692 per million = 1 in 371

Per Shot	Ent Dose	Beam HVL	Male Cancer Risk	Female Cancer Risk
AP	0.450 R	2.4 mm Al	None	440 per million
LAT	1.108 R	2.6 mm Al		492 per million

AGE 20   Ovaries, dose CE: 605 mrads
HYSTEROSALPINGOGRAPHY   Embryo, dose CE: 783 mrads

Common Exam (CE): Five AP and one LAT
                     (Also FLU and spot films)
Rate of future *leukemia* from Common Exam:
         Females: 14 per million = 1 in 71,420
Rate of future *cancer* from Common Exam: **(Smokers)**
         Females: 2,095 per million = 1 in 477   (CE × 1.00)

Per Shot	Ent Dose	Beam HVL	Male Cancer Risk	Female Cancer Risk
AP	0.545 R	2.4 mm Al	None	381 per million
LAT	1.343 R	2.6 mm Al		190 per million

All values are for the Common Exam

Age 25, Hysterosalpingo.	Cancer Rate...............	*(Lowering Factor)*
Females: 2,070 per million = 1 in 483		(Age 20 × 0.988)
Age 30, Hysterosalpingo.	Cancer Rate...............	*(Lowering Factor)*
Females: 1,829 per million = 1 in 547		(Age 20 × 0.873)
Age 35, Hystersalpingo.	Cancer Rate...............	*(Lowering Factor)*
Females: 1,305 per million = 1 in 766		(Age 20 × 0.623)
Age 40, Hysterosalpingo.	Cancer Rate...............	*(Lowering Factor)*
Females: 819 per million = 1 in 1,221		(Age 20 × 0.391)
Age 45, Hysterosalpingo.	Cancer Rate...............	*(Lowering Factor)*
Females: 369 per million = 1 in 2,710		(Age 20 × 0.176)
Age 50, Hysterosalpingo.	Cancer Rate...............	*(Lowering Factor)*
Females: 36 per million = 1 in 27,800		(Age 20 × 0.017)
Age 55, Hysterosalpingo.	Cancer Rate...............	*(Lowering Factor)*
Females: 25 per million = 1 in 40,000		(Age 20 × 0.012)

INTRAVENOUS PYELOGRAM (I.V.P.)

Contrast Medium: Yes. An organically bound iodine compound given intravenously.

Fluoroscopy and Spot Films: No.

Length of Field: In adults, field center is at the level of the bi-iliac crests, and (in the AP exam) field center is at body midline. The field length is 43.2 cm, so it extends from approximately the xiphoid process to 5.5 cm below the pubic symphysis. The pediatric exams are adjusted to encompass the same organ regions, except of course for the "Kidneys-AP" shots (see below for field).

Organs Generating Most Cancer Risk:
    Males: Prostate, large intestine, bladder, stomach, pancreas, rectum.
    Females: Large intestine, corpus uteri, stomach, pancreas, bladder,
        breasts. (The breasts are *more* at risk in pediatric exams because of
        the "Kidneys-AP" shot.)

Special Comments:
- Note that the Common Exam is different for pediatric and adult ages.
- The "Kidneys-AP" shot extends vertically "from diaphragm to 2.5 cm below umbilicus" for all pediatric ages, according to Rosenstein and co-workers (1979).
- In this exam, and several others, a particularly steep decrease in risk from the LAT shot occurs as age advances from 10 to 20 years old. See the last "Special Comment," Barium Enema Exam.

AGE NEW   Testes, dose CE: 15 mrads
I.V.P. (INTRAVENOUS PYELOGRAM)   Ovaries, dose CE: 167 mrads

Common Exam (CE): Two AP and two "Kidneys-AP"
                    (Total: 4 shots)
Rate of future *leukemia* from Common Exam:
            Males: 8 per million = 1 in 125,000
            Females: 5 per million = 1 in 200,000
Rate of future *cancer* from Common Exam:
            Males: 3,568 per million = 1 in 280
            Females: 3,833 per million = 1 in 261

Per Shot	Ent Dose	Beam HVL	Male Cancer Risk	Female Cancer Risk
AP	0.117 R	2.5 mm Al	1,089 per million	1,043 per million
PA	0.086 R	2.5 mm Al	602 per million	642 per million
LAT	0.103 R	2.6 mm Al	656 per million	806 per million
OBL-AP	0.179 R	2.6 mm Al	1,595 per million	1,615 per million
Kid'y-AP	0.130 R	2.5 mm Al	695 per million	874 per million

AGE 1   Testes, dose CE: 16 mrads
I.V.P. (INTRAVENOUS PYELOGRAM)   Ovaries, dose CE: 156 mrads

Common Exam (CE): Two AP and two "Kidneys-AP"
                    (Total: 4 shots)
Rate of future *leukemia* from Common Exam:
            Males: 9 per million = 1 in 111,000
            Females: 5 per million = 1 in 200,000
Rate of future *cancer* from Common Exam:
            Males: 3,726 per million = 1 in 268
            Females: 4,029 per million = 1 in 248

Per Shot	Ent Dose	Beam HVL	Male Cancer Risk	Female Cancer Risk
AP	0.144 R	2.5 mm Al	1,162 per million	1,113 per million
PA	0.107 R	2.5 mm Al	621 per million	652 per million
LAT	0.127 R	2.6 mm Al	631 per million	787 per million
OBL-AP	0.221 R	2.6 mm Al	1,620 per million	1,644 per million
Kid'y-AP	0.161 R	2.5 mm Al	701 per million	902 per million

AGE 5   Testes, dose CE: 20 mrads
I.V.P. (INTRAVENOUS PYELOGRAM)   Ovaries, dose CE: 187 mrads

Common Exam (CE): Two AP and two "Kidneys-AP"
                    (Total: 4 shots)
Rate of future *leukemia* from Common Exam:
            Males: 12 per million = 1 in 83,300
            Females: 7 per million = 1 in 143,000

Rate of future *cancer* from Common Exam:
  Males: 5,032 per million = 1 in 199
  Females: 5,141 per million = 1 in 194

Per Shot	Ent Dose	Beam HVL	Male Cancer Risk	Female Cancer Risk
AP	0.243 R	2.5 mm Al	1,615 per million	1,462 per million
PA	0.180 R	2.5 mm Al	852 per million	836 per million
LAT	0.215 R	2.6 mm Al	794 per million	906 per million
OBL-AP	0.372 R	2.6 mm Al	2,192 per million	2,113 per million
Kid'y-AP	0.271 R	2.5 mm Al	901 per million	1,108 per million

AGE 10   Testes, dose CE: 22 mrads
I.V.P. (INTRAVENOUS PYELOGRAM)   Ovaries, dose CE: 239 mrads

Common Exam (CE): Two AP and two "Kidneys-AP)
            (Total: 4 shots)
Rate of future *leukemia* from Common Exam:
  Males: 14 per million = 1 in 71,400
  Females: 9 per million = 1 in 111,000
Rate of future *cancer* from Common Exam:
  Males: 5,790 per million = 1 in 173
  Females: 5,604 per million = 1 in 178

Per Shot	Ent Dose	Beam HVL	Male Cancer Risk	Female Cancer Risk
AP	0.367 R	2.5 mm Al	1,863 per million	1,588 per million
PA	0.272 R	2.5 mm Al	956 per million	890 per million
LAT	0.324 R	2.6 mm Al	838 per million	915 per million
OBL-AP	0.563 R	2.6 mm Al	2,404 per million	2,242 per million
Kid'y-AP	0.410 R	2.5 mm Al	1,032 per million	1,214 per million

AGE 15   Testes, dose CE: 19 mrads
I.V.P. (INTRAVENOUS PYELOGRAM)   Ovaries, dose CE: 284 mrads

Common Exam (CE): Two AP and two "Kidneys-AP"
            (Total: 4 shots)
Rate of future *leukemia* from Common Exam:
  Males: 15 per million = 1 in 66,700
  Females: 9 per million = 1 in 111,000
Rate of future *cancer* from Common Exam:
  Males: 3,260 per million = 1 in 307
  Females: 3,059 per million = 1 in 327

Age 15, I.V.P. *(continued)*

Per Shot	Ent Dose	Beam HVL	Male Cancer Risk	Female Cancer Risk
AP	0.491 R	2.5 mm Al	1,054 per million	868 per million
PA	0.364 R	2.5 mm Al	469 per million	425 per million
LAT	0.434 R	2.6 mm Al	300 per million	308 per million
OBL-AP	0.753 R	2.6 mm Al	1,140 per million	1,024 per million
Kid'y-AP	0.548 R	2.5 mm Al	576 per million	662 per million

AGE 20
I.V.P. (INTRAVENOUS PYELOGRAM)

Testes, dose CE: 50 mrads
Ovaries, dose CE: 692 mrads
Embryo, dose CE: 935 mrads

Common Exam (CE): Five AP and one OBL-AP
(Total: 6 shots)
Rate of future *leukemia* from Common Exam:
Males: 24 per million = 1 in 41,700
Females: 15 per million = 1 in 66,700
Rate of future *cancer* from Common Exam: **(Smokers)**
Males: 5,792 per million = 1 in 173   (CE × 1.02)
Females: 4,828 per million = 1 in 207   (CE × 1.02)

Per Shot	Ent Dose	Beam HVL	Male Cancer Risk	Female Cancer Risk
AP	0.595 R	2.5 mm Al	976 per million	808 per million
PA	0.441 R	2.5 mm Al	386 per million	343 per million
LAT	0.526 R	2.6 mm Al	135 per million	134 per million
OBL-AP	0.913 R	2.6 mm Al	912 per million	788 per million

All values are for the Common Exam

Age 25, I.V.P.   Cancer Rate............... *(Lowering Factor)*
        Males: 5,757 per million = 1 in 174   (Age 20 × 0.994)
        Females: 4,770 per million = 1 in 210   (Age 20 × 0.988)
Age 30, I.V.P.   Cancer Rate............... *(Lowering Factor)*
        Males: 4,946 per million = 1 in 202   (Age 20 × 0.854)
        Females: 4,215 per million = 1 in 237   (Age 20 × 0.873)
Age 35, I.V.P.   Cancer Rate............... *(Lowering Factor)*
        Males: 3,539 per million = 1 in 282   (Age 20 × 0.611)
        Females: 3,008 per million = 1 in 332   (Age 20 × 0.623)
Age 40, I.V.P.   Cancer Rate............... *(Lowering Factor)*
        Males: 2,155 per million = 1 in 464   (Age 20 × 0.372)
        Females: 1,888 per million = 1 in 530   (Age 20 × 0.391)
Age 45, I.V.P.   Cancer Rate............... *(Lowering Factor)*
        Males: 938 per million = 1 in 1,066   (Age 20 × 0.162)
        Females: 850 per million = 1 in 1,176   (Age 20 × 0.176)
Age 50, I.V.P.   Cancer Rate............... *(Lowering Factor)*
        Males: 87 per million = 1 in 11,500   (Age 20 × 0.015)
        Females: 82 per million = 1 in 12,200   (Age 20 × 0.017)
Age 55, I.V.P.   Cancer Rate............... *(Lowering Factor)*
        Males: 58 per million = 1 in 17,200   (Age 20 × 0.010)
        Females: 58 per million = 1 in 17,200   (Age 20 × 0.012)

KNEE

Contrast Medium: No.

Fluoroscopy and Spot Films: No.

Length of Field: Body part. See below.

Organs Generating Most Cancer Risk:
   Males: Lymphatic tissues (generating lymphoma, Hodgkin's Disease, and
      multiple myeloma), connective tissue, skin, bone.
   Females: Same.

Special Comments:
   • Cancer and leukemia risks are for examination of *one* knee joint, with
      the field including one third of the lower leg and one third of the femur.
   • Cancer risk is based on the approximation that 4.89% of body bone is in
      this defined field for one knee joint.
   • Because the risk will be virtually identical regardless of the beam's
      direction, the table provides one entry for "any" shot.

AGE NEW   Testes, dose CE: < 1 mrad
KNEE   Ovaries, dose CE: < 1 mrad

Common Exam (CE): One AP, one LAT, and
                  one OBL (Total: 3 shots)
Rate of future *leukemia* from Common Exam:
            Males: 1 per million = 1 in one million
            Females: 0.6 per million = 1 in 1.7 million
Rate of future *cancer* from Common Exam:
            Males: 11 per million = 1 in 90,900
            Females: 12 per million = 1 in 83,333

Per Shot	Ent Dose	Beam HVL	Male Cancer Risk	Female Cancer Risk
Any	0.051 R	2.4 mm Al	3.8 per million	3.9 per million

AGE 1   Testes, dose CE: < 1 mrad
KNEE   Ovaries, dose CE: < 1 mrad

Common Exam (CE): One AP, one LAT, and
                  one OBL (Total: 3 shots)
Rate of future *leukemia* from Common Exam:
            Males: 1 per million = 1 in one million
            Females: 0.6 per million = 1 in 1.7 million
Rate of future *cancer* from Common Exam:
            Males: 13 per million = 1 in 76,900
            Females: 13 per million = 1 in 76,900

Age 1, Knee *(continued)*

Per Shot	Ent Dose	Beam HVL	Male Cancer Risk	Female Cancer Risk
Any	0.063 R	2.4 mm Al	4.2 per million	4.3 per million

AGE 5   Testes, dose CE: < 1 mrad
KNEE   Ovaries, dose CE: < 1 mrad

Common Exam (CE): One AP, one LAT, and
                      one OBL (Total: 3 shots)
Rate of future *leukemia* from Common Exam:
          Males: 1.1 per million = 1 in 909,000
          Females: 0.7 per million = 1 in 1.4 million
Rate of future *cancer* from Common Exam:
          Males: 17 per million = 1 in 58,800
          Females: 17 per million = 1 in 58,800

Per Shot	Ent Dose	Beam HVL	Male Cancer Risk	Female Cancer Risk
Any	0.106 R	2.4 mm Al	5.8 per million	5.5 per million

AGE 10   Testes, dose CE: < 1 mrad
KNEE   Ovaries, dose CE: < 1 mrad

Common Exam (CE): One AP, one LAT, and
                      one OBL (Total: 3 shots)
Rate of future *leukemia* from Common Exam:
          Males: 1 per million = 1 in one million
          Females: 0.7 per million = 1 in 1.4 million
Rate of future *cancer* from Common Exam:
          Males: 20 per million = 1 in 50,000
          Females: 18 per million = 1 in 55,600

Per Shot	Ent Dose	Beam HVL	Male Cancer Risk	Female Cancer Risk
Any	0.160 R	2.4 mm Al	6.7 per million	6.1 per million

AGE 15   Testes, dose CE: < 1 mrad
KNEE   Ovaries, dose CE: < 1 mrad

Common Exam (CE): One AP, one LAT, and
                      one OBL (Total: 3 shots)
Rate of future *leukemia* from Common Exam:
          Males: 0.6 per million = 1 in 1.7 million
          Females: 0.4 per million = 1 in 2.5 million

Rate of future *cancer* from Common Exam:
          Males: 11 per million = 1 in 90,900
          Females: 10 per million = 1 in 100,000

Per Shot	Ent Dose	Beam HVL	Male Cancer Risk	Female Cancer Risk
Any	0.214 R	2.4 mm Al	3.7 per million	3.3 per million

AGE 20   Testes, dose CE: < 1 mrad
KNEE   Ovaries, dose CE: < 1 mrad
                                                      Embryo, dose CE: < 1 mrad

Common Exam (CE): One AP, one LAT, and
                  one OBL (Total: 3 shots)
Rate of future *leukemia* from Common Exam:
          Males: < 0.1 per million = < 1 in ten million
          Females: < 0.1 per million = < 1 in ten million
Rate of future *cancer* from Common Exam: **(Smokers)**
          Males: 10 per million = 1 in 100,000   (CE × 1.00)
          Females: 8.6 per million = 1 in 116,000   (CE × 1.00)

Per Shot	Ent Dose	Beam HVL	Male Cancer Risk	Female Cancer Risk
Any	0.260 R	2.4 mm Al	3.3 per million	2.9 per million

All values are for the Common Exam

Age 30, Knee   Cancer Rate............... *(Lowering Factor)*
          Males: 8.5 per million = 1 in 118,000   (Age 20 × 0.854)
          Females: 7.5 per million = 1 in 133,000   (Age 20 × 0.873)
Age 40, Knee   Cancer Rate............... *(Lowering Factor)*
          Males: 3.7 per million = 1 in 270,000   (Age 20 × 0.372)
          Females: 3.4 per million = 1 in 294,000   (Age 20 × 0.391)
Age 50, Knee   Cancer Rate............... *(Lowering Factor)*
          Males: 0.15 per million = 1 in 6.7 million   (Age 20 × 0.015)
          Females: 0.15 per million = 1 in 6.7 million   (Age 20 × 0.017)

K.U.B. (KIDNEY-URETER-BLADDER)

Contrast Medium: No.

Fluoroscopy and Spot Films: No.

Length of Field: In the adult, the field center is at the bi-iliac crest and the body midline. The field (total length = 43.2 cm) extends vertically from the xiphoid process of the sternum down to 5 cm below the pubic symphysis. All pediatric

K.U.B. *(continued)*

calculations for this exam assume that the field length is adjusted to encompass only the same body region and organs.

Organs Generating Most Cancer Risk:
   Males: Bladder, prostate, large intestine, stomach, pancreas, rectum.
   Females: Large intestine, corpus uteri, bladder, stomach, pancreas, cervix.

Special Comment:
   • The Common Exam varies with age.

AGE NEW   Testes, dose CE: 9 mrads
K.U.B. (KIDNEY-URETER-BLADDER)   Ovaries, dose CE: 71 mrads

Common Exam (CE): One AP
                      (Total: 1 shot)
Rate of future *leukemia* from Common Exam:
         Males: 3 per million = 1 in 333,000
         Females: 2 per million = 1 in 500,000
Rate of future *cancer* from Common Exam:
         Males: 1,260 per million = 1 in 794
         Females: 1,229 per million = 1 in 814

Per Shot	Ent Dose	Beam HVL	Male Cancer Risk	Female Cancer Risk
AP	0.130 R	2.5 mm Al	1,260 per million	1,229 per million
PA	0.082 R	2.4 mm Al	544 per million	580 per million
LAT	0.411 R	2.5 mm Al	2,433 per million	3,011 per million
OBL-PA	0.116 R	2.4 mm Al	1,215 per million	1,441 per million

AGE 1   Testes, dose CE: 10 mrads
K.U.B. (KIDNEY-URETER-BLADDER)   Ovaries, dose CE: 59 mrads

Common Exam (CE): One AP
                      (Total: 1 shot)
Rate of future *leukemia* from Common Exam:
         Males: 3 per million = 1 in 333,000
         Females: 2 per million = 1 in 500,000
Rate of future *cancer* from Common Exam:
         Males: 1,344 per million = 1 in 744
         Females: 1,288 per million = 1 in 776

Per Shot	Ent Dose	Beam HVL	Male Cancer Risk	Female Cancer Risk
AP	0.161 R	2.5 mm Al	1,344 per million	1,288 per million
PA	0.101 R	2.4 mm Al	574 per million	563 per million
LAT	0.507 R	2.5 mm Al	2,339 per million	2,942 per million
OBL-PA	0.296 R	2.4 mm Al	1,195 per million	1,421 per million

AGE 5
K.U.B. (KIDNEY-URETER-BLADDER)

Testes, dose CE: 23 mrads
Ovaries, dose CE: 162 mrads

Common Exam (CE): One AP and one Erect Abdomen-AP
(Total: 2 shots)
Rate of future *leukemia* from Common Exam:
      Males: 9 per million = 1 in 111,000
      Females: 5 per million = 1 in 200,000
Rate of future *cancer* from Common Exam:
      Males: 3,517 per million = 1 in 284
      Females: 3,288 per million = 1 in 304

Per Shot	Ent Dose	Beam HVL	Male Cancer Risk	Female Cancer Risk
AP	0.271 R	2.5 mm Al	1,869 per million	1,691 per million
PA	0.171 R	2.4 mm Al	788 per million	720 per million
LAT	0.856 R	2.5 mm Al	2,940 per million	3,386 per million
OBL-PA	0.498 R	2.4 mm Al	1,583 per million	1,727 per million
Erect AP	0.271 R	2.5 mm Al	1,648 per million	1,597 per million

AGE 10
K.U.B. (KIDNEY-URETER-BLADDER)

Testes, dose CE: 25 mrads
Ovaries, dose CE: 220 mrads

Common Exam (CE): One AP and one Erect Abdomen-AP
(Total: 2 shots)
Rate of future *leukemia* from Common Exam:
      Males: 11 per million = 1 in 90,900
      Females: 7 per million = 1 in 143,000
Rate of future *cancer* from Common Exam:
      Males: 4,052 per million = 1 in 247
      Females: 3,603 per million = 1 in 278

Per Shot	Ent Dose	Beam HVL	Male Cancer Risk	Female Cancer Risk
AP	0.410 R	2.5 mm Al	2,155 per million	1,838 per million
PA	0.258 R	2.4 mm Al	884 per million	766 per million
LAT	1.294 R	2.5 mm Al	3,106 per million	3,420 per million
OBL-PA	0.754 R	2.4 mm Al	1,615 per million	1,770 per million
Erect AP	0.410 R	2.5 mm Al	1,897 per million	1,765 per million

AGE 15
K.U.B. (KIDNEY-URETER-BLADDER)

Testes, dose CE: 22 mrads
Ovaries, dose CE: 221 mrads

Common Exam (CE): One AP and one Erect Abdomen-AP
(Total: 2 shots)
Rate of future *leukemia* from Common Exam:
      Males: 11 per million = 1 in 90,900
      Females: 7 per million = 1 in 143,000

Age 15, K.U.B. *(continued)*

Rate of future *cancer* from Common Exam:
          Males: 2,396 per million = 1 in 417
          Females: 2,044 per million = 1 in 489

Per Shot	Ent Dose	Beam HVL	Male Cancer Risk	Female Cancer Risk
AP	0.548 R	2.5 mm Al	1,221 per million	1,003 per million
PA	0.346 R	2.4 mm Al	433 per million	363 per million
LAT	1.730 R	2.5 mm Al	1,113 per million	1,155 per million
OBL-PA	1.008 R	2.4 mm Al	864 per million	670 per million
Erect AP	0.548 R	2.5 mm Al	1,175 per million	1,041 per million

AGE 20
K.U.B. (KIDNEY-URETER-BLADDER)

Testes, dose CE: 11 mrads
Ovaries, dose CE: 134 mrads
Embryo, dose CE: 178 mrads

Common Exam (CE): One AP
          (Total: 1 shot)
Rate of future *leukemia* from Common Exam:
          Males: 4 per million = 1 in 250,000
          Females: 2.5 per million = 1 in 400,000
Rate of future *cancer* from Common Exam: **(Smokers)**
          Males: 1,169 per million = 1 in 855   (CE × 1.02)
          Females: 936 per million = 1 in 1,068   (CE × 1.02)

Per Shot	Ent Dose	Beam HVL	Male Cancer Risk	Female Cancer Risk
AP	0.664 R	2.5 mm Al	1,169 per million	936 per million
PA	0.419 R	2.4 mm Al	348 per million	309 per million
LAT	2.097 R	2.5 mm Al	503 per million	504 per million
OBL-PA	1.222 R	2.4 mm Al	688 per million	598 per million

All values are for the Common Exam

Age 25, K.U.B.   Cancer Rate. . . . . *(Lowering Factor)*
          Males: 1,162 per million = 1 in 861   (Age 20 × 0.994)
          Females: 925 per million = 1 in 1,081   (Age 20 × 0.988)
Age 30, K.U.B.   Cancer Rate. . . . . *(Lowering Factor)*
          Males: 998 per million = 1 in 1,002   (Age 20 × 0.854)
          Females: 817 per million = 1 in 1,224   (Age 20 × 0.873)
Age 35, K.U.B.   Cancer Rate. . . . . *(Lowering Factor)*
          Males: 714 per million = 1 in 1,401   (Age 20 × 0.611)
          Females: 583 per million = 1 in 1,715   (Age 20 × 0.623)
Age 40, K.U.B.   Cancer Rate. . . . . *(Lowering Factor)*
          Males: 435 per million = 1 in 2,299   (Age 20 × 0.372)
          Females: 366 per million = 1 in 2,732   (Age 20 × 0.391)

Age 45, K.U.B.   Cancer Rate . . . . *(Lowering Factor)*
       Males: 189 per million = 1 in 5,291   (Age 20 × 0.162)
       Females: 165 per million = 1 in 6,061   (Age 20 × 0.176)
Age 50, K.U.B.   Cancer Rate . . . . *(Lowering Factor)*
       Males: 18 per million = 1 in 55,600   (Age 20 × 0.015)
       Females: 16 per million = 1 in 62,500   (Age 20 × 0.017)
Age 55, K.U.B.   Cancer Rate . . . . *(Lowering Factor)*
       Males: 12 per million = 1 in 83,300   (Age 20 × 0.010)
       Females: 11 per million = 1 in 90,900   (Age 20 × 0.012)

LOWER LEG: TIBIA AND FIBULA

Contrast Medium: No.

Fluoroscopy and Spot Films: No.

Length of Field: Body part.

Organs Generating Most Cancer Risk:
   Males: Lymphatic tissues (generating lymphomas, multiple myelomas,
      and Hodgkin's Disease), skin, connective tissue, bone.
   Females: Same.

Special Comments:
- Cancer and leukemia risks are for examination of *one* lower leg.
- Cancer risk is based on the approximation that 6.2% of body bone is in the lower leg on one side of the body.
- Because the risk will be virtually identical regardless of the beam's direction, the table provides one entry for "either" shot.

AGE NEW   Testes, dose CE: < 1 mrad
LOWER LEG: TIBIA AND FIBULA   Ovaries, dose CE: < 1 mrad

Common Exam (CE): One AP and one LAT
                 (Total: 2 shots)
Rate of future *leukemia* from Common Exam:
      Males: 0.9 per million = 1 in 1.1 million
      Females: 0.6 per million = 1 in 1.7 million
Rate of future *cancer* from Common Exam:
      Males: 11 per million = 1 in 90,900
      Females: 11 per million = 1 in 90,900

Per Shot	*Ent Dose*	*Beam HVL*	*Male Cancer Risk*	*Female Cancer Risk*
Either	0.051 R	2.4 mm Al	5.5 per million	5.5 per million

AGE 1
LOWER LEG: TIBIA AND FIBULA

Testes, dose CE: < 1 mrad
Ovaries, dose CE: < 1 mrad

Common Exam (CE): One AP and one LAT
(Total: 2 shots)
Rate of future *leukemia* from Common Exam:
    Males: 0.9 per million = 1 in 1.1 million
    Females: 0.6 per million = 1 in 1.7 million
Rate of future *cancer* from Common Exam:
    Males: 12 per million = 1 in 83,300
    Females: 11 per million = 1 in 90,900

Per Shot	Ent Dose	Beam HVL	Male Cancer Risk	Female Cancer Risk
Either	0.063 R	2.4 mm Al	6.1 per million	5.5 per million

AGE 5
LOWER LEG: TIBIA AND FIBULA

Testes, dose CE: < 1 mrad
Ovaries, dose CE: < 1 mrad

Common Exam (CE): One AP and one LAT
(Total: 2 shots)
Rate of future *leukemia* from Common Exam:
    Males: 1.1 per million = 1 in 909,000
    Females: 0.7 per million = 1 in 1.4 million
Rate of future *cancer* from Common Exam:
    Males: 17 per million = 1 in 58,800
    Females: 16 per million = 1 in 62,500

Per Shot	Ent Dose	Beam HVL	Male Cancer Risk	Female Cancer Risk
Either	0.106 R	2.4 mm Al	8.4 per million	8 per million

AGE 10
LOWER LEG: TIBIA AND FIBULA

Testes, dose CE: < 1 mrad
Ovaries, dose CE: < 1 mrad

Common Exam (CE): One AP and one LAT
(Total: 2 shots)
Rate of future *leukemia* from Common Exam:
    Males: 1 per million = 1 in one million
    Females: 0.6 per million = 1 in 1.7 million
Rate of future *cancer* from Common Exam:
    Males: 19 per million = 1 in 52,600
    Females: 18 per million = 1 in 55,600

Per Shot	Ent Dose	Beam HVL	Male Cancer Risk	Female Cancer Risk
Either	0.160 R	2.4 mm Al	9.7 per million	8.8 per million

AGE 15
LOWER LEG: TIBIA AND FIBULA

Testes, dose CE: < 1 mrad
Ovaries, dose CE: < 1 mrad

Common Exam (CE): One AP and one LAT
(Total: 2 shots)
Rate of future *leukemia* from Common Exam:
    Males: 0.6 per million = 1 in 1.7 million
    Females: 0.4 per million = 1 in 2.5 million
Rate of future *cancer* from Common Exam:
    Males: 11 per million = 1 in 90,900
    Females: 10 per million = 1 in 100,000

Per Shot	Ent Dose	Beam HVL	Male Cancer Risk	Female Cancer Risk
Either	0.214 R	2.4 mm Al	5.4 per million	4.8 per million

AGE 20
LOWER LEG: TIBIA AND FIBULA

Testes, dose CE: < 1 mrad
Ovaries, dose CE: < 1 mrad
Embryo, dose CE: < 1 mrad

Common Exam (CE): One AP and one LAT
(Total: 2 shots)
Rate of future *leukemia* from Common Exam:
    Males: < 0.1 per million = < 1 in 10 million
    Females: < 0.1 per million = < 1 in 10 million
Rate of future *cancer* from Common Exam: **(Smokers)**
    Males: 9.6 per million = 1 in 104,000   (CE × 1.00)
    Females: 8.3 per million = 1 in 120,000   (CE × 1.00)

Per Shot	Ent Dose	Beam HVL	Male Cancer Risk	Female Cancer Risk
Either	0.260 R	2.4 mm Al	4.8 per million	4.15 per million

All values are for the Common Exam

Age 30, Lower Leg   Cancer Rate................ *(Lowering Factor)*
        Males: 8.2 per million = 1 in 122,000   (Age 20 × 0.854)
        Females: 7.2 per million = 1 in 139,000   (Age 20 × 0.873)
Age 40, Lower Leg   Cancer Rate................ *(Lowering Factor)*
        Males: 3.6 per million = 1 in 278,000   (Age 20 × 0.372)
        Females: 3.2 per million = 1 in 313,000   (Age 20 × 0.391)
Age 50, Lower Leg   Cancer Rate................ *(Lowering Factor)*
        Males: 0.14 per million = 1 in 7.1 million   (Age 20 × 0.015)
        Females: 0.14 per million = 1 in 7.1 million   (Age 20 × 0.017)

LUMBAR SPINE—WIDE

Contrast Medium: No.

Fluoroscopy and Spot Films: No.

Length of Field: The field center is 5.5 cm above the bi-iliac crest and at the body midline in the AP shot. In the LAT shot, field center is moved 5 cm to the patient's rear. The field length is 43.2 cm, so it extends from 5 cm above the xiphoid process to the level of the pubic symphysis.

Organs Generating Most Cancer Risk:
  Males: Prostate, stomach, bladder, large intestine, pancreas, kidney.
  Females: Large intestine, corpus uteri, breasts, stomach, pancreas, ovaries.

Special Comments:
- This exam is designated as "wide" not to suggest that its field is any wider than normal (see Section 2 of this chapter), but rather to help distinguish it from the Lumbar Spine—Narrow Exam, which follows.
- In this exam, and several others, a particularly steep decrease in risk from the LAT shot occurs as age advances from 10 to 20 years old. See the last "Special Comment," Barium Enema Exam.

AGE NEW   Testes, dose CE: 14 mrads
LUMBAR SPINE—WIDE   Ovaries, dose CE: 451 mrads

Common Exam (CE): One AP, one LAT, and
                         one OBL-PA (Total: 3 shots)
Rate of future *leukemia* from Common Exam:
          Males: 43 per million = 1 in 23,300
          Females: 27 per million = 1 in 37,000
Rate of future *cancer* from Common Exam:
          Males: 7,824 per million = 1 in 128
          Females: 8,068 per million = 1 in 124

Per Shot	Ent Dose	Beam HVL	Male Cancer Risk	Female Cancer Risk
AP	0.173 R	2.4 mm Al	1,547 per million	1,545 per million
PA	0.106 R	2.5 mm Al	725 per million	688 per million
LAT	0.627 R	2.6 mm Al	4,733 per million	4,920 per million
OBL-PA	0.218 R	2.5 mm Al	1,544 per million	1,603 per million

AGE 1   Testes, dose CE: 15 mrads
LUMBAR SPINE—WIDE   Ovaries, dose CE: 434 mrads

Common Exam (CE): One AP, one LAT, and
                         one OBL-PA (Total: 3 shots)

Rate of future *leukemia* from Common Exam:
          Males: 40 per million = 1 in 25,000
          Females: 25 per million = 1 in 40,000
Rate of future *cancer* from Common Exam:
          Males: 7,910 per million = 1 in 126
          Females: 8,221 per million = 1 in 122

Per Shot	Ent Dose	Beam HVL	Male Cancer Risk	Female Cancer Risk
AP	0.214 R	2.4 mm Al	1,709 per million	1,697 per million
PA	0.131 R	2.5 mm Al	757 per million	714 per million
LAT	0.774 R	2.6 mm Al	4,638 per million	4,906 per million
OBL-PA	0.269 R	2.5 mm Al	1,563 per million	1,618 per million

AGE 5   Testes, dose CE: 16 mrads
LUMBAR SPINE—WIDE   Ovaries, dose CE: 615 mrads

Common Exam (CE): One AP, one LAT, and
                    one OBL-PA (Total: 3 shots)
Rate of future *leukemia* from Common Exam:
          Males: 53 per million = 1 in 18,900
          Females: 33 per million = 1 in 30,300
Rate of future *cancer* from Common Exam:
          Males: 10,335 per million = 1 in 97
          Females: 10,201 per million = 1 in 98

Per Shot	Ent Dose	Beam HVL	Male Cancer Risk	Female Cancer Risk
AP	0.361 R	2.4 mm Al	2,448 per million	2,303 per million
PA	0.221 R	2.5 mm Al	1,035 per million	907 per million
LAT	1.305 R	2.6 mm Al	5,830 per million	5,905 per million
OBL-PA	0.453 R	2.5 mm Al	2,057 per million	1,993 per million

AGE 10   Testes, dose CE: 17 mrads
LUMBAR SPINE—WIDE   Ovaries, dose CE: 792 mrads

Common Exam (CE): One AP, one LAT, and
                    one OBL-PA (Total: 3 shots)
Rate of future *leukemia* from Common Exam:
          Males: 58 per million = 1 in 17,200
          Females: 36 per million = 1 in 27,800
Rate of future *cancer* from Common Exam:
          Males: 11,144 per million = 1 in 90
          Females: 10,650 per million = 1 in 94

Age 10, Lumbar Spine, Wide *(continued)*

Per Shot	Ent Dose	Beam HVL	Male Cancer Risk	Female Cancer Risk
AP	0.545 R	2.4 mm Al	2,818 per million	2,518 per million
PA	0.338 R	2.5 mm Al	1,159 per million	952 per million
LAT	1.974 R	2.6 mm Al	6,166 per million	6,067 per million
OBL-PA	0.685 R	2.5 mm Al	2,160 per million	2,065 per million

AGE 15
LUMBAR SPINE—WIDE

Testes, dose CE: 11 mrads
Ovaries, dose CE: 636 mrads

Common Exam (CE): One AP, one LAT, and
            one OBL-PA (Total: 3 shots)
Rate of future *leukemia* from Common Exam:
        Males: 51 per million = 1 in 19,600
        Females: 32 per million = 1 in 31,250
Rate of future *cancer* from Common Exam:
        Males: 4,520 per million = 1 in 221
        Females: 4,332 per million = 1 in 231

Per Shot	Ent Dose	Beam HVL	Male Cancer Risk	Female Cancer Risk
AP	0.729 R	2.4 mm Al	1,544 per million	1,340 per million
PA	0.446 R	2.5 mm Al	562 per million	446 per million
LAT	2.639 R	2.6 mm Al	2,045 per million	2,151 per million
OBL-PA	0.916 R	2.5 mm Al	931 per million	841 per million

AGE 20
LUMBAR SPINE—WIDE

Testes, dose CE: 7 mrads
Ovaries, dose CE: 376 mrads
Embryo, dose CE: 370 mrads

Common Exam (CE): One AP, one LAT, and
            one OBL-PA (Total: 3 shots)
Rate of future *leukemia* from Common Exam:
        Males: 28 per million = 1 in 35,700
        Females: 18 per million = 1 in 55,600
Rate of future *cancer* from Common Exam: **(Smokers)**
        Males: 3,031 per million = 1 in 330   (CE × 1.19)
        Females: 2,883 per million = 1 in 347   (CE × 1.09)

Per Shot	Ent Dose	Beam HVL	Male Cancer Risk	Female Cancer Risk
AP	0.884 R	2.4 mm Al	1,422 per million	1,211 per million
PA	0.541 R	2.5 mm Al	453 per million	361 per million
LAT	3.199 R	2.6 mm Al	974 per million	1,114 per million
OBL-PA	1.110 R	2.5 mm Al	635 per million	558 per million

All values are for the Common Exam

Age 25, Lumbar Sp. Wide   Cancer Rate............... *(Lowering Factor)*
      Males: 3,013 per million = 1 in 332   (Age 20 × 0.994)
      Females: 2,848 per million = 1 in 351   (Age 20 × 0.988)
Age 30, Lumbar Sp. Wide   Cancer Rate............... *(Lowering Factor)*
      Males: 2,588 per million = 1 in 386   (Age 20 × 0.854)
      Females: 2,517 per million = 1 in 397   (Age 20 × 0.873)
Age 35, Lumbar Sp. Wide   Cancer Rate............... *(Lowering Factor)*
      Males: 1,852 per million = 1 in 540   (Age 20 × 0.611)
      Females: 1,796 per million = 1 in 557   (Age 20 × 0.623)
Age 40, Lumbar Sp. Wide   Cancer Rate............... *(Lowering Factor)*
      Males: 1,128 per million = 1 in 886   (Age 20 × 0.372)
      Females: 1,127 per million = 1 in 887   (Age 20 × 0.391)
Age 45, Lumbar Sp. Wide   Cancer Rate............... *(Lowering Factor)*
      Males: 491 per million = 1 in 2,037   (Age 20 × 0.162)
      Females: 507 per million = 1 in 1,972   (Age 20 × 0.176)
Age 50, Lumbar Sp. Wide   Cancer Rate............... *(Lowering Factor)*
      Males: 45 per million = 1 in 22,200   (Age 20 × 0.015)
      Females: 49 per million = 1 in 20,400   (Age 20 × 0.017)
Age 55, Lumbar Sp. Wide   Cancer Rate............... *(Lowering Factor)*
      Males: 30 per million = 1 in 33,300   (Age 20 × 0.010)
      Females: 35 per million = 1 in 28,600   (Age 20 × 0.012)

LUMBAR SPINE—NARROW

Contrast Medium: No.

Fluoroscopy and Spot Films: No.

Length of Field: The vertical dimensions of the field are identical with those of the Wide Exam.

Organs Generating Most Cancer Risk:
    Males: Prostate, bladder, stomach, large intestine, kidney, pancreas.
    Females: Corpus uteri, large intestine, breasts, stomach, bladder, cervix
    uteri.

Special Comments:
- The field width extends only about 8.9 cm to either side of field center.
- The cancer risks from this exam should be contrasted with those from the Lumbar Spine—Wide Exam. Of course, the choice between wide and narrow fields depends also upon what information is required from the exam.

AGE NEW   Testes, dose CE: 13 mrads
LUMBAR SPINE—NARROW   Ovaries, dose CE: 336 mrads

Common Exam (CE): One AP-Narrow, one LAT-Narrow,
              and one OBL-PA-*Wide*
Rate of future *leukemia* from Common Exam:
        Males: 31 per million = 1 in 32,300
        Females: 20 per million = 1 in 50,000
Rate of future *cancer* from Common Exam:
        Males: 5,447 per million = 1 in 184
        Females: 4,948 per million = 1 in 202

Per Shot	Ent Dose	Beam HVL	Male Cancer Risk	Female Cancer Risk
AP-Nar	0.173 R	2.4 mm Al	1,253 per million	1,082 per million
LAT-Nar	0.627 R	2.6 mm Al	2,650 per million	2,263 per million
OBL-PA-Wi	0.218 R	2.5 mm Al	1,544 per million	1,603 per million

AGE 1   Testes, dose CE: 14 mrads
LUMBAR SPINE—NARROW   Ovaries, dose CE: 323 mrads

Common Exam (CE): One AP-Narrow, one LAT-Narrow,
              and one OBL-PA-*Wide*
Rate of future *leukemia* from Common Exam:
        Males: 28 per million = 1 in 35,700
        Females: 17 per million = 1 in 58,800
Rate of future *cancer* from Common Exam:
        Males: 5,544 per million = 1 in 180
        Females: 5,063 per million = 1 in 198

Per Shot	Ent Dose	Beam HVL	Male Cancer Risk	Female Cancer Risk
AP-Nar	0.214 R	2.4 mm Al	1,384 per million	1,188 per million
LAT-Nar	0.774 R	2.6 mm Al	2,597 per million	2,257 per million
OBL-PA-Wi	0.269 R	2.5 mm Al	1,563 per million	1,618 per million

AGE 5   Testes, dose CE: 15 mrads
LUMBAR SPINE—NARROW   Ovaries, dose CE: 458 mrads

Common Exam (CE): One AP-Narrow, one LAT-Narrow,
              and one OBL-PA-*Wide*
Rate of future *leukemia* from Common Exam:
        Males   37 per million = 1 in 27,000
        Females: 23 per million = 1 in 43,500

Rate of future *cancer* from Common Exam:
        Males: 7,305 per million = 1 in 137
        Females: 6,321 per million = 1 in 158

Per Shot	Ent Dose	Beam HVL	Male Cancer Risk	Female Cancer Risk
AP-Nar	0.361 R	2.4 mm Al	1,983 per million	1,612 per million
LAT-Nar	1.305 R	2.6 mm Al	3,265 per million	2,716 per million
OBL-PA-Wi	0.453 R	2.5 mm Al	2,057 per million	1,993 per million

AGE 10   Testes, dose CE: 16 mrads
LUMBAR SPINE—NARROW   Ovaries, dose CE: 590 mrads

Common Exam (CE): One AP-Narrow, one LAT-Narrow,
                and one OBL-PA-*Wide*
Rate of future *leukemia* from Common Exam:
        Males: 41 per million = 1 in 24,400
        Females: 26 per million = 1 in 38,500
Rate of future *cancer* from Common Exam:
        Males: 7,896 per million = 1 in 127
        Females: 6,619 per million = 1 in 151

Per Shot	Ent Dose	Beam HVL	Male Cancer Risk	Female Cancer Risk
AP-Nar	0.545 R	2.4 mm Al	2,283 per million	1,763 per million
LAT-Nar	1.974 R	2.6 mm Al	3,453 per million	2,791 per million
OBL-PA-Wi	0.685 R	2.5 mm Al	2,160 per million	2,065 per million

AGE 15   Testes, dose CE: 10 mrads
LUMBAR SPINE—NARROW   Ovaries, dose CE: 474 mrads

Common Exam (CE): One AP-Narrow, one LAT-Narrow,
                and one OBL-PA-*Wide*
Rate of future *leukemia* from Common Exam:
        Males: 36 per million = 1 in 27,800
        Females: 22 per million = 1 in 45,500
Rate of future *cancer* from Common Exam:
        Males: 3,327 per million = 1 in 301
        Females: 2,768 per million = 1 in 361

Age 15, Lumbar Spine—Narrow *(continued)*

Per Shot	Ent Dose	Beam HVL	Male Cancer Risk	Female Cancer Risk
AP-Nar	0.729 R	2.4 mm Al	1,251 per million	938 per million
LAT-Nar	2.639 R	2.6 mm Al	1,145 per million	989 per million
OBL-PA-Wi	0.916 R	2.5 mm Al	931 per million	841 per million

AGE 20
LUMBAR SPINE—NARROW

Testes, dose CE: 7 mrads
Ovaries, dose CE: 280 mrads
Embryo, dose CE: 348 mrads

Common Exam (CE): One AP-Narrow, one LAT-Narrow,
                        and one OBL-PA-*Wide*
Rate of future *leukemia* from Common Exam:
            Males: 20 per million = 1 in 50,000
            Females: 13 per million = 1 in 76,900
Rate of future *cancer* from Common Exam: **(Smokers)**
            Males: 2,332 per million = 1 in 429   (CE × 1.15)
            Females: 1,918 per million = 1 in 521   (CE × 1.09)

Per Shot	Ent Dose	Beam HVL	Male Cancer Risk	Female Cancer Risk
AP-Nar	0.884 R	2.4 mm Al	1,152 per million	848 per million
LAT-Nar	3.199 R	2.6 mm Al	545 per million	512 per million
OBL-PA-Wi	1.110 R	2.5 mm Al	635 per million	558 per million

All values are for the Common Exam

Age 25, Lumbar Sp. Narrow   Cancer Rate............... *(Lowering Factor)*
            Males: 2,318 per million = 1 in 431   (Age 20 × 0.994)
            Females: 1,895 per million = 1 in 528   (Age 20 × 0.988)
Age 30, Lumbar Sp. Narrow   Cancer Rate............... *(Lowering Factor)*
            Males: 1,992 per million = 1 in 502   (Age 20 × 0.854)
            Females: 1,674 per million = 1 in 597   (Age 20 × 0.873)
Age 35, Lumbar Sp. Narrow   Cancer Rate............... *(Lowering Factor)*
            Males: 1,425 per million = 1 in 702   (Age 20 × 0.611)
            Females: 1,195 per million = 1 in 837   (Age 20 × 0.623)
Age 40, Lumbar Sp. Narrow   Cancer Rate............... *(Lowering Factor)*
            Males: 868 per million = 1 in 1,152   (Age 20 × 0.372)
            Females: 750 per million = 1 in 1,333   (Age 20 × 0.391)
Age 45, Lumbar Sp. Narrow   Cancer Rate............... *(Lowering Factor)*
            Males: 378 per million = 1 in 2,646   (Age 20 × 0.162)
            Females: 338 per million = 1 in 2,959   (Age 20 × 0.176)
Age 50, Lumbar Sp. Narrow   Cancer Rate............... *(Lowering Factor)*
            Males: 35 per million = 1 in 28,600   (Age 20 × 0.015)
            Females: 33 per million = 1 in 30,300   (Age 20 × 0.017)
Age 55, Lumbar Sp. Narrow   Cancer Rate............... *(Lowering Factor)*
            Males: 23 per million = 1 in 43,500   (Age 20 × 0.010)
            Females: 23 per million = 1 in 43,500   (Age 20 × 0.012)

LUMBO-SACRAL SPINE

Contrast Medium: No.

Fluoroscopy and Spot Films: No.

Length of Field: The field center is at the level of the bi-iliac crests, in the body midline. The field length is 43.2 cm, so it extends vertically from the level of the xiphoid process to 5.5 cm below the pubic symphysis.

Organs Generating Most Cancer Risk:
   Males: Prostate, stomach, bladder, large intestine, kidney, pancreas.
   Females: Corpus uteri, large intestine, stomach, ovaries, pancreas,
      rectum.

Special Comment:
   • In this exam, and several others, a particularly steep decrease in risk
   from the LAT shot occurs as age advances from 10 to 20 years old. See
   the last "Special Comment," Barium Enema Exam.

AGE NEW   Testes, dose CE: 73 mrads
LUMBO-SACRAL SPINE   Ovaries, dose CE: 642 mrads

Common Exam (CE): One AP, one LAT, and
                  one OBL-PA (Total: 3 shots)
Rate of future *leukemia* from Common Exam:
         Males: 52 per million = 1 in 19,200
         Females: 33 per million = 1 in 30,300
Rate of future *cancer* from Common Exam:
         Males: 8,156 per million = 1 in 123
         Females: 9,207 per million = 1 in 109

Per Shot	Ent Dose	Beam HVL	Male Cancer Risk	Female Cancer Risk
AP	0.178 R	2.4 mm Al	1,621 per million	1,630 per million
PA	0.382 R	2.4 mm Al	2,370 per million	2,466 per million
LAT	0.682 R	2.6 mm Al	4,514 per million	5,539 per million
OBL-PA	0.315 R	2.5 mm Al	2,021 per million	2,038 per million

AGE 1   Testes, dose CE: 77 mrads
LUMBO-SACRAL SPINE   Ovaries, dose CE: 659 mrads

Common Exam (CE): One AP, one LAT, and
                  one OBL-PA (Total: 3 shots)
Rate of future *leukemia* from Common Exam:
         Males: 49 per million = 1 in 20,400
         Females: 31 per million = 1 in 32,300
Rate of future *cancer* from Common Exam:
         Males: 8,070 per million = 1 in 124
         Females: 9,209 per million = 1 in 108

Age 1, Lumbo-Sacral Spine *(continued)*

Per Shot	Ent Dose	Beam HVL	Male Cancer Risk	Female Cancer Risk
AP	0.220 R	2.4 mm Al	1,729 per million	1,782 per million
PA	0.472 R	2.4 mm Al	2,443 per million	2,503 per million
LAT	0.842 R	2.6 mm Al	4,339 per million	5,412 per million
OBL-PA	0.389 R	2.5 mm Al	2,002 per million	2,015 per million

AGE 5
LUMBO-SACRAL SPINE

Testes, dose CE: 84 mrads
Ovaries, dose CE: 877 mrads

Common Exam (CE): One AP, one LAT, and
              one OBL-PA (Total: 3 shots)
Rate of future *leukemia* from Common Exam:
        Males: 65 per million = 1 in 15,400
        Females: 40 per million = 1 in 25,000
Rate of future *cancer* from Common Exam:
        Males: 10,512 per million = 1 in 95
        Females: 11,328 per million = 1 in 88

Per Shot	Ent Dose	Beam HVL	Male Cancer Risk	Female Cancer Risk
AP	0.372 R	2.4 mm Al	2,404 per million	2,414 per million
PA	0.796 R	2.4 mm Al	3,354 per million	3,211 per million
LAT	1.420 R	2.6 mm Al	5,455 per million	6,472 per million
OBL-PA	0.655 R	2.5 mm Al	2,653 per million	2,442 per million

AGE 10
LUMBO-SACRAL SPINE

Testes, dose CE: 86 mrads
Ovaries, dose CE: 1,121 mrads

Common Exam (CE): One AP, one LAT, and
              one OBL-PA (Total: 3 shots)
Rate of future *leukemia* from Common Exam:
        Males: 75 per million = 1 in 13,300
        Females: 47 per million = 1 in 21,300
Rate of future *cancer* from Common Exam:
        Males: 11,288 per million = 1 in 88
        Females: 11,755 per million = 1 in 85

Per Shot	Ent Dose	Beam HVL	Male Cancer Risk	Female Cancer Risk
AP	0.562 R	2.4 mm Al	2,773 per million	2,623 per million
PA	1.204 R	2.4 mm Al	3,761 per million	3,418 per million
LAT	2.147 R	2.6 mm Al	5,762 per million	6,627 per million
OBL-PA	0.991 R	2.5 mm Al	2,753 per million	2,505 per million

AGE 15
LUMBO-SACRAL SPINE

Testes, dose CE: 56 mrads
Ovaries, dose CE: 900 mrads

Common Exam (CE): One AP, one LAT, and
                    one OBL-PA (Total: 3 shots)
Rate of future *leukemia* from Common Exam:
        Males: 70 per million = 1 in 14,300
        Females: 44 per million = 1 in 22,700
Rate of future *cancer* from Common Exam:
        Males: 4,861 per million = 1 in 206
        Females: 4,597 per million = 1 in 218

Per Shot	Ent Dose	Beam HVL	Male Cancer Risk	Female Cancer Risk
AP	0.752 R	2.4 mm Al	1,570 per million	1,381 per million
PA	1.610 R	2.4 mm Al	1,847 per million	1,634 per million
LAT	2.871 R	2.6 mm Al	2,066 per million	2,194 per million
OBL-PA	1.325 R	2.5 mm Al	1,225 per million	1,022 per million

AGE 20
LUMBO-SACRAL SPINE

Testes, dose CE: 40 mrads
Ovaries, dose CE: 543 mrads
Embryo, dose CE: 527 mrads

Common Exam (CE): One AP, one LAT, and
                    one OBL-PA (Total: 3 shots)
Rate of future *leukemia* from Common Exam:
        Males: 46 per million = 1 in 21,700
        Females: 29 per million = 1 in 34,500
Rate of future *cancer* from Common Exam: **(Smokers)**
        Males: 3,402 per million = 1 in 294   (CE × 1.03)
        Females: 2,970 per million = 1 in 337   (CE × 1.02)

Per Shot	Ent Dose	Beam HVL	Male Cancer Risk	Female Cancer Risk
AP	0.911 R	2.4 mm Al	1,502 per million	1,204 per million
PA	1.952 R	2.4 mm Al	1,485 per million	1,319 per million
LAT	3.480 R	2.6 mm Al	926 per million	928 per million
OBL-PA	1.606 R	2.5 mm Al	974 per million	838 per million

All values are for the Common Exam

Age 25, Lumbo-Sacral Spine   Cancer Rate................ *(Lowering Factor)*
            Males: 3,381 per million = 1 in 296   (Age 20 × 0.994)
            Females: 2,934 per million = 1 in 341   (Age 20 × 0.988)
Age 30, Lumbo-Sacral Spine   Cancer Rate............... *(Lowering Factor)*
            Males: 2,905 per million = 1 in 344   (Age 20 × 0.854)
            Females: 2,593 per million = 1 in 386   (Age 20 × 0.873)

Lumbo-Sacral Spine *(continued)*

Age 35, Lumbo-Sacral Spine   Cancer Rate............... *(Lowering Factor)*
        Males: 2,079 per million = 1 in 481   (Age 20 × 0.611)
        Females: 1,850 per million = 1 in 540   (Age 20 × 0.623)
Age 40, Lumbo-Sacral Spine   Cancer Rate............... *(Lowering Factor)*
        Males: 1,266 per million = 1 in 790   (Age 20 × 0.372)
        Females: 1,161 per million = 1 in 861   (Age 20 × 0.391)
Age 45, Lumbo-Sacral Spine   Cancer Rate............... *(Lowering Factor)*
        Males: 551 per million = 1 in 1,815   (Age 20 × 0.162)
        Females: 523 per million = 1 in 1,912   (Age 20 × 0.176)
Age 50, Lumbo-Sacral Spine   Cancer Rate............... *(Lowering Factor)*
        Males: 51 per million = 1 in 19,600   (Age 20 × 0.015)
        Females: 50 per million = 1 in 20,000   (Age 20 × 0.017)
Age 55, Lumbo-Sacral Spine   Cancer Rate............... *(Lowering Factor)*
        Males: 34 per million = 1 in 29,400   (Age 20 × 0.010)
        Females: 36 per million = 1 in 27,800   (Age 20 × 0.012)

NECK—SOFT TISSUE

Special Comment:
- For this exam, the cancer risks provided with the Cervical Spine Exam should simply be converted, by the usual methods demonstrated in Chapter 4, for whatever entrance doses and beam qualities are selected.

PELVIS

Contrast Medium: No.

Fluoroscopy and Spot Films: No.

Length of Field: The field center is 8.0 cm below the bi-iliac crests, at body midline. The field length is 35.6 cm for the AP shot, so it extends vertically from 10 cm above the bi-iliac crests to 10 cm below the pubic symphysis, and hence includes the testes. The LAT shot is 43.2 cm in length, extending from 8 cm below the xiphoid to 5 cm below testes center.

Organs Generating Most Cancer Risk:
    Males: Prostate, bladder, rectum, large intestine, other genital organs, and lymphatic tissue (generating lymphomas, multiple myelomas, and Hodgkin's Disease).
    Females: Corpus uteri, bladder, cervix uteri, ovaries, rectum, large intestine.

Special Comments:
- Testes shielding should be considered.
- The biggest benefit from shielding would be reduction in genetic risk

rather than cancer risk from this exam, because the testes do not account for a big share of the exam's cancer risk.
- The Common Exam changes with age.
- In this exam, and several others, a particularly steep decrease in risk from the LAT shot occurs as age advances from 10 to 20 years old. See the last "Special Comment," Barium Enema Exam.

AGE NEW Testes, dose CE: 220 mrads
PELVIS Ovaries, dose CE: 82 mrads

Common Exam (CE): Two AP
                    (Total: 2 shots)
Rate of future *leukemia* from Common Exam:
        Males: 5 per million = 1 in 200,000
        Females: 3 per million = 1 in 333,000
Rate of future *cancer* from Common Exam:
        Males: 1,226 per million = 1 in 816
        Females: 1,234 per million = 1 in 810

Per Shot	Ent Dose	Beam HVL	Male Cancer Risk	Female Cancer Risk
AP	0.107 R	2.4 mm Al	613 per million	617 per million
PA	0.060 R	2.4 mm Al	241 per million	244 per million
LAT	0.263 R	2.6 mm Al	771 per million	1,264 per million
OBL-AP	0.283 R	2.6 mm Al	1,317 per million	1,608 per million

AGE 1 Testes, dose CE: 230 mrads
PELVIS Ovaries, dose CE: 90 mrads

Common Exam (CE): Two AP
                    (Total: 2 shots)
Rate of future *leukemia* from Common Exam:
        Males: 5 per million = 1 in 200,000
        Females: 3 per million = 1 in 333,000
Rate of future *cancer* from Common Exam:
        Males: 1,350 per million = 1 in 741
        Females: 1,160 per million = 1 in 862

Per Shot	Ent Dose	Beam HVL	Male Cancer Risk	Female Cancer Risk
AP	0.132 R	2.4 mm Al	675 per million	580 per million
PA	0.075 R	2.4 mm Al	242 per million	249 per million
LAT	0.325 R	2.6 mm Al	737 per million	1,227 per million
OBL-AP	0.349 R	2.6 mm Al	1,389 per million	1,482 per million

AGE 5
PELVIS

Testes, dose CE: 249 mrads
Ovaries, dose CE: 160 mrads

Common Exam (CE): Two AP
(Total: 2 shots)
Rate of future *leukemia* from Common Exam:
      Males: 8 per million = 1 in 125,000
      Females: 5 per million = 1 in 200,000
Rate of future *cancer* from Common Exam:
      Males: 1,902 per million = 1 in 526
      Females: 1,554 per million = 1 in 643

Per Shot	Ent Dose	Beam HVL	Male Cancer Risk	Female Cancer Risk
AP	0.222 R	2.4 mm Al	951 per million	777 per million
PA	0.126 R	2.4 mm Al	316 per million	303 per million
LAT	0.548 R	2.6 mm Al	910 per million	1,433 per million
OBL-AP	0.589 R	2.6 mm Al	1,889 per million	1,898 per million

AGE 10
PELVIS

Testes, dose CE: 182 mrads
Ovaries, dose CE: 198 mrads

Common Exam (CE): Two AP
(Total: 2 shots)
Rate of future *leukemia* from Common Exam:
      Males: 7 per million = 1 in 143,000
      Females: 4 per million = 1 in 250,000
Rate of future *cancer* from Common Exam:
      Males: 2,170 per million = 1 in 461
      Females: 1,664 per million = 1 in 601

Per Shot	Ent Dose	Beam HVL	Male Cancer Risk	Female Cancer Risk
AP	0.336 R	2.4 mm Al	1,085 per million	832 per million
PA	0.190 R	2.4 mm Al	349 per million	322 per million
LAT	0.829 R	2.6 mm Al	952 per million	1,476 per million
OBL-AP	0.890 R	2.6 mm Al	2,142 per million	2,004 per million

AGE 15
PELVIS

Testes, dose CE: 110 mrads
Ovaries, dose CE: 202 mrads

Common Exam (CE): Two AP
(Total: 2 shots)
Rate of future *leukemia* from Common Exam:
      Males: 8 per million = 1 in 125,000
      Females: 5 per million = 1 in 200,000
Rate of future *cancer* from Common Exam:
      Males: 1,194 per million = 1 in 838
      Females: 880 per million = 1 in 1,136

Per Shot	Ent Dose	Beam HVL	Male Cancer Risk	Female Cancer Risk
AP	0.450 R	2.4 mm Al	597 per million	440 per million
PA	0.254 R	2.4 mm Al	166 per million	150 per million
LAT	1.108 R	2.6 mm Al	370 per million	492 per million
OBL-AP	1.190 R	2.6 mm Al	1,115 per million	927 per million

AGE 20
PELVIS

Testes, dose CE: 41 mrads
Ovaries, dose CE: 105 mrads
Embryo, dose CE: 145 mrads

Common Exam (CE): One AP
(Total: 1 shot)
Rate of future *leukemia* from Common Exam:
    Males: 3 per million = 1 in 333,000
    Females: 2 per million = 1 in 500,000
Rate of future *cancer* from Common Exam: **(Smokers)**
    Males: 553 per million = 1 in 1,808   (CE × 1.00)
    Females: 381 per million = 1 in 2,625   (CE × 1.00)

Per Shot	Ent Dose	Beam HVL	Male Cancer Risk	Female Cancer Risk
AP	0.545 R	2.4 mm Al	553 per million	381 per million
PA	0.308 R	2.4 mm Al	132 per million	123 per million
LAT	1.343 R	2.6 mm Al	135 per million	190 per million
OBL-AP	1.443 R	2.6 mm Al	1,004 per million	828 per million

All values are for the Common Exam

Age 25, Pelvis   Cancer Rate............... *(Lowering Factor)*
    Males: 550 per million = 1 in 1,818   (Age 20 × 0.994)
    Females: 374 per million = 1 in 2,674   (Age 20 × 0.988)
Age 30, Pelvis   Cancer Rate............... *(Lowering Factor)*
    Males: 472 per million = 1 in 2,119   (Age 20 × 0.854)
    Females: 333 per million = 1 in 3,003   (Age 20 × 0.873)
Age 35, Pelvis   Cancer Rate............... *(Lowering Factor)*
    Males: 338 per million = 1 in 2,959   (Age 20 × 0.611)
    Females: 237 per million = 1 in 4,219   (Age 20 × 0.623)
Age 40, Pelvis   Cancer Rate............... *(Lowering Factor)*
    Males: 206 per million = 1 in 4,854   (Age 20 × 0.372)
    Females: 149 per million = 1 in 6,711   (Age 20 × 0.391)
Age 45, Pelvis   Cancer Rate............... *(Lowering Factor)*
    Males: 90 per million = 1 in 11,100   (Age 20 × 0.162)
    Females: 67 per million = 1 in 14,925   (Age 20 × 0.176)
Age 50, Pelvis   Cancer Rate............... *(Lowering Factor)*
    Males: 8.2 per million = 1 in 122,000   (Age 20 × 0.015)
    Females: 6.5 per million = 1 in 154,000   (Age 20 × 0.017)
Age 55, Pelvis   Cancer Rate............... *(Lowering Factor)*
    Males: 5.5 per million = 1 in 182,000   (Age 20 × 0.010)
    Females: 4.6 per million = 1 in 217,000   (Age 20 × 0.012)

RETROGRADE PYELOGRAM

Contrast Medium: Yes. An organically bound iodine compound, injected via catheter in the urethra and bladder.

Fluoroscopy and Spot Films: Sometimes.
If FLU is used, the cancer and leukemia risks are additional to those given here from the films. Please see Chapter 6 for calculating risks from FLU.

Length of Field: In adults, the field center is at the level of the bi-iliac crests, and for the AP shot, at body midline. The field length is 43.2 cm, so it extends from approximately the xiphoid process to 5.5 cm below the pubic symphysis. For the "Kidneys-AP" shot (pediatric ages), see below.

Organs Generating Most Cancer Risk:
> *Males:* Prostate, large intestine, bladder, stomach, pancreas, rectum.
> *Females:* Large intestine, corpus uteri, stomach, pancreas, bladder,
> breasts. (The breasts are *more* at risk in pediatric exams because of the "Kidneys-AP" shots.)

Special Comments:
- The shots of the Common Exam differ for the pediatric and adult ages.
- The "Kidneys-AP" shot extends vertically "from diaphragm to 2.5 cm below umbilicus" for all pediatric ages, according to Rosenstein and co-workers (1979).

AGE NEW   Testes, dose CE: 10 mrads
RETROGRADE PYELOGRAM   Ovaries, dose CE: 167 mrads

Common Exam (CE): Two AP and two "Kidneys-AP"
(Total: 4 shots)
Rate of future *leukemia* from Common Exam:
> Males: 5 per million = 1 in 200,000
> Females: 3 per million = 1 in 333,000
Rate of future *cancer* from Common Exam:
> Males: 3,568 per million = 1 in 280
> Females: 3,833 per million = 1 in 261

Per Shot	Ent Dose	Beam HVL	Male Cancer Risk	Female Cancer Risk
AP	0.117 R	2.5 mm Al	1,089 per million	1,043 per million
Kid'y-AP	0.130 R	2.5 mm Al	695 per million	874 per million

AGE 1
RETROGRADE PYELOGRAM

Testes, dose CE: 11 mrads
Ovaries, dose CE: 156 mrads

Common Exam (CE): Two AP and two "Kidneys-AP"
(Total: 4 shots)
Rate of future *leukemia* from Common Exam:
Males: 6 per million = 1 in 167,000
Females: 3.6 per million = 1 in 278,000
Rate of future *cancer* from Common Exam:
Males: 3,726 per million = 1 in 268
Females: 4,029 per million = 1 in 248

Per Shot	Ent Dose	Beam HVL	Male Cancer Risk	Female Cancer Risk
AP	0.144 R	2.5 mm Al	1,162 per million	1,113 per million
Kid'y-AP	0.161 R	2.5 mm Al	701 per million	902 per million

AGE 5
RETROGRADE PYELOGRAM

Testes, dose CE: 14 mrads
Ovaries, dose CE: 187 mrads

Common Exam (CE): Two AP and two "Kidneys-AP"
(Total: 4 shots)
Rate of future *leukemia* from Common Exam:
Males: 8 per million = 1 in 125,000
Females: 5 per million = 1 in 200,000
Rate of future *cancer* from Common Exam:
Males: 5,032 per million = 1 in 199
Females: 5,141 per million = 1 in 194

Per Shot	Ent Dose	Beam HVL	Male Cancer Risk	Female Cancer Risk
AP	0.243 R	2.5 mm Al	1,615 per million	1,462 per million
Kid'y-AP	0.271 R	2.5 mm Al	901 per million	1,108 per million

AGE 10
RETROGRADE PYELOGRAM

Testes, dose CE: 15 mrads
Ovaries, dose CE: 239 mrads

Common Exam (CE): Two AP and two "Kidneys-AP"
(Total: 4 shots)
Rate of future *leukemia* from Common Exam:
Males: 9 per million = 1 in 111,000
Females: 5.5 per million = 1 in 182,000
Rate of future *cancer* from Common Exam:
Males: 5,790 per million = 1 in 173
Females: 5,604 per million = 1 in 178

Age 10, Retrograde Pyelogram *(continued)*

Per Shot	*Ent Dose*	*Beam HVL*	*Male Cancer Risk*	*Female Cancer Risk*
AP	0.367 R	2.5 mm Al	1,863 per million	1,588 per million
Kid'y-AP	0.410 R	2.5 mm Al	1,032 per million	1,214 per million

AGE 15   Testes, dose CE: 13 mrads
RETROGRADE PYELOGRAM   Ovaries, dose CE: 284 mrads

Common Exam (CE): Two AP and two "Kidneys-AP"
                     (Total: 4 shots)
Rate of future *leukemia* from Common Exam:
          Males: 9 per million = 1 in 111,000
          Females: 5.5 per million = 1 in 182,000
Rate of future *cancer* from Common Exam:
          Males: 3,260 per million = 1 in 307
          Females: 3,059 per million = 1 in 327

Per Shot	*Ent Dose*	*Beam HVL*	*Male Cancer Risk*	*Female Cancer Risk*
AP	0.491 R	2.5 mm Al	1,054 per million	868 per million
Kid'y-AP	0.548 R	2.5 mm Al	576 per million	662 per million

AGE 20   Testes, dose CE: 34 mrads
RETROGRADE PYELOGRAM   Ovaries, dose CE: 460 mrads
                                                        Embryo, dose CE: 612 mrads

Common Exam (CE): Four AP
                     (Total: 4 shots)
Rate of future *leukemia* from Common Exam:
          Males: 15 per million = 1 in 66,700
          Females: 9 per million = 1 in 111,000
Rate of future *cancer* from Common Exam: **(Smokers)**
          Males: 3,904 per million = 1 in 256   (CE × 1.02)
          Females: 3,232 per million = 1 in 309   (CE × 1.02)

Per Shot	*Ent Dose*	*Beam HVL*	*Male Cancer Risk*	*Female Cancer Risk*
AP	0.595 R	2.5 mm Al	976 per million	808 per million

All values are for the Common Exam

Age 25, Retrograde Pyelo.   Cancer Rate................ *(Lowering Factor)*
          Males: 3,880 per million = 1 in 258   (Age 20 × 0.994)
          Females: 3,193 per million = 1 in 313   (Age 20 × 0.988)

Age 30, Retrograde Pyelo.   Cancer Rate................ *(Lowering Factor)*
     Males: 3,334 per million = 1 in 300   (Age 20 × 0.854)
     Females: 2,822 per million = 1 in 354   (Age 20 × 0.873)
Age 35, Retrograde Pyelo.   Cancer Rate................ *(Lowering Factor)*
     Males: 2,385 per million = 1 in 419   (Age 20 × 0.611)
     Females: 2,014 per million = 1 in 496   (Age 20 × 0.623)
Age 40, Retrograde Pyelo.   Cancer Rate................ *(Lowering Factor)*
     Males: 1,452 per million = 1 in 689   (Age 20 × 0.372)
     Females: 1,264 per million = 1 in 791   (Age 20 × 0.391)
Age 45, Retrograde Pyelo.   Cancer Rate................ *(Lowering Factor)*
     Males: 632 per million = 1 in 1,582   (Age 20 × 0.162)
     Females: 569 per million = 1 in 1,757   (Age 20 × 0.176)
Age 50, Retrograde Pyelo.   Cancer Rate................ *(Lowering Factor)*
     Males: 58 per million = 1 in 17,240   (Age 20 × 0.015)
     Females: 55 per million = 1 in 18,180   (Age 20 × 0.017)
Age 55, Retrograde Pyelo.   Cancer Rate................ *(Lowering Factor)*
     Males: 39 per million = 1 in 25,600   (Age 20 × 0.010)
     Females: 39 per million = 1 in 25,600   (Age 20 × 0.012)

RIBS

Contrast Medium: No.

Fluoroscopy and Spot Films: No.

Length of Field: The field center is 9.5 cm below the sternal notch. The field length is 43.2 cm, so it extends from 19 cm below the vertex of the skull down to approximately 2.5 cm below the xiphoid process.

Organs Generating Most Cancer Risk:
    Males: Stomach, bronchi, kidneys, pancreas, large intestine.
    Females: Breasts, large intestine, bronchi, stomach, pancreas, kidneys.
    (The breasts account for over 50% of the total cancer risk from this examination.)

AGE NEW   Testes, dose CE: < 1 mrad
RIBS   Ovaries, dose CE: 3 mrads

Common Exam (CE): One AP, one PA, and one OBL-PA
                  (Total: 3 shots)
Rate of future *leukemia* from Common Exam:
     Males: 7 per million = 1 in 143,000
     Females: 4 per million = 1 in 250,000
Rate of future *cancer* from Common Exam:
     Males: 942 per million = 1 in 1,062
     Females: 1,736 per million = 1 in 576

Age New, Ribs *(continued)*

Per Shot	Ent Dose	Beam HVL	Male Cancer Risk	Female Cancer Risk
AP	0.070 R	2.2 mm Al	273 per million	812 per million
PA	0.057 R	2.4 mm Al	201 per million	243 per million
LAT	0.036 R	3.0 mm Al	246 per million	373 per million
OBL-PA	0.123 R	2.4 mm Al	468 per million	681 per million

AGE 1　　　　　　　　　　　　　　Testes, dose CE: < 1 mrad
RIBS　　　　　　　　　　　　　　Ovaries, dose CE: 3 mrads

Common Exam (CE): One AP, one PA, one OBL-PA
　　　　　　　　　(Total: 3 shots)
Rate of future *leukemia* from Common Exam:
　　　　　Males:　　　8 per million = 1 in 125,000
　　　　　Females:　　5 per million = 1 in 200,000
Rate of future *cancer* from Common Exam:
　　　　　Males:　　1,017 per million = 1 in 983
　　　　　Females: 1,900 per million = 1 in 526

Per Shot	Ent Dose	Beam HVL	Male Cancer Risk	Female Cancer Risk
AP	0.086 R	2.2 mm Al	298 per million	935 per million
PA	0.070 R	2.4 mm Al	217 per million	258 per million
LAT	0.045 R	3.0 mm Al	240 per million	382 per million
OBL-PA	0.152 R	2.4 mm Al	502 per million	707 per million

AGE 5　　　　　　　　　　　　　　Testes, dose CE: < 1 mrad
RIBS　　　　　　　　　　　　　　Ovaries, dose CE: 4 mrads

Common Exam (CE): One AP, one PA, and one OBL-PA
　　　　　　　　　(Total: 3 shots)
Rate of future *leukemia* from Common Exam:
　　　　　Males:　　　11 per million = 1 in 90,900
　　　　　Females:　　7 per million = 1 in 143,000
Rate of future *cancer* from Common Exam:
　　　　　Males:　　1,410 per million = 1 in 709
　　　　　Females: 2,539 per million = 1 in 394

Per Shot	Ent Dose	Beam HVL	Male Cancer Risk	Female Cancer Risk
AP	0.146 R	2.2 mm Al	429 per million	1,285 per million
PA	0.118 R	2.4 mm Al	305 per million	336 per million
LAT	0.076 R	3.0 mm Al	313 per million	496 per million
OBL-PA	0.256 R	2.4 mm Al	676 per million	918 per million

AGE 10   Testes, dose CE: $<$ 1 mrad
RIBS   Ovaries, dose CE: 3 mrads

Common Exam (CE): One AP, one PA, and one OBL-PA
                     (Total: 3 shots)
Rate of future *leukemia* from Common Exam:
          Males: 13 per million = 1 in 76,900
          Females: 8 per million = 1 in 125,000
Rate of future *cancer* from Common Exam:
          Males: 1,579 per million = 1 in 633
          Females: 2,747 per million = 1 in 364

Per Shot	Ent Dose	Beam HVL	Male Cancer Risk	Female Cancer Risk
AP	0.220 R	2.2 mm Al	498 per million	1,437 per million
PA	0.178 R	2.4 mm Al	343 per million	354 per million
LAT	0.115 R	3.0 mm Al	329 per million	510 per million
OBL-PA	0.387 R	2.4 mm Al	738 per million	956 per million

AGE 15   Testes, dose CE: $<$1 mrad
RIBS   Ovaries, dose CE: 2.5 mrad

Common Exam (CE): One AP, one PA, and one OBL-PA
                     (Total: 3 shots)
Rate of future *leukemia* from Common Exam:
          Males: 13 per million = 1 in 76,900
          Females: 8 per million = 1 in 125,000
Rate of future *cancer* from Common Exam:
          Males: 784 per million = 1 in 1,276
          Females: 1,408 per million = 1 in 710

Per Shot	Ent Dose	Beam HVL	Male Cancer Risk	Female Cancer Risk
AP	0.294 R	2.2 mm Al	278 per million	817 per million
PA	0.238 R	2.4 mm Al	179 per million	169 per million
LAT	0.153 R	3.0 mm Al	123 per million	228 per million
OBL-PA	0.517 R	2.4 mm Al	327 per million	422 per million

AGE 20   Testes, dose CE: $<$ 1 mrad
RIBS   Ovaries, dose CE: $<$ 1 mrad
                                              Embryo, dose CE: $<$ 1 mrad

Common Exam (CE): One AP, one PA, and one OBL-PA
                     (Total: 3 shots)
Rate of future *leukemia* from Common Exam:
          Males: 11 per million = 1 in 90,900
          Females: 7 per million = 1 in 143,000

Age 20, Ribs *(continued)*

Rate of future *cancer* from Common Exam: (Smokers)
      Males: 681 per million = 1 in 1,468   (CE × 2.70)
      Females: 1,214 per million = 1 in 824   (CE × 1.60)

Per Shot	Ent Dose	Beam HVL	Male Cancer Risk	Female Cancer Risk
AP	0.357 R	2.2 mm Al	275 per million	774 per million
PA	0.289 R	2.4 mm Al	161 per million	129 per million
LAT	0.186 R	3.0 mm Al	69 per million	154 per million
OBL-PA	0.627 R	2.4 mm Al	245 per million	311 per million

All values are for the Common Exam

Age 25, Ribs   Cancer Rate............... *(Lowering Factor)*
      Males: 677 per million = 1 in 1,477   (Age 20 × 0.994)
      Females: 1,199 per million = 1 in 834   (Age 20 × 0.988)
Age 30, Ribs   Cancer Rate............... *(Lowering Factor)*
      Males: 582 per million = 1 in 1,718   (Age 20 × 0.854)
      Females: 1,060 per million = 1 in 943   (Age 20 × 0.873)
Age 35, Ribs   Cancer Rate............... *(Lowering Factor)*
      Males: 416 per million = 1 in 2,404   (Age 20 × 0.611)
      Females: 756 per million = 1 in 1,323   (Age 20 × 0.623)
Age 40, Ribs   Cancer Rate............... *(Lowering Factor)*
      Males: 253 per million = 1 in 3,952   (Age 20 × 0.372)
      Females: 475 per million = 1 in 2,105   (Age 20 × 0.391)
Age 45, Ribs   Cancer Rate............... *(Lowering Factor)*
      Males: 110 per million = 1 in 9,091   (Age 20 × 0.162)
      Females: 214 per million = 1 in 4,673   (Age 20 × 0.176)
Age 50, Ribs   Cancer Rate............... *(Lowering Factor)*
      Males: 10 per million = 1 in 100,000   (Age 20 × 0.015)
      Females: 21 per million = 1 in 47,600   (Age 20 × 0.017)
Age 55, Ribs   Cancer Rate............... *(Lowering Factor)*
      Males: 7 per million = 1 in 143,000   (Age 20 × 0.010)
      Females: 14 per million = 1 in 71,400   (Age 20 × 0.012)

SCAPULA

Contrast Medium: No.

Fluoroscopy and Spot Films: No.

Length of Field: The field length is 30.5 cm, and extends from the level of the larynx to approximately 2.5 cm below the xiphoid process. The field center is 4.8 cm below the sternal notch, and 13.6 cm away from the body midline. Because the width of the field is 25.4 cm, the field does not reach fully to body midline.

Organs Generating Most Cancer Risk:
>   *Males:* Bronchi, larynx, male breast, lymphatic tissue, esophagus.
>   *Females:* Breast, bronchi, lymphatic tissue.

Special Comments:
- Cancer and leukemia risks are for examination of *one* scapula.
- In the male, more than 50% of the cancer risk from this exam arises in the bronchi.
- In the female, 85%–90% of the cancer risk from this exam arises in the breast.

AGE NEW   Testes, dose CE: < 1 mrad
SCAPULA   Ovaries, dose CE: < 1 mrad

Common Exam (CE): One AP
>   (Total: 1 shot)

Rate of future *leukemia* from Common Exam:
>   Males: 0.2 per million = 1 in 5 million
>   Females: 0.1 per million = 1 in 10 million

Rate of future *cancer* from Common Exam:
>   Males: 17 per million = 1 in 58,800
>   Females: 101 per million = 1 in 9,900

Per Shot	Ent Dose	Beam HVL	Male Cancer Risk	Female Cancer Risk
AP	0.038 R	2.2 mm Al	17 per million	101 per million

AGE 1   Testes, dose CE: < 1 mrad
SCAPULA   Ovaries, dose CE: < 1 mrad

Common Exam (CE): One AP
>   (Total: 1 shot)

Rate of future *leukemia* from Common Exam:
>   Males: 0.2 per million = 1 in 5 million
>   Females: 0.1 per million = 1 in 10 million

Rate of future *cancer* from Common Exam:
>   Males: 18 per million = 1 in 55,600
>   Females: 117 per million = 1 in 8,550

Per Shot	Ent Dose	Beam HVL	Male Cancer Risk	Female Cancer Risk
AP	0.047 R	2.2 mm Al	18 per million	117 per million

AGE 5
SCAPULA

Testes, dose CE: < 1 mrad
Ovaries, dose CE: < 1 mrad

Common Exam (CE): One AP
(Total: 1 shot)
Rate of future *leukemia* from Common Exam:
        Males: 0.2 per million = 1 in 5 million
        Females: 0.1 per million = 1 in 10 million
Rate of future *cancer* from Common Exam:
        Males: 26 per million = 1 in 38,460
        Females: 161 per million = 1 in 6,210

Per Shot	Ent Dose	Beam HVL	Male Cancer Risk	Female Cancer Risk
AP	0.080 R	2.2 mm Al	26 per million	161 per million

AGE 10
SCAPULA

Testes, dose CE: < 1 mrad
Ovaries, dose CE: < 1 mrad

Common Exam (CE): One AP
(Total: 1 shot)
Rate of future *leukemia* from Common Exam:
        Males: 0.3 per million = 1 in 3.3 million
        Females: 0.2 per million = 1 in 5 million
Rate of future *cancer* from Common Exam:
        Males: 29 per million = 1 in 34,500
        Females: 184 per million = 1 in 5,440

Per Shot	Ent Dose	Beam HVL	Male Cancer Risk	Female Cancer Risk
AP	0.120 R	2.2 mm Al	29 per million	184 per million

AGE 15
SCAPULA

Testes, dose CE: < 1 mrad
Ovaries, dose CE: < 1 mrad

Common Exam (CE): One AP
(Total: 1 shot)
Rate of future *leukemia* from Common Exam:
        Males: 0.3 per million = 1 in 3.3 million
        Females: 0.2 per million = 1 in 5 million
Rate of future *cancer* from Common Exam:
        Males: 16 per million = 1 in 62,500
        Females: 103 per million = 1 in 9,710

Per Shot	Ent Dose	Beam HVL	Male Cancer Risk	Female Cancer Risk
AP	0.161 R	2.2 mm Al	16 per million	103 per million

AGE 20   Testes, dose CE: < 1 mrad
SCAPULA   Ovaries, dose CE: < 1 mrad
_____   Embryo, dose CE: < 1 mrad

Common Exam (CE): One AP
                    (Total: 1 shot)
Rate of future *leukemia* from Common Exam:
          Males: 0.4 per million = 1 in 2.5 million
          Females: 0.25 per million = 1 in 4 million
Rate of future *cancer* from Common Exam: **(Smokers)**
          Males: 16 per million = 1 in 62,500   (CE × 5.97)
          Females: 99 per million = 1 in 10,100   (CE × 1.37)

Per Shot	Ent Dose	Beam HVL	Male Cancer Risk	Female Cancer Risk
AP	0.195 R	2.2 mm Al	16 per million	99 per million

All values are for the Common Exam

Age 25, Scapula   Cancer Rate. . . . . *(Lowering Factor)*
          Males: 16 per million = 1 in 62,500   (Age 20 × 0.994)
          Females: 98 per million = 1 in 10,200   (Age 20 × 0.988)
Age 30, Scapula   Cancer Rate. . . . . *(Lowering Factor)*
          Males: 14 per million = 1 in 71,430   (Age 20 × 0.854)
          Females: 86 per million = 1 in 11,630   (Age 20 × 0.873)
Age 35, Scapula   Cancer Rate. . . . . *(Lowering Factor)*
          Males: 9.8 per million = 1 in 102,000   (Age 20 × 0.611)
          Females: 62 per million = 1 in 16,100   (Age 20 × 0.623)
Age 40, Scapula   Cancer Rate. . . . . *(Lowering Factor)*
          Males: 6.0 per million = 1 in 167,000   (Age 20 × 0.372)
          Females: 39 per million = 1 in 25,600   (Age 20 × 0.391)
Age 45, Scapula   Cancer Rate. . . . . *(Lowering Factor)*
          Males: 2.6 per million = 1 in 385,000   (Age 20 × 0.162)
          Females: 17 per million = 1 in 58,800   (Age 20 × 0.176)
Age 50, Scapula   Cancer Rate. . . . . *(Lowering Factor)*
          Males: 0.24 per million = 1 in 4.2 million   (Age 20 × 0.015)
          Females: 1.5 per million = 1 in 667,000   (Age 20 × 0.017)
Age 55, Scapula   Cancer Rate. . . . . *(Lowering Factor)*
          Males: 0.16 per million = 1 in 6.2 million   (Age 20 × 0.010)
          Females: 1.2 per million = 1 in 833,000   (Age 20 × 0.012)

_____

SHOULDER
_____

Contrast Medium: No.

Fluoroscopy and Spot Films: No.

Length of Field: The field length is 30.5 cm, and extends from 1 cm below the external acoustic meatus to 4 cm above the xiphoid process. The field center is at

Shoulder *(continued)*
the vertical level of the sternal notch and, for the AP or PA shot, 15.3 cm to one side of the body midline. Because the field width is 25.4 cm, it extends only to within about 2 cm of the body midline.

Organs Generating Most Cancer Risk:
   Males: Bronchi, male breast, lymphatic tissues, kidney, skin.
   Females: Breast, bronchi.

Special Comments:
   - Cancer and leukemia risks are for examination of *one* shoulder.
   - In the female, the breast accounts for more than 85% of the cancer risk from this exam.
   - Breast shielding should be considered for this exam to the extent it is compatible with the needed image of the shoulder.
   - This exam is one of several in which the resulting cancer risk for females would be markedly reduced whenever the PA beam direction could replace the AP direction.
   - The notable disparity in risk among the AP, PA, and LAT shots results not only from differences in entrance dose, beam quality, and beam direction, but also from differences in the field. The AP and PA shots irradiate only one side of the body whereas the LAT shot customarily irradiates both.

AGE NEW   Testes, dose CE: < 1 mrad
SHOULDER   Ovaries, dose CE: < 1 mrad

Common Exam (CE): One AP
                      (Total: 1 shot)
Rate of future *leukemia* from Common Exam:
          Males: 0.2 per million = 1 in 5 million
          Females: 0.1 per million = 1 in 10 million
Rate of future *cancer* from Common Exam:
          Males: 12 per million = 1 in 83,300
          Females: 81 per million = 1 in 12,350

Per Shot	Ent Dose	Beam HVL	Male Cancer Risk	Female Cancer Risk
AP	0.038 R	2.2 mm Al	12 per million	81 per million
PA	0.029 R	2.1 mm Al	9.6 per million	16 per million
LAT	0.191 R	2.5 mm Al	430 per million	506 per million
OBL-PA	0.060 R	2.3 mm Al	66 per million	84 per million

AGE 1   Testes, dose CE: < 1 mrad
SHOULDER   Ovaries, dose CE: < 1 mrad

Common Exam (CE): One AP
                      (Total: 1 shot)

Rate of future *leukemia* from Common Exam:
　　　　　Males:　　0.2 per million = 1 in 5 million
　　　　　Females: 0.1 per million = 1 in 10 million
Rate of future *cancer* from Common Exam:
　　　　　Males:　　13 per million = 1 in 76,900
　　　　　Females: 93 per million = 1 in 10,750

Per Shot	Ent Dose	Beam HVL	Male Cancer Risk	Female Cancer Risk
AP	0.047 R	2.2 mm Al	13 per million	93 per million
PA	0.036 R	2.1 mm Al	10 per million	17 per million
LAT	0.236 R	2.5 mm Al	433 per million	516 per million
OBL-PA	0.074 R	2.3 mm Al	67 per million	86 per million

AGE 5　　　　　　　　　　　　　　　Testes, dose CE: < 1 mrad
SHOULDER　　　　　　　　　　　　　Ovaries, dose CE: < 1 mrad

Common Exam (CE): One AP
　　　　　　　　　(Total: 1 shot)
Rate of future *leukemia* from Common Exam:
　　　　　Males:　　0.2 per million = 1 in 5 million
　　　　　Females:　0.1 per million = 1 in 10 million
Rate of future *cancer* from Common Exam:
　　　　　Males:　　17 per million = 1 in 58,800
　　　　　Females: 126 per million = 1 in 7,940

Per Shot	Ent Dose	Beam HVL	Male Cancer Risk	Female Cancer Risk
AP	0.080 R	2.2 mm Al	17 per million	126 per million
PA	0.060 R	2.1 mm Al	13 per million	20 per million
LAT	0.397 R	2.5 mm Al	560 per million	642 per million
OBL-PA	0.125 R	2.3 mm Al	86 per million	106 per million

AGE 10　　　　　　　　　　　　　　Testes, dose CE: < 1 mrad
SHOULDER　　　　　　　　　　　　　Ovaries, dose CE: < 1 mrad

Common Exam (CE): One AP
　　　　　　　　　(Total: 1 shot)
Rate of future *leukemia* from Common Exam:
　　　　　Males:　　0.3 per million = 1 in 3.3 million
　　　　　Females:　0.2 per million = 1 in 5 million
Rate of future *cancer* from Common Exam:
　　　　　Males:　　19 per million = 1 in 52,600
　　　　　Females: 146 per million = 1 in 6,850

Age 10, Shoulder *(continued)*

Per Shot	Ent Dose	Beam HVL	Male Cancer Risk	Female Cancer Risk
AP	0.120 R	2.2 mm Al	19 per million	146 per million
PA	0.091 R	2.1 mm Al	15 per million	55 per million
LAT	0.601 R	2.5 mm Al	603 per million	668 per million
OBL-PA	0.189 R	2.3 mm Al	93 per million	109 per million

AGE 15
SHOULDER

Testes, dose CE: < 1 mrad
Ovaries, dose CE: < 1 mrad

Common Exam (CE): One AP
                    (Total: 1 shot)
Rate of future *leukemia* from Common Exam:
          Males: 0.3 per million = 1 in 3.3 million
          Females: 0.2 per million = 1 in 5 million
Rate of future *cancer* from Common Exam:
          Males: 9.9 per million = 1 in 101,000
          Females: 80 per million = 1 in 12,500

Per Shot	Ent Dose	Beam HVL	Male Cancer Risk	Female Cancer Risk
AP	0.161 R	2.2 mm Al	9.9 per million	80 per million
PA	0.122 R	2.1 mm Al	8.3 per million	9.9 per million
LAT	0.804 R	2.5 mm Al	254 per million	305 per million
OBL-PA	0.252 R	2.3 mm Al	39 per million	50 per million

AGE 20
SHOULDER

Testes, dose CE: < 1 mrad
Ovaries, dose CE: < 1 mrad
Embryo, dose CE: < 1 mrad

Common Exam (CE): One AP
                    (Total: 1 shot)
Rate of future *leukemia* from Common Exam:
          Males: 0.3 per million = 1 in 3.3 million
          Females: 0.2 per million = 1 in 5 million
Rate of future *cancer* from Common Exam: **(Smokers)**
          Males: 9.6 per million = 1 in 104,000   (CE × 6.33)
          Females: 77 per million = 1 in 13,000   (CE × 1.27)

Per Shot	Ent Dose	Beam HVL	Male Cancer Risk	Female Cancer Risk
AP	0.195 R	2.2 mm Al	9.6 per million	77 per million
PA	0.148 R	2.2 mm Al	5.3 per million	6.0 per million
LAT	0.974 R	2.5 mm Al	153 per million	222 per million
OBL-PA	0.306 R	2.3 mm Al	27 per million	36 per million

All values are for the Common Exam

Age 30, Shoulder   Cancer Rate............... *(Lowering Factor)*
         Males: 8.2 per million = 1 in 122,000   (Age 20 × 0.854)
         Females: 66 per million = 1 in 15,200   (Age 20 × 0.873)
Age 40, Shoulder   Cancer Rate............... *(Lowering Factor)*
         Males: 3.6 per million = 1 in 278,000   (Age 20 × 0.372)
         Females: 30 per million = 1 in 33,300   (Age 20 × 0.391)
Age 50, Shoulder   Cancer Rate............... *(Lowering Factor)*
         Males: 0.14 per million = 1 in 7.1 million   (Age 20 × 0.015)
         Females: 1.3 per million = 1 in 769,000   (Age 20 × 0.017)

SKULL

Contrast Medium: No.

Fluoroscopy and Spot Films: No.

Length of Field: In the adult, the field center is at the nasion and the body midline for the AP shot. The field length is 30.5 cm, so it extends from above the vertex of the skull to approximately the level of the larynx. For the pediatric exams, adjustments are made to encompass the same regions, and the Towne's shot (see below) is often used.

Organs Generating Most Cancer Risk:
    Males: Brain, lips, tongue, larynx, mouth, pharynx.
    Females: Brain, thyroid, mouth, tongue, salivary glands, pharynx.

Special Comments:
- The Common Exam changes three times with age. The cancer risk will change because of this feature alone, aside from the effects of age.
- The Towne's projection is a special one often used in pediatric exams. It is an AP shot, but the X-ray beam is at a 30° angle away from perpendicular to the supine patient. The beam enters the head at a higher position than it exits, and points caudad (toward the lower part or tail of the body).

AGE NEW   Testes, dose CE: < 1 mrad
SKULL   Ovaries, dose CE: < 1 mrad

Common Exam (CE): One AP, one LAT, and
                   one Towne's AP (Total: 3 shots)
Rate of future *leukemia* from Common Exam:
         Males: 3 per million = 1 in 333,000
         Females: 2 per million = 1 in 500,000
Rate of future *cancer* from Common Exam:
         Males: 419 per million = 1 in 2,390
         Females: 299 per million = 1 in 3,340

Age New, Skull *(continued)*

Per Shot	Ent Dose	Beam HVL	Male Cancer Risk	Female Cancer Risk
AP	0.094 R	2.4 mm Al	152 per million	123 per million
PA	0.087 R	2.4 mm Al	134 per million	86 per million
LAT	0.055 R	2.3 mm Al	113 per million	67 per million
Towne's	0.094 R	2.4 mm Al	154 per million	109 per million

AGE 1
SKULL

Testes, dose CE: < 1 mrad
Ovaries, dose CE: < 1 mrad

Common Exam (CE): One AP, two LAT, and
one Towne's AP (Total: 4 shots)
Rate of future *leukemia* from Common Exam:
Males: 3 per million = 1 in 333,000
Females: 2 per million = 1 in 500,000
Rate of future *cancer* from Common Exam:
Males: 548 per million = 1 in 1,825
Females: 366 per million = 1 in 2,730

Per Shot	Ent Dose	Beam HVL	Male Cancer Risk	Female Cancer Risk
AP	0.116 R	2.4 mm Al	159 per million	118 per million
PA	0.107 R	2.4 mm Al	133 per million	87 per million
LAT	0.068 R	2.3 mm Al	118 per million	68 per million
Towne's	0.116 R	2.4 mm Al	153 per million	112 per million

AGE 5
SKULL

Testes, dose CE: < 1 mrad
Ovaries, dose CE: < 1 mrad

Common Exam (CE): One PA, two LAT, and
one Towne's AP (Total: 4 shots)
Rate of future *leukemia* from Common Exam:
Males: 4 per million = 1 in 250,000
Females: 2.5 per million = 1 in 400,000
Rate of future *cancer* from Common Exam:
Males: 746 per million = 1 in 1,340
Females: 455 per million = 1 in 2,200

Per Shot	Ent Dose	Beam HVL	Male Cancer Risk	Female Cancer Risk
AP	0.196 R	2.4 mm Al	238 per million	173 per million
PA	0.181 R	2.4 mm Al	198 per million	119 per million
LAT	0.115 R	2.3 mm Al	162 per million	95 per million
Towne's	0.196 R	2.4 mm Al	224 per million	146 per million

AGE 10
SKULL

Testes, dose CE: < 1 mrad
Ovaries, dose CE: < 1 mrad

Common Exam (CE): One PA, two LAT, and
one Towne's AP (Total: 4 shots)
Rate of future *leukemia* from Common Exam:
      Males: 5 per million = 1 in 200,000
      Females: 3 per million = 1 in 333,000
Rate of future *cancer* from Common Exam:
      Males: 818 per million = 1 in 1,222
      Females: 471 per million = 1 in 2,123

Per Shot	Ent Dose	Beam HVL	Male Cancer Risk	Female Cancer Risk
AP	0.296 R	2.4 mm Al	263 per million	180 per million
PA	0.273 R	2.4 mm Al	212 per million	125 per million
LAT	0.174 R	2.3 mm Al	167 per million	94 per million
Towne's	0.296 R	2.4 mm Al	272 per million	158 per million

AGE 15
SKULL

Testes, dose CE: < 1 mrad
Ovaries, dose CE: < 1 mrad

Common Exam (CE): One AP, two LAT, and
one Towne's AP (Total: 4 shots)
Rate of future *leukemia* from Common Exam:
      Males: 6 per million = 1 in 167,000
      Females: 4 per million = 1 in 250,000
Rate of future *cancer* from Common Exam:
      Males: 455 per million = 1 in 2,200
      Females: 248 per million = 1 in 4,030

Per Shot	Ent Dose	Beam HVL	Male Cancer Risk	Female Cancer Risk
AP	0.396 R	2.4 mm Al	158 per million	98 per million
PA	0.365 R	2.4 mm Al	120 per million	67 per million
LAT	0.233 R	2.3 mm Al	86 per million	46 per million
Towne's	0.396 R	2.4 mm Al	163 per million	89 per million

AGE 20
SKULL

Testes, dose CE: < 1 mrad
Ovaries, dose CE: < 1 mrad
Embryo, dose CE: < 1 mrad

Common Exam (CE): One AP, one PA, and
two LAT (Total: 4 shots)
Rate of future *leukemia* from Common Exam:
      Males: 6 per million = 1 in 167,000
      Females: 4 per million = 1 in 250,000

Age 20, Skull *(continued)*

Rate of future *cancer* from Common Exam: (Smokers)
      Males: 401 per million = 1 in 2,495   (CE × 1.01)
      Females: 236 per million = 1 in 4,240   (CE × 1.02)

Per Shot	Ent Dose	Beam HVL	Male Cancer Risk	Female Cancer Risk
AP	0.480 R	2.4 mm Al	144 per million	88 per million
PA	0.443 R	2.4 mm Al	113 per million	64 per million
LAT	0.282 R	2.3 mm Al	72 per million	42 per million
OBL-PA	0.221 R	2.4 mm Al	59 per million	34 per million

All values are for the Common Exam

Age 25, Skull   Cancer Rate............... *(Lowering Factor)*
      Males: 398 per million = 1 in 2,510   (Age 20 × 0.994)
      Females: 233 per million = 1 in 4,290   (Age 20 × 0.988)
Age 30, Skull   Cancer Rate............... *(Lowering Factor)*
      Males: 342 per million = 1 in 2,925   (Age 20 × 0.854)
      Females: 206 per million = 1 in 4,850   (Age 20 × 0.873)
Age 35, Skull   Cancer Rate............... *(Lowering Factor)*
      Males: 245 per million = 1 in 4,080   (Age 20 × 0.611)
      Females: 147 per million = 1 in 6,800   (Age 20 × 0.623)
Age 40, Skull   Cancer Rate............... *(Lowering Factor)*
      Males: 149 per million = 1 in 6,710   (Age 20 × 0.372)
      Females: 92 per million = 1 in 10,870 (Age 20 × 0.391)
Age 45, Skull   Cancer Rate............... *(Lowering Factor)*
      Males: 65 per million = 1 in 15,400 (Age 20 × 0.162)
      Females: 42 per million = 1 in 23,800 (Age 20 × 0.176)
Age 50, Skull   Cancer Rate............... *(Lowering Factor)*
      Males: 6.0 per million = 1 in 167,000 (Age 20 × 0.015)
      Females: 4.0 per million = 1 in 250,000 (Age 20 × 0.017)
Age 55, Skull   Cancer Rate............... *(Lowering Factor)*
      Males: 4.0 per million = 1 in 250,000 (Age 20 × 0.010)
      Females: 2.8 per million = 1 in 357,000 (Age 20 × 0.012)

SMALL BOWEL SERIES

Contrast Medium: Yes. Barium sulfate suspension, administered by mouth.

Fluoroscopy and Spot Films: Yes. Cancer risk from FLU and spot films are additional to those given in the tables. Please see Chapter 6 for calculation of FLU risk.

Length of Field: In the adult, the field center is at the bi-iliac crests and the body midline. The field length is 43.2 cm, so it extends from approximately the xiphoid process to 5 cm below the pubic symphysis. Pediatric fields are adjusted to encompass the same regions.

Organs Generating Most Cancer Risk:
  Males: Prostate, kidneys, large intestine, bladder, rectum, stomach.
  Females: Corpus uteri, large intestine, kidneys, ovaries, cervix, rectum.

Special Comments:
  • The AP shot for this exam, which is taken before administration of the contrast medium, is commonly identical with the AP of the K.U.B. Exam.
  • The cancer risk from the PA shots has been adjusted for partial shielding of some abdominal organs from the X-ray beam by the barium sulfate.

AGE NEW   Testes, dose CE: 53 mrads
SMALL BOWEL SERIES   Ovaries, dose CE: 311 mrads

Common Exam (CE): One AP and four PA
                    (Total: 5 shots)
Rate of future *leukemia* from Common Exam:
        Males: 33 per million = 1 in 30,300
        Females: 21 per million = 1 in 47,600
Rate of future *cancer* from Common Exam:
        Males: 5,044 per million = 1 in 198
        Females: 5,057 per million = 1 in 198

Per Shot	Ent Dose	Beam HVL	Male Cancer Risk	Female Cancer Risk
AP	0.130 R	2.5 mm Al	1,260 per million	1,229 per million
PA	0.107 R	2.9 mm Al	946 per million	957 per million

AGE 1   Testes, dose CE: 58 mrads
SMALL BOWEL SERIES   Ovaries, dose CE: 309 mrads

Common Exam (CE): One AP and four PA
                    (Total: 5 shots)
Rate of future *leukemia* from Common Exam:
        Males: 32 per million = 1 in 31,300
        Females: 20 per million = 1 in 50,000
Rate of future *cancer* from Common Exam:
        Males: 5,292 per million = 1 in 189
        Females: 5,356 per million = 1 in 187

Per Shot	Ent Dose	Beam HVL	Male Cancer Risk	Female Cancer Risk
AP	0.161 R	2.5 mm Al	1,344 per million	1,288 per million
PA	0.133 R	2.9 mm Al	987 per million	1,017 per million

AGE 5
SMALL BOWEL SERIES

Testes, dose CE: 65 mrads
Ovaries, dose CE: 413 mrads

Common Exam (CE): One AP and four PA
(Total: 5 shots)
Rate of future *leukemia* from Common Exam:
        Males: 49 per million = 1 in 20,400
        Females: 31 per million = 1 in 32,260
Rate of future *cancer* from Common Exam:
        Males: 7,357 per million = 1 in 136
        Females: 6,819 per million = 1 in 147

Per Shot	*Ent Dose*	*Beam HVL*	*Male Cancer Risk*	*Female Cancer Risk*
AP	0.271 R	2.5 mm Al	1,869 per million	1,691 per million
PA	0.224 R	2.9 mm Al	1,372 per million	1,282 per million

AGE 10
SMALL BOWEL SERIES

Testes, dose CE: 69 mrads
Ovaries, dose CE: 528 mrads

Common Exam (CE): One AP and four PA
(Total: 5 shots)
Rate of future *leukemia* from Common Exam:
        Males: 57 per million = 1 in 17,550
        Females: 36 per million = 1 in 27,800
Rate of future *cancer* from Common Exam:
        Males: 8,235 per million = 1 in 121
        Females: 7,182 per million = 1 in 139

Per Shot	*Ent Dose*	*Beam HVL*	*Male Cancer Risk*	*Female Cancer Risk*
AP	0.410 R	2.5 mm Al	2,155 per million	1,838 per million
PA	0.338 R	2.9 mm Al	1,520 per million	1,336 per million

AGE 15
SMALL BOWEL SERIES

Testes, dose CE: 52 mrads
Ovaries, dose CE: 591 mrads

Common Exam (CE): One AP and four PA
(Total: 5 shots)
Rate of future *leukemia* from Common Exam:
        Males: 53 per million = 1 in 18,900
        Females: 33 per million = 1 in 30,300
Rate of future *cancer* from Common Exam:
        Males: 4,229 per million = 1 in 236
        Females: 3,555 per million = 1 in 281

Per Shot	Ent Dose	Beam HVL	Male Cancer Risk	Female Cancer Risk
AP	0.548 R	2.5 mm Al	1,221 per million	1,003 per million
PA	0.452 R	2.9 mm Al	752 per million	638 per million

AGE 20
SMALL BOWEL SERIES

Testes, dose CE: 40 mrads
Ovaries, dose CE: 570 mrads
Embryo, dose CE: 566 mrads

Common Exam (CE): One AP and four PA
                          (Total: 5 shots)
Rate of future *leukemia* from Common Exam:
         Males: 36 per million = 1 in 27,800
         Females: 23 per million = 1 in 43,500
Rate of future *cancer* from Common Exam: **(Smokers)**
         Males: 3,649 per million = 1 in 274   (CE × 1.71)
         Females: 2,972 per million = 1 in 336   (CE × 1.41)

Per Shot	Ent Dose	Beam HVL	Male Cancer Risk	Female Cancer Risk
AP	0.664 R	2.5 mm Al	1,169 per million	936 per million
PA	0.548 R	2.9 mm Al	620 per million	509 per million

All values are for the Common Exam

Age 25, Small Bowel   Cancer Rate............... *(Lowering Factor)*
         Males: 3,627 per million = 1 in 276   (Age 20 × 0.994)
         Females: 2,936 per million = 1 in 341   (Age 20 × 0.988)
Age 30, Small Bowel   Cancer Rate............... *(Lowering Factor)*
         Males: 3,116 per million = 1 in 321   (Age 20 × 0.854)
         Females: 2,595 per million = 1 in 385   (Age 20 × 0.873)
Age 35, Small Bowel   Cancer Rate............... *(Lowering Factor)*
         Males: 2,230 per million = 1 in 448   (Age 20 × 0.611)
         Females: 1,852 per million = 1 in 540   (Age 20 × 0.623)
Age 40, Small Bowel   Cancer Rate............... *(Lowering Factor)*
         Males: 1,357 per million = 1 in 737   (Age 20 × 0.372)
         Females: 1,162 per million = 1 in 861   (Age 20 × 0.391)
Age 45, Small Bowel   Cancer Rate............... *(Lowering Factor)*
         Males: 591 per million = 1 in 1,692   (Age 20 × 0.162)
         Females: 523 per million = 1 in 1,912   (Age 20 × 0.176)
Age 50, Small Bowel   Cancer Rate............... *(Lowering Factor)*
         Males: 55 per million = 1 in 18,200   (Age 20 × 0.015)
         Females: 51 per million = 1 in 19,600   (Age 20 × 0.017)
Age 55, Small Bowel   Cancer Rate............... *(Lowering Factor)*
         Males: 36 per million = 1 in 27,800   (Age 20 × 0.010)
         Females: 36 per million = 1 in 27,800   (Age 20 × 0.012)

THORACIC SPINE—WIDE

Contrast Medium: No.

Fluoroscopy and Spot Films: No.

Length of Field: The field length is 43.2 cm in the adult, and extends vertically from approximately the level of the larynx to approximately 9 cm above the bi-iliac crests. The field center is 7.6 cm above the xiphoid process and, in the AP and PA shots, at the body midline. In the LAT shot, the field center is 5 cm to the patient's rear. For pediatric exams, the fields are adjusted to encompass the same organ regions as in the adult.

Organs Generating Most Cancer Risk:
   Males: Stomach, bronchi, pancreas, larynx, esophagus, large intestine.
   Females: Breasts, stomach, pancreas, bronchi, large intestine, kidneys.

Special Comments:
   • This exam is designated "wide" not to suggest that its field is any wider than normal (see Section 2 of this chapter), but rather to help distinguish it from the "narrow" and "special" exams, which follow.
   • For the female, the PA shot confers a much lower cancer risk than the AP shot. Please see Thoracic Spine—Special Exam.

AGE NEW   Testes, dose CE: 1 mrad
THORACIC SPINE—WIDE   Ovaries, dose CE: 5 mrads

Common Exam (CE): One AP and one LAT
                         (Total: 2 shots)
Rate of future *leukemia* from Common Exam:
            Males: 11 per million = 1 in 90,900
            Females: 7 per million = 1 in 143,000
Rate of future *cancer* from Common Exam:
            Males: 1,736 per million = 1 in 576
            Females: 2,530 per million = 1 in 395

Per Shot	Ent Dose	Beam HVL	Male Cancer Risk	Female Cancer Risk
AP	0.130 R	2.4 mm Al	508 per million	1,605 per million
PA	0.101 R	2.5 mm Al	334 per million	449 per million
LAT	0.286 R	2.4 mm Al	1,228 per million	925 per million
OBL-PA	0.148 R	2.4 mm Al	550 per million	549 per million

AGE 1
THORACIC SPINE—WIDE

Testes, dose CE: 1 mrad
Ovaries, dose CE: 6 mrads

Common Exam (CE): One AP and one LAT
               (Total: 2 shots)
Rate of future *leukemia* from Common Exam:
        Males: 11 per million = 1 in 90,900
        Females: 7 per million = 1 in 143,000
Rate of future *cancer* from Common Exam:
        Males: 1,798 per million = 1 in 556
        Females: 2,741 per million = 1 in 365

Per Shot	Ent Dose	Beam HVL	Male Cancer Risk	Female Cancer Risk
AP	0.161 R	2.4 mm Al	572 per million	1,804 per million
PA	0.125 R	2.5 mm Al	358 per million	476 per million
LAT	0.353 R	2.4 mm Al	1,226 per million	937 per million
OBL-PA	0.182 R	2.4 mm Al	565 per million	570 per million

AGE 5
THORACIC SPINE—WIDE

Testes, dose CE: 1 mrad
Ovaries, dose CE: 7 mrad

Common Exam (CE): One AP and one LAT
               (Total: 2 shots)
Rate of future *leukemia* from Common Exam:
        Males: 14 per million = 1 in 71,400
        Females: 9 per million = 1 in 111,000
Rate of future *cancer* from Common Exam:
        Males: 2,363 per million = 1 in 423
        Females: 3,653 per million = 1 in 274

Per Shot	Ent Dose	Beam HVL	Male Cancer Risk	Female Cancer Risk
AP	0.271 R	2.4 mm Al	805 per million	2,523 per million
PA	0.211 R	2.5 mm Al	500 per million	614 per million
LAT	0.595 R	2.4 mm Al	1,558 per million	1,130 per million
OBL-PA	0.308 R	2.4 mm Al	749 per million	715 per million

AGE 10
THORACIC SPINE—WIDE

Testes, dose CE: < 1 mrad
Ovaries, dose CE: 6.3 mrad

Common Exam (CE): One AP and one LAT
               (Total: 2 shots)
Rate of future *leukemia* from Common Exam:
        Males: 16 per million = 1 in 62,500
        Females: 10 per million = 1 in 100,000

Age 10, Thoracic Spine—Wide *(continued)*

Rate of future *cancer* from Common Exam:
Males: 2,576 per million = 1 in 388
Females: 3,908 per million = 1 in 256

Per Shot	Ent Dose	Beam HVL	Male Cancer Risk	Female Cancer Risk
AP	0.410 R	2.4 mm Al	925 per million	2,788 per million
PA	0.319 R	2.5 mm Al	559 per million	640 per million
LAT	0.900 R	2.4 mm Al	1,651 per million	1,120 per million
OBL-PA	0.465 R	2.4 mm Al	813 per million	734 per million

AGE 15
THORACIC SPINE—WIDE

Testes, dose CE: < 1 mrad
Ovaries, dose CE: 4.5 mrad

Common Exam (CE): One AP and one LAT
(Total: 2 shots)
Rate of future *leukemia* from Common Exam:
Males: 14 per million = 1 in 71,400
Females: 9 per million = 1 in 111,000
Rate of future *cancer* from Common Exam:
Males: 1,134 per million = 1 in 882
Females: 1,953 per million = 1 in 512

Per Shot	Ent Dose	Beam HVL	Male Cancer Risk	Female Cancer Risk
AP	0.548 R	2.4 mm Al	515 per million	1,554 per million
PA	0.426 R	2.5 mm Al	292 per million	294 per million
LAT	1.203 R	2.4 mm Al	619 per million	399 per million
OBL-PA	0.622 R	2.4 mm Al	362 per million	307 per million

AGE 20
THORACIC SPINE—WIDE

Testes, dose CE: < 1 mrad
Ovaries, dose CE: < 1 mrad
Embryo, dose CE: 1.4 mrad

Common Exam (CE): One AP and one LAT
(Total: 2 shots)
Rate of future *leukemia* from Common Exam:
Males: 10 per million = 1 in 100,000
Females: 5 per million = 1 in 200,000
Rate of future *cancer* from Common Exam: **(Smokers)**
Males: 784 per million = 1 in 1,276   (CE × 2.75)
Females: 1,645 per million = 1 in 608   (CE × 1.46)

Per Shot	Ent Dose	Beam HVL	Male Cancer Risk	Female Cancer Risk
AP	0.664 R	2.4 mm Al	437 per million	1,421 per million
PA	0.517 R	2.5 mm Al	259 per million	225 per million
LAT	1.458 R	2.4 mm Al	347 per million	224 per million
OBL-PA	0.754 R	2.4 mm Al	267 per million	211 per million

All values are for the Common Exam

Age 25, Thoracic Sp. Wide   Cancer Rate............... *(Lowering Factor)*
        Males: 779 per million = 1 in 1,285   (Age 20 × 0.994)
        Females: 1,625 per million = 1 in 615   (Age 20 × 0.988)
Age 30, Thoracic Sp. Wide   Cancer Rate............... *(Lowering Factor)*
        Males: 670 per million = 1 in 1,492   (Age 20 × 0.854)
        Females: 1,436 per million = 1 in 696   (Age 20 × 0.873)
Age 35, Thoracic Sp. Wide   Cancer Rate............... *(Lowering Factor)*
        Males: 479 per million = 1 in 2,088   (Age 20 × 0.611)
        Females: 1,025 per million = 1 in 976   (Age 20 × 0.623)
Age 40, Thoracic Sp. Wide   Cancer Rate............... *(Lowering Factor)*
        Males: 292 per million = 1 in 3,425   (Age 20 × 0.372)
        Females: 643 per million = 1 in 1,555   (Age 20 × 0.391)
Age 45, Thoracic Sp. Wide   Cancer Rate............... *(Lowering Factor)*
        Males: 127 per million = 1 in 7,875   (Age 20 × 0.162)
        Females: 290 per million = 1 in 3,450   (Age 20 × 0.176)
Age 50, Thoracic Sp. Wide   Cancer Rate............... *(Lowering Factor)*
        Males: 12 per million = 1 in 83,300   (Age 20 × 0.015)
        Females: 28 per million = 1 in 35,700   (Age 20 × 0.017)
Age 55, Thoracic Sp. Wide   Cancer Rate............... *(Lowering Factor)*
        Males: 8 per million = 1 in 125,000   (Age 20 × 0.010)
        Females: 20 per million = 1 in 50,000   (Age 20 × 0.012)

THORACIC SPINE—NARROW

Contrast Medium: No.

Fluoroscopy and Spot Films: No.

Length of Field: The field length is the same as for the Thoracic Spine—Wide Exam, but the field width (see below) is much reduced.

Organs Generating Most Cancer Risk:
    Males: Stomach, bronchi, larynx, pancreas, esophagus.
    Females: Breasts, stomach, pancreas, bronchi.

Thoracic Spine—Narrow *(continued)*

Special Comments:
- For the AP-Narrow and PA-Narrow shots, the field center is at body midline, but the field width is only 17.8 cm, so it extends only 8.9 cm from the midline in either direction. The LAT-Narrow shot, with field center 5 cm to the patient's rear, extends forward of the field center only 7.5 cm, so its edge is still 7.5 cm from the anterior chest wall.
- The cancer risks from this exam should be compared with those from the Wide Exam and the Special Exam. The choice, of course, involves weighing particular diagnostic information against cancer risk.

AGE NEW   Testes, dose CE: < 1 mrad
THORACIC SPINE—NARROW   Ovaries, dose CE: 3.9 mrad

Common Exam (CE): One AP-Narrow and
　　　　　　　　　　　　one LAT-Narrow (Total: 2 shots)
Rate of future *leukemia* from Common Exam:
　　　　　Males:　　　6 per million = 1 in 167,000
　　　　　Females:　　4 per million = 1 in 250,000
Rate of future *cancer* from Common Exam:
　　　　　Males:　　1,057 per million = 1 in 946
　　　　　Females: 1,341 per million = 1 in 746

Per Shot	*Ent Dose*	*Beam HVL*	*Male Cancer Risk*	*Female Cancer Risk*
AP-Nar	0.130 R	2.4 mm Al	320 per million	851 per million
LAT-Nar	0.286 R	2.4 mm Al	737 per million	490 per million
PA-Nar	0.101 R	2.5 mm Al	210 per million	238 per million

AGE 1   Testes, dose CE: <1 mrad
THORACIC SPINE—NARROW   Ovaries, dose CE: 4.7 mrad

Common Exam (CE): One AP-Narrow and
　　　　　　　　　　　　one LAT-Narrow (Total: 2 shots)
Rate of future *leukemia* from Common Exam:
　　　　　Males:　　　6 per million = 1 in 167,000
　　　　　Females:　　4 per million = 1 in 250,000
Rate of future *cancer* from Common Exam:
　　　　　Males:　　1,096 per million = 1 in 912
　　　　　Females: 1,453 per million = 1 in 688

Per Shot	*Ent Dose*	*Beam HVL*	*Male Cancer Risk*	*Female Cancer Risk*
AP-Nar	0.161 R	2.4 mm Al	360 per million	956 per million
LAT-Nar	0.353 R	2.4 mm Al	736 per million	497 per million
PA-Nar	0.125 R	2.5 mm Al	226 per million	252 per million

AGE 5
THORACIC SPINE—NARROW

Testes, dose CE: 1 mrad
Ovaries, dose CE: 5.5 mrads

Common Exam (CE): One AP-Narrow and
one LAT-Narrow (Total: 2 shots)
Rate of future *leukemia* from Common Exam:
Males: 8 per million = 1 in 125,000
Females: 5 per million = 1 in 200,000
Rate of future *cancer* from Common Exam:
Males: 1,442 per million = 1 in 693
Females: 1,936 per million = 1 in 516

Per Shot	Ent Dose	Beam HVL	Male Cancer Risk	Female Cancer Risk
AP-Nar	0.271 R	2.4 mm Al	507 per million	1,337 per million
LAT-Nar	0.595 R	2.4 mm Al	935 per million	599 per million
PA-Nar	0.211 R	2.5 mm Al	315 per million	325 per million

AGE 10
THORACIC SPINE—NARROW

Testes, dose CE: 1 mrad
Ovaries, dose CE: 4.9 mrad

Common Exam (CE): One AP-Narrow and
one LAT-Narrow (Total: 2 shots)
Rate of future *leukemia* from Common Exam:
Males: 10 per million = 1 in 100,000
Females: 6 per million = 1 in 167,000
Rate of future *cancer* from Common Exam:
Males: 1,574 per million = 1 in 635
Females: 2,072 per million = 1 in 483

Per Shot	Ent Dose	Beam HVL	Male Cancer Risk	Female Cancer Risk
AP-Nar	0.410 R	2.4 mm Al	583 per million	1,478 per million
LAT-Nar	0.900 R	2.4 mm Al	991 per million	594 per million
PA-Nar	0.319 R	2.5 mm Al	352 per million	339 per million

AGE 15
THORACIC SPINE—NARROW

Testes, dose CE: < 1 mrad
Ovaries, dose CE: 3.5 mrad

Common Exam (CE): One AP-Narrow and
one LAT-Narrow (Total: 2 shots)

Age 15, Thoracic Spine—Narrow (continued)

Rate of future *leukemia* from Common Exam:
   Males: 8 per million = 1 in 125,000
   Females: 5 per million = 1 in 200,000
Rate of future *cancer* from Common Exam:
   Males: 695 per million = 1 in 1,439
   Females: 1,034 per million = 1 in 967

Per Shot	Ent Dose	Beam HVL	Male Cancer Risk	Female Cancer Risk
AP-Nar	0.548 R	2.4 mm Al	324 per million	823 per million
LAT-Nar	1.203 R	2.4 mm Al	371 per million	211 per million
PA-Nar	0.426 R	2.5 mm Al	184 per million	156 per million

AGE 20
THORACIC SPINE—NARROW

Testes, dose CE: < 1 mrad
Ovaries, dose CE: < 1 mrad
Embryo, dose CE: < 1 mrad

Common Exam (CE): One AP-Narrow and
       one LAT-Narrow (Total: 2 shots)
Rate of future *leukemia* from Common Exam:
   Males: 6 per million = 1 in 167,000
   Females: 3 per million = 1 in 333,000
Rate of future *cancer* from Common Exam: **(Smokers)**
   Males: 483 per million = 1 in 2,070 (CE × 2.42)
   Females: 872 per million = 1 in 1,147 (CE × 1.44)

Per Shot	Ent Dose	Beam HVL	Male Cancer Risk	Female Cancer Risk
AP-Nar	0.664 R	2.4 mm Al	275 per million	753 per million
LAT-Nar	1.458 R	2.4 mm Al	208 per million	119 per million
PA-Nar	0.517 R	2.5 mm Al	163 per million	119 per million

All values are for the Common Exam

Age 25, Thor. Sp. Narrow   Cancer Rate............... *(Lowering Factor)*
   Males: 480 per million = 1 in 2,083 (Age 20 × 0.994)
   Females: 862 per million = 1 in 1,160 (Age 20 × 0.988)
Age 30, Thor. Sp. Narrow   Cancer Rate............... *(Lowering Factor)*
   Males: 412 per million = 1 in 2,427 (Age 20 × 0.854)
   Females: 761 per million = 1 in 1,314 (Age 20 × 0.873)
Age 35, Thor. Sp. Narrow   Cancer Rate............... *(Lowering Factor)*
   Males: 295 per million = 1 in 3,390 (Age 20 × 0.611)
   Females: 543 per million = 1 in 1,842 (Age 20 × 0.623)
Age 40, Thor. Sp. Narrow   Cancer Rate............... *(Lowering Factor)*
   Males: 180 per million = 1 in 5,556 (Age 20 × 0.372)
   Females: 341 per million = 1 in 2,932 (Age 20 × 0.391)

Age 45, Thor. Sp. Narrow   Cancer Rate............... *(Lowering Factor)*
    Males: 78 per million = 1 in 12,820   (Age 20 × 0.162)
    Females: 153 per million = 1 in 6,536   (Age 20 × 0.176)

Age 50, Thor. Sp. Narrow   Cancer Rate............... *(Lowering Factor)*
    Males: 7 per million = 1 in 143,000   (Age 20 × 0.015)
    Females: 15 per million = 1 in 66,700   (Age 20 × 0.017)

Age 55, Thor. Sp. Narrow   Cancer Rate............... *(Lowering Factor)*
    Males: 5 per million = 1 in 200,000   (Age 20 × 0.010)
    Females: 10 per million = 1 in 100,000   (Age 20 × 0.012)

THORACIC SPINE—SPECIAL

Contrast Medium: No.

Fluoroscopy and Spot Films: No.

Length of Field: The field length is the same as for the Wide Exam and the Narrow Exam.

Organs Generating Most Cancer Risk:
    Males: Bronchi, stomach, pancreas, kidney, larynx, esophagus.
    Females: Breasts, pancreas, bronchi, stomach, kidneys.

Special Comments:
- This Special Exam differs from the Wide Exam by substituting the PA-Wide shot for the AP-Wide shot. The Special Exam illustrates an advantage, especially for females, in risk reduction compared with the Wide Exam (see tabulation below), and corroborates the work of Nash and co-workers (1979), Gray and co-workers (1983), and Taylor and co-workers (1979, and 1983 in Johns and Cunningham).
- Even further reduction in risk from this exam should be possible in cases which permit the use of still another combination of shots: the PA-Narrow and the LAT-Narrow. We shall call such an exam the Least Risk Exam in the tabulation below. Of course, advantages in risk reduction disappear in cases where PA or narrow shots cannot deliver the needed diagnostic information, or lead to many re-takes due to uncertain positioning of a patient.
- The comparison below illustrates how new exams, under contemplation, can be evaluated for consequent cancer risk by using information from one or several tables (the "mix-and-match" power):

Thoracic Spine—Special *(continued)*

Common Exam	Exam's Cancer Risk for Newborn Females	Exam's Cancer Risk for 10-Year-Old Females	Exam's Cancer Risk for 20-Year-Old Females
WIDE: One AP-Wide + one LAT-Wide	2,530 per million	3,908 per million	1,645 per million
NARROW: One AP-Narrow + one LAT-Narrow	1,341 per million	2,072 per million	872 per million
SPECIAL: One PA-Wide + one LAT-Wide	1,374 per million	1,760 per million	449 per million
LEAST RISK: One PA-Narrow + one LAT-Narrow	728 per million	933 per million	238 per million

AGE NEW
THORACIC SPINE—SPECIAL

Testes, dose CE: < 1 mrad
Ovaries, dose CE: 4.9 mrads

Common Exam (CE): One PA-Wide and
one LAT-Wide (Total: 2 shots)
Rate of future *leukemia* from Common Exam:
        Males: 12 per million = 1 in 83,300
        Females: 7 per million = 1 in 143,000
Rate of future *cancer* from Common Exam:
        Males: 1,562 per million = 1 in 640
        Females: 1,374 per million = 1 in 728

Per Shot	Ent Dose	Beam HVL	Male Cancer Risk	Female Cancer Risk
PA-Wi	0.101 R	2.5 mm Al	334 per million	449 per million
LAT-Wi	0.286 R	2.4 mm Al	1,228 per million	925 per million
PA-Nar	0.101 R	2.5 mm Al	210 per million	238 per million

AGE 1
THORACIC SPINE—SPECIAL

Testes, dose CE: < 1 mrad
Ovaries, dose CE: 5.8 mrads

Common Exam (CE): One PA-Wide and
　　　　　　　　one LAT-Wide (Total: 2 shots)
Rate of future *leukemia* from Common Exam:
　　　　Males:　　　13 per million = 1 in 76,900
　　　　Females:　　 8 per million = 1 in 125,000
Rate of future *cancer* from Common Exam:
　　　　Males:　　1,584 per million = 1 in 631
　　　　Females: 1,413 per million = 1 in 708

Per Shot	Ent Dose	Beam HVL	Male Cancer Risk	Female Cancer Risk
PA-Wi	0.125 R	2.5 mm Al	358 per million	476 per million
LAT-Wi	0.353 R	2.4 mm Al	1,226 per million	937 per million
PA-Nar	0.125 R	2.5 mm Al	226 per million	252 per million

AGE 5
THORACIC SPINE—SPECIAL

Testes, dose CE: < 1 mrad
Ovaries, dose CE: 6.8 mrads

Common Exam (CE): One PA-Wide and
　　　　　　　　one LAT-Wide (Total: 2 shots)
Rate of future *leukemia* from Common Exam:
　　　　Males:　　　17 per million = 1 in 58,800
　　　　Females:　　10 per million = 1 in 100,000
Rate of future *cancer* from Common Exam:
　　　　Males:　　2,058 per million = 1 in 486
　　　　Females: 1,744 per million = 1 in 573

Per Shot	Ent Dose	Beam HVL	Male Cancer Risk	Female Cancer Risk
PA-WI	0.211 R	2.5 mm Al	500 per million	614 per million
LAT-Wi	0.595 R	2.4 mm Al	1,558 per million	1,130 per million
PA-Nar	0.211 R	2.5 mm Al	315 per million	325 per million

AGE 10
THORACIC SPINE—SPECIAL

Testes, dose CE: < 1 mrad
Ovaries, dose CE: 6.1 mrads

Common Exam (CE): One PA-Wide and
　　　　　　　　one LAT-Wide (Total: 2 shots)
Rate of future *leukemia* from Common Exam:
　　　　Males:　　　19 per million = 1 in 52,600
　　　　Females:　　12 per million = 1 in 83,300
Rate of future *cancer* from Common Exam:
　　　　Males:　　2,210 per million = 1 in 452
　　　　Females: 1,760 per million = 1 in 568

Age 10, Thoracic Spine—Special *(continued)*

Per Shot	Ent Dose	Beam HVL	Male Cancer Risk	Female Cancer Risk
PA-Wi	0.319 R	2.5 mm Al	559 per million	640 per million
LAT-Wi	0.900 R	2.4 mm Al	1,651 per million	1,120 per million
PA-Nar	0.319 R	2.5 mm Al	352 per million	339 per million

AGE 15　　　　　　　　　　　　　　Testes, dose CE: < 1 mrad
THORACIC SPINE—SPECIAL　　　　Ovaries, dose CE: 4.4 mrads

Common Exam (CE): One PA-Wide and
　　　　　　　　　one LAT-Wide (Total: 2 shots)
Rate of future *leukemia* from Common Exam:
　　　　Males:　　17 per million = 1 in 58,800
　　　　Females: 11 per million = 1 in 90,900
Rate of future *cancer* from Common Exam:
　　　　Males:　　911 per million = 1 in 1,098
　　　　Females: 693 per million = 1 in 1,443

Per Shot	Ent Dose	Beam HVL	Male Cancer Risk	Female Cancer Risk
PA-Wi	0.426 R	2.5 mm Al	292 per million	294 per million
LAT-Wi	1.203 R	2.4 mm Al	619 per million	399 per million
PA-Nar	0.426 R	2.5 mm Al	184 per million	156 per million

AGE 20　　　　　　　　　　　　　　Testes, dose CE: < 1 mrad
THORACIC SPINE—SPECIAL　　　　Ovaries, dose CE: < 1 mrad
　　　　　　　　　　　　　　　　　　Embryo, dose CE: 1.3 mrad

Common Exam (CE): One PA-Wide and
　　　　　　　　　one LAT-Wide (Total: 2 shots)
Rate of future *leukemia* from Common Exam:
　　　　Males:　　12 per million = 1 in 83,300
　　　　Females:　 8 per million = 1 in 125,000
Rate of future *cancer* from Common Exam:　　　　**(Smokers)**
　　　　Males:　　606 per million = 1 in 1,650　　(CE × 2.98)
　　　　Females: 449 per million = 1 in 2,227　　(CE × 2.76)

Per Shot	Ent Dose	Beam HVL	Male Cancer Risk	Female Cancer Risk
PA-Wi	0.517 R	2.5 mm Al	259 per million	225 per million
LAT-Wi	1.458 R	2.4 mm Al	347 per million	224 per million
PA-Nar	0.517 R	2.5 mm Al	163 per million	119 per million

All values are for the Common Exam

Age 25, Thor. Sp. Special　　　Cancer Rate.................. *(Lowering Factor)*
　　　　Males:　　602 per million = 1 in 1,661　　(Age 20 × 0.994)
　　　　Females: 444 per million = 1 in 2,252　　(Age 20 × 0.988)

Age 30, Thor. Sp. Special   Cancer Rate................ *(Lowering Factor)*
       Males: 518 per million = 1 in 1,930   (Age 20 × 0.854)
       Females: 392 per million = 1 in 2,551   (Age 20 × 0.873)
Age 35, Thor. Sp. Special   Cancer Rate................ *(Lowering Factor)*
       Males: 370 per million = 1 in 2,703   (Age 20 × 0.611)
       Females: 280 per million = 1 in 3,571   (Age 20 × 0.623)
Age 40, Thor. Sp. Special   Cancer Rate................ *(Lowering Factor)*
       Males: 225 per million = 1 in 4,444   (Age 20 × 0.372)
       Females: 176 per million = 1 in 5,682   (Age 20 × 0.391)
Age 45, Thor. Sp. Special   Cancer Rate................ *(Lowering Factor)*
       Males: 98 per million = 1 in 10,200   (Age 20 × 0.162)
       Females: 79 per million = 1 in 12,660   (Age 20 × 0.176)
Age 50, Thor. Sp. Special   Cancer Rate................ *(Lowering Factor)*
       Males: 9 per million = 1 in 111,000   (Age 20 × 0.015)
       Females: 8 per million = 1 in 125,000   (Age 20 × 0.017)
Age 55, Thor. Sp. Special   Cancer Rate................ *(Lowering Factor)*
       Males: 6 per million = 1 in 167,000   (Age 20 × 0.010)
       Females: 5 per million = 1 in 200,000   (Age 20 × 0.012)

UPPER GASTRO-INTESTINAL EXAM
("Upper G.I. Series")

Contrast Medium: Yes. Barium sulfate suspension, given by mouth.

Fluoroscopy and Spot Films: Yes. The cancer risks from FLU and spot films are additional to the risks presented here from the films. Please see Chapter 6 for FLU calculations.

Length of Field: For adults, the field length is 43.2 cm, and extends from 4 cm below the sternal notch to 6 cm below the bi-iliac crests. The field center is 6.6 cm below the xiphoid process. In the AP and PA shots, the center is 4.3 cm to the left of body midline; in the LAT shot, it is 3.0 cm forward of body midline (toward the front of the patient). Fields for the pediatric exams are adjusted to encompass the same organ regions.

Organs Generating Most Cancer Risk:
    Males: Kidneys, large intestine, stomach, bronchi, pancreas, liver.
    Females: Large intestine, kidneys, pancreas, breasts, stomach, bronchi.

Special Comments:
- Dose estimates to specific organs took account of the shielding provided by the barium sulfate itself.
- In this exam, and several others, a particularly steep decrease in risk from the LAT shot occurs as age advances from 10 to 20 years old. See the last "Special Comment," Barium Enema Exam.

AGE NEW   Testes, dose CE: 2 mrads
UPPER GASTRO-INTESTINAL SERIES   Ovaries, dose CE: 36 mrads

Common Exam (CE): One AP, one PA, one
                      LAT, and two OBL-PA (Total: 5 shots)
Rate of future *leukemia* from Common Exam:
    Males: 43 per million = 1 in 23,260
    Females: 27 per million = 1 in 37,040
Rate of future *cancer* from Common Exam:
    Males: 3,773 per million = 1 in 265
    Females: 3,887 per million = 1 in 257

Per Shot	*Ent Dose*	*Beam HVL*	*Male Cancer Risk*	*Female Cancer Risk*
AP	0.126 R	2.8 mm Al	537 per million	591 per million
PA	0.107 R	2.9 mm Al	546 per million	559 per million
LAT	0.225 R	3.0 mm Al	1,092 per million	1,137 per million
OBL-PA	0.152 R	2.9 mm Al	799 per million	800 per million

AGE 1   Testes, dose CE: 2 mrads
UPPER GASTRO-INTESTINAL SERIES   Ovaries, dose CE: 42 mrads

Common Exam (CE): One AP, one PA, one
                      LAT, and two OBL-PA (Total: 5 shots)
Rate of future *leukemia* from Common Exam:
    Males: 41 per million = 1 in 24,390
    Females: 26 per million = 1 in 38,460
Rate of future *cancer* from Common Exam:
    Males: 3,829 per million = 1 in 261
    Females: 4,080 per million = 1 in 236

Per Shot	*Ent Dose*	*Beam HVL*	*Male Cancer Risk*	*Female Cancer Risk*
AP	0.155 R	2.8 mm Al	599 per million	680 per million
PA	0.133 R	2.9 mm Al	577 per million	604 per million
LAT	0.278 R	3.0 mm Al	1,085 per million	1,154 per million
OBL-PA	0.187 R	2.9 mm Al	784 per million	821 per million

AGE 5   Testes, dose CE: 2 mrads
UPPER GASTRO-INTESTINAL SERIES   Ovaries, dose CE: 53 mrads

Common Exam (CE): One PA, one PA, one
                      LAT, and two OBL-PA (Total: 5 shots)
Rate of future *leukemia* from Common Exam:
    Males: 57 per million = 1 in 17,540
    Females: 36 per million = 1 in 27,780

Rate of future *cancer* from Common Exam:
      Males: 5,051 per million = 1 in 198
      Females: 5,066 per million = 1 in 197

Per Shot	Ent Dose	Beam HVL	Male Cancer Risk	Female Cancer Risk
AP	0.262 R	2.8 mm Al	865 per million	924 per million
PA	0.224 R	2.9 mm Al	804 per million	772 per million
LAT	0.469 R	3.0 mm Al	1,324 per million	1,323 per million
OBL-PA	0.316 R	2.9 mm Al	1,029 per million	1,023 per million

AGE 10
                                    Testes, dose CE: 2 mrads
UPPER GASTRO-INTESTINAL SERIES   Ovaries, dose CE: 63 mrads

Common Exam (CE): One AP, one PA, one
                  LAT, and two OBL-PA (Total: 5 shots)
Rate of future *leukemia* from Common Exam:
      Males: 64 per million = 1 in 15,630
      Females: 40 per million = 1 in 25,000
Rate of future *cancer* from Common Exam:
      Males: 5,448 per million = 1 in 184
      Females: 4,981 per million = 1 in 201

Per Shot	Ent Dose	Beam HVL	Male Cancer Risk	Female Cancer Risk
AP	0.395 R	2.8 mm Al	996 per million	1,015 per million
PA	0.338 R	2.9 mm Al	894 per million	794 per million
LAT	0.709 R	3.0 mm Al	1,356 per million	1,218 per million
OBL-PA	0.478 R	2.9 mm Al	1,101 per million	977 per million

AGE 15
                                    Testes, dose CE: 2 mrads
UPPER GASTRO-INTESTINAL SERIES   Ovaries, dose CE: 63 mrads

Common Exam (CE): One AP, one PA, one
                  LAT, and two OBL-PA (Total: 5 shots)
Rate of future *leukemia* from Common Exam:
      Males: 54 per million = 1 in 18,520
      Females: 34 per million = 1 in 29,410
Rate of future *cancer* from Common Exam:
      Males: 2,515 per million = 1 in 398
      Females: 2,240 per million = 1 in 446

Age 15, Upper Gastro-Intestinal Series *(continued)*

Per Shot	Ent Dose	Beam HVL	Male Cancer Risk	Female Cancer Risk
AP	0.529 R	2.8 mm Al	550 per million	546 per million
PA	0.452 R	2.9 mm Al	459 per million	384 per million
LAT	0.948 R	3.0 mm Al	504 per million	454 per million
OBL-PA	0.638 R	2.9 mm Al	501 per million	428 per million

AGE 20
UPPER GASTRO-INTESTINAL SERIES

Testes, dose CE: 1 mrad
Ovaries, dose CE: 61 mrads
Embryo, dose CE: 43 mrads

Common Exam (CE): One AP, one PA, one
LAT, and two OBL-PA (Total: 5 shots)
Rate of future *leukemia* from Common Exam:
　　　　Males:　　38 per million = 1 in 26,320
　　　　Females:　24 per million = 1 in 41,700
Rate of future *cancer* from Common Exam:　　　　(Smokers)
　　　　Males:　1,850 per million = 1 in 540　　(CE × 2.11)
　　　　Females: 1,585 per million = 1 in 631　　(CE × 1.65)

Per Shot	Ent Dose	Beam HVL	Male Cancer Risk	Female Cancer Risk
AP	0.641 R	2.8 mm Al	490 per million	470 per million
PA	0.548 R	2.9 mm Al	394 per million	308 per million
LAT	1.149 R	3.0 mm Al	242 per million	223 per million
OBL-PA	0.774 R	2.9 mm Al	362 per million	292 per million

All values are for the Common Exam

Age 25, Upper G.I. Series　　Cancer Rate............... *(Lowering Factor)*
　　　　Males:　1,839 per million = 1 in 544　　(Age 20 × 0.994)
　　　　Females: 1,566 per million = 1 in 638　　(Age 20 × 0.988)
Age 30, Upper G.I. Series　　Cancer Rate............... *(Lowering Factor)*
　　　　Males:　1,580 per million = 1 in 633　　(Age 20 × 0.854)
　　　　Females: 1,384 per million = 1 in 722　　(Age 20 × 0.873)
Age 35, Upper G.I. Series　　Cancer Rate............... *(Lowering Factor)*
　　　　Males:　1,130 per million = 1 in 885　　(Age 20 × 0.611)
　　　　Females:　987 per million = 1 in 1,013　　(Age 20 × 0.623)
Age 40, Upper G.I. Series　　Cancer Rate............... *(Lowering Factor)*
　　　　Males:　688 per million = 1 in 1,453　　(Age 20 × 0.372)
　　　　Females:　620 per million = 1 in 1,613　　(Age 20 × 0.391)
Age 45, Upper G.I. Series　　Cancer Rate............... *(Lowering Factor)*
　　　　Males:　300 per million = 1 in 3,333　　(Age 20 × 0.162)
　　　　Females:　279 per million = 1 in 3,584　　(Age 20 × 0.176)

Age 50, Upper G.I. Series   Cancer Rate............... *(Lowering Factor)*
            Males: 28 per million = 1 in 35,700   (Age 20 × 0.015)
            Females: 27 per million = 1 in 37,000   (Age 20 × 0.017)
Age 55, Upper G.I. Series   Cancer Rate............... *(Lowering Factor)*
            Males: 18 per million = 1 in 55,600   (Age 20 × 0.010)
            Females: 19 per million = 1 in 52,600   (Age 20 × 0.012)

WRIST INCLUDING HAND

Contrast Medium: No.

Fluoroscopy and Spot Films: No.

Length of Field: Body part.

Organs Generating Most Cancer Risk:
    Males: Lymphatic tissue (generating lymphomas, multiple myelomas, and
        Hodgkin's Disease), skin, connective tissue, bone.
    Females: Same.

Special Comments:
- Cancer and leukemia risks are for examination of *one* wrist plus hand.
- Risk is calculated for "any" shot, regardless of beam direction. Of course, when entrance dose or beam quality is altered for different beam directions, the risk can be adjusted by the usual methods demonstrated in Chapter 4, Sections 11 and 12.
- Cancer risk is based on the estimate that 1.37% of the body bone is in each wrist plus hand.

AGE NEW   Testes, dose CE: < 1 mrad
WRIST INCLUDING HAND   Ovaries, dose CE: < 1 mrad

Common Exam (CE): One AP, one LAT, and
                    one OBL (Total: 3 shots)
Rate of future *leukemia* from Common Exam:
            Males: 0.3 per million = 1 in 3.3 million
            Females: 0.2 per million = 1 in 5 million
Rate of future *cancer* from Common Exam:
            Males: 4.0 per million = 1 in 250,000
            Females: 4.0 per million = 1 in 250,000

Per Shot	*Ent Dose*	*Beam HVL*	*Male Cancer Risk*	*Female Cancer Risk*
Any	0.050 R	2.2 mm Al	1.3 per million	1.3 per million

AGE 1
WRIST INCLUDING HAND

Testes, dose CE: < 1 mrad
Ovaries, dose CE: < 1 mrad

Common Exam (CE): One AP, one LAT, and
                  one OBL (Total: 3 shots)
Rate of future *leukemia* from Common Exam:
        Males: 0.3 per million = 1 in 3.3 million
        Females: 0.2 per million = 1 in 5 million
Rate of future *cancer* from Common Exam:
        Males: 4.5 per million = 1 in 222,000
        Females: 4.5 per million = 1 in 222,000

Per Shot	*Ent Dose*	*Beam HVL*	*Male Cancer Risk*	*Female Cancer Risk*
Any	0.062 R	2.2 mm Al	1.5 per million	1.5 per million

AGE 5
WRIST INCLUDING HAND

Testes, dose CE: < 1 mrad
Ovaries, dose CE: < 1 mrad

Common Exam (CE): One AP, one LAT, and
                  one OBL (Total: 3 shots)
Rate of future *leukemia* from Common Exam:
        Males: 0.4 per million = 1 in 2.5 million
        Females: 0.25 per million = 1 in 4 million
Rate of future *cancer* from Common Exam:
        Males: 6.0 per million = 1 in 167,000
        Females: 5.8 per million = 1 in 172,400

Per Shot	*Ent Dose*	*Beam HVL*	*Male Cancer Risk*	*Female Cancer Risk*
Any	0.105 R	2.2 mm Al	2.0 per million	1.92 per million

AGE 10
WRIST INCLUDING HAND

Testes, dose CE: < 1 mrad
Ovaries, dose CE: < 1 mrad

Common Exam (CE): One AP, one LAT, and
                  one OBL (Total: 3 shots)
Rate of future *leukemia* from Common Exam:
        Males: 0.4 per million = 1 in 2.5 million
        Females: 0.25 per million = 1 in 4 million
Rate of future *cancer* from Common Exam:
        Males: 7.0 per million = 1 in 143,000
        Females: 6.4 per million = 1 in 156,000

Per Shot	Ent Dose	Beam HVL	Male Cancer Risk	Female Cancer Risk
Any	0.158 R	2.2 mm Al	2.33 per million	2.13 per million

AGE 15
WRIST INCLUDING HAND

Testes, dose CE: < 1 mrad
Ovaries, dose CE: < 1 mrad

Common Exam (CE): One AP, one LAT, and
one OBL (Total: 3 shots)
Rate of future *leukemia* from Common Exam:
Males: 0.2 per million = 1 in 5 million
Females: 0.1 per million = 1 in 10 million
Rate of future *cancer* from Common Exam:
Males: 3.6 per million = 1 in 278,000
Females: 3.2 per million = 1 in 313,000

Per Shot	Ent Dose	Beam HVL	Male Cancer Risk	Female Cancer Risk
Any	0.212 R	2.2 mm Al	1.2 per million	1.05 per million

AGE 20
WRIST INCLUDING HAND

Testes, dose CE: <1 mrad
Ovaries, dose CE: <1 mrad
Embryo, dose CE: <1 mrad

Common Exam (CE): One AP, one LAT, and
one OBL (Total: 3 shots)
Rate of future *leukemia* from Common Exam:
Males: < 0.1 per million = < 1 in 10 million
Females: < 0.1 per million = < 1 in 10 million
Rate of future *cancer* from Common Exam: **(Smokers)**
Males: 3.2 per million = 1 in 312,000   (CE × 1.00)
Females: 2.8 per million = 1 in 357,000   (CE × 1.00)

Per Shot	Ent Dose	Beam HVL	Male Cancer Risk	Female Cancer Risk
Any	0.257 R	2.2 mm Al	1.06 per million	0.92 per million

All values are for the Common Exam

Age 30, Wrist incl. Hand   Cancer Rate............... *(Lowering Factor)*
Males: 2.7 per million = 1 in 370,000   (Age 20 × 0.854)
Females: 2.4 per million = 1 in 417,000   (Age 20 × 0.873)
Age 40, Wrist incl. Hand   Cancer Rate............... *(Lowering Factor)*
Males: 1.2 per million = 1 in 833,000   (Age 20 × 0.372)
Females: 1.1 per million = 1 in 909,000   (Age 20 × 0.391)
Age 50, Wrist incl. Hand   Cancer Rate............... *(Lowering Factor)*
Males: 0.05 per million = 1 in 20 million   (Age 20 × 0.015)
Females: 0.05 per million = 1 in 20 million   (Age 20 × 0.017)

CHAPTER 6

Fluoroscopy as an Additional Procedure

Those common diagnostic examinations which sometimes or always use fluoroscopy, in addition to their radiographic films, are so noted in the tables of Chapters 5 and 7. Because the ionizing radiation delivered by fluoroscopy is identical in producing health effects, *rad for rad,* with the radiation delivered by the making of films, risk assessment for such examinations must take both fluoroscopy and films into account.

However, the prevailing assumption has been that the risk from fluoroscopic procedures is difficult or nearly impossible to evaluate. We no longer agree. The purpose of this chapter is to demonstrate a method which will provide an extremely useful "first cut" at evaluating the cancer risk contributed by the fluoroscopic part of diagnostic X-ray examinations.

First, an easily made error needs prevention. A report might say, for example, that the entrance dose from an entire fluoroscopic procedure is 5 roentgens (free-in-air), and that the combination of all *films* taken before, during, or after the fluoroscopy delivers an entrance dose of 2.7 roentgens (FIA). The *wrong* conclusion would be that the total entrance dose from the combined radiographic plus fluoroscopic procedure is 7.7 roentgens (FIA). Such a combination of doses would be utterly misleading. It is never appropriate to combine entrance doses for exposures covering different regions of the body, or different amounts of the same region.

Suppose the radiographic entrance dose of 2.7 roentgens applies to a field 14 by 17 inches, or 238 square inches, while the fluoroscopic entrance dose of 5 roentgens applies to a field size (beam area) of 4 by 4 inches, or 16 square inches. If the same region of the body is at issue and the area examined fluoroscopically is much smaller, the cancer risk *per roentgen of entrance dose* will also be much smaller.

The appropriate procedure is always to calculate the separate cancer risks from the radiography and from the fluoroscopy, and then to combine the *cancer risks,* not the entrance doses.

Here we shall demonstrate a reasonable method for evaluating the cancer risk associated with fluoroscopy; the method also makes it possible to evaluate the risk from the many small "spot films" often taken during such procedures.

Section 1: What the Fluoroscopy Tables Mean

By far the most common use of fluoroscopy is for examination of the abdominal and pelvic organs: segments of the gastro-intestinal tract, the urinary system, and the fallopian tubes (oviducts). Also common is its use for special examinations of the thorax (chest) and for guidance of catheters in angiographies. The overwhelming share of all fluoroscopic exams can be evaluated by this chapter's Fluoroscopy Tables (FLU Tables), which cover all segments of the thorax, abdomen, and pelvis.

We use the term "abdomen" from here on to refer to the *entire* trunk below the diaphragm: abdomen plus pelvis. This use follows from our treatment of the abdomen plus pelvis as a single region, and from space limitations in the FLU Tables.

The previous chapters have emphasized that the cancer risk, from a given entrance dose, is definitely not uniform throughout the body. Consequently, in order to evaluate the risk from fluoroscopies, we need to ascertain how the cancer risk varies for each segment of the thorax and abdomen.

We have divided the thorax into four quadrants of equal area—left upper, right upper, left lower, and right lower—and we have done the same for the abdomen. Then the risk from irradiating an *entire* quadrant with 1 roentgen of entrance dose has been evaluated by the same method used to evaluate the risk from irradiating any other field. Details of the method are provided in Chapter 19.

We have made separate risk calculations for the four quadrants of the thorax, the four quadrants of the abdomen, plus a special "central pelvic" area. It turns out that all four quadrants of the thorax confer such similar cancer risk per roentgen of entrance dose that they should be considered the same, for all practical purposes. But within the *abdomen,* the risk is quite different from one quadrant to another.

In fact, for the abdomen, additional data are presented in the FLU Tables for what we call the central pelvic region, an area the same size as the standard four abdominal quadrants, but located centrally in the lower abdomen with half in each lower quadrant. Because the cancer risk per roentgen of entrance dose is much higher from this special region than from the standard four abdominal quadrants, it deserves the special evaluation.

We have calculated, for the usual age intervals and for non-smokers of both sexes, what the cancer risk is from exposing each full quadrant of the thorax and abdomen to one roentgen of entrance dose free-in-air. We have made the calculations for both the anterior-posterior and the posterior-anterior beam directions. These values are presented in the Fluoroscopy Tables, located at the end of this chapter.

These tables provide a basic reference source enabling users to evaluate risks from all fluoroscopic exams of the torso done with AP and PA beams.

With the FLU Tables at hand, users can go on to estimate cancer risk from various fluoroscopic X-ray procedures, whatever their dose rate, duration, field size (beam size), or beam quality. Obviously, beam size and total time of exposure are two crucial variables in raising or lowering the cancer risk from fluoroscopy, so in Section 2, we shall show how they are handled with the FLU Tables.

Section 2: How to Use the Fluoroscopy Tables

Checklist of Considerations

When estimating the cancer risk from various fluoroscopic exams, it is useful to have a standard checklist of steps. Following them in sequence assures that no necessary consideration has been left out of the calculation. For fluoroscopy, a suggested checklist follows.

Step 1, Beam Direction and Risk per Roentgen: The beam direction determines which part of the FLU Table to use:

(a) The upper half for anterior-posterior (AP), or

(b) The lower half for posterior-anterior (PA).

The cancer risk per entrance roentgen found there is *the basic number* which will be successively and simply modified, to fit particular conditions, in steps which follow.

Step 2, Total Entrance Dose in Roentgens (FIA): Two considerations determine the total entrance dose:

(a) Roentgens of entrance dose per minute of operation (dose rate), and

(b) Total time of operation in a quadrant.

The total entrance dose is (a) times (b). It will be either higher or lower, by some factor, than the reference total entrance dose of 1.0 roentgen FIA used in all the FLU Tables. In Step 2, the cancer risk from Step 1 is adjusted for any total entrance dose other than 1.0 roentgen FIA by exactly the same method demonstrated in Chapter 4, Section 11, and in the examples which follow.

Step 3, Beam Quality: All the FLU Tables apply to a reference beam quality of 2.3 mm Al HVL. In Step 3, the cancer risk from Step 2 is adjusted for beam qualities other than 2.3 mm Al by exactly the same method demonstrated in Chapter 4, Section 12, and in the examples which follow.

Step 4, Size of the Whole Relevant Quadrant: This will differ for patients in different age-sex categories, of course. Areas of quadrants for a male and female "reference" patient are provided at the top of each FLU Table.

Step 5, Size of Area Actually Examined (Beam Size): This is determined by the fluoroscopist, and can be provided only by him or her. Past experience will most often make it possible for the fluoroscopist to *estimate,* in advance of a contemplated exam, the likely beam size (as well as all the other items in this checklist).

Step 6, Lowering Factor for the Area Exposed: In virtually every case, the area fluoroscoped will be smaller than the area of a full quadrant. The appropriate lowering factor must be obtained to adjust the cancer risk from Step 3, which applies to irradiation of an *entire* quadrant. The lowering factor is simply the value provided in Step 5 divided by the value obtained (from the FLU Table) in Step 4. The lowering factor = (area fluoroscoped) / (area of whole quadrant).

During fluoroscopy, of course, the beam is moved around by the fluoroscopist; many different parts of a quadrant may be exposed at different moments. Nevertheless, very good risk estimates can be made, thanks to a reasonable approximation: the cancer risk *within* a single quadrant is uniform.

Ages Beyond 20 Years

Steps 1 through 6 should be performed *directly* on the applicable cancer risk found for ages 30, 40, or 50 in the FLU Tables (Step 1). No reference to the age-20 entry is necessary for older ages.

More Than One Quadrant Exposed

When a fluoroscopic beam is larger than one whole quadrant or when a beam (regardless of its size) exposes more than one quadrant, the risks from each exposed quadrant are simply calculated *separately* and then added together, as demonstrated in Example 2 below.

Automatic Devices

Fluoroscopic equipment today frequently has automatic features, such as a beam intensity which varies with either the size of beam or the thickness of the patient. Ardran and Crooks (in Ansell, 1976), both of the British Atomic Energy Research Establishment at Harwell, recommend the use of R-cm² dose-meters, which measure exposures in roentgens times square centimeters (R × cm²). They comment (p. 420): "Without such equipment, radiologists may be unaware of the magnitude of the dose they are delivering."

If such meters are used, how can the checklist be used to evaluate cancer risk? The fluoroscopist will only have to estimate the average beam area (in square centimeters) which he or she used in a quadrant. Then the entrance dose in roentgens can be retrieved from the R × cm² measurement provided by the meter, by simple division: (R × cm²) / (cm²) = R. Thus, the data for all six checklist items will be at hand.

A Useful Habit

If one reviews each of the six checklist items in evaluating risk from a fluoroscopic examination, all relevant considerations will have been taken into account. We shall illustrate with some examples.

Example 1: A Single Quadrant Involved

A man 20 years old needs fluoroscopy in the left lower quadrant of the thorax. The machine to be used will give an entrance dose of 3.5 roentgens FIA per minute, and the expected total time of fluoroscopic examination is 2 minutes. The beam will be directed from anterior to posterior, and the beam area is expected to be about 75 cm². Beam quality will be 2.3 mm Al HVL. What is the estimated cancer risk from this exam?

ANSWER: Step 6 will provide the answer.

Step 1, Beam Direction and Risk per Roentgen: Because this is an AP procedure, we use the upper half of the FLU Table for 20-year-old males, and we extract the cancer risk: 54 per million for *any* of the thoracic quadrants, from 1 roentgen of entrance dose.

Step 2, Total Entrance Dose: (3.5 roentgens per minute) × (2 minutes) = 7.0 roentgens FIA. Therefore, the cancer risk in Step 1 has to be adjusted by a raising factor of (7.0 R / 1.0 R) or 7.0. So 7.0 × 54 cancers per million = 378 cancers per million.

Step 3, Beam Quality: Because Example 1 is illustrating the same beam quality used as the "reference" beam quality in the FLU Tables, no adjustment is needed. Users have no need to consult Special Table D (Chapter 21) unless they have two *different* beam qualities to look up in it. So in this example, we carry down *378 per million* from Step 2.

Step 4, Size of Whole Relevant Quadrant: The FLU Table provides this at the top as 228.8 cm².

Step 5, Size of Area Actually Examined (Beam Size): This was provided (by the fluoroscopist) as an estimated 75 cm².

Step 6, Lowering Factor for the Area Exposed: This is the fluoroscoped area divided by the area of the full quadrant: 75 cm² / 228.8 cm² = 0.328. So 0.328 is multiplied by the adjusted cancer risk already obtained in Step 3: 0.328 × 378 cancers per million = 124 cancers per million (or 1 chance in 8,065 of getting cancer from the exam).

Smoking Factor: If this patient were a smoker, we would find the male smoking factor for thoracic FLU exams in Section 4, immediately preceding the first FLU Table. It is 6.84 for the anterior-posterior exam, so we would raise the cancer risk per million (not the "1 chance in 8,065" expression) accordingly: 6.84 × 124 per million = 848 per million, or 1 chance in 1,179.

Example 2: Two Quadrants Involved

Abdominal fluoroscopy is being done for a 15-year-old male. The entrance exposure-rate is 3.0 roentgens FIA per minute at a beam quality of 2.4 mm Al HVL. The fluoroscopist uses a beam of 90 cm² during the entire examination, and needs it for 3.0 minutes in the abdomen's upper left quadrant and for 2.2 minutes in the right upper quadrant. What is the cancer risk from the entire fluoroscopic procedure if the AP beam direction is used?

ANSWER: Because the exam irradiates two different quadrants of the abdomen, we must handle each part separately. Then, as the last step, we shall add the cancer risks from the two parts.

Left Upper Quadrant

Step 1, Beam Direction and Risk per Roentgen: Because this is an AP procedure, again we use the upper half of the FLU Table. From the table for 15-year-old males, we extract the cancer risk: 426 per million for the *abdomen's* left upper quadrant, from 1 roentgen of entrance dose.

Step 2, Total Entrance Dose: (3.0 roentgens per minute) × (3.0 minutes) = 9.0 roentgens FIA for this quadrant. Therefore, the cancer risk in Step 1 has to be adjusted by a raising factor of (9.0 / 1.0) or 9.0. So 9.0 × 426 per million yields an adjusted cancer risk of 3,834 per million.

Step 3, Beam Quality: Because 2.4 mm Al HVL is a higher beam quality than the 2.3 used in the FLU Tables, we know the cancer risk must go *up*. We need a raising factor (a value greater than 1.0) for the risk in Step 2. We create the factor from Special Table D by the method demonstrated in Chapter 4, Section 12. We look up *two* entries, and divide the bigger one by the smaller one. The entry for the beam quality used—2.4 mm Al HVL—is 1.05. The entry for the FLU Table's reference beam quality—2.3 mm—is 1.00. We divide 1.05 by 1.00, which yields 1.05 of course, and we multiply it times the cancer risk from Step 2. So 1.05 × 3,834 per million = 4,026 per million.

Step 4, Size of the Whole Relevant Quadrant: The FLU Table provides this as 278 cm².

Step 5, Size of the Area Actually Examined (Beam Size): This was provided (by the fluoroscopist) as 90 cm².

Step 6, Lowering Factor for the Area Exposed: This is the area fluoroscoped divided by the area of the full quadrant: 90 cm² / 278 cm² = 0.324. So 0.324 is multiplied by the adjusted cancer risk obtained in Step 3: 0.324 × 4,026 per million = 1,304 per million as the cancer risk from *this* quadrant.

Right Upper Quadrant

Step 1, Beam Direction and Risk per Roentgen: Again using the AP section of the FLU Table for 15-year-old males, we extract the cancer risk for *this* quadrant: 294 per million.

Step 2, Total Entrance Dose: (3.0 roentgens per minute) × (2.2 minutes) = 6.6 roentgens FIA for this quadrant. The cancer risk from 1 roentgen is adjusted: 6.6 × 294 per million = 1,940 per million.

Step 3, Beam Quality: The raising factor is 1.05, as it was for the other quadrant, since the beam quality is the same. It is applied to the risk just obtained in Step 2: 1.05 × 1,940 per million = 2,037 per million.

Step 4, Size of the Whole Relevant Quadrant: Each quadrant of the abdomen is the same size. For the reference patient in this case, the FLU Table provides 278 cm² again.

Step 5, Size of the Area Actually Examined (Beam Size): This was provided (by the fluoroscopist) as 90 cm².

Step 6, Lowering Factor for the Area Exposed: In this example, it is the same as for the other quadrant: 90 cm² / 278 cm² = 0.324. It is applied to the adjusted cancer risk obtained in Step 3: 0.324 × 2,037 per million = 660 per million as the cancer risk from *this* quadrant.

Final Step: Combination

To obtain the lifetime risk of later cancer resulting from this fluoroscopic procedure, the risks from both quadrants have to be combined. *They differ by nearly 2-fold.* The risk from the left upper quadrant + the risk from the right upper quadrant = 1,304 + 660 = 1,964 (per million) = 1 chance in 509.

If films are taken before, during, or after this fluoroscopic procedure, the risk per million which they confer would be added to 1,964. Therefore, we do not round off the number (see Chapter 5, Section 2).

Section 3: Some Special Considerations for Fluoroscopy

Opportunities to Reduce Dose

When speaking of dose reduction, radiologists mean reducing the total ionizing energy transferred to human tissue. Therefore, dose reduction follows reduction in dose rate, beam size (field size), or duration of the patient's exposure to the beam. But there is *no* merit to any of these reductions if one of them nullifies the ability of the fluoroscopist to obtain the needed diagnostic information. Only he or she can make such a judgment during an exam. Big reductions in dose are really achieved *prior* to an exam, as a result of equipment maintenance (Chapter 16), training, and forethought.

With respect to fluoroscopic doses, Ardran and Crooks (p. 420 in Ansell, 1976) of the Atomic Energy Research Establishment at Harwell, offer many important observations, including the five which follow:

1. "The tendency to use unnecessarily large beams during fluoroscopy, particularly the use of rectangular fields, completely over-covering a circular image intensifier, is prevalent."

2. "In the past it was essential to use small beams during fluoroscopy, in order that the scatter might be reduced and the contrast enhanced, so as to have an acceptable image. With modern television systems the contrast can be enhanced electronically and the necessity for small beams from this point of view is now not so great. This means that frequently higher radiation exposures in terms of $R \times cm^2$ are given for the fluoroscopy with modern equipment than used to be given without image intensification."

3. "The use of $R\text{-}cm^2$ dose meters is recommended. . . . to train radiologists, since this gives them an immediate indication of the beneficial effects of speed and of keeping the beam size small."

4. "Likewise, it must be remembered that fluoroscopic exposures

(measured in terms of R × cm²) with a small beam can often result in less radiation than that caused by one large radiograph."

5. "Measurements have shown that for examinations of the gastro-intestinal tract, it depends on the radiologist and the nature of the case as to whether the largest proportion of the dose is given by fluoroscopy or by the associated radiography (27)." (The sequence is altered, but all quotes are from page 420.)

Biggest Benefits: Care in the Central Pelvic Region

We wish to call attention to the especially high hazard from fluoroscopy (or any other X-ray procedure) involving the central pelvic region. If we examine the FLU Table for, say, the 20-year-old females, we find the following cancer risks from the AP beam direction, per roentgen of en-trance dose at a beam quality of 2.3 mm Al HVL:

Abdomen for Whole Quadrant	Cancer Risk per Roentgen FIA
Left Upper	254 per million
Right Upper	206 per million
Left Lower	427 per million
Right Lower	394 per million
Central Pelvic	676 per million

Since every 10% reduction in dose translates into a 10% reduction in risk, clearly the central pelvic region pays bigger health bonuses than any other abdominal quadrant in return for reductions in beam intensity, beam size, and beam duration. In fact, the bonuses are more than 3-fold higher from the central pelvic region than from the right upper quadrant.

Avoiding Nonsensical Generalizations

It would be a big mistake to consider "fluoroscopy" simply as an entity with respect to delayed side-effects like cancer. The risks are vastly differ-ent for different circumstances. The following comparison illustrates a huge disparity resulting simply from age and beam direction:

Beam Direction	Age of Patient	Abdominal Quadrant Examined	Cancer Risk from 1 Roentgen Entrance Dose
Anterior-posterior	Female, age 1	Whole right lower quadrant	2,287 per million
Posterior-anterior	Female, age 50	The same	3.1 per million

There is a factor of 2,287 / 3.1 or 738-fold separating these two risk values for examination of the *same* abdominal quadrant. We make this comparison to point out the lack of wisdom in generalized statements about the danger or safety of fluoroscopy, or any other X-ray procedure.

Meaningful numbers can now replace misleading generalizations. Numbers for risk can incorporate the crucial differences of age-sex category, particular quadrants fluoroscoped, dose rate, dose duration, beam size, beam direction, and even beam quality.

Section 4: Rules Followed in the Fluoroscopy Tables

Separate tables are provided for nine ages. The following statements apply to every table.

Two-Part Tables: The upper half of each table applies when the anterior-posterior (AP) beam direction is used; the lower half, when the posterior-anterior (PA) beam direction is used.

The Term "Abdomen": This refers here to the entire region below the thorax—in other words, the abdomen and pelvis as one entity (see Section 1 of this chapter).

Reference Area and Dose: All risk values apply to a total entrance dose, to an entire quadrant, of 1.0 roentgen free-in-air (FIA) at a beam quality of 2.3 mm aluminum half-value layer (HVL).

Risk Values: The risks are expressed, as they are in Chapter 5 and elsewhere, as the rate of later cancer per million such exams. After such risks have been adjusted by the six-step checklist, they can be converted to the "1 chance in 2,000" type of expression by using the "recipe" boxed in Chapter 1.

Smoking Factors: The risks are for non-smokers. For thoracic FLU exams, the raising factor for *male smokers* is approximately 6.84 for the AP exam and 6.89 for the PA exam. For *female smokers,* the raising factor is 1.32 for the AP exam and 4.14 for the PA exam. The reason for the large difference is the prominence of breast-cancer risk in the female's AP exam (Chapter 4, Section 6). These factors would be applied to raise the risk per million appropriately.

Left and Right Sides: Left and right refer to the patient's left and right sides, not the fluoroscopist's.

Section 5: The Fluoroscopy Tables (pp. 188–196)

Area of a *full* thoracic quadrant:
    Males = 29.08 cm²   Females = 26.17 cm²
Area of a *full* abdominal quadrant (also central pelvis):
    Males = 39.38 cm²   Females = 35.44 cm²

Males   THORAX—AP Age New

Left Upper	*Right Upper*
248.93	248.93
per million	per million
Left Lower	*Right Lower*
248.93	248.93
per million	per million

Females   THORAX—AP Age New

Left Upper	*Right Upper*
2278.5	2278.5
per million	per million
Left Lower	*Right Lower*
2278.5	2278.5
per million	per million

Males   ABDOMEN—AP Age New

Left Upper	*Right Upper*
1701.8	1366.4
per million	per million
Left Lower	*Right Lower*
2892.7	2767.4
per million	per million

Central Pelvic
5037.2
per million

Females ABDOMEN—AP Age New

Left Upper	*Right Upper*
1509.9	1477.5
per million	per million
Left Lower	*Right Lower*
2748.3	2583.9
per million	per million

Central Pelvic
4551.0
per million

Males   THORAX—PA Age New

Left Upper	*Right Upper*
321.65	321.65
per million	per million
Left Lower	*Right Lower*
321.65	321.65
per million	per million

Females   THORAX—PA Age New

Left Upper	*Right Upper*
607.88	607.88
per million	per million
Left Lower	*Right Lower*
607.88	607.88
per million	per million

Males   ABDOMEN—PA Age New

Left Upper	*Right Upper*
1284.5	1162.3
per million	per million
Left Lower	*Right Lower*
1742.0	1641.2
per million	per million

Central Pelvic
2812.8
per million

Females ABDOMEN—PA Age New

Left Upper	*Right Upper*
1143.7	1139.4
per million	per million
Left Lower	*Right Lower*
2039.7	1907.4
per million	per million

Central Pelvic
3246.2
per million

AGE 1, FLUOROSCOPY

Area of a *full* thoracic quadrant:

Males = 60.8 cm²   Females = 54.72 cm²

Area of a *full* abdominal quadrant (also central pelvis):

Males = 84.28 cm²   Females = 75.85 cm²

Males   THORAX—AP   Age 1

Left Upper 224.28 per million	*Right Upper* 224.28 per million
Left Lower 224.28 per million	*Right Lower* 224.28 per million

Males   ABDOMEN—AP   Age 1

Left Upper 1538.5 per million	*Right Upper* 1197.5 per million
Left Lower 2610.3 per million	*Right Lower* 2494.5 per million

Central Pelvic

4538.5

per million

Females   THORAX—AP   Age 1

Left Upper 2082.6 per million	*Right Upper* 2082.6 per million
Left Lower 2082.6 per million	*Right Lower* 2082.6 per million

Females   ABDOMEN—AP   Age 1

Left Upper 1345.6 per million	*Right Upper* 1284.2 per million
Left Lower 2437.1 per million	*Right Lower* 2287.1 per million

Central Pelvic

4020.6

per million

Males   THORAX—PA   Age 1

Left Upper 279.05 per million	*Right Upper* 279.05 per million
Left Lower 279.05 per million	*Right Lower* 279.05 per million

Males   ABDOMEN—PA   Age 1

Left Upper 1095.4 per million	*Right Upper* 999.38 per million
Left Lower 1465.2 per million	*Right Lower* 1384.0 per million

Central Pelvic

2385.3

per million

Females   THORAX—PA   Age 1

Left Upper 504.85 per million	*Right Upper* 504.85 per million
Left Lower 504.85 per million	*Right Lower* 504.85 per million

Females   ABDOMEN—PA   Age 1

Left Upper 954.10 per million	*Right Upper* 952.60 per million
Left Lower 1697.5 per million	*Right Lower* 1592.2 per million

Central Pelvic

2727.3

per million

AGE 5, FLUOROSCOPY

Area of a *full* thoracic quadrant:
Males = 100.88 cm²   Females = 90.79 cm²
Area of a *full* abdominal quadrant (also central pelvis):
Males = 139.7 cm²   Females = 125.73 cm²

Males   THORAX—AP   Age 5

Left Upper 191.73 per million	*Right Upper* 191.73 per million
Left Lower 191.73 per million	*Right Lower* 191.73 per million

Females   THORAX—AP   Age 5

Left Upper 1738.4 per million	*Right Upper* 1738.4 per million
Left Lower 1738.4 per million	*Right Lower* 1738.4 per million

Males   ABDOMEN—AP   Age 5

Left Upper 1306.1 per million	*Right Upper* 989.44 per million
Left Lower 2171.9 per million	*Right Lower* 2071.3 per million

Central Pelvic
3758.9
per million

Females   ABDOMEN—AP   Age 5

Left Upper 1100.5 per million	*Right Upper* 1026.8 per million
Left Lower 1947.0 per million	*Right Lower* 1821.1 per million

Central Pelvic
3185.3
per million

Males   THORAX—PA   Age 5

Left Upper 226.83 per million	*Right Upper* 226.83 per million
Left Lower 226.83 per million	*Right Lower* 226.83 per million

Females   THORAX—PA   Age 5

Left Upper 383.73 per million	*Right Upper* 383.73 per million
Left Lower 383.73 per million	*Right Lower* 383.73 per million

Males   ABDOMEN—PA   Age 5

Left Upper 901.42 per million	*Right Upper* 827.86 per million
Left Lower 1168.2 per million	*Right Lower* 1105.3 per million

Central Pelvic
1913.6
per million

Females   ABDOMEN—PA   Age 5

Left Upper 748.72 per million	*Right Upper* 750.76 per million
Left Lower 1309.5 per million	*Right Lower* 1230.8 per million

Central Pelvic
2119.2
per million

AGE 10, FLUOROSCOPY

Area of a *full* thoracic quadrant:
Males = 135.13 cm²   Females = 121.61 cm²
Area of a *full* abdominal quadrant (also central pelvis):
Males = 211.95 cm²   Females = 190.76 cm²

Males THORAX—AP Age 10		Females THORAX—AP Age 10	
Left Upper 139.63 per million	*Right Upper* 139.63 per million	*Left Upper* 1285.9 per million	*Right Upper* 1285.9 per million
Left Lower 139.63 per million	*Right Lower* 139.63 per million	*Left Lower* 1285.9 per million	*Right Lowe* 1285.9 per million

Males ABDOMEN—AP Age 10		Females ABDOMEN—AP Age 10	
Left Upper 994.86 per million	*Right Upper* 740.85 per million	*Left Upper* 796.54 per million	*Right Upper* 735.52 per million
Left Lower 1691.7 per million	*Right Lower* 1612.9 per million	*Left Lower* 1439.9 per million	*Right Lower* 1346.0 per million
Central Pelvic 2936.6 per million		*Central Pelvic* 2361.4 per million	

Males THORAX—PA Age 10		Females THORAX—PA Age 10	
Left Upper 153.73 per million	*Right Upper* 153.73 per million	*Left Upper* 252.58 per million	*Right Upper* 252.58 per million
Left Lower 153.73 per million	*Right Lower* 153.73 per million	*Left Lower* 252.58 per million	*Right Lower* 252.58 per million

Males ABDOMEN—PA Age 10		Females ABDOMEN—PA Age 10	
Left Upper 654.97 per million	*Right Upper* 614.61 per million	*Left Upper* 512.21 per million	*Right Upper* 525.52 per million
Left Lower 846.59 per million	*Right Lower* 801.15 per million	*Left Lower* 905.58 per million	*Right Lower* 851.41 per million
Central Pelvic 1401.0 per million		*Central Pelvic* 1479.2 per million	

Area of a *full* thoracic quadrant:
Males = 185.43 cm²   Females = 166.88 cm²
Area of a *full* abdominal quadrant (also central pelvis):
Males = 277.98 cm²   Females = 250.18 cm²

Males   THORAX—AP   Age 15

Left Upper 64.85 per million	*Right Upper* 64.85 per million
Left Lower 64.85 per million	*Right Lower* 64.85 per million

Females   THORAX—AP   Age 15

Left Upper 554.75 per million	*Right Upper* 554.75 per million
Left Lower 554.75 per million	*Right Lower* 554.75 per million

Males   ABDOMEN—AP   Age 15

Left Upper 425.71 per million	*Right Upper* 294.29 per million
Left Lower 712.4 per million	*Right Lower* 676.9 per million

Central Pelvic
1226.1
per million

Females   ABDOMEN—AP   Age 15

Left Upper 328.99 per million	*Right Upper* 285.08 per million
Left Lower 572.53 per million	*Right Lower* 531.61 per million

Central Pelvic
921.52
per million

Males   THORAX—PA   Age 15

Left Upper 63.88 per million	*Right Upper* 63.88 per million
Left Lower 63.88 per million	*Right Lower* 63.88 per million

Females   THORAX—PA   Age 15

Left Upper 86.95 per million	*Right Upper* 86.95 per million
Left Lower 86.95 per million	*Right Lower* 86.95 per million

Males   ABDOMEN—PA   Age 15

Left Upper 249.29 per million	*Right Upper* 241.85 per million
Left Lower 297.0 per million	*Right Lower* 282.86 per million

Central Pelvic
497.7
per million

Females   ABDOMEN—PA   Age 15

Left Upper 184.66 per million	*Right Upper* 193.84 per million
Left Lower 308.55 per million	*Right Lower* 292.25 per million

Central Pelvic
512.4
per million

AGE 20, FLUOROSCOPY

Area of a *full* thoracic quadrant:
      Males = 228.75 cm²   Females = 205.88 cm²

Area of a *full* abdominal quadrant (also central pelvis):
      Males = 344 cm²   Females = 309.6 cm²

Males THORAX—AP Age 20		Females THORAX—AP Age 20	
Left Upper 53.68 per million	*Right Upper* 53.68 per million	*Left Upper* 447.13 per million	*Right Upper* 447.13 per million
Left Lower 53.68 per million	*Right Lower* 53.68 per million	*Left Lower* 447.13 per million	*Right Lower* 447.13 per million

Males ABDOMEN—AP Age 20		Females ABDOMEN—AP Age 20	
Left Upper 335.98 per million	*Right Upper* 215.38 per million	*Left Upper* 253.96 per million	*Right Upper* 206.18 per million
Left Lower 552.32 per million	*Right Lower* 523.22 per million	*Left Lower* 426.81 per million	*Right Lower* 393.86 per million
Central Pelvic 944.26 per million		*Central Pelvic* 675.68 per million	

Males THORAX—PA Age 20		Females THORAX—PA Age 20	
Left Upper 46.88 per million	*Right Upper* 46.88 per million	*Left Upper* 53.35 per million	*Right Upper* 53.35 per million
Left Lower 46.88 per million	*Right Lower* 46.88 per million	*Left Lower* 53.35 per million	*Right Lower* 53.35 per million

Males ABDOMEN—PA Age 20		Females ABDOMEN—PA Age 20	
Left Upper 174.85 per million	*Right Upper* 176.62 per million	*Left Upper* 123.11 per million	*Right Upper* 133.3 per million
Left Lower 187.4 per million	*Right Lower* 180.04 per million	*Left Lower* 193.26 per million	*Right Lower* 184.93 per million
Central Pelvic 321.23 per million		*Central Pelvic* 329.9 per million	

AGE 30, FLUOROSCOPY

Area of a *full* thoracic quadrant:

    Males = 228.75 cm²   Females = 205.88 cm²

Area of a *full* abdominal quadrant (also central pelvis):

    Males = 344 cm²   Females = 309.6 cm²

Males	THORAX—AP	Age 30	Females	THORAX—AP	Age 30
Left Upper 45.88 per million	*Right Upper* 45.88 per million		*Left Upper* 390.41 per million	*Right Upper* 390.41 per million	
Left Lower 45.88 per million	*Right Lower* 45.88 per million		*Left Lower* 390.41 per million	*Right Lower* 390.41 per million	

Males	ABDOMEN—AP	Age 30	Females	ABDOMEN—AP	Age 30
Left Upper 287.20 per million	*Right Upper* 184.11 per million		*Left Upper* 221.75 per million	*Right Upper* 180.03 per million	
Left Lower 472.14 per million	*Right Lower* 447.26 per million		*Left Lower* 372.67 per million	*Right Lower* 343.90 per million	
Central Pelvic 807.18 per million			*Central Pelvic* 589.97 per million		

Males	THORAX—PA	Age 30	Females	THORAX—PA	Age 30
Left Upper 40.07 per million	*Right Upper* 40.07 per million		*Left Upper* 46.58 per million	*Right Upper* 46.58 per million	
Left Lower 40.07 per million	*Right Lower* 40.07 per million		*Left Lower* 46.58 per million	*Right Lower* 46.58 per million	

Males	ABDOMEN—PA	Age 30	Females	ABDOMEN—PA	Age 30
Left Upper 149.47 per million	*Right Upper* 150.98 per million		*Left Upper* 107.49 per million	*Right Upper* 116.39 per million	
Left Lower 160.19 per million	*Right Lower* 153.90 per million		*Left Lower* 168.75 per million	*Right Lower* 161.47 per million	
Central Pelvic 274.61 per million			*Central Pelvic* 288.05 per million		

AGE 40, FLUOROSCOPY

Area of a *full* thoracic quadrant:
      Males = 228.75 cm²   Females = 205.88 cm²
Area of a *full* abdominal quadrant (also central pelvis):
      Males = 344 cm²   Females = 309.6 cm²

Males   THORAX—AP   Age 40

Left Upper 19.98 per million	*Right Upper* 19.98 per million
Left Lower 19.98 per million	*Right Lower* 19.98 per million

Females   THORAX—AP   Age 40

Left Upper 174.68 per million	*Right Upper* 174.68 per million
Left Lower 174.68 per million	*Right Lower* 174.68 per million

Males   ABDOMEN—AP   Age 40

Left Upper 125.08 per million	*Right Upper* 80.18 per million
Left Lower 205.62 per million	*Right Lower* 194.78 per million

Central Pelvic
351.53
per million

Females ABDOMEN—AP   Age 40

Left Upper 99.21 per million	*Right Upper* 80.55 per million
Left Lower 166.74 per million	*Right Lower* 153.87 per million

Central Pelvic
263.96
per million

Males   THORAX—PA   Age 40

Left Upper 17.45 per million	*Right Upper* 17.45 per million
Left Lower 17.45 per million	*Right Lower* 17.45 per million

Females   THORAX—PA   Age 40

Left Upper 20.84 per million	*Right Upper* 20.84 per million
Left Lower 20.84 per million	*Right Lower* 20.84 per million

Males   ABDOMEN—PA   Age 40

Left Upper 65.09 per million	*Right Upper* 65.75 per million
Left Lower 69.77 per million	*Right Lower* 67.03 per million

Central Pelvic
119.59
per million

Females   ABDOMEN—PA   Age 40

Left Upper 48.09 per million	*Right Upper* 52.08 per million
Left Lower 75.50 per million	*Right Lower* 72.25 per million

Central Pelvic
128.88
per million

Area of a *full* thoracic quadrant:
Males = 228.75 cm²   Females = 205.88 cm²

Area of a *full* abdominal quadrant (also central pelvis):
Males = 344 cm²   Females = 309.6 cm²

Males   THORAX—AP   Age 50

Left Upper	*Right Upper*
0.80	0.80
per million	per million
Left Lower	*Right Lower*
0.80	0.80
per million	per million

Females   THORAX—AP   Age 50

Left Upper	*Right Upper*
7.60	7.60
per million	per million
Left Lower	*Right Lower*
7.60	7.60
per million	per million

Males   ABDOMEN—AP   Age 50

Left Upper	*Right Upper*
5.00	3.21
per million	per million
Left Lower	*Right Lower*
8.23	7.79
per million	per million

Central Pelvic
14.07
per million

Females   ABDOMEN—AP   Age 50

Left Upper	*Right Upper*
4.32	3.51
per million	per million
Left Lower	*Right Lower*
7.26	6.70
per million	per million

Central Pelvic
11.49
per million

Males   THORAX—PA   Age 50

Left Upper	*Right Upper*
0.70	0.70
per million	per million
Left Lower	*Right Lower*
0.70	0.70
per million	per million

Females   THORAX—PA   Age 50

Left Upper	*Right Upper*
0.91	0.91
per million	per million
Left Lower	*Right Lower*
0.91	0.91
per million	per million

Males   ABDOMEN—PA   Age 50

Left Upper	*Right Upper*
2.60	2.63
per million	per million
Left Lower	*Right Lower*
2.79	2.68
per million	per million

Central Pelvic
4.79
per million

Females   ABDOMEN—PA   Age 50

Left Upper	*Right Upper*
2.09	2.27
per million	per million
Left Lower	*Right Lower*
3.29	3.14
per million	per million

Central Pelvic
5.61
per million

CHAPTER 7

Common Angiographies

The use of angiography, to study the blood's circulation in a region or in a specific organ, has become an important part of diagnostic radiology. The usual procedure uses both films and fluoroscopy, as well as a contrast agent.

A recent and elegant development called digital subtraction angiography, discussed briefly in Chapter 15, does not use film to receive the images from the X-ray beam. Nevertheless, this book's methods, for assessing the resulting cancer risk, are fully applicable to any procedure done with digital subtraction angiography. Cancer risk from diagnostic radiology results from the energy transferred by the X-ray beam to human tissue, a transfer which has already occurred *before* the residual beam reaches whatever image-maker is on the patient's far side. Backscatter from image-receiving equipment is a negligible factor in the patient's dose; a very small fraction of the initial X-ray beam ever reaches such equipment.

Sometimes very large entrance doses are reported for angiographic procedures. An erroneous impression, exaggerating the risk, results unless it is emphasized that such doses often apply to areas very much smaller than field sizes in routine X-ray exams. To make *correct* risk evaluations, the size of the irradiated areas needs proper attention.

For the convenience of this book's users, we have calculated risks from five common angiographic exams, done under typical conditions. While Chapters 5 and 6 enable their users to evaluate the cancer risks from virtually any angiographic procedure, Chapter 7 provides a handy shortcut for many circumstances.

197

Section 1: Derivation of the Tables
for Five Common Angiographies

Webster, Alpert, and Brownell (1974) have published a very comprehensive study of angiographic procedures for pediatric patients; we base our analyses upon it because the study applies to "procedures in use in one large general hospital, which uses techniques believed to be typical."

These workers present data which make it possible not only to ascertain the entrance exposures, but also to derive the separate amounts of body exposed by the films and by the fluoroscopy, for patients age 1 through age 15. We have extrapolated the Webster-type data to permit evaluation of angiographic procedures for the newborn and for people over age 15.

Although we had to make some approximations and assumptions in order to provide the tables which follow, we know that these tables provide very reasonable and useful approximations of the risk from exams performed under similar conditions.

Section 2: Rules Followed in the Angiography Tables

The following statements apply to every table.

Separate Risks: The cancer risks from films and fluoroscopy (FLU) are provided separately, and the risk stated for the Common Exam is their sum.

Risks from FLU: The risk entries for fluoroscopy in the tables already take account of all the factors involved in Steps 1 through 6 described in the previous chapter. The field size is provided by the tables as a piece of information, *not* as a call for any calculation or other action by the user.

Origin of Dose Figures: These entrance doses are *not* derived by the standard pediatric lowering factors presented in Table 3, Chapter 5; the angiographic doses are derived from the data of Webster and co-workers (1974) for these specific exams.

Entrance Dose from FILMS: The entry for the entrance dose from FILMS is *not* the dose per individual shot; this entry is the sum from all the films made during the Common Exam. Entrance doses can be *validly* added whenever the field, beam direction, and beam quality remain constant, or nearly so. The human evidence (see Chapter 2, Myth 10) indicates that, when the issue is the induction of cancer by ionizing radiation, the irradiated organs just do not "care" whether a given dose of energy is transferred all at once or with interruptions (with several separate shots, for instance).

Adjustment for Other Doses: For exams done with other entrance doses, risks can be adjusted in the usual way, demonstrated in Chapter 4, Section 11.

Adjustment for Other Beam Qualities: The risks have been calculated for a beam quality of 2.3 mm Al HVL. For any other beam quality, the risks can be adjusted in the usual way, demonstrated in Chapter 4, Section 12.

Smoking Issue: The risks are for non-smokers.

Section 3: The Tables for Common Angiographies

ANGIOCARDIOGRAPHY

Contrast Medium: Yes. Organically bound iodine compound administered by catheter intra-arterially.

Fluoroscopy and Spot Films: Yes.

Length of Field: See the individual ages for field sizes.

Organs Generating Most Cancer Risk:
    Males: Bronchi, stomach, kidney, large intestine, pancreas, larynx.
    Females: Breasts, bronchi, large intestine, stomach, kidneys, pancreas.

Special Comment:
- The cancer risk *falls* from age 1 to age 5 for angiocardiography, in contrast to the pattern in Chapter 5, because a smaller *fraction* of chest area is exposed in the 5-year-old than in the 1-year-old by this exam.

AGE NEW　　　　　　　　　　　　　　　　Testes, dose CE: < 1 mrad
ANGIOCARDIOGRAPHY　　　　　　　　　Ovaries, dose CE: 1.2 mrads

Common Exam (CE): Forty films
                  (20 AP and 20 LAT) with
                  FLU (PA) thirty minutes
Field size, FILMS: 0.8 of chest area exposed
Field size, FLU: 0.11 of chest area exposed

Age New, Angiocardiography *(continued)*

Rate of future *leukemia* from Common Exam:
>   Males: 60 per million = 1 in 16,700
>   Females: 38 per million = 1 in 26,300

Rate of future *cancer* from Common Exam:
>   Males: 10,783 per million = 1 in 93
>   Females: 19,825 per million = 1 in 50

Sum	Ent Dose	Beam HVL	Male Cancer Risk	Female Cancer Risk
FILMS	1.85 R	2.3 mm Al	5,790 per million	13,536 per million
FLU	15.44 R	2.3 mm Al	4,993 per million	6,289 per million

AGE 1
ANGIOCARDIOGRAPHY

Testes, dose CE: < 1 mrad
Ovaries, dose CE: < 1 mrad

Common Exam (CE): Forty films
>   (20 AP and 20 LAT) with
>   FLU (PA) thirty minutes

Field size, FILMS: 0.75 of chest area exposed
Field size, FLU: 0.104 of chest area exposed
Rate of future *leukemia* from Common Exam:
>   Males: 78 per million = 1 in 12,800
>   Females: 49 per million = 1 in 20,400

Rate of future *cancer* from Common Exam:
>   Males: 9,853 per million = 1 in 101
>   Females: 18,212 per million = 1 in 55

Sum	Ent Dose	Beam HVL	Male Cancer Risk	Female Cancer Risk
FILMS	2.06 R	2.3 mm Al	4,674 per million	11,840 per million
FLU	17.65 R	2.3 mm Al	5,179 per million	6,372 per million

AGE 5
ANGIOCARDIOGRAPHY

Testes, dose CE: <1 mrad
Ovaries, dose CE: 1.5 mrads

Common Exam (CE): Forty films
>   (20 AP and 20 LAT) with
>   FLU (PA) thirty minutes

Field size, FILMS: 0.38 of chest area exposed
Field size, FLU: 0.09 of chest area exposed
Rate of future *leukemia* from Common Exam:
>   Males: 84 per million = 1 in 11,900
>   Females: 52 per million = 1 in 19,200

Rate of future *cancer* from Common Exam:
>   Males: 8,387 per million = 1 in 119
>   Females: 12,483 per million = 1 in 80

Sum	Ent Dose	Beam HVL	Male Cancer Risk	Female Cancer Risk
FILMS	2.43 R	2.3 mm Al	2,527 per million	5,783 per million
FLU	26.47 R	2.3 mm Al	5,860 per million	6,700 per million

AGE 10
ANGIOCARDIOGRAPHY

Testes, dose CE: < 1 mrad
Ovaries, dose CE: 1.3 mrads

Common Exam (CE): Forty films
                 (20 AP and 20 LAT) with
                 FLU (PA) thirty minutes
Field size, FILMS: 0.35 of chest area exposed
Field size, FLU: 0.09 of chest area exposed
Rate of future *leukemia* from Common Exam:
         Males: 63 per million = 1 in 15,900
         Females: 40 per million = 1 in 25,000
Rate of future *cancer* from Common Exam:
         Males: 8,586 per million = 1 in 116
         Females: 12,762 per million = 1 in 78

Sum	Ent Dose	Beam HVL	Male Cancer Risk	Female Cancer Risk
FILMS	4.19 R	2.3 mm Al	2,630 per million	6,357 per million
FLU	37.50 R	2.3 mm Al	5,956 per million	6,405 per million

AGE 15
ANGIOCARDIOGRAPHY

Testes, dose CE: < 1 mrad
Ovaries, dose CE: 1.1 mrads

Common Exam (CE): Forty films
                 (20 AP and 20 LAT) with
                 FLU (PA) thirty minutes
Field size, FILMS: 0.35 of chest area exposed
Field size, FLU: 0.09 of chest area exposed
Rate of future *leukemia* from Common Exam:
         Males: 82 per million = 1 in 12,200
         Females: 51 per million = 1 in 19,600
Rate of future *cancer* from Common Exam:
         Males: 4,256 per million = 1 in 235
         Females: 6,154 per million = 1 in 162

Sum	Ent Dose	Beam HVL	Male Cancer Risk	Female Cancer Risk
FILMS	5.29 R	2.3 mm Al	1,150 per million	3,198 per million
FLU	48.53 R	2.3 mm Al	3,106 per million	2,956 per million

AGE 20
ANGIOCARDIOGRAPHY

Testes, dose CE: < 1 mrad
Ovaries, dose CE: < 1 mrad
Embryo, dose CE: < 1 mrad

Common Exam (CE): Forty films
                 (20 AP and 20 LAT) with
                 FLU (PA) thirty minutes
Field size, FILMS: 0.35 of chest area exposed
Field size, FLU: 0.09 of chest area exposed
Rate of future *leukemia* from Common Exam:
        Males: 88 per million = 1 in 11,400
        Females: 55 per million = 1 in 18,200
Rate of future *cancer* from Common Exam: **(Smokers)**
        Males: 3,481 per million = 1 in 287   (CE × 3.07)
        Females: 4,723 per million = 1 in 212   (CE × 1.97)

Sum	Ent Dose	Beam HVL	Male Cancer Risk	Female Cancer Risk
FILMS	6.25 R	2.3 mm Al	968 per million	2,676 per million
FLU	51.47 R	2.3 mm Al	2,513 per million	2,047 per million

All values are for the Common Exam

Age 25, Angiocardiography   Cancer Rate............... *(Lowering Factor)*
        Males: 3,460 per million = 1 in 289   (Age 20 × 0.994)
        Females: 4,666 per million = 1 in 214   (Age 20 × 0.988)
Age 30, Angiocardiography   Cancer Rate............... *(Lowering Factor)*
        Males: 2,973 per million = 1 in 336   (Age 20 × 0.854)
        Females: 4,123 per million = 1 in 242   (Age 20 × 0.873)
Age 35, Angiocardiography   Cancer Rate............... *(Lowering Factor)*
        Males: 2,127 per million = 1 in 470   (Age 20 × 0.611)
        Females: 2,942 per million = 1 in 340   (Age 20 × 0.623)
Age 40, Angiocardiography   Cancer Rate............... *(Lowering Factor)*
        Males: 1,295 per million = 1 in 772   (Age 20 × 0.372)
        Females: 1,847 per million = 1 in 541   (Age 20 × 0.391)
Age 45, Angiocardiography   Cancer Rate............... *(Lowering Factor)*
        Males: 564 per million = 1 in 1,773   (Age 20 × 0.162)
        Females: 831 per million = 1 in 1,203   (Age 20 × 0.176)
Age 50, Angiocardiography   Cancer Rate............... *(Lowering Factor)*
        Males: 52 per million = 1 in 19,200   (Age 20 × 0.015)
        Females: 80 per million = 1 in 12,500   (Age 20 × 0.017)
Age 55, Angiocardiography   Cancer Rate............... *(Lowering Factor)*
        Males: 35 per million = 1 in 28,600   (Age 20 × 0.010)
        Females: 57 per million = 1 in 17,500   (Age 20 × 0.012)

CELIAC (LIVER) ANGIOGRAPHY

Contrast Medium: Yes. Organically bound iodine compound administered by catheter intra-arterially.

Fluoroscopy and Spot Films: Yes.

Length of Field: See the individual ages for field sizes.

Organs Generating Most Cancer Risk:
  Males: Prostate, large intestine, bladder, stomach, pancreas, rectum.
  Females: Large intestine, corpus uteri, stomach, cervix uteri, bladder, pancreas.

AGE NEW   Testes, dose CE: 104 mrads
CELIAC ANGIOGRAPHY   Ovaries, dose CE: 993 mrads

Common Exam (CE): Two series, each of 15
                        AP films (Total: 30 films)
                        with FLU (PA) five minutes
Field size, FILMS: 1.0 of area exposed
Field size, FLU: 0.5 of area exposed
Rate of future *leukemia* from Common Exam:
        Males: 91 per million = 1 in 11,000
        Females: 57 per million = 1 in 17,500
Rate of future *cancer* from Common Exam:
        Males: 19,644 per million = 1 in 51
        Females: 19,228 per million = 1 in 52

Sum	Ent Dose	Beam HVL	Male Cancer Risk	Female Cancer Risk
FILMS	1.47 R	2.3 mm Al	13,006 per million	12,694 per million
FLU	2.57 R	2.3 mm Al	6,638 per million	6,534 per million

AGE 1   Testes, dose CE: 102 mrads
CELIAC ANGIOGRAPHY   Ovaries, dose CE: 942 mrads

Common Exam (CE): Two series, each of 15
                        AP films (Total: 30 films)
                        with FLU (PA) five minutes
Field size, FILMS: 1.0 of area exposed
Field size, FLU: 0.5 of area exposed
Rate of future *leukemia* from Common Exam:
            Males: 79 per million = 1 in 12,700
            Females: 49 per million = 1 in 20,400

Age 1, Celiac Angiography *(continued)*

Rate of future *cancer* from Common Exam:
        Males: 18,355 per million = 1 in 54
        Females: 17,913 per million = 1 in 56

Sum	Ent Dose	Beam HVL	Male Cancer Risk	Female Cancer Risk
FILMS	1.54 R	2.3 mm Al	12,128 per million	11,878 per million
FLU	2.94 R	2.3 mm Al	6,227 per million	6,035 per million

AGE 5
CELIAC ANGIOGRAPHY

Testes, dose CE: 147 mrads
Ovaries, dose CE: 1,609 mrads

Common Exam (CE): Two series, each of 15
               films (Total: 30 films)
               with FLU (PA) five minutes
Field size, FILMS: 1.0 of area exposed
Field size, FLU: 0.25 of area exposed
Rate of future *leukemia* from Common Exam:
        Males: 84 per million = 1 in 11,900
        Females: 52 per million = 1 in 19,200
Rate of future *cancer* from Common Exam:
        Males: 26,635 per million = 1 in 38
        Females: 25,059 per million = 1 in 40

Sum	Ent Dose	Beam HVL	Male Cancer Risk	Female Cancer Risk
FILMS	3.31 R	2.3 mm Al	22,228 per million	20,865 per million
FLU	4.41 R	2.3 mm Al	4,407 per million	4,194 per million

AGE 10
CELIAC ANGIOGRAPHY

Testes, dose CE: 341 mrads
Ovaries, dose CE: 4,485 mrads

Common Exam (CE): Two series, each of 15
               films (Total: 30 films)
               with FLU (PA) five minutes
Field size, FILMS: 1.0 of area exposed
Field size, FLU: 0.25 of area exposed
Rate of future *leukemia* from Common Exam:
        Males: 177 per million = 1 in 5,650
        Females: 111 per million = 1 in 9,000
Rate of future *cancer* from Common Exam:
        Males: 60,868 per million = 1 in 16
        Females: 53,752 per million = 1 in 19

Sum	Ent Dose	Beam HVL	Male Cancer Risk	Female Cancer Risk
FILMS	11.03 R	2.3 mm Al	56,372 per million	49,625 per million
FLU	6.25 R	2.3 mm Al	4,496 per million	4,127 per million

AGE 15
CELIAC ANGIOGRAPHY

Testes, dose CE: 339 mrads
Ovaries, dose CE: 5,345 mrads

Common Exam (CE): Two series, each of 15
                  AP films (Total: 30 films)
                  with FLU (PA) 5 minutes
Field size, FILMS: 1.0 of area exposed
Field size, FLU: 0.25 of area exposed
Rate of future *leukemia* from Common Exam:
          Males: 199 per million = 1 in 5,030
          Females: 124 per million = 1 in 8,060
Rate of future *cancer* from Common Exam:
          Males: 38,612 per million = 1 in 26
          Females: 32,071 per million = 1 in 31

Sum	Ent Dose	Beam HVL	Male Cancer Risk	Female Cancer Risk
FILMS	16.91 R	2.3 mm Al	36,465 per million	30,159 per million
FLU	8.09 R	2.3 mm Al	2,147 per million	1,912 per million

AGE 20
CELIAC ANGIOGRAPHY

Testes, dose CE: 275 mrads
Ovaries, dose CE: 4,656 mrads
Embryo dose CE: 5,342 mrads

Common Exam (CE): Two series, each of 15
                  AP films (Total: 30 films)
                  with FLU (PA) 5 minutes
Field size, FILMS: 1.0 of area exposed
Field size, FLU: 0.25 of area exposed
Rate of future *leukemia* from Common Exam:
          Males: 144 per million = 1 in 6,940
          Females: 90 per million = 1 in 11,100
Rate of future *cancer* from Common Exam: (Smokers)
          Males: 31,109 per million = 1 in 32   (CE × 1.02)
          Females: 25,834 per million = 1 in 39   (CE × 1.02)

Sum	Ent Dose	Beam HVL	Male Cancer Risk	Female Cancer Risk
FILMS	18.38 R	2.3 mm Al	29,535 per million	24,503 per million
FLU	8.82 R	2.3 mm Al	1,574 per million	1,331 per million

Celiac Angiography *(continued)*

All values are for the Common Exam

Age 25, Celiac Angio'y   Cancer Rate............... *(Lowering Factor)*
        Males: 30,922 per million = 1 in 32   (Age 20 × 0.994)
        Females: 25,524 per million = 1 in 39   (Age 20 × 0.988)
Age 30, Celiac Angio'y   Cancer Rate............... *(Lowering Factor)*
        Males: 26,567 per million = 1 in 38   (Age 20 × 0.854)
        Females: 22,553 per million = 1 in 44   (Age 20 × 0.873)
Age 35, Celiac Angio'y   Cancer Rate............... *(Lowering Factor)*
        Males: 19,008 per million = 1 in 53   (Age 20 × 0.611)
        Females: 16,094 per million = 1 in 62   (Age 20 × 0.623)
Age 40, Celiac Angio'y   Cancer Rate............... *(Lowering Factor)*
        Males: 11,572 per million = 1 in 86   (Age 20 × 0.372)
        Females: 10,101 per million = 1 in 99   (Age 20 × 0.391)
Age 45, Celiac Angio'y   Cancer Rate............... *(Lowering Factor)*
        Males: 5,040 per million = 1 in 198   (Age 20 × 0.162)
        Females: 4,547 per million = 1 in 220   (Age 20 × 0.176)
Age 50, Celiac Angio'y   Cancer Rate............... *(Lowering Factor)*
        Males: 467 per million = 1 in 2,141   (Age 20 × 0.015)
        Females: 439 per million = 1 in 2,278   (Age 20 × 0.017)
Age 55, Celiac Angio'y   Cancer Rate............... *(Lowering Factor)*
        Males: 311 per million = 1 in 3,215   (Age 20 × 0.010)
        Females: 310 per million = 1 in 3,226   (Age 20 × 0.012)

CEREBRAL ANGIOGRAPHY

Contrast Medium: Yes. Organically bound iodine compound administered by catheter intra-arterially.

Fluoroscopy and Spot Films: Yes.

Length of Field: See the individual ages for field sizes.

Organs Generating Most Cancer Risk:
    Males: Larynx, brain, lips, pharynx, tongue, mouth tissues.
    Females: Thyroid, brain, breasts, bronchi, mouth tissues, tongue.

AGE NEW   Testes, dose CE: < .1 mrad
CEREBRAL ANGIOGRAPHY   Ovaries, dose CE: < 1 mrad

Common Exam (CE): Biplane, 48 films
                      (24 AP and 24 LAT) with
                      FLU (PA) six minutes
Field size, FILMS: Full head and neck
Field size, FLU: Lower half of neck and upper half of chest

Rate of future *leukemia* from Common Exam:
        Males: 138 per million = 1 in 7,250
        Females: 86 per million = 1 in 11,600
Rate of future *cancer* from Common Exam:
        Males: 12,517 per million = 1 in 80
        Females: 9,968 per million = 1 in 100

Sum	Ent Dose	Beam HVL	Male Cancer Risk	Female Cancer Risk
FILMS	5.56 R	2.3 mm Al	10,469 per million	7,387 per million
FLU	1.99 R	2.3 mm Al	2,048 per million	2,581 per million

AGE 1
CEREBRAL ANGIOGRAPHY

Testes, dose CE: < 1 mrad
Ovaries, dose CE: < 1 mrad

Common Exam (CE): Biplane, 48 films
                      (24 AP and 24 LAT) with
                      FLU (PA) six minutes
Field size, FILMS: Full head and neck
Field size, FLU: Lower half of neck and upper half of chest
Rate of future *leukemia* from Common Exam:
        Males: 104 per million = 1 in 9,600
        Females: 65 per million = 1 in 15,400
Rate of future *cancer* from Common Exam:
        Males: 11,469 per million = 1 in 87
        Females: 8,925 per million = 1 in 112

Sum	Ent Dose	Beam HVL	Male Cancer Risk	Female Cancer Risk
FILMS	6.18 R	2.3 mm Al	9,683 per million	6,634 per million
FLU	2.21 R	2.3 mm Al	1,786 per million	2,291 per million

AGE 5
CEREBRAL ANGIOGRAPHY

Testes, dose CE: < 1 mrad
Ovaries, dose CE: < 1 mrad

Common Exam (CE): Biplane 48 films
                      (24 AP and 24 LAT) with
                      FLU (PA) six minutes
Field size, FILMS: Full head and neck
Field size, FLU: Lower half of neck and upper half of chest
Rate of future *leukemia* from Common Exam:
        Males: 139 per million = 1 in 7,200
        Females: 87 per million = 1 in 11,500
Rate of future *cancer* from Common Exam:
        Males: 13,201 per million = 1 in 76
        Females: 9,652 per million = 1 in 104

Age 5, Cerebral Angiography *(continued)*

Sum	Ent Dose	Beam HVL	Male Cancer Risk	Female Cancer Risk
FILMS	8.38 R	2.3 mm Al	11,058 per million	7,377 per million
FLU	3.53 R	2.3 mm Al	2,143 per million	2,275 per million

AGE 10   Testes, dose CE: < 1 mrad
CEREBRAL ANGIOGRAPHY   Ovaries, dose CE: < 1 mrad

Common Exam (CE): Biplane 48 films
                      (24 AP and 24 LAT) with
                      FLU (PA) six minutes
Field size, FILMS: Full head and neck
Field size, FLU: Lower half of neck and upper half of chest
Rate of future *leukemia* from Common Exam:
          Males: 113 per million = 1 in 8,850
          Females: 71 per million = 1 in 14,100
Rate of future *cancer* from Common Exam:
          Males: 10,962 per million = 1 in 91
          Females: 7,816 per million = 1 in 128

Sum	Ent Dose	Beam HVL	Male Cancer Risk	Female Cancer Risk
FILMS	8.82 R	2.3 mm Al	8,863 per million	5,662 per million
FLU	5.29 R	2.3 mm Al	2,099 per million	2,154 per million

AGE 15   Testes, dose CE: < 1 mrad
CEREBRAL ANGIOGRAPHY   Ovaries, dose CE: < 1 mrad

Common Exam (CE): Biplane 48 films
                      (24 AP and 24 LAT) with
                      FLU (PA) six minutes
Field size, FILMS: Full head and neck
Field size, FLU: Lower half of neck and upper half of chest
Rate of future *leukemia* from Common Exam:
          Males: 113 per million = 1 in 8,850
          Females: 71 per million = 1 in 14,100
Rate of future *cancer* from Common Exam:
          Males: 5,129 per million = 1 in 195
          Females: 3,608 per million = 1 in 277

Sum	Ent Dose	Beam HVL	Male Cancer Risk	Female Cancer Risk
FILMS	9.71 R	2.3 mm Al	3,922 per million	2,543 per million
FLU	7.06 R	2.3 mm Al	1,207 per million	1,065 per million

AGE 20
CEREBRAL ANGIOGRAPHY

Testes, dose CE: < 1 mrad
Ovaries, dose CE: < 1 mrad
Embryo, dose CE: < 1 mrad

Common Exam (CE): Biplane 48 films
(24 AP and 24 LAT) with
FLU (PA) six minutes
Field size, FILMS: Full head and neck
Field size, FLU: Lower half of neck and upper half of chest
Rate of future *leukemia* from Common Exam:
Males: 103 per million = 1 in 9,700
Females: 65 per million = 1 in 15,400
Rate of future *cancer* from Common Exam: **(Smokers)**
Males: 4,236 per million = 1 in 236   (CE × 2.1)
Females: 2,915 per million = 1 in 343   (CE × 2.0)

Sum	*Ent Dose*	*Beam HVL*	*Male Cancer Risk*	*Female Cancer Risk*
FILMS	10.29 R	2.3 mm Al	3,143 per million	2,064 per million
FLU	8.09 R	2.3 mm Al	1,093 per million	851 per million

All values are for the Common Exam

Age 25, Cerebral Angio'y   Cancer Rate............... *(Lowering Factor)*
Males: 4,210 per million = 1 in 238   (Age 20 × 0.994)
Females: 2,880 per million = 1 in 347   (Age 20 × 0.988)
Age 30, Cerebral Angio'y   Cancer Rate............... *(Lowering Factor)*
Males: 3,618 per million = 1 in 276   (Age 20 × 0.854)
Females: 2,545 per million = 1 in 393   (Age 20 × 0.873)
Age 35, Cerebral Angio'y   Cancer Rate............... *(Lowering Factor)*
Males: 2,588 per million = 1 in 386   (Age 20 × 0.611)
Females: 1,816 per million = 1 in 551   (Age 20 × 0.623)
Age 40, Cerebral Angio'y   Cancer Rate............... *(Lowering Factor)*
Males: 1,576 per million = 1 in 634   (Age 20 × 0.372)
Females: 1,140 per million = 1 in 877   (Age 20 × 0.391)
Age 45, Cerebral Angio'y   Cancer Rate............... *(Lowering Factor)*
Males: 686 per million = 1 in 1,460   (Age 20 × 0.162)
Females: 513 per million = 1 in 1,950   (Age 20 × 0.176)
Age 50, Cerebral Angio'y   Cancer Rate............... *(Lowering Factor)*
Males: 64 per million = 1 in 15,630   (Age 20 × 0.015)
Females: 50 per million = 1 in 20,000   (Age 20 × 0.017)
Age 55, Cerebral Angio'y   Cancer Rate............... *(Lowering Factor)*
Males: 42 per million = 1 in 23,800   (Age 20 × 0.010)
Females: 35 per million = 1 in 28,600   (Age 20 × 0.012)

PULMONARY ARTERIOGRAPHY

Contrast Medium: Yes. Organically bound iodine compound administered by catheter intra-arterially.

Fluoroscopy and Spot Films: Yes.

Length of Field: See the individual ages for field sizes.

Organs Generating Most Cancer Risk:
Males: Stomach, bronchi, pancreas, large intestine, liver, esophagus.
Females: Breasts, large intestine, stomach, bronchi, pancreas, liver.

Special Comment:
- The markedly lower risk from FLU than from FILMS results mainly from the difference in risk between the AP and PA beam directions, not from the difference in entrance doses.

AGE NEW
PULMONARY ARTERIOGRAPHY

Testes, dose CE: < 1 mrad
Ovaries, dose CE: < 1 mrad

Common Exam (CE): Thirty AP films, with
FLU (PA) 1.5 minutes
Field size, FILMS: 1.0 of chest area exposed
Field size, FLU: 0.5 of chest area exposed
Rate of future *leukemia* from Common Exam:
Males: 49 per million = 1 in 20,400
Females: 31 per million = 1 in 32,300
Rate of future *cancer* from Common Exam:
Males: 9,327 per million = 1 in 107
Females: 24,762 per million = 1 in 40

Sum	Ent Dose	Beam HVL	Male Cancer Risk	Female Cancer Risk
FILMS	1.84 R	2.3 mm Al	7,987 per million	23,050 per million
FLU	0.81 R	2.3 mm Al	1,340 per million	1,712 per million

AGE 1
PULMONARY ARTERIOGRAPHY

Testes, dose CE: < 1 mrad
Ovaries, dose CE: < 1 mrad

Common Exam (CE): Thirty AP films, with
FLU (PA) 1.5 minutes
Field size, FILMS: 1.0 of chest area exposed
Field size, FLU: 0.42 of chest area exposed
Rate of future *leukemia* from Common Exam:
Males: 47 per million = 1 in 21,300
Females: 30 per million = 1 in 33,300

Rate of future *cancer* from Common Exam:
      Males: 9,481 per million = 1 in 105
      Females: 26,743 per million = 1 in 37

Sum	Ent Dose	Beam HVL	Male Cancer Risk	Female Cancer Risk
FILMS	2.21 R	2.3 mm Al	8,420 per million	25,388 per million
FLU	0.88 R	2.3 mm Al	1,061 per million	1,355 per million

AGE 5
PULMONARY ARTERIOGRAPHY

Testes, dose CE: < 1 mrad
Ovaries, dose CE: < 1 mrad

Common Exam (CE): Thirty AP films, with
               FLU (PA) 1.5 minutes
Field size, FILMS: 0.55 of chest area exposed
Field size, FLU: 0.22 of chest area exposed
Rate of future *leukemia* from Common Exam:
      Males: 49 per million = 1 in 20,400
      Females: 31 per million = 1 in 32,300
Rate of future *cancer* from Common Exam:
      Males: 8,790 per million = 1 in 114
      Females: 24,613 per million = 1 in 41

Sum	Ent Dose	Beam HVL	Male Cancer Risk	Female Cancer Risk
FILMS	4.71 R	2.3 mm Al	7,992 per million	23,691 per million
FLU	1.32 R	2.3 mm Al	798 per million	922 per million

AGE 10
PULMONARY ARTERIOGRAPHY

Testes, dose CE: < 1 mrad
Ovaries, dose CE: < 1 mrad

Common Exam (CE): Thirty AP films, with
               FLU (PA) 1.5 minutes
Field size, FILMS: 0.55 of chest area exposed
Field size, FLU: 0.22 of chest area exposed
Rate of future *leukemia* from Common Exam:
      Males: 37 per million = 1 in 27,000
      Females: 23 per million = 1 in 43,500
Rate of future *cancer* from Common Exam:
      Males: 10,318 per million = 1 in 97
      Females: 28,335 per million = 1 in 35

Age 10, Pulmonary Arteriography *(continued)*

Sum	Ent Dose	Beam HVL	Male Cancer Risk	Female Cancer Risk
FILMS	7.5 R	2.3 mm Al	9,509 per million	27,487 per million
FLU	1.91 R	2.3 mm Al	809 per million	848 per million

AGE 15
PULMONARY ARTERIOGRAPHY

Testes, dose CE: < 1 mrad
Ovaries, dose CE: < 1 mrad

Common Exam (CE): Thirty AP films, with
FLU (PA) 1.5 minutes
Field size, FILMS: 0.55 of chest area exposed
Field size, FLU: 0.22 of chest area exposed
Rate of future *leukemia* from Common Exam:
    Males: 56 per million = 1 in 17,900
    Females: 35 per million = 1 in 28,600
Rate of future *cancer* from Common Exam:
    Males: 6,283 per million = 1 in 159
    Females: 17,678 per million = 1 in 56

Sum	Ent Dose	Beam HVL	Male Cancer Risk	Female Cancer Risk
FILMS	11.69 R	2.3 mm Al	5,914 per million	17,317 per million
FLU	2.43 R	2.3 mm Al	369 per million	361 per million

AGE 20
PULMONARY ARTERIOGRAPHY

Testes, dose CE: < 1 mrad
Ovaries, dose CE: < 1 mrad
Embryo, dose CE: < 1 mrad

Common Exam (CE): Thirty AP films, with
FLU (PA) 1.5 minutes
Field size, FILMS: 0.55 of chest area exposed
Field size, FLU: 0.22 of chest area exposed
Rate of future *leukemia* from Common Exam:
    Males: 60 per million = 1 in 16,700
    Females: 38 per million = 1 in 26,300
Rate of future *cancer* from Common Exam: (Smokers)
    Males: 5,535 per million = 1 in 181   (CE × 3.24)
    Females: 14,969 per million = 1 in 67   (CE × 1.40)

Sum	Ent Dose	Beam HVL	Male Cancer Risk	Female Cancer Risk
FILMS	12.50 R	2.3 mm Al	5,230 per million	14,707 per million
FLU	2.65 R	2.3 mm Al	305 per million	262 per million

All values are for the Common Exam

Age 25, Pulmonary Arter'y   Cancer Rate............... *(Lowering Factor)*
        Males: 5,502 per million = 1 in 182   (Age 20 × 0.994)
        Females: 14,789 per million = 1 in 68   (Age 20 × 0.988)
Age 30, Pulmonary Arter'y   Cancer Rate............... *(Lowering Factor)*
        Males: 4,727 per million = 1 in 212   (Age 20 × 0.854)
        Females: 13,068 per million = 1 in 76   (Age 20 × 0.873)
Age 35, Pulmonary Arter'y   Cancer Rate............... *(Lowering Factor)*
        Males: 3,382 per million = 1 in 296   (Age 20 × 0.611)
        Females: 9,326 per million = 1 in 107   (Age 20 × 0.623)
Age 40, Pulmonary Arter'y   Cancer Rate............... *(Lowering Factor)*
        Males: 2,059 per million = 1 in 486   (Age 20 × 0.372)
        Females: 5,568 per million = 1 in 180   (Age 20 × 0.391)
Age 45, Pulmonary Arter'y   Cancer Rate............... *(Lowering Factor)*
        Males: 897 per million = 1 in 1,115   (Age 20 × 0.162)
        Females: 2,634 per million = 1 in 380   (Age 20 × 0.176)
Age 50, Pulmonary Arter'y   Cancer Rate............... *(Lowering Factor)*
        Males: 83 per million = 1 in 12,000   (Age 20 × 0.015)
        Females: 254 per million = 1 in 3,900   (Age 20 × 0.017)
Age 55, Pulmonary Arter'y   Cancer Rate............... *(Lowering Factor)*
        Males: 55 per million = 1 in 18,200   (Age 20 × 0.010)
        Females: 180 per million = 1 in 5,600   (Age 20 × 0.012)

RENAL ANGIOGRAPHY

Contrast Medium: Yes. Organically bound iodine compound administered by catheter intra-arterially.

Fluoroscopy and Spot Films: Yes.

Length of Field: See the individual ages for field sizes.

Organs Generating Most Cancer Risk:
    Males: Large intestine, kidney, stomach, prostate, pancreas, bladder.
    Females: Large intestine, kidney, stomach, pancreas, corpus uteri, liver.

AGE NEW   Testes, dose CE: 19 mrads
RENAL ANGIOGRAPHY   Ovaries, dose CE: 195 mrads

Common Exam (CE): Two series, each of 10
                    AP films (Total: 20 films)
                    with FLU (PA) four minutes
Field size, FILMS: 0.25 of abdomen exposed
Field size, FLU: 0.5 of abdomen exposed

Age New, Renal Angiography (continued)

Rate of future *leukemia* from Common Exam:
  Males: 52 per million = 1 in 19,200
  Females: 33 per million = 1 in 30,300
Rate of future *cancer* from Common Exam:
  Males: 6,500 per million = 1 in 154
  Females: 6,532 per million = 1 in 153

Sum	Ent Dose	Beam HVL	Male Cancer Risk	Female Cancer Risk
FILMS	0.93 R	2.3 mm Al	1,390 per million	1,502 per million
FLU	2.21 R	2.3 mm Al	5,110 per million	5,030 per million

AGE 1
RENAL ANGIOGRAPHY

Testes, dose CE: 17 mrads
Ovaries, dose CE: 144 mrads

Common Exam (CE): Two series, each of 10
              AP films (Total: 20 films)
              with FLU (PA) four minutes
Field size, FILMS: 0.21 of abdomen exposed
Field size, FLU: 0.47 of abdomen exposed
Rate of future *leukemia* from Common Exam:
  Males: 44 per million = 1 in 22,700
  Females: 27 per million = 1 in 37,000
Rate of future *cancer* from Common Exam:
  Males: 5,712 per million = 1 in 175
  Females: 5,656 per million = 1 in 177

Sum	Ent Dose	Beam HVL	Male Cancer Risk	Female Cancer Risk
FILMS	1.03 R	2.3 mm Al	1,186 per million	1,230 per million
FLU	2.35 R	2.3 mm Al	4,526 per million	4,426 per million

AGE 5
RENAL ANGIOGRAPHY

Testes, dose CE: 10 mrads
Ovaries, dose CE: 111 mrads

Common Exam (CE): Two series, each of 10
              AP films (Total: 20 films)
              with FLU (PA) four minutes
Field size, FILMS: 0.11 of entire abdomen
Field size, FLU: 0.24 of entire abdomen
Rate of future *leukemia* from Common Exam:
  Males: 31 per million = 1 in 32,300
  Females: 19 per million = 1 in 52,600
Rate of future *cancer* from Common Exam:
  Males: 5,077 per million = 1 in 197
  Females: 4,520 per million = 1 in 221

Sum	Ent Dose	Beam HVL	Male Cancer Risk	Female Cancer Risk
FILMS	2.21 R	2.3 mm Al	1,568 per million	1,464 per million
FLU	3.53 R	2.3 mm Al	3,509 per million	3,056 per million

AGE 10
RENAL ANGIOGRAPHY

Testes, dose CE: 9 mrads
Ovaries, dose CE: 155 mrads

Common Exam (CE): Two series, each of 10
AP films (Total: 20 films)
with FLU (PA) four minutes
Field size, FILMS: 0.085 of entire abdomen
Field size, FLU: 0.24 of entire abdomen
Rate of future *leukemia* from Common Exam:
Males: 38 per million = 1 in 26,300
Females: 24 per million = 1 in 41,700
Rate of future *cancer* from Common Exam:
Males: 5,358 per million = 1 in 187
Females: 4,596 per million = 1 in 218

Sum	Ent Dose	Beam HVL	Male Cancer Risk	Female Cancer Risk
FILMS	3.53 R	2.3 mm Al	1,697 per million	1,473 per million
FLU	5.00 R	2.3 mm Al	3,661 per million	3,123 per million

AGE 15
RENAL ANGIOGRAPHY

Testes, dose CE: 6 mrads
Ovaries, dose CE: 144 mrads

Common Exam (CE): Two series, each of 10
AP films (Total: 20 films)
with FLU (PA) four minutes
Field size, FILMS: 0.085 of entire abdomen
Field size, FLU: 0.24 of entire abdomen
Rate of future *leukemia* from Common Exam:
Males: 41 per million = 1 in 24,400
Females: 26 per million = 1 in 38,500
Rate of future *cancer* from Common Exam:
Males: 2,912 per million = 1 in 343
Female: 2,385 per million = 1 in 419

Sum	Ent Dose	Beam HVL	Male Cancer Risk	Female Cancer Risk
FILMS	5.51 R	2.3 mm Al	1,073 per million	881 per million
FLU	6.47 R	2.3 mm Al	1,839 per million	1,504 per million

AGE 20
RENAL ANGIOGRAPHY

Testes, dose CE: 3 mrads
Ovaries, dose CE: 119 mrads
Embryo, dose CE: 106 mrads

Common Exam (CE): Two series, each of 10
AP films (Total: 20 films)
with FLU (PA) four minutes
Field size, FILMS: 0.085 of entire abdomen
Field size, FLU: 0.24 of entire abdomen
Rate of future *leukemia* from Common Exam:
        Males: 38 per million = 1 in 26,300
        Females: 24 per million = 1 in 41,700
Rate of future *cancer* from Common Exam: **(Smokers)**
        Males: 2,442 per million = 1 in 410   (CE × 1.05)
        Females: 1,898 per million = 1 in 527   (CE × 1.04)

Sum	Ent Dose	Beam HVL	Male Cancer Risk	Female Cancer Risk
FILMS	6.61 R	2.3 mm Al	978 per million	786 per million
FLU	7.35 R	2.3 mm Al	1,464 per million	1,112 per million

All values are for the Common Exam

Age 25, Renal Angiography   Cancer Rate . . . . *(Lowering Factor)*
        Males: 2,427 per million = 1 in 412   (Age 20 × 0.994)
        Females: 1,875 per million = 1 in 533   (Age 20 × 0.988)
Age 30, Renal Angiography   Cancer Rate . . . . *(Lowering Factor)*
        Males: 2,085 per million = 1 in 480   (Age 20 × 0.854)
        Females: 1,657 per million = 1 in 604   (Age 20 × 0.873)
Age 35, Renal Angiography   Cancer Rate . . . . *(Lowering Factor)*
        Males: 1,492 per million = 1 in 670   (Age 20 × 0.611)
        Females: 1,182 per million = 1 in 846   (Age 20 × 0.623)
Age 40, Renal Angiography   Cancer Rate . . . . *(Lowering Factor)*
        Males: 908 per million = 1 in 1,101   (Age 20 × 0.372)
        Females: 742 per million = 1 in 1,348   (Age 20 × 0.391)
Age 45, Renal Angiography   Cancer Rate . . . . *(Lowering Factor)*
        Males: 396 per million = 1 in 2,525   (Age 20 × 0.162)
        Females: 334 per million = 1 in 2,994   (Age 20 × 0.176)
Age 50, Renal Angiography   Cancer Rate . . . . *(Lowering Factor)*
        Males: 36 per million = 1 in 27,780   (Age 20 × 0.015)
        Females: 32 per million = 1 in 31,250   (Age 20 × 0.017)
Age 55, Renal Angiography   Cancer Rate . . . . *(Lowering Factor)*
        Males: 24 per million = 1 in 41,700   (Age 20 × 0.010)
        Females: 23 per million = 1 in 43,480   (Age 20 × 0.012)

CHAPTER 8

Mammography

Mammography is a diagnostic radiology procedure dedicated to the idea that X-rays used this way can detect *early* malignant changes in the breast and can help physicians to diagnose breast cancer at a time in its development when other techniques would fail or would be equivocal.

Section 1: The Individual's Benefit versus Risk Judgment

The Controversy over Benefit

With respect to the benefit from this examination, disagreement persists. The issue is not whether mammography can pick up early but real breast cancer which *also* could be discovered by other means not carrying a radiation hazard. Rather, the issue is whether the mammographic procedure can detect some early but true breast cancers which might prove "curable," whereas other procedures would *miss* such cases. There are studies which claim it can. We do not intend to enter that controversy here. Instead, our purpose is to evaluate the mammographic procedures in use with respect to the risk of breast cancer *caused* by the procedures' radiation. The physician, radiologist, and patient can use such information in making their own benefit-risk judgments.

A second question is expense. Doing the mammographic procedure might be less expensive than doing a complete medical history and examination of a woman, so mammography might be a good screening procedure on a cost basis. But the woman who is worried sufficiently about breast cancer to ask for screening might also be the woman who would prefer to sacrifice money in order to avoid breast irradiation.

Progress in Reducing Doses

In mammography's early development, it gave breast tissue much higher doses than is the case currently. In the 1970s, people began to appreciate that ionizing radiation can *cause* breast cancer. As a result, the mammographic procedure was called into question on the grounds that the aggregate injury from examining millions of women, especially those under age 50, might be greater than the benefit which the procedure could possibly achieve.

Recently, there has been renewed interest in mammography, with the suggestion that the procedure be considered for wider use, because the dose—on the average—has come down markedly from what it was during the height of the controversy. However, mammographic doses vary greatly from one institution to another, and from one method to another.

Section 2: Derivation of Risk Values for Mammography

As a result of the national survey program known as "Breast Exposure: Nationwide Trends" (the BENT program), information is now available about the entrance doses received by the breasts from two major methods of mammography, performed with procedures and conditions reported as typical in 1978.

From these data, we calculated the breast cancer risk from each method of mammography for women from 20 years through 55 years of age. We have made these estimates for the "average" breast, widely estimated to be 6 centimeters thick under compression (Logan, in Bassett and Gold, 1982). There are 2.54 centimeters in one inch (see "Centimeter" in Glossary).

The risk values are provided in the Main Mammography Table at the end of this chapter. In addition, risk values can be obtained for the "small" breast, estimated to be 4 cm thick under compression, and for the "large" breast, estimated to be 8 cm thick under compression. The method is demonstrated in Sections 3 and 4 of this chapter.

We think that the best measure of breast dose to use for estimating cancer risk from mammography is the average dose absorbed by the entire breast. Some workers suggest that the "midbreast" dose is the appropriate measure. However, the epidemiological evidence which reveals cancer risks from breast irradiation is based upon *average* absorbed breast dose, so we think it most appropriate to use that measure here.

In the mammographic procedure, *two* exposures of each breast are almost invariably made. In the craniocaudad shot, the beam direction runs from head to foot, and in the mediolateral shot, the beam irradiates the breast from the center of the body to the side. Rosenstein (1980) has estimated that the average conditions and exposures are virtually identical for the two directions of the beam, and so we shall treat the two shots no differently from each other. Moreover, the two different methods of mammography use the *same* shots, even though they take them with different equipment.

One type of equipment receives the X-ray image on a plate called a xerox, rather than on film, so its use is called xero-radiography. The other type of equipment uses film with a screen which intensifies the image, so its use is called the film-screen mode or method.

Rosenstein (1980) has provided data on two important variables regarding both xero-radiography which uses the *tungsten* target X-ray tube, and the film-screen mode which uses the *molybdenum* target X-ray tube. From him, we obtain the average values, as of 1978, for entrance dose free-in-air to the breast per shot, and for beam quality. Table 4 shows these values, which apply equally to the craniocaudad and the mediolateral shots.

Table 4 is just the start of the calculation, of course, because the average dose *absorbed* by the breasts is what determines their cancer risk from each shot. We have derived values for the absorbed dose from the basic data of Hammerstein and co-workers (1979); Table 5 shows them.

Lastly, any estimation of cancer risk requires accounting for age at exposure. Table 6 does so.

Table 4. Average Entrance Doses and Beam Qualities for Mammography, as of 1978

Xero-Radiography with Tungsten Target X-Ray Tube:
Entrance Dose = 0.89 roentgen free-in-air
Beam Quality = 1.5 mm Aluminum HVL
Film-Screen Mode with Molybdenum Target X-Ray Tube:
Entrance Dose = 0.73 roentgen free-in-air
Beam Quality = 0.6 mm Aluminum HVL

SOURCE: Based on Rosenstein, 1980.

Table 5. Relationship of Average Absorbed Breast Dose to Beam Quality, per One Roentgen of Entrance Dose Free-in-Air

Asterisks: They denote the average beam quality used in the United States as of 1978 (Rosenstein).

Application: All the entries for absorbed dose are values below 1.0, and will be used as lowering factors.

Half-Value Layer: For the film-screen mode, the *HVL*—which is a property of the beam—is still measured in mm aluminum even though the filters used on the X-ray machine were made of molybdenum.

Beam Quality in mm Al HVL	Average Absorbed Breast Dose in Rads per One Roentgen Entrance Dose FIA (4 cm thickness)	Average Absorbed Breast Dose in Rads per One Roentgen Entrance Dose FIA (6 cm thickness)	Average Absorbed Breast Dose in Rads per One Roentgen Entrance Dose FIA (8 cm thickness)
For Xero-Radiography with tungsten target X-ray tube			
0.3	0.219	0.149	0.114
0.4	0.261	0.182	0.142
0.5	0.284	0.204	0.161
0.6	0.309	0.227	0.179
0.7	0.345	0.253	0.200
0.8	0.371	0.280	0.220
0.9	0.386	0.300	0.235
1.0	0.406	0.315	0.250
1.1	0.428	0.337	0.267
1.2	0.453	0.358	0.288
1.3	0.484	0.383	0.310
1.4	0.516	0.410	0.332
1.5*	0.530	0.422	0.345
1.6	0.544	0.438	0.359
For Film-Screen Mode with molybdenum target X-ray tube			
0.3	0.167	0.113	0.087
0.4	0.174	0.121	0.095
0.5	0.225	0.162	0.128
0.6*	0.255	0.187	0.147
0.7	0.302	0.222	0.175
0.8	0.339	0.256	0.201
0.9	0.356	0.276	0.217
1.0	0.377	0.292	0.232
1.1	0.400	0.315	0.250

SOURCE: These tables were derived from the basic data of Hammerstein and co-workers (1979), particularly their Figures 4 and 5.

Table 6. Future Breast Cancer Rate from One Rad, by Age at Exposure

Absorbed Dose: The average dose = 1 rad to each breast (the breast-pair), and the rates represent the combined risk generated by *both* breasts from the radiation exposure, not by *each* breast.

Relationship: These values are also found in Special Table B, Chapter 21.

From exposure at age 20:	2,432 per million
From exposure at age 25:	2,402 per million
From exposure at age 30:	2,124 per million
From exposure at age 35:	1,516 per million
From exposure at age 40:	950 per million
From exposure at age 45:	428 per million
From exposure at age 50:	41 per million
From exposure at age 55:	29 per million

With Tables 4, 5, and 6 the ingredients are all at hand to find out what the risk is, so no one anymore need weigh benefits against risks of unknown magnitude. In the next section, we will demonstrate how we used Tables 4, 5, and 6 to obtain the entries for age 20 in the Main Mammography Table, which is located at the end of this chapter. Entries for other ages were obtained in a similar manner. The risk values in the Main Mammography Table are, of course, from average entrance doses and average beam qualities. One can also obtain the risk matching *any* entrance dose or beam quality, by using Tables 5 and 6, as we will demonstrate in Sections 3 and 4 of this chapter.

Section 3: A Checklist and Demonstration

In order to calculate cancer risks from mammography, when such risks are not in the Main Mammography Table, it is very useful to have a standard checklist of steps. Such a checklist is provided below.

Step 1, Assembly of Data: If the items below have been listed, the calculation can be done in a moment, in one unbroken operation.

a. Age of the woman examined.
b. Size of breasts (small, average, large).
c. Method (xerox-tungsten or film-screen-molybdenum).
d. Number of shots to the breast-pair.
e. Entrance dose per shot.
f. Beam quality.

Step 2, Absorbed Dose per Shot: This is the entrance dose from Step 1-e times the lowering factor found in Table 5. It applies to the *pair* of breasts.

Step 3, Risk per Shot: This is the absorbed dose obtained in Step 2 times the risk per rad from Table 6. It applies to the *pair* of breasts.

Step 4, Risk from All Shots: This is the risk value from Step 3 times the number of shots per breast-pair from Step 1-d. If only one breast is examined, the risk obtained in Step 4 must be multiplied by 0.5.

Obtaining Two Entries for the Main Mammography Table

We will demonstrate here how the two entries for age 20, in the Main Mammography Table, were obtained. Users who need values which are not in that table would follow exactly the same steps to obtain them.

Step 1, Assembly of Data: For this illustration, the data will match the specifications for the Main Mammography Table.

   a. Age is 20 years.
   b. Size of breasts is near average, or 6 cm thick under compression.
   c. Methods are both xero-radiography and film-screen mode.
   d. Number of shots is the customary two per breast-pair (two of each breast).
   e. Entrance dose is the average, from Table 4.
   Xerox Mode: 0.89 roentgen FIA.
   Film-Screen Mode: 0.73 roentgen FIA.
   f. Beam quality is the average, from Table 4.
   Xerox Mode: 1.5 mm Al HVL.
   Film-Screen Mode: 0.6 mm Al HVL.

Step 2, Absorbed Dose per Shot: This is Step 1-e times the lowering factor found in Table 5.
Xerox Mode: (0.89 R) $\times$ (0.422 rads per R) = 0.376 rads per shot.
Film-Screen Mode: (0.73 R) $\times$ (0.187 rads per R) = 0.137 rads per shot.

Step 3, Risk per Shot: This is the value from Step 2 times the risk per rad from Table 6.
Xerox Mode: (0.376 rads per shot) $\times$ (2,432 cancers per million, per rad) = 914.43 cancers per million, per shot.
Film-Screen Mode: (0.137 rads per shot) $\times$ (2,432 cancers per million, per rad) = 333.18 cancers per million, per shot.

Step 4, Risk from All Shots: This is the value from Step 3 times the number of shots per breast-pair.

Xerox Mode: (914.43 cancers per million, per shot) × (2 shots) = 1,829 cancers per million, or 1 chance in 547. And this is the risk value entered in the Main Mammography Table at the end of this chapter.

Film-Screen Mode: (333.18 cancers per million, per shot) × (2 shots) = 666 cancers per million, or 1 chance in 1,502. This value, too, is in the Main Mammography Table.

Section 4: "But in My Clinic . . ."— Some Questions and Answers

---

Question 1: For My Clinic, How Would I Modify the Main Table?

I run a clinic where we use xero-radiography, but with much lower doses than average. For instance, for the small breast, we might use an entrance dose of 0.43 roentgen, with a beam quality of 1.2 mm aluminum half-value layer instead of 1.5 mm. Most of the women we examine are age 50 or older. How would I modify the Main Mammography Table to find out risks for my particular patients?

ANSWER: In Chapters 4, 6, and 7, we made conversions and adjustments on cancer rates taken from main tables. Not so, with mammography. The values in the Main Mammography Table should not be adjusted. Instead, the calculations just start from scratch and move down through Steps 1 through 4, as demonstrated in the previous section. With ten lines on a pad of paper, or one unbroken operation on a pocket calculator, it is done. We will use a few extra lines below to insert reminders.

Step 1, Assembly of Data:

a. Age = 50 years.
b. Breast size = small, or 4 cm thick.
c. Method = xerox-tungsten.
d. Number of shots = 2 per breast-pair.
e. Entrance dose = 0.43 R per shot.
f. Beam quality = 1.2 mm Al HVL.

Step 2, Absorbed Dose per Shot: This is Step 1-e times the lowering factor from Table 5. So (0.43 R) × (0.453 rads per R) = 0.1948 rads per shot.

Step 3, Risk per Shot: This is the answer from Step 2 times the risk per rad from Table 6. So (0.1948 rads per shot) × (41 cancers per million, per rad) = 7.986 cancers per million, per shot.

Step 4, Risk from All Shots: This is the answer from Step 3 times the number of shots per breast-pair. So (7.986 cancers per million, per shot) × (2 shots) = 16 cancers per million (rounded off), or 1 chance in 62,500.

Question 2: Why Choose the Riskier Method?

Examining the Main Mammography Table, I notice that the cancer risk is over twice as high from xero-radiography as from the film-screen method. Why would anyone choose to use xero-radiography?

ANSWER: Many radiologists are convinced that they get much better diagnostic information from the xero-radiography method, and that this benefit justifies the higher cancer risk. We describe a test related to this issue in Section 5 of this chapter.

Question 3: Are Such Low Beam Qualities Correct?

I'm wondering about the beam qualities you show for mammography in Table 5, because they are so much lower than the ones in Chapter 5. Am I right? And is Table 5 really right?

ANSWER: Yes, and yes. The beam qualities found useful for mammography are indeed much lower than for most of the routine films and exams.

Section 5: Is the Diagnostic Information Better from One Technique than from Another?

No doubt radiologists have quite a range of opinions about the best way to *test* the diagnostic quality of information from X-ray exams. We report on one method below, but we do not imply that it is the only one.

Fitzgerald and co-workers (1981) surveyed mammographic practice in 61 National Health Service Centers in Great Britain between July 1976 and June 1977. In addition to assessing the surface doses received by patients, they endeavored to assess the quality of the diagnostic information from four different methods (Table 7) of making the examinations.

To test image quality, phantoms were loaded with test pieces which had various shapes, sizes, and compositions corresponding to "water-like, adipose-like, and calcification-like" and simulating female breast tissue. Radiographs of the phantoms were made by each of the four methods. Both physicists and radiologists studied the resulting images to detect the test pieces. They worked out an "image score" for quality, with the best possible value equal to 78. The results are in Table 7.

Table 7. Comparison of Image Quality from Four Types of Mammography

Type of Dose: This table reports *surface* dose to a simulated breast, not
average absorbed dose.
Asterisks: They denote the types of equipment combination covered
in Tables 4 and 5 of this chapter. However, the Fitzgerald study
does not provide beam qualities for the data in Table 7.

Type of Tube-Target and Image-Receptor	Mean Surface Dose ± standard deviation (in rads)	Mean Image Score ± standard deviation (in score units)
*Molybdenum Target with Film Receptor	1.19 ± 0.98	33.0 ± 3.7
Tungsten Target with Film Receptor	0.59 ± 0.30	24.7 ± 5.2
Molybdenum Target with Xerox Receptor	3.26 ± 0.94	40.9 ± 3.0
*Tungsten Target with Xerox Receptor	0.89 ± 0.43	39.4 ± 3.6

As we know from Table 5 of this chapter, beam quality is a major determinant for breasts of their average *absorbed* dose from a given surface dose. In the absence of beam-quality information for Table 7, it is not possible to say whether one method gives a better image score than another for the *same* average absorbed breast dose, which means for the same risk.

But what can be said is that, under the clinical conditions in use in those 61 British centers, the mean image score was definitely the best from xero-radiography with both molybdenum and tungsten target X-ray tubes. The combination of *film* with tungsten target scored so much lower that Fitzgerald and co-workers questioned whether its use at all was justified in clinical practice. Moreover, they found that the combination's poor performance seemed *not* related to the special characteristics of the film used, and *not* related to the presence or absence of a screen. Tungsten targets with *xerox* receptors yielded far superior image scores than did tungsten targets with either the film-screen combination or the film alone.

The tungsten-xerox and the molybdenum-xerox combinations yielded image scores within 4% of each other (39.4 and 40.9). But the surface dose of 3.26 rads for the molybdenum-xerox system is much higher than the 0.89 rads for the tungsten-xerox system. It might well appear that the tungsten-xerox system achieves nearly the same image quality with a much lower dose.

But this appearance could be deceptive if (and we repeat: if) the molybdenum-xerox system could use a much lower beam quality than the tungsten-xerox system. Although the beam qualities were not reported for Table 7, in general the beam qualities used with molybdenum-target tubes have indeed been lower than those used with tungsten-target tubes. If the beam quality used in the molybdenum-xerox system were much lower than in the tungsten-xerox system, then the difference in average absorbed breast doses would be much smaller than the big difference in surface doses. A useful inquiry might compare the image quality from the two xerox systems under circumstances delivering the *same* average absorbed breast dose and thus conferring the *same* risk.

Section 6: Rules Followed in the Main Mammography Table

Separate values are provided for eight ages and for the Common Exam done by two methods. The following statements apply to every value.

Common Exam: The Common Exam consists of 2 shots (craniocaudad and mediolateral) to each breast, or 2 shots per breast-pair.

Expression of Risk: The cancer risk is expressed, as it is throughout this book, as the rate of cases resulting from a million such exams, and also as a number compared with 1.0.

Specific Type of Cancer: In this table, the only type of cancer considered is breast cancer. In mammography, the dose to organs other than the breasts is so small, as Rosenstein (1980) has pointed out, that other organs contribute cancer risks which are simply negligible by comparison.

Risk per Pair: The table shows the combined risk generated by both breasts, not by each breast. If only one breast is examined, the risk would be reduced to half.

Breast Size: The risks apply to women with breasts of average size: 6 cm thick under compression (Logan, 1982). The risk for 4-cm and 8-cm breasts ("small" and "large") can also be easily obtained by the steps demonstrated in Section 4 of this chapter.

Doses and Beam Qualities: The ones used in the table for each method are the ones found to be average in the United States as of 1978.

Repeated Exams: A woman's aggregate risk from several exams done at various ages can be obtained by adding the risk *per million* (never the "1 in 547" type of expression).

Rounding Off: For reasons given early in Chapter 5, we minimize the rounding off of risk values.

Section 7: The Main Mammography Table

Xero-Radiography with Tungsten-Target X-Ray Tube

Entrance Dose = 0.89 roentgens, free-in-air
Beam Quality = 1.5 mm Al half-value layer

Age at exam	Resulting Rate of Future Breast Cancer
20 years	1,829 per million = 1 chance in 547
25 years	1,806 per million = 1 chance in 554
30 years	1,597 per million = 1 chance in 626
35 years	1,140 per million = 1 chance in 877
40 years	714 per million = 1 chance in 1,401
45 years	322 per million = 1 chance in 3,106
50 years	31 per million = 1 chance in 32,258
55 years	22 per million = 1 chance in 45,455

Film-Screen Mammography with Molybdenum Target X-Ray Tube

Entrance Dose = 0.73 roentgens, free-in-air
Beam Quality = 0.6 mm Al half-value layer

Age at exam	Resulting Rate of Future Breast Cancer
20 years	666 per million = 1 chance in 1,502
25 years	658 per million = 1 chance in 1,520
30 years	582 per million = 1 chance in 1,718
35 years	415 per million = 1 chance in 2,410
40 years	260 per million = 1 chance in 3,846
45 years	117 per million = 1 chance in 8,547
50 years	11 per million = 1 chance in 90,909
55 years	8 per million = 1 chance in 125,000

CHAPTER 9

Dental X-Ray Examinations

Our objective for dental radiographic examinations is the same as for all other diagnostic X-ray exams: to evaluate the resulting risks of cancer and leukemia, of damaging an embryo in utero, and of genetic injury to children subsequently conceived by the person examined. The last two potential risks from dental exams turn out to be negligible, because the radiation dose to embryo, testes, and ovaries is so very small (please see tables at the end of this chapter). However, an exception to this statement could result from a "leaky" X-ray machine, so it is an attractive practice to protect all of a patient's organs below the jaw with an easily-used lead apron and collar.

Section 1: The Basis of the Risk Tables

To determine the cancer and leukemia risks resulting from dental X-rays, we need two types of dose information: (a) the usual entrance doses, and (b) the number of rads, per roentgen of entrance dose free-in-air, absorbed by the organs in the head and neck, as well as some estimate of dose received by organs below the neck from internal scatter. The first is easy, the second a bit more complicated.

   Entrance doses in dental X-ray exams have decreased markedly dur-

228

ing the past thirty years, partly due to the use of fast films. According to the 1977 NEXT study (see Wochos and Cameron, 1977, 1979), the average entrance dose in the United States is 0.580 roentgens free-in-air, for both the peri-apical and the bitewing shots. They both are intra-oral shots—the film is held inside the mouth—but for the bitewing shot, the film is positioned to show the crowns of some upper and lower teeth on one film, whereas the peri-apical film is positioned to show entire teeth (lower or upper, but not both on the same film) *including* the tips of their roots in the jawbone.

To determine the rads per entrance roentgen, we have found two publications especially useful: the studies by Greer (1972) and by Wall and co-workers (1979). With a combination of information from these two sources, plus an estimate of our own for organs below the neck, we could arrive at reasonable values for the rads per entrance roentgen.

Rads per Entrance Roentgen: A Synthesis

The Greer study was designed to evaluate the effects of cone type and beam quality upon the doses received by the structures in the head and neck during a full-mouth X-ray examination. Using a phantom and thermoluminescent dosimeters, Greer did show small variations in absorbed doses from changes in kilovoltage and type of cone.

For this book, we used his results from an 11.75-inch plastic open-end cone with a lead lining, with which lead washers collimated the diameter of the beam to 2.75 inches at the end of the cone.

Greer provides data for skin doses where the beam enters and exits, and for the thyroid gland, mandible, submandibular glands, parotid glands, maxillary sinus, base of tongue, corneal surface, and sella turcica. But no data are presented for the active bone marrow, from which the leukemia risk can be evaluated.

Wall and co-workers provide data for doses to some other structures in the head and neck and for active bone marrow.

Because both sets of data on rads per roentgen include the tongue, we could use the tongue as a common reference site to normalize one set of data to the other, after both sets were adjusted appropriately to the same beam quality. To the resulting list of absorbed doses, we supplied values for organs below the neck, which are irradiated only by internal scatter (see Chapter 19).

Lastly, we converted the data from a full-mouth exam into values for a *single* dental film, since most dental X-ray exams involve only one or a few shots.

Although obviously shots from the right side, left side, and front, or from higher or lower levels with respect to the teeth, put different tissues into the X-ray beam, the resulting cancer risk hardly differs from one shot to another. This is partly because the human head has the same organs on each side, and partly because circular beams blur the differences in shots by irradiating more area than appears on the rectangular films. It is a very sensible approximation, in our opinion, to consider the risk from any single intra-oral film to be the same, for a given patient.

The final results obtained for rads per entrance roentgen, for a single dental film, are provided in Table 8.

Table 8. Rads to an Adult per Entrance Roentgen from One Average Dental Film

Beam Quality: Beam quality = 2.3 mm Al half-value layer.

Brain: The brain dose was estimated by using half of Greer's value for sella turcica. If this fraction overestimates the brain dose, it will not overestimate the resulting cancer risk by much, because the brain is not among the top sources of risk from this exam (see Section 5 of this chapter).

Gonads: The dose to ovaries and testes would be even lower than to abdominal organs.

Diffuse Organs: Doses to such widely distributed organs as lymphatic tissues, connective tissue, skin, bone, and bone marrow are based upon energy delivered in the head region divided by the total body mass of the particular organs (see Section 1 of this chapter).

Organ	Rads per 1.0 roentgen, free-in-air
Floor of mouth	0.167
Thyroid	0.0092
Salivary glands	0.112
Tongue	0.167
Eyes	0.287
Brain	0.0066
Lips	0.691
Esophagus	0.0005
Pharynx	0.029
Larynx	0.0092
Bronchi	0.001
Other respiratory organs	0.001
Abdominal organs	0.0001
Breast-pair	0.001
Lymphatic tissues	0.0099
Bone, skin, connective tissue	0.0129
Entire active bone marrow	0.0099

Leukemia Risk: The Active Bone Marrow

In Table 8, the value for active bone marrow dose is several times higher than that given by Shleien, who based an estimate on the 1970 national survey. He showed (1977):

Dental (anterior teeth) 0.0029 rads for entrance dose of 1.11 roentgens.

Dental (posterior teeth) 0.0008 rads for entrance dose of 1.17 roentgens.

Even though his entrance doses are not free-in-air (that is, they include backscatter), it is still obvious that our doses from the analysis of the Greer and Wall data are much higher for active bone marrow. We do not know the reason for this disparity. We have used the bone-marrow dose we derived from Greer and Wall for our estimates of leukemia risk in the tables for Dental Exams, and we wish users to know that the risks for *leukemia* would be several times lower if we had used Shleien's rads-per-roentgen values.

Some Confusion over "the Dose from a Dental X-Ray"

Shleien's value of 2.9 millirads (0.0029 rads), as the dose to the active bone marrow from a shot of the front teeth, is the value cited in some leaflets just as "the dose from a dental X-ray." Such leaflets, by failing to distinguish between the active marrow dose (2.9 millirads) and the corresponding entrance dose (approximately 1,000 millirads of skin dose), are bound to create some confusion.

The enormous disparity in dose occurs mostly because the dose delivered to the active bone marrow, during a single dental X-ray, is delivered to only a tiny *fraction* of the body's entire active marrow. But the dose is quite properly averaged over the body's *entire* active marrow because that "organ" is believed to be uniformly leukemogenic. It would be the same if it were possible for an X-ray shot to deliver 1 rad to ¼ of of the stomach. The dose to the *entire* stomach would be reported as ¼ rad, if stomach tissue is considered to be about uniformly cancer-prone. In fact, it is not possible, due to internal scattering of energy (see Chapters 10 and 19), to deliver 1 rad exclusively to ¼ of the stomach; but for a widely distributed "organ" such as the bone marrow, it nearly is.

Section 2: The Full-Mouth Dental Exam

The number of single films taken during the Full-Mouth Dental Exam varies from place to place, and from patient to patient. One of us recently wanted a Full-Mouth Exam, and the routine version included 27 separate films. Greer used 21. Some exams, especially for children, use fewer.

Because the tables at the end of this chapter include the *single* intra-oral film, the risk from any Full-Mouth Exam—no matter which number of single films it uses—can be readily obtained by simple multiplication. We have done the calculation for a Full-Mouth Exam consisting of 16 single films as a demonstration, but we do not imply that 16 represents some standard number. The number varies.

Full-Mouth Dental Exam Compared with Skull Exam

Many users of this book may be surprised that a 16-film Full-Mouth Dental Exam confers a cancer risk which is about 2-fold worse than a full Skull Exam (Chapter 5). In the dental office, each film looks so very small compared with the whole skull. But when the numbers for comparative cancer risk are analyzed, they make perfect sense.

First, the cancer risks from the Full-Mouth Dental Exam are based on 16 films, compared with 4 films for the usual Skull Exam. Second, the dental films focus 16 times on the pharynx and buccal cavity sites, whose combined rate of spontaneous cancer is far greater than the brain's spontaneous rate. Third, the area really exposed during each dental X-ray is larger than the tiny film reveals, because the film fits *within* a circular beam which is 2.75 inches in diameter, as suggested below:

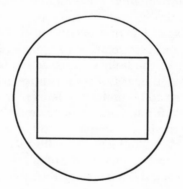

And lastly, the cancer values from the dental films are based on a higher entrance dose than the entrance doses for the skull films.

The risk from frequent Full-Mouth Exams is certainly not trivial for younger people (especially males), and therefore we call attention to two opportunities to lower the risk *without* giving up the perfectly obvious benefits which dental X-rays can confer. One opportunity is for dental offices to take the low-cost, practical steps discussed in Chapter 16 to measure their doses and reduce them (unless the doses are already well below average), and then to speak up so that people will know how to *find* those particular offices. The other opportunity is for patients and parents to avoid any office where they or their children might possibly receive doses 50-fold and even 100-fold higher than necessary (Section 4 of this chapter). Neither remedy means giving up *any* desirable dental X-ray exams.

Section 3: Pantomography
Compared with Single Films

The pantomographic technique, used in dental radiography, provides an image of the entire set of teeth on a single film, with all teeth visible from root to crown. The whole process takes only a minute or two to complete, and requires little expertise on the part of the operator because the alignment of the X-ray tube and the film is automatic.

Wall and co-workers point out that the most widely used technique for acquiring similar diagnostic information involves taking between 11 and 14 intra-oral films, each of which requires the operator accurately to align the X-ray tube, the patient, and the film. But, as we shall see below, the notion that extra-oral pantomographic film and intra-oral single films deliver similar diagnostic information is hotly under challenge.

The various brands of pantomographic equipment operate somewhat differently, but the basic principle is the same in that the X-ray tube and film cassette, which are horizontally opposite each other on either side of the patient's head, rotate around the head so that a narrow beam of X-ray scans simultaneously across the patient's teeth and the film. Among the brands, differences in beam geometry and scanning motions may significantly affect the distribution of absorbed dose within different parts of the head.

In addition to pantomography's attractive simplicity of operation, the claim is widely made that the technique delivers a smaller net dose of radiation than conventional Full-Mouth Exams. It is acknowledged that *some* organs may receive higher doses from some pantomographic techniques than they do from conventional radiography, but the claim is made that the net dose to organs of the head and neck is lower, and therefore the cancer risk is lower.

Valachovic and Lurie (1980) have questioned whether the use of pantomography really results in lower radiation doses from dentistry. They assert that, in practice, it probably *increases* the "radiation burden," and they show little enthusiasm for pantomography in dentistry:

It is our contention that although there are specific clinical indications for an extra-oral panoramic film, the vast majority of panoramic radiographs taken in the United States are inappropriate, unnecessary, and potentially inaccurate and confusing. Extra-oral panoramic radiology substantially adds to the population radiation burden with little if any concomitant benefit to the patients. (p. 141.)

Their objection, over and above their severe doubt that the dose is truly any lower than from conventional film systems, is that the diagnostic quality of information achieved simply is not good enough. They state:

Perhaps the greatest excess contribution to the patient radiation exposure from panoramic radiography occurs when suspected positive findings on panoramic films generally require additional plain films [conventional intra-oral films] to be taken. These films are needed to clearly demonstrate and define suspicious positive findings which are poorly shown on the panoramic film due to its inherent distortion. The plain films usually could have been ordered at the outset if a thorough clinical and historical evaluation were obtained, and would have demonstrated the pathology without the need for the panoramic film. Additionally, panoramic artifacts in the midline and molar regions suggest the presence of pathology and require plain films which reveal nothing more than normal anatomy. (p. 142.)

Wall and co-workers emphatically confirm that the conventional intra-oral technique does deliver superior diagnostic detail. But they are favorably impressed with the utility of the pantomographic technique, and suggest that its use as a screening method can significantly reduce the number of conventional films needed.

Section 4: The Hundred-Fold Variation in Dose

The controversy over whether pantomography does or does not deliver a lower dose than a full-mouth intra-oral exam hinges, in part, on comparability in procedures. For example, if one technique is using the best high-speed films and the other is not, then an inherent superiority of one over the other cannot be tested. Moreover, if one ponders the information in Table 9 below, which reports a 100-fold range in doses from intra-oral films, one has to ask about pantomography: lower doses than *whose* intra-oral films?

Wochos and Cameron, in their analysis of NEXT data for the years

Table 9. Variation in Entrance Doses for Dental Films

| Number of Institutions Studied | Projection | Exposure (Roentgens Free-in-Air) | | |
		Mean	Standard Deviation	Maximum/ Minimum
1,408	Dental Bitewing	0.650	0.727	100 to 1
759	Dental Periapical	0.644	0.696	100 to 1

Note: Mean exposure fell to 0.580 R when data from 1975 had been analyzed (1979 paper).

1972–1974, reported in 1977 and 1979 on the very wide range in entrance dose among facilities for ostensibly the same procedure. Table 9 shows their values (1977) for the common single films.

With a standard deviation exceeding the mean itself, it is no mystery that certain workers are skeptical about claims that one technique produces a lower dose than another in practice. So much depends upon who is doing each procedure, and with what equipment and film.

Wochos and Cameron found another very important point, namely that measured entrance doses were markedly lower with increased peak kilovoltage, at least up to 80 kVp. They recommend that the higher voltage be used, provided image quality is not sacrificed.

In their 1979 paper, in which they provide additional analysis of NEXT data, Wochos and Cameron show that, for dental bitewing shots, the ratio of actually measured dose to theoretical dose (assumed or calculated) ranges from 0.1 to 4.0. In other words, they found that true doses ranged from 10 times *lower* than calculated from manuals, to 4 times *higher.* They attribute this 40-fold range to X-ray units whose calibration has become misadjusted with respect to peak kilovoltage, milliamperage, or both.

Because calculated doses can be so grossly misleading, Wochos and Cameron strongly recommend that doses simply be measured, with inexpensive pen dosimeters or thermoluminescent dosimeters (see Chapter 16 of this book). Getting *reliable* information about the true magnitude of entrance doses is an essential part of *minimizing* such doses for the patients, in both dentistry and medicine.

Section 5: Rules Followed
in the Tables for Dental Exams

There are two sets of tables. The first provides risk information about a single intra-oral film, and the second, about a Full-Mouth Exam consisting of 16 single films. Both sets of tables begin at age 5.

The Basic Shot: The risk is treated as equal from all individual intra-oral films, regardless of which part of the dentition is examined (Section 1 of this chapter).

Type of Cone: Risks are based on the use of an 11.75-inch plastic open-end cone with a lead lining (Section 1 of this chapter).

Field Size: Field size for adults is a circular beam with a diameter of 2.75 inches.

Multiple Shots: The risk from exams consisting of 2, 5, 8, or any other number of shots can be obtained by simply multiplying the risk from the Single Film Exam by the number of shots. Such multiplication is performed always on the *risk per million,* never on the "1 in 2,000" type of expression. *Example:* the cancer risk to a 15-year-old male from 7 single films would be 7 × 67 per million = 469 per million. By the "recipe" boxed in Chapter 1, the risk can also be stated as 1 chance in 2,132.

Full-Mouth Exam: The risk from a Full-Mouth Exam consisting of *more* than 16 shots can be obtained in the same way just demonstrated above. *Example:* the cancer risk to a 15-year-old male resulting from 21 single films would be 21 × 67 per million = 1,407 per million = 1 chance in 711. Another way is to multiply the aggregate risk from 16 films (the entry in the Full-Mouth Exam table) by the appropriate raising factor, which is the actual number of shots divided by 16. *Example:* 1,072 per million from the Full-Mouth Exam table × (21 shots / 16 shots) = 1,072 per million × 1.3125 = 1,407 per million.

Organs Generating Most Cancer Risk:

Males: Lips, tongue, mouth, eyes, pharynx.

Females: Mouth, lips, tongue, eyes, salivary glands, lymphatic tissues.

Section 6: The Tables for the Dental Exams

AGE 5
DENTAL—SINGLE FILM

Testes, dose CE: < < 1 mrad
Ovaries, dose CE: < < 1 mrad

Common Exam (CE): Bitewing or peri-apical
Rate of future *leukemia* from Common Exam:
        Males: 0.69 per million = 1 in 1.4 million
        Females: 0.44 per million = 1 in 2.3 million

Rate of future *cancer* from Common Exam:
      Males: 101 per million = 1 in 9,900
      Females: 50 per million = 1 in 20,000

Per Shot	Ent Dose	Beam HVL	Male Cancer Risk	Female Cancer Risk
Basic	0.237 R	2.3 mm Al	101 per million	50 per million

AGE 10
DENTAL—SINGLE FILM

Testes, dose CE: < < 1 mrad
Ovaries, dose CE: < < 1 mrad

Common Exam (CE): Bitewing or peri-apical
Rate of future *leukemia* from Common Exam:
      Males: 0.88 per million = 1 in 1.1 million
      Females: 0.56 per million = 1 in 1.8 million
Rate of future *cancer* from Common Exam:
      Males: 107 per million = 1 in 9,350
      Females: 46 per million = 1 in 21,740

Per Shot	Ent Dose	Beam HVL	Male Cancer Risk	Female Cancer Risk
Basic	0.358 R	2.3 mm Al	107 per million	46 per million

AGE 15
DENTAL—SINGLE FILM

Testes, dose CE: < < 1 mrad
Ovaries, dose CE: < < 1 mrad

Common Exam (CE): Bitewing or peri-apical
Rate of future *leukemia* from Common Exam:
      Males: 1 per million = 1 in one million
      Females: 0.63 per million = 1 in 1.6 million
Rate of future *cancer* from Common Exam:
      Males: 67 per million = 1 in 14,930
      Females: 26 per million = 1 in 38,500

Per Shot	Ent Dose	Beam HVL	Male Cancer Risk	Female Cancer Risk
Basic	0.478 R	2.3 mm Al	67 per million	26 per million

AGE 20
DENTAL—SINGLE FILM

Testes, dose CE: < < 1 mrad
Ovaries, dose CE: < < 1 mrad
Embryo, dose CE: < < 1 mrad

Common Exam (CE): Bitewing or peri-apical
Rate of future *leukemia* from Common Exam:
      Males: 1.1 per million = 1 in 909,000
      Females: 0.7 per million = 1 in 1.4 million

Age 20, Dental—Single Film *(continued)*

Rate of future *cancer* from Common Exam: (Smokers)
       Males: 70 per million = 1 in 14,300   (CE × 1.03)
       Females: 26 per million = 1 in 38,500   (CE × 1.05)

Per Shot	Ent Dose	Beam HVL	Male Cancer Risk	Female Cancer Risk
Basic	0.580 R	2.3 mm Al	70 per million	26 per million

All values are for the Common Exam—Single Film

Age 25, Dental—One Film   Cancer Rate.............. *(Lowering Factor)*
       Males: 70 per million = 1 in 14,300   (Age 20 × 0.994)
       Females: 26 per million = 1 in 38,500   (Age 20 × 0.988)
Age 30, Dental—One Film   Cancer Rate.............. *(Lowering Factor)*
       Males: 60 per million = 1 in 16,700   (Age 20 × 0.854)
       Females: 23 per million = 1 in 43,500   (Age 20 × 0.873)
Age 35, Dental—One Film   Cancer Rate.............. *(Lowering Factor)*
       Males: 43 per million = 1 in 23,260   (Age 20 × 0.611)
       Females: 16 per million = 1 in 62,500   (Age 20 × 0.623)
Age 40, Dental—One Film   Cancer Rate.............. *(Lowering Factor)*
       Males: 26 per million = 1 in 38,500   (Age 20 × 0.372)
       Females: 10 per million = 1 in 100,000   (Age 20 × 0.391)
Age 45, Dental—One Film   Cancer Rate.............. *(Lowering Factor)*
       Males: 11 per million = 1 in 90,900   (Age 20 × 0.162)
       Females: 4.6 per million = 1 in 217,000   (Age 20 × 0.176)
Age 50, Dental—One Film   Cancer Rate.............. *(Lowering Factor)*
       Males: 1.0 per million = 1 in one million   (Age 20 × 0.015)
       Females: 0.4 per million = 1 in 2.5 million   (Age 20 × 0.017)
Age 55, Dental—One Film   Cancer Rate.............. *(Lowering Factor)*
       Males: 0.7 per million = 1 in 1.4 million   (Age 20 × 0.010)
       Females: 0.3 per million = 1 in 3.3 million   (Age 20 × 0.012)

AGE 5   Testes, dose CE: 1 mrad
DENTAL—FULL MOUTH   Ovaries, dose CE: 1 mrad

Common Exam (CE): 16 single shots
Rate of future *leukemia* from Common Exam:
       Males: 11 per million = 1 in 90,900
       Females: 7 per million = 1 in 143,000
Rate of future *cancer* from Common Exam:
       Males: 1,616 per million = 1 in 619
       Females: 800 per million = 1 in 1,250

AGE 10
DENTAL—FULL MOUTH

Testes, dose CE: 1 mrad
Ovaries, dose CE: 1 mrad

Common Exam (CE): 16 single shots
Rate of future *leukemia* from Common Exam:
        Males: 14 per million = 1 in 71,400
        Females: 9 per million = 1 in 111,000
Rate of future *cancer* from Common Exam:
        Males: 1,712 per million = 1 in 584
        Females: 736 per million = 1 in 1,359

AGE 15
DENTAL—FULL MOUTH

Testes, dose CE: < 1 mrad
Ovaries, dose CE: < 1 mrad

Common Exam (CE): 16 single shots
Rate of future *leukemia* from Common Exam:
        Males: 16 per million = 1 in 62,500
        Females: 10 per million = 1 in 100,000
Rate of future *cancer* from Common Exam:
        Males: 1,072 per million = 1 in 933
        Females: 416 per million = 1 in 2,400

AGE 20
DENTAL—FULL MOUTH

Testes, dose CE: < 1 mrad
Ovaries, dose CE: < 1 mrad
Embryo, dose CE: < 1 mrad

Common Exam (CE): 16 single shots
Rate of future *leukemia* from Common Exam:
        Males: 18 per million = 1 in 55,600
        Females: 11 per million = 1 in 90,900
Rate of future *cancer* from Common Exam: **(Smokers)**
        Males: 1,120 per million = 1 in 893   (CE × 1.03)
        Females: 416 per million = 1 in 2,400   (CE × 1.05)

All values are for the Common Exam—Full Mouth

Age 25, Dental—16 Films   Cancer Rate . . . . *(Lowering Factor)*
        Males: 1,113 per million = 1 in 898   (Age 20 × 0.994)
        Females: 411 per million = 1 in 2,433   (Age 20 × 0.988)
Age 30, Dental—16 Films   Cancer Rate . . . . *(Lowering Factor)*
        Males: 956 per million = 1 in 1,046   (Age 20 × 0.854)
        Females: 363 per million = 1 in 2,755   (Age 20 × 0.873)
Age 35, Dental—16 Films   Cancer Rate . . . . *(Lowering Factor)*
        Males: 684 per million = 1 in 1,462   (Age 20 × 0.611)
        Females: 259 per million = 1 in 3,861   (Age 20 × 0.623)

Dental—Full Mouth *(continued)*

Age 40, Dental—16 Films   Cancer Rate............... *(Lowering Factor)*
        Males: 417 per million = 1 in 2,398   (Age 20 × 0.372)
        Females: 163 per million = 1 in 6,135   (Age 20 × 0.391)
Age 45, Dental—16 Films   Cancer Rate............... *(Lowering Factor)*
        Males: 181 per million = 1 in 5,525   (Age 20 × 0.162)
        Females: 73 per million = 1 in 13,699   (Age 20 × 0.176)
Age 50, Dental—16 Films   Cancer Rate............... *(Lowering Factor)*
        Males: 17 per million = 1 in 58,800   (Age 20 × 0.015)
        Females: 7.1 per million = 1 in 140,800   (Age 20 × 0.017)
Age 55, Dental—16 Films   Cancer Rate............... *(Lowering Factor)*
        Males: 11 per million = 1 in 90,900   (Age 20 × 0.010)
        Females: 5 per million = 1 in 200,000   (Age 20 × 0.012)

CHAPTER 10

Computed (Axial) Tomography Scanning

The examination in diagnostic radiology which produces images of a transverse cross-section of the body, usually in slices about 1 centimeter (10 millimeters) thick, has become familiar under the abbreviation of C.A.T. Scan (sometimes C.T. Scan). This chapter provides a method for estimating future cancer risk from any such examination.

Although C.A.T. scanning equipment has been available for clinical use for a relatively short time, individuals and institutions have produced a number of excellent papers carefully evaluating dosimetry and image quality from the various machines. Perry and Bridges, and McCullough, Payne, Baker, Houser, and Reese were among the pioneers in this effort. In a recent paper from four collaborating institutions, Shope, Morgan, Showalter, Pentlow, Rothenberg, White, and Speller (1982) have reported in detail on the dosimetry, *under usual conditions of clinical practice,* from one or more scanner instruments produced by ten different manufacturers. The instruments have quite different operating parameters.

One of the major differences, involving the X-ray tube's motion, has consequences for the distribution of the dose. In some scanners, the X-ray tube moves through an arc of only 180°, which produces a slice with very uneven surface doses. In some other scanners, the tube moves through an arc of 360°, which produces a slice with more nearly uniform surface doses. Section 3 of this chapter will consider surface dose in more detail.

We will begin, however, by explaining the meaning and derivation of the tables which are located at the end of this chapter, and which are named the Isolated Slice Tables. They tell the future cancer risk from irradiating any isolated slice of the body when the slice's average dose is 1.0 rad. Then we will demonstrate simplified steps for the following procedures:

- How to estimate average doses for isolated slices in clinical practice (Section 3);
- How to estimate the associated dose inevitably scattered into adjacent slices on both sides of an examined slice (Section 4);
- How to evaluate the resulting cancer risk, with scattered dose included, from a scan which examines only one slice (Section 5);
- How to evaluate the cancer risk from any scan which examines multiple slices (Section 6).

Section 1:
Derivation of the Isolated Slice Tables

The meaning of the Isolated Slice Tables arises, of course, from their derivation—which we will explain by discussing a male patient of age 20 years.

Special Table A in Chapter 21 shows the cancer risk generated by each of his organs due to a dose of one rad absorbed by the entire organ or organ system. (Special Table B shows the information for females.) It should be well noted here that the risks in Table A (and B) are from an *absorbed* dose of 1.0 rad, not from an entrance dose, and they apply to *entire* organs or organ systems. For C.A.T. scanning, we must deal with risks from irradiated *slices* of organs rather than from organs irradiated in their entirety. Therefore, we need appropriate lowering factors for the entries in Table A.

The first step is to ascertain what *fraction* of each organ resides in each successive 1-centimeter slice of an adult male. Let us start with the highest point or vertex of his skull, and then move 1 centimeter at a time along his body's craniocaudad (head-to-tail) axis until we reach the lowest part of his pelvis. We choose 1 centimeter because the slices used clinically are of that order (some as thin as 3 millimeters, and others as thick as 14 millimeters). Moreover, 1 centimeter will provide the most convenient unit when our findings are adjusted for slices of other widths.

By consulting an atlas of anatomy, we can learn the vertical dimensions for each and every organ of the average person's head, thorax, abdomen, and pelvis. (Non-average individuals are discussed later.)

Let us suppose that a particular organ starts at 3 centimeters from the vertex and extends to 6 centimeters from the vertex. Then its vertical dimension would be 3 centimeters. If the organ were a perfect cube of 3 centimeters along every edge, then a dose of one rad absorbed by a slice *one* centimeter thick would produce a cancer risk equal to *one-third* of the entry for cancer risk in Special Table A. The lowering factor would be 0.33 for that particular organ.

But nature seems unconcerned with human convenience, and so we won't find any organ which is a perfect cube. For example, the liver and pancreas have shapes quite different from the cube. We must therefore take account of every organ's shape as we go from one centimeter to the next. For the liver, the slices nearer to the head contain a much larger fraction of the organ than do the more distant slices, due to the liver's wedge-like shape. The same is true for the pancreas; a larger share of the pancreas is encompassed in slices nearer to the head than in those more distant.

The lowering factors needed for the risks in Special Table A are no different, in principle, for irregularly shaped organs than for perfect cubes. The issue is, what *fraction* of the total organ is present in a particular slice to be scanned? Of course, a more refined treatment—not practical at this time—would take into account anything known about regions of an organ which generate the organ's spontaneous cancer at *different* rates. But we will make the approximation that each organ is uniformly cancer-prone. This simplifying assumption seems reasonable in every case, especially for organs which are scanned nearly in their entirety during a multi-scan examination.

Therefore, whenever a particular slice encompasses, for example, one-fifth (or 0.2) of an organ's entire mass, and whenever that slice absorbs one rad, then we will say that the partial organ in the slice will generate a cancer risk equal to one-fifth (or 0.2) of the rate entered in Special Table A for the whole organ. The appropriate lowering factor for Table A's entry would be 0.20 in such a case.

To derive the Isolated Slice Tables, we have estimated what fraction of each organ of the head, thorax, abdomen, and pelvis resides in each 1-centimeter slice (from vertex of the head to the base of the pelvis) for adults and for ages 5, 10 and 15 years.

To derive an entry for one slice in one table, the second step is to obtain the separate cancer risk generated by *each* partial organ irradiated within that one slice. So for each partial organ in the slice, the corresponding entry in Special Table A (or B) is multiplied by the fraction of the organ irradiated.

The third and final step, to obtain the cancer risk arising from the whole slice, is *addition* of all the risks contributed separately by the partial organs.

Seeing for Oneself

Both the second and third steps can be clearly seen by any reader who turns now to the Isolated Slice Table for age-20 males, at the end of this chapter. Let us consider the slice at position 23-24 cm. The total cancer risk, in the column near the far right, is given as 85 (per million). And this is the sum of the entries to its left: 21 from thyroid, 52 from larynx, 5 from esophagus, 4 from lymphatic tissues, and 3 from bone, connective tissue, and skin = 85 (per million).

Readers who examine Chapter 19 will quickly realize that the Isolated Slice Tables are derived according to the same principles as all the other tables in this book.

For C.A.T. scanning, however, a special approximation has been made, and it is this: all the partial organs located within a scanned slice receive the *same average dose* regardless of where they reside within that slice. It will be clear, from Section 3 of this chapter, that this simplifying assumption is not as good for 180° scanners as it is for 360° models. However, at this stage of scanning's development, the assumption seems reasonable to us because it permits the provision of "first cut" risk estimates for immediate use in countless benefit-risk decisions.

The procedures, calculations, and approximations described above, in combination, make it possible to produce tables of cancer risk per 1-centimeter slice, from the vertex to the base of the pelvis, for males and females of all ages, for any average dose absorbed. We have chosen one rad as the reference dose for the Isolated Slice Tables at the end of this chapter. For actual exams, if the average dose in a slice is greater than one rad, the cancer risk simply goes up in direct proportion; if it is below one rad, the risk goes down in direct proportion.

As noted in this chapter's introduction, the tables' entries do not show the full cancer risk from scans of a single slice because they exclude the risk induced in adjacent slices. The word "isolated" in the name of the tables may serve as a reminder. The risk added by the two slices on each side of a scanned slice is not negligible. The combined dose to these four slices can be about equal to the dose which the scanned slice absorbs, as Section 4 of this chapter shows. How much the dose increment adds to the cancer risk depends, in each case, on what organs which were located in the *scanned* slice may have disappeared two centimeters away, and which other organs may have appeared. For instance, if the reader returns to the Isolated Slice Table for age-20 males, and compares the slice at position 23–24 cm with the slice at position 24–25 cm, he or she will see the disappearance of the larynx and the appearance of the bronchi (lungs).

Patients of Other Sizes

The Isolated Slice Tables might appear at first glance to apply only to people of exactly the same length. Not at all. Physicians hardly rely on tape measures to locate organs, and so they will certainly be able to identify which lines in the tables correspond with patients, regardless of their length. The first thing which physicians and other users must look for in the Isolated Slice Tables is a column showing the upper and lower edges of an organ to be scanned; they should pay no attention at first to the columns showing the distance from the vertex.

An example will illustrate. If a user is interested in estimating the cancer risk from scanning the top side of a 20-year-old male's liver, he or she simply finds the row in the age-20 male table where the liver appears: the row at 46–47 cm. The risk for that row, 31 cancers per million, applies no matter how far the top side of a particular patient's liver actually lies from his vertex. Only slight errors will be introduced by using the tables for patients of various lengths.

If the situation warrants, even those errors can be eliminated. The key is for the user of the Isolated Slice Tables to note that the total for every column matches the entry for the same organ in Special Table A or B (Chapter 21) for the corresponding age-sex category. For instance, in the age-20 male Isolated Slice Table, the total cancer risk at the bottom of the *stomach* column is 333 (per million) from an absorbed dose of 1.0 rad. In Special Table A, the corresponding entry is also a stomach-cancer rate per absorbed rad of 333 per million for age-20 males. The Isolated Slice Table has simply divided the risk from irradiating the *whole* stomach into shares appropriate for 1-cm slices. The way to adjust a table for a particularly tall person is to distribute the total risks from the exposed organs over more slices; for very short people, over fewer slices.

Users who redistribute an organ's risk over more (or fewer) centimeters have a simple way to prevent errors: check the vertical totals, which should not change. Of course, the *horizontal* totals for single slices may very well change; the whole purpose of the adjustment is to obtain new risks per slice for non-standard patients.

Some patients have an organ in a peculiar *position.* In the human, the positions of the stomach, large intestine, uterus, and female breast vary within limits. We have used the same generalization about the female breast as Meschan (1973): we locate none of it below the diaphragm. For patients with an organ unusually located, it would be very easy to adjust the risk per slice by moving whole columns up or down a few centimeters and adding horizontally along the affected rows to obtain adjusted values for the "Totals" column near the far right.

Section 2:
Risks Which Differ by a Factor of 11,200

Some remarkable information emerges from the column of total risks near the far right of each Isolated Slice Table. There is eye-popping variation in riskiness among slices within one person (one table).

For instance, more than a 10-fold difference occurs in the head of a male adult. In the table for the 20-year-old male, very close to the vertex we find the first risk as 5 cancers per million, from one rad absorbed by the slice between 1–2 cm. If we ask where the 5 comes from, a search of all the columns from left to right shows that 4 come from a small fraction of the brain (far left column) and that 1 comes from the combined bone, connective tissue, and skin in that slice. When we move down to the position 9–10 cm from the vertex, the total cancer risk jumps to 30 cancers per million due to the cancer risks from brain, eyes, lymphatic tissues, bone, connective tissue, and skin. In the slice 11–12 cm from the vertex, the total cancer risk per rad rises to 66 per million because the risks from the buccal cavity and nasopharynx are quite appreciable, and their sum grossly exceeds what is subtracted as the brain's contribution is decreasing.

In a similar manner, we can examine how total cancer risk varies for each successive slice, and observe the relatively large variation as contributions from some organs disappear and those from other organs come in.

At 49–50 cm from the vertex, the marked increase to a total cancer risk of 100 per million is the result of major contributions to risk from stomach, liver, and pancreas. At 86–87 cm from the vertex, the prostate enters the slice and increases the risk enormously to a total of 1,035 cancers per million.

The reader may have noticed that, per slice, the bronchi contribute less risk than several other organs. There are two reasons. First, all the tabulations in this book are for non-smokers. Second, the lungs are distributed among many slices, so their contribution to cancer risk is likewise distributed; the *total* at the bottom of the bronchi column matches expectation.

For the 20-year-old female, the Isolated Slice Table tells a different story about future cancer risk from C.A.T. scans delivering an average dose of 1 rad to a 1-cm slice. Between 26 and 38 cm from the vertex, where the central part of the breast is located, the risk rises to 251 per million per slice. In the slices between positions 49 and 52, the contribution from the pancreas produces a relatively large risk per slice, and again between 59 and 64 cm there is a bulge in risk because of contributions from the stomach, large intestine, and kidney. The region between 79 and 88 cm from the vertex also has high values per slice because of the cancer risk contributed by the rectum, bladder, uterus (cervix and corpus) and ovaries. In the two slices between 85 and 87 cm from the vertex, the total cancer risk per slice rises to 364 per million, the highest value for slices anywhere in the 20-year-old female, from the vertex to the base of the pelvis.

For every age-sex category, the totals at the bottoms of all the columns let us compare how much different organs or organ systems can contribute to cancer risk from C.A.T. scanning.

The tables for the pediatric years show the cancer risks per slice to be higher, of course. Not only does the risk of cancer per rad rise with decreasing age, but each 1-centimeter slice encompasses a larger fraction of each particular organ as we consider younger and younger ages.

Examination of the Isolated Slice Tables can leave no doubt that the particular region scanned makes a very large difference, for the patient, in the risk of serious delayed side-effects. For the 20-year-old male, the cancer risk per slice per rad ranges from 5 per million to 1,035 per million, more than a 200-fold difference. For the 20-year-old female, the range is from 4 per million to 364 per million, roughly a 90-fold difference in risk per slice.

What becomes obvious is that it is inappropriate to speak about "the cancer risk from C.A.T. scanning" without clearly specifying *what* region of *whose* body is being scanned.

Only Numbers Tell the Story

It would be hard to overestimate the value of destroying the myth that a particular *type* of diagnostic X-ray procedure produces the largest hazard of future cancer. Previous chapters demonstrated the huge range of risk from other procedures.

The same point can be strikingly illustrated for C.A.T. scanning by comparing the total future cancer risks per slice per rad for the *least* sensitive torso region of a male 50 years old and the *most* sensitive torso region of a male 5 years old.

For the male 50 years old, at 44–45 cm from the vertex, near the lowest border of the esophagus, the risk per slice per rad is 0.27 cancers per million. This is 1 chance in 3.7 million. For the male 5 years old, at 55–56 cm from the vertex, where the prostate gland is located, the risk per slice per rad is 3,035 cancers per million. This is 1 chance in 330. Risks from scattered dose are excluded in both examples.

The risk from a single torso slice scanned can be 3,035 / 0.27, or *about 11,200 times higher* in one region of a male 5 years old than it is in another region of a male 50 years old.

Section 3:
Estimating Dose within an Isolated Slice

Scanning equipment in use falls into two major categories: in one, the X-ray tube moves through an arc of 180 degrees, and in the other, through 360 degrees. There are also some variations on these possibilities. Shope and co-workers (1982) point out that some of the nominally 360° systems may expose the patient during more than a 360° rotation of the source (the X-ray beam). This phenomenon, known as "overscan," results in exposure of narrow regions to higher doses than expected. Some other operating modes of 360° scanners expose the patient during less than 360° of source rotation. Shope points out that then the dose distribution resembles the distribution from the 180° systems, even though the scanner is a 360° machine.

The 360° scanner, when really scanning over the whole 360°, produces a rather uniform surface or near-surface radiation dose, since all parts of a slice's surface are near the X-ray source at some point during the rotation. From 180° scanners, the distribution of the near-surface dose is much less uniform, of course.

From both types of scanners, the dose at the center of the slice is of course lower than the dose near most surfaces (see the diagrams). The size of the dose difference is affected, as we shall see, by the diameter of the slice and the low density of the lungs.

The size of the difference has a consequence for estimates of cancer risk. When we take an *average* of a slice's center dose and its mean near-surface dose, the smaller the difference between the two doses, the better their average approximates the true doses received everywhere throughout the slice.

Shope and co-workers (1982) conducted dosimetry studies using several scanners, several scanning modes, and several types of phantom (head, torso, and a special thorax model). From their Figure 5, for a torso model of Plexiglas, we have the types of diagram shown in Figures 1 and 2.

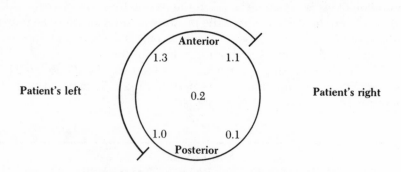

Figure 1

Scanner Type: EMI CT 5005 is operating in the 180° mode, with a
1.3-cm slice. The arc outside the phantom shows the travel of the
X-ray tube.

Phantom Type: The body is a Plexiglas phantom of 32 cm diameter.

Dose Distribution: The doses were measured 1 cm inside the surface
and at the center of the slice. All doses are in rads.

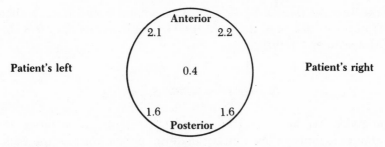

Figure 2

Scanner Type: General Electric CT/T 8800 is operating in the 360°
  mode, with a 1.0-cm slice.
Phantom Type: The body is a Plexiglas phantom of 32 cm diameter.
Dose Distribution: The doses were measured 1 cm inside the surface
  and at the center of the slice. All doses are in rads.

In the 360° scanning mode, the near-surface doses are lower in the
patient's back (both measurements = 1.6 rads) than in the front (2.1 and
2.2 rads) because the support structures underneath the patient absorb
some of the energy in beams entering from the back. Nevertheless, the
360° scanning mode clearly produces a much more uniform dose near the
surface than does the 180° mode.

Abdominal-Pelvic Dose—360° Scanning

The following procedure will produce a reasonable approximation of the
average dose absorbed by organs in any region below the chest from
360° scanning. We shall use Figure 2 to illustrate.
  First, we average the four near-surface doses:

$$\frac{2.1 + 2.2 + 1.6 + 1.6}{4} = 1.88 \text{ rads}$$

as the mean near-surface dose. Next, we average the mean near-surface
dose of 1.88 rads and the center dose of 0.4 rads:

$$\frac{1.88 + 0.4}{2} = 1.14 \text{ rads}$$

as the average dose.
  We consider this a very reasonable first approximation of the average
dose received by all the partial organs in that slice. Section 1 of this chapter
showed that the Isolated Slice Tables provide cancer-risk values if all the
fractional organs in a 1-cm slice absorb an average dose of 1 rad. So if a

slice receives the dose of 1.14 rads just calculated from Figure 2, then the table's entry would need multiplication by 1.14. Section 5 of this chapter provides a fuller context.

Thorax Dose—360° Scanning

Shope and co-workers point out that, at the center of a special *thorax* phantom containing a low-density material which imitates the lung, the dose is very much closer to the near-surface dose than Figure 2 shows for the *body* phantom containing tissue-equivalent Plexiglas. They suggest that, for the same near-surface dose, the center dose in the thorax would be about three times higher than in the abdomen.

Using Figure 2 again, we therefore raise the center dose for the thorax to about 1.2 rads, then average it with the mean near-surface dose of 1.88 rads, and obtain an average absorbed dose of 1.54 rads, which must be exceedingly close to the dose actually experienced by the organs within the chest.

Head Dose—360° Scanning

Figure 3 below comes from the data of Shope and co-workers for head scanning with the 360° system.

As expected for a body region with a small diameter, the center dose for the head is much closer to the near-surface doses than it was in the abdominal-pelvic body phantom. However, the near-surface dose to the left anterior region is 3.0 rads, a measurement higher than the other

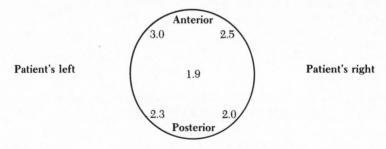

Figure 3
Scanner Type: Ohio Nuclear Delta is operating in the 360° mode, with a 1.0-cm slice.
Phantom Type: The head is a Plexiglas phantom of 16 cm diameter.
Dose Distribution: The doses were measured 1 cm inside the surface and at the center of the slice. All doses are in rads.

near-surface doses. The reason cited by Shope and co-workers is "over-scan." The dose disparity would not occur in most 360° head scans.

The first step toward obtaining the average dose per slice for head scans is, as usual, to average the four near-surface doses. With Figure 3 serving as an illustration, that operation yields a mean near-surface dose of 2.45 rads, which we average in the second step with the center dose of 1.9 rads. The result is an average absorbed dose of 2.18 rads to all the fractional organs in a particular slice.

For head and neck scanning, this procedure should yield very good approximations indeed.

Effect from Body-Size and Age

The head phantom demonstrates that the difference between a slice's center dose and mean near-surface dose is small when the slice's diameter is small. Evidence confirms logic on this matter. Similarly, one can antici-pate that there will be a much smaller difference between center and near-surface doses when the abdomen or pelvis of a child (or small adult) is scanned than when the same region of a large adult is scanned. The smaller the person scanned, the more nearly do all organs in a slice receive the same dose, and the more closely does a slice's average dose match the doses truly received by each organ.

Average Doses—180° Scanning

We will use the same two steps for 180° as for 360° scanning: finding the mean near-surface dose, and then averaging it with the center dose. We will refer back to Figure 1 earlier in this section to provide an illustration of a 180° scan.

Averaging the four near-surface doses (1.3, 1.1, 1.0, and 0.1 rads), we obtain a mean near-surface dose of 0.9 rad. Averaging that and the center dose of 0.2 rad, we obtain an average dose for the slice of 0.55 rad.

In this illustration, the dose to organs in the left anterior region will be underestimated the most, and the dose to the right posterior organs will be overestimated the most. The consequently overestimated and under-estimated cancer risks from the fractional organs in those regions will tend to balance each other out, but will not do it perfectly. That is why we have higher confidence in this risk-estimating procedure for 360° scans than for 180° scans.

Nevertheless, it is reasonable to treat this first approximation of aver-age dose per slice as satisfactory, even for the 180° scans, given all the other uncertainties associated with variations in equipment and even in organ positions from person to person.

Doses as Illustrative

The doses we have cited earlier, from Shope and co-workers, represent measured doses delivered by particular machines to phantoms under circumstances which the researchers describe as usual conditions of clinical practice. The doses may or may not be typical. No one claims that they represent nationwide averages from all types of machines on all sizes of patients.

It is likely that the situation prevailing in C.A.T. scanning is similar to the situation prevailing in fluoroscopy and routine X-ray films: huge ranges in dose used for the same exams (Chapters 6, 9, 16).

Section 4: Dose to Adjacent, Unscanned Slices

When we have obtained the average dose to an isolated scanned slice, we have not yet addressed the totality of the dose. In reality, a slice cannot be isolated. It is impossible to prevent radiation from scattering into areas

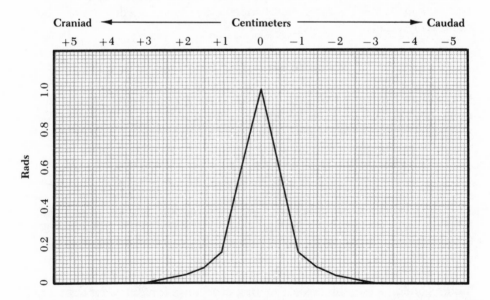

Figure 4-ns. *Dose Profile of a Single-Slice Scan.* This figure shows the *near-surface* distribution of X-rays along the body when a 1-cm slice is scanned. This curve is purely illustrative; such curves vary with different scanners. The maximum dose illustrated is 1.0 rad, which is received at the midline of the scanned slice. The doses in the adjacent unscanned 1-cm slices (+1, +2, −1, −2) come from internal scatter.

of the body above and below the slice which is being scanned. The dose to each 1-cm slice immediately adjacent is much lower than it is to the slice being scanned, but it is not negligible, and its magnitude depends upon the particular scanner used. A very much lower dose is received by tissues *two* centimeters away from the slice being scanned. For slices *three* centimeters away on each side of the scanned slice, Shope and co-workers report that the dose from internal scatter is negligible for the near-surface regions and somewhat larger in the center region. Such terms as "low" are not absolute, of course; they simply indicate a magnitude *relative* to the dose in the scanned slice.

Since internal scatter has a significant impact on cancer risk from C.A.T. scanning, we are not entitled to walk away from this problem just because it is messy. Instead, we will provide some simplifying assumptions which we think have practical value.

We will start by referring to two figures commonly called dose profiles: Figure 4-ns (ns for near-surface) and Figure 4-ctr (ctr for center). Dose profiles vary for beams from different types of equipment, and must be provided for particular machines by manufacturers or radiation physicists. Our figures are simply illustrative, and are based on McCullough and Payne (1978), from their discussion of multi-slice scans. McCullough and

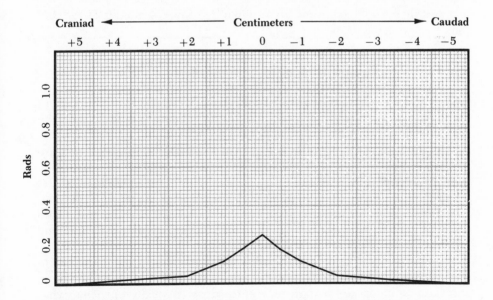

Figure 4-ctr. *Dose Profile of a Single-Scan Slice.* This figure shows the dose distribution at the *center* of the body from the same scan illustrated in Figure 4-ns. The maximum dose is 0.24 rad, which is received at the midline of the scanned slice. The doses in the adjacent unscanned 1-cm slices (+1, +2, +3, −1, −2, −3) come from internal scatter.

Payne show a range of 0.5 to 19.5 rads as the maximum surface dose for single-slice scans in various scanning modes. Shope and co-workers (1982) observed, in their study of actual clinical practice, a range of below 0.5 rad to about 10 rads as the maximum surface dose for a single-slice scan. Our Figure 4-ns depicts a maximum surface dose of 1.0 rad.

Information from the Dose Profiles

Figure 4-ns shows how the near-surface dose is distributed along the craniocaudad axis, from a single-slice scan, when the maximum near-surface dose is 1.0 rad. The scanned slice is named as "ground 0"; the three 1-cm slices above it, toward the head, are named $+1$, $+2$, and $+3$, and the three 1-cm slices below it, toward the feet, are named -1, -2, and -3. Figure 4-ctr shows the corresponding information for the slice's center dose.

It is obvious from Figure 4-ns that the near-surface dose is not uniform along the line from head to tail, even within the scanned slice; the maximum of 1.0 rad occurs at the scanned slice's midline. (Note that a midline along the head-tail axis has nothing to do with the center of the body or the center dose.) The *average* near-surface dose for the scanned slice is determined from the area under its part of the dose-profile curve, and turns out to be 0.75 rad from this beam. For the center dose of the scanned slice, the maximum value shown by Figure 4-ctr is 0.24 rad, but the average is 0.21 rad.

Uses of the Information

With respect to estimating cancer risk, there are three key points about dose profiles. First, when the dose profile for a beam is known, then the relative magnitude of the average doses it delivers to the scanned slice and to the adjacent slices can also be known; we shall demonstrate this immediately below. Second, because those relative magnitudes are fixed, their ratios provide fixed lowering factors which are applicable to the scanned slice's average dose, no matter what it may be; we shall demonstrate this, too. Third, just one analysis of a profile provides dose ratios which can be used again and again for scans done by that machine; one need not start "from scratch" for each exam.

In Section 3 of this chapter, we showed a two-step process for obtaining a slice's *average* dose: first we obtained the mean near-surface dose, and then we averaged it with the center dose. With dose profiles, what happens is the same, except that the average near-surface dose and the average center dose are determined by areas under the curves. Then these two numbers are averaged. We shall use Figures 4-ns and 4-ctr to illustrate.

For the *scanned* slice, Figure 4-ns provides an average near-surface dose of 0.75 rad and an average center dose of 0.21 rad, so the average dose to the whole scanned slice is 0.48 rad. Using the dose profiles in exactly the same way for adjacent slices, we find the following:

Slice	Average Near-Surface Dose	Average Center Dose	Average Dose to Whole Slice
Scanned slice	0.75 rad	0.21 rad	0.48 rad
+1 or −1	0.2 rad	0.12 rad	0.16 rad
+2 or −2	0.09 rad	0.04 rad	0.065 rad
+3 or −3	negligible	negligible	negligible

These average doses to the adjacent slices enable us to obtain the lowering factors applicable to *any* average dose received by the scanned slice from a particular exam. We obtain the two lowering factors by simple division, as follows:

Slice	Average Dose to Whole Slice	Dose to Unscanned Slice Divided by Dose to Scanned Slice = Lowering Factor
Scanned slice	0.48 rad	——
+1 or −1	0.16 rad	0.16 / 0.48 = 0.33 as the factor
+2 or −2	0.065 rad	0.065 / 0.48 = 0.135 as the factor

To illustrate how to apply these lowering factors, let us suppose that a one-slice exam is contemplated. The radiology staff reports that this machine delivers an average dose to the scanned slice of about 1.75 rads. In a moment, we also know the approximate average dose to the adjacent slices:

Slice	Average Dose to Scanned Slice Times the Lowering Factor = Average Dose to Unscanned Slice
Scanned slice	Average Dose = 1.75 rads (from Radiology)
+1 or −1	Average Dose = 1.75 rads × 0.33 = 0.58 rad
+2 or −2	Average Dose = 1.75 rads × 0.135 = 0.24 rad

As we will show in this chapter's next sections, the average dose to the scanned slice, the lowering factors, and the Isolated Slice Tables at the end of this chapter are the only three ingredients required to evaluate the cancer risk from both single-slice and multi-slice C.A.T. Scan examinations.

Section 5: Incremental Risk
from Adjacent, Unscanned Slices

This section demonstrates the final step which produces the estimated cancer risk from any single-slice scan. This estimate takes account of the incremental risk arising from the unscanned slices.

Tables 10 and 11, which follow, may be useful as models. We use Table 10 to illustrate a scan in the bladder region of a 20-year-old male, and Table 11 to illustrate a scan in his kidney region. Both illustrations presume a scanner with the dose profile shown in Figures 4-ns and 4-ctr. To facilitate comparison, both tables presume the same average dose to the scanned slice: 1.75 rads. The entries in Column 4 for Cancer Rate per Rad come directly from the Isolated Slice Table for 20-year-old males at the end of this chapter. Entries in the Isolated Slice Tables are equally applicable to slices which receive their doses directly from scanning and to slices which receive their doses only from scatter. *The slices don't know the difference.*

How important is the risk generated by scatter into the adjacent, unscanned slices? In Table 10, the adjacent slices added substantially to

Table 10. Cancer Risk from a 1-Slice Bladder Scan

Patient = 20-year-old male, non-smoker
Slice Width = 1 cm
Average Absorbed Dose in Scanned Slice = 1.75 rads (from Radiology)
Lowering Factor for +1 and −1 Slices = 0.33
Lowering Factor for +2 and −2 Slices = 0.135
Column 3: The dose entries come from its middle entry (boxed) multiplied by the appropriate lowering factor.
Column 4: The entries come without alteration from the Isolated Slice Table for 20-year-old males.
Column 5: The entries come from multiplying Column 3 times Column 4.

(1) Slice	(2) Distance from Vertex	(3) Average Dose in Rads	(4) Cancer Rate per Rad	(5) Cancer Risk from the Slice
+2 cm	83–84 cm	0.24	129 per million	31.0 per million
+1 cm	84–85 cm	0.58	187 per million	108.5 per million
Scanned	85–86 cm	1.75	252 per million	441.0 per million
−1 cm	86–87 cm	0.58	1,035 per million	600.3 per million
−2 cm	87–88 cm	0.24	1,034 per million	248.2 per million

Total cancer risk from this single-slice exam = 1,429 per million = 1 chance in 700

Table 11. Cancer Risk from a 1-Slice Kidney Region Scan

Patient = 20-year-old male, non-smoker
Slice Width = 1 cm
Average Absorbed Dose in Scanned Slice = 1.75 rads (from Radiology)
Lowering Factor for +1 and −1 Slices = 0.33
Lowering Factor for +2 and −2 Slices = 0.135

(1)	*(2)*	*(3)*	*(4)*	*(5)*
Slice	*Distance from Vertex*	*Average Dose in Rads*	*Cancer Rate per Rad*	*Cancer Risk from the Slice*
+2 cm	53–54 cm	0.24	92 per million	22.1 per million
+1 cm	54–55 cm	0.58	93 per million	53.9 per million
Scanned	55–56 cm	1.75	93 per million	162.8 per million
−1 cm	56–57 cm	0.58	93 per million	53.9 per million
−2 cm	57–58 cm	0.24	94 per million	22.6 per million

Total cancer risk from this single-slice exam
= 315.3 per million
= 1 chance in 3,172

the risk: 1,429 minus 441 = 988 cancers per million from the adjacent slices. In this case, the unscanned slices contributed far *more* to the overall cancer risk than did the scanned slice, because the adjacent slices on one side involved the high-risk region containing the prostate. In Table 11, also, the unscanned slices caused a big share of the risk: 315.3 minus 162.8 = 152.5 cancers per million, an incremental risk nearly as large as the risk from the scanned slice. Obviously, serious errors would result from neglecting the radiation-induced cancer risk arising in unscanned slices due to scattered dose.

Section 6: Evaluating Risk from Multi-Slice Exams

Many C.A.T. Scan exams involve more than one slice. If five slices are scanned, not only does the central slice provide radiation to adjacent slices, but the adjacent slices each receive their own dose and provide some radiation to the central slice. In Figures 5-ns and 5-ctr, the overlapping curves show the way the five slices add radiation to each other.

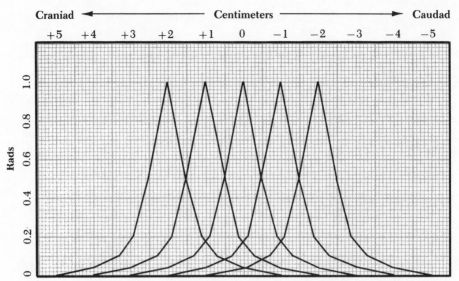

Figure 5-ns. *Dose Profile of a Multi-Slice Scan.* This figure shows the near-surface distribution of dose from scanning five adjacent 1-cm slices. Each of the five scans distributes dose into adjacent slices in the same manner as does the single scan depicted in Figure 4-ns because, in Figure 5-ns, each separate scan is identical to the one in Figure 4-ns except for its location.

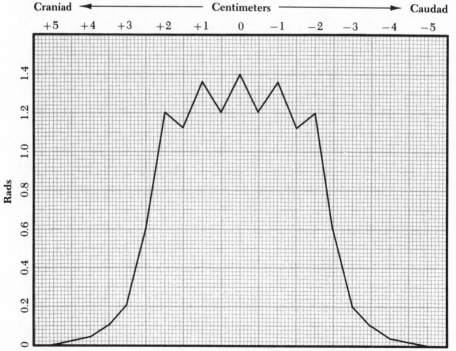

Figure 6-ns. *Dose Profile of a Multi-Slice Scan.* This figure shows exactly the same information as Figure 5-ns, but the doses which overlapped in Figure 5-ns have been piled on top of each other here. The maximum near-surface dose in all five scanned slices now *exceeds* 1.0 rad because each scanned slice receives scattered dose from adjacent scanned slices.

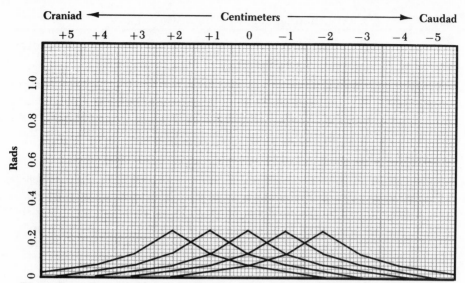

Figure 5-ctr. *Dose Profile of a Multi-Slice Scan.* This figure shows the dose distribution at the *center* of the body from the same multi-slice scan illustrated in Figure 5-ns. Each of the five separate scans is exactly like the one illustrated in Figure 4-ctr except for its location.

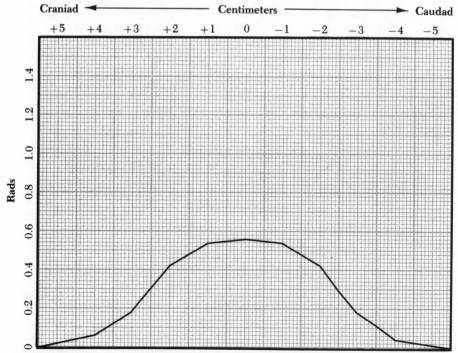

Figure 6-ctr. *Dose Profile of a Multi-Slice Scan.* This figure shows exactly the same information as Figure 5-ctr, but the doses which overlapped in Figure 5-ctr have been piled on top of each other here. The maximum center dose in all five scanned slices now *exceeds* 0.24 rad because each scanned slice receives scattered dose from adjacent scanned slices.

A comparison of Figure 5-ns with Figure 4-ns, and Figure 5-ctr with Figure 4-ctr, readily shows that in these illustrations, the five adjacent slices are each scanned with the same maximum near-surface dose (1.0 rad) and the same maximum center dose (0.24 rad). But this need not be the case. If the doses varied from slice to slice, the general procedure would still be the same for obtaining the aggregate cancer risk from the five-slice exam.

The curves in Figures 6-ns and 6-ctr result from adding up the doses which *overlap* in Figures 5-ns and 5-ctr, and making the sums visible. Although these composite curves are quite popular in the literature and can lead to the right answers concerning cancer risk, we are going to produce the same right answers by a method (Table 12) which is probably far easier to follow and far more general in its applicability. We have tested both methods, and they give the same answer, as they must.

Table 12. Cancer Risk from a 5-Slice Kidney Region Scan

Patient: A 20-year-old male, non-smoker

Slice Width: 1 cm per slice, five slices

Dose: Average absorbed dose in scanned slice = 1.75 rads in each, when treated as separate single-slice exams as in Table 11.

Specificity: This table, like Tables 10 and 11, is illustrative only. Actual doses, and lowering factors for dose (from dose profiles), differ from one facility to another.

> *From Scanning cm 53–54:*
>
> Total Cancer Risk = 321.3 per million
>
> *From Scanning cm 54–55:*
>
> Total Cancer Risk = 314.5 per million
>
> *From Scanning cm 55–56:*
>
> Total Cancer Risk = 315.3 per million
>
> *From Scanning cm 56–57:*
>
> Total Cancer Risk = 313.7 per million
>
> *From Scanning cm 57–58:*
>
> Total Cancer Risk = 318.9 per million

> *From the Entire 5-Slice Scan:*
>
> Total Cancer Risk = 1,583.7 per million
> = 1 chance in 631

SOURCE: The entry for position 55–56 is the total from Table 11. The four other values were obtained in similar tables *not* presented here.

They *must* give the same answer because, when a certain amount of ionizing radiation is "poured" into certain slices of a certain human body, it will distribute itself in only one way. Its distribution among the slices will be the same whether it is poured in all at once during a single multi-slice exam, or whether it is poured into those slices by scanning each slice *on different days.* Therefore the risk from a five-slice scan can be obtained by treating it like five separate single-slice scans, and adding up the risks. In other words, one makes five tables like Table 10 or Table 11, and then adds up the risks as demonstrated in Table 12.

We did an experiment to see how long such a method would take. First, we referred back to Table 11 in which the only slice scanned was at position 55–56 cm. We asked, what would be the risk from an exam in that region if slices 53–54, 54–55, 56–57, and 57–58 were also scanned for the same patient? One of us (EO'C) used a hand-calculator and a pad of ruled paper to make four more tables similar to Table 11. It took her ten minutes to complete all four, and this rate was *not* the consequence of practice, since she had done only one such table before. We conclude that our method for obtaining the risk from multi-slice scans is not onerous.

The cancer risk from the five-slice kidney scan described above is presented in Table 12: 1,584 per million, or 1 chance in 631. There are two reasons that 1,584 per million is so close to 5 times the center-slice total of 315.3 per million (from Table 11). When one consults the Isolated Slice Table from positions 51–52 through 59–60, the near-right "Totals" column shows that the cancer risk per slice in that whole region varies only slightly. One slice is much like another in terms of risk. The second reason is that this illustration presumed the *same average dose* in every slice.

Two Suggestions

We conclude this section with two suggestions. The second is the more important one.

More Distant Slices: When the beam whose profile is used in Figures 4, 5, and 6 is strengthened, then scattered radiation from the scanned slice will reach more than 2 centimeters beyond the scanned slice, although neither the shape of the dose profile nor the lowering factors for the $+1$, -1, $+2$, and -2 slices will change. It is a simple matter, for any beam, to use a dose profile from a relatively high dose in order to establish the additional lowering factors applicable to the $+3$ and -3 slices and beyond (Section 4 of this chapter). Inclusion of the dose scattered to the more distant slices will prevent underestimates of the cancer risk from exams performed with relatively high doses.

Clarity about Dose: For evaluating risk from multi-slice C.A.T. Scans, a very useful habit would be always to specify whether the average dose to a scanned slice *includes* or *excludes* the dose contributed to it by adjacent scanned slices.

Our method asks for the average dose to a scanned slice *before* the addition of dose increments from adjacent scanned slices. Confusion and error will occur if the method is applied to average doses which already include the contributions from adjacent scanned slices.

Woe will also fall upon anyone who carelessly applies the method to a near-surface dose or to a center dose. The method applies to the *average* dose in a single scanned slice, excluding the dose increments it receives from adjacent scanned slices.

Section 7:
Rules Followed in the Isolated Slice Tables

Detailed tables are provided for males and females at ages 5, 10, 15, and 20. Summary tables for ages 30, 40, and 50 are based on the familiar lowering factors from the tables of Chapter 5. Details for ages above 20 are taken from the age-20 table, as in Chapter 5 also. The following statements apply to all the Isolated Slice Tables.

Risk per Million: Like the other tables in this book, the numbers in these tables express risk as cancers per million. These tables, however, omit the words "per million" in order to achieve "fit." The only numbers in these tables which are *not* "per million" cancer risks are the numbers on both sides which describe the location of each slice in centimeters from the vertex.

Horizontal Totals: Each entry for the cancer risk in the "Totals" column near the far right is simply the sum of the entries in its own row across the page. It is the "Totals" column which supplies the entries needed for risk calculations. Nevertheless, it is *not* the first column which a user needs to consult. First the user needs to consult the columns for the particular organs involved in a contemplated scan, locate the organs' upper and lower edges, and thus identify the applicable rows (Section 1 of this chapter).

Vertical Totals: Each total at the bottom of a column is derived from Special Table A or B of Chapter 21, and represents the cancer risk per million when the *entire* organ (or organ system) absorbs a dose of 1.0 rad. The following organs, found in Special Tables A and B, are omitted from the Isolated Slice Tables or are combined with other organs:

"Other Respiratory" (both sexes) is omitted.
"Other Genital" (males only) is omitted.
"Other Genital" (females) is combined with cervix + corpus.
"Other Endocrine" (both sexes) is omitted.
"Other Gastro-intestinal, Unspecified" (both sexes) is combined with small intestine.
"All Other, Unspecified" (both sexes) is omitted.

The reason for omitting some is that it is hard to know the craniocaudad distribution of these cancers. They represent a diffuse "background" risk which will occur in addition to the much larger contributions per slice from the specified organs.

The Zeroes: The many zeroes in various columns exist because these tables, like no others in this book, evaluate the risk arising within an isolated area. If no part of a particular organ resides in a given slice, such an organ simply cannot contribute to the risk arising "geographically" from that slice of the body.

Average Absorbed Dose: The cancer risks per 1-cm slice apply when 1.0 rad is the *average* absorbed dose in that slice. These tables do not apply to near-surface doses or center doses. They apply to an average dose of 1.0 rad absorbed by an isolated slice, *before* the addition of dose increments from adjacent scanned slices.

Beam Quality: Beam quality is not specified for these tables because the dose is an absorbed dose, not an entrance dose; it does not matter to the organs how the energy got there.

Effect of Smoking: The risks provided for the chest area are for non-smokers, as usual. Scans irradiating the lungs would result in higher risks for smokers.

Section 8: The Isolated Slice Tables (pp. 264–281)

AGE 5, Males, ISOLATED SLICE TABLE

Position (cm)	0–1	1–2	2–3	3–4	4–5	5–6	6–7	7–8	8–9	9–10	10–11	11–12	12–13	13–14	14–15	15–16	16–17	17–18	18–19	19–20	20–21	21–22	22–23	23–24	24–25	25–26	26–27	27–28
TOTALS	0	29	86	96	96	98	96	96	96	68	51	155	239	239	240	242	242	84	202	274	286	303	103	103	165	170	170	170
Prostate	0	0	0	0	0	0	0	0	0	0	0	0	0	0	0	0	0	0	0	0	0	0	0	0	0	0	0	0
Bladder	0	0	0	0	0	0	0	0	0	0	0	0	0	0	0	0	0	0	0	0	0	0	0	0	0	0	0	0
Kidney	0	0	0	0	0	0	0	0	0	0	0	0	0	0	0	0	0	0	0	0	0	0	0	0	0	0	0	0
Pancreas	0	0	0	0	0	0	0	0	0	0	0	0	0	0	0	0	0	0	0	0	0	0	0	0	0	0	0	0
Liver	0	0	0	0	0	0	0	0	0	0	0	0	0	0	0	0	0	0	0	0	0	0	0	0	0	0	0	0
Rectum	0	0	0	0	0	0	0	0	0	0	0	0	0	0	0	0	0	0	0	0	0	0	0	0	0	0	0	0
Large Intestine	0	0	0	0	0	0	0	0	0	0	0	0	0	0	0	0	0	0	0	0	0	0	0	0	0	0	0	0
Small Intestine & Other G.I.	0	0	0	0	0	0	0	0	0	0	0	0	0	0	0	0	0	0	0	0	0	0	0	0	0	0	0	0
Stomach	0	0	0	0	0	0	0	0	0	0	0	0	0	0	0	0	0	0	0	0	0	0	0	0	0	0	0	0
Bone, Connective, Skin	0	11	11	11	11	11	11	11	11	11	11	11	11	11	12	12	12	12	12	12	12	12	12	12	12	12	12	12
Lymphatic Tissues	0	0	0	8	18	18	18	18	18	18	18	18	18	18	23	23	23	23	23	23	23	23	23	23	23	28	28	28
Breast-Pair	0	0	0	0	0	0	0	0	0	0	0	0	0	0	0	0	0	0	0	0	1	6	6	6	6	6	6	6
Bronchi	0	0	0	0	0	0	0	0	0	0	0	0	0	0	0	0	0	0	0	0	11	23	32	32	32	94	94	94
Esophagus	0	0	0	0	0	0	0	0	0	0	0	0	0	0	16	30	30	30	30	30	30	30	30	30	0	0	0	0
Larynx	0	0	0	0	0	0	0	0	0	0	0	0	151	151	151	151	0	0	0	0	0	0	0	0	0	0	0	0
Thyroid	0	0	0	0	0	0	0	0	0	0	0	0	0	0	0	58	58	58	0	0	0	0	0	0	0	0	0	0
Pharynx	0	0	0	0	0	0	0	0	39	52	52	52	49	49	49	0	0	0	0	0	0	0	0	0	0	0	0	0
Buccal Organs	0	0	0	0	0	0	0	0	68	158	158	158	158	0	0	0	0	0	0	0	0	0	0	0	0	0	0	0
Eyes	0	0	0	0	0	0	19	22	19	0	0	0	0	0	0	0	0	0	0	0	0	0	0	0	0	0	0	0
Brain/C.N.S.	0	18	67	69	67	67	67	20	0	0	0	0	0	0	0	0	0	0	0	0	0	0	0	0	0	0	0	0
Position (cm)	0–1	1–2	2–3	3–4	4–5	5–6	6–7	7–8	8–9	9–10	10–11	11–12	12–13	13–14	14–15	15–16	16–17	17–18	18–19	19–20	20–21	21–22	22–23	23–24	24–25	25–26	26–27	27–28

Age range	Brain	Eyes	Bucc	Phary	Thyro	Lary	Esoph	Bronc	Br'st	Lymph	B-C-S	Stom	SmInt	LgInt	Rec'm	Liver	Pancr	Kid'y	Bladd	Prost	Body
28–29	0	0	0	0	0	0	0	0	0	28	12	0	0	0	0	0	0	0	0	0	170
29–30	0	0	0	0	0	0	30	94	6	28	13	0	0	0	0	0	0	0	0	0	170
30–31	0	0	0	0	0	0	30	94	5	28	13	0	0	0	0	0	0	0	0	0	152
31–32	0	0	0	0	0	0	17	94	0	28	13	0	0	0	0	0	0	0	0	0	152
32–33	0	0	0	0	0	0	17	94	0	28	13	0	0	0	0	0	0	0	0	0	140
33–34	0	0	0	0	0	0	7	47	0	28	13	47	0	0	0	45	176	20	0	0	372
34–35	0	0	0	0	0	0	0	43	0	28	13	96	0	0	0	45	176	45	0	0	446
35–36	0	0	0	0	0	0	0	43	0	28	13	96	0	0	0	45	176	75	0	0	457
36–37	0	0	0	0	0	0	0	24	0	28	13	96	4	90	0	45	111	80	0	0	467
37–38	0	0	0	0	0	0	0	0	0	28	13	96	8	90	0	45	61	80	0	0	406
38–39	0	0	0	0	0	0	0	0	0	29	13	96	8	90	0	30	61	80	0	0	402
39–40	0	0	0	0	0	0	0	0	0	29	13	96	9	230	0	25	55	80	0	0	537
40–41	0	0	0	0	0	0	0	0	0	29	13	96	9	230	0	25	25	60	0	0	507
41–42	0	0	0	0	0	0	0	0	0	29	13	96	9	230	0	25	0	25	0	0	472
42–43	0	0	0	0	0	0	0	0	0	29	13	96	9	225	0	15	0	0	0	0	442
43–44	0	0	0	0	0	0	0	0	0	29	13	30	9	175	0	10	0	0	0	0	291
44–45	0	0	0	0	0	0	0	0	0	30	13	0	9	230	0	10	0	0	0	0	177
45–46	0	0	0	0	0	0	0	0	0	30	13	0	9	125	0	10	0	0	0	0	177
46–47	0	0	0	0	0	0	0	0	0	30	13	0	9	125	0	0	0	0	0	0	177
47–48	0	0	0	0	0	0	0	0	0	30	13	0	9	125	0	0	0	0	0	0	207
48–49	0	0	0	0	0	0	0	0	0	30	13	0	9	155	0	0	0	0	0	0	145
49–50	0	0	0	0	0	0	0	0	0	30	13	0	9	93	0	0	0	0	0	0	132
50–51	0	0	0	0	0	0	0	0	0	30	13	0	8	80	0	0	0	0	0	0	127
51–52	0	0	0	0	0	0	0	0	0	30	13	0	8	75	0	0	0	0	0	0	275
52–53	0	0	0	0	0	0	0	0	0	30	13	0	8	50	0	0	0	0	174	0	760
53–54	0	0	0	0	0	0	0	0	0	30	13	0	6	0	270	0	0	0	439	0	825
54–55	0	0	0	0	0	0	0	0	0	30	13	0	0	0	335	0	0	0	439	0	3035
55–56	0	0	0	0	0	0	0	0	0	30	13	0	0	0	335	0	0	0	439	2212	2839
56–57	0	0	0	0	0	0	0	0	0	30	13	0	0	0	335	0	0	0	250	2211	23
57–58	0	0	0	0	0	0	0	0	0	10	13	0	0	0	0	0	0	0	0	0	23
TOTALS	442	60	858	342	174	604	417	1039	60	1397	701	941	167	2418	1275	375	841	705	1741	4423	18980
	Brain	Eyes	Bucc	Phary	Thyro	Lary	Esoph	Bronc	Br'st	Lymph	B-C-S	Stom	SmInt	LgInt	Rec'm	Liver	Pancr	Kid'y	Bladd	Prost	Body

Age 5 Male

AGE 5, Females, ISOLATED SLICE TABLE

Position (cm)	0–1	1–2	2–3	3–4	4–5	5–6	6–7	7–8	8–9	9–10	10–11	11–12	12–13	13–14	14–15	15–16	16–17	17–18	18–19	19–20	20–21	21–22	22–23	23–24	24–25	25–26	26–27	27–28
TOTALS	0	21	75	85	85	85	85	60	63	93	120	121	120	124	123	51	72	229	390	1022	847	847	888	892	892	892	892	892
Ovaries	0	0	0	0	0	0	0	0	0	0	0	0	0	0	0	0	0	0	0	0	0	0	0	0	0	0	0	0
Uterus (corpus & cervix) & Other Genital	0	0	0	0	0	0	0	0	0	0	0	0	0	0	0	0	0	0	0	0	0	0	0	0	0	0	0	0
Bladder	0	0	0	0	0	0	0	0	0	0	0	0	0	0	0	0	0	0	0	0	0	0	0	0	0	0	0	0
Kidney	0	0	0	0	0	0	0	0	0	0	0	0	0	0	0	0	0	0	0	0	0	0	0	0	0	0	0	0
Pancreas	0	0	0	0	0	0	0	0	0	0	0	0	0	0	0	0	0	0	0	0	0	0	0	0	0	0	0	0
Liver	0	0	0	0	0	0	0	0	0	0	0	0	0	0	0	0	0	0	0	0	0	0	0	0	0	0	0	0
Rectum	0	0	0	0	0	0	0	0	0	0	0	0	0	0	0	0	0	0	0	0	0	0	0	0	0	0	0	0
Large Intestine	0	0	0	0	0	0	0	0	0	0	0	0	0	0	0	0	0	0	0	0	0	0	0	0	0	0	0	0
Small Intestine & Other G.I.	0	0	0	0	0	0	0	0	0	0	0	0	0	0	0	0	0	0	0	0	0	0	0	0	0	0	0	0
Stomach	0	0	0	0	0	0	0	0	0	0	0	0	0	0	0	0	0	0	0	0	0	0	0	0	0	0	0	0
Bone, Connective, Skin	0	11	11	11	11	11	11	11	11	11	11	11	12	12	12	12	12	12	12	12	12	12	12	12	12	12	12	12
Lymphatic Tissues	0	0	6	16	16	16	16	16	16	16	16	16	17	22	22	22	22	22	22	22	22	22	22	22	22	26	26	26
Breast-Pair	0	0	0	0	0	0	0	0	0	0	0	0	0	0	0	0	0	0	0	0	150	775	775	775	775	775	775	775
Bronchi	0	0	0	0	0	0	0	0	0	0	0	0	0	0	0	0	0	0	0	0	10	18	25	25	66	66	66	66
Esophagus	0	0	0	0	0	0	0	0	0	0	0	0	0	0	0	0	0	0	0	8	13	13	13	13	13	13	13	13
Larynx	0	0	0	0	0	0	0	0	0	0	0	0	0	0	0	0	0	30	30	30	29	0	0	0	0	0	0	0
Thyroid	0	0	0	0	0	0	0	0	0	0	0	0	0	0	0	0	0	0	152	153	153	0	0	0	0	0	0	0
Pharynx	0	0	0	0	0	0	0	0	14	14	18	18	18	17	17	17	0	0	0	0	0	0	0	0	0	0	0	0
Buccal Organs	0	0	0	0	0	0	0	32	75	75	73	73	72	0	0	0	0	0	0	0	0	0	0	0	0	0	0	0
Eyes	0	0	0	0	0	0	0	20	22	20	0	0	0	0	0	0	0	0	0	0	0	0	0	0	0	0	0	0
Brain/C.N.S.	0	10	58	58	58	58	58	58	13	0	0	0	0	0	0	0	0	0	0	0	0	0	0	0	0	0	0	0
Position (cm)	0–1	1–2	2–3	3–4	4–5	5–6	6–7	7–8	8–9	9–10	10–11	11–12	12–13	13–14	14–15	15–16	16–17	17–18	18–19	19–20	20–21	21–22	22–23	23–24	24–25	25–26	26–27	27–28

Age 5 Female	Brain	Eyes	Bucc	Phary	Thyro	Lary	Esoph	Bronc	Br'st	Lymph	B-C-S	Stom	SmInt	LgInt	Rec'm	Liver	Pancr	Kid'y	Bladd	Uter	Ovar	Body
28-29	0	0	0	0	0	0	13	67	750	26	12	0	0	0	0	0	0	0	0	0	0	868
29-30	0	0	0	0	0	0	12	67	492	26	13	0	0	0	0	0	0	0	0	0	0	610
30-31	0	0	0	0	0	0	12	57	0	26	13	0	0	0	0	0	0	0	0	0	0	103
31-32	0	0	0	0	0	0	12	57	0	26	13	0	0	0	0	0	0	0	0	0	0	103
32-33	0	0	0	0	0	0	7	23	0	26	13	0	0	0	0	50	170	13	0	0	0	119
33-34	0	0	0	0	0	0	0	23	0	26	13	39	0	0	0	50	170	24	0	0	0	334
34-35	0	0	0	0	0	0	0	23	0	26	13	64	0	0	0	50	170	45	0	0	0	370
35-36	0	0	0	0	0	0	0	11	0	26	13	64	0	0	0	50	106	52	0	0	0	379
36-37	0	0	0	0	0	0	0	0	0	26	13	64	4	120	0	35	56	52	0	0	0	435
37-38	0	0	0	0	0	0	0	0	0	26	13	64	8	120	0	30	56	52	0	0	0	374
38-39	0	0	0	0	0	0	0	0	0	26	13	64	9	126	0	30	54	52	0	0	0	376
39-40	0	0	0	0	0	0	0	0	0	26	13	64	9	240	0	30	25	52	0	0	0	488
40-41	0	0	0	0	0	0	0	0	0	26	13	64	9	240	0	16	0	40	0	0	0	460
41-42	0	0	0	0	0	0	0	0	0	27	13	19	9	240	0	11	0	15	0	0	0	421
42-43	0	0	0	0	0	0	0	0	0	27	13	0	9	235	0	10	0	0	0	0	0	399
43-44	0	0	0	0	0	0	0	0	0	27	13	0	9	195	0	10	0	0	0	0	0	288
44-45	0	0	0	0	0	0	0	0	0	28	13	0	9	250	0	0	0	0	0	0	0	310
45-46	0	0	0	0	0	0	0	0	0	28	13	0	9	160	0	0	0	0	0	0	0	210
46-47	0	0	0	0	0	0	0	0	0	28	13	0	9	255	0	0	0	0	0	0	0	305
47-48	0	0	0	0	0	0	0	0	0	28	13	0	9	210	0	0	0	0	0	0	0	305
48-49	0	0	0	0	0	0	0	0	0	28	13	0	9	130	0	0	0	0	0	0	0	260
49-50	0	0	0	0	0	0	0	0	0	28	13	0	9	90	0	0	0	0	0	0	598	778
50-51	0	0	0	0	0	0	0	0	0	28	13	0	9	90	0	0	0	0	0	0	599	739
51-52	0	0	0	0	0	0	0	0	0	28	13	0	8	70	0	0	0	0	0	0	0	843
52-53	0	0	0	0	0	0	0	0	0	28	13	0	8	0	0	0	0	0	80	703	0	1103
53-54	0	0	0	0	0	0	0	0	0	28	13	0	6	0	241	0	0	0	170	903	0	1363
54-55	0	0	0	0	0	0	0	0	0	28	13	0	0	0	295	0	0	0	170	903	0	1417
55-56	0	0	0	0	0	0	0	0	0	28	13	0	0	0	295	0	0	0	170	903	0	1214
56-57	0	0	0	0	0	0	0	0	0	28	13	0	0	0	295	0	0	0	79	702	0	415
57-58	0	0	0	0	0	0	0	0	0	8	8	0	0	0	0	0	0	0	0	0	0	21
TOTALS	371	62	400	133	458	119	184	695	7592	1295	702	634	169	3026	1126	422	807	449	669	4114	1197	24624

AGE 10, Males, ISOLATED SLICE TABLE

Position (cm)	0-1	1-2	2-3	3-4	4-5	5-6	6-7	7-8	8-9	9-10	10-11	11-12	12-13	13-14	14-15	15-16	16-17	17-18	18-19	19-20	20-21	21-22	22-23	23-24	24-25	25-26	26-27	27-28	28-29	29-30	30-31	31-32	32-33	33-34
TOTALS	0	14	26	49	72	74	74	74	89	42	115	161	159	159	165	165	165	59	156	213	219	234	66	66	128	128	129	129	129	129	130	130	81	76
Prostate	0	0	0	0	0	0	0	0	0	0	0	0	0	0	0	0	0	0	0	0	0	0	0	0	0	0	0	0	0	0	0	0	0	0
Bladder	0	0	0	0	0	0	0	0	0	0	0	0	0	0	0	0	0	0	0	0	0	0	0	0	0	0	0	0	0	0	0	0	0	0
Kidney	0	0	0	0	0	0	0	0	0	0	0	0	0	0	0	0	0	0	0	0	0	0	0	0	0	0	0	0	0	0	0	0	0	0
Pancreas	0	0	0	0	0	0	0	0	0	0	0	0	0	0	0	0	0	0	0	0	0	0	0	0	0	0	0	0	0	0	0	0	0	0
Liver	0	0	0	0	0	0	0	0	0	0	0	0	0	0	0	0	0	0	0	0	0	0	0	0	0	0	0	0	0	0	0	0	0	0
Rectum	0	0	0	0	0	0	0	0	0	0	0	0	0	0	0	0	0	0	0	0	0	0	0	0	0	0	0	0	0	0	0	0	0	0
Large Intestine	0	0	0	0	0	0	0	0	0	0	0	0	0	0	0	0	0	0	0	0	0	0	0	0	0	0	0	0	0	0	0	0	0	0
Small Intestine & Other G.I.	0	0	0	0	0	0	0	0	0	0	0	0	0	0	0	0	0	0	0	0	0	0	0	0	0	0	0	0	0	0	0	0	0	0
Stomach	0	0	0	0	0	0	0	0	0	0	0	0	0	0	0	0	0	0	0	0	0	0	0	0	0	0	0	0	0	0	0	0	0	0
Bone, Connective, Skin	0	5	5	5	5	5	7	7	7	7	7	7	7	7	7	7	7	7	7	7	7	7	7	7	7	7	7	7	8	8	8	9	9	9
Lymphatic Tissues	0	0	0	0	10	10	10	10	10	10	10	10	10	10	17	17	17	17	17	17	17	17	17	17	18	18	18	18	18	18	18	18	18	18
Breast-Pair	0	0	0	0	0	0	0	0	0	0	0	0	0	0	0	0	0	0	0	0	0	0	1	4	4	4	4	4	4	4	4	4	4	0
Bronchi	0	0	0	0	0	0	0	0	0	0	0	0	0	0	0	0	0	0	0	5	18	18	18	80	80	80	80	80	80	80	31	30	0	0
Esophagus	0	0	0	0	0	0	0	0	0	0	0	0	0	0	0	0	0	0	10	20	20	20	20	20	19	19	19	19	19	19	19	19	0	0
Larynx	0	0	0	0	0	0	0	0	0	0	0	0	0	0	0	0	0	0	122	122	122	121	0	0	0	0	0	0	0	0	0	0	0	0
Thyroid	0	0	0	0	0	0	0	0	0	0	0	0	0	0	0	0	0	0	0	47	47	47	0	0	0	0	0	0	0	0	0	0	0	0
Pharynx	0	0	0	0	0	0	0	0	0	0	27	36	36	36	35	35	35	35	0	0	0	0	0	0	0	0	0	0	0	0	0	0	0	0
Buccal Organs	0	0	0	0	0	0	0	0	0	0	55	108	106	106	106	106	106	0	0	0	0	0	0	0	0	0	0	0	0	0	0	0	0	0
Eyes	0	0	0	0	0	0	0	0	16	17	16	0	0	0	0	0	0	0	0	0	0	0	0	0	0	0	0	0	0	0	0	0	0	0
Brain/C.N.S.	0	9	21	34	57	57	57	57	56	8	0	0	0	0	0	0	0	0	0	0	0	0	0	0	0	0	0	0	0	0	0	0	0	0
Position (cm)	0-1	1-2	2-3	3-4	4-5	5-6	6-7	7-8	8-9	9-10	10-11	11-12	12-13	13-14	14-15	15-16	16-17	17-18	18-19	19-20	20-21	21-22	22-23	23-24	24-25	25-26	26-27	27-28	28-29	29-30	30-31	31-32	32-33	33-34

Age 10 — Male

Age	Brain	Eyes	Bucc	Phary	Thyro	Lary	Esoph	Bronc	Br'st	Lymph	B-C-S	Stom	SmInt	LgInt	Rec'm	Liver	Pancr	Kid'y	Bladd	Prost	Body
34–35	0	0	0	0	0	0	19	30	0	18	9	0	0	0	0	0	0	0	0	0	76
35–36	0	0	0	0	0	0	8	10	0	18	9	0	0	0	0	0	0	0	0	0	45
36–37	0	0	0	0	0	0	8	10	0	18	9	0	0	0	0	35	0	0	0	0	80
37–38	0	0	0	0	0	0	0	10	0	18	9	30	0	0	0	35	145	20	0	0	102
38–39	0	0	0	0	0	0	0	9	0	18	9	70	0	0	0	35	145	30	0	0	306
39–40	0	0	0	0	0	0	0	9	0	18	9	70	0	0	0	35	145	68	0	0	316
40–41	0	0	0	0	0	0	0	0	0	18	9	70	2	45	0	35	95	68	0	0	392
41–42	0	0	0	0	0	0	0	0	0	18	9	70	4	45	0	20	45	68	0	0	329
42–43	0	0	0	0	0	0	0	0	0	18	9	70	6	45	0	18	45	69	0	0	279
43–44	0	0	0	0	0	0	0	0	0	18	9	70	6	45	0	17	43	69	0	0	279
44–45	0	0	0	0	0	0	0	0	0	18	9	70	6	135	0	16	15	68	0	0	366
45–46	0	0	0	0	0	0	0	0	0	18	9	70	6	135	0	16	0	68	0	0	337
46–47	0	0	0	0	0	0	0	0	0	18	9	70	6	135	0	10	0	30	0	0	316
47–48	0	0	0	0	0	0	0	0	0	18	9	70	6	130	0	10	0	10	0	0	273
48–49	0	0	0	0	0	0	0	0	0	18	9	29	6	101	0	10	0	0	0	0	183
49–50	0	0	0	0	0	0	0	0	0	18	9	0	6	130	0	10	0	0	0	0	173
50–51	0	0	0	0	0	0	0	0	0	18	9	0	6	75	0	0	0	0	0	0	108
51–52	0	0	0	0	0	0	0	0	0	18	9	0	6	75	0	0	0	0	0	0	109
52–53	0	0	0	0	0	0	0	0	0	18	9	0	6	75	0	0	0	0	0	0	109
53–54	0	0	0	0	0	0	0	0	0	19	9	0	6	75	0	0	0	0	0	0	109
54–55	0	0	0	0	0	0	0	0	0	19	9	0	6	75	0	0	0	0	0	0	109
55–56	0	0	0	0	0	0	0	0	0	19	9	0	6	75	0	0	0	0	0	0	108
56–57	0	0	0	0	0	0	0	0	0	19	9	0	5	75	0	0	0	0	0	0	108
57–58	0	0	0	0	0	0	0	0	0	19	9	0	5	75	0	0	0	0	0	0	106
58–59	0	0	0	0	0	0	0	0	0	19	9	0	5	73	0	0	0	0	0	0	134
59–60	0	0	0	0	0	0	0	0	0	20	9	0	5	100	0	0	0	0	0	0	119
60–61	0	0	0	0	0	0	0	0	0	20	10	0	5	85	0	0	0	0	0	0	75
61–62	0	0	0	0	0	0	0	0	0	20	10	0	5	40	0	0	0	0	0	0	75
62–63	0	0	0	0	0	0	0	0	0	20	10	0	5	40	0	0	0	0	0	0	158
63–64	0	0	0	0	0	0	0	0	0	20	10	0	5	33	155	0	0	0	90	0	358
64–65	0	0	0	0	0	0	0	0	0	20	10	0	5	33	291	0	0	0	290	0	475
65–66	0	0	0	0	0	0	0	0	0	20	10	0	0	0	291	0	0	0	290	0	611
66–67	0	0	0	0	0	0	0	0	0	20	10	0	0	0	291	0	0	0	290	0	
67–68	0	0	0	0	0	0	0	0	0	20	10	0	0	0	0	0	0	0	294	1784	2399
68–69	0	0	0	0	0	0	0	0	0	20	10	0	0	0	0	0	0	0	294	1783	2254
69–70	0	0	0	0	0	0	0	0	0	10	9	0	0	0	0	0	0	0	150	0	19
TOTALS	356	49	693	275	141	487	336	838	49	1127	566	759	135	1950	1028	302	678	568	1404	3567	15308

AGE 10, Females, ISOLATED SLICE TABLE

Position (cm)	0–1	1–2	2–3	3–4	4–5	5–6	6–7	7–8	8–9	9–10	10–11	11–12	12–13	13–14	14–15	15–16	16–17	17–18	18–19	19–20	20–21	21–22	22–23	23–24	24–25	25–26	26–27	27–28	28–29	29–30	30–31	31–32	32–33	33–34
TOTALS	0	11	22	41	59	61	61	60	74	39	62	76	76	77	83	83	82	82	35	49	169	173	179	140	740	783	784	786	797	795	785	785	185	50
Ovaries	0	0	0	0	0	0	0	0	0	0	0	0	0	0	0	0	0	0	0	0	0	0	0	0	0	0	0	0	0	0	0	0	0	0
Uterus (corpus & cervix) & Other Genital	0	0	0	0	0	0	0	0	0	0	0	0	0	0	0	0	0	0	0	0	0	0	0	0	0	0	0	0	0	0	0	0	0	0
Bladder	0	0	0	0	0	0	0	0	0	0	0	0	0	0	0	0	0	0	0	0	0	0	0	0	0	0	0	0	0	0	0	0	0	0
Kidney	0	0	0	0	0	0	0	0	0	0	0	0	0	0	0	0	0	0	0	0	0	0	0	0	0	0	0	0	0	0	0	0	0	0
Pancreas	0	0	0	0	0	0	0	0	0	0	0	0	0	0	0	0	0	0	0	0	0	0	0	0	0	0	0	0	0	0	0	0	0	0
Liver	0	0	0	0	0	0	0	0	0	0	0	0	0	0	0	0	0	0	0	0	0	0	0	0	0	0	0	0	0	0	0	0	0	0
Rectum	0	0	0	0	0	0	0	0	0	0	0	0	0	0	0	0	0	0	0	0	0	0	0	0	0	0	0	0	0	0	0	0	0	0
Large Intestine	0	0	0	0	0	0	0	0	0	0	0	0	0	0	0	0	0	0	0	0	0	0	0	0	0	0	0	0	0	0	0	0	0	0
Small Intestine & Other G.I.	0	0	0	0	0	0	0	0	0	0	0	0	0	0	0	0	0	0	0	0	0	0	0	0	0	0	0	0	0	0	0	0	0	0
Stomach	0	0	0	0	0	0	0	0	0	0	0	0	0	0	0	0	0	0	0	0	0	0	0	0	0	0	0	0	0	0	0	0	0	0
Bone, Connective, Skin	0	5	5	5	5	5	7	7	7	7	7	7	7	7	7	7	7	7	7	7	7	7	7	7	7	7	7	7	8	8	8	8	8	8
Lymphatic Tissues	0	0	0	8	8	8	8	8	8	8	8	8	8	15	15	15	15	15	15	15	15	15	15	15	16	16	16	16	16	16	16	16	16	16
Breast-Pair	0	0	0	0	0	0	0	0	0	0	0	0	0	0	0	0	0	0	0	0	0	0	0	100	700	700	712	710	712	700	700	100	0	0
Bronchi	0	0	0	0	0	0	0	0	0	0	0	0	0	0	0	0	0	0	0	0	3	10	10	53	53	53	53	53	53	18	17	0	0	0
Esophagus	0	0	0	0	0	0	0	0	0	0	0	0	0	0	0	0	0	0	0	4	7	7	7	8	8	8	8	8	8	8	8	8	8	8
Larynx	0	0	0	0	0	0	0	0	0	0	0	0	0	0	0	0	0	0	0	0	23	23	23	23	0	0	0	0	0	0	0	0	0	0
Thyroid	0	0	0	0	0	0	0	0	0	0	0	0	0	0	0	0	0	0	0	0	117	118	117	0	0	0	0	0	0	0	0	0	0	0
Pharynx	0	0	0	0	0	0	0	0	0	0	10	13	13	14	13	13	13	13	0	0	0	0	0	0	0	0	0	0	0	0	0	0	0	0
Buccal Organs	0	0	0	0	0	0	0	0	0	21	48	48	48	48	48	47	0	0	0	0	0	0	0	0	0	0	0	0	0	0	0	0	0	0
Eyes	0	0	0	0	0	15	17	15	0	0	0	0	0	0	0	0	0	0	0	0	0	0	0	0	0	0	0	0	0	0	0	0	0	0
Brain/C.N.S.	0	6	17	28	46	46	46	45	44	7	0	0	0	0	0	0	0	0	0	0	0	0	0	0	0	0	0	0	0	0	0	0	0	0
Position (cm)	0–1	1–2	2–3	3–4	4–5	5–6	6–7	7–8	8–9	9–10	10–11	11–12	12–13	13–14	14–15	15–16	16–17	17–18	18–19	19–20	20–21	21–22	22–23	23–24	24–25	25–26	26–27	27–28	28–29	29–30	30–31	31–32	32–33	33–34

Age 10 Female

Age	Brain	Eyes	Bucc	Phary	Thyro	Lary	Esoph	Bronc	Br st	Lymph	B-C-S	Stom	SmInt	LgInt	Rec'm	Liver	Pancr	Kid'y	Bladd	Uter	Ovar	Body
34-35	0	0	0	0	0	0	8	0	0	16	8	0	0	0	0	0	0	0	0	0	0	49
35-36	0	0	0	0	0	0	8	17	0	16	8	0	0	0	0	0	0	0	0	0	0	37
36-37	0	0	0	0	0	0	4	5	0	16	8	0	0	0	0	36	0	0	0	0	0	69
37-38	0	0	0	0	0	0	0	5	0	16	8	20	0	0	0	36	137	12	0	0	0	85
38-39	0	0	0	0	0	0	0	5	0	16	8	42	2	65	0	36	137	15	0	0	0	256
39-40	0	0	0	0	0	0	0	5	0	16	8	45	4	65	0	36	137	43	0	0	0	262
40-41	0	0	0	0	0	0	0	5	0	16	8	45	5	65	0	36	87	43	0	0	0	352
41-42	0	0	0	0	0	0	0	0	0	16	8	45	5	65	0	22	38	43	0	0	0	290
42-43	0	0	0	0	0	0	0	0	0	16	8	45	5	165	0	20	38	43	0	0	0	240
43-44	0	0	0	0	0	0	0	0	0	16	9	45	5	165	0	19	36	43	0	0	0	239
44-45	0	0	0	0	0	0	0	0	0	16	9	45	5	165	0	18	10	43	0	0	0	337
45-46	0	0	0	0	0	0	0	0	0	16	9	45	5	165	0	18	0	43	0	0	0	311
46-47	0	0	0	0	0	0	0	0	0	16	9	45	6	125	0	12	0	12	0	0	0	295
47-48	0	0	0	0	0	0	0	0	0	17	9	45	6	145	0	12	0	5	0	0	0	265
48-49	0	0	0	0	0	0	0	0	0	17	9	20	6	85	0	12	0	0	0	0	0	193
49-50	0	0	0	0	0	0	0	0	0	17	9	0	6	80	0	12	0	0	0	0	0	189
50-51	0	0	0	0	0	0	0	0	0	17	9	0	6	80	0	0	0	0	0	0	0	117
51-52	0	0	0	0	0	0	0	0	0	17	9	0	6	80	0	0	0	0	0	0	0	112
52-53	0	0	0	0	0	0	0	0	0	17	9	0	6	80	0	0	0	0	0	0	0	112
53-54	0	0	0	0	0	0	0	0	0	17	9	0	5	80	0	0	0	0	0	0	0	112
54-55	0	0	0	0	0	0	0	0	0	17	9	0	5	80	0	0	0	0	0	0	0	112
55-56	0	0	0	0	0	0	0	0	0	18	9	0	5	80	0	0	0	0	0	0	0	112
56-57	0	0	0	0	0	0	0	0	0	18	9	0	5	80	0	0	0	0	0	0	0	111
57-58	0	0	0	0	0	0	0	0	0	18	9	0	5	115	0	0	0	0	0	0	0	111
58-59	0	0	0	0	0	0	0	0	0	18	9	0	5	85	0	0	0	0	0	0	0	111
59-60	0	0	0	0	0	0	0	0	0	18	9	0	5	55	0	0	0	0	0	0	0	147
60-61	0	0	0	0	0	0	0	0	0	18	9	0	0	55	0	0	0	0	0	0	460	577
61-62	0	0	0	0	0	0	0	0	0	18	9	0	0	55	0	0	0	0	0	0	460	547
62-63	0	0	0	0	0	0	0	0	0	18	9	0	0	45	0	0	0	0	47	632	0	719
63-64	0	0	0	0	0	0	0	0	0	18	9	0	0	0	0	0	0	0	133	632	0	766
64-65	0	0	0	0	0	0	0	0	0	18	9	0	0	0	0	0	0	0	133	632	0	842
65-66	0	0	0	0	0	0	0	0	0	18	9	0	0	0	115	0	0	0	131	632	0	907
66-67	0	0	0	0	0	0	0	0	0	18	9	0	0	0	250	0	0	0	70	631	0	1039
67-68	0	0	0	0	0	0	0	0	0	18	9	0	0	0	250	0	0	0	0	0	0	347
68-69	0	0	0	0	0	0	0	0	0	18	8	0	0	0	250	0	0	0	0	0	0	276
69-70	0	0	0	0	0	0	0	0	0	8	6	0	0	0	0	0	0	0	0	0	0	14
TOTALS	285	48	308	102	352	92	141	534	5834	995	540	487	130	2325	865	325	620	345	514	3159	920	18921
	Brain	Eyes	Bucc	Phary	Thyro	Lary	Esoph	Bronc	Br st	Lymph	B-C-S	Stom	SmInt	LgInt	Rec'm	Liver	Pancr	Kid'y	Bladd	Uter	Ovar	Body

AGE 15, Males, ISOLATED SLICE TABLE

Position (cm)	0–1	1–2	2–3	3–4	4–5	5–6	6–7	7–8	8–9	9–10	10–11	11–12	12–13	13–14	14–15	15–16	16–17	17–18	18–19	19–20	20–21	21–22	22–23	23–24	24–25	25–26	26–27	27–28	28–29	29–30	30–31	31–32	32–33	33–34	34–35	35–36	36–37	37–38	38–39	39–40	40–41
TOTALS	0	5	9	15	24	29	29	29	29	36	31	49	69	69	70	70	70	71	71	70	72	75	99	99	105	22	24	24	25	47	47	49	49	49	49	50	50	49	47	47	31
Prostate	0	0	0	0	0	0	0	0	0	0	0	0	0	0	0	0	0	0	0	0	0	0	0	0	0	0	0	0	0	0	0	0	0	0	0	0	0	0	0	0	0
Bladder	0	0	0	0	0	0	0	0	0	0	0	0	0	0	0	0	0	0	0	0	0	0	0	0	0	0	0	0	0	0	0	0	0	0	0	0	0	0	0	0	0
Kidney	0	0	0	0	0	0	0	0	0	0	0	0	0	0	0	0	0	0	0	0	0	0	0	0	0	0	0	0	0	0	0	0	0	0	0	0	0	0	0	0	0
Pancreas	0	0	0	0	0	0	0	0	0	0	0	0	0	0	0	0	0	0	0	0	0	0	0	0	0	0	0	0	0	0	0	0	0	0	0	0	0	0	0	0	0
Liver	0	0	0	0	0	0	0	0	0	0	0	0	0	0	0	0	0	0	0	0	0	0	0	0	0	0	0	0	0	0	0	0	0	0	0	0	0	0	0	0	0
Rectum	0	0	0	0	0	0	0	0	0	0	0	0	0	0	0	0	0	0	0	0	0	0	0	0	0	0	0	0	0	0	0	0	0	0	0	0	0	0	0	0	0
Large Intestine	0	0	0	0	0	0	0	0	0	0	0	0	0	0	0	0	0	0	0	0	0	0	0	0	0	0	0	0	0	0	0	0	0	0	0	0	0	0	0	0	0
Small Intestine & Other G.I.	0	0	0	0	0	0	0	0	0	0	0	0	0	0	0	0	0	0	0	0	0	0	0	0	0	0	0	0	0	0	0	0	0	0	0	0	0	0	0	0	0
Stomach	0	0	0	0	0	0	0	0	0	0	0	0	0	0	0	0	0	0	0	0	0	0	0	0	0	0	0	0	0	0	0	0	0	0	0	0	0	0	0	0	0
Bone, Connective, Skin	0	1	1	1	1	2	2	2	2	2	2	2	2	2	2	3	3	3	3	3	3	3	3	3	3	3	3	3	3	3	3	3	3	3	3	4	4	4	4	4	4
Lymphatic Tissues	0	0	0	0	0	0	5	5	5	5	5	5	5	5	5	5	5	6	6	6	6	6	6	7	7	7	7	7	7	7	7	7	7	7	7	8	8	8	8	8	8
Breast-Pair	0	0	0	0	0	0	0	0	0	0	0	0	0	0	0	0	0	0	0	0	0	0	0	0	0	1	1	2	2	2	3	3	3	2	2	2	1	0	0	0	0
Bronchi	0	0	0	0	0	0	0	0	0	0	0	0	0	0	0	0	0	0	0	0	0	0	0	0	0	6	6	6	6	28	28	29	29	29	29	29	29	28	28	12	12
Esophagus	0	0	0	0	0	0	0	0	0	0	0	0	0	0	0	0	0	0	0	0	0	6	6	6	6	7	7	7	7	7	7	7	7	7	7	7	7	7	7	7	7
Larynx	0	0	0	0	0	0	0	0	0	0	0	0	0	0	0	0	0	0	0	0	60	60	60	60	0	0	0	0	0	0	0	0	0	0	0	0	0	0	0	0	0
Thyroid	0	0	0	0	0	0	0	0	0	0	0	0	0	0	0	0	0	0	0	0	23	23	23	0	0	0	0	0	0	0	0	0	0	0	0	0	0	0	0	0	0
Pharynx	0	0	0	0	0	0	0	0	0	0	11	16	16	16	16	16	16	13	0	0	0	0	0	0	0	0	0	0	0	0	0	0	0	0	0	0	0	0	0	0	0
Buccal Organs	0	0	0	0	0	0	0	0	0	0	0	0	20	46	46	46	46	46	46	45	0	0	0	0	0	0	0	0	0	0	0	0	0	0	0	0	0	0	0	0	0
Eyes	0	0	0	0	0	0	0	0	7	10	7	0	0	0	0	0	0	0	0	0	0	0	0	0	0	0	0	0	0	0	0	0	0	0	0	0	0	0	0	0	0
Brain/C.N.S.	0	4	8	14	22	22	22	22	22	14	4	0	0	0	0	0	0	0	0	0	0	0	0	0	0	0	0	0	0	0	0	0	0	0	0	0	0	0	0	0	0

| Position (cm) | 0–1 | 1–2 | 2–3 | 3–4 | 4–5 | 5–6 | 6–7 | 7–8 | 8–9 | 9–10 | 10–11 | 11–12 | 12–13 | 13–14 | 14–15 | 15–16 | 16–17 | 17–18 | 18–19 | 19–20 | 20–21 | 21–22 | 22–23 | 23–24 | 24–25 | 25–26 | 26–27 | 27–28 | 28–29 | 29–30 | 30–31 | 31–32 | 32–33 | 33–34 | 34–35 | 35–36 | 36–37 | 37–38 | 38–39 | 39–40 | 40–41 |

Age 15, Male

Age	Body	Prost	Bladd	Kid'y	Panc	Liver	Rec'm	LgInt	SmInt	Stom	B-C-S	Lymph	Br'st	Bronc	Esoph	Lary	Thyro	Phary	Bucc	Eyes	Brain
41–42	31	0	0	0	0	0	0	0	0	0	4	8	0	0	0	0	0	0	0	0	0
42–43	45	0	0	0	0	15	0	0	0	0	4	8	0	12	7	0	0	0	0	0	0
43–44	37	0	0	0	0	15	0	0	0	0	4	8	0	12	6	0	0	0	0	0	0
44–45	36	0	0	0	0	15	0	0	0	16	4	8	0	4	6	0	0	0	0	0	0
45–46	128	0	0	7	74	15	0	0	0	20	4	8	0	4	5	0	0	0	0	0	0
46–47	139	0	0	14	74	15	0	0	0	33	4	8	0	4	0	0	0	0	0	0	0
47–48	184	0	0	26	74	15	0	0	1	33	4	8	0	4	0	0	0	0	0	0	0
48–49	132	0	0	26	35	8	0	17	1	33	4	8	0	4	0	0	0	0	0	0	0
49–50	113	0	0	26	17	7	0	17	2	33	4	8	0	0	0	0	0	0	0	0	0
50–51	114	0	0	26	17	7	0	17	2	33	4	8	0	0	0	0	0	0	0	0	0
51–52	114	0	0	26	17	7	0	17	2	33	4	8	0	0	0	0	0	0	0	0	0
52–53	157	0	0	26	17	7	0	17	2	33	4	8	0	0	0	0	0	0	0	0	0
53–54	145	0	0	26	9	7	0	68	2	33	4	8	0	0	0	0	0	0	0	0	0
54–55	145	0	0	26	0	4	0	68	2	33	4	8	0	0	0	0	0	0	0	0	0
55–56	126	0	0	26	0	4	0	68	2	24	4	8	0	0	0	0	0	0	0	0	0
56–57	107	0	0	16	0	4	0	68	2	12	4	8	0	0	0	0	0	0	0	0	0
57–58	66	0	0	9	0	4	0	68	3	6	4	8	0	0	0	0	0	0	0	0	0
58–59	77	0	0	0	0	0	0	46	3	0	4	8	0	0	0	0	0	0	0	0	0
59–60	42	0	0	0	0	0	0	63	3	0	4	8	0	0	0	0	0	0	0	0	0
60–61	42	0	0	0	0	0	0	28	3	0	4	8	0	0	0	0	0	0	0	0	0
61–62	42	0	0	0	0	0	0	28	3	0	4	8	0	0	0	0	0	0	0	0	0
62–63	42	0	0	0	0	0	0	28	3	0	4	8	0	0	0	0	0	0	0	0	0
63–64	43	0	0	0	0	0	0	28	3	0	4	8	0	0	0	0	0	0	0	0	0
64–65	43	0	0	0	0	0	0	28	3	0	4	8	0	0	0	0	0	0	0	0	0
65–66	43	0	0	0	0	0	0	28	3	0	4	8	0	0	0	0	0	0	0	0	0
66–67	43	0	0	0	0	0	0	28	3	0	4	8	0	0	0	0	0	0	0	0	0
67–68	43	0	0	0	0	0	0	28	3	0	4	8	0	0	0	0	0	0	0	0	0
68–69	43	0	0	0	0	0	0	28	2	0	4	8	0	0	0	0	0	0	0	0	0
69–70	42	0	0	0	0	0	0	28	2	0	4	7	0	0	0	0	0	0	0	0	0
70–71	41	0	0	0	0	0	0	27	2	0	4	7	0	0	0	0	0	0	0	0	0
71–72	50	0	0	0	0	0	0	36	0	0	4	7	0	0	0	0	0	0	0	0	0
72–73	44	0	0	0	0	0	0	30	0	0	4	7	0	0	0	0	0	0	0	0	0
73–74	27	0	0	0	0	0	0	14	0	0	4	7	0	0	0	0	0	0	0	0	0
74–75	27	0	0	0	0	0	0	14	0	0	4	7	0	0	0	0	0	0	0	0	0
75–76	22	0	0	0	0	0	0	9	0	0	4	7	0	0	0	0	0	0	0	0	0
76–77	76	0	54	0	0	0	78	9	0	0	4	7	0	0	0	0	0	0	0	0	0
77–78	154	0	132	0	0	0	143	9	0	0	4	7	0	0	0	0	0	0	0	0	0
78–79	221	0	132	0	0	0	143	0	0	0	4	7	0	0	0	0	0	0	0	0	0
79–80	286	0	132	0	0	0	143	0	0	0	4	7	0	0	0	0	0	0	0	0	0
80–81	1165	879	132	0	0	0	0	0	0	0	4	7	0	0	0	0	0	0	0	0	0
81–82	1143	879	110	0	0	0	0	0	0	0	4	7	0	0	0	0	0	0	0	0	0
82–83	11	0	0	0	0	0	0	0	0	0	4	7	0	0	0	0	0	0	0	0	0
TOTALS	7547	1758	692	280	334	149	507	962	67	375	279	555	24	413	166	240	69	136	341	24	176

Position (cm)	0–1	1–2	2–3	3–4	4–5	5–6	6–7	7–8	8–9	9–10	10–11	11–12	12–13	13–14	14–15	15–16	16–17	17–18	18–19	19–20	20–21	21–22	22–23	23–24	24–25	25–26	26–27	27–28	28–29	29–30	30–31	31–32	32–33	33–34	34–35	35–36	36–37	37–38	38–39	39–40	40–41
TOTALS	0	4	8	11	19	23	23	23	30	26	27	31	32	32	32	33	33	32	11	20	76	77	81	15	126	166	241	255	255	320	320	320	320	320	320	138	30	29	19	19	
Ovaries																																									
Uterus (corpus & cervix) & other genital																																									
Bladder																																									
Kidney																																									
Pancreas																																									
Liver																																									
Rectum																																									
Large intestine																																									
Small intestine & other G.I.																																									
Stomach																																									
Bone, connective, skin	0	1	1	1	1	2	2	2	2	2	2	2	2	2	2	2	2	2	2	2	2	2	2	2	2	2	3	3	3	3	3	3	3	3	3	3	3	3	3	3	3
Lymphatic tissues	0	0	0	0	0	4	4	4	4	4	4	4	4	4	4	5	5	5	5	5	5	6	6	6	6	6	6	6	6	6	6	6	6	6	6	6	6	6	6	6	6
Breast-pair																										110	150	225	225	225	290	290	290	290	290	108					
Bronchi																					4	4	4	4	18	18	18	18	18	18	18	18	18	17	7	7					
Esophagus																					2	2	2	2	2	3	3	3	3	3	3	3	3	3	3	3	3				
Larynx																					11	11	11	11																	
Thyroid																				56	56	56																			
Pharynx								3	6	6	6	6	6	6	4																										
Buccal organs										8	19	20	20	20	20	20	19																								
Eyes								7	9	7																															
Brain/C.N.S.	0	3	7	10	17	17	17	17	17	11	3																														

| Position (cm) | 0–1 | 1–2 | 2–3 | 3–4 | 4–5 | 5–6 | 6–7 | 7–8 | 8–9 | 9–10 | 10–11 | 11–12 | 12–13 | 13–14 | 14–15 | 15–16 | 16–17 | 17–18 | 18–19 | 19–20 | 20–21 | 21–22 | 22–23 | 23–24 | 24–25 | 25–26 | 26–27 | 27–28 | 28–29 | 29–30 | 30–31 | 31–32 | 32–33 | 33–34 | 34–35 | 35–36 | 36–37 | 37–38 | 38–39 | 39–40 | 40–41 |

Age 15 Female

Age	Brain	Eyes	Bucc	Phary	Thyro	Lary	Esoph	Bronc	Br'st	Lymph	B-C-S	Stom	SmInt	LgInt	Rec'm	Liver	Pancr	Kid'y	Bladd	Uter	Ovar	Body
41-42	0	0	0	0	0	0	3	7	0	7	3	0	0	0	0	0	0	0	0	0	0	20
42-43	0	0	0	0	0	0	2	7	0	7	3	0	0	0	0	16	0	0	0	0	0	35
43-44	0	0	0	0	0	0	2	2	0	7	3	0	0	0	0	16	0	0	0	0	0	30
44-45	0	0	0	0	0	0	2	2	0	7	4	0	0	0	0	16	0	0	0	0	0	31
45-46	0	0	0	0	0	0	0	2	0	7	4	10	0	0	0	16	66	4	0	0	0	109
46-47	0	0	0	0	0	0	0	2	0	7	4	12	0	0	0	16	66	8	0	0	0	115
47-48	0	0	0	0	0	0	0	2	0	7	4	20	0	0	0	16	66	15	0	0	0	130
48-49	0	0	0	0	0	0	0	0	0	7	4	20	1	18	0	8	31	15	0	0	0	104
49-50	0	0	0	0	0	0	0	0	0	7	4	21	1	18	0	7	15	15	0	0	0	88
50-51	0	0	0	0	0	0	0	0	0	7	4	21	2	18	0	7	15	15	0	0	0	89
51-52	0	0	0	0	0	0	0	0	0	7	4	21	2	18	0	7	15	16	0	0	0	90
52-53	0	0	0	0	0	0	0	0	0	7	4	21	2	18	0	7	14	16	0	0	0	89
53-54	0	0	0	0	0	0	0	0	0	7	4	21	2	78	0	7	8	16	0	0	0	143
54-55	0	0	0	0	0	0	0	0	0	7	4	20	2	78	0	4	0	15	0	0	0	130
55-56	0	0	0	0	0	0	0	0	0	7	4	20	2	78	0	4	0	15	0	0	0	130
56-57	0	0	0	0	0	0	0	0	0	7	4	15	2	78	0	4	0	10	0	0	0	120
57-58	0	0	0	0	0	0	0	0	0	7	4	7	2	78	0	4	0	5	0	0	0	107
58-59	0	0	0	0	0	0	0	0	0	7	4	3	2	55	0	0	0	0	0	0	0	71
59-60	0	0	0	0	0	0	0	0	0	7	4	0	2	76	0	0	0	0	0	0	0	89
60-61	0	0	0	0	0	0	0	0	0	7	4	0	2	32	0	0	0	0	0	0	0	45
61-62	0	0	0	0	0	0	0	0	0	7	4	0	2	32	0	0	0	0	0	0	0	45
62-63	0	0	0	0	0	0	0	0	0	7	4	0	2	32	0	0	0	0	0	0	0	45
63-64	0	0	0	0	0	0	0	0	0	7	4	0	2	32	0	0	0	0	0	0	0	45
64-65	0	0	0	0	0	0	0	0	0	7	4	0	3	32	0	0	0	0	0	0	0	46
65-66	0	0	0	0	0	0	0	0	0	7	4	0	2	32	0	0	0	0	0	0	0	45
66-67	0	0	0	0	0	0	0	0	0	7	4	0	2	32	0	0	0	0	0	0	0	45
67-68	0	0	0	0	0	0	0	0	0	7	4	0	2	32	0	0	0	0	0	0	0	45
68-69	0	0	0	0	0	0	0	0	0	7	4	0	2	32	0	0	0	0	0	0	0	45
69-70	0	0	0	0	0	0	0	0	0	7	4	0	2	32	0	0	0	0	0	0	0	45
70-71	0	0	0	0	0	0	0	0	0	7	4	0	3	32	0	0	0	0	0	0	0	46
71-72	0	0	0	0	0	0	0	0	0	7	4	0	3	46	0	0	0	0	0	0	0	60
72-73	0	0	0	0	0	0	0	0	0	7	4	0	3	34	0	0	0	0	0	0	0	48
73-74	0	0	0	0	0	0	0	0	0	7	4	0	2	17	0	0	0	0	0	0	219	249
74-75	0	0	0	0	0	0	0	0	0	7	4	0	2	17	0	0	0	0	0	0	220	250
75-76	0	0	0	0	0	0	0	0	0	6	4	0	2	11	0	0	0	0	0	232	0	255
76-77	0	0	0	0	0	0	0	0	0	6	4	0	2	11	0	0	0	0	20	255	0	298
77-78	0	0	0	0	0	0	0	0	0	6	4	0	2	10	0	0	0	0	47	255	0	324
78-79	0	0	0	0	0	0	0	0	0	6	4	0	0	0	62	0	0	0	47	255	0	374
79-80	0	0	0	0	0	0	0	0	0	6	4	0	0	0	117	0	0	0	47	255	0	429
80-81	0	0	0	0	0	0	0	0	0	6	4	0	0	0	117	0	0	0	47	255	0	429
81-82	0	0	0	0	0	0	0	0	0	6	3	0	0	0	117	0	0	0	37	0	0	163
82-83	0	0	0	0	0	0	0	0	0	6	3	0	0	0	0	0	0	0	0	0	0	9
TOTALS	136	23	146	49	168	44	67	255	2783	474	257	232	62	1109	413	155	296	165	245	1507	439	8586
	Brain	Eyes	Bucc	Phary	Thyro	Lary	Esoph	Bronc	Br'st	Lymph	B-C-S	Stom	SmInt	LgInt	Rec'm	Liver	Pancr	Kid'y	Bladd	Uter	Ovar	Body

AGE 20, Males, ISOLATED SLICE TABLE

Position (cm)	Brain/C.N.S.	Eyes	Buccal Organs	Pharynx	Thyroid	Larynx	Esophagus	Bronchi	Breast-Pair	Lymphatic Tissues	Bone, Connective, Skin	Stomach	Small Intestine & Other G.I.	Large Intestine	Rectum	Liver	Pancreas	Kidney	Bladder	Prostate	TOTALS	Position (cm)
0–1	0	0	0	0	0	0	0	0	0	0	0	0	0	0	0	0	0	0	0	0	0	0–1
1–2	4	0	0	0	0	0	0	0	0	0	1	0	0	0	0	0	0	0	0	0	5	1–2
2–3	8	0	0	0	0	0	0	0	0	0	1	0	0	0	0	0	0	0	0	0	9	2–3
3–4	12	0	0	0	0	0	0	0	0	0	1	0	0	0	0	0	0	0	0	0	13	3–4
4–5	18	0	0	0	0	0	0	0	0	4	2	0	0	0	0	0	0	0	0	0	20	4–5
5–6	18	0	0	0	0	0	0	0	0	4	2	0	0	0	0	0	0	0	0	0	20	5–6
6–7	18	0	0	0	0	0	0	0	0	4	2	0	0	0	0	0	0	0	0	0	24	6–7
7–8	18	0	0	0	0	0	0	0	0	4	2	0	0	0	0	0	0	0	0	0	24	7–8
8–9	18	0	0	0	0	0	0	0	0	4	2	0	0	0	0	0	0	0	0	0	24	8–9
9–10	18	6	0	0	0	0	0	0	0	4	2	0	0	0	0	0	0	0	0	0	30	9–10
10–11	18	8	0	0	0	0	0	0	0	4	2	0	0	0	0	0	0	0	0	0	32	10–11
11–12	4	6	38	12	0	0	0	0	0	4	2	0	0	0	0	0	0	0	0	0	66	11–12
12–13	2	0	38	13	0	0	0	0	0	4	2	0	0	0	0	0	0	0	0	0	59	12–13
13–14	0	0	38	14	0	0	0	0	0	4	2	0	0	0	0	0	0	0	0	0	58	13–14
14–15	0	0	38	14	0	0	0	0	0	4	3	0	0	0	0	0	0	0	0	0	59	14–15
15–16	0	0	38	14	0	0	0	0	0	4	3	0	0	0	0	0	0	0	0	0	59	15–16
16–17	0	0	38	14	0	0	0	0	0	4	3	0	0	0	0	0	0	0	0	0	59	16–17
17–18	0	0	38	14	0	0	0	0	0	4	3	0	0	0	0	0	0	0	0	0	59	17–18
18–19	0	0	37	13	0	0	0	0	0	4	3	0	0	0	0	0	0	0	0	0	57	18–19
19–20	0	0	0	13	0	0	0	0	0	4	3	0	0	0	0	0	0	0	0	0	20	19–20
20–21	0	0	0	0	0	54	5	0	0	4	3	0	0	0	0	0	0	0	0	0	66	20–21
21–22	0	0	0	0	0	54	5	0	0	4	3	0	0	0	0	0	0	0	0	0	66	21–22
22–23	0	0	0	0	21	54	5	0	0	4	3	0	0	0	0	0	0	0	0	0	87	22–23
23–24	0	0	0	0	21	52	5	0	0	4	3	0	0	0	0	0	0	0	0	0	85	23–24
24–25	0	0	0	0	20	0	5	5	0	6	3	0	0	0	0	0	0	0	0	0	39	24–25
25–26	0	0	0	0	0	0	5	5	0	6	3	0	0	0	0	0	0	0	0	0	19	25–26
26–27	0	0	0	0	0	0	5	5	1	6	3	0	0	0	0	0	0	0	0	0	20	26–27
27–28	0	0	0	0	0	0	5	5	1	6	3	0	0	0	0	0	0	0	0	0	20	27–28
28–29	0	0	0	0	0	0	6	26	2	6	3	0	0	0	0	0	0	0	0	0	43	28–29
29–30	0	0	0	0	0	0	6	26	2	6	3	0	0	0	0	0	0	0	0	0	43	29–30
30–31	0	0	0	0	0	0	5	26	2	6	3	0	0	0	0	0	0	0	0	0	42	30–31
31–32	0	0	0	0	0	0	5	26	2	6	3	0	0	0	0	0	0	0	0	0	42	31–32
32–33	0	0	0	0	0	0	5	26	2	6	3	0	0	0	0	0	0	0	0	0	42	32–33
33–34	0	0	0	0	0	0	5	26	2	6	3	0	0	0	0	0	0	0	0	0	42	33–34
34–35	0	0	0	0	0	0	5	26	2	6	3	0	0	0	0	0	0	0	0	0	42	34–35
35–36	0	0	0	0	0	0	5	26	2	6	3	0	0	0	0	0	0	0	0	0	42	35–36
36–37	0	0	0	0	0	0	5	26	1	6	3	0	0	0	0	0	0	0	0	0	41	36–37
37–38	0	0	0	0	0	0	5	26	1	6	3	0	0	0	0	0	0	0	0	0	41	37–38
38–39	0	0	0	0	0	0	5	26	1	6	3	0	0	0	0	0	0	0	0	0	41	38–39
39–40	0	0	0	0	0	0	5	11	0	6	3	0	0	0	0	0	0	0	0	0	25	39–40
40–41	0	0	0	0	0	0	5	11	0	6	3	0	0	0	0	0	0	0	0	0	25	40–41
41–42	0	0	0	0	0	0	5	11	0	6	3	0	0	0	0	0	0	0	0	0	25	41–42
42–43	0	0	0	0	0	0	5	11	0	6	3	0	0	0	0	0	0	0	0	0	25	42–43
43–44	0	0	0	0	0	0	5	3	0	7	3	0	0	0	0	0	0	0	0	0	18	43–44

Age 20 — Male

Age	Brain	Eyes	Bucc	Phary	Thyro	Lary	Esoph	Bronc	Br'st	Lymph	B-C-S	Stom	SmInt	LgInt	Rec'm	Liver	Pancr	Kid'y	Bladd	Prost	Body
44–45	0	0	0	0	0	0	0	0	0	7	3	0	0	0	0	0	0	0	0	0	18
45–46	0	0	0	0	0	0	5	3	0	7	3	0	0	0	0	0	0	0	0	0	18
46–47	0	0	0	0	0	0	5	3	0	7	3	0	0	0	0	0	0	0	0	0	31
47–48	0	0	0	0	0	0	5	3	0	7	3	0	0	0	0	0	0	0	0	0	31
48–49	0	0	0	0	0	0	5	3	0	7	3	0	0	0	0	0	0	0	0	0	31
49–50	0	0	0	0	0	0	5	0	0	7	3	10	0	0	0	13	62	5	0	0	100
50–51	0	0	0	0	0	0	0	0	0	7	3	15	0	0	0	13	61	15	0	0	114
51–52	0	0	0	0	0	0	0	0	0	7	3	23	0	0	0	13	61	21	0	0	128
52–53	0	0	0	0	0	0	0	0	0	7	3	23	0	0	0	13	31	21	0	0	92
53–54	0	0	0	0	0	0	0	0	0	7	3	23	0	16	0	13	15	21	0	0	92
54–55	0	0	0	0	0	0	0	0	0	7	3	24	0	16	0	13	15	21	0	0	93
55–56	0	0	0	0	0	0	0	0	0	7	3	24	0	16	0	7	15	21	0	0	93
56–57	0	0	0	0	0	0	0	0	0	7	3	24	1	16	0	6	15	21	0	0	93
57–58	0	0	0	0	0	0	0	0	0	7	3	24	1	16	0	6	15	21	0	0	94
58–59	0	0	0	0	0	0	0	0	0	7	3	24	1	16	0	6	8	21	0	0	84
59–60	0	0	0	0	0	0	0	0	0	7	3	24	1	63	0	6	0	21	0	0	123
60–61	0	0	0	0	0	0	0	0	0	7	3	24	2	63	0	6	0	21	0	0	123
61–62	0	0	0	0	0	0	0	0	0	7	3	23	2	63	0	3	0	14	0	0	115
62–63	0	0	0	0	0	0	0	0	0	7	3	23	2	63	0	3	0	5	0	0	107
63–64	0	0	0	0	0	0	0	0	0	7	3	15	2	63	0	3	0	0	0	0	94
64–65	0	0	0	0	0	0	0	0	0	7	3	10	2	44	0	3	0	0	0	0	67
65–66	0	0	0	0	0	0	0	0	0	7	3	0	3	25	0	3	0	0	0	0	38
66–67	0	0	0	0	0	0	0	0	0	7	3	0	3	25	0	3	0	0	0	0	38
67–68	0	0	0	0	0	0	0	0	0	7	3	0	3	25	0	0	0	0	0	0	38
68–69	0	0	0	0	0	0	0	0	0	7	3	0	3	25	0	0	0	0	0	0	38
69–70	0	0	0	0	0	0	0	0	0	7	3	0	2	25	0	0	0	0	0	0	37
70–71	0	0	0	0	0	0	0	0	0	7	3	0	2	25	0	0	0	0	0	0	37
71–72	0	0	0	0	0	0	0	0	0	7	3	0	2	25	0	0	0	0	0	0	37
72–73	0	0	0	0	0	0	0	0	0	7	3	0	2	25	0	0	0	0	0	0	37
73–74	0	0	0	0	0	0	0	0	0	7	3	0	2	25	0	0	0	0	0	0	37
74–75	0	0	0	0	0	0	0	0	0	7	3	0	2	25	0	0	0	0	0	0	37
75–76	0	0	0	0	0	0	0	0	0	7	3	0	2	25	0	0	0	0	0	0	37
76–77	0	0	0	0	0	0	0	0	0	6	3	0	2	25	0	0	0	0	0	0	36
77–78	0	0	0	0	0	0	0	0	0	6	3	0	2	34	0	0	0	0	0	0	45
78–79	0	0	0	0	0	0	0	0	0	6	3	0	2	29	0	0	0	0	0	0	40
79–80	0	0	0	0	0	0	0	0	0	6	3	0	1	10	0	0	0	0	0	0	21
80–81	0	0	0	0	0	0	0	0	0	6	3	0	1	10	0	0	0	0	0	0	20
81–82	0	0	0	0	0	0	0	0	0	6	3	0	0	6	0	0	0	0	46	0	16
82–83	0	0	0	0	0	0	0	0	0	6	3	0	0	6	0	0	0	0	114	0	61
83–84	0	0	0	0	0	0	0	0	0	6	3	0	0	6	0	0	0	0	114	0	129
84–85	0	0	0	0	0	0	0	0	0	6	3	0	0	0	64	0	0	0	114	0	187
85–86	0	0	0	0	0	0	0	0	0	6	3	0	0	0	129	0	0	0	114	0	252
86–87	0	0	0	0	0	0	0	0	0	6	3	0	0	0	129	0	0	0	114	783	1035
87–88	0	0	0	0	0	0	0	0	0	6	3	0	0	0	129	0	0	0	0	782	1034
88–89	0	0	0	0	0	0	0	0	0	6	3	0	0	0	0	0	0	0	0	0	9
TOTALS	156	20	303	121	62	214	147	368	21	495	248	333	59	856	451	133	298	249	616	1565	6715

AGE 20, Females, ISOLATED SLICE TABLE

Position (cm)	0-1	1-2	2-3	3-4	4-5	5-6	6-7	7-8	8-9	9-10	10-11	11-12	12-13	13-14	14-15	15-16	16-17	17-18	18-19	19-20	20-21	21-22	22-23	23-24	24-25	25-26	26-27	27-28	28-29	29-30	30-31	31-32	32-33	33-34	34-35	35-36	36-37	37-38	38-39	39-40	40-41	41-42	42-43	43-44
TOTALS	0	4	7	9	16	16	20	20	26	28	36	29	28	29	29	28	28	28	28	10	18	18	67	65	61	12	139	139	248	248	249	250	250	251	251	250	153	153	153	18	18	18	17	12
Ovaries	0	0	0	0	0	0	0	0	0	0	0	0	0	0	0	0	0	0	0	0	0	0	0	0	0	0	0	0	0	0	0	0	0	0	0	0	0	0	0	0	0	0	0	0
Uterus (corpus & cervix) & Other Genital	0	0	0	0	0	0	0	0	0	0	0	0	0	0	0	0	0	0	0	0	0	0	0	0	0	0	0	0	0	0	0	0	0	0	0	0	0	0	0	0	0	0	0	0
Bladder	0	0	0	0	0	0	0	0	0	0	0	0	0	0	0	0	0	0	0	0	0	0	0	0	0	0	0	0	0	0	0	0	0	0	0	0	0	0	0	0	0	0	0	0
Kidney	0	0	0	0	0	0	0	0	0	0	0	0	0	0	0	0	0	0	0	0	0	0	0	0	0	0	0	0	0	0	0	0	0	0	0	0	0	0	0	0	0	0	0	0
Pancreas	0	0	0	0	0	0	0	0	0	0	0	0	0	0	0	0	0	0	0	0	0	0	0	0	0	0	0	0	0	0	0	0	0	0	0	0	0	0	0	0	0	0	0	0
Liver	0	0	0	0	0	0	0	0	0	0	0	0	0	0	0	0	0	0	0	0	0	0	0	0	0	0	0	0	0	0	0	0	0	0	0	0	0	0	0	0	0	0	0	0
Rectum	0	0	0	0	0	0	0	0	0	0	0	0	0	0	0	0	0	0	0	0	0	0	0	0	0	0	0	0	0	0	0	0	0	0	0	0	0	0	0	0	0	0	0	0
Large Intestine	0	0	0	0	0	0	0	0	0	0	0	0	0	0	0	0	0	0	0	0	0	0	0	0	0	0	0	0	0	0	0	0	0	0	0	0	0	0	0	0	0	0	0	0
Small Intestine & Other G.I.	0	0	0	0	0	0	0	0	0	0	0	0	0	0	0	0	0	0	0	0	0	0	0	0	0	0	0	0	0	0	0	0	0	0	0	0	0	0	0	0	0	0	0	0
Stomach	0	0	0	0	0	0	0	0	0	0	0	0	0	0	0	0	0	0	0	0	0	0	0	0	0	0	0	0	0	0	0	0	0	0	0	0	0	0	0	0	0	0	0	0
Bone, Connective, Skin	0	1	1	1	2	2	2	2	2	2	2	2	2	2	2	2	2	2	2	2	2	2	2	2	2	2	2	2	2	2	2	2	2	2	2	2	3	3	3	3	3	3	3	3
Lymphatic Tissues	0	0	0	0	0	4	4	4	4	4	4	4	4	4	4	4	4	4	4	4	5	5	5	5	5	5	5	5	5	5	5	5	5	5	5	5	5	5	5	5	5	5	5	5
Breast-Pair	0	0	0	0	0	0	0	0	0	0	0	0	0	0	0	0	0	0	0	0	0	0	0	0	0	0	127	127	224	224	225	225	225	225	225	224	127	127	127	0	0	0	0	0
Bronchi	0	0	0	0	0	0	0	0	0	0	0	0	0	0	0	0	0	0	0	0	0	0	0	0	0	0	3	3	15	15	15	16	16	16	16	16	15	15	7	7	7	2	0	0
Esophagus	0	0	0	0	0	0	0	0	0	0	0	0	0	0	0	0	0	0	0	0	2	2	2	2	2	2	2	2	2	2	2	2	2	2	2	2	2	2	2	2	2	3	2	2
Larynx	0	0	0	0	0	0	0	0	0	0	0	0	0	0	0	0	0	0	10	10	10	8	0	0	0	0	0	0	0	0	0	0	0	0	0	0	0	0	0	0	0	0	0	0
Thyroid	0	0	0	0	0	0	0	0	0	0	0	0	0	0	0	0	0	0	0	0	0	0	49	49	49	0	0	0	0	0	0	0	0	0	0	0	0	0	0	0	0	0	0	0
Pharynx	0	0	0	0	0	0	0	4	5	5	5	5	5	5	5	4	0	0	0	0	0	0	0	0	0	0	0	0	0	0	0	0	0	0	0	0	0	0	0	0	0	0	0	0
Buccal Organs	0	0	0	0	0	0	0	0	0	0	17	17	17	18	18	17	17	17	0	0	0	0	0	0	0	0	0	0	0	0	0	0	0	0	0	0	0	0	0	0	0	0	0	0
Eyes	0	0	0	0	0	0	6	8	6	6	0	0	0	0	0	0	0	0	0	0	0	0	0	0	0	0	0	0	0	0	0	0	0	0	0	0	0	0	0	0	0	0	0	0
Brain/C.N.S.	0	3	6	8	14	14	14	14	14	14	3	1	0	0	0	0	0	0	0	0	0	0	0	0	0	0	0	0	0	0	0	0	0	0	0	0	0	0	0	0	0	0	0	0
Position (cm)	0-1	1-2	2-3	3-4	4-5	5-6	6-7	7-8	8-9	9-10	10-11	11-12	12-13	13-14	14-15	15-16	16-17	17-18	18-19	19-20	20-21	21-22	22-23	23-24	24-25	25-26	26-27	27-28	28-29	29-30	30-31	31-32	32-33	33-34	34-35	35-36	36-37	37-38	38-39	39-40	40-41	41-42	42-43	43-44

Age 20 — Female

Age	Brain	Eyes	Bucc	Phary	Thyro	Lary	Esoph	Bronc	Br'st	Lymph	B-C-S	Stom	SmInt	LgInt	Rec'm	Liver	Paner	Kid'y	Bladd	Uter	Ovar	Body
44–45	0	0	0	0	0	0	2	2	0	5	3	0	0	0	0	0	0	0	0	0	0	12
45–46	0	0	0	0	0	0	2	2	0	5	3	0	0	0	0	0	0	0	0	0	0	10
46–47	0	0	0	0	0	0	2	2	0	5	3	0	0	0	0	14	0	0	0	0	0	24
47–48	0	0	0	0	0	0	2	2	0	5	3	0	0	0	0	14	0	0	0	0	0	24
48–49	0	0	0	0	0	0	2	2	0	6	3	0	0	0	0	13	0	3	0	0	0	24
49–50	0	0	0	0	0	0	0	0	0	6	3	6	0	0	0	13	56	10	0	0	0	87
50–51	0	0	0	0	0	0	0	0	0	6	3	9	0	0	0	13	56	11	0	0	0	97
51–52	0	0	0	0	0	0	0	0	0	6	3	14	1	0	0	7	56	11	0	0	0	103
52–53	0	0	0	0	0	0	0	0	0	6	3	14	2	14	0	6	28	12	0	0	0	69
53–54	0	0	0	0	0	0	0	0	0	6	3	14	2	20	0	6	11	12	0	0	0	67
54–55	0	0	0	0	0	0	0	0	0	6	3	15	2	20	0	6	11	12	0	0	0	75
55–56	0	0	0	0	0	0	0	0	0	6	3	15	2	20	0	6	11	12	0	0	0	75
56–57	0	0	0	0	0	0	0	0	0	6	3	15	2	20	0	6	11	12	0	0	0	75
57–58	0	0	0	0	0	0	0	0	0	6	3	15	3	20	0	3	7	12	0	0	0	75
58–59	0	0	0	0	0	0	0	0	0	6	3	15	3	71	0	3	0	11	0	0	0	68
59–60	0	0	0	0	0	0	0	0	0	6	3	14	3	71	0	3	0	11	0	0	0	112
60–61	0	0	0	0	0	0	0	0	0	6	3	14	2	71	0	3	0	3	0	0	0	110
61–62	0	0	0	0	0	0	0	0	0	6	3	13	2	71	0	3	0	0	0	0	0	111
62–63	0	0	0	0	0	0	0	0	0	6	3	9	2	71	0	3	0	0	0	0	0	102
63–64	0	0	0	0	0	0	0	0	0	6	3	6	2	49	0	0	0	0	0	0	0	95
64–65	0	0	0	0	0	0	0	0	0	6	3	0	2	27	0	0	0	0	0	0	0	66
65–66	0	0	0	0	0	0	0	0	0	5	3	0	2	27	0	0	0	0	0	0	0	38
66–67	0	0	0	0	0	0	0	0	0	5	3	0	2	27	0	0	0	0	0	0	0	37
67–68	0	0	0	0	0	0	0	0	0	5	3	0	2	27	0	0	0	0	0	0	0	37
68–69	0	0	0	0	0	0	0	0	0	5	3	0	2	27	0	0	0	0	0	0	0	37
69–70	0	0	0	0	0	0	0	0	0	5	3	0	2	27	0	0	0	0	0	0	0	37
70–71	0	0	0	0	0	0	0	0	0	5	3	0	2	27	0	0	0	0	0	0	0	37
71–72	0	0	0	0	0	0	0	0	0	5	3	0	2	27	0	0	0	0	0	0	0	37
72–73	0	0	0	0	0	0	0	0	0	5	3	0	1	27	0	0	0	0	0	0	0	37
73–74	0	0	0	0	0	0	0	0	0	5	3	0	1	27	0	0	0	0	0	0	0	37
74–75	0	0	0	0	0	0	0	0	0	5	3	0	1	27	0	0	0	0	0	0	0	37
75–76	0	0	0	0	0	0	0	0	0	5	3	0	1	42	0	0	0	0	0	0	0	51
76–77	0	0	0	0	0	0	0	0	0	5	3	0	0	34	0	0	0	0	0	0	0	43
77–78	0	0	0	0	0	0	0	0	0	5	3	0	0	15	0	0	0	0	0	0	0	266
78–79	0	0	0	0	0	0	0	0	0	5	3	0	0	15	0	0	0	0	0	0	0	267
79–80	0	0	0	0	0	0	0	0	0	5	3	0	0	7	0	0	0	0	0	0	192	167
80–81	0	0	0	0	0	0	0	0	0	5	3	0	0	7	0	0	0	0	0	0	192	244
81–82	0	0	0	0	0	0	0	0	0	5	3	0	0	7	0	0	0	0	0	167	0	268
82–83	0	0	0	0	0	0	0	0	0	5	3	0	0	0	52	0	0	0	0	230	0	313
83–84	0	0	0	0	0	0	0	0	0	5	3	0	0	0	103	0	0	0	16	230	0	364
84–85	0	0	0	0	0	0	0	0	0	5	3	0	0	0	103	0	0	0	40	230	0	364
85–86	0	0	0	0	0	0	0	0	0	5	3	0	0	0	103	0	0	0	40	230	0	149
86–87	0	0	0	0	0	0	0	0	0	5	3	0	0	0	0	0	0	0	40	230	0	8
87–88	0	0	0	0	0	0	0	0	0	5	3	0	0	0	0	0	0	0	40	0	0	0
88–89	0	0	0	0	0	0	0	0	0	5	3	0	0	0	0	0	0	0	38	0	0	0
TOTALS	119	20	138	43	147	38	59	223	2432	415	225	203	55	969	361	135	258	144	214	1317	384	7899

279

AGES 20, 30, 40, 50: Summaries for Males and Females, ISOLATED SLICE TABLES
Cancer risks for males (M) are on left; risks for females (F) are on right

Position	Age 20-M	Age 30-M	Age 40-M	Age 50-M
0-1	0	0	0	0
1-2	5	4	2	0.08
2-3	9	8	3	0.14
3-4	13	11	5	0.20
4-5	20	17	7	0.30
5-6	20	17	7	0.30
6-7	24	20	9	0.36
7-8	24	20	9	0.36
8-9	24	20	9	0.36
9-10	30	26	11	0.45
10-11	32	27	12	0.48
11-12	66	56	25	0.99
12-13	59	50	22	0.89
13-14	58	50	22	0.87
14-15	59	50	22	0.89
15-16	59	50	22	0.89
16-17	59	50	22	0.89
17-18	59	50	22	0.89
18-19	57	49	21	0.86
19-20	20	17	7	0.30
20-21	66	56	25	0.99
21-22	66	56	25	0.99
22-23	87	74	32	1.31
23-24	85	73	32	1.28
24-25	39	33	15	0.59
25-26	19	16	7	0.29
26-27	20	17	7	0.30
27-28	20	17	7	0.30
28-29	43	37	16	0.65
29-30	43	37	16	0.65
30-31	42	36	16	0.63
31-32	42	36	16	0.63
32-33	42	36	16	0.63
33-34	42	36	16	0.63
34-35	42	36	16	0.63
35-36	42	36	16	0.63
36-37	41	35	15	0.62
37-38	41	35	15	0.62
38-39	41	35	15	0.62
39-40	25	21	9	0.38
40-41	25	21	9	0.38
41-42	25	21	9	0.38
42-43	25	21	9	0.38

Position	Age 20-F	Age 30-F	Age 40-F	Age 50-F
0-1	0	0	0	0
1-2	4	3	2	0.07
2-3	7	6	3	0.12
3-4	9	8	4	0.15
4-5	16	14	6	0.27
5-6	16	14	6	0.27
6-7	20	17	8	0.34
7-8	20	17	8	0.34
8-9	20	17	8	0.34
9-10	26	23	10	0.44
10-11	28	24	11	0.48
11-12	36	31	14	0.61
12-13	29	25	11	0.49
13-14	28	24	11	0.48
14-15	29	25	11	0.49
15-16	29	25	11	0.49
16-17	28	24	11	0.48
17-18	28	24	11	0.48
18-19	28	24	11	0.48
19-20	10	9	4	0.17
20-21	18	16	7	0.31
21-22	18	16	7	0.31
22-23	67	58	26	1.14
23-24	65	57	25	1.11
24-25	61	53	24	1.04
25-26	12	10	5	0.20
26-27	139	121	54	2.36
27-28	139	121	54	2.36
28-29	248	217	97	4.22
29-30	248	217	97	4.22
30-31	249	217	97	4.23
31-32	250	218	98	4.25
32-33	250	218	98	4.25
33-34	250	218	98	4.25
34-35	250	218	98	4.25
35-36	249	217	97	4.23
36-37	152	133	59	2.58
37-38	152	133	59	2.58
38-39	152	133	59	2.58
39-40	17	15	7	0.29
40-41	17	15	7	0.29
41-42	18	16	7	0.31
42-43	17	15	7	0.29

CANCERS PER MILLION	Age 20-M	Age 30-M	Age 40-M	Age 50-M	Age 20-F	Age 30-F	Age 40-F	Age 50-F
43–44	18	15	7	0.27	12	10	5	0.20
44–45	18	15	7	0.27	12	10	5	0.20
45–46	18	15	7	0.27	12	10	5	0.20
46–47	31	26	12	0.47	26	23	10	0.44
47–48	31	26	12	0.47	26	23	10	0.44
48–49	31	26	12	0.47	26	23	10	0.44
49–50	100	85	37	1.50	87	76	34	1.48
50–51	114	97	42	1.71	97	85	38	1.65
51–52	128	109	48	1.92	103	90	40	1.75
52–53	92	79	34	1.38	69	60	27	1.17
53–54	92	79	34	1.38	67	58	26	1.14
54–55	93	79	35	1.40	75	65	29	1.28
55–56	93	79	35	1.40	75	65	29	1.28
56–57	93	79	35	1.40	75	65	29	1.28
57–58	94	80	35	1.41	75	65	29	1.28
58–59	84	72	31	1.26	68	59	27	1.16
59–60	123	105	46	1.85	112	98	44	1.90
60–61	123	105	46	1.85	110	96	43	1.87
61–62	115	98	43	1.73	111	97	43	1.89
62–63	107	91	40	1.61	102	89	40	1.73
63–64	94	80	35	1.41	95	83	37	1.62
64–65	67	57	25	1.01	66	58	26	1.12
65–66	38	32	14	0.57	38	33	15	0.65
66–67	38	32	14	0.57	37	32	14	0.63
67–68	38	32	14	0.57	37	32	14	0.63
68–69	38	32	14	0.57	37	32	14	0.63
69–70	37	32	14	0.56	37	32	14	0.63
70–71	37	32	14	0.56	37	32	14	0.63
71–72	37	32	14	0.56	37	32	14	0.63
72–73	37	32	14	0.56	37	32	14	0.63
73–74	37	32	14	0.56	37	32	14	0.63
74–75	37	32	14	0.56	37	32	14	0.63
75–76	37	32	14	0.56	37	32	14	0.63
76–77	36	31	13	0.54	37	32	14	0.63
77–78	45	38	17	0.68	51	45	20	0.87
78–79	40	34	15	0.60	43	38	17	0.73
79–80	21	18	8	0.30	216	189	84	3.67
80–81	20	17	7	0.24	216	189	84	3.67
81–82	16	14	6		183	160	72	3.11
82–83	61	52	23	0.92	261	228	102	4.44
83–84	129	110	48	1.94	285	249	111	4.85
84–85	187	160	70	2.81	330	288	129	5.61
85–86	252	215	94	3.78	381	333	149	6.48
86–87	1,035	884	385	15.5	381	333	149	6.48
87–88	1,034	883	385	15.5	149	130	58	2.53
88–89	9	8	3	0.14	8	7	3	0.14
CANCERS PER MILLION	6715	5735	2498	100.73	7899	6896	3089	134.28

281

CHAPTER 11

Leukemia
as a Delayed Effect

Both in Hiroshima and in Nagasaki, the death rate from leukemia for the period October 1950 to December 1972 exceeds that expected on the basis of Japanese national rates, even for the group of people estimated to have been exposed to doses of less than 10 rad. . . . (Sir E.E. Pochin [1976], National Radiological Protection Board, England)

We treat the risk of leukemia separately from the risk of other cancers because its time sequence, following exposure to ionizing radiation, is totally different from the comparable time sequence for solid cancers (Chapter 18).

When individuals in a group are exposed one time to ionizing radiation, the group's rate of excess leukemia resulting from the irradiation reaches its peak about 7.5 years later. (This interval changes, of course, if members of a group are exposed more than once, over an extended period of time.) After 7.5 years, excess cases in a 1-exposure group continue to appear, but the magnitude of the excess declines. In the Hiroshima-Nagasaki experience, the excess cases are virtually absent some 30 years following exposure. By contrast, for the various solid cancers discussed in this book, the rate of excess cases peaks some forty years following the radiation exposure.

On the average, therefore, if people are irradiated at the same age, each case of radiation-induced leukemia represents a much more serious loss of lifespan to the individual who develops it, than does each fatal radiation-induced cancer case, because the leukemia occurs so much sooner.

During the unfolding period of the Hiroshima-Nagasaki evidence, upon which this chapter's analysis is based, very few of the leukemia cases had a long survival period. Hence, the incidence rate and the mortality rate for leukemia were essentially identical in the study of A-bomb survivors. We shall treat the leukemia data from Hiroshima-Nagasaki as incidence data.

Recent therapeutic efforts with leukemia mean that some of the cases which would have been quickly fatal in earlier years may now have a fairly long life expectancy.

This chapter covers the following main topics:

- Definition and magnitude of "Leukemia Dose" (Section 1);
- The leukemia risk from any type of X-ray exam (Section 2);
- The consequence of six marrow-rads (Section 3);
- Lessons from a Mayo Clinic study (Section 4);
- Lessons from an Ontario pediatric study (Section 5);
- Information as a deadly weapon (Section 6).

Section 1: The Magnitude of the U.S. "Leukemia Doses"

A detailed analysis of the rates at which ionizing radiation produces leukemia has been presented in *Radiation and Human Health* (Gofman, 1981), and we will use the results from that analysis in this section.

Whole-Body Leukemia Dose

We will use the term "Whole-Body Leukemia Dose" in analyzing the expected rate of excess leukemia from ionizing radiation exposure. One Whole-Body Leukemia Dose is the dose of ionizing radiation which will cause one extra case of leukemia among an exposed group of people.

The dose is expressed in terms of "marrow-rads," which can best be understood from the meaning of "person-rads." One person who absorbs 1 rad yields what is called 1 person-rad, and 12 people who each absorb 5 rads yield 60 person-rads. A person-rad is simply the number of persons times the number of rads. Person-rads can be added: 1 person-rad plus 60 person-rads = 61 person-rads. The same convention is used when the dose to only one *part* of the body is at issue, such as lung-rads, stomach-rads, or marrow-rads. Such terms refer, of course, to absorbed doses, not entrance doses.

It is customary, and sensible, to use the absorbed dose to the active bone marrow of the whole body as the relevant dose for leukemia calculations. This is partly because a large share of the radiation-induced leukemia cases results from irradiating the bone marrow, and partly because one can approximate that the dose to the active bone marrow provides a good indicator of a similar dose to any other widely distributed leukemia-susceptible cells.

No Discernible Age Trend

The evidence from Hiroshima-Nagasaki is such that we cannot discern a definitive trend of susceptibility to radiation-induced leukemia by age at exposure. We doubt that any new evidence, at least in the foreseeable future, is going to make it possible to ascertain whether or not any real age trends exist for radiation-induced leukemia, as they clearly do for radiation-induced cancers of other types. Therefore, we must consider the full range of data, all ages combined, from the Hiroshima-Nagasaki studies.

Doses per excess case of leukemia among the A-bomb survivors range among the various age groups between 5,000 and 15,000 marrow-rads. We will use the mid-value of 10,000 marrow-rads as the Whole-Body Leukemia Dose—the aggregate dose which produces one case of radiation-induced leukemia in an irradiated group.

Higher Spontaneous Rate among Males

The Whole-Body Leukemia Dose of 10,000 marrow-rads is derived from data combining males and females. We need separate values for each, however. The leukemia consequences of irradiation are more severe for males than females because males have the higher rate of *spontaneous* leukemia. Therefore, males will develop more leukemia per marrow-rad, which means that *fewer* marrow-rads will induce a case. This is another way of saying that males will have a *lower* Whole-Body Leukemia Dose than females.

In the calculation which follows, we assume that an observation which holds for all other malignancies produced by ionizing radiation also holds for leukemia: there is no difference between males and females in the *percent increase* of the disease per rad of irradiation.

Obtaining Separate Leukemia Doses
for Males and Females

How do we go about obtaining separate Whole-Body Leukemia Doses for males and females? We must start with Japan, because the comparisons of rates among irradiated and non-irradiated people are based on observations made *there*.

For Japan, the age-adjusted spontaneous leukemia rates for 1974–1975 were 4.2 per 100,000 per year for males, and 3.1 per 100,000 per year for females. From these rates, we create a lowering factor (3.1 / 4.2) and use it below to distribute the one Whole-Body Leukemia Dose of 10,000 marrow-rads appropriately between males and females in a population composed equally of each sex. Readers who have consulted Chapter 22 will have little trouble following the calculations in this chapter.

Let d = the female Whole-Body Leukemia Dose in marrow-rads.

Then (3.1 / 4.2) × (d) = the male Whole-Body Leukemia Dose = 0.738d.

Because the average of the two doses must equal what was *observed*, namely 10,000 marrow-rads per excess leukemia, we must say:

$$\frac{d + 0.738d}{2} = 10,000. \text{ So } \frac{1.738d}{2} = 10,000. \text{ So } 0.869d = 10,000.$$

Lastly, d = 11,507 = the female Whole-Body Leukemia Dose, in marrow-rads. And because 0.738d (above) = the *male* Whole-Body Leukemia Dose, we simply multiply 0.738 × 11,507 to get it: 8,492 marrow-rads. We shall not round off here, until we have considered the U.S. population.

The Leukemia Doses for American Males and Females

The age-adjusted leukemia rate is spontaneously higher among U.S. males than among Japanese males: 6.9 per 100,000 for Americans and 4.2 per 100,000 for Japanese. A higher spontaneous rate means a larger number of cases per marrow-rad, so the Whole-Body Leukemia Dose for U.S. males will be *lower* than for Japanese males. We need to multiply the Japanese Leukemia Dose by a lowering factor (a number smaller than 1.0), and we have the appropriate factor: (4.2 / 6.9) = 0.6087. So the Whole-Body Leukemia Dose for U.S. males = 0.6087 × 8,492 marrow rads = 5,169 marrow-rads. We will round this off further to 5,000 marrow-rads.

The spontaneous leukemia rate also is higher among U.S. females than among Japanese females: 4.3 per 100,000 for Americans and 3.1 per 100,000 for Japanese. Again we can use the ratio of the rates as our lowering factor for the Japanese Leukemia Dose. So the Whole-Body Leukemia Dose for U.S. females = (3.1 / 4.3) × (11,507 marrow-rads) = 8,296 marrow-rads. We will round this off further to 8,000 marrow rads. In our opinion, the goodness of the data does not justify any closer approximations than these:

For U.S. Males: 5,000 marrow-rads per leukemia.
For U.S. Females: 8,000 marrow-rads per leukemia.

Section 2: Leukemia Risk from Any Type of X-Ray Exam

If we know that one additional case of leukemia is expected per 5,000 marrow-rads absorbed by a group of U.S. males, we can also know what the risk of leukemia is from *one* marrow-rad absorbed by that group. The answer is easily obtained because there is a linear relationship between radiation dose and leukemia production (R&HH). If *one* additional case is caused per 5,000 marrow-rads, it follows that only a fraction of a case (1 / 5,000 or 0.0002 case) is caused by *one* marrow-rad. We can express that statement as an equation in which the division line stands for the word "per":

$$\frac{1 \text{ leukemia case}}{5,000 \text{ marrow-rads}} = \frac{0.0002 \text{ leukemia case}}{1 \text{ marrow-rad}}$$

Exactly the same information can be expressed otherwise, in the familiar manner: the male risk from 1 rad absorbed by all his active bone marrow is 200 per million, or 1 chance in 5,000. For U.S. females:

$$\frac{1 \text{ leukemia case}}{8,000 \text{ marrow-rads}} = \frac{0.000125 \text{ leukemia case}}{1 \text{ marrow-rad}}$$

Expressed in the familiar manner, the female risk from 1 rad absorbed by all her active bone marrow is 125 per million, or 1 chance in 8,000. For easy reference, we have boxed these values in Table 13.

Table 13 is the basis for the entries entitled "Rate of future leukemia from Common Exam" in this book's risk tables. For every diagnostic examination evaluated in Chapters 5, 7, and 9, we have obtained or estimated the whole-body marrow dose in rads.

Active bone marrow progressively recedes from the extremities of the limbs, as children move toward adulthood. Consequently, the active bone marrow is less widely distributed and more concentrated in the adult. On the other hand, bone marrow in the young is more accessible to the X-ray beam. We have tried to take both effects into account in estimating marrow-rads per exam at various ages.

Table 13. Leukemia Risk from Any Type of X-Ray Exam

The Proper Marrow Dose: For the first term in the equations below, the proper dose depends on the fraction of the marrow irradiated. For example, if an exam exposes one-fifth of the body's active bone marrow to 1.0 rad, the first term would be 0.2 marrow-rad per exam. When only a fraction of the whole body's active marrow is irradiated, that fraction *must* be used as the lowering factor which will lower the risk appropriately.

For Males, United States:
    Risk of Leukemia per Exam =
    (marrow-rads per exam) × (200 per million, per marrow-rad)
For Females, United States:
    Risk of Leukemia per Exam =
    (marrow-rads per exam) × (125 per million, per marrow-rad)

Using the equations from Table 13, we translated marrow-doses per exam into separate leukemia risks for males and females. Because there seems to be *no lessening* of risk with advancing age, the leukemia risks stated in the age-20 section of a table should be used for ages over 20 without applying any lowering factor. The lowering factors in the tables are for cancer risks only.

One Marrow-Rad As an Unusual Dose

It is not as easy as some researchers seem to think for an adult to accumulate 1.0 whole-body marrow-rad from diagnostic X-ray exams—unless, of course, he or she steps into a facility using entrance doses 10-fold or 20-fold above average (Chapter 16). So if researchers are interested in testing the leukemia risks from average entrance doses, they need to note that it takes *all* of the following exams to add up to about 1 marrow-rad for an adult (Kereiakes and Rosenstein, 1980, pp. 210, 211):

1. Barium Enema (excluding marrow dose from FLU)
2. Cervical Spine
3. Chest
4. Cholecystogram (excluding marrow dose from FLU)
5. Full Spine Chiropractic
6. Hip (one)

    7. I.V.P.
    8. K.U.B.
    9. Lumbo-Sacral Spine
 10. Pelvis
 11. Ribs
 12. Shoulder (one)
 13. Skull
 14. Thoracic Spine
 15. Upper G.I. (excluding marrow dose from FLU)

This list is purely illustrative; an infinite variety of combinations could also add up to 1 marrow-rad. If we imagine 5,000 males who each have this extraordinary medical history, we have a group representing 5,000 marrow-rads, and we can expect *one* excess case of leukemia to occur.

Is it any wonder that small epidemiologic studies at average diagnostic doses are virtually precluded, even before they start, from proving anything at all? We will return to this important issue in Sections 4, 5, and 6 of this chapter.

Section 3: The Consequence of Six Marrow-Rads

Spontaneous leukemia is a rare disease. But, for the person who develops leukemia, it is not rare at all—it is there, and it is very serious.

Because of the rarity of spontaneous leukemia, it turns out that we expect only one radiation-induced case per 5,000 marrow-rads among U.S. males, and only one radiation-induced case per 8,000 marrow-rads among U.S. females. However, in another sense, leukemia is very *easily* induced by ionizing radiation.

That other sense is understood by asking, how big a dose would *double* the frequency of this dreaded disease in the United States? The answer: an average dose of only 6 marrow-rads would increase the frequency by 100%. In other words, a person's risk of leukemia is doubled *by 6 marrow-rads.*

The Doubling Dose for Leukemia

Analysis of the large experience recorded in the leukemia registries of Hiroshima and Nagasaki has led to the conclusion that, when males and females are considered together, there is a 17% increase in the leukemia rate for every rad delivered to the whole-body active bone marrow. Therefore, 6 marrow-rads increase the leukemia rate by $6 \times 17\% = 102\%$ (a doubling). Twelve marrow-rads add about 200% to the spontaneous rate, and 18 marrow-rads add about 300% to the spontaneous rate.

The name for the dose which *doubles* the spontaneous rate—adds 100% to it—is the doubling dose. Two doubling doses add 200% to the spontaneous rate. Three doubling doses add 300% to the spontaneous rate.

As we stated earlier in this chapter, radiation's effect in producing leukemia virtually stops before the thirtieth year after exposure, so leukemia's doubling dose applies to approximately the twenty-five year period after irradiation. Doubling doses for other malignancies must specify a duration, too, if confusion is to be avoided.

Discovering the Connection of Radiation and Leukemia

Radiologists themselves provided the first evidence that X-rays increase the frequency of leukemia; the discovery was made by studying the rate of leukemia among such physicians. In the 1940s, March (1944) demonstrated that radiologists developed leukemia with a higher frequency than did other physicians. Because the radiologists received their radiation in divided doses over a long period of time, it is reasonable to conclude that the radiation effect for leukemia was indeed cumulative. A combination of small doses had a large effect.

Later, in the 1950s, overwhelming evidence that radiation induces excess leukemia became available in the series of atomic bomb survivors, and also in the series of patients who had received therapeutic radiation to their spines for the disease known as ankylosing spondylitis. But in both groups, the doses per exposure were very large compared with the divided doses which the radiologists experienced.

Hope springs eternal, and soon the experience of the radiologists was ignored. We began to hear that the Hiroshima-Nagasaki and spondylitic data told us only about "high doses delivered rapidly." Those who hoped that doses at diagnostic levels might not be leukemogenic also forgot, however, about Stewart's classic studies demonstrating excess leukemia in children irradiated in-utero (Chapter 12), with doses as low as 0.25 to 1.5 rads.

Looking Again at Evidence

Hope is a glorious thing. So it is natural and useful that medical investigators continue to re-examine whether or not radiation doses in the diagnostic range produce leukemia.

Two recent studies have addressed this question. Both report finding *no* provable excess leukemia. As we will show (Sections 4 and 5 of this chapter), both studies are so badly flawed as to be totally useless in addressing the question which they attempted to answer. They have, therefore, provided what we consider to be seriously false reassurance both to the medical profession and to patients concerning the true leukemia risk from ionizing radiation.

Section 4: The Mayo Clinic Study by Linos and Co-Workers

Linos and co-workers at the Mayo Clinic published the paper "Low Dose Radiation and Leukemia" in *The New England Journal of Medicine* (1980). In it, they report their conclusions and some of their data. They say at the beginning of their paper in the abstract (p. 1101):

> No statistically significant increase was found in the risk of developing leukemia after radiation doses of 0 to 300 rads (3 Gy) to the bone marrow when these amounts were administered in small doses over long periods of time, as in routine medical care.

To find out that there is no leukemia risk at all from "routine medical care" would be welcome news indeed—if it were true. It comes as something of a shock to read the *conclusion* of the same paper (p. 1105):

> Consequently, we maintain that low levels of exposure to medical radiation most probably did not increase the risk of leukemia in this community, but that if it did, the factor of increase is almost surely less than 2.0.

The Mayo investigators are saying that the size of their sample, and their manner of conducting the study, were so designed that, if low-dose medical radiation were nearly doubling the rate of leukemia in a community, they could have missed the effect with their study.

Nevertheless, their abstract plus the first half of the cited conclusion are almost certain to leave most readers with a false sense of reassurance.

The Practical Questions

Because a set of extensive data from Japan already exists on leukemia induction by radiation, useful questions to study would be, is there any reason *not* to use those observations? Would the Hiroshima-Nagasaki evidence *overestimate* the leukemia risk per marrow-rad if doses were divided and relatively low, as they are in diagnostic X-ray exams? Can we prove a *lower* leukemia risk per marrow-rad from diagnostic radiology than the 17% increase per marrow-rad observed at Hiroshima-Nagasaki?

One can begin by asking, if the effect per marrow-rad is just as severe as indicated by the Hiroshima-Nagasaki data, how big would the effect be from routine diagnostic X-rays on the leukemia rate in a U.S. community?

It is stated (BEIR III, 1980) that the average marrow dose received by U.S. adults from diagnostic radiology is 0.077 marrow-rads per year. It is even less for children, but giving the Mayo study some help, we will use the adult value of 0.077. The 17% increase in leukemia per marrow-rad from Hiroshima-Nagasaki data is an average value, males and females combined, for the 25-year period following exposure. In order to make a valid comparison, we must use the average annual American marrow-dose from diagnostic radiology for a 25-year period, rather than for a single year. If, on the average, Americans each absorb 0.077 marrow-rads every year from such procedures, the total dose received during each 25-year period is 1.925 marrow-rads per person.

The Existing Consistency

If diagnostic radiation is as potent in producing leukemia as was the rapidly delivered radiation at Hiroshima and Nagasaki, then we would expect that an American population would show (in an appropriately designed study) the following increase in leukemia incidence: 1.925 marrow-rads $\times$ 17% increase per marrow-rad = 32.7%. And if diagnostic radiation were *twice* as potent as bomb radiation per marrow-rad (but we are not suggesting that it is), the increase in leukemia frequency would be 65.4%.

But all that the Mayo investigators can say is that, if the effect were a 100% increase (a doubling of the spontaneous rate), they could have missed it. In effect, they have acknowledged that their study has nothing to say about effects as serious per marrow-rad as at Hiroshima and Nagasaki, and in fact, has little to say about effects even *twice* as bad.

In summary, the Mayo study in no way conflicts with the studies of the bomb survivors. Both sets of data are compatible. Therefore, no contradiction exists between the Mayo study and this book, which uses the bomb-survivor data. The Mayo study provides no reason whatsoever to think that diagnostic radiation is any less serious than the values in this book indicate.

Section 5: The Ontario Study by Spengler and Co-Workers

The second study which purports to challenge the leukemogenic potency of diagnostic radiation is that of Spengler and co-workers (1983) in the journal *Pediatrics*. Entitled "Cancer Mortality Following Cardiac Catheterization: A Preliminary Follow-up Study of 4,891 Irradiated Children," the paper says at the outset, in its abstract (p. 235): "The preliminary

findings did not demonstrate a significant leukemia risk arising from diagnostic catheterization."

Many readers mistakenly assume, when a paper reports finding "no
significant effect," that this means the effect is absent. Such an assumption
can be utterly wrong. If a study has too few subjects, or too small an
average dose, or too short a follow-up time, then proof of a statistically
significant effect may be impossible to obtain *even when the effect is huge.*

Spengler and co-workers have appropriately labeled their paper a
"preliminary follow-up study," and they do recognize its great shortcom-
ings. For instance, they admit that "Actual radiation doses for the children
were not readily available for this preliminary study." And near the conclusion of their paper, they state: "In essence, the size of our cohort is not
sufficient to detect accurately a low-dose radiation effect."

These are straightforward admissions of two of the study's serious
limitations, but the admissions are probably not sufficient to undo the
harm which can come from misunderstandings of the abstract.

The same question we asked about the Mayo study needs asking
again: does this study from Ontario, Canada indicate any lesser leukemogenic effect per marrow-rad from diagnostic radiation than was observed
per marrow-rad at Hiroshima and Nagasaki?

How to Test the Question

Because no actual dose measurements were made for the Ontario children, Spengler and co-workers provide some estimates of entrance dose,
which are similar to the entrance doses derived for Chapter 7 of this book
from the data of Webster and co-workers. Spengler and co-workers also
provide an estimate of absorbed chest dose, which also seems reasonable.
But they provide no estimate of field size, which is crucial for estimating
marrow-rads per exam. Consequently, their paper enables no one to estimate the dose which is relevant to the effect (leukemia) which they are
testing.

One is forced to look elsewhere. We are going to use Webster's data
for a complete catheterization plus cardiac angiogram series; these are the
data we analyzed for the Angiocardiography table in Chapter 7, Section
3. Because the field size is given for each age, it was possible to estimate
marrow-rads per exam.

Is it a reasonable approximation to apply these marrow-rads to the
Ontario children, in spite of the wide range of doses used in diagnostic
radiology? We say yes. First of all, it is clearly superior to no data at all for
marrow-rads. Secondly, the entrance doses based on Webster's data are
strikingly similar to the "exposure" of 25–30 rads guesstimated for the
Ontario series in the Spengler paper. And thirdly, the approximation is

likely to be close to the truth because we are not mixing "apples and oranges." We are combining data from two *leading* medical centers.

The Ontario study reports on children who had cardiac catheterization procedures all as patients at the Hospital for Sick Children in Toronto between 1946 and 1968. Spengler and co-workers state (p. 236), "The cardiac catheterization laboratory at the hospital was, and still remains, the major pediatric cardiology referral facility of its type serving the Province of Ontario."

Toronto, Canada, is a metropolis with fully modern medical centers, and we can presume that the leading hospital in this field would have used procedures comparable to those at equivalent centers in the United States, such as Boston's renowned Massachusetts General Hospital (M.G.H.), which was the source of the data for Webster and co-workers (1974).

If the data from M.G.H. are not a good match for the Ontario children, the approximation is more likely to overestimate the average marrow dose to the Ontario children than to underestimate it. Some of the Ontario exams occurred as early as 1946, and both Spengler and Webster comment that the *duration* of procedures has steadily increased over the years due to the increasingly complex studies which such angiograms perform. Therefore, marrow-rads per exam are likely to be higher from the M.G.H. data than they really were for the early Ontario exams.

Using the data derived from Webster, we can provide the doses to bone marrow from the Angiocardiography Exam which uses 40 radiographic films (biplane AP and lateral) and 30 minutes of fluoroscopy:

Age	Dose from Films and FLU Combined
Newborn	0.300 marrow-rad
1 year	0.388 marrow-rad
5 years	0.419 marrow-rad
10 years	0.317 marrow-rad
15 years	0.408 marrow-rad

The distribution of age and sex among the Ontario children was given by the Spengler paper as the following:

	Total Number	Age Group 0 to 4 Years	Age Group 5 to 9 Years	Age Group 10+ Years
Males	2,703	1,477	735	491
Females	2,188	935	731	522

For the group 0–4 years old, we will use a marrow dose halfway between the values for newborns and age 5, or 0.360 marrow-rads. For the group 5–9 years old, we will use a marrow dose halfway between the values for ages 5 and 10, or 0.368 marrow-rads. For the group 10 years and older, we will use the values for the 15-year-olds, or 0.408 marrow-rads. We need to obtain the *average* marrow doses for males and females:

$$Males \frac{(1{,}477 \times 0.360) + (735 \times 0.368) + (491 \times 0.408)}{1{,}477 + 735 + 491} = 0.371 \text{ marrow-rads}$$

$$Females \frac{(935 \times 0.360) + (731 \times 0.368) + (522 \times 0.408)}{935 + 731 + 522} = 0.374 \text{ marrow-rads}$$

Applying the Bomb-Survivor Evidence

Now we will calculate how much one would expect leukemia to increase *from the doses above,* if diagnostic radiation and bomb radiation are equally potent per marrow-rad.

Among the bomb survivors, males and females combined, there was a 17% increase in leukemia per marrow-rad, during the 25-year period following exposure in Hiroshima and Nagasaki. But the Ontario children were followed up for a shorter time: an average of 13.8 years for males and 13.3 years for females. Because the incidence of leukemia peaks about 7.5 years after exposure and then tapers off with a long tail, for any short follow-up period, the percentage increase is *higher* than the average for the entire 25 years. For the male group with 13.8 years of follow-up, the Japanese experience predicts a 27.3% increase in leukemia per marrow-rad. For the female group with the slightly shorter follow-up of 13.3 years, the curve predicts a 27.8% increase per marrow-rad.

We are now in a position to apply a very useful technique for solving this and similar problems by figuring out the *relative* magnitudes of two quantities, when we are fortunate enough to have the actual magnitude of *one* of them. We can say in this case:

Let w = the expected leukemia rate *with* the angiocardiograms.

Let w_0 = the spontaneous leukemia rate *without* the angiocardiograms.

Because Spengler and co-workers will provide the actual magnitude of w_0, we can provide the magnitude of w from the bomb-survivor data if we can just state the *relative* magnitudes of w and w_0. How many times bigger will w be than w_0? The following equation simply states in symbols and numbers what is obvious in words: the leukemia rate for the irradiated males (w) is equal to the spontaneous rate (w_0) plus whatever increment in the spontaneous rate (w_0) is caused by the dose in rads (0.371 marrow-rad) times the percent increase per rad (27.3% or 0.273).

$$w = w_0 + w_0(0.371 \text{ marrow-rad} \times 0.273 \text{ per marrow-rad})$$

$$w = w_0 + (w_0 \times 0.10128)$$

$$w = w_0 + 0.10128\ w_0$$

$$w = 1.101w_0\ \text{(rounded off)}$$

The last and shortest equation tells us that w is 1.101 times bigger than w_0. In other words, *whatever* the spontaneous rate of leukemia is without the angiograms, the rate predicted for the catheterized male children is 1.101 times higher (or about 10% higher).

For females, the procedure is the same:

$$w = w_0 + w_0(0.374\ \text{marrow-rad} \times 0.278\ \text{per marrow-rad})$$

$$w = w_0 + (w_0 \times 0.104)$$

$$w = w_0 + 0.104w_0$$

$$w = 1.104w_0$$

So, whatever the spontaneous rate of leukemia is without the angiograms, the rate predicted for the irradiated female children is 1.104 times higher. The raising factor is 1.104 for the females, and 1.101 for the males.

Did Spengler and co-workers observe *less* leukemia than the bomb-survivor studies predict? More? The same?

Spengler and co-workers present the following values from Ontario vital statistics for the leukemia cases (deaths) expected among the studied children during the follow-up period, if the radiation exposure had *no* effect. These are the appropriate *spontaneous* values for such an interval.

The Male Cohort, If Unirradiated:	1.22 leukemia deaths
The Female Cohort, If Unirradiated:	0.66 leukemia deaths
The Total Group, If Unirradiated:	1.88 leukemia deaths

When we apply the raising factors of 1.101 and 1.104 to the spontaneous values above, we find out the number of leukemia deaths which the *irradiated* cohorts will show if bomb radiation and diagnostic radiation have equal potency in producing leukemia:

The Male Cohort, Irradiated:	
1.22 deaths × 1.101 =	1.34 leukemia deaths
The Female Cohort, Irradiated:	
0.66 deaths × 1.104 =	0.73 leukemia deaths
The Total Group, Irradiated =	2.07 leukemia deaths

The number of leukemia deaths actually observed in the irradiated children was three. But no one should interpret the observation of 3.0 cases as any indication that diagnostic X-rays are even *more* potent than bomb radiation per marrow-rad. The random fluctuations of small numbers rule out such an interpretation.

The proper conclusion is simply that the observations made in the Ontario study are completely consistent with diagnostic radiation and bomb radiation having *equal* effects per marrow-rad. The Ontario study certainly does not prove a lower lower leukemia risk per marrow-rad from diagnostic radiology than from the Hiroshima-Nagasaki experience. The Spengler paper in no way challenges the leukemia risks presented in this book.

The Important Lesson

Although the abstract of the Spengler paper may suggest to the unwary that even angiocardiography (with many films and lengthy fluoroscopy) probably produces no leukemia risk for children, in reality, the evidence from that same paper is completely consistent with a very large increase in risk: 27.5% per marrow-rad during the 13.5 years following exposure.

It is particularly unfortunate that the probability of misunderstanding and consequent injury is intensified in a section entitled "Commentaries" in the same issue of *Pediatrics*. Comments on the Spengler study are provided by Robert Brent, a consultant to the BEIR Committee. He repeats the suggestion that "The investigators were unable to demonstrate a significant leukemia risk . . . for diagnostic radiation exposure." We are distressed that Brent did not do appropriate calculations before making a pronouncement which is so likely to mislead its readers.

The important lesson, from Sections 4 and 5 of this chapter, is the same one we described in Chapters 1 and 2. In science, when different investigators report findings which appear to contradict each other, the contradiction is not real. There is only one reality, no matter how dimly we humans perceive it at a given time.

Section 6: Information as a Deadly Weapon

Our objective in this book is to make for the reader *the best estimate we can* about the risk of developing cancer, leukemia, and other health injuries as a result of diagnostic X-ray examinations. We do not suggest that diagnostic exams are "bad" or "good" for people. As we stressed in the very first chapter, the judgment of whether or not an X-ray exam is good for a particular person must be made by physician and patient with full consideration of the risk from *not* having the examination.

It is only natural for all humans involved in some way with medicine and dentistry to hope that a tool as useful as diagnostic radiology will be harmless, or nearly so. We are no exceptions. We wish that all the risks we have evaluated in various chapters of this book were lower than they are. But hopes and opinions which fly in the face of evidence and logic can do only *harm* to humans.

We consider it a disservice for anyone either to overestimate or to underestimate the true risks from diagnostic X-rays. False findings and misleading pronouncements in the health sciences can be deadly weapons, literally. Words can kill. In fact, words which mislead people can kill *many* more humans than a bridge, a dam, or an automobile which is designed defectively.

We encourage scientists to keep probing and testing the goodness of data in the field of low-level radiation. But when a study is done which is far too small or too short (or both) to detect *anything,* and then such a study serves as a basis for widely circulated pronouncements that diagnostic radiation is showing "no significant effect" upon cancer and leukemia risks, that study can contribute nothing but confusion for millions of patients and their physicians on a matter of life and death.

CHAPTER 12

Injuries
to an Embryo or Fetus
from X-Rays

Following the work of Dr. Alice Stewart and others, it is now almost universally accepted that radiation to the fetus can cause leukemia or other neoplastic disease. (G.M. Ardran and H.E. Crooks [1976], Atomic Energy Research Establishment, Harwell, England [pp. 433–34])

It seems certain that irradiation of the embryo or fetus can cause major defects at birth. Among these, small head size and diminished intelligence are the most frequent. (Dr. Gilbert W. Beebe [1980], Clinical Epidemiology Division, National Cancer Institute, Washington, D.C.)

Our purpose here is to evaluate the health effects of diagnostic X-rays upon the embryo in-utero. For this reason, in the age-20 section of the Common Exam tables, we have provided the dose received by an embryo when a pregnant woman has one of the exams. The work of Rosenstein on dosimetry has been particularly helpful.

The embryo dose in the tables of this book applies to the early stages of pregnancy, up to approximately two months. We assume that, when a woman knows she is pregnant, she and her physicians will definitely avoid exposing her abdomen except in situations of overriding necessity. If such exposures occur, the risks per whole-body rad absorbed by the fetus are heavy, as the reader will see for himself or herself in this chapter. Of course, the dose to the embryo, provided in a table's age-20 section, is not altered by the actual age of the pregnant woman.

If an abdominal exam must be done during a well-advanced pregnancy, the whole-body dose to the fetus will be less uniform than it would be during the first two months. Estimates of absorbed fetal dose in such cases can be made for different beam directions by using Special Table C, when *actual* entrance doses are known.

Diagnostic pelvimetry, generally performed late in pregnancy, has been reported to deliver the following range of doses to the fetus:

Webster and co-workers (1974):	4 rads
Laws (1983):	0.6 to 4 rads
Robinson (1983) reporting on	
Great Britain's 1977 average	
for obstetric exams:	0.325 rads

Distinct Types of Risk

This chapter examines several distinct types of risk to the unborn child from X-ray exams:

- Permanently reduced body size (Section 1);
- Nonspecific infant mortality during the first year of life, and often during the first week (Section 2);
- Risk of the special childhood cancers (embryomata), plus leukemia, during the first 15 years of life (Section 3);
- Risk of the familiar adult cancers during the entire lifespan (Section 4);
- Risk of severe mental retardation (Section 5);
- Risk of a huge group of disorders customarily called "congenital anomalies," meaning any type of marked deviation from normal. Congenital abnormalities include major and minor defects of the eyes, heart, blood-vessel system, undescended testes (cryptorchidism), and skeletal deformities (Section 6).

Section 1: A Lasting Reduction in Body Height and Weight

Wood and co-workers (1967) demonstrated that there was a small, but statistically significant, effect of in-utero radiation at Hiroshima and Nagasaki in reducing average height and weight among the irradiated children. This effect persisted for the first 17 years of life, and after that, further follow-up study was not possible.

Within the limited data, it was not possible to demonstrate any connection between the stage of gestation and the radiation's effect on size. By contrast, the Hiroshima-Nagasaki data show that in-utero exposure to radiation early in gestation was far more potent in producing defective brain development than the same exposure late in gestation. This suggests that different mechanisms account for the body-size and the brain effects.

The data are not sufficient on reduced body size to approximate any dose-response curve for this effect. Therefore we have no basis for expecting the effect to occur, or not to occur, from radiation doses at the diagnostic level. We can only say that, if an effect occurs at all at such dose levels, it must be quite small.

Section 2: Nonspecific Infant Mortality

Reliable quantitative evidence is very scarce for comparing in-utero radiation to excess infant mortality from nonspecific causes during the first year of life. We will rely on the data reported from Hiroshima-Nagasaki by Kato (1971). He found an excess infant mortality rate for in-utero irradiation of 0.54% per rad, or 0.54 per 100 per rad. When the rate is expressed in our familiar way, it is a risk of infant mortality per rad of 5,400 per million, or 1 chance in 185 per *fetal* rad. Thus the risk refers not to an entrance dose received by a mother, but rather to a whole-body rad absorbed by the unborn child.

We have deep reservations concerning any application of this finding to in-utero doses at the diagnostic levels reported in this book. There are two reasons.

First, there are no data specifically from the low-dose group in the Hiroshima-Nagasaki studies of infant mortality. Direct evidence at very low doses most definitely exists for the risks of cancer and mental retardation discussed later in this chapter, but not for nonspecific infant mortality.

Second, Kato found that the infant mortality was higher from irradiation in the third trimester of pregnancy than in either of the earlier trimesters. This observation suggests that the mortality is *not* caused by the arising of large clusters of defective cells from single injured cells, because if it were, the effect would almost certainly be larger from exposure during the earlier stages of pregnancy than during the later stages (Section 6 of this chapter). The mechanism accounting for the mortality is simply not known at this time.

For *unknown* mechanisms, there is no basis in medical science for automatically assuming (in the absence of any comparable observations) that an effect is proportional to dose (the linear dose-response curve).

No one is presently in a position to assert that the rate of 5,400 per million, per fetal rad, applies equally to all dose levels. All that can be said for now is that doses in the range of diagnostic X-rays *may or may not* increase the rate of nonspecific infant mortality during the first year of life. If such doses do increase the nonspecific mortality rate, the increase per rad is uncertain, but the seriousness of the stakes is self-evident.

Section 3: Childhood Cancers and Leukemia between Ages 0–15

Stewart and co-workers (1956) initiated the remarkable work showing that, when mothers have diagnostic radiation during pregnancy, their offspring show approximately a 50% increase in the risk of cancer or leukemia during the first 10 years of life (later studies extended this to the first 15 years). For investigating effects much beyond age 15, the method is not a powerful one, so effects lasting longer are considered separately in Section 4 of this chapter.

Later investigations by Stewart and Kneale (1970) showed that the risk of childhood cancer or leukemia was proportional to radiation dose (the linear dose-response curve) in the general region of 0.25 to 1.5 rads absorbed by the fetus. The substance, method, and validity of these studies are discussed in detail elsewhere (R&HH, Gofman, 1981).

The findings of Stewart's in-utero studies have been independently confirmed by additional studies (MacMahon, 1962; Newcombe and McGregor, 1971; Holford, 1975; Mole, 1974, 1979). We consider them scientifically solid. Their meaning, with respect to the common X-ray examinations evaluated in this book, is set forth below.

How to Use the Evidence

To determine risk in a particular case, three pieces of information are needed:

1. The spontaneous risk of childhood cancer and leukemia without in-utero irradiation;
2. The Stewart factor of a 50% increase per rad absorbed by the fetus;
3. The fetal dose per diagnostic X-ray exam.

In the United States, the sum of the spontaneous death rates from cancer plus leukemia, during the first 15 years of life, is about 6 per 100,000 children per year. Over 15 years, the spontaneous death rate for both diseases combined would be (15 years) × (6 cases per 100,000 per year) = 90 per 100,000 children. Expressed in our customary way, the spontaneous risk over all 15 years would be 900 per million, or 1 chance in 1,111.

Now that all three pieces of information are at hand, they can be applied to a real-world problem.

Typical Problem

A woman is near-term in a pregnancy. Because of questions concerning vaginal delivery versus caesarian section in this case, the woman's pelvic dimensions are examined by X-ray. Three shots are taken. Each delivers about 250 millirads to the fetus. The total dose to the fetus is 750 millirads, or 0.75 rad as the average whole-body dose. What is the child's added risk of fatal malignant disease in the first 15 years of life?

ANSWER: Without in-utero irradiation, the child would have a spontaneous risk of 900 per million for such malignant disease. One fetal rad increases the spontaneous risk 50%, which means an additional risk of (0.50) × (900 per million). But in this case, the fetal dose is less than a whole rad, so we know the added risk will be proportionally less. The additional risk from this exam is (0.75 rad) × (0.50 per rad) × (900 per million) = 338 per million, or 1 chance in 2,959 due to the exam.

The General Formula

The same format can be used to obtain the child's risk from *any* type of diagnostic X-ray exam. The formula is boxed, for easy relocation, as Table 14-A.

We think the Stewart factor of 50% incremental risk per fetal rad needs no adjustment for early versus late pregnancy. There is considerable debate over whether or not the evidence shows a much higher effect in the first trimester than in the two later trimesters (BEIR-III, pp. 543–47). Unless some definitive evidence turns up in favor of treating the first

---

Table 14-A. Risk of Fatal Childhood Cancer and Leukemia from In-Utero Irradiation

Risk per Exam =	(embryo or fetal dose in rads) × (0.5 per rad) × (900 per million). And abbreviated:
Risk per Exam =	(embryo or fetal dose) × (450 per million).

trimester differently from the other two, we recommend applying 50% per fetal rad to all three.

Section 4: Adult-Type Cancers during Full Lifespan

The Stewart study addresses special childhood cancers plus leukemias which occur during the first 15 years of life. From other studies, we know that adult-type cancers induced from radiation exposure of infants (not fetuses) reach their peak rate of occurrence some 40 years after exposure (R&HH). It is reasonable to assume that, *in this respect,* infants are no different when they are still in the womb than they are known to be shortly after leaving the womb. If this approximation is made, then the *lifetime* cancer risk from X-ray doses received by the infant in-utero can be readily estimated.

How to Estimate the Risk

We will assume the infant in-utero and the newborn infant are equally vulnerable to cancer induction by radiation; however, the approximation may underestimate the risk from in-utero exposure. The question becomes, how sensitive is the newborn?

The answer lies in the risk totals at the bottom of Special Table A for males and Special Table B for females (Chapter 21). Those tables provide the additional cancer rate per organ, when it absorbs 1 rad. And when every organ absorbs 1 rad, the effect is equivalent to 1 rad of *whole-body* dose. Thus the totals provide the information we seek for most cases of in-utero exposure. From the tables:

For the Newborn Male: 1 rad of whole-body exposure confers an additional lifetime cancer risk of 22,743 per million, or 1 chance in 44. This is cancer incidence, not mortality.

For the Newborn Female: 1 rad of whole-body exposure confers an additional lifetime cancer risk of 30,005 per million, or 1 chance in 33. This is cancer incidence, not mortality.

The method of applying these risk values (for newborns) to infants in-utero is like the one demonstrated in the previous section, except that we take the child's sex into account too.

Illustrative Problem

A fetus receives a whole-body dose of 0.75 rad during her mother's pelvimetry exam. What will be the child's resulting risk of getting a radiation-induced cancer sometime during her lifetime?

ANSWER: The risk which this exposure adds is (0.75 rad) × (30,005 per million, per rad) = 22,504 per million, or 1 chance in 44.

The General Formula

The formula is simple for finding the lifetime cancer risk from any diagnostic X-ray exam, for the person who receives whole-body exposure in-utero. It is boxed, for easy relocation, as Table 14-B.

Table 14-B. Lifetime Risk of Cancer (Incidence)
from In-Utero Irradiation

Dose: In the equations below, the dose is the whole-body dose in rads absorbed by the embryo or fetus.

Male, Risk per Exam =
(embryo or fetal dose) × (22,743 per million)
Female, Risk per Exam =
(embryo or fetal dose) × (30,005 per million)

A comparison of Tables 14-A and 14-B shows that the risk of developing cancer as an adult from in-utero irradiation dwarfs the risk of developing cancer and leukemia in childhood from the same exposure. On the other hand, each fatal cancer or leukemia in childhood causes a far, far greater loss of lifespan than does each fatal adult cancer.

The huge disparity in risks per fetal rad results only in small part from comparing an incidence rate with a mortality rate. The overwhelming reason for the disparity is the difference in the *spontaneous* mortality rates: 900 per million for fatal childhood cancer and leukemia over 15 childhood years, compared with approximately 150,000 per million for fatal adult cancer, among non-smokers, for the lifespan.

Section 5: Severe Mental Retardation
from In-Utero Exposure

We need the same three types of information to evaluate the risk of mental retardation as we needed in Section 3 to evaluate the risk of childhood cancer and leukemia:

1. The spontaneous risk without in-utero irradiation;
2. The percent increase (in the spontaneous risk) per rad absorbed by the embryo or fetus; we shall continue calling both doses *fetal* rads;
3. The fetal dose per diagnostic X-ray exam.

Percent Increase per Rad

The value for the percent increase per fetal rad comes directly from the Hiroshima-Nagasaki evidence presented by Wood and co-workers (1967), Miller and Blot (1972), Blot and Miller (1973), Miller and Mulvihill (1976), and the analysis of it in *Radiation and Human Health.*

There are two types of data from those reports: for profound mental retardation and for small head-size. The head-size is not a cosmetic problem like a giant nose or protruding ears. As Miller and Blot point out, "The main stimulus to skull growth is brain growth." Microcephaly and mental retardation are closely associated (BEIR-III, p. 584–85). Very small head-size reflects the failure of the brain to develop fully.

The frequency of small head-size among children irradiated in-utero at Hiroshima and Nagasaki was reported by Miller and Blot. Their study included only the worst cases—those whose head circumferences were initially at least two standard deviations below average and remained at least one standard deviation below average during the years of follow-up. The researchers found that the radiation effect was very much greater per fetal rad among children irradiated during the first 17 weeks of gestation than among those who were longer in the womb.

During the first 17 weeks, the radiation exposure increased the spontaneous rate by between 10.1% and 45.4% per fetal rad, in the dose range of 5 to 121 fetal rads. The increment per rad was 19.4% in the 5-rad dose-group. When Hiroshima was considered alone, the findings were similar: at the fetal dose of 7.25 rads, the percent increment was 27.6% per rad.

Mental retardation was also studied directly (Wood and co-workers, 1967; Blot and Miller, 1973). The only children who were classified as mentally retarded were those who were unable to perform simple calculations, to make conversation, to care for themselves, or were completely unmanageable or had to be institutionalized. Even with these extreme criteria, and in spite of the inclusion of children irradiated well beyond 17 weeks of gestation, the findings show that radiation increased the frequency of mental retardation from 9.8% to 28.5% per fetal rad, in the dose range of 13.7 to 121 fetal rads.

It is reasonable to assume that, if cases of somewhat less profound mental retardation had been included in the study, a radiation effect would have been provable at even lower doses, as it was for small head-size. For instance, if the frequency of mental retardation is increasing at the rate of 20% per fetal rad, then 5 rads make the doubling dose (Chapter 11, Section 3). But within a group of fixed size (like the group receiving 5 fetal rads), it is just harder to prove a true doubling of a spontaneously rare event (like severe mental retardation) than a true doubling of a spontaneously more common event (like milder retardation).

Choice of the Value to Use for Diagnostic X-Rays

The findings on risk per fetal rad are so similar for serious mental retardation and for small head-size that we are going to treat them as the same. At a dose of 5 fetal rads, a 19.4% increase per rad in the frequency of small head-size was observed. We will treat this rate as the most likely rate of a serious degree of mental retardation from irradiation in-utero, if the exposure occurs during the first 17 weeks of gestation.

No direct evidence proves that this rate occurs at total doses of 1.0 fetal rad or less, but other evidence and logic strongly suggest that it does. One cell with an injured library of instructions (genes and chromosomes) can produce clusters of defective cells which, in turn, can produce congenital anomalies. Ionizing radiation injures genes and chromosomes right down to the lowest doses, and what may be the most common type of injury—deletion of a whole piece—is known to be directly proportional to dose. Therefore, it is scientifically reasonable to assume that the risk of serious mental retardation, induced by in-utero irradiation during the first 17 weeks of gestation, is proportional to dose right down to the lowest conceivable doses. Any *other* assumption would be enormously irresponsible, in our opinion. (Additional information in Section 6.)

Having settled on 19.4% per fetal rad as the percent increase in the spontaneous risk, we must now turn attention to the two additional pieces of information needed in order to evaluate the risk from any diagnostic X-ray exam.

Fetal Dose per Exam

One piece is the fetal dose received during particular X-ray examinations of a pregnant woman. This information is provided for the first 8 weeks of gestation as "embryo dose," in millirads, in this book's tables of Common Exams. For 9–17 weeks, very good estimates can be made from the appropriate entries in Special Table C (Chapter 21), which provides millirads per entrance roentgen for five different beam directions. As will be seen in the illustrative problems below, millirads need to be converted to rads. *Example:* 486 millirads = 0.486 rad.

Spontaneous Rate of Serious Retardation

The final piece of needed information is the spontaneous rate of serious mental retardation in the *absence* of in-utero exposure to X-rays. The rate for severe retardation among the comparable group of Japanese children who were in-utero at the time of the atomic bombing, and who were *not* irradiated, is 4.7 per 1,000 (R&HH, p. 738). This rate, expressed in our customary manner, is 4,700 per million, or 1 in 213. This rate is consistent with the famous Trimble and Doughty study (1974), done in British Columbia, whose findings are summarized in Tables 1 through 9 of UNSCEAR 1977 (pp. 514–19). We will treat 4,700 per million as the spontaneous rate of serious mental retardation.

The General Formula

The risk of serious mental retardation resulting from in-utero whole-body exposure to X-rays during the first 17 weeks of gestation is the product of three values: (the fetal dose in rads) × (the percent increase per rad in the spontaneous risk) × (the spontaneous risk per million). Therefore, whenever an embryo or fetus absorbs 1.0 rad of whole-body dose during those 17 weeks, the risk is (1.0 rad) × (0.194 per rad) × (4,700 per million) = 912 per million, or 1 in 1,096. The last two terms will remain the same no matter how the dose varies, so they can be multiplied together and rounded off a little.

The resulting formula for evaluating the risk from any diagnostic X-ray exam is boxed as Table 15 for easy relocation. The risk, like the other risks in this book, is *additional* to the spontaneous risk.

Table 15. Risk of Serious Mental Retardation from In-Utero Irradiation during the First 17 Weeks of Gestation

Risk per Exam = (fetal whole-body dose, in rads) × (912 per million, per rad)

Applications of the Formula

Two illustrations will show the vast difference in risk from different exams.

Illustrative Problem: An I.V.P. Exam

A 24-year-old woman is unaware that she is 4 weeks pregnant when she has an Intravenous Pyelogram (I.V.P.) Exam. What risk of serious mental retardation does the exam confer upon her child in-utero?

ANSWER: From Chapter 5, we find that the complete I.V.P. Exam under average conditions gives an embryo dose of 935 millirads, or 0.935 rad. The dose is applicable for women of all ages; no lowering factor is applied for mothers over age 20 because what matters here is the embryo. We simply apply the formula from Table 15. The child's risk of serious mental retardation from the exam = (0.935 rad) × (912 per million, per rad) = 853 per million, or 1 chance in 1,172.

Illustrative Problem: A Thoracic Spine Exam

A woman 26 years of age is unaware that she is pregnant when she suffers a chest injury in an automobile accident. Her physician orders a Thoracic Spine Exam. What is her child's risk of serious mental retardation from the exam?

ANSWER: The table for the Thoracic Spine—Wide Exam, in Chapter 5, shows the embryo dose as 1.4 millirads, or 0.0014 rads. Therefore, the child's risk of serious mental retardation from the exam = (0.0014 rad) × (912 per million, per rad) = 1.3 per million, or 1 chance in 769,000.

The Risk of Less Severe Mental Handicaps

It is very probable, for reasons given at the end of Section 6, that the same injury rate applies to *all* degrees of mental handicap, from mild to profound. If that be the case, then the risk of mild and moderate mental handicaps as well as the very severe ones can be evaluated. Users of this book who wish to consider *all* degrees of mental handicap, with respect to contemplated X-ray exams, must modify Table 15 in the manner shown below.

Modification of Table 15

Suppose that inclusion of the milder cases of mental handicap triples the *spontaneous* rate from 4,700 per million to 14,100 per million (or 1 per 71 people). From the derivation of Table 15, it is clear that this assumption means a tripling of the risk per exam. If a reader has good reason to use some factor higher or lower than 3.0, the illustration which follows should of course be adapted accordingly. Otherwise:

The risk per exam of some sort of mental handicap from in-utero radiation during the first 17 weeks of gestation = (fetal dose in rads) × (percent increase in the spontaneous rate, per rad) × (spontaneous rate per million). And when values are inserted, the risk = (fetal dose in rads) × (0.194 per rad) × (14,100 per million). When the last two terms, which do not change, are combined, it becomes an obvious tripling of Table 15:

$$Risk\ per\ Exam = \text{(fetal whole-body dose, in rads)}$$
$$\times\ (2{,}735\ \text{per million, per rad})$$

The answers provided by this equation would include *both* the mild and severe cases of mental retardation, and all degrees between.

Section 6: Other Radiation-Induced Congenital Anomalies

Among humans, the only major congenital anomaly *proven* to be inducible by in-utero exposure to moderate or low doses of ionizing radiation is defective development of the central nervous system (C.N.S.). However, the absence of a positive study demonstrating other radiation effects does not necessarily mean that the effects are absent. It can just as easily mean that no study which is inherently capable of proving the effects has ever been undertaken.

Although we are assigning no quantitative values in this book to radiation effects not yet demonstrated in the human at or near diagnostic dose levels, we are providing this section so that the reader will be fairly warned that there are most probably *numerous* serious problems, besides defective brain development, which are induced by in-utero exposure to radiation, right down to the lowest conceivable doses. A large body of experimental animal data shows that in-utero radiation exposure indeed induces other anomalies.

Then why have they not been proven radiation-inducible in humans, too? Why have the radiation studies which proved the effect upon the central nervous system not simultaneously proven an excess of other anomalies? The probable reason may be found in the spontaneous frequencies, which differ. When other congenital anomalies appear spontaneously (without in-utero irradiation), mental retardation and other C.N.S. disorders are a feature which characterizes *many different* syndromes. In other words, the spontaneous frequency of C.N.S. defects seems to be higher than the spontaneous frequency of other types of congenital defects. As demonstrated by some leukemia studies (Chapter 11), when a disease (or anomaly) is spontaneously rare and the number of cases per million is small, it can be virtually impossible to detect a radiation effect even when the effect is huge.

Reasons for Expecting a Radiation Effect at the Lowest Doses

The conclusion that in-utero radiation exposure of humans induces congenital defects, right down to the lowest doses, rests on two main premises.

First: Ionizing radiation, even at extremely low doses and dose rates, breaks human chromosomes and inflicts enduring chromosomal injuries. This premise is not speculation. Even in the 1-rad region of dose, there is evidence (reviewed in R&HH). In addition, preliminary studies reported by the Atomic Energy Commission (1970, pp. 1360–62) showed that the effect was measurable among some Alaskan eskimos whose cumulative dose at the time, from atomic fallout, was estimated to be only 1 rad.

Second: In-utero breakage of chromosomes, followed by loss (deletion) of whole pieces of chromosomes, accounts for many of the spontaneous congenital anomalies. This premise is made speculative only because we have chosen the word "many" instead of "some." The fact that in-utero deletions do cause *some* serious congenital anomalies has been proven by any reasonable standard of proof (evidence reviewed in R&HH). The consequences of in-utero deletions can be extremely severe for the child, as indicated below.

Some Serious Deletion Syndromes

The Cri-du-Chat Syndrome: Characterized by profound mental handicaps and psychomotor retardation, microcephaly, growth failure, low-set ears, and a strange mewing cry which gave the syndrome its name.

The Wolf-Hirschhorn Deletion Syndrome: Characterized by severe mental handicaps, delayed psychomotor development, growth failure, and multiple malformations (palate, lips, heart, urinary tract, and bones for instance).

The 13-q Deletion Syndrome: Characterized by mild to profound mental handicap, coloboma of the iris and other eye defects, and a grossly excessive rate of the rare eye cancer, retinoblastoma, in one or both eyes.

Although the three syndromes above share many common features, each is characterized by a piece missing from a *different* chromosome.

Can anyone be sure, however, that the chromosome deletions which characterize these syndromes occurred in-utero and were not inherited from one of the parents? Also, why are so few such syndromes recognized to be caused by deletions, if the second key premise is valid? These two questions, whose answers are related to each other, are important.

Mosaicism: a Source of Answers and Caution

Time of Deletion: Many congenital anomalies are indistinguishable from inherited anomalies. The latter result from injuries to genes and chromosomes which occur before conception (in the ovum or sperm of a parent or more distant ancestor) or, far less often, immediately after conception (before divisions of the fertilized ovum).

When a chromosome deletion is inherited, it *must* be present in every single cell of the recipient's body, except the sex cells (where in the post-meiotic stages, it will be present in only half). The proof that a chromosome deletion occurred in-utero is the observation that the deletion is *not* found in cells sampled from some of the child's organs; the deletion is found replicated in cells from only some of the child's organs or in only some cells of a single organ.

The phenomenon of at least two different chromosomal patterns in the same individual is called mosaicism, and the newborns who display it are called mosaics. *Their chromosomal injury occurred in-utero.*

Failure of Recognition: There are very good reasons to believe that mosaics are far more common than is presently recognized medically.

First, until recently, not many people suspected that mosaicism might explain a large share of congenital anomalies. Consequently, there has been little effort made to find out whether an abnormal child is a mosaic or not. Only during the last 15 years or so did investigators ask if the four known autosomal trisomies (Down's Syndrome, Edward's Syndrome, Patau's Syndrome, and Schmid-Fraccaro Syndrome) could occur as mosaics. *All* of them do (Zellweger and Simpson, 1977).

Second, the techniques for studying chromosomal patterns are still expensive, crude, and incapable of detecting small deletions. By comparison, detecting trisomies is very, very easy.

Third, cells from *many* different organs of each abnormal child would have to be tested in order to determine whether mosaicism exists, and if so, to what extent. The simple non-finding of a chromosome deletion, trisomy, or other chromosome aberration in a sample of blood, bone marrow, or skin *by no means* indicates the absence of mosaicism.

Similarly, a positive finding in one of these samples in no way demonstrates that the aberration occurs in every system and is inherited. Of course, if a sample from a parent shows the identical chromosome aberration, inheritance can be presumed certain.

The Importance of Trimester

In view of the strength of the two key premises, it is likely and bordering on certainty that in-utero exposures to ionizing radiation do increase the frequency of mosaic newborns, with congenital defects ranging from mild to severe. If this is true, then the trimester of exposure can be expected to make a very large difference with respect to additional anomalies besides C.N.S. defects. We will review why this expectation makes sense.

A pregnancy starts with a single cell. Every other cell (an estimated 40 trillion of them in a human adult) is a descendant of that one cell. The human develops from the original cell by divisions, the one cell becoming two, the two becoming four, and so forth, in a series of "generations." The original cell disappears forever when it first divides.

It is believed that only the very earliest generations of cells are "totipotent," which is a type of omnipotence; each totipotent cell can develop into *any* part of the developing embryo. Later generations of cells differentiate (specialize) and become ancestors of cells with only *certain* types of functions. Such cells might be called "multipotent." A fully specialized cell, which might be called "unipotent," produces only cells having functions identical to its own. At least this seems to be the case when such cells are in their natural environment; what a fully specialized cell might do elsewhere, in a laboratory or under other unusual conditions, may be quite extraordinary.

As far as anyone presently knows, totipotent, multipotent, and fully specialized cells—notwithstanding their different functions—all share identical chromosomes and genes.

There must be more multipotent cells early in gestation than later, and each multipotent cell may be ancestral to cells in more than one organ. A radiation-induced deletion in such a cell, if the cell survives and is still able to divide, will have far-reaching consequences.

Diminishing Consequences

As gestation progresses, each cell—whether multipotent or unipotent—is ancestral to fewer and fewer descendants. By the time a fetus weighs 3.5 pounds, each cell (on the *average*) will be ancestral to only two cells before a 7-pound newborn baby is "ready." By contrast, the same type of approximation indicates that, when a 7-pound infant is born, the single original cell has already been ancestral to about 2 trillion cells.

The enormous disparity in the number of descendants suggests that, if a cell suffers a radiation-induced deletion of a piece of chromosome late in gestation, and if the cell survives and someday divides, the injury will be passed to many fewer descendants than if a cell sustains the same injury early in gestation.

This reasoning suggests also that the so-called "minor" congenital defects could be results of chromosomal deletions which occur late in pregnancy, when each deletion can affect only a *small* share of the mosaic infant's cells.

How Dose Relates to Severity and Likelihood

When one thinks about the *severity* of congenital anomalies, two separate variables need to be distinguished with respect to in-utero deletions of parts of chromosomes. One is *when* during gestation a deletion occurs, because the timing helps determine how many descendant cells will be affected. The other is *how big* the piece of lost chromosome is, because size determines how many genes are lost and just how handicapped each descendant cell will be.

Neither of these important variables is affected by the magnitude of the radiation dose.

However, when one thinks about the *probability* of congenital anomalies, in the full range of their severity, then the relationship between deletions and dose becomes extremely important. The size of the dose determines the number of chromosomal breaks which occurs and the probability of lost pieces. There is no doubt that the likelihood of chromosomal deletions in a group of irradiated cells is *directly proportional to the size of the radiation dose,* at least for any dose range pertinent to diagnostic X-ray exams.

CHAPTER 13

Heritable Injuries Induced by Radiation

At this time, there still exists a wide range of uncertainty about the "cost," per rad, in genetic (heritable) disorders experienced by the offspring of irradiated parents.

The term "genetic disorders" includes not only the physical problems caused by mutations of single genes, but also those due to multi-gene aberrations such as the loss of whole sections of DNA (by deletion of a piece of chromosome), a section's migration to the wrong position (following a chromosome break), the presence of extra genetic material (for instance, a trisomy), and other abnormalities which result in an imbalance of genetic material in a cell.

The key distinction, required to classify an injury of genetic material as a "genetic injury," is that the resulting aberration be *heritable* from a parent to a child and more distant generations. If the very same genetic injury occurs to a child in-utero, then this child will be a mosaic (Chapter 12). If the child's gonads escape the injury, this individual cannot transmit the genetic injury to his or her own children.

Clinically, nonetheless, the mosaic individual may appear to have the same disorders as the person who inherited the problems.

314

Section 1: The Reasons
for the Wide Range of Uncertainty

One of the important reasons that there is so much uncertainty, which we share, about the rate of heritable genetic disorders per rad of radiation dose to the gonads is that, when the question is studied, no one really knows yet what he or she is looking for.

We do not yet know which disorders have a genetic cause, let alone know if the suspected genetic injury occurred in-utero or earlier. Although we are quite proficient these days at counting and recording medical disorders, we have only the vaguest notion which ones have been inherited, or "partly inherited." The latter are the so-called irregularly inherited diseases, a vaguely defined classification now containing some major killers such as heart disease. Two important consequences of our ignorance need stating here.

First: Because we do not know which particular disorders are heritable, we do not know the spontaneous rate of inherited disorders. The estimated spontaneous incidence used by the BEIR and UNSCEAR committees incorporates an estimate of 90,000 per million for the spontaneous rate of the irregularly inherited diseases. Gofman (1981) suggests that the true rate for that category alone is probably closer to 450,000 per million than to 90,000. On the other hand, there may be exaggerations in the rates of some other disorders (perhaps the trisomies, for instance) which are presently presumed to be overwhelmingly inherited. It could turn out that many cases now counted as inherited are actually cases of mosaicism. Table 16-A reflects a 4.5-fold range in the estimates of spontaneous risk of genetic disorder.

Table 16-A. Rate of Heritable Injuries per Rad, per Generation

Dose: The dose of 1.0 rad refers to a gonadal dose accumulated by each parent prior to conceiving a child—1.0 rad by the father plus 1.0 rad by the mother.

Spontaneous Rate of All Heritable Disorders, Defects and Diseases Combined (range of estimates)	Incremental Number of Cases from One Rad per Person, per Generation		
	UNSCEAR (1977)	*BEIR-III (1980)*	*R&HH (1981)*
105,100 to 467,100 per million live births	196 per million	74 to 1,132 per million	191 to more than 20,000 per million

SOURCE: Table 16-A is abbreviated from Table 76 in *Radiation and Human Health.*

Second: Because we do not know the spontaneous rate of inherited disorders, we cannot measure how much the spontaneous rate is increased by a gonadal radiation exposure of 1.0 rad. It is hardly surprising that the estimates of genetic risk per rad per person per generation are as different as indicated in Table 16-A.

In view of the obvious uncertainties, we think the fairest and most helpful thing to do for users of this book is to present the possible consequences per rad derived from both extremes of Table 16-A.

Applicable Risk Rates and Doses

The range of risk will be from 37 per million live births per rad to 10,000 per million live births per rad. We are cutting the table's risk rates in half because they are based on *both* parents having accumulated 1.0 rad, and we will be analyzing the risk when *one* parent has specific diagnostic X-ray examinations.

In both the low-risk estimates and the high-risk estimates, the incremental risk includes many disorders which first appear in adult life and are not seen in the infant. Many people seem to think of genetic disorders as only the ones which are obvious shortly after birth, but that belief is mistaken.

It is customary to treat gonadal doses as cumulative and the risk to children subsequently conceived as proportional to the *total* dose accumulated by either parent before the conception. In the absence of evidence to the contrary, the logic for this, which lies in the nature of the reproductive process, seems compelling. There is no evidence at the present time suggesting that a parent's age at gonadal irradiation changes the effect upon children conceived later.

Therefore, to estimate a child's risk of genetic damage from diagnostic radiology, the doses to ovaries and testes from *all* pre-conception X-ray examinations must be considered.

Section 2: Assessing the Heritable Risk from Specific X-Ray Exams

---

For each common diagnostic X-ray examination evaluated in Chapters 5 and 7, the tables provide the dose to testes and ovaries. The following problems illustrate how to apply such information in practice, to estimate the range of expected effects upon the children from future pregnancies.

Problem 1: an I.V.P. Exam

At age 20, a woman has an Intravenous Pyelogram. Six years later, she becomes pregnant. She expresses her worry that the radiation exposure from the I.V.P. Exam may damage her child. What is the likelihood?

ANSWER: In the table for the I.V.P. Exam in Chapter 5, we find the dose to the ovaries, which is always in the age-20 section for adults of any age. It is estimated at 692 millirads, or 0.692 rad. Clearly, the child's incremental risk per exam = (a parent's gonadal dose in rads) × (the risk per gonadal rad). We want to obtain probabilities from both ends of the range derived from Table 16-A.

For the Low Estimate: The child's risk will be (0.692 rad) × (37 per million, per rad) = 25.6 per million, or 1 chance in 39,062.

For the High Estimate: Since the rad units will "cancel each other out," we can abbreviate. The child's risk will be (0.692) × (10,000 per million) = 6,920 per million, or 1 chance in 144.

Problem 2: a Full-Mouth Dental Exam

At age 23, a woman has a Full-Mouth Dental Exam of 27 films. Two years later, she becomes pregnant and asks how bad the risk to her child will be from the recent dental exam. How bad is it?

ANSWER: In the table for the Full-Mouth Dental Exam in Chapter 9, we find the dose to the ovaries in the age-20 section. It is estimated at less than 1 millirad for a 16-film exam. This is a 27-film exam, which could put the ovarian dose closer to 2 millirads than to 1.0. Again, we want to provide the range of risk.

For the Low Estimate: The child's incremental risk of a genetic disorder will be (0.002) × (37 per million) = 0.074 per million, or 1 chance in 13.5 million.

For the High Estimate: The child's risk will be (0.002) × (10,000 per million) = 20 per million, or 1 chance in 50,000.

The General Formula

Table 16-B, boxed for easy relocation, provides the formulas used above for low and high estimates; they reflect the range of uncertainties demonstrated in Table 16-A. When users are applying the formulas to actual cases, the following reminders may help prevent errors.

Shielding of Testes: The tables of Common Exams provide the dose to *unshielded* testes; shielding can significantly lower the dose when the testes would otherwise be in the direct beam.

Table 16-B. Likelihood of Heritable Injury per Diagnostic X-Ray Exam

Child's Incremental Risk (Low Estimate) per Exam =
   (a parent's gonadal dose from exam, in rads) × (37 per
   million, per rad).
Child's Incremental Risk (High Estimate) per Exam =
   (a parent's gonadal dose from exam, in rads) × (10,000 per
   million, per rad).

Ages below 20 Years: In the tables of Common Exams, for all ages above age 20, the gonadal dose is in the age-20 section. But below age 20, separate gonadal doses must be used. They change with age because of the changing entrance doses, the changing absorbed dose per entrance roentgen, and changing distance of ovaries and testes from the center of the field, and (sometimes) the changing shots which compose the Common Exam.

Several Exams: A child's incremental risk is proportional to the sum of gonadal doses from all of his or her parents' diagnostic exams before the child's conception. Because a parent's age at irradiation would not alter the risk for the child, the dose from a combination of earlier exams can be treated like a *single* exam with the formulas of Table 16-B.

Section 3: An Unnecessary Burden of Guilt

Guilt is a real-world problem which we have frequently encountered, from mothers and fathers alike, when they have a child with an obvious genetic defect. "I know I should not have had those full-mouth dental X-rays just two years before the birth of our child. If only I had not had that exam, our child would not have this problem."

Let us suppose that the situation is the one illustrated above in Problem 2. First of all, these parents are incorrect in assuming that the short time (2 years) between exam and birth is relevant at all. Secondly, like most people, they obviously do not realize the very high frequency of spontaneous genetic disorders having nothing at all to do with medical or dental X-rays. Even the lower figure for spontaneous heritable defects, on the left side of Table 16-A, is 105,100 per million live births. This means that we must expect a major or minor genetic defect in one out of every ten live births.

How to Be Realistic about Causes

In Problem 2, the high estimate of the child's incremental risk from the mother's Dental Exam is 20 per million. That value is derived from a spontaneous frequency of 467,100 per million and a large risk per rad. The child's *total* risk is always the sum of the spontaneous risk plus the risk from the exam: 467,100 per million + 20 per million = 467,120 per million. The fraction contributed by the Dental Exam is 20 per 467,120, or 1 part in 23,356. In other words, their child's genetic problem is about 23,000 times more likely to have been caused by something *other* than the mother's Dental Exam than by it.

The low estimate of the child's incremental risk in Problem 2 is 0.074 per million. Again, the child's *total* risk of having genetic damage is the sum of the spontaneous risk plus the risk from the exam: 105,100 per million + 0.074 per million = 105,100.074 per million. The fractional causation of the genetic defect by the exam is therefore 0.074 parts per 105,100.074, or 1 part per 1.4 million. The child's genetic problem is about 1.4 million times more likely *not* to have been caused by the exam than by it.

We think this issue needs to be understood. And only the numbers can tell the story.

Many parents needlessly blame and punish themselves for being responsible for their child's genetic disorder when the basis for such guilt is essentially nonexistent. And we know of some exceedingly poorly-based lawsuits which suggest that radiation is responsible for a defect, when the odds are overwhelming that radiation had nothing to do with producing the defect.

Many people have made it clear to us that they assume children must almost *certainly* suffer a genetic disorder as a result of virtually *any* diagnostic X-ray exam taken by their parents. But this is a mistaken assumption, far from the truth. The risk varies enormously among the the different exams, as demonstrated by Problems 1 and 2 above, and the risk will be proportional to the aggregate gonadal dose from *all* such exams prior to conception.

Section 4:
Some Aggregate Genetic Impacts from X-Rays

In view of the uncertainties described in Section 1 of this chapter, it would be reckless to bet *against* the higher risk formula in Table 16-B. Although it is not "solid," we will show in Section 5 of this chapter why the higher risk needs to be taken very, very seriously in diagnostic radiology nevertheless.

Comparing Individuals and Populations

We will refer back, now, to Problem 1 dealing with the I.V.P. Exam. The high estimate indicates that, all by itself, this exam created a risk to a child conceived later of 6,920 per million (1 in 144). If the child does have a genetic defect, it is the result of the spontaneous risk plus the risk from the exam: 467,100 per million + 6,920 per million = 474,020 per million. The fractional causation from the exam is therefore 6,920 parts per 474,020, or 1 part per 69. The parents and the physicians should not be too quick to blame themselves.

On the other hand, there is clearly no reason whatsoever for any complacency about exams which irradiate either the ovaries or the testes. A rate of 6,920 per million (the high estimate) means that when a million I.V.P. Exams have been done on women who will later have a child, there will be 6,920 children born with radiation-induced disorders *in addition to* the disorders which they might well have had anyway. That is, as we said in Chapter 1, "a heap of misery."

The Importance of Gonadal Shielding and Beam Collimation

It is obviously important to shield the testes from direct beams—during the Hip and Femur Exams, for instance. Even for men who will be fathering no children in the future, shielding reduces the risk of testicular *cancer*. When the ovaries can be similarly shielded with leaded covers, both genetic risk and cancer risk are reduced.

But no amount of external shielding can prevent doses to ovaries and testes from radiation internally scattered. For that problem, by far the most effective measure to reduce both genetic risk and cancer risk is to collimate beams so that field sizes are reduced to the smallest area capable of producing the needed diagnostic information. We can use the ovaries to illustrate four different degrees of effect:

1. If the ovaries must sit fully in the field of the direct beam, there can be virtually no reduction in the scattered dose which they receive.

2. If reducing the field size places the ovaries near the edge of the field, but still in the direct beam, their dose from scatter will be reduced; the reason is that some adjacent organs are thereby moved outside the direct beam and therefore receive less radiation to scatter back into the ovaries (Chapter 19, Section 2).

3. If reducing the field size can place the ovaries just outside the field of the direct beam, they will still receive substantial amounts of scattered radiation, but far less than if they were in the direct beam.

4. If reducing the field size can place the ovaries several centimeters outside the edge of the direct beam, their dose from internal scatter will be substantially reduced (Chapter 10, Section 4).

Shaping a Child's Destiny

Earlier in this section, we considered the genetic impact of just one exam, the I.V.P., which delivers a relatively high dose to the ovaries. Even higher are the ovarian doses from certain exams involving abdominal fluoroscopy, such as Celiac Angiography, Barium Enema, Small Bowel Series, and Hysterosalpingography (examination of the uterus and fallopian tubes).

The fact that relatively high ovarian doses are unavoidable in some exams makes it all the more important to reduce them in *other* kinds of exams whenever possible.

The young child who needs only a K.U.B. Exam today may be the same individual who needs an I.V.P. Exam ten years later and a Lumbar Spine Exam three years after that. And each such exam *counts* in the destiny of some child not yet conceived.

Section 5: Two Reasons for Special Caution

The Heritable Cancers: How Many?

Recent research, concerning heritable cancers which appear causally linked to heritable chromosomal aberrations, may have large implications for diagnostic radiology. The evidence and logic which support this caution are fully presented in *Radiation and Human Health;* only a very brief synopsis follows.

Point 1: At low doses, ionizing radiation has been proven to cause transfer of chromosome pieces between chromosomes (translocations).

Point 2: At low doses, radiation has been proven to cause breakage and subsequent loss of a piece of chromosome (deletions).

Point 3: Both types of chromosomal injury are proven to be heritable.

Point 4: Both types of chromosomal injury, when they are carried in all (or most) cells of a person, predict that the carrier is very likely to develop specific types of cancer. This has been proven for one specific type of translocation, two specific types of deletion, and three specific types of cancer—Wilm's tumor, retinoblastoma, and renal cell carcinoma. Below, we will describe only the extraordinary incidence of the kidney cancer among the members of one family.

Inherited Translocation and Kidney Cancer

A family studied by Cohen and co-workers (1979) is suffering with a virtual epidemic of renal cell carcinoma. The inquiry began when one member of the family with the cancer in both kidneys mentioned that several relatives, in three consecutive generations, also had renal cell carcinoma. It turned out that 10 adults in this one family had this particular type of cancer. Six of the 10 had it in both kidneys, and 8 of the 10 were showing two or more foci of the cancer per affected kidney.

Chromosomes from the peripheral blood leukocytes of 22 adult family members of the second and third generation were studied (karyotypic analysis). Twelve showed no chromosomal aberrations. Ten of the 22 showed a balanced chromosome *translocation* between the short arm of chromosome 3 and the long arm of chromosome 8. Karyotypic analysis was possible on only 8 of the 10 cancer cases—and all 8 showed the translocation.

The Cohen work is recent, and the question arises: do cancers other than this kidney cancer have a basis in heritable chromosome translocations? We hope that many investigators are keeping the Cohen findings in mind whenever they suspect that one type of cancer may be occurring with unusual frequency in a family.

Translocations with Leukemias and Lymphomas

Major advances in the identification of specific translocations associated with (and probably causal of) several blood-cell malignancies have recently been reported (Croce, 1985). Not only is there the well known chromosome 9;22 translocation which is found with chronic myelogenous leukemia, but now other specific translocations have been identified for the following blood cancers:

8;21 with acute myelogenous leukemia;
15;17 with acute promyelocytic leukemia;
11;19 with acute monocytic leukemia, acute myelomonocytic leukemia;
1;19 with pre-B-cell leukemia;
8;14 and 8;22 and 2;8 with Burkitt lymphoma, acute lymphocytic leukemia of the B-cell type (L3);
11;14 with chronic lymphocytic leukemia, diffuse large- and small-cell lymphoma, multiple myeloma, acute lymphocytic leukemia of the T-cell type;
14;18 with follicular lymphoma;
4;11 with acute lymphocytic leukemia.

Deletions, Eye Cancer, and Wilm's Tumor

Karyotypic analysis is also producing important results connecting partially *deleted* chromosomes with specific types of cancer. People who have part of the long arm of chromosome 13 deleted have many problems, including mental retardation and the extraordinary rate of 20 per 100 of the eye cancer, retinoblastoma (Zellweger and Simpson, 1977). People with an interstitial deletion of the short arm of chromosome 11 also have many problems, including aniridia (failure of the iris to develop), abnormal genitalia, and a very high rate of Wilm's tumor. Riccardi and co-workers (1978) studied six people with the triad of problems and found that all had the interstitial deletion of chromosome 11. Riccardi studied one pair of twins, and both showed the deletion, which indicates that it was inherited. One twin already had a Wilm's tumor.

The Irregularly Inherited Diseases: a Speculation

The irregularly inherited diseases are those which geneticists declare to possess an inherited "component." However, the component's pattern of inheritance appears "irregular" and confusing. Into this category fall many major constitutional and degenerative diseases such as anemia, diabetes, schizophrenia, epilepsy, atherosclerosis, ulcer, and cancer (BEIR-I, p. 56).

It seems quite possible (Gofman, 1981) that the inherited component of these diseases could be chromosomal translocations and partial deletions. It is an inherent characteristic of these lesions that their size varies enormously from one case to another. This would result in exactly what is observed clinically so often: variation in severity, variation in the associated problems, and overlap between different syndromes. For the geneticists, the picture would appear messy indeed, by comparison with the orderly single-gene diseases.

The Low-Risk and High-Risk Formulas

The technologies for detecting chromosomal translocations and deletions are still crude, but improving. Techniques remain too poor to discern deletions of a small part of a chromosome's arm; the missing piece must be relatively large to be detected.

As the research tools improve in this field, it may turn out that several types of cancer—possibly *many* types—can be caused by presently unrecognized translocations and partial deletions of chromosomes, with some fraction of such injuries occurring in sperm precursors or ovum precursors, and passing successfully through "nature's filter" into the offspring of the parent in whom the injury occurred.

The fact that both types of chromosomal injury are very easily induced by ionizing radiation at low doses needs remembering, with respect to diagnostic X-rays.

If it turns out that chromosome translocations and partial deletions also help cause the huge class of irregularly inherited diseases, then the implications for diagnostic radiology are even bigger.

As long as the uncertainties persist, we think it would be *highly imprudent* to rely on the low-risk formula from Table 16-B.

CHAPTER 14

Does Irradiation Cause Premature Aging?

An idea which has persisted for decades is that radiation may accelerate aging, by contributing to virtually *all* of the health problems associated with aging.

Our examination of the world evidence does not convince us that any aging effect, other than the induction of cancer and leukemia, has been proven to exist. We did not dismiss this issue lightly, because a real effect of radiation in accelerating aging (in ways additional to malignancy production) could be of great consequence. Therefore, we wish to explain *why* we find no acceptable reason for assigning any numerical risk from diagnostic X-ray examinations (after birth) for this supposed effect.

Section 1: The Inherent Weakness of Anecdotal Evidence

We hear statements about a whole host of symptoms occurring in members of groups which are presumed to have had excessive exposure to ionizing radiation, although measurements of possible doses received (if any) are seldom available. If exposure were certain, such evidence would be the type called "anecdotal." Would it be capable of proving anything?

All human populations experience a host of symptoms, physical changes with age, and ill health from many diseases. Therefore, the observation that various individuals have health problems proves exactly nothing about radiation being responsible, unless the problems among an adequate series of irradiated people can be compared for *excessive age-specific frequency* with the same problems among a comparable series of unirradiated people. Anecdotal evidence on such an issue is simply incapable of proving anything.

Scientifically valid studies have proved beyond doubt that low-dose radiation exposure causes increased rates of human cancer. It is regrettable that some opportunities were not taken to perform equally valid studies on health effects *other* than cancer and leukemia for population groups known to have been exposed. Such studies would not have been easy to do, but without them, we are totally unable to comment on the many illnesses and symptoms alleged hither and yon to have been caused by ionizing radiation.

On the other hand, if the various alleged symptoms, physical infirmities, and diseases were truly caused by radiation, it is reasonable to expect that irradiated groups would have an *excess age-specific mortality,* wholly aside from the excess cancer and leukemia effects. In the absence of evidence comparing death rates among irradiated and non-irradiated groups from each and every infirmity, we can look for an excess rate by comparing the *aggregate* non-cancer mortality rates for exposed and unexposed groups. We will consider two such investigations.

Section 2: The Evidence from Hiroshima-Nagasaki, and its Critics

In what is clearly the largest population sample yet studied, namely the Hiroshima-Nagasaki bomb survivors, the following finding was reported by Beebe, Land, and Kato (1978, p. 4): "Thus far the mortality experience of the Japanese A-bomb survivors suggests that the life-shortening effect of whole-body human exposure to ionizing radiation derives from its carcinogenic effect, not from any acceleration of the aging process."

Beebe and co-workers point out carefully that the appropriateness of the A-bomb survivors, as a study group, has been challenged on the ground that these people are survivors of a major catastrophe. They cite the criticisms of Stewart (1973) and Rotblat (1977).

We have examined the extensive tabulations of non-cancer mortalities for Hiroshima-Nagasaki in the paper of Beebe and co-workers. If radiation increases the frequency of deaths from non-malignancies, one should detect a dose-related effect (in both linear and non-linear situations): the higher the dose, the more frequent the effect. With respect to malignancies, that is exactly what is found among the survivors of Hiroshima-Nagasaki in the various dose-groups. But with respect to non-cancer diseases, no internally consistent evidence of dose-related excess mortality among the survivors is seen.

In almost any human series studied, however, if one breaks the data into enough small subdivisions, the operation necessarily introduces some random fluctuations in the "findings," and then one will certainly see dips, spikes, and supposed effects from some variable appearing sporadically in one category or another. If such numbers are taken seriously and analyzed for internal "trends," the result will be a literature filling up with unreliable findings and overstated conclusions. Statistical over-massage is a serious disease among scientists.

When we ask for a solid indication of a dose-related radiation effect upon mortality other than malignancy, it is simply not there at this time in the Japanese data. Our own examination of the evidence leads us to concur with Beebe and co-workers on this issue. The Japanese data provide no reason whatsoever to assign any risk value for premature aging from diagnostic doses of radiation.

We are well aware that Stewart and Kneale (1984) would take issue with our view. Their view is that radiation exposure must be increasing non-cancer mortality among the Hiroshima-Nagasaki survivors, and that the effect is *obscured* by the competing (opposing) effects of (a) a possible selection of hardy individuals by the disaster itself, and (b) a possible dose-related residual bone-marrow injury which balances out this hardiness. We just do not think support for their speculations is provided yet by the evidence.

We have also considered the evidence from a very different study. Its subjects are people who are presumed to have received their radiation exposure in a series of small doses, and who are not survivors of a catastrophe: the radiologists themselves.

Section 3: The Evidence Comparing Radiologists with Other Physicians

A series of reports about radiologists is often cited as "proof" that radiation increases the rates not only of cancer and leukemia, but also other serious or fatal diseases such as stroke, cardio-vascular-renal disease, hypertensive disease, and diabetes. As we shall see, the data themselves may point to a different conclusion—namely, that low-dose radiation exposure has no effect beyond the increase in cancer and leukemia. (The studies did not investigate genetic or congenital effects.)

The Choice of Control Group: Matanowski and co-workers (1975a, 1975b) compared mortality rates for several cohorts of radiologists with the rates for other physician specialists. The concept behind the study is that, if the various categories of specialists have different average exposures to ionizing radiation, then they should show different rates of diseases related to radiation exposure. But suppose the specialists would have shown different rates of those diseases even in the *absence* of radiation exposure. How could the researchers know what group of physicians would show the disease rates which radiologists *would* show, if radiologists were *not* exposed to radiation? In this type of study, as in all others, the choice of control group is crucial.

Matanowski and co-workers elected, in the papers cited, to use ophthalmologists as the control group for testing three other groups of physicians who are presumed to receive more occupational radiation exposure than do ophthalmologists: radiologists, internists, and otolaryngologists (ear-nose-throat specialists). We agree it is very likely that the ophthalmologists had lower average exposures to radiation than the radiologists, but we find no reason offered for believing that they are otherwise a suitable control group.

However, we need not dismiss the whole study on that basis, because the study provides, internally, data on two other possible control groups for the radiologists: the internists and the otolaryngologists. The internists, for instance, may well have had higher occupational radiation exposures than either the otolaryngologists or the ophthalmologists, but if the radiologists had an even higher exposure than the internists, and if radiation causes non-cancer mortality, then the radiologists should show higher non-cancer mortality rates than the internists—if the rates would have been similar in the two groups *without* radiation exposure. The same could be said about comparing radiologists with otolaryngologists.

Instead of comparing the radiologists only with the ophthalmologists, we will make the two additional comparisons and examine the results for consistency.

Relative Size of Doses: How will we know if the radiologists really had higher radiation exposures than any of the three other groups? The ratio of the cancer rates will tell us. From many other studies, independent of these, it is already known that radiation exposure increases cancer mortality. Therefore, Matanowski's data on cancer rates among the four groups can serve as the indicator of the groups' relative radiation doses.

The issue at hand is not whether radiation increases the frequency of cancer, which has already been proven, but whether radiation *also* increases the frequency of non-cancer causes of death. What can we conclude on this issue from the Matanowski reports?

Comparison of Ratios: Data from the studies are provided in Table 17. In Part 3 of the table, we have provided the simple ratios (derived from the table's Part 1) which show how many times higher the cancer rate is for the radiologists than it is for the other three types of physicians. In Part 4 of the table, we have provided the simple ratios (derived from the table's Part 2) which show how many times higher—or lower—the non-cancer mortality rate is for the radiologists than it is for the other three groups. The ratios tell a story quite different from "proof" of a non-cancer effect from radiation.

Analysis of the Results: What we see in Part 3 of Table 17 is that radiologists show a higher cancer mortality in 8 out of 8 ratios. Radiologists have a higher cancer rate than all other type of physicians in the study, even in the youngest cohort (1940–1949 entry into the field). These ratios provide probable confirmation that the radiologists truly received higher occupational doses. If *only* the ophthalmologists were used as a control group, we should wonder whether the radiologists' higher cancer rate was either just a statistical fluke or the result of some variable unrelated to radiation.

Now comes the key question: do the radiologists also show a higher *non-cancer* mortality rate than the physicians who received less radiation exposure? Has radiation produced other health threats for the radiologists besides cancer?

Part 4 of Table 17 suggests that radiation exposure makes little or no difference at all to the radiologists' non-cancer mortality. Four ratios are *above* the control groups', and four ratios are *below.* One could do elaborate statistical analyses on the ratios, because their individual weight varies with the size and age of each sample, but inspection and common sense are sometimes far preferable. That is the case here, because there is no way of knowing which control group is the best match for radiologists, and the relative size of the radiation doses is so crudely estimated.

If radiation does cause both a cancer and non-cancer effect, then the ratios in Part 4 of Table 17 should be highest exactly where they are highest in Part 3. Where the cancer ratio is high, the non-cancer ratio should be high also.

But there are enough exceptions to suggest random chance. An obvious exception is the pair of Radiol/Ophthal ratios (3.2 and 0.99) in the 1940–1949 cohort. And there are others. The 1940–1949 Radiol/Otolary non-cancer ratio should be higher than the Radiol/Inter ratio, because the corresponding cancer ratios in Part 3 predict it. But the opposite is true; it is lower (0.89 versus 0.96). Likewise, if a non-cancer effect exists, the 1930–1939 Radiol/Inter non-cancer ratio should be higher than the Radiol/Otolary ratio, because the corresponding cancer ratios in Part 3 predict it. But the opposite is true; it is lower (0.91 versus 1.14).

Table 17. Comparison of Causes of Death in Radiologists vs. Other Physicians

> *Cohorts:* Cohorts are those who entered the field in the same decade. Data are from Matanowski and co-workers, 1975a (Table 3) and 1975b (Table 1).
>
> *Combination:* In the 1920–1929 cohort, the data could not be separated for the otolaryngologists and the ophthalmologists.
>
> *Rates:* Entries are age- and time-adjusted death rates per 1,000 person-years.
>
> *Follow-up:* The 1920–1929 cohort includes data from all ages of follow-up; the 1930–1939 cohort, through age 74; the 1940–1949 cohort, through age 64.
>
> *Abbreviations:* "Radiol" stands for radiologists; "Inter" for internists; "Otolary" for otolaryngologists; "Ophthal" for ophthalmologists.

Part 1: Cancer Mortality Rate

Cohort	Radiol	Inter	Otolary	Ophthal
1920–1929	3.2	2.1	1.7	
1930–1939	2.5	1.6	1.8	1.4
1940–1949	1.6	1.2	0.9	0.5

Part 2: Non-Cancer Mortality Rate

1920–1929 Cohort

Diabetes	0.28	0.20	0.15	
Cardiovascular-renal	11.64	10.31	9.1	
Stroke	1.65	1.24	1.44	
Hypertensive disease	0.96	0.73	0.73	
Pneumonia	0.66	0.76	0.42	
Suicide	0.50	0.37	0.31	
Accidents	0.80	0.89	0.34	
Sum of the non-cancer death rates	16.49	14.50	12.49	

1930–1939 Cohort

Diabetes	0.05	0.04	0.14	0.05
Cardiovascular-renal	7.54	7.56	6.04	6.06
Stroke	0.78	0.90	0.78	0.46
Hypertensive disease	0.26	0.54	0.34	0.40
Pneumonia	0.05	0.32	0.23	0.0
Suicide	0.17	0.35	0.34	0.28
Accidents	0.55	0.59	0.37	0.27
Sum of the non-cancer death rates	9.40	10.30	8.24	7.52

Table 17. Part 2: Non-Cancer Mortality Rate *(Continued)*

1940–1949 Cohort	Radiol	Inter	Otolary	Ophthal
Diabetes	0.09	0.03	0.19	0.0
Cardiovascular-renal	3.77	3.62	3.95	3.53
Stroke	0.29	0.33	0.44	0.11
Hypertensive disease	0.18	0.23	0.08	0.15
Pneumonia	0.0	0.13	0.04	0.06
Suicide	0.29	0.22	0.30	0.37
Accidents	0.25	0.50	0.45	0.69
Sum of the non-cancer death rates	4.87	5.06	5.45	4.91

NOTE: In Part 2's individual categories, jumpiness of the horizontal entries suggests the worrisome role of random fluctuation when data are finely subdivided. Rates of suicide and accidents, included in Matanowski's study, are not necessarily *unrelated* to radiation, if radiation increases diseases which contribute to such events.

Part 3: Cancer Ratios, Radiologists vs. Others

Cohort	Radiol/ Inter	Radiol/ Otolary		Radiol/ Ophthal
1920–1929	1.52		1.88	
1930–1939	1.56	1.39		1.79
1940–1949	1.33	1.78		3.2

Part 4: Non-Cancer Ratios, Radiologists vs. Others

Cohort				
1920–1929	1.14		1.32	
1930–1939	0.91	1.14		1.25
1940–1949	0.96	0.89		0.99*

NOTE: In Part 4, the ratio with the asterisk would be 1.12 if suicide and accidents had been excluded; such an exclusion would barely alter the other ratios.

After inspecting the data, we certainly cannot share Matanowski and co-workers' conclusions (1975a, p. 196) that it is "reasonable" to conclude that radiation causes a "non-specific aging effect," resulting in life shortening among the radiologists.

These studies do not *rule out* a very small effect of radiation on non-cancer mortality, but they indicate that if indeed any such effect exists, it must be small compared with radiation's effect on *cancer* mortality.

Section 4: Summary on Premature Aging

Two separate studies, each capable of clearly showing a cancer effect from radiation, cannot show a non-cancer effect. We find that the available evidence is thin to nonexistent in support of a premature aging effect from radiation, other than the undeniable cancer-leukemia effect so strongly proven by a multitude of studies.

But the absence of a convincing positive study does not necessarily mean the absence of effect. What it seems to mean under these circumstances is that, if radiation causes premature aging, the effect must be quite small per rad compared with radiation's effect on cancer and leukemia. Moreover, if a premature aging effect exists, it might or might not operate at diagnostic levels of radiation exposure.

CHAPTER 15

Risks Unrelated to Radiation: Contrast Agents

Diagnostic X-ray examinations can be divided into two major groups. The first is composed of all the exams in which the X-ray beam itself is the only thing which enters the body. Such exams are considered "non-invasive" because a fully conscious person is examined without any local or general anesthetic, and no substance of any sort is given to the examined person by mouth, by injection, by enema, or by retrograde introduction into the urinary tract. In the other major groups of exams, artificial contrast agents are introduced into the body. The use of contrast agents sometimes has side-effects totally unrelated to radiation. This chapter briefly reviews some of them in the following sequence:

- The need for contrast agents (Section 1);
- Exams of the gastro-intestinal tract (Section 2);
- Exams of the urinary tract (Section 3);
- Exams of the gallbladder (Section 4);
- Side-effects from angiographies (Section 5);
- Intravenous digital subtraction angiographies (Section 6).

Section 1: The Need for Contrast Agents

If the same amount of energy reached a diagnostic film everywhere, the film would be uniformly exposed and would yield no image at all. A radiograph produces diagnostic information to the extent that it is unevenly exposed. Behind parts of the body which absorb virtually 100% of the X-ray beam, a film remains unexposed and clear; behind other parts, it blackens and turns opaque to various degrees. Even when non-film receptors for the image are used, the exposure principle is the same.

The key to information is the fact that specific body structures absorb the X-ray beam to a different degree than do surrounding tissues or organs. Consequently, by *enhancing* the contrast among structures of the body with respect to their absorption of X-rays, modern diagnostic radiology is able to obtain greatly increased diagnostic information in many circumstances.

A Natural Contrast Medium: In the bones, calcium salts provide a natural, built-in contrast material, which makes it unnecessary to *add* any contrast medium when bones are studied radiographically. Indeed, the reason that radiography can detect bone defects which are related either to loss or increment of the bones' calcium content is that such bones show a marked difference in their absorption of radiation.

In non-bony regions, calcium compounds are sometimes deposited as part of a pathologic process. Such depositions provide the natural contrast medium, calcium, which facilitates radiologic diagnosis. Mammography depends, in part, upon calcium-containing structures in the abnormal breast. Certain arterial diseases and kidney stones can be diagnosed by detecting calcium deposits where they should not be.

The Importance of Atomic Number: The contrast provided for radiologists by naturally occurring ionic calcium is due to a law of physics: elements of high atomic number absorb X-rays to a greater extent than do elements of low atomic number. Therefore calcium (atomic number = 20) blocks the passage of an X-ray beam to a much greater extent than do the elements hydrogen (atomic number = 1), carbon (atomic number = 6), nitrogen (atomic number = 7), and oxygen (atomic number = 8), which constitute the bulk of non-bony human tissues.

The Artificial Contrast Media

In many regions of the body, including cardiac chambers, arteries, and various segments of the urinary and gastro-intestinal tracts, there is no natural agent like calcium to provide radiographic contrast. When diagnostic information is required for such regions, it is necessary to introduce into the picture (literally) a chemical agent which can provide the otherwise missing contrast.

Most chemical elements of high atomic number are too toxic even to be considered, however. The radioactive element thorium (atomic number = 90) was effective as an artificial contrast medium, but its use in diagnostic radiology has been abandoned because the element's own radioactivity produced a variety of cancers in patients.

Iodine as a Contrast Agent: Iodine (atomic number = 53) is one of the very few elements of high atomic number which play a role in normal biochemistry and physiology; the various thyroid hormones all contain iodine within their molecules. Although toxicity rules out iodide ion and free iodine as contrast agents, chemical compounds which bind the iodine within their molecules can be used successfully.

These compounds, which are introduced into the body by mouth, by catheter, or by injection into vessels, have indeed proved capable of providing enough iodine, for the amounts taken in, to give very good radiographic contrast. Organic compounds containing iodine are currently being used in millions of diagnostic radiology examinations throughout the world. Side-effects will be briefly reviewed in Sections 3, 4, and 5 of this chapter.

Barium as a Contrast Agent: A second element in widespread use for diagnostic radiology is barium (atomic number = 56). While the ability of barium to provide radiographic contrast is excellent, the toxicity of free barium ions is extreme. This rules out barium compounds which could conceivably release barium ions to body tissues. Barium sulfate, a compound of exceedingly low solubility, is used successfully as a common contrast agent.

Countless millions of gastro-intestinal examinations are conducted by using liquid suspensions of barium sulfate. Patients take quite large quantities orally (the "barium swallow" and the "barium meal") or by enema. So few barium ions are released by this compound that barium poisoning is not a problem. Some of the non-toxic side-effects which occasionally accompany barium sulfate are reviewed briefly in Section 2 of this chapter.

The Three Types of Side-Effects

In current practice, the iodine-compounds and barium sulfate overwhelmingly dominate in the field of contrast media. Using them may involve certain unwanted side-effects, however. Just as cancer and leukemia are delayed side-effects which occur among only *some* patients from the radiation, so the side-effects from the chemicals occur only among *some* patients. Numerous studies have been conducted to ascertain the frequencies of such side-effects, and we will report many of the findings in this chapter. The side-effects fall into three main classes.

Chemical: Problems can originate with the contrast agent itself.

Mechanical: Problems can arise from the mechanics of placing the contrast agent where it is needed in the body. The swallowing of a chemical creates no problems of a mechanical nature, of course. But the successful introduction of iodine-containing contrast media, intravenously and intra-arterially, either by needle or by catheter, takes plenty of skill and experience (and some luck), as we shall see in Section 5 of this chapter. There can be even fatal side-effects simply from the mechanical procedures required to introduce the compound into the body in the right concentration at the right place at the right time.

Anesthetic: Problems can also arise from anesthesia, local or general. Anesthesia certainly does *not* accompany all uses of contrast media. But sophisticated procedures today can place contrast agents into almost any body region one might imagine, and sometimes it is necessary to use local or general anesthesia in order to render the procedure acceptable. When an anesthetic is used, its own toxicity becomes a third risk factor. However, the field of side-effects, from very mild to fatal, as an aftermath of anesthesia is a large subject by itself. This chapter will not discuss it at all.

A Valuable Source

For the information in the next four sections of this chapter, we are all in debt to the various contributors to the elegant book *Complications in Diagnostic Radiology,* edited by G. Ansell (1976), as well as to the numerous investigators whose studies the contributors cite.

Section 2: Examinations of the Gastrointestinal Tract

Solidification: A "not uncommon" side-effect from barium sulfate in the barium meal exam (Upper G.I. Series) has been described by Ansell as follows (p. 335): "Minor degrees of barium impaction are not uncommon in routine barium meal examinations and patients may suffer considerable discomfort from the passage of rock-like masses of hardened barium. It is good practice to warn patients of the possible constipation effects of barium and to advise the use of a laxative or liquid paraffin when necessary."

The formation of hard deposits of barium sulfate is a side-effect which means that this contrast agent is no longer chosen for urography. Even in the colon, stasis of barium sulfate has occasionally produced serious obstruction, requiring surgery for correction.

Perforation: A very different side-effect from the barium enema exam has been described also. Perforation of the colon has occurred in a small proportion of cases, with serious or even fatal consequences when the perforation permits infusion of the barium sulfate into the peritoneal or retroperitoneal spaces.

Ansell stated that this complication is "not excessively rare" and cited a recent survey of some 250,000 barium enemas. Intraperitoneal rupture occurred in 15 cases, and extraperitoneal rupture occurred in 6 cases. When the combined incidence of 21 per 250,000 is expressed in our customary way, it is a risk of 84 per million, or 1 chance in 12,000. In a much smaller (and therefore less reliable) series of 10,000 enemas, there were 4 cases of intraperitoneal rupture, or a rate of 400 per million.

The status of the patient's colon, specifically the presence of pathology *prior* to the exam, must increase both the likelihood of a diagnostic exam and the likelihood of complications.

Section 3: Examinations of the Urinary Tract

Millions of urographic exams using iodine-containing contrast media are done worldwide. Reports on the toxic side-effects include the following information about the Intravenous Pyelogram (I.V.P. Exam).

"Minor" Reactions

In a British survey of more than 300,000 I.V.P. exams in the United Kingdom, reactions classified as "minor" included nausea, retching, slight vomiting, feeling of heat, limited urticaria, mild pallor or sweating, itchy skin rashes, arm pain, and sneezing. Ansell did not compute the rate. He reports that in a survey of 40,000 urograms at the Ochsner Clinic, the incidence of "mild" reactions was 8%, or 80,000 per million. In a survey of some 30,000 patients who had the exam at the Mayo Clinic, the incidence of "minor" and "trivial" reactions was estimated at 5.1%, or 51,000 per million. The reactions classed as trivial included mild hot flush, metallic taste in the mouth, mild nausea, cough, sneezing, and tingling of the skin. In a smaller series which Ansell cited, Davies and co-workers (1975) reported similar "trivial" symptoms following 59% of the urograms, or a rate of 590,000 per million. Symptoms listed as trivial by Davies and co-workers included unpleasant sensations in the perineal area such as burning, a feeling of wetness, or a desire to empty the rectum or bladder, accompanied by a false sensation of having done so. The occurrence of trivial side-effects appeared to Davies and co-workers to be related to the dose and speed of the iodine compound's injection.

"Intermediate" Reactions

In the U.K. survey mentioned above, symptoms of "intermediate" serious-ness included faintness, severe vomiting, extensive urticaria, edema of the face or glottis, broncho-spasm, dyspnea, chills, chest pain, abdominal pain, and headache. Intermediate symptoms occurred in 142 out of 318,500 urograms. Expressed in our customary way, the rate was 446 per million, or 1 in 2,242. In the Mayo Clinic series cited above (30,000 examinations), the rate of "moderate" reactions was about 8,900 per million, or 1 in 112.

"Severe" Reactions

In the U.K. survey, "severe" meant that there was often fear for the patient's life. Severe reactions included severe vascular collapse, loss of consciousness, pulmonary edema, cardiac arrest, a syndrome resembling myocardial infarction, and cardiac arrhythmias. The incidence rate was 24 severe reactions out of 318,500 urograms, and among these, 8 resulted in death. The incidence of 24 severe reactions in that series is a rate of approximately 75 per million, or 1 in 13,300.

In the Mayo Clinic series (30,000 urograms), only one-third of the reactions classified as severe were considered life-threatening. The rate of severe reactions was reported at about 909 per million, or 1 in 1,100.

The rate among *children* of acute reactions to intravenous pyelogra-phy was studied by Gooding and co-workers (1975). They found the over-all incidence rate of reactions (all degrees of severity) to be 3.4%, or 34,000 per million, with the rate of severe reactions estimated at 400 per million, or 1 in 2,500.

Mortality Rates: The rates of death (all ages) from reactions have been studied in several countries.

- 25 per million, or 1 per 40,000 examinations in the U.K. survey;
- 16.5 per million, or 1 per 61,000 exams in a French study;
- 12 per million, or 1 per 85,000 exams in an Italian study;

- 20 per million, or 1 per 50,000 exams in a U.S. study by Fischer (1972).

Trends: Whether the rate of severe complications is rising or falling is very difficult to determine, as Ansell points out, because there is a trend toward accepting sicker patients for urography, and also possibly toward using higher dosage. Neither trend would mean that the exam is any more hazardous than it used to be, if equivalent conditions could be compared. Differences both in conditions of examination and in classification of reactions surely contribute to the difference in *rates* of reactions reported in various series from various places.

Blood Pressure: Among the severe reactions, Ansell found that hypotension with circulatory collapse was by far the outstanding feature; it was manifest in 35% of the cases of severe reaction. In fact, the *majority* of severe reactions included the fall in blood pressure, although circulatory collapse was not always present.

Why and When?

Ansell states that the real mechanism underlying the reactions to contrast media used in I.V.P. Exams is still not understood, but that it does not appear to be of classical allergic nature. He says (p. 6), "Reactions are unpredictable and usually occur during the injection or within the following five to ten minutes. However, occasionally, they may be delayed in onset."

Retrograde Pyelography

For patients having known or presumed sensitivity to contrast media, but also having an urgent need for a urographic exam, retrograde pyelography has been used. Studies have found that absorption of the contrast agent into the systemic circulation does occur, but it is very low compared with its circulation following intravenous use of the agent.

Retrograde Urethrocystography

Inflammation of the urethra and bladder was sometimes a side-effect from this procedure, but Ansell found it difficult to estimate how much of the reaction was due to the contrast medium and how much to the local anesthetic.

Section 4: Examinations of the Gallbladder

Oral Cholecystography: Iodine-containing contrast media are administered by mouth in millions of examinations of the gallbladder. Ansell reports that major complications are "relatively uncommon," but that approximately 50% of patients suffer mild or moderate effects such as nausea, with or without vomiting, diarrhea, headache, abdominal pain, difficulty with urination, dizziness, or urticaria. Ansell also states that severe hypotensive collapse is rare.

Intravenous Cholecystography: Ansell reports that the side-effects from intravenous use of contrast media in cholecystography are similar to the ones from intravenous urography. He says, "However, the reactions following intravenous cholangiography are frequently more severe." Hypotensive collapse and bronchospasm are features of the severe reactions. Comparing the rates of severe reactions from the intravenous gallbladder and I.V.P. exams, Ansell states that the rate is about 8 times higher from intravenous cholangiography than from intravenous urography.

For cholecystography, with iodipamide as the contrast agent injected intravenously, the following rates of reaction were reported in the U.K. survey (Ansell, 1970):

Intermediate reactions: 1,429 per million, or 1 in 700.
Severe reactions: 625 per million, or 1 in 1,600.
Death: 200 per million, or 1 in 5,000.

Section 5: Side-Effects from Angiographies

A Caution about Reported Rates: The relatively sophisticated radiological procedures which use contrast agents have provided abundant new information which is diagnostically important. Consequently, such procedures are used for patients with very serious diseases, often in an advanced state of development, even though such patients may be much less able to tolerate the contrast medium than people who are less ill—and less desperately in need of the exam. Some seriously ill patients have a very high risk of dying whether or not they have an exam requiring a contrast agent. Therefore, it is almost certain that some unhappy outcomes are falsely attributed to the exam. In fact, Herlinger (1976) reports that it has been customary to attribute any death which occurs during angiography, or within the subsequent 48 hours, to the examination.

Baum and co-workers (1966) decided to compare the rate and type of fatal events which occurred during the 48 hours *before* cancelled angiographies with the rate within 48 hours *following* such exams. Herlinger comments on that study, "There was surprising similarity, indicating that the pre-existing disease and not the angiogram bore responsibility for most angiographic fatalities in more recent years."

Problems of Mechanical Origin

The rate of complications arising from the mechanics of introducing the contrast medium is related to the skill and experience of the team doing the examination, and also to luck. We will see why this is so as we review four types of complications which can result from the procedure of putting the contrast agent into the appropriate blood vessel or heart chamber. They are perforation, hematoma formation, thrombosis, and embolism, and the consequent health effects.

Perforation. One type of perforation occurs when an injection pierces the intimal lining of the artery and delivers the contrast agent into the wall of the artery instead of into the lumen. The result can be that the artery's lumen actually closes and blood is virtually denied to the regions which the artery normally supplies.

A related but different type of perforation begins the same way but results in arterial dissection. The injected material moves along *inside* the wall of the artery for quite a distance, causes pressure upon some branches of the artery, and thereby compromises the blood supply to organs which the branches supply. Complications such as dissection may be more likely among people having diseased arteries than among others.

Hematoma Formation. Hematomas, which are accumulations of blood in tissues *outside* the blood-vessel system, can result from perforating the artery during introduction of the contrast medium, either by needle or catheter. Secondary effects, such as pressure on nerves with consequent loss of nerve function in a region, can and do occur.

Thrombosis. Thrombosis, which is blood clotting within the arterial system, is another event which can compromise blood delivery to the organs supplied by the impaired artery. Because thrombotic tendency appears to be accentuated by any injury of a vessel's endothelial lining, it is hardly surprising that thrombosis has been a hazard in angiographic procedures which use catheters. However, thrombosis is a much smaller hazard from such procedures than it used to be, thanks to extensive improvements in the fashioning and use of catheters over the past two decades.

Embolism. A thrombus which stays at its site of origin may hardly compromise circulation at all, if sufficient lumen is still available to let an adequate flow of blood past the thrombus. But if the thrombus does not adhere firmly to the arterial wall, it can break off, travel in the arterial flow, and reach a region of smaller diameter, where it can totally occlude the blood supply. This is embolism, or embolization, a feared complication in all intravascular procedures.

A blood clot is not the only traveling hazard which can cause embolism; plaque and air bubbles can do it, too.

Some patients have severe degrees of the disease atherosclerosis in the arterial wall. If a needle or catheter pierces a diseased artery, pieces of the atherosclerotic plaque can be released from the wall into the vessel's lumen, migrate to a region of lesser diameter, and finally occlude an important arterial branch. Lundervold and Engeset, in their chapter on cerebral angiography and its complications in Ansell's book, state the situation very well (p. 176):

> *Technical problems* are a more common cause of complications in cerebral angiography than the new contrast media used. A meticulous technique by a well-trained neuroradiologist is therefore essential. The most common causes of serious complications are intramural injection which may completely occlude the injected vessel, and embolization from an atheromatous plaque after puncturing a diseased vessel wall. (Emphasis in the original.)

Their comments would apply not only to *cerebral* angiography, but to additional types as well.

Air bubbles also are capable of causing embolism. When a contrast medium is infused into an artery, air may enter the solution unless the infusion system is carefully connected. The hazard is that air bubbles may travel to narrow arterial branches and provoke occlusion with serious consequences. The frequency with which authors discuss this possibility suggests that, in practice, it may be a substantial problem.

Problems of Chemical Origin

In a small fraction of cases, the intra-arterial injection of contrast medium by needle or catheter may result in serious adverse effects whose true cause is not readily evident. For the understanding of some possible explanations, we will briefly review the way such injection is performed.

Importance of the Agent's Concentration: If the outlines of arterial branches need visualization in a diagnostic examination, sufficient contrast agent must be *present* in the examined branches. Because normal blood flow dilutes the bolus of injected contrast medium, enough medium must be injected so that, even after the inevitable dilution, enough concentration remains in the vessel under study to absorb X-rays efficiently. Otherwise, there is no way for the radiologist to see the vessel's outlines.

The necessity of coping with dilution has led to rather concentrated solutions and fairly rapid injection of the iodine-containing contrast agent. But the more injected and the faster the injection, the greater the chance that a local high concentration will provoke a nasty effect. Therefore, work never ends on the goal of reducing the toxicity of contrast media.

Serious reactions considered to be somehow associated with high *local* concentration of the contrast agent have occurred in angiography of the cerebral vessels, the cardiopulmonary vessels, the renal arteries, and others. The precise mechanisms which cause such reactions remain uncertain and subjects of speculation, but no one doubts that the adverse reactions have occurred.

Aortography. In aortography, cases have been reported of serious spinal cord damage and paraplegia, which Herlinger (1976, in the Ansell book, p. 56) has attributed as follows:

The tragic complication of paraplegia may result from the entry of a high concentration or of a large bolus of contrast medium into vessels supplying the spinal cord.

Herlinger says that this unplanned access of the medium to the spinal cord may be the result of either (a) the contrast medium gaining unplanned access to the anterior spinal artery, or (b) the medium becoming diverted into the spinal vascular bed due to an obstruction in the aorta or iliac arteries. There is also the suspicion that a high concentration of the iodine-containing compound may injure the endothelial lining of blood vessels and may overwhelm the normal barrier in the spinal vasculature between the blood and the central nervous system (C.N.S.). The result would be the access—which would otherwise never occur—of toxic material to tissues of the spinal cord.

Frequency of Complications: Herlinger (1976, p. 57) stated:

McAfee reported major neurological complications in 0.22 percent of examinations using older, more toxic contrast media. Such complications, however, do still occur at the present time, and it is believed that published reports do not reflect the real incidence. We have been fortunate enough not to encounter a single example.

The risk of 0.22 percent, expressed in our customary fashion, is 2,200 per million, or 1 chance in 450, but the rate is not necessarily applicable to current practice with less toxic contrast media.

Cardiac Catheterization. Neurological complications have been reported also from cardiac catheterization—insertion of a catheter into the heart and some of its arteries—with and without accompanying angiocardiography. Swan's early report (1968) gave a figure of 24 neurological complications in a series of 12,367 examinations, which is a rate of 1,940 per million, or 1 chance in about 500. Of the 24 patients, 11 sustained generalized cerebral dysfunction, and 13 had C.N.S. complications with focal signs, according to Saunders and Dow (1976). The focal signs were either left or right hemiparesis (paralysis of half the body).

Saunders and Dow suspected that embolisms may have caused the reactions, but that chemical possibilities needed consideration too. Some possibilities were (a) a direct effect upon the brain possibly due to the very high concentration of contrast medium, and (b) possible disturbance of circulation in the brain due to the hyperosmolality of the contrast medium, whose high concentration of ions might pull fluid from tissues into the vessels.

Cerebral Angiography. In cerebral angiography, also, adverse side-effects upon the central nervous system have definitely occurred; their range is described by Lundervold and Engeset (1976, in the Ansell book, p. 151):

> These include a whole range of central nervous disorders from transient motor or sensory deficit to decerebration and death. Their incidence varies among reviews because of differences in definition of complications, contrast agents, techniques, and patient selections. Since the pioneers in this field started, there has been much improvement in technique and contrast media. With current contrast media and technique, permanent complications, including death, occur with an incidence of about 1–3 percent. Surveys indicate a death occurring in an average of one in every 250 cerebral angiograms, compared with only one in every 40,000 urograms.

These rates of C.N.S. injury associated with cerebral angiography can be expressed, of course, in our customary way.

Incidence: from 10,000 per million (1 chance in 100) to 30,000 per million (1 chance in 33).

Death: 4,000 per million (1 chance in 250).

Concentration and Speed: Lundervold and Engeset warn (p. 154):

The substances now in clinical use produce little alteration of the blood-brain barrier in normal concentrations, amount, and rate of injection, but if given in too high a dosage or concentration, or too fast, serious brain damage and even death may occur.

Acute Renal Failure

Talner (1976) reported that there can be renal complications from non-renal angiography, including mesenteric and celiac angiography, angiocardiography, aortography, peripheral arteriography, and spinal arteriography. Among the complications, acute renal failure (kidney failure) is the most serious and clinically the most significant. Within 24 hours following angiography, urinary output may diminish and, in some cases, continue decreasing until it ceases completely (anuria). Incidence data differ greatly from one report to another.

- Lang (1963) reported only 2 cases among more than 11,000 percutaneous retrograde arteriograms; this is a rate of 182 per million, or 1 in 5,500.
- Robertson and co-workers (1969) reported no cases in 1,750 angiographies.
- The Mayo Clinic experience between 1968 and 1972 was 1 case per 1,000 angiographic procedures (Port and co-workers, 1974); this is a rate of 1,000 per million, or 1 in 1,000.

While the use of large volumes of contrast media is cited as one possible cause of renal failure associated with various types of angiographies, investigators admit that the true cause remains obscure. They are puzzled, for instance, by the fact that in more than 2,700 bilateral *renal* arteriograms at the Mayo Clinic, not even one patient developed renal failure (Port and co-workers, 1974).

Human Error

All the authors who discuss adverse side-effects from contrast media in various angiographic exams say that they suspect over-injection, by error, in at least some of the cases. The suspicion is natural; how could this one type of procedure escape human error? The harm caused by such errors will become less, if the contrast agents become less toxic. Some of the risks from angiography described in this section can be reduced also by a technique which we will describe, with pleasure, in the next section.

Section 6: Intravenous Digital Subtraction Angiography

The evidence in Sections 2, 3, 4, and 5 of this chapter indicates that injecting iodine-containing contrast media into arteries carries a higher risk than using equivalent agents either intravenously or orally. A technique which permits angiographies to be conducted successfully with *intravenous* injections is in operation at the Lahey Clinic near Boston and at some other medical centers.

The principles of the technique, described by Robel (1982), are simple. Although injecting a contrast agent intravenously results in its great dilution before it reaches the arterial system, the agent can still deliver a faint image of the arterial system one wishes to study. But in a regular radiograph, the faint image is lost among all the other information. If the other information could be removed (subtracted out), the faint image would remain isolated, available for electronic intensification, and at hand as useful diagnostic information. Thanks to computers and electronics, it can be done now.

With the Lahey Clinic's system, for instance, fluoroscopic images are digitized—that is, each point in an image is converted into a number by the computer. Such numbers are convertible back to images, of course. For angiography, a first set of images of the vessels under study is recorded *before* introduction of any contrast medium; this first set contains also bone and soft tissue. After the intravenous injection of a contrast agent, a second set of images is made; this set contains everything in the first set *plus* the faint image provided by the diluted contrast agent.

Both before and after the injection, all areas except those containing some contrast agent give the same image (and same digits) in the first and second sets. Therefore, when the computer subtracts the first set from the second set, the result leaves a third set of digitized images which show only the contrast material inside the blood vessels.

Not only does the technique obtain the needed information from intravenous injection, but the images can be manipulated by computer to achieve the desired contrast. Even color. It is the prediction of Dr. Scholz at the Lahey Clinic that digital radiography will revolutionize diagnostic radiology much as the C.A.T. scanner did in the 1970s. "The 1990s will see the end of X-ray film as we know it," he predicts.

Whether or not that prediction comes true, we rejoice in this fine application of science and technology to reduce the hazard of useful diagnostic examinations.

CHAPTER 16

Low-Cost Ways
to Reduce Dose and Risk

In earlier chapters, we have evaluated the risk of cancer, leukemia, and other diseases from exposure to diagnostic X-rays. Because it is clear that X-ray examinations can provide important benefits in medical diagnosis, it would seem sensible for everyone concerned—radiologists, referring physicians, dentists, patients, and parents—to cooperate in retaining the benefits while simultaneously reducing the hazards.

The news on this issue is very good. Several teams of dedicated researchers, whom we will describe in this chapter, have provided the practical information which enables very large reductions in dose and therefore in risk to be achieved. Johns and Cunningham, members of one of the most capable teams in the world, say in the fourth edition of their classic book *The Physics of Radiology* (1983, p. 557):

> We have evidence (Taylor, 1979) that the dose from diagnostic radiology can be reduced by a factor of at least 3 with little work and by a factor of 10 or more if all conditions are optimized.

This is not a "blue sky" claim from speculators. Johns, Cunningham, and Taylor have worked for many years in cooperation with people throughout the Canadian radiology profession, and they have repeatedly *demonstrated* in busy X-ray facilities how to achieve the large reduction in dose which they talk about. And they do it with whatever equipment a facility

347

already has; no major purchases of new equipment are involved. Some key aspects of their successful program are discussed in Section 2 of this chapter.

In the United States, the world renowned Mayo Clinic in Rochester, Minnesota, is one of the institutions making serious efforts to measure and reduce doses in all its radiologic examinations. A leading contributor there to those efforts is Dr. Joel Gray, a radiation physicist. Dr. Gray (1984, p. 96) comments about offices which will not tell patients the dose:

> My feeling is that if they won't tell you, they don't know, and
> if they don't know, they could be among the facilities delivering
> a hundred times the necessary dose.

At the end of Section 1, we will examine the huge range of doses which patients receive for the same examination in various facilities (Tables 19 and 20).

The purpose of this chapter is to provide a summary—a sort of checklist—of low-cost ways to measure and reduce dose. By reducing dose, we mean transferring less energy to human tissues. Therefore, dose reduction involves not only entrance doses but also size of the areas exposed. The sequence is as follows:

- Measurement of entrance dose (Section 1);
- Reduction of entrance dose (Section 2);
- Reduction of field size (Section 3);
- Choice of beam direction (Section 4);
- Exams for scoliosis patients—a spectacular achievement in dose reduction (Section 5).

Section 1: Measurement of Entrance Dose

It should be obvious that the first step in any facility's program of dose reduction is to learn how big its current doses actually are. It turns out that calculation of doses is no substitute for measurement, and that measurement is easy and inexpensive.

Measured Doses Compared with Calculated Doses

Many medical and dental facilities never measure entrance doses; instead, they calculate them from tables of peak kilovoltage (kVp), milliampere-seconds (mAs), and filtration. But direct measurements have proven that such calculated doses are often seriously in error.

For instance, in Chapter 9 we summarized the findings reported by Wochos and Cameron about dental X-rays. They showed that doses which were measured instead of calculated ranged from 0.1 to 4.0 times the calculated dose—a factor of 40 for the range. They found the situation similar for a variety of other examinations.

From the extremely useful NEXT studies sponsored by the U.S. Bureau of Radiological Health, Wochos and Cameron (1977) had the raw data from which they obtained the range of disagreement between calculated doses (from kVp and mAs) and true doses measured with thermoluminescent dosimeters (TLDs). The comparison is shown in Table 18.

Wochos and Cameron comment that "the wide variation in the ratio of measured to expected output indicates that many X-ray units are out of calibration in regard to kVp or mA."

In a later paper (1979, p. 134), Wochos, Detorie, and Cameron make a recommendation:

> We feel it is important to have the patient exposure measured for each X-ray unit. Two X-ray units operated with supposedly the same filtration and at the same kVp and mAs do not necessarily deliver the same patient exposure. The exposure can be adequately measured with inexpensive pen dosimeters or on-patient TLDs.

Writing in 1982, Suntharalingam says (p. 998):

> A recent survey (1980) on the current status of clinical applications of thermoluminescent dosimetry in the United States in-

Table 18. Comparison of Measured vs. Calculated Entrance Doses

Ratios: The ratios are measured dose divided by theoretical dose, where the theoretical value is obtained from kilovoltage, milliampere-seconds, and manuals.

Number of Institutions Studied	Type of Examination	Lowest Ratio	Highest Ratio	Total Range
1,434	PA Chest Radiograph	0.1	4.0	40-fold
126	LAT Skull Radiograph	0.2	4.0	20-fold
491	The K.U.B. Radiograph or AP Abdomen	0.1	4.0	40-fold
95	AP Retrograde Pyelogram	0.2	4.0	20-fold
52	AP Thoracic Spine	0.2	4.0	20-fold
210	AP Cervical Spine	0.1	4.0	40-fold
634	AP Lumbo-Sacral Spine	0.1	4.0	40-fold
31	AP Full Spine Radiograph	0.3	4.0	13-fold

dicated that about one-half of the facilities surveyed use TLD for dose measurements in diagnostic radiology.

Radiation Monitoring by Mail

When a radiologic office wants to reduce entrance doses, it must first be able to measure them. To facilitate such measurements anywhere in the United States and in foreign countries too, Radiation Monitoring by Mail was established in 1975 as a public service operation by the Department of Medical Physics at the University of Wisconsin Medical School. The address is:

Radiation Monitoring by Mail, University of Wisconsin
Room 1530 Medical Physics Laboratories
1300 University Avenue
Madison, Wisconsin 53706, U.S.A.
The telephone number is 608 / 262-6320.

Radiation Monitoring by Mail provides TLD crystals with instructions for measuring dose during any type of diagnostic X-ray exam (including but not limited to dental exams, C.A.T. Scans, mammography, chest, and lower spine exams). The tiny TLD crystals (2 per patient) are taped to the skin, and they do not interfere with the X-ray process. After exposure, the X-ray office mails the set of crystals back to the monitoring service, which "reads" them and mails a written report giving the doses within two weeks after receipt.

A fee is set which reimburses the Medical Physics Department for costs. As of January 1985, the fee for a 5-patient set including 10 TLDs, instructions, and the written report, was $55.00 ($11.00 per patient). The service for dental TLDs (5) cost $40.00. The service is available to facilities outside the United States, too.

In Canada, a by-mail service for measuring doses to patients (and staff) has been organized by Dr. Kenneth Taylor. The address is:

Kenneth W. Taylor, Ph.D.
Starmil Imaging Science, Inc.
299 Evans Avenue
Toronto, Ontario M8Z 1K2, Canada
The telephone number is 416 / 978-5503.

Making It Easy: With such a service available, it would be hard to imagine any reason why entrance doses should not be knowable at every place giving medical and dental X-rays. There is simply no need to depend on calculations which may be introducing very large mistakes about dose, such as calling the dose 10 times as high as it truly is, or 4 times lower.

In addition, as this book goes to press, a company in Rochester, New York, is introducing a TLD-based monitoring system which allows the patient to keep track of his or her own radiation exposure from medical and dental X-rays as well as environmental radiation. Members enrolled in the program will be supplied with a credit-card-sized monitor carrying multiple TLDs. One TLD is permanently mounted to measure background radiation exposure from the environment. The other TLDs are used for measuring dose during specific X-ray exams. The fee charged for enrollment will include reading the TLDs and reporting to the member the radiation exposure from X-ray examinations and background sources. More information on this program is available from the following group:

Personal Monitoring Technologies, Inc.
1030 First Federal Plaza
Rochester, New York 14614, U.S.A.
The telephone number is 716 / 232-1600.

Contacting Expert Help

An important reason for the unreliability of entrance doses which are calculated (instead of measured) is the frequency with which X-ray units become out of calibration. Calibration can be corrected by the service of a qualified radiological physicist, who can also help maintain the quality-control measures which assure optimal images, reduced need for retakes, and minimal exposure of patients.

Dr. Robert Barish, an associate professor of radiology at the New York University School of Medicine, recommends (1984, p. 97) that direct quality assurance measurements on X-ray facilities be conducted at least once each year by a qualified radiological physicist.

Help in testing and maintaining equipment is available by mail from both the Wisconsin and Ontario groups already mentioned. For instance, the Wisconsin group offers a service which measures the half-value layer of an X-ray unit; also, it rents quality control equipment (including a phantom for testing and improving image quality in mammography).

The Ontario group has organized a by-mail service which can monitor X-ray and light beam collimation, focal spot size, peak kilovoltage, screen performance, film processing conditions, and more. The service supplies a radiologic office with simple phantoms, test objects, film packets, and instructions for their use by the staff; afterwards, these items are returned to Starmil Imaging for analysis and a written report. In addition, Dr. Taylor's group is available to make independent on-site tests of expensive pieces of equipment before they are replaced (sometimes unnecessarily), to test the performance of new equipment before it is accepted, and to educate staff members in the safe use of equipment and in the quality-control techniques which produce improved images with minimal patient (and staff) exposures.

In California, an effective program is helping both hospitals and private offices (medical, dental, and chiropractic) to measure and reduce doses; it is led by Jack Signorella, C.R.T., Ed.M. The address is:

Jack Signorella, Director
Radiologic Technology Program, Cabrillo College
6500 Soquel Avenue
Aptos, California 95003, U.S.A.
The telephone number is 408 / 425-6256.

The contacts mentioned in this section are illustrative; they certainly do not comprise an exhaustive directory of help in this field. According to the American Association of Physicists in Medicine, state and local health departments have lists of qualified radiological physicists.

Ranges of Entrance Dose for Specific Exams

The Wochos-Cameron study of doses, found during the NEXT survey, is most illuminating. The data in Table 19 are taken from their publication (1977).

Operators on the high side of the average probably have little or no idea that they are delivering high doses, because a high entrance dose does not automatically result in an overexposed film.

In view of this enormous range which characterizes entrance doses in the United States, it is easy to understand the basis of a statement by Dr. Edward Webster (1984, p. 96), an expert radiologic physicist at the Massachusetts General Hospital:

> When a woman arrives at a doctor's office for a mammogram,
> she has no way of knowing whether she's getting three hundred
> or three thousand millirads.

Canada shows a similarly great variation in entrance doses from one place to another. Taylor and co-workers reported the ranges they measured in Toronto for diagnostic procedures in 1978. Table 20 provides a sample of their measurements.

Taylor and co-workers made the following comment about their measurements: "There is ample evidence that this problem occurs in most X-ray installations throughout the world and is not just a problem in Ontario."

They are correct. The situation is even worse in the United States, as we noted above. Suntharalingam (1982, p. 992) commented this way on the wide range of doses observed during the NEXT studies in the United States: "The wide range in these exposure values for the same type of

Table 19. Dose Ranges for Specific Exams, United States

Abbreviations: The abbreviations for milli-roentgen and millirad are, respectively, mR and mrad.

Lowest Dose: Wochos and Cameron provide maximum dose and the ratio of maximum to minimum dose; instead of trying to read minimum values from their drawings, we divided their maximum values by the ratio to obtain the entries for the Lowest Dose column.

Number of Institutions	Examination	Entrance Dose in Milli-Roentgens (mR)			
		Mean Value	*Standard Deviation*	*Highest Dose*	*Lowest Dose*
1,433	Chest PA	23	29	2,300	3
126	Skull LAT	270	343	2,700	13
491	K.U.B. or Abdomen AP	562	341	2,900	22
95	Retrograde Pyelogram AP	594	282	1,400	93
52	Thoracic Spine AP	690	585	3,200	64
210	Cervical Spine AP	228	299	2,600	7
634	Lumbo-Sacral Spine AP	792	545	5,500	11
31	Full Spine	291	150	700	50
70	Feet	210	306	2,000	29
1,408	Dental Bitewing	650	727	6,800	68
759	Dental Periapical	644	696	7,500	75

Table 20. Dose Ranges for Specific Exams, Canada

Procedure	*Range of Exposures in Roentgens*
Chest	0.02 to 0.15
Barium Meal (Upper G.I. Series)	1.6 to 90
Barium Enema (Lower G.I. Series)	16 to 128
Intravenous Pyelogram	1.3 to 41
Gallbladder	4 to 48

SOURCE: Table 16–5 in Johns and Cunningham (1983, p. 648).

examination is a result of the wide variation in exposure factors and techniques that are used by the different facilities. It should be pointed out that these data do not reflect the corresponding diagnostic quality of the images obtained, and in many cases patient dose can be reduced without loss of pertinent diagnostic information."

The Size of Proven Reductions in Entrance Dose

It is essentially self-evident, from the wide range of entrance doses which are providing acceptable information to radiologists in both the United States and Canada, that there is ample room for greatly reducing the average entrance dose *without* losing acceptable quality in images.

Logic is fortified by evidence on this matter. Taylor's Canadian team has proven in the field that the projected dose reductions can really be obtained without any loss of image quality. Taylor and co-workers have been promoting a dose-reduction program among Ontario radiologists. They have been invited to radiological facilities, have ascertained which operations delivered doses much higher than necessary, have made the appropriate corrections, and have found that the radiologists could not perceive any loss in the quality of the diagnostic information produced *after* dose reduction compared with its quality *before,* at much higher doses to the patients. Table 21 shows how the minimum entrance doses which some radiologists have achieved compare with the average exposures in Ontario for late 1979.

Taylor and colleagues urge that radiologists try to reduce doses to their patients to the levels already achieved by the radiologists participating in the dose-reduction program—or even lower.

Dr. Harold Johns, in the course of giving the Richards Memorial Lecture in 1979, expressed an opinion about how *not* to approach this goal, and we vigorously agree. He warned (Johns and Cunningham, 1983, p. 650): "If regulatory bodies set maximum levels above which the exposures must not go, then there will be a tendency for service technologists to set their machines to those levels, in spite of the fact that it is possible to work with much lower exposure rates. Thus, setting a legal limit may be an unwise step, if we are really interested in reducing dose."

Table 21. Dose Reduction Achievements for Specific Exams, Ontario

Examination	Minimum Exposure Used (mR)	Average Dose Used (mR) in 1979
Skull Lateral	100	265
Cervical Spine AP	90	140
Thoracic Spine AP	260	460
Chest PA	8	25
Lumbar Spine AP	180	620
Lumbar Spine Lateral	500	2,445
Abdomen AP (K.U.B.)	190	530
Intravenous Pyelogram	150	600

SOURCE: Table 16-6 in Johns and Cunningham (1983, p. 650).

Section 2: Reduction of Entrance Dose

It is not our purpose to give detailed, step-by-step instructions here on how to reduce entrance doses without any loss of diagnostic information. Instead, we wish to mention two excellent sources for such information; we recommend them highly for their authenticity and magnificent clarity in the specific measures they explain.

- Chapter 16, "Diagnostic Radiology," prepared by Drs. Taylor, Yaffe, Fenster, and Holloway in collaboration with Drs. Johns and Cunningham in the book *The Physics of Radiology, Fourth Edition* (1983).
- Chapter 19, "Radiation Problems" (the section therein entitled "Methods of Dose Reduction"), prepared by Drs. Ardran and Crooks in the book edited by Dr. G. Ansell, *Complications in Diagnostic Radiology* (1976).

In addition, journals continue to yield new articles on techniques for specific exams which reduce their dose. Such articles provided the information in Section 5 of this chapter, for instance.

The purpose of Section 2 is to identify many of the major factors found by Taylor and his associates to be very important for achieving dose reduction, together with their assessment of the magnitude of reduction associated with specific measures. The chapter by Taylor and colleagues is, as we have emphasized, based on real-world experience, not on speculation.

Choice of Beam Direction

For certain procedures, an AP beam direction is commonly used. In a gastro-intestinal examination, Taylor and associates indicate that, compared to the AP direction, the PA direction can produce the same exposure of the film while *lowering* the dose received by centrally-placed abdominal organs by 3-fold. We would approach this problem by comparing the final cancer risk from the two shots, since reducing risk is the goal of reducing dose. The tables in Chapters 5 and 6 make it very easy to compare the risks from AP and PA shots, and such comparisons may stimulate a new look at the relative merits of customary beam directions. But it is the radiologist who must judge whether reversing beam direction sacrifices necessary image quality.

How Films Are Processed

Taylor and colleagues point out that how the film is developed will affect the exposures required for the examination. In Ontario hospitals, they found by direct experience that for films of the *same* nominal speed, the exposure required to produce an optical density of 1.0 could vary by a *factor of 3* according to the chemistry and conditions used for processing the film. When the wrong chemistry can require using an entrance dose three times higher than otherwise necessary, this step in radiology must be regarded as a potential source of significant dose reductions.

Selection of Optimal Screen-Film Combinations

Taylor and colleagues showed that different combinations of screen and film led to a variation in the required exposure by a *factor of 6.* Proper choices are another big way to reduce dose.

Choice of Filter

Taylor and colleagues point out that, in the past, most radiography used aluminum filters to harden the beam (raise the beam quality). They showed that rare earth or tungsten filters can reduce exposure by as much as a *factor of 2,* with no significant change in image contrast. One drawback they mention on this issue is that a higher load occurs on the X-ray tube. This field, which is currently an active one, is bringing improved filters to market; some may do even better than cutting dose in half.

Reduction of Dose Rate in Fluoroscopy

There is excellent agreement between the recommendations from Taylor and co-workers concerning fluoroscopy and those recommendations from Ardran and Crooks already mentioned in Chapter 6.

In Taylor and co-workers' study (1979) of 30 radiological facilities in Ontario, excessive dose rate and excessive total time accounted for a huge range in entrance doses for several common fluoroscopic examinations. Their key findings on dose rate are three.

Before: Facilities using high fluoroscopic exposure-rates obtained no better diagnostic quality than the facilities using low dose rates.

After: The radiologists were just as satisfied with the diagnostic images after Taylor and colleagues lowered dose rates as before.

Intensifying Screens: Excessively high dose rates were closely associated with the use of older cadmium-sulfide intensifying screens; in terms of reduced dose rate, cesium-iodide types were preferable. (Ardran and Crooks note that image-intensifier systems, which deteriorate with use, need periodic checking.)

Acceptance of 70 mm and 100 mm Fluorography

With modern image intensifiers, the radiologist can take a 70 mm to 100 mm film rather than a larger radiograph during fluoroscopy. Taylor and co-workers found that a common cause of high doses was the use of full-sized film when the 70 mm to 100 mm picture from the image-intensifier system produced satisfactory diagnostic information.

Proper Maintenance of Fluoroscopy Equipment

There are several special tests which Taylor and colleagues use in checking the output of X-ray equipment. Some of these tests, now available through radiological physicists, show up serious additional sources of unsuspected and unnecessary exposure to patients. As we shall relate, a patient can receive more dose while the fluoroscope is "off" than while it is "on," if its decay performance has been checked in only routine ways.

In their work, Taylor and colleagues found that one of the important features requiring measurement was the waveform of the X-ray yield as a function of time. In one machine, a malfunctioning milliampere stabilizer resulted in a continuous increase in milliamperage—and therefore in X-ray dose to the patient—during the course of an exposure. In another, too high a temperature for the tube filament was used, which resulted in an initial high peak exposure, followed after the first second by falling temperature and dose, thanks to control circuits. But even though the fluoroscopist stopped the exposure at 4 seconds, the X-ray yield *continued,* due to the gradual discharge of the high-voltage circuit. The dose did not fall to zero until 12 seconds after "termination."

As Taylor states (1983, p. 656):

> The initial spike and the long decay should not have been present and more than doubled the dose to the patient. Furthermore, the radiation emitted during the tail could not be seen because the television tube is automatically blanked at the termination of fluoroscopy. Thus the patient was being irradiated without the radiologist's knowledge. Usual methods of quality

control that measure steady state conditions do not detect these transients. These transients are commonly found in fluoroscopy but are seldom investigated. The long decay can be eliminated by using higher mA and lower kV or, better, by discharging the high tension circuit with a load resistance that is automatically connected into the circuit at the end of fluoroscopy. Ironically, the conscientious radiologist who might use high kV and a series of 2-second exposures would in fact deliver to the patient three times the radiation in the 'off' periods as in the 'on' time. *This is a serious problem, since half the machines in clinical use studied in our survey had one or both of these faults present.* (Emphasis added.)

If *half* the facilities in a survey show such equipment defects, it is clear that much greater use needs to be made of the services of qualified radiologic physicists. We consider it fortunate that the radiology profession has available talented physicists with the knowledge, equipment, and desire to help prevent unnecessary patient exposures.

Section 3: Reduction in Field Size

Collimation to Body Part

There is universal agreement that there is *never* a reason to use a beam size larger than the film size in a diagnostic examination. If beam size exceeds film size, many tissues will be irradiated totally unnecessarily, and the cancer risk will be increased for no offsetting benefit whatsoever.

But there is more to consider. Often the film is larger than the part of the body being examined. There is no justification for having the beam size any larger than the part of the body being examined, so beams should always be collimated to body part.

From the discussions in Chapter 19, we must expect that collimation would make little or no difference in dose to organs fully in the field, but would make a large difference in dose to organs at the periphery of the field. Rosenstein, Beck, and Warner (1979) observed precisely this effect. They have provided, for several pediatric examinations, calculations comparing collimations to body part and to film size; from their Table 15 (p. 41), we take the following data from the AP Abdomen Exam of infants one year old. For both collimations, the beam quality was 2.5 mm Al HVL.

Their data illustrate the value of collimating to body part rather than to film size. The ovary, which is fully in the field of the abdominal shot, is the only organ whose dose is *not* reduced by proper collimation.

Organ	AP Abdomen	
	Collimation to Body Part	Collimation to Film Size
	Field size at image receptor = 7.1 × 8.3 inches	Field size at image receptor = 10 × 12 inches
	mrads per R entrance dose	mrads per R entrance dose
Testes	105	1,070
Ovaries	370	370
Thyroid	not detectable	9
Active bone marrow	100	140
Lungs	48	255

Caution about Underestimates: Our tables evaluate risks based on absorbed organ doses. The tables will *underestimate* risks at facilities which collimate to film size regardless of the patient's size.

Pediatric Exams: Collimation to body part makes an especially great difference for the pediatric examinations. In view of the high sensitivity of newborns and young children to induction of cancer by radiation (Table 2 in Chapter 3), the professionals managing in pediatric exams to achieve the smallest useful fields deserve to feel good about their efforts.

Fluoroscopic Exams: In Chapters 6 and 7, we showed how the risk from fluoroscopies is not necessarily higher than from the routine films of the same examination, if the beam size during fluoroscopy can be kept small. The effect of small field size on cancer risk is illustrated by the tables for celiac, cerebral, and pulmonary arteriography, where the risk from the films *exceeds* the risk from the fluoroscopy, due to the small area fluoroscoped (Chapter 7).

The Choice of Circular or Rectangular Field

There is no automatic advantage from circular collimation compared with rectangular. What counts in terms of risk is not the shape of the beam, but its area. In an abdominal exam, for instance, if the coning or collimation is circular, and if *all* of the circular field shows on the film (diagram, next page), then the exposed area is automatically smaller than it would be, had the *entire* film been exposed. But in intra-oral dental radiography, the circular coning generally covers a much larger area than the small rectangular film (diagram, right side), because it is otherwise difficult to be sure the desired area is covered.

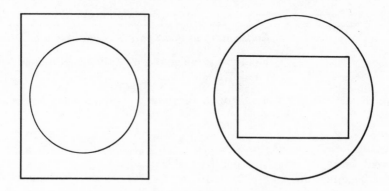

Avoiding Particular Organs

It is a general principle for dose reduction, whether achieved by collimating (coning down) or by using a lead shielding apron, that if we prevent exposure of the organs which generate the most cancer, we achieve the best results for the patient. Therefore, we will list the organs which spontaneously generate the most cancer, in order of decreasing numbers. For smokers, the lungs (bronchi) would head the lists.

For Nonsmoking Males, United States: Prostate, large intestine, urinary bladder, rectum, buccal cavity including pharynx, lungs, stomach, pancreas, kidneys, and larynx.

For Nonsmoking Females, United States: Breasts, large intestine, corpus uteri, ovaries, cervix uteri, rectum, pancreas, lungs, urinary bladder, buccal cavity including pharynx, thyroid, and kidneys.

Interested readers will see that the two lists are consistent with Special Tables A and B (Chapter 21), whose entries are directly related to spontaneous cancer rates. The reason we have omitted melanomas and lymphomas in the lists above is that only a small fraction of the "organs" from which they arise can be exposed during single diagnostic examinations.

Genetic Risk: In terms of reducing genetic injuries, of course the testes should be shielded or kept out of the field whenever possible; the same is true (but less often achievable) for the ovaries. No shielding can prevent internal scatter from reaching these organs, but the farther they are from the field, the less scatter will reach them.

In-Utero Risk: To reduce the risk of several types of injury to the embryo in-utero, it is evident that the uterus should be exposed as little as possible in a woman who is possibly pregnant, or known to be.

Section 4: Choice of Beam Direction

Beam direction, already mentioned in Section 2 of this chapter and in earlier chapters, deserves additional emphasis because the choice can make a very big difference in the dose absorbed by the most cancer-prone organs. Just how big those differences are is clearly seen in Special Table C of Chapter 21. It shows for the "reference adult" how many millirads are absorbed by each separate organ, per roentgen of entrance dose, for the AP, PA, LAT, OBL-AP, and OBL-PA beam directions. Tables in Chapters 5 and 6 convert those differences in absorbed dose into the corresponding differences in cancer risk.

The tables of Chapter 5 make it possible to compare risk from different beam directions at the *customary* entrance doses and beam qualities. The tables of Chapter 6 make it possible to compare risk from AP and PA beam directions at a *fixed* entrance dose and beam quality, for each of 9 sections of the torso.

For exams involving the chest and breasts, the potential, great advantage of PA shots instead of AP shots for females is outstanding, as is the potential, great advantage for both males and females of PA shots instead of AP shots of the abdomen and especially of the pelvis. We say "potential" because there is *no* advantage in situations where the needed diagnostic information would be lost by reversing beam direction.

Section 5: Exams for Scoliosis Patients— A Spectacular Achievement in Dose Reduction

It pleases us to report here on what has been accomplished at some facilities in reducing dose and risk from X-ray exams of the spine, by a combination of measures including change in beam direction, use of shielding, and improved choice of film-screen combination. These achievements are especially important for patients with the relatively common deformity known as idiopathic adolescent scoliosis, a lateral curvature of the spine. According to Moe (1979), an estimated 5% to 10% of American children have this disorder.

Successes of the Case Western Reserve Team

Nash, Gregg, Brown, and Pillai (1979), colleagues at Case Western Reserve, called attention to the serious problem of excessive radiation dosage accumulated by female scoliosis patients during the course of one of the disorder's common treatments, the Milwaukee Brace treatment. As Nash and co-workers pointed out, adolescent girls would be monitored with some 20 X-ray films, plus retakes, or a total of 22 radiographs during the average three-year treatment period. Most films were taken as AP shots. Having made their own measurements, Nash and co-workers estimated an average entrance dose of 1.13 roentgens for the AP shots used, and 1.78 roentgens for the lateral shots. From their estimates of dose to organs, they concluded (p. 371) that "given an average of twenty-two roentgenograms over a three-year Milwaukee Brace-treatment program," the risk of breast cancer due to X-ray radiation rose "from 140 to 290 per million (110 percent)."

A Doubled Risk of Breast Cancer: We need not question here whether the Nash team used the best value for risk per breast-rad; that subject is covered near the end of Chapter 2. The point is that these investigators concluded that monitoring the scoliosis therapy with diagnostic X-rays was *more than doubling* the patients' risk of later breast cancer, the most common cancer of all among nonsmoking women. Moreover, Nash and co-workers noted that "many scoliosis patients may require more roentgenograms than the average scoliosis patient postulated in this study."

Steps Which Reduced Breast Dose

Nash and colleagues decided to do something about this situation. They proved in a series of scoliosis patients that shifting beam direction from anterior-posterior to posterior-anterior could reduce the breast cancer risk *by a factor of 28.* * Their conclusion is in extremely reasonable accord with the values we obtain for breast dose by applying Special Tables C and D (Chapter 21) to the *typical* AP and PA entrance doses provided in the age-15 Wide *Thoracic* Spine Exam (Chapter 5).

For the AP Beam: (0.548 R of entrance dose) × (0.693 rad of breast dose per R) × (1.05 raising factor for 2.4 mm Al HVL) = 0.399 rad of breast dose.

For the PA Beam: (0.426 R of entrance dose) × (0.037 rad of breast dose per R) × (1.19 raising factor for 2.5 mm Al HVL) = 0.019 rad of breast dose.

Ratio of Doses and Therefore Risk: 0.399 rad / 0.019 rad = 21.

Image Quality: Significantly, the Nash team reported that the X-ray

---

*We believe there is a typographical error in Nash *et al* on page 373 concerning the breast exposure in the AP projection. We assume their number is meant to be 620 millirems rather than 62 millirems; the former value fits the value in their Table 1 and the rest of their paper.

films obtained from the PA beam direction proved technically satisfactory for routine scoliosis care.

Lateral and Narrow Shots: For the lateral shots, Nash and colleagues found that using a lead shawl to shield the breast tissue was very effective in reducing dose to the breasts. This feature, they point out, is particularly important for patients who also have kyphosis (humpback curvature) and who need more lateral shots, which require higher entrance doses.

Elsewhere in this book (Chapter 5), we called attention to the marked reduction in cancer risk from the Thoracic and Lumbar Spine Exams when the beam is collimated to a narrow field but still provides a good view of the spine. Nash and co-workers agree, but warn that if this method is attempted by a technician lacking sufficient experience, part of the spine might be obscured, and then additional shots might be required. They recommend the narrower films for experienced technicians.

Reduction in Overall Dose

This team did not focus only on the dose to the breasts. Nash and co-workers also indicated that the overall dose could be reduced *by a factor of 8* with a combination of other measures, especially choosing the right screen-film combination.

Their study is a classic illustration that investigators who pay attention to measuring dose in diagnostic radiology can arrive at procedures which significantly reduce the cancer risk for patients.

Successes of the Mayo Clinic Team

Additional work on the risk from X-rays for scoliosis patients has been done by Gray, Hoffman, and Peterson at the Mayo Clinic. In an extensive study (1983), they report on how they used the following combination of measures to reduce dose:

- A posterior-anterior beam direction;
- Specially designed leaded acrylic filters;
- A high-speed screen-film system;
- A breast-shield;
- Additional filtration in the X-ray tube collimator.

The technical reader should definitely consult their fine paper for the details. Here, we report only their overall conclusions, which are impressive, to state the case very mildly.

A 69-Fold Reduction in Breast Dose

We quote Gray and co-workers (p. 5):

> Dosimeter measurements of the exposure to the thyroid, breast, and abdominal areas were made on an Alderson phantom. They revealed an eightfold reduction in abdominal exposure for both the posteroanterior and lateral radiographs. There was a twentyfold reduction in exposure to the thyroid for the posteroanterior radiograph from 100 to less than 5 milliroentgens and for the lateral radiograph there was a 100-fold reduction from 618 to six milliroentgens. For the breasts there was a sixty-nine fold reduction from 344 to less than five milliroentgens for the posteroanterior radiograph and a fifty-five fold reduction from 277 to less than five milliroentgens for the lateral radiograph. These reductions in exposure were obtained without significant loss in the quality of the radiographs and in most instances with an improvement in the over-all quality of the radiograph due to the more uniform exposure.

The Invisible Bonds of Goodwill

Patients being treated for scoliosis are patients at a very vulnerable age for induction of cancer by radiation. Few of them may ever know the names of the individuals on these two research teams, but they will nevertheless be in their debt.

If the teams' accomplishments also inspire widespread efforts with respect to other types of exams, too, then *many, many millions* of patients will benefit from their work.

CHAPTER 17

Assessing
the Aggregate Cancers
from Diagnostic X-Rays

In Chapter 16, we reported the overwhelming evidence that many diagnostic examinations, both in dentistry and medicine, are being conducted with unnecessarily large radiation doses to the patient. We were pleased to report on the dedicated work, by radiologists and physicists in radiology, which has proven beyond doubt that doses in diagnostic radiology can be reduced by a factor of between 3 and 10 without any loss in the diagnostic quality of the examinations.

- "But is it worth the effort to reduce these doses?" one might ask. The proper answer to that question is another question.
- "What would you think of preventing more than 1.5 million unnecessary cancers in the U.S. population over the next 30 years (one generation)?"

We will show in Section 1 that this enormous contribution to public health in the cancer field is truly what can be accomplished if Americans take the advice of the teams, described in the previous chapter, about how to obtain an easy, three-fold average reduction in dose from diagnostic examinations.

365

Section 1: How Many Cancers Can Be Prevented?
The Quantitative Evidence

The first step toward determining how many cancers could be prevented is to determine how many cancers are being produced by the *current* techniques used in diagnostic radiology. To do this, we need three items of information.

1. The Population Size. Because we are speaking of the next 30 years, it is reasonable to consider an equilibrium population for the United States of about 250 million persons.

2. The Cancer Consequences per Common Exam. The radiation dose and the cancer consequences from the various medical and dental X-ray exams, performed under average conditions today, are essential items of information; they are presented in Chapters 5 and 9 of this book. The values we need here are the cancer consequences from the Common Exam (not from single shots). For the average Dental Exam, we will use an estimate of 5 films, a value derived from data presented by Shleien (1977).

3. The Frequency of Various Exams at Various Ages. Shleien (1977) has provided the number of examinations per 100 persons of each age, both for dental and medical X-rays (summarized in Table 1 of this book). For the frequencies of specific exams, we have two important sources.

For Pediatric Ages: For each of the pediatric ages from newborns up through age 15 years, Beck and Rosenstein (1979) show what percentage of examined patients received each kind of examination. By combining their data with the total frequency of diagnostic exams per 100 persons per year by ages (from Shleien), we can obtain the number of examinations of every type per 100 persons per year, for each pediatric age. And from U.S. vital statistics, we know how many males and females are present in an equilibrium population at each age (demonstrated for males in R&HH, Table 3). So we arrive at the actual number of exams of every type being performed annually at each of the pediatric ages.

For Adult Ages: Kereiakes and Rosenstein (1980) provide quantitative data showing, for the 17 most common diagnostic X-ray exams, how the number of exams is distributed among adults. By combining their information with the frequency of exams from Shleien, and with the number of people in each adult age category from vital statistics, we can calculate the number of examinations of each of the 17 types given in the United States per year. (We use the value for 20-year-olds for Shleien's 15–24 year age-group.)

The Consequences of Current Practice

By the method just described, we arrive at the results presented in Table 22, which shows how many cancers are being induced annually by dental and medical diagnostic radiology, not including diagnostic nuclear medicine.

Table 22. Cancers Induced per Year by Dental and Medical Diagnostic X-Ray Exams, United States

Age Group (Years)	DENTAL Diagnostic Radiology: Cancers Induced per Year	
	Males	*Females*
Under 15 years of age	2,756	1,207
15–24 years of age	2,681	1,006
25–34 years of age	2,158	845
35–44 years of age	767	305
45–54 years of age	24	10
Total, All Ages, from Dental Radiology	8,386	3,373

Age Group (Years)	MEDICAL Diagnostic X-Rays: Cancers Induced per Year	
	Males	*Females*
Under 15 years of age	4,686	4,809
15–24 years of age	10,559	10,049
25–34 years of age	11,843	11,593
35–44 years of age	5,842	5,954
45–54 years of age	247	278
Total, All Ages, from Medical Diagnostic X-Rays	33,177	32,683

All Ages	Combined Cancers Induced per Year	
Total from Dental and Medical X-Rays, by Sex	41,563	36,056
Total from Dental and Medical X-Rays, Sexes Combined	77,619	

A Reasonable Estimate?

We did an extra check on the reasonableness of this sum of 78,000 cancers (rounded off) induced annually from the combination of medical and dental diagnostic X-rays. We asked, what *average* whole-body dose does this figure imply for each person in a mixed-age population of 250 million nonsmokers?

To find the answer, we increased the value of 3,771 cancer deaths per million people per rad (Chapter 2, discussion with Myth 12) to adjust for incidence of cancer instead of mortality, and then lowered it the appropriate amount for a completely nonsmoking population. These adjustments gave us a value of 6,491 cancers occurring per million nonsmokers, if each received 1 rad, for a population sample of mixed ages distributed like an equilibrium population.

If 6,491 cancers occur when 1 million person-rads of whole-body dose are delivered to nonsmokers of mixed ages, this can be stated as 1 million person-rads per 6,491 cancers, or 1 million person-rads / 6,491 cancers, or 154.1 person-rads per cancer.

In Table 22, we estimated 78,000 cancers induced per year from medical and dental diagnostic X-rays. The corresponding whole-body dose delivery to the population would be, from above, (154.1 person-rads per cancer) × (78,000 cancers) = 12 million person-rads. Therefore, for an equilibrium population of 250 million people, the average annual whole-body dose from combined medical and dental X-ray exams would be 12 million person-rads / 250 million persons = 0.048 rad, or 48 millirads.

Elsewhere, Shleien (1977) has approximated the average bone-marrow dose (including adults and children) as 77 millirads from medical plus dental diagnostic procedures for the year 1970. Shleien included fluoroscopy in his estimate, whereas we did not. Also, Shleien presumably based his dose estimate on typical beam collimations, whereas our dose estimate is derived from risk estimates which assume collimation is more nearly made to body part instead of to film size. For these reasons, Shleien's value for *our* parameters would be lower than the 77 millirads he reported.

We are confident that our whole-body dose is in a very reasonable range.

Some Important Points about the Estimate

Persistence of Smoking: All calculations for Table 22 were made on the basis of a nonsmoking population, as were the tables in this book. Cigarette smoking has been declining continually, and may well decline even more. If not, the use of a nonsmoking population for Table 22 would make 78,000 cancers per year an underestimate.

Beam Collimation: All calculations assumed the universal practice of beam collimation more nearly to body part than to film size for medical X-rays. This is not currently the case, and makes 78,000 cancers per year somewhat too low a number to match the real annual cost of diagnostic radiology.

Less Common Exams: Rosenstein's list of 17 common examinations taken by adults obviously does not include a wide variety of additional exams. Not included, for instance, were angiographies and C.A.T. Scans. Although the excluded exams are each relatively infrequent, they collectively add to the risk. We therefore raised all our adult cancer estimates for Table 22 by a factor of 1.2 to take this into account.

Induction vs. Appearance: The numbers and total in Table 22 refer to the cancers *induced* each year. Radiation induced cancers do not appear in the same year in which they are induced. Only a very small fraction of those induced by X-rays appear during the first 10 years after irradiation, and thereafter the rate of appearance (per million persons irradiated) increases every year for some 40 years, after which the rate is expected to decline (Chapter 18).

Beyond Age 55: We have neglected any cancers induced in patients who are over age 55 at the time of the X-ray, since no evidence suggests that they occur (R&HH).

Additional Exclusions: We have *not* included, of course, leukemias, embryo injuries, and genetic costs in these calculations; the estimate in Table 22 represents exclusively the aggregate cancer consequences. Excluded, too, are additional cancers from diagnostic procedures used in nuclear medicine.

The Prevention of 1.5 Million Cancers

This chapter began by announcing the opportunity to prevent *1.5 million* unnecessary cancers per generation (30 years). The derivation of that figure is simple.

At the current rate of induction (78,000 cases per year), diagnostic X-ray exams during 30 years would induce (78,000 cancers per year) × (30 years) = 2,340,000 cancers.

In Chapter 16, we reported why a 3-fold reduction in dose from such exams should be readily achievable, and why a much larger reduction would be achievable with some additional effort—all without losing any of the benefits of the diagnostic information. If the dose is reduced by a factor of 3, the cancers induced would also be reduced by that same factor. Therefore, Americans would be able to eliminate two-thirds of the cancers now being induced by diagnostic X-rays, while one-third would still be induced. In 30 years, Americans would prevent (⅔) × (2,340,000 cancers) = 1,560,000 cancers.

Aside from cessation of cigarette smoking, the authors of this book are aware of nothing on the horizon which would eliminate as many cancers as the single action of reducing the dosage in medical and dental diagnostic radiology.

Unlike other recommendations, dose reduction would not even require giving up beloved habits and pleasures. In terms of economic resources, the services of well-trained and independent radiologic physicists to check and adjust equipment (including film developers) would be far less costly than the enormous medical bill for 1.5 million cancer casualties. In terms of people's *most* valued resources—such as health, time, and affection—the opportunity is priceless.

Section 2: How Might We Accomplish This? The Issue of Human Rights

Because the potential benefits from reducing doses are so vast and appealing, we predict that some good-hearted people will use this book to agitate for more governmental regulation of X-ray doses and procedures. We emphatically oppose such regulation as a very dangerous way to achieve dose reduction.

If ever we allow government to make everything which would be *good* for people *compulsory,* we will have abolished human freedom. The same extinction of freedom will occur if ever we allow government to *ban* everything *bad* for people. When obesity, failure to exercise, table salt, eggs, megavitamins, "empty calories," football, bicycles, rock-climbing, construction work, fire-fighting, and "workaholic" behavior are banned as health hazards—along with excessive X-ray doses—we will surely recognize the tyrannical implications of thoughtlessly supporting government regulation "for people's own good."

Although there is no doubt that unnecessarily high X-ray doses seriously injure people and that dose reduction would be good for people, the use of government force to achieve that goal would violate the fundamental human right-and-duty. That right-and-duty can be defined in a single sentence.

The Basic Human Right-and-Duty, Defined

The basic human right, from which all other genuine human rights derive, is the right of all peaceable individuals to hold themselves and their own property free from human-caused intrusion, force, and fraud, *provided* they also accept the sacrifices necessary to secure successfully the identical right for all other peaceable individuals.

The Crucial Barrier to Tyranny

The basic human right-and-duty provides no exemption for agents of any government. As humans, their freedom to pass laws and impose regulations is defined and *limited* by the basic human right-and-duty. Their rights—which by definition are claims entitling people to *make* other people behave in certain ways—are no different or greater than the rights of other peaceable citizens. If an act would be wrong for an *individual* to do, the act also is wrong for a government or any other *group* of individuals to do. The fundamental barrier to tyranny in free societies is the principle that, both in and out of government, all non-aggressors (peaceable individuals) have exactly the same basic human right-and-duty.

The Definition Applied to X-Ray Exams

When medical or dental X-ray exams are not forced upon anyone, they are purely voluntary transactions between consenting individuals. Therefore, the government has no right whatsoever to intrude into the terms or conditions of X-ray examinations. For voluntary transactions, the government's only legitimate role relates to the basic human duty: helping to protect peaceable individuals from force and fraud in its many forms, from false claims to breach of promise.

In a free society, when people choose behavior which intrudes on no one else's body or other property, such behavior is in a class by itself. Voluntary behavior is neither in a class with behavior imposed on innocent people by their duty to help defend the system of human rights, nor is it in a class with behavior imposed on innocent people by aggressors—for instance, muggers and polluters. Both muggers and polluters violate the basic human right-and-duty by causing intrusions upon the bodies and other properties of peaceable people who did *not* consent to such intrusions and who have *no duty* to consent.

To interfere with the freedom of muggers, polluters, and other aggressors, is not only a right but a duty. To interfere with the freedom of peaceable individuals, who may choose risky activities which impose no intrusion on anyone else, is a *violation* of their basic human right. If each single violation seems too trivial to resist, violations proliferate. They interfere with freedom in all voluntary activities somewhere: employment agreements, contracts of every type, trade, recreation, speech, publishing, worship, assembly, and so forth. The aggregate impact of trivial violations is the abolition of human freedom.

To achieve reduced X-ray doses, it is neither proper nor necessary to let government violate the basic human right-and-duty. If people do not want reduced X-ray doses, what right does anyone have to force this benefit on them?

The Power of Desire

Dose reduction will occur spontaneously, without any use of human force, if people want it. And they do.

There are plenty of physicians and dentists who are concerned about X-ray doses. Many have already demonstrated this by voluntarily abandoning some high-dose practices, and by voluntarily figuring out doses from the new C.A.T. Scans and other procedures. We have heard from a *few thousand* radiologists who apparently have not been fooled by a lavish campaign from other quarters to deny and obscure the evidence about the hazard from low-dose radiation. A very powerful force in that campaign has been the government itself.

The Careful Professional: A far larger effort to reduce X-ray doses might have already occurred in medicine and dentistry if there had been no such campaign. It is remarkable that there are so many professionals making efforts to reduce doses *anyway.*

Physicians and dentists enjoy more than monetary gain from their work; there is an emotional bonus from helping people, and professionals are well aware that this bonus turns sour if their services later inflict unnecessary misery on some of their patients. Therefore, whether or not their patients demand reduced doses, physicians and dentists will tend to reduce doses whenever they become convinced of the hazard.

The Careful Referral: For the same reasons and without compulsion, referring physicians who ask their patients to take X-ray exams elsewhere will learn to search out the X-ray services whose measured doses are below, not above, average. A multitude of patients and parents are starting to press for careful referrals.

The attitudes of patients about self-injury do differ, of course. It is a fact that millions of people do smoke and do drive without fastening seat belts. Yet even adults who claim they might as well make no effort to avoid health hazards—because they are certain to die "anyway" sometime—turn on the light before starting down a pitch-dark flight of stairs. Given a choice between going to a high-dose or a low-dose X-ray facility, even they might choose the low-dose place.

The Careful Patient: Many adults are not at all casual about trying to keep their health. They jog, they diet, they give up smoking, they give up beloved foods or alcohol, they buy good tires, and they give their personal attention to lowering unnecessary risks of all sizes. Their attitude is, "A little here, a little there—it all adds up, for *me!*"

They do not see 1 chance in 5,000 (or 200 per million) as a negligible risk, especially if it is repeated ten or twenty times. They would see no sense in volunteering every year to play Russian roulette, even if there were 5,000 chambers in the gun and only one randomly-located chamber were loaded. Twenty years of this suicidal game would yield 1 chance in 250 of deadly consequences.

Given the choice of getting the benefits of diagnostic X-rays from a high-dose or a low-dose facility, such people would surely choose the low-dose place. To the extent that they are actively seeking it out and spreading the word, their search automatically confers the benefits of reduced doses on many others, too.

The Careful Parent: Perhaps more than anyone else, conscientious parents who object to the forced exposure of their children to asbestos, lead, dioxin, PCBs, EDB, and other pollutants in drinking water and air, are determined to avoid risks of a voluntary nature—such as unnecessarily high X-ray doses. Such parents do not want to be the type whose own carelessness inflicts upon their children a 16-fold higher risk of later cancer from a needed X-ray exam than necessary (Chapter 4, Example 10).

More and more such parents are seeking out physicians and dentists who measure and know the X-ray doses given in their offices. Such physicians and dentists rapidly gain a competitive advantage, because word spreads that "They measure doses and really know what they are doing in that office."

Hospitals are beginning to perceive the advantage. We have received reports (not confirmed by us directly) that some California hospitals have been advertising the fact that their X-ray doses are 30% below the national average.

The Triumph of Free People

Because so many dose-givers and dose-receivers are pressing for lower X-ray doses, reduction will continue happening. It may happen more quickly because of this book. It will happen in freedom and without government intrusions and force.

The benefits will be automatically shared by children with careless parents and by all other patients, too, because lower doses will become common practice. Thanks simply to those who *do* care, millions of cases of future misery will never have to occur.

CHAPTER 18

Four Fundamental Generalizations Concerning Induction of Cancer by Radiation

Twenty years ago, the kinds of simplifying and unifying calculations which now make it possible to evaluate the cancer risk from diagnostic radiology would not have been possible. One reason is that so much of the human epidemiological evidence now available was absent then. But even a mountain of data is unusable unless people can find the regularities in it and formulate generalizations ("laws") which confer reliable predictive power on anyone who applies them.

Early pioneers in this field saw the outlines of some important generalizations even when the data were far less extensive than now. Outstanding are the contributions made by Court-Brown and Doll (1965) in their studies of the ankylosing spondylitis cases in Great Britain, and by Stewart and co-workers (1956) in their studies of the cancer and leukemia consequences from in-utero irradiation. Those studies inspired the generalizations which underlie the practical calculations of this book.

Section 1: The Three Initial Generalizations, and a Fourth

Gofman and Tamplin (1969–1970) first stated three generalizations concerning radiation carcinogenesis in the following manner.

Generalization 1: "All forms of cancer, in all probability, can be increased by ionizing radiation, and the correct way to describe the phenomenon is either in terms of the dose required to double the spontaneous mortality rate for each cancer, or alternatively, of the (percent) increase in mortality rate of such cancers per rad of exposure."

Generalization 2: "All forms of cancer show closely similar doubling doses and closely similar percentage increases in cancer mortality rate per rad."

Generalization 3: "Youthful subjects require less radiation to increase the (cancer) mortality rate by a specified fraction than do adults."

It is gratifying that all of the evidence which has accumulated since the three generalizations were published in this form has provided support for their correctness and usefulness. In other words, the three "laws" have been correctly predicting what is being found. They apply to incidence as well as mortality.

Recently, it has become evident that a fourth generalization should be added (Gofman, 1983, p. 9). It concerns the time intervals (so-called "latency periods") between irradiation and the clinical appearance of malignancies.

Generalization 4: "The peak percent increase in cancer rate per rad is reached grossly earlier for such high LET radiations as alpha-particle irradiation in contrast to the time to reach peak percents for low LET radiation."

Practical Implications of the New "Law"

Medical and dental X-rays are low LET radiations. LET is an abbreviation for *linear energy transfer.* As X-rays pass through body tissue, they tear electrons from their atoms, endow them with unnaturally immense energies, and transform them into tiny bullets traveling through tissue. Such electrons do their damage by breaking chemical bonds at random and by causing the formation of new bonds which would otherwise not occur. In the course of committing this mayhem, the high-speed electrons are transferring to the tissues a portion of their energy for every millimeter they travel. The amount of energy transferred per millimeter by a low LET radiation is small *by comparison* with the amount transferred per millimeter by alpha particles. That is why alpha-particle radiation is known as high LET radiation.

As investigators have been unraveling the dose-effect relationship of ionizing radiation and cancer induction, they have received epidemiologic evidence from some groups irradiated only by low LET radiation, some by a mixture of high and low LET radiations, and still others almost wholly by high LET radiations. The evaluation of delayed consequences, per rad, is very strongly influenced by the *speed* at which the malignancies appear during a limited (rather than lifespan) follow-up.

Unless we appreciate that these speeds are very different from high LET radiation than from low LET radiation, some drastically erroneous conclusions can be drawn concerning the cancer-inducing potency of various radiations, including diagnostic X-ray radiation. Such erroneous conclusions would be better avoided.

Section 2: Quantitative Estimates for Two Sets of Latencies

Using the evidence which has become available, we list below the time of the peak occurrence of radiation-induced cancer and leukemia in groups exposed to low LET and high LET radiations.

Low LET Radiations: X-Rays, Gamma Rays, Beta Particles

Leukemia: The rate of radiation-induced leukemia in a group reaches a peak about 7.5 years after irradiation, if the exposure occurs at a single time. Of course, latency times within a group are not all the same; without some earlier and later cases in a distribution, there would be no *peak* frequency at 7.5 years. The farther we move away from the peak in either direction, the smaller the proportion of leukemia cases found along the distribution curve.

When someone says that radiation-induced leukemia does not occur until two years after irradiation, all he or she means is that the relative number of cases occurring *before* two years is probably small. There is no reason why some cannot occur sooner. The interval depends only on the time between divisions of the altered (malignant) cells which are successful. If that time is short in an individual, a leukemia can become clinically manifest far earlier than the peak occurrence time observed in a whole series of irradiated individuals.

Cancers Other than Leukemias: For radiation-induced cases of cancer other than leukemia, the rate in a group reaches a peak about 40 years after irradiation, if the exposure occurs at a single time. As with leukemias, there is a distribution of shorter and longer latencies. Relatively few of the total excess cases occur during the early period after a group's exposure. The number of cases progressively increases as the time is approaching 40 years after irradiation.

In principle, there is nothing which precludes a small fraction of the total cases from occurring in even less than a year following exposure. In a small exposed group, however, not enough early cases can exist to demonstrate statistical significance; hence, it is common to assert than none at all have occurred during the early period. But that assertion is unproven.

High LET Radiations: Alpha Particles and Neutrons

Leukemia: There are not enough data to reveal whether the interval between exposure and peak occurrence of radiation-induced leukemia cases is shorter after high LET radiation than after low LET radiation.

Cancers Other than Leukemias: The evidence clearly indicates that radiation-induced cancers occur with a peak frequency which is much earlier following high LET radiation than low LET radiation. One of us (Gofman, 1983) has estimated that the frequency of cancers induced by alpha-particle irradiation reaches its peak in the neighborhood of seven to eight years following the exposure. The evidence for this is strong in several independent series which show the time distribution of excess cancers resulting from alpha-particle irradiation. These series include:

a. The uranium miners (Lundin and co-workers, 1971);
b. The patients treated with radium-224 (Mays and Spiess, 1978);
c. The radium-dial painters (Stehney and co-workers, 1978).

Evaluating Future Studies

We hope that this additional generalization (Generalization 4) will prove useful to researchers studying cancer induction by radiation, as they evaluate new studies which will appear in future literature.

Section 3: Caution about RBE Factors

Generalization 4 necessarily calls into question the practice of assigning special raising factors, such as 10 and 20, for the so-called *relative biological effectiveness* (RBE) of high LET radiation compared with low LET in inducing malignancies. A major part of the RBE of high LET radiation probably results from the massive shift forward in time for the cancers induced.

Is there anything else to the RBE? Unfortunately, there seems to be no high LET series, *with adequately measured doses in rads,* to permit direct comparison with a low LET series on this matter. If high LET radiations have no special potency at all compared with low LET types, except in shortening the latency period for cancer (and causing a concomitantly greater loss of lifespan per fatal case), then there would be no justification for using the customary raising factors of 10 or 20 to estimate the number of cancer cases resulting from high LET exposure.

The validity of using such factors (and the rem unit) is an important and intriguing question needing an answer, in the future, from evidence.

Section 4: A Speculation about the Observed Age-Factor

Two major functions of science are (1) to determine what the facts truly are and (2) to endeavor to understand why and how they come to be as they are.

One of the most solid facts of medical science is that ionizing radiation is indeed a cause of cancer and leukemia. But no one yet knows why or how radiation acts to induce either one of these diseases. Another solid observation is that youthful subjects require less radiation to increase the cancer mortality rate by a specified fraction or percentage than do adults (Generalization 3). But no one yet knows why.

We wish it to be entirely clear that what follows is a speculation, which someone else may wish to test or may already be testing somewhere. Speculation, recognized for what its limitations are, is a very useful part of scientific endeavor, as described in (2) above.

Puzzling and Meaningful Differences? For years, one of us (JWG) has been asked, "But *why* are the young the most sensitive to getting cancer from radiation exposure?" Also, "Why is a similar scale of sensitivity by age *not* found for the induction of leukemia by radiation?"

One speculative answer can be stated as an additional question: could it be that the rate of healthy cell division (either for body growth or for cell replacement) is the key?

There are two reality-checks which make that particular speculative answer seem unreasonable. First, we observe that sensitivity to radiation carcinogenesis *continues* to fall in adults after their body growth has ceased. Second, the yield of radiation-induced cancers is *very different* from two organs—the small intestine and the large intestine—which replace some of their old cells at very similar and especially rapid rates.

A different speculation may fit the facts better. The key may lie in the percentage of cells in an organ (at any age) which are still totipotent or nearly so (multipotent).

A Step toward an Explanation? Let us speculate that (a) the percentage of multipotent cells falls as age advances, and that (b) multipotency is related to carcinogenesis and leukemogenesis.

Then the observed age sensitivity for *cancer* production would follow. But no age-related trend is discernible for radiation-induced *leukemia.*

Leukemia is associated with cells of the active bone marrow. These cells are, and remain throughout life, multipotent—that is, they produce a variety of cells with different structures and functions: lymphocytes, eosinophiles, basophiles, neutrophilic granulocytes, red cell precursors, and megakaryocytes (the origin of platelets).

Therefore, if (a) and (b) are true, we would *expect* to observe little or no age-related trend for the radiation induction of leukemia.

In a sense, our suggestion is a variant of an old, old idea about cancer production, namely the "embryonic rest" concept that cancer arises from undifferentiated cells which have persisted beyond gestation.

CHAPTER 19

The Method Used to Produce the Cancer-Risk Tables

Three main ingredients were required to produce the cancer-risk tables in this book. One was an organ's cancer risk per absorbed rad (Section 1 of this chapter). The second was the appropriate number of rads per irradiated organ from a given exam (Section 2). The third was the product of the first and second: the cancer risk per X-ray exam (Section 3).

It turned out that dosimetry was, by far, the most difficult problem to solve in preparing this book. Before any computation of *risk* could begin, it was necessary to figure out absorbed doses per entrance roentgen for every separate organ irradiated directly and indirectly by each shot separately, for every different exam, and for six different ages (body sizes). Accordingly, the bulk of this chapter (Section 2) relates the method and sources used to handle the dosimetry.

Section 1: Cancer Risk per Rad

The cancer risk from exposure to ionizing radiation can be expressed in either of two ways: (1) the total number of cancers induced by radiation, irrespective of the fraction which prove lethal, or (2) the number which are fatal. This book deals with the former.

Derivation of Special Tables A and B

In *Radiation and Human Health* (Gofman, 1981), the worldwide epidemiological evidence relating absorbed dose of radiation and risk of future cancer death has been analyzed. That analysis led to a systematic evaluation, by age and sex, of rads per future cancer death for every *type* of human cancer (Tables 29 and 30, R&HH).

For *this* book, we converted rads per future cancer death into future cancer deaths per rad; the arithmetic is demonstrated in Chapter 22, Section 7. Then we converted cancer deaths per rad into cancer *incidence* per rad, by using the ratio of a particular cancer's incidence rate to its mortality rate (Table 33, R&HH). The results are shown by Special Tables A and B in Chapter 21 of this book.

Stability of the Ratios: A few of the reported incidence-to-mortality ratios (for pharyngeal cancer, for instance) have fluctuated over time. Such fluctuations up and down can be expected for some of the cancers in the years ahead, too. The great bulk of the ratios, however, have been quite stable over time. It would take a dramatic change in the incidence-to-mortality ratio of some of the major cancers, with the changes *confirmed* by at least a decade of reporting, in order to invoke an appreciable change in this book's tables.

This Book's Handling of Skin Cancer: Users of this book's tables should know that they incorporate only the risk of malignant melanoma, among the skin cancers. Melanoma is a life-threatening disease, with an incidence-to-mortality ratio of about 1.92 for males and about 2.77 for females.

This Book's Handling of Lung Cancer: In order to provide cancer-risk estimates in this book for nonsmokers (the predominant and growing part of the U.S. population), we used two approximations. First is the customary one that smokers show a "spontaneous" rate of fatal lung cancer 10-fold higher than nonsmokers. Second is the approximation that the *current* mortality rates from lung cancer in the United States are arising from age cohorts in which 50% of males and 25% of females customarily smoked. By factoring out the "contributions" which smokers make to the current lung-cancer death rates, we were able to arrive at reasonable estimates of lung-cancer incidence among an otherwise comparable non-smoking population.

For users of this book who do smoke, we have provided special factors with each X-ray exam to indicate how many times more likely they are than nonsmokers to get cancer from that particular exam.

Section 2: Figuring Out the Rads

The Goal: Average Dose in Rads per Organ

The "rad" unit of dose is an abbreviation for *radiation absorbed dose.* One rad represents the absorption of 100 ergs of energy per gram of tissue. A dose in rads has no time factor in it; rather, it represents the total dose received, whether it has been delivered over seconds, milliseconds, weeks, months, or years.

A thick organ, even when fully in a beam's exposure field, absorbs a non-uniform dose because of its varying depth with respect to the incident photons. It is the organ's *average* absorbed dose which we want for this book's computations.

When the total energy absorbed in the organ is determined (in ergs), this total energy is divided by the total mass of the organ (in grams). The result is the average quantity of energy in ergs absorbed by each gram of tissue. In order to convert ergs to rads, this quantity is then divided by 100 ergs per gram. The answer is what we seek: the *average* dose in rads absorbed throughout an organ. (For X-rays, the conversion factor from rads to rems is 1.0 or unity, so the rem and rad units could be used interchangeably in this book.)

Attention to Every Irradiated Organ

Serious investigators of cancer induction in humans by ionizing radiation generally agree now that virtually all organs which spontaneously develop cancer also develop radiation-induced cancer (Chapter 2). This means that, in order to evaluate the cancer consequences from a diagnostic X-ray procedure, it is *not* good enough to know the average dose absorbed by only one organ or a few "organs of interest" in the main X-ray beam. Rather, it is essential to know what dose is received directly and indirectly by *all* irradiated organs, including those lying outside the field of the collimated X-ray beam.

The Importance of Internally Scattered Dose: Rosenstein (1976a) has pointed out, and Cohen (1972) before him has shown, that approximately

75% of the dose to ovaries lying 10 centimeters deep within the body, from a beam centered above them, is due to photons *scattered* into the ovaries from surrounding tissues within the primary beam. This huge contribution from scatter is not caused by poor collimation or by objects outside the body. Instead, it results from scattering *within* the body, both of primary photons in the beam and of Compton degraded photons. The phenomenon cannot be eliminated.

The consequence is that, even when organs lie near but not in the collimated field, they can still receive sizeable radiation doses. If such organs happen to be ones having the high spontaneous rates of cancer (see lists in Chapter 16, Section 3), the cancer risk arising from organs ir- radiated *outside* the field can exceed the risk arising from organs within the field, as illustrated in Chapter 10, Section 5.

Dose from scatter drops off rapidly with distance. The farther an organ lies from the edge of the X-ray field, the lower is the internally scattered dose it receives. From examinations of the skull or teeth, for example, the dose to organs such as testis, ovary, uterus, or prostate is exceedingly low.

Important Sources of Dose Information

It is evident from the considerations above that, for evaluating the true cancer risk from any particular X-ray exam or combination of exams, it is necessary to know the doses absorbed by *all* the organs which receive appreciable radiation. This is the real problem. To what extent does this information exist?

The literature contains many efforts to provide, for specific diagnos- tic procedures, the doses absorbed both inside and outside the beam's direct field. But most such reports are relevant only for the conditions of the reporting institution in terms of tube-to-film distances, peak kilovolt- age, 3-phase versus 1-phase current, and so forth. Information of much more general usefulness was needed for this book, and has come from two major types of studies.

The first type uses phantoms (dummies) which simulate body compo- sition, including proper placement of materials corresponding to lung tissue, solid tissues, bone, and bone marrow. Thermoluminescent dosime- ters are placed at various positions within the phantom, and they record the doses associated with a certain skin entrance-dose from a beam of specified collimated dimensions. In some instances we use such studies, but for the most part they do not lend themselves to the scope of this project.

A different approach to dosimetry has been used in the past decade, in the excellent work of investigators at the Oak Ridge National Laborato- ries, and in the magnificent work of Rosenstein and others in the Bureau of Radiological Health, part of the U.S. Department of Health and Human Services (formerly Health, Education, and Welfare). Their procedure is known mathematically as a Monte Carlo method.

These workers have developed and applied a computer program which uses a simulated human phantom and a simulated broad beam of X-rays of various energies striking the phantom from the directions generally used in diagnostic X-ray examinations. Applying the physics of photoelectric absorption of incident photons and the physics of Compton scattering, the investigators can calculate the final energy deposition in all organ-regions of the phantom, both inside and outside the X-ray field, at any depth, from a certain number of photons incident upon specified areas of the phantom's surface (skin). The Monto Carlo calculations take account both of the energy deposited in tissues directly from the primary beam and of energy delivered by scatter from other regions of the body.

Once the computer code is written, the limitations on making dose estimates for various organs and beams are basically money and computer time. One result is that the accuracy of doses is not as high for organs relatively distant from the primary X-ray field as for organs in the primary field. For a given input of simulated photons, relatively few reach the more distant regions, so unless more computer time is used, there is a "small numbers problem" making doses for distant organs relatively less reliable than for in-field organs.

An Organ Here, an Organ There

The tabular data provided by Rosenstein in his various publications are enormously rich and helpful for our present purposes. The only difficulty is that, at the time Rosenstein undertook his work, there was interest in only a very limited number of organs: bone marrow, thyroid, ovaries, testes, uterus (for dose to embryos), and later breast and lung. For our purposes, we also need doses to brain, buccal tissues, esophagus, stomach, pancreas, kidneys, liver, large intestine, prostate, and essentially every other organ of the body.

Fortunately, Jones, Auxier, and Snyder at the Oak Ridge Laboratory have published a superbly useful paper entitled "Dose to Standard Reference Man from External Sources of Monoenergetic Photons" (1973). They studied photons, by the Monte Carlo method, for energies from 50 keV (keV = 1 thousand electron-volts) to 10 meV (meV = 1 million electron-volts) incident upon a simulated human phantom.

Since the *average* energy of the photons in the vast majority of diagnostic X-ray beams is in the range of 25–40 keV (even though the *peak* kilovoltage can be 100 keV or more), it was necessary to convert the Oak Ridge findings into figures applicable at much lower average energies (lower beam qualities) than the 50 keV of their lower limit. Here again,

Rosenstein's studies were enormously helpful because he provided tissue-to-air (approximately rads-to-roentgens) ratios as a function of X-ray energies from 20 keV through 80 keV. These ratios helped us convert the Oak Ridge data into values applicable for the customary energies and beam qualities used in diagnostic radiology.

A huge increment in needed information is achieved from the Oak Ridge studies. Dose estimates become available for AP, PA, and lateral (left to right) beam directions for all of the following organs: the adrenals, bladder, clavicles, stomach, upper large intestine, lower large intestine, small intestine, heart, kidneys, liver, pancreas, pelvis, ribs, scapulae, spine, skin, spleen, and thymus.

With these data added to Rosenstein's, we come close to having most of the information needed to evaluate the dose, for adults, to each and every organ from various X-ray procedures. It is readily possible to make very reasonable estimates of dose to the remaining organs, with the help of a good cross-sectional anatomy book and the information about doses to nearby organs from Rosenstein and from Jones and co-workers.

Derivation of Special Table C

What we are driving toward are the doses *absorbed* by every irradiated organ, when any particular entrance dose incident upon a patient has been measured: in short, Special Table C of Chapter 21.

In most matters (and probably in all), information must be linked with well-defined reference points, or else it is useless. So the values of absorbed doses per organ must be related to a well-defined position of the organ in the exposure field, to a "reference" body-size, and to a specific entrance dose and beam quality. We must define the standards used for each.

"Fully in the Field" as a Standard

The values in Special Table C refer to an organ's absorbed dose per entrance roentgen when that organ is *fully in the field*. This standard means that the absorbed dose is stable and reliable, because the organ's dose from internal scatter will not go up even if the size of the field goes up. The organ has already "got" all the scatter it can get, for all *practical* purposes.

Careful use of our two main sources makes this standard possible. In the case of the Rosenstein studies, so many different shots and exams are considered that one or more provide estimates of the full-field doses for the organs which he evaluated. In the Jones and co-workers' studies with broad beams, the fields are very large (40 by 70 centimeters) for the AP and PA beam directions, and we can safely regard the organs for which they provide doses as well centered in the beam.

The Standards for Body Size

We would like, ideally, to have direct Monte Carlo evaluations for the full-field dose to every organ in the body, for all ages, and for a great variety of height-weight combinations. But such information is not likely to become available in the near future. In the interim, this book uses reasonable approximations derived from our major sources.

For adults, the studies by both Jones and Rosenstein used an idealized human phantom, the "reference adult" (Special Table C). Obviously not all adults have the same dimensions, but differences among adults are of less concern than the great differences between adults and children 1, 5, and 10 years old.

For pediatric ages, Rosenstein has provided extremely useful information by his extension of the Monte Carlo studies to a variety of X-ray exams given to children who are newborn, 1, and 5 years old. From his work, one can derive full-field doses for some AP, PA, and lateral shots of lungs, breasts, bone marrow, uterus, ovaries, testes, and thyroid. Since the Jones studies do not provide data applicable to the pediatric groups, we extended the Rosenstein values to additional organs by anatomical analysis.

We derived full-field values for the age-groups of 10 and 15 years by interpolation, coupled with scaling factors for the overall body dimensions as a function of age. We would much prefer not to have had to make any interpolations, but without them, it would be impossible to provide any useful estimates *at all* concerning risks from X-ray exams taken between the ages of 5 and 20.

One day, very likely, all this book's pediatric estimates can be sharpened, with the help of future studies using either the Monte Carlo method or dosimeter measurements in phantoms which correspond to the pediatric body sizes. Meanwhile, the pediatric values in this book provide information of practical usefulness in making millions and millions of benefit-risk judgments.

The Standard for Entrance Dose

In the practice of diagnostic radiology, the measurement which is easily made is the skin or entrance dose. But in the literature, reports are not always as clear as they should be about whether or not the measurement included backscatter from the patient's body.

Rosenstein is explicit in his tabulations. He presents all his tabulations in terms of "Entrance Dose Free in Air," which is the dose measured in roentgens where the surface of the body would be, but without a body in place. Thus his measured entrance dose has no contribution from any radiation scattered back to the surface from the body tissues.

Some others report skin or entrance dose, measured in rads, at the skin surface with a body or phantom in place. Such measurements include an important contribution from radiation scattered back to the surface. The contribution from backscattering, which varies with beam quality, is in the range of 25% to 35% of the measured total. Therefore, one must know—if trying to compare results from one study to another—whether entrance doses were measured with or without backscatter. The conversion of one type of measurement to the other is demonstrated in Chapter 3, Section 4.

In this book, all *entrance* doses are given in roentgens free-in-air (FIA). The data from the studies by Jones and co-workers were converted to this format, too, with the help of tables from Harrison (1981) providing backscatter factors for beams of various qualities and for fields of various sizes.

The Standard for Beam Quality

The entries in Special Table C show the doses in millirads which organs absorb when they are fully in the field of a beam delivering an entrance dose of 1.0 roentgen FIA, at a beam quality of 2.3 mm Al HVL. (The Glossary defines beam quality and half-value layer.)

A beam quality of 2.3 mm Al HVL corresponds to an *average* energy of 30 keV for the X-ray photons—a typical value even when the *peak* kilovoltage of an X-ray machine is set in the neighborhood of 85 to 100 keV.

To compute risks from Common Exams (Chapter 5), a method is needed to convert the values in Special Table C for *other* beam qualities often reported in Kereiakes and Rosenstein (1980). Special Table D provides the conversion factors used by us, and available for use by others, with the simple method demonstrated in Chapter 4, Section 12.

The Derivation of Special Table D

It is well appreciated, in the field of diagnostic radiology, that X-ray examinations are conducted under quite a variety of circumstances with respect to peak kilovoltage of the beam, amount of filtration with aluminum or other materials, and voltage-controlling systems (such as full-wave rectification or not, three-phase electrical supply or one-phase).

As a net result, the beam quality varies from one installation to another. Even within the same institution, beam quality will be purposely varied from one beam direction to another, or from one patient to another.

Nevertheless, inspection of the Common Exam tables in Chapter 5 shows that the average beam quality used in practice, nationwide, is in the vicinity of 2.3 mm Al HVL—sometimes higher and sometimes lower. A higher ("harder") beam quality means that, on the average, organs will absorb higher doses per roentgen of entrance dose than in Special Table C; a lower beam quality will give lower average absorbed doses per roentgen.

Making a Simplification: It is inherent in the physics of radiation absorption, as a function of beam quality, that there cannot truly be a *single* adjustment factor for organs lying at unequal depths from the beam's entry surface. But we have ascertained that very *reasonable* single values, applicable to all organs at once, can be obtained and well used.

A highly refined adjustment accounting for dose change with beam-quality change would require a separate Monte Carlo evaluation for every organ, for every beam direction, and for every age. Rosenstein found the computer requirements to be massive, even for a very limited list of organs. His tabulations do provide, for several diagnostic beam qualities and for six different organs, the dose absorbed per entrance roentgen from AP, PA, and lateral beam directions.

Our simplification, for making a *single* adjustment for all organs at once, uses the approximation that all organs lie in the same plane as the uterus, relative to beam direction. Therefore, the factors in Special Table D overestimate the true absorbed dose for organs lying more superficially than our reference depth, are just right for most organs, and are underestimates for organs lying more deeply than our reference depth.

Testing the Simplification: We expected these problems to be readily tolerable for three reasons. First, the factors do not apply at all when the beam quality is 2.3 mm Al HVL. Second, the dose and corresponding risk from most Common Exams come from more than one shot; often two or three beam directions are involved, which means that over- and underestimates tend to cancel each other. Third, even within a single shot, the overall risk from the shot is the *sum* of the risks to organs lying above the reference depth, at the reference depth, and below the reference depth, so a balancing occurs.

We were able to test our expectation that using a single factor would introduce negligible error, thanks to Rosenstein's work (1980) which shows how the dose absorbed by each organ he studied responded, separately, to changes in beam quality. There was excellent agreement, well within the range of experimental error, between the risk values obtained with our shortcut (Special Table D) and the risk values obtained by making separate adjustments for each organ with change in beam quality.

The factors in Special Table D were determined by studying the tissue-to-air ratios from the Monte Carlo method (Rosenstein, 1976a). Some single values are slightly out of line, but we have elected not to smooth out such "glitches," most of which occurred at beam qualities seldom used in diagnostic X-ray exams.

The Last Big Issue of Dosimetry

Another determination must be made about dose to different organs from the same shot, and this determination has far greater impact on risk estimates than slight variations in beam quality. It can be best described in Section 3, however, when we explain the entries in Column 6 of our standard computer printout.

Section 3: Cancer Risk per Examination

In this section, the AP shot of the K.U.B. Exam, for a female at age 20, will serve occasionally as an illustration of how each entry of cancer risk was determined for this book's tables of Common Exams, ages 0 through 20. From Chapter 5's K.U.B. Exam, we see that a 20-year-old woman has a cancer risk of 936 per million (or 1 chance in 1,068) from the AP shot when the entrance dose is 0.664 roentgen FIA and the beam quality is 2.5 mm Al HVL. We will trace how the value of 936 per million originates.

For every shot evaluated in this book (with exceptions such as Mammograms, Chapter 8), the same standard format was used to determine cancer risk. Each of well over 1,000 computer printouts contains the following columns.

Column 1: List of Organs

This column contains no numbers. It contains the names of all organs listed in Special Tables A and B—33 entries for males or 35 for females. The last entry, "all other and unspecified," is included in spite of its vagueness because it is a sizeable and potentially deadly category, with an incidence-to-mortality ratio close to 1.0.

Column 2: Risk per Rad

This column contains, for one age-sex category, the cancer incidence rates which will arise from each organ when it absorbs 1 rad at a beam quality of 2.3 mm Al HVL. These entries come from either Special Table A or Special Table B.

Column 2's entries (33 if male, 35 if female) are the *basic risk entries* which will each be raised or lowered by four separate factors (in successive columns) as we determine the net yield of cancers from each organ from the particular shot under analysis. All of Column 2's entries show risk per dose (1.0 rad). All four adjustments to be made are adjustments of dosimetry from 1.0 rad to some other absorbed dose. Because cancer risk is directly proportional to absorbed dose, some of the same adjustments in these columns are treated in Chapter 4 as adjustments directly to risk.

Column 3: Rads per Roentgen

This column states the rads absorbed by each organ from 1.0 roentgen of entrance dose, if the organ is well centered in the field. These entries are values from one column of Special Table C, after conversion from millirads to rads. Because all these entries are numbers below 1.0, they will operate as *lowering* factors on the risks in Column 2.

However, there are no entries in Special Table C for three widely distributed cancer sources: the lymphatic system, the category of bone, connective tissue, and skin, and the class of sites reported as "all other and unspecified." For the lymphatic system, we applied rads-per-roentgen ratios which we obtained for bone marrow in shots evaluated by Kereiakes and Rosenstein. Part of the lymphatic system is within the bone marrow. For this and other reasons, whatever rads-per-roentgen ratio we entered for one, we also consistently entered for the other. For bone, connective tissue, and skin, we raised the lymphatic ratio by 1.3 (30%) due to the greater accessibility of these "organs" to the X-ray photons. These approximations cannot introduce much error into the risk values for any shot because the very diffusion of these systems (and of the "all other and unspecified" category) makes each a minor contributor to cancer risk *per shot.*

Certainly not all the organs in Column 1 are fully in the field. Column 6 provides the entries which take this fact into account.

With regard to the testes, they are not in Special Table C because they are *fully* in the field so rarely during diagnostic X-ray exams. Their absorbed doses were specially estimated for every Common Exam on the basis of the customary fields if no shielding were used. The proper use of shielding will provide various amounts of protection, which can be easily measured and confirmed by TLDs.

Column 4: Entrance Dose in Roentgens

This column states the typical entrance dose in roentgens FIA. When the dose is greater than Column 3's reference value of 1.0 roentgen, the entry in Column 4 acts as a *raising* factor for the cancer risks in Column 2. When the entry is less than 1.0 roentgen, it acts as a *lowering* factor.

For the AP shot of the K.U.B. Exam for an age-20 female, the entry is a lowering factor: 0.664 roentgen FIA.

Column 5: Beam Quality

This column states the appropriate adjustment factor, from Special Table D, for beam qualities other than 2.3 mm Al HVL.

For the AP shot of the K.U.B. Exam, for instance, the customary beam quality is 2.5 mm Al HVL. Therefore, a *raising* factor must be created from the ratio of two values in the AP column of Special Table D. For 2.5 mm Al, the entry is 1.10. For 2.3 mm Al, the entry is 1.00, of course. So the ratio entered in Column 5 is 1.10 / 1.00, which means a raising factor of 1.10 for the cancer risks in Column 2. A factor of 1.10 corresponds with a 10% increment.

Column 6: Organ's Relation to Field

This column states the fraction of an organ's full-field dose (per entrance roentgen) which applies to a particular shot. Therefore, the entries are either 1.0 (100%), or a number less than 1.0. When the entry is below 1.0, it operates as a *lowering* factor for the risks in Column 2.

The first step in determining an entry for Column 6 was to ascertain the customary boundaries of the exposure field, which we determined from standard references such as Kereiakes and Rosenstein (1980), Greenfield (1973), Jacobi (1977), and others. In Chapter 5 of this book, we state the dimensions of the examined area in the introduction to each exam.

From the boundaries of the field, we determined which of the organs listed in Column 1 are well centered in the field. Their entries in Column 6 are 1.0 (100%). For organs too distant from the boundaries of the field to receive any internally scattered dose (for instance, the eyes in the K.U.B. Exam), the entries are each zero, because *no* incremental cancer risk will arise from them due to this shot. In other words, the zero entries in Column 6 deal with all unirradiated organs by completely eliminating them from participation.

Obtaining the Fractional Entries: For all other organs in Column 1, an appropriate fraction of the full-field absorbed dose (see Column 3) has to be determined. Here, tables such as Table 102 in the Kereiakes and Rosenstein book (1980) were very useful. For instance, for the AP shot of the K.U.B. Exam, their table shows the relative doses absorbed by ovaries, thyroid, active bone marrow, uterus, and lungs, when the boundaries of the field are the customary ones for adults. Their values are based on the Monte Carlo studies, of course.

If their table provides a value of 20 millirads per roentgen (after adjustment to 2.3 mm Al HVL), and if Special Table C provides a full-field value for the same organ of 100 millirads per roentgen, then we know that the effective fraction of the full-field dose for that organ from this shot is 20 / 100, or 0.2. This fraction becomes a reference point for estimating fractions for organs at *other* distances.

There are many organs neither evaluated by Kereiakes and Rosenstein nor fully in the field, such as the rectum in the AP shot of the K.U.B. Exam. Its lowest portion lies close to the *edge* of the field, so it would be incorrect to assign it 100% of its full-field absorbed dose. We assigned it the fraction 0.9 in this shot.

In a similar fashion, fractions were assigned in Column 6 for each organ whose entry was neither 1.0 nor zero. Also, according to field size, we made estimates of the appropriate fractions to enter for each of the three diffusely distributed cancer sources: the lymphatic system, the category of bone, connective tissue and skin, and the class of sites reported as "all other and unspecified."

Column 7: Net Risk per Organ

This column, like all the previous columns, contains 33 entries for males or 35 for females. In fact, every entry in Column 7 is simply the product of (Column 2) × (Column 3) × (Column 4) × (Column 5) × (Column 6). The product for each row is the net risk that the shot will induce a cancer in the organ of that row.

The Sum of Column 7: Risk per Shot

The sum of the entries in Column 7, for the AP shot of the K.U.B. Exam for an age-20 woman, is 936 per million. That is one piece of information entered in the risk table for the K.U.B. Exam, Chapter 5.

For every other shot and Common Exam evaluated, the risk was determined by the same method.

Handling of Ages above and below 20 Years

For adults above the age of 20, we have made the assumptions already described in Chapter 3, Section 2. The age-20 risks were simply reduced by the lowering factors for age. The occasional need to use these age factors again, for special adjustments, is explained and demonstrated in Chapter 4, Section 15.

For the pediatric ages (below 20 years), nothing so simple was acceptable, for all the reasons mentioned in Chapter 3, Sections 2, 3, and 5, and also in this chapter. Completely independent analyses were needed and were made for each pediatric age-sex category.

There is one exception to that statement: the narrow fields for the spine and esophagus (barium swallow) exams. The risk value from each narrow shot was obtained by full analysis for the 20-year male and 20-year female in the normal fashion. Then, not in the usual fashion, the value for the corresponding shot at each younger age was obtained as follows: a lowering factor was computed by dividing the cancer risk from the narrow shot at age 20 by the risk from the wide shot at age 20. This lowering factor was then applied to the corresponding wide shot at each younger age.

Section 4: How Good is the Method?

In this chapter and in earlier ones, we have identified some uncertainties in human knowledge which remain and which affect the issue at hand: evaluation of the health effects from diagnostic X-ray examinations. We have described the approximations which are necessarily incorporated into the risk estimates in this book.

For anyone who is unfamiliar with the use of approximations in science, we point out an important fact: it is exceedingly unlikely, in an effort such as this one, that approximations will all operate in the same direction. Certainly *not all* the approximations will produce underestimates, and certainly *not all* the approximations will produce overestimates. On the contrary, various approximations will work in opposite directions and tend to cancel each other out.

Confidence is justified that the risk values provided in this book are indeed close to the truth.

CHAPTER 20

Applying This Book beyond the United States

This book provides quantitative tables of frequency for three different types of delayed side-effects from diagnostic X-rays: mental retardation, heritable injuries, and malignancies. To what extent are the tables applicable in other countries?

Section 1: Risks of Mental Retardation and Heritable Injuries

The risk estimates concerning mental retardation from in-utero irradiation (Table 15) and concerning heritable injuries (Table 16-B) can be applied in other countries without modification, in our opinion. Although both tables derive from the spontaneous rates of these two problems (mental retardation and inherited health problems), and although the spontaneous rates undoubtedly are reported to differ in various countries, we do not believe the reported differences are meaningful. The reason is simple: both kinds of problems are very poorly defined. Therefore, differences in reported spontaneous rates cannot be meaningful.

Section 2: Risk of Leukemias

The risk estimates provided with each exam in Chapters 5, 7, and 9 were derived by the method shown in Chapter 11. The U.S. mortality rate from spontaneous leukemia in 1974–75 entered into the computation. For males, it was 6.9 per 100,000; and for females, 4.3 per 100,000.

For a different population, the risk estimates per exam need only one adjustment. They need to be multiplied by the ratio of the leukemia death rate in the "new" population over the rate in the United States. The use of this ratio incorporates the approximation that the leukemia *incidence* rates would yield a ratio similar to the mortality ratio.

Illustrative Problem

A 30-year-old male, in a population whose death rate for males from spontaneous leukemia is 6.3 per 100,000, has the Wide Thoracic Spine Exam. What is his leukemia risk from that exam?

ANSWER: The first step is to ascertain what his risk would be if he were an American. In Chapter 5, we find that the leukemia risk for age-20 males is 10 per million from the Wide Thoracic Spine Exam. With respect to leukemia risk, no lowering factor for age is used at ages above 20. Thus the risk for an age-30 American male would be 10 per million also.

In the "new" population, the spontaneous leukemia risk is 6.3 / 6.9, or 0.913 times lower than in the United States. Therefore, the leukemia risk per exam must be lowered by the same ratio: (10 per million) $\times$ (0.913) = 9 per million. That is the answer. Answers for any other population and any other X-ray exam would be obtained in a similar way.

Section 3: Risk of Cancers

An important difference between cancer and leukemia, which affects the applicability of this book to populations in lands other than the United States, is the difference in the *duration* of the effect from radiation. The cancer effect is known to be still climbing in an irradiated group up to 40 years following a single radiation exposure, it is presumed to peak 40 years after the irradiation, and then it is expected to endure in gradually lessening strength for the remaining lifespan. In great contrast, the leukemia effect from radiation peaks about 7.5 years after a single exposure, begins to lessen after that, and is virtually gone by 25 to 30 years after irradiation.

Population Differences in Life Expectancy

These very different durations of radiation effect have an obvious implication for populations whose average life expectancy at birth is only 50 years. People's lifetime risk of cancer from X-ray exams taken at age 35, for instance, will be grossly *lower* in a population where most people are dead from non-cancer causes by the age of 50, compared with the risk in a population whose average life expectancy at birth is 70 to 80 years. In the first population, there is a high chance that irradiated people will not live long enough to reach the ages when the *spontaneous* rate of cancer begins to climb, and since radiation acts to increase the *spontaneous* cancer rate, such populations will have lesser lifetime cancer risks from diagnostic radiology.

The cancer risks used to compute the risks per X-ray exam in this book were developed in *Radiation and Human Health.* The methods used in that book are valid for determining cancer risk from radiation exposure for any population, anywhere, provided they are applied to the population's own data concerning (1) length of average lifespan and (2) the spontaneous, age-specific, cancer mortality rate.

The average life expectancy should be considered first. This book can yield useful estimates of cancer risk per exam in any population where the life expectancy at birth is in the range of 65 to 80 years. But if the life expectancy is shorter, the help of the source book (R&HH) would be required to make the cancer risk-tables in this book applicable. There is no reliable shortcut.

The Age-Specific Cancer Mortality Rate

The rate of spontaneous cancer rises steeply as people grow older, and the *shape* of the steeply rising curve which represents this observation can be presumed to be approximately the same everywhere. When this approximation is used and when the age-specific rate of cancer mortality is known for the *same* age in two populations, then the ratio of the two rates at that age describes the relative rates at *all* ages when the one population is compared with the other. Such rates at the same age are called "standardized age-specific cancer mortality rates," and they must not be confused with rates which have been adjusted for other purposes (such as rates which have been adjusted for the distribution of *ages* in two different populations).

The cancer risks tabulated in this book are directly proportional to the standardized age-specific cancer mortality rate, as demonstrated in Table 3 of R&HH. The rate used for U.S. males was 50 per 100,000 *at age 40;* and for females, 58.0 per 100,000 *at age 40.*

How to Extend Applicability

For a population whose standardized age-specific cancer mortality rates are close to the U.S. rates above, *and* whose average life expectancy at birth lies between 65 and 80 years, this book's cancer risk-tables need no adjustment at all. They provide useful approximations as they stand.

If average life expectancy is in the "right" range but the standardized age-specific cancer mortality rates are not close to the U.S. rates above, then the cancer risks in this book need one simple adjustment: they need to be multiplied by the ratio of the *non-U.S.* age-specific cancer mortality rate over the rate of 50 (for males) or 58 (for females).

Illustrative Problem

A 30-year-old female, in a population where the standardized age-specific cancer mortality rate for age-40 females is 49.2 per 100,000, needs an I.V.P. Exam. What is her cancer risk from this exam?

ANSWER: The first step is to ascertain what her risk would be if she were an American. Chapter 5 shows that her risk would be 4,215 per million, or 1 in 237. The adjustment factor is the standardized rate in the "new" population (49.2) over the comparable U.S. rate from above (58.0). Therefore, this patient's cancer risk from the I.V.P. Exam is (49.2 / 58.0) × (4,215 per million) = 3,575 per million, or 1 chance in 280.

Answers for any other exam, in any other population which "qualifies" on the life expectancy issue, would be obtained in a comparable, simple fashion. A population need not be the entire population of a country. A population is any group at all whose pertinent rates on the two important variables—life expectancy and age-specific cancer mortality rates—are known. The adjustment above incorporates the approximation that the incidence-to-mortality ratios on the whole do not differ much from country to country.

Different Spontaneous Rates of Particular Cancers

The rate of a *specific* type of cancer may be grossly different in some countries than in the United States. If a really big difference occurs for a site which is a leading contributor to the spontaneous U.S. cancer rate (Chapter 16, listing in Section 3), then this book's risk values, for an exam whose risk arises primarily from that site, will be "off" for a non-U.S. population. Those exams are readily identified by using the Common Exam's introduction, where "Organs Generating Most Cancer Risk" are listed.

Because the cancer risk per exam arises from *many* organs, very few exams can be much affected by different spontaneous rates for a single organ. But it can happen.

How Big an Effect? For instance, in the Barium Swallow Exam, the breasts account for about 55% of the cancer risk for U.S. females. Suppose that in a "new" population, the spontaneous rate of breast cancer were only half as high as it is in the United States. Then *half* of the breast cancer risk from the Barium Swallow Exam would not occur. Therefore, the overall risk from the exam would be 27.5% lower for women in the "new" population than for women in the United States.

CHAPTER 21

The Special Tables

This chapter presents four tables whose derivation was explained in Chapter 19, and whose application to specific exams has been discussed in several earlier chapters. They are Special Tables A, B, C, and D.

Special Table A (for Males) and
Special Table B (for Females):
Cancer Rates per Rad, by Specific Organs

The Content: Entries show cancer incidence rates per million caused by absorption of one rad by an entire organ (or organ system). This is one of relatively few tables in the book where dose is *not* an entrance or skin dose; in Special Tables A and B, one rad is an *absorbed* average dose received by an entire organ. Dose is often described by its recipient, as in "marrow-rad" (Chapter 11) or "bladder-rad" (below).

Risks for Individuals and Groups: Tables A and B, like all others in this book, can be used to evaluate risk both for individuals and for groups of individuals. *Illustration:* For males at age 20, the risk per rad of future bladder cancer is 616 per million (Table A). This means that the individual 20-year-old male whose bladder absorbs 1.0 rad has a personal risk of 616 per million, or 1 chance in 1,623 of having bladder cancer in the future as a consequence of the radiation exposure. It also means that there will be 616 bladder cancers if 1 million age-20 males each receives 1.0 bladder-rad, or if 2 million age-20 males each receives 0.5 bladder-rad, or if 500,000 age-20 males each receives 2.0 bladder-rads.

Subtotals in the Tables: For convenience, subtotals are provided for certain groups of organs, such as the Buccal Cavity + Pharynx, Digestive Organs, Respiratory Organs, and so on. One can add up group entries or individual entries, but not both in the *same* addition.

Whole-Body Exposure: The total risk per million from all organs combined is equivalent to the risk from 1.0 rad of whole-body exposure (absorbed dose, not entrance dose). This equivalency is illustrated in Chapter 12, Section 4. Whole-body doses rarely occur from diagnostic X-rays except for embryos and fetuses.

Smoking Issue: Entries for Bronchi + Lungs are for non-smokers.

Ages: Entries for ages 25–55 begin immediately following ages 0–20. As in all other tables in the book, age is the age at the time of radiation exposure.

Derivation: Special Tables A and B are derived in the same way demonstrated in Tables 29 and 30 of *Radiation and Human Health* (Gofman, 1981), except that for Special Tables A and B, adjustments have been made for non-smokers and for cancer incidence instead of mortality.

Special Table A. (For Males:) Cancer Rates per Rad, by Specific Organs

Organ Site Irradiated	0 yrs	1 yr	5 yrs	10 yrs	15 yrs	20 yrs
Buccal Cavity + Pharynx	*1334*	*1317*	*1201*	*966*	*478*	*424*
Lips	298	294	268	216	107	95
Tongue	239	236	215	173	86	76
Salivary Glands	95	94	86	69	34	30
Floor of Mouth	95	94	86	69	34	30
Other Sites, Mouth	227	224	204	164	81	72
Pharynx	380	375	342	275	136	121
Eyes	*67*	*66*	*60*	*49*	*24*	*21*
Brain and C.N.S.	*491*	*485*	*442*	*356*	*176*	*156*
Digestive Organs	*7152*	*7062*	*6434*	*5188*	*2559*	*2277*
Esophagus	463	457	417	336	166	147
Stomach	1046	1033	941	759	374	333
Small Intestine	89	88	80	65	32	28
Large Intestine	2688	2655	2418	1950	962	856
Rectum	1417	1400	1275	1028	507	451
Liver + Biliary	417	411	375	302	149	133
Pancreas	935	923	841	678	334	298
Other, Unspecified	97	95	87	70	35	31
Respiratory Organs	*1976*	*1951*	*1777*	*1433*	*706*	*629*
Larynx	672	663	604	487	240	214
Bronchi + Lungs	1155	1141	1039	838	413	368
Other, Unspecified	149	147	134	108	53	47
Breast Pair, Males	*67*	*66*	*60*	*49*	*24*	*21*
Urinary Organs	*2718*	*2684*	*2446*	*1972*	*972*	*865*
Bladder	1935	1911	1741	1404	692	616
Kidney + Related	783	773	705	568	280	249
Genital Organs	*5289*	*5223*	*4758*	*3838*	*1891*	*1684*
Prostate	4916	4855	4423	3567	1758	1565
Other Unspecified	373	368	335	271	133	119
Endocrine Glands	*231*	*228*	*208*	*168*	*82*	*74*
Thyroid	194	191	174	141	69	62
Other Endocrine	37	37	34	27	13	12
Blood, Lymph Tissues	*1551*	*1533*	*1395*	*1125*	*555*	*493*
Hodgkin's Disease	306	302	275	222	109	97
Multiple Myeloma	349	345	314	253	125	111
Other Lymphomas	896	886	806	650	321	285
Bone, Skin, Connective	*784*	*774*	*706*	*569*	*280*	*249*
Bone	82	81	74	60	29	26
Connective Tissue	187	184	168	135	67	59
Skin (Melanoma esp.)	515	509	464	374	184	164
All Other, Unspecified	*1083*	*1070*	*975*	*786*	*387*	*345*
Totals, per Million *All Organs Combined*	*22743*	*22459*	*20462*	*16499*	*8134*	*7238*

Organ Site Irradiated	25 yrs	30 yrs	35 yrs	40 yrs	45 yrs	50 yrs	55 yrs
Buccal Cavity + Pharynx	*422*	*364*	*260*	*157*	*69*	*6.3*	*4.3*
Lips	94	81	58	35	15	1.4	1.0
Tongue	76	65	46	28	12	1.1	0.8
Salivary Glands	30	26	19	11	5	0.4	0.3
Floor of Mouth	30	26	19	11	5	0.5	0.3
Other Sites, Mouth	72	62	44	27	12	1.1	0.7
Pharynx	120	104	74	45	20	1.8	1.2
Eyes	*21*	*18*	*13*	*8*	*3*	*0.3*	*0.2*
Brain and C.N.S.	*155*	*134*	*95*	*58*	*25*	*2.3*	*1.6*
Digestive Organs	*2262*	*1946*	*1391*	*848*	*370*	*34.1*	*23.2*
Esophagus	146	126	90	55	24	2.2	1.5
Stomach	331	285	203	124	54	5.0	3.4
Small Intestine	28	24	17	11	5	0.4	0.3
Large Intestine	850	731	523	319	139	13	8.7
Rectum	448	386	276	168	73	7	4.6
Liver + Biliary	132	113	81	49	22	2	1.4
Pancreas	296	254	182	111	48	4	3.0
Other, Unspecified	31	27	19	11	5	0.5	0.3
Respiratory Organs	*624*	*537*	*385*	*235*	*103*	*9.4*	*6.5*
Larynx	212	183	131	80	35	3.2	2.2
Bronchi + Lungs	365	314	225	137	60	5.5	3.8
Other, Unspecified	47	40	29	18	8	0.7	0.5
Breast Pair, Males	*21*	*18*	*13*	*8*	*3*	*0.3*	*0.2*
Urinary Organs	*860*	*739*	*528*	*322*	*140*	*12.9*	*8.8*
Bladder	612	526	376	229	100	9.2	6.3
Kidney + Related	248	213	152	93	40	3.7	2.5
Genital Organs	*1673*	*1438*	*1028*	*627*	*273*	*24.8*	*17.2*
Prostate	1555	1337	956	583	254	23	16
Other, Unspecified	118	101	72	44	19	1.8	1.2
Endocrine Glands	*73*	*63*	*45*	*27*	*12*	*1.1*	*0.7*
Thyroid	61	53	38	23	10	0.9	0.6
Other Endocrine	12	10	7	4.4	1.9	0.2	0.1
Blood, Lymph Tissues	*490*	*422*	*301*	*183*	*80*	*7.4*	*5.0*
Hodgkin's Disease	97	83	59	36	16	1.4	1.0
Multiple Myeloma	110	95	68	41	18	1.7	1.1
Other Lymphomas	283	244	174	106	46	4.3	2.9
Bone, Skin, Connective	*248*	*213*	*152*	*93*	*41*	*3.7*	*2.6*
Bone	26	22	16	10	4	0.4	0.3
Connective Tissue	59	51	36	22	10	0.9	0.6
Skin (Melanoma esp.)	163	140	100	61	27	2.4	1.7
All Other, Unspecified	*343*	*295*	*211*	*128*	*56*	*5.1*	*3.5*
Totals, per Million *All Organs Combined*	*7192*	*6187*	*4422*	*2694*	*1175*	*107.7*	*73.8*

A

401

Special Table B. (For Females:) Cancer Rates per Rad, by Specific Organs

B

Organ Site Irradiated	0 yrs	1 yr	5 yrs	10 yrs	15 yrs	20 yrs
Buccal Cavity + Pharynx	*622*	*607*	*534*	*411*	*196*	*172*
Lips	33	32	28	22	10	9
Tongue	131	128	113	87	41	36
Salivary Glands	87	85	74	57	27	24
Floor of Mouth	43	42	37	29	14	12
Other Sites, Mouth	173	169	149	114	55	48
Pharynx	155	151	133	102	49	43
Eyes	*72*	*71*	*62*	*48*	*23*	*20*
Brain + C.N.S.	*432*	*422*	*371*	*285*	*136*	*119*
Digestive Organs	*7420*	*7241*	*6368*	*4893*	*2334*	*2040*
Esophagus	214	209	184	141	67	59
Stomach	739	721	634	487	232	203
Small Intestine	82	80	70	54	26	23
Large Intestine	3526	3440	3026	2325	1109	969
Rectum	1312	1280	1126	865	413	361
Liver + Biliary	492	480	422	325	155	135
Pancreas	940	918	807	620	296	258
Other, Unspecified	115	113	99	76	36	32
Respiratory Organs	*1031*	*1006*	*884*	*680*	*325*	*284*
Larynx	139	136	119	92	44	38
Bronchi + Lungs	810	790	695	534	255	223
Other, Unspecified	82	80	70	54	26	23
Breast Pair, Females	*8849*	*8634*	*7592*	*5834*	*2783*	*2432*
Urinary Organs	*1304*	*1272*	*1118*	*859*	*410*	*358*
Bladder	780	761	669	514	245	214
Kidney + Related	524	511	449	345	165	144
Genital Organs	*6185*	*6038*	*5311*	*4079*	*1946*	*1701*
Cervix Uteri	1309	1278	1123	863	412	360
Corpus Uteri	3114	3038	2672	2053	979	856
Ovaries	1395	1362	1197	920	439	384
Other, Unspecified	367	360	319	243	116	101
Endocrine Glands	*566*	*552*	*486*	*374*	*178*	*156*
Thyroid	533	520	458	352	168	147
Other Endocrine	33	32	28	22	10	9
Blood, Lymph Tissues	*1508*	*1471*	*1293*	*994*	*474*	*414*
Hodgkin's Disease	246	240	211	162	77	68
Multiple Myeloma	362	353	310	238	114	99
Other Lymphomas	900	878	772	594	283	247
Bone, Skin, Connective	*823*	*803*	*705*	*542*	*259*	*226*
Bone	66	64	56	43	21	18
Connective Tissue	165	161	141	109	52	45
Skin (Melanoma esp.)	592	578	508	390	186	163
All Other, Unspecified	*1193*	*1164*	*1024*	*786*	*375*	*328*
Totals, per Million *All Organs Combined*	*30005*	*29281*	*25748*	*19785*	*9439*	*8250*

Organ Site Irradiated	25 yrs	30 yrs	35 yrs	40 yrs	45 yrs	50 yrs	55 yrs
Buccal Cavity + Pharynx	*170*	*150*	*108*	*68*	*30.2*	*2.9*	*2.0*
Lips	9	8	6	4	1.6	0.2	0.1
Tongue	36	32	23	14	6.4	0.6	0.4
Salivary Glands	24	21	15	9	4.2	0.4	0.3
Floor of Mouth	12	10	7	5	2.1	0.2	0.1
Other Sites, Mouth	47	42	30	19	8.4	0.8	0.6
Pharynx	42	37	27	17	7.5	0.7	0.5
Eyes	*20*	*17*	*12*	*8*	*3.5*	*0.4*	*0.2*
Brain + C.N.S.	*117*	*104*	*74*	*46*	*21*	*2.0*	*1.4*
Digestive Organs	*2014*	*1781*	*1272*	*797*	*358.6*	*34.2*	*23.8*
Esophagus	58	51	37	23	10	1.0	0.7
Stomach	201	177	127	79	36	3.5	2.4
Small Intestine	22	20	14	9	4	0.4	0.3
Large Intestine	957	846	604	379	171	16.0	11.0
Rectum	356	315	225	141	63	6.1	4.3
Liver + Biliary	134	118	84	53	24	2.3	1.6
Pancreas	255	226	161	101	45	4.4	3.1
Other, Unspecified	31	28	20	12	5.6	0.5	0.4
Respiratory Organs	*280*	*247*	*177*	*111*	*49.7*	*4.9*	*3.4*
Larynx	38	33	24	15	6.7	0.7	0.5
Bronchi + Lungs	220	194	139	87	39	3.8	2.6
Other, Unspecified	22	20	14	8.8	4	0.4	0.3
Breast Pair, Females	*2402*	*2124*	*1516*	*950*	*428*	*41.0*	*29.0*
Urinary Organs	*354*	*313*	*224*	*140*	*63*	*6.0*	*4.2*
Bladder	212	187	134	84	38	3.6	2.5
Kidney + Related	142	126	90	56	25	2.4	1.7
Genital Organs	*1679*	*1485*	*1059*	*665*	*299*	*29.3*	*20.0*
Cervix Uteri	355	314	224	141	63	6.1	4.3
Corpus Uteri	845	747	533	334	151	15.0	10.0
Ovaries	379	335	239	150	67	6.5	4.5
Other, Unspecified	100	89	63	40	18	1.7	1.2
Endocrine Glands	*154*	*136*	*97*	*61*	*27.6*	*2.7*	*1.8*
Thyroid	145	128	91	57	26	2.5	1.7
Other Endocrine	9	8	5.6	3.5	1.6	0.2	0.1
Blood, Lymph Tissues	*409*	*362*	*258*	*162*	*73*	*7.0*	*4.9*
Hodgkin's Disease	67	59	42	26	12	1.1	0.8
Multiple Myeloma	98	87	62	39	17	1.7	1.2
Other Lymphomas	244	216	154	97	44	4.2	2.9
Bone, Skin, Connective	*224*	*198*	*140*	*89*	*40*	*3.9*	*2.6*
Bone	18	16	11	7.1	3.2	0.3	0.2
Connective Tissue	45	40	28	18	8.0	0.8	0.5
Skin (Melanoma esp.)	161	142	101	64	29	2.8	1.9
All Other, Unspecified	*324*	*286*	*204*	*128*	*58*	*5.6*	*3.9*
Totals, per Million							
All Organs Combined	*8147*	*7203*	*5141*	*3225*	*1451.6*	*139.9*	*97.2*

Special Table C. Absorbed Dose by Specific Organs,
per Roentgen of Entrance Dose

C

Organ Doses: Entries are in *millirads* of average dose absorbed by
each organ if the organ is *fully* in the field of the direct beam
(Chapter 19).

Entrance Dose: Entrance dose is 1.0 roentgen free-in-air, at a beam
quality of 2.3 mm Al HVL (30 keV). All entries can be adjusted
for other entrance doses and beam qualities by the usual methods of Chapter 4, because absorbed dose and cancer risk are
directly proportional to each other.

Beam Directions: Five separate beam directions are provided. For
lateral and oblique shots, the calculations for this table are based
on beams directed from the patient's left to right (LR).

The Reference Adult: This table applies to a "reference adult" (weight
= 70 kilograms; height = 174 centimeters).

Specific Organ	Beam AP	Beam PA	Beam LAT-LR	Beam OBL-AP	Beam OBL-PA
Stomach	678	76	163	421	120
Bladder	642	62	29	336	46
Heart	476	61	53	265	57
Thymus	618	43	15	317	29
Liver + Biliary	455	163	6	231	85
Upper Lg. Intestine	396	72	20	208	46
Lower Lg. Intestine	247	100	33	140	67
Small Intestine	309	110	34	172	72
Lung (Male)	360	335	131	246	233
Lung (Female)	282	359	152	217	256
Uterus	257	114	33	245	74
Ovaries	190	128	45	118	87
Pancreas	235	132	56	146	94
Kidneys	70	763	89	80	426
Spleen	167	425	37	269	398
Adrenals	56	441	30	43	235
Brain	367	367	367	367	367
Esophagus-Cervical	167	92	163	165	128
Esophagus-Thoracic	266	92	85	176	89
Buccal Tissues	390	150	390	390	270
Pharynx	266	92	266	266	179
Larynx	250	92	163	207	128
Prostate	260	115	33	147	74
Eyes	700	30	100	400	65
Rectum	160	150	33	97	91
Breast Pair (Male)	765	37	183	474	110
Breast Pair (Fem)	693	37	183	438	110
Thyroid	743	66	110	427	88

Effect upon Risk: Changes in beam quality cause changes in absorbed dose per entrance roentgen. Since risk is directly proportional to dose, when beam quality *differs* from the one shown in a table for a Common Exam, the risk in that table will need appropriate raising or lowering.

Using Two Entries: To create the appropriate raising or lowering factor for a special beam quality, a ratio is taken from *two* entries found in Special Table D, as demonstrated in Chapter 4, Section 12. Both entries must come from the same column (same beam direction).

Entries for Oblique Shots: The adjustment factors for OBL-AP beams are the average of the AP and LAT entries; for the OBL-PA beams, they are the average of the PA and LAT entries.

Derivation: The derivation of Special Table D is described in Chapter 19.

Beam Quality in mm Al, HVL	Adjustment Factors				
	AP Beam	PA Beam	LAT Beam	OBL-AP Beam	OBL-PA Beam
1.9	0.73	0.63	0.67	0.70	0.65
2.0	0.79	0.69	0.73	0.76	0.71
2.1	0.90	0.83	0.85	0.875	0.84
2.2	0.95	0.94	0.93	0.94	0.935
2.3	1.00	1.00	1.00	1.00	1.00
2.4	1.05	1.10	1.09	1.07	1.095
2.5	1.10	1.19	1.19	1.145	1.19
2.6	1.15	1.27	1.28	1.215	1.275
2.7	1.20	1.42	1.37	1.285	1.395
2.8	1.27	1.52	1.47	1.37	1.495
2.9	1.32	1.57	1.55	1.435	1.56
3.0	1.34	1.64	1.61	1.475	1.625
3.1	1.41	1.74	1.67	1.54	1.705
3.2	1.49	1.86	1.75	1.62	1.805
3.3	1.58	2.00	1.85	1.715	1.925

A Guide to Factors and Ratios

The most basic rules of arithmetic explain everything which users of this book will be seeing and doing, so we shall state some of them for real, positive numbers.

1. Any positive number divided by itself equals 1.0.
2. Any positive number divided or multiplied by 1.0 will still yield itself.
3. Any positive number multiplied by a number less than 1.0, will yield a number smaller than itself.
4. Any positive number multiplied by a number greater than 1.0, will yield a number larger than itself.
5. Any positive number divided by a smaller number will yield a value greater than 1.0.
6. Any positive number divided by a larger number will yield a value smaller than 1.0.

NOTE: A fraction, such as ⅖ or 0.4, "qualifies" as a positive number, and therefore it fits Rules 1 through 6 above. So do *unknown* positive numbers represented by letters such as "D" or "K." But *zero* is a special value which does *not* qualify as a positive number.

7. The relative size of any two positive values can be easily compared by dividing one of them by the other (taking a ratio).

8. When an equation is true, the *total value* of everything on one side of the equal sign is identical with the *total value* of everything on the other side. Each entire side can be regarded as a single value which is equal to the value on the other side, no matter how different the sides may look.

9. When identical things are done to the total value on each side of an equation, the two values may change, but they remain identical *with each other.*

Rules 1 through 9, which anyone can easily confirm with simple numbers such as 10 or 12, will be cited in this chapter by their numbers. These rules also come in handy to explain everyday problems having nothing at all to do with X-rays.

Section 1: Three Common Types of Need

Three types of need inspire the great bulk of everyday "math," and they account for what users of this book will see and do.

One common need is to convert a value which you already have into a new and truly different value suitable for new and different circumstances. That is what we are doing (starting in Chapter 4, Section 4) with lowering factors for ages above 20 years, for instance.

Another type of common need is to obtain a value you do not yet have at all, in any form. That is what we are doing every time we create a special lowering factor or raising factor for risk (as in Chapter 4, Sections 11, 12, and 15), to suit a new dose or a new beam quality.

A third common need is to change the *appearance* or expression of a value without changing its true value—its meaning—at all. That is what we are doing (starting in Chapter 4, Section 1) when we convert a risk of 746 per million into a risk of 1 per 1,340, or 1 chance in 1,340.

Telling Right from Wrong: A useful habit to develop is to keep asking yourself which kind of need you are trying to meet. If you have trouble answering yourself at first, don't give up. Trial and error will usually tell you. Try something and then ask, "Did I get a new value from an old value? Or just an old value in a new disguise? Or a new value I never had before at all?" With a little practice, you will really know what you are doing, and what is most important in practical terms, you will be able to tell a right answer from a wrong one.

Section 2: The Raising and Lowering Factors

For ages *above 20 years,* all the tables for Common Exams in Chapter 5 provide lowering factors for use if (and only if) some adjustments need making for a new dose, new beam quality, or new combination of shots. In Chapter 10 on C.A.T. Scanning, lowering factors were illustrated for the risk contributed by slices lying outside the direct beam.

It is no accident that all lowering factors are values below 1.0. Rule 3 makes it so. Likewise, all raising factors have to be values above 1.0. Rule 4 makes it so.

Section 3: Why Ratios Work as Factors

The convertibility of the risk values in this book to fit almost any conceivable circumstance is one of their great merits. In Chapter 4, Sections 11, 12, and 15, such conversions were demonstrated but not explained. In every case, we were multiplying the old risk by a ratio. But why?

The explanation lies in the simple nature of a ratio. A ratio is a device by which the relative magnitudes of two numbers are compared. The two numbers are made into a fraction, and then the fraction is simplified by division, which converts the bottom of the fraction into the number 1.0. In ratios, the 1.0 in the fraction's bottom is almost never expressed because a 1.0 in that position has no effect at all upon the value (Rule 2).

Directly Proportional Risks: Cancer risk is directly proportional to radiation dose (Chapters 2 and 19). Higher dose means higher risk, but how much higher? Suppose an entrance dose is raised from 0.712 R used in a risk-table to 0.984 R used for a particular patient. We take a ratio of the new dose over the old dose: 0.984 R / 0.712 R = 1.382. This ratio tells us that the number 0.984 is *1.382 times bigger* than 0.712. And that is why 1.382 is the correct raising factor for risk in this case. If dose is made 1.382 times bigger, then the matching risk (which is directly proportional to dose) will also become 1.382 times bigger.

The principle is exactly the same if the entrance dose is lowered from 0.984 R to 0.712 R. Lower dose means lower risk, but how much lower? Again we take the ratio of the new dose over the old dose: 0.712 R / 0.984 R = 0.724. This ratio tells us that the number 0.712 is *0.724 times smaller* than 0.984. The corresponding risk will be 0.724 times smaller, and therefore 0.724 is the correct lowering factor in this case.

Choosing Tops and Bottoms: In this book, you will always know *in advance* whether the adjustment you are making is going to raise the risk or lower it, or raise a dose or lower a dose. Consequently, you will always know whether you need to create a raising factor or a lowering factor. By Rules

5 and 6, you will immediately know which number belongs on the top of a fraction and which number belongs on the bottom. When you need a raising factor, the *smaller* number must go on the bottom (Rule 5). When you need a lowering factor, the *bigger* number must go on the bottom (Rule 6). These rules are in complete harmony with the "new value over old value" rule, which works too.

Section 4: Why "Risk per Million" Converts to "One Chance In"

When we wish to convert the risk of 578 per million into something more comprehensible, the "recipe" boxed in Chapter 1 instructed us to divide 1,000,000 by 578 and to say "1 in" (or "1 per") before the answer.

Why does a rate of 578 per million = 1 per 1,730? Let it be emphasized that a dividing line can always be substituted for the word "per." Therefore, we can also say that 578 / 1,000,000 = 1 / 1,730. In this pair of equal rates, 578 has been replaced on the top of the lefthand fraction by the far more comprehensible 1.0 in the righthand fraction.

How did the 1.0 get there? We simply divided *both* the top and the bottom of the fraction (578 / 1,000,000) by 578. *When 578 is divided by 578, we obtain the 1.0 we like on top (Rule 1).* When 1,000,000 is divided by 578, we obtain 1,730 on the bottom. This handy division changed the appearance of the quantity (578 / 1,000,000) into something more desirable (1 / 1,730) without changing its value (its meaning). Thanks to Rule 2, its meaning remained unchanged. Because 578 / 578 = 1.0, the whole quantity of (578 / 1,000,000) was just divided by 1.0, in effect.

To comprehend a risk, we need to know its magnitude *relative* to some comprehensible standard. It is hard to grasp how many times smaller 578 is than 1,000,000. By converting 578 per 1,000,000 into the equal rate of 1 per 1,730, we discover that 578 is 1,730 times smaller than 1,000,000. The relative magnitudes of 1.0 and 1,730 are obvious. A risk of 1 chance in 1,730 has a meaning which is instantly clear.

(If the ratio of 1 per 1,730 is "carried out" by division, it is a ratio of 0.000578; this step need not be done.)

Section 5: An Accident at Age 20 Instead of Age 50

In Chapter 4, Section 9, Example 17, we illustrated the aggregate risk from nine X-ray exams taken by a man who was in a car wreck at age 50. His aggregate risk of later cancer from the exams was 77 per million, or

1 chance in about 13,000. Suppose he had had the same accident and exams at age 20. We could look up the risks from each different exam in the age-20 sections and add them up, of course. Or we could perform a shortcut, thanks to ratios and lowering factors.

First of all, we know that the risk at age 20 will be higher, due to the greater sensitivity at younger ages. In fact, we know (Chapter 3) that all the cancer risks in the tables for males at age 50 are simply the risks for males at age 20 multiplied by the lowering factor of 0.015. So we know that 77 per million = (mystery risk at age 20) × (0.015).

So how do we reverse the multiplication? By division, of course. Rule 9 tells us that if we do identical things to each side of the equation above, we cannot alter its meaning. So we will divide *each* side by 0.015. We get 5,133 = (mystery risk at age 20) × (1.0).

That is our answer. The risk at age 20 would have been 5,133 per million, or 1 chance in 195.

Reciprocals as Shortcuts: People who work with numbers all the time use reciprocals as a shortcut. The reciprocal of any positive number is just 1.0 divided by that number. The reciprocal of the lowering factor 0.015 is 1 / 0.015, or 66.666.

Dividing by a number is the same as multiplying by its reciprocal. Rule 2 makes it so. The 1.0 *in that position* cannot change the value of a numerator, such as 77. So, 77 / 0.015 = 77 × (1 / 0.015). To solve the preceding problem, some people would say, "Just multiply 77 per million by the reciprocal of the lowering factor which created it in the first place." Indeed, 77 × 66.666 yields 5,133 too.

Section 6: Why Does the Risk Peak at Age 10?

As noted in Chapter 3, Section 2, the cancer risk from X-ray exams often (not always) peaks at age 10 in the tables, even though newborns and 1-year-olds are *more* sensitive to radiation injury. The peak at age 10 results from the fact that the sensitivity is falling at a lower rate than the pediatric doses are rising.

How can we tell which is the bigger rate? The handy device is the ratio, again. From Table 2 in Chapter 3, we can find out the rate at which the sensitivity is falling between age 5 and age 10, for instance. For males, the sensitivity is (1.38 / 1.11) = *1.24 times lower* at age 10 than at age 5. From Table 3 in Chapter 5, we see that the customary entrance dose is (0.617 / 0.408) = *1.51 times higher* at age 10 than at age 5. Since 1.51 is a bigger number than 1.24, we can expect that the increased dose will raise the risk more than the decreased sensitivity will lower it, if all other influences on the risk are the same at both ages.

Between ages 10 and 15, the picture changes. The sensitivity is (2.80 / 1.38) = *2.03 times lower* at age 15 than at age 10. The dose is

(0.825 / 0.617) = *1.34 times higher* at age 15 than at age 10. Since the age effect prevails over the dose effect now, we can expect the cancer risk to start falling.

How much bigger is the change in sensitivity than the change in dose, between ages 10 and 15? A ratio of the two ratios can tell us: (2.03 / 1.34) = 1.51 times bigger. There is nothing handier than a ratio for comparing the magnitude of two values.

Section 7: How to Deal with Strange Rates

By "strange rates," we mean any rate which is expressed with a base not comparable to the base with which you are working. For instance, in Chapter 15 we were converting rates such as *24 per 12,367* and *0.22 percent* into rates per million, the base chosen for this book. Rates with the same base (a common denominator) can be compared regardless of the base's particular size. Very popular sizes are 1.0, 100, and 1,000,000. People who lack the "know-how" to convert rates to a common base often feel dreadfully uncertain whether one rate is higher or lower than another.

A most comforting power is conferred upon everyone by Rule 1: any positive number divided by itself yields a 1.0. Right away, this rule tells you that you can get a comprehensible 1.0 for at least one of the two numbers in any rate. (In any rate which appears to have only *one* number, the other number is 1.0 already; 50 miles per gallon means 50 miles per 1.0 gallon.)

How to Get a 1.0 in Tops or Bottoms

The power of Rule 1 can be demonstrated by getting a 1.0 from the rate of 0.22 percent. Of course "percent" means per hundred, so 0.22% = 0.22 per hundred = (0.22 / 100). You are now able to get a 1.0 from whichever half of that fraction you wish.

If you aim Rule 1 at 0.22 and divide 0.22 by itself, you have 1.0 *in the top* of the fraction. To prevent the value of the fraction from changing, you must divide the bottom by 0.22 also: 100 / 0.22 = 454.5. Thus your converted rate is 1 per 454.5.

If you aim Rule 1 at 100 and divide 100 by itself, you have 1.0 *in the bottom* of the fraction. To prevent the value of the fraction from changing, you must divide the top by 100 also: 0.22 / 100 = 0.0022. Thus your converted rate is 0.0022 per 1.0. Depending on the problem at hand, this answer might be telling the rate of brain injury per exam, gallons of gas burned per mile, or dollar–cost per sheet of paper.

With this procedure, any "strange" rate can be converted to a rate per 1.0.

How to Get a Rate per Million

Anyone who can get a 1.0 where he or she wants it can also get a million, at will, with just one additional step. Indeed, you can easily convert the "strange" rate of 24 per 12,367 to a rate of 1,941 per million. First you divide both the bottom and top of the fraction (24 / 12,367) by 12,367, which yields the rate per 1.0. Then you multiply both the top and bottom of the resulting fraction by 1,000,000, which yields the rate per million. If you do the parts which involve 1.0 in your head and save the calculator for (24 / 12,367) $\times$ (1,000,000), you can make the conversion in an unbroken operation.

Seeing the Mate for Every Rate

There can be a choice in bottoms, since every rate has a mate. For a rate of 24 children per 12,367 lollipops, there is also a rate of 12,367 lollipops per 24 children. You just choose the rate with the most meaning for the situation: 0.00194 children per lollipop, or 515 lollipops per child.

    This easy convertibility was used, for Chapter 19, to change rads per 1.0 cancer into cancers per 1.0 rad. It all starts with the power of Rule 1 to produce a 1.0 wherever you need it.

Section 8: How to Recognize Some Disguised Numbers

There exists a simple source of big confusion among people who do not need to work with numbers all the time. They just do not expect that the very same value can take on dozens of different appearances. After such people start expecting this to happen, dealing with numbers becomes a lot more comfortable for them. The skill of recognizing the same value in its many disguises takes practice, but the *expectation* of disguises is enough to prevent much confusion, too.

Recognizing Division Disguised as Multiplication

Suppose we consider the need to average four near-surface doses, as in Chapter 10, Section 3. We had the expression

$$\frac{2.1 + 2.2 + 1.6 + 1.6}{4} = 1.88.$$

But such two-layered fractions create costly nuisances in typesetting. Flat lines are more desirable. So the reader must be prepared to recognize division even when it is disguised as multiplication. The very same expression above could be expressed on one line as

$$(0.25) \times (2.1 + 2.2 + 1.6 + 1.6) = 1.88.$$

What's happened? In Section 5 of this chapter, we showed that dividing by a number is the same as multiplying by its reciprocal. Rule 2 makes it so. Therefore, instead of *dividing* the sum of the four doses by 4, as instructed by the two-layered equation, we can *multiply* their sum by ¼, which is the decimal fraction 0.25 (as any calculator will confirm). A reciprocal as a decimal fraction makes it easy to convert the original expression —which had four numbers all perched on a line above the divisor 4—into (0.25) × (the string of numbers) = 1.88, sitting neatly on one line.

Such conversions of division into multiplication become more difficult to recognize, of course, with numbers less familiar than 4. Suppose you (as a reader) expect a quantity to be divided by 1.284. Instead, you find the quantity being multiplied by 0.7788. The same maneuver just described above has been performed. The reciprocal of 1.284 = 1 / 1.284 = 0.7788. Multiplication by the reciprocal of 1.284 has replaced division by 1.284.

How can you test 0.7788 to find out whose reciprocal it might be? You know that (1 / mystery number) = 0.7788. If you invoke Rule 2, you can put a 1.0 under 0.7788. Then (1 / mystery number) = 0.7788 / 1. If next you invoke Rule 9, you can flip both fractions: (mystery number / 1) = 1 / 0.7788 = 1.284. The shortcut is obvious: just divide 1 by whatever number you wish to test.

Division is *frequently* expressed as multiplication, and it can bewilder anyone who is not expecting it.

Recognizing the Substitution of Identical Values

Even simple values can take on dozens of different appearances, and the number of disguises rises toward infinity due to substitutions.

Suppose that "w" stands for a positive value of unknown size, as it did in Chapter 11, Section 5. You might need to recognize that (0.77w), and (1w − 0.23w), and (w − 0.23w), and also w(1 − 0.23) are all *identical* values, just expressed differently. Therefore, one is very likely to be substituted for another without explanation.

Now suppose that w = 3q. Then the quantity 3q can be substituted anywhere that w appears, because their values are identical. Suddenly 0.77w could disappear and 2.31q could take its place because 0.77w = 0.77 × w = 0.77 × 3q = 2.31q.

People who have difficulty in following such changes are *not* "hopeless when it comes to math." They simply lack practice. And it would be senseless for them to hope that others would stop using disguises and

substitutions, because these changes are what enable some otherwise un-
solvable problems to be *solved*.

Finding a 1.0 in Unwelcome Places

As a result of the process called *factoring out,* a 1.0 will often pop up
where the unpracticed reader does not expect it or welcome it. Rules 1
and 2 can lessen the distress. A mysterious 1.0 often means that some value
has been divided by itself (Rule 1). And that means some other quantity
—probably nearby—must have been multiplied by the same value (Rule
2); otherwise, the meaning of the expression would have been altered.

Example: In Chapter 11, Section 5, it was shown that $w = w_o +$
$(w_o \times 0.10128)$. But a reader might well encounter the same equation
elsewhere looking very different: $w = w_o(1 + 0.10128)$.

Following Instructions: An inexperienced reader, confused by the 1
in the equation, can often find relief through trial and error. Why not try
doing what the righthand side tells us to do? It instructs us to multiply
both 1 *and* 0.10128 by w_o, and the operation yields:

$$w = 1w_o + 0.10128w_o$$

Since $0.10128w_o$ is the same as $(w_o \times 0.10128)$, we can substitute:

$$w = w_o + (w_o \times 0.10128)$$

The two equations which looked so different are truly the same.

Understanding the 1.0: But where did the 1 come from in the equation $w = w_o (1 + 0.10128)$? We start the answer with the equation from
Chapter 11, Section 5:

$$w = w_o + (w_o \times 0.10128)$$

After the multiplication is performed inside the parenthesis, we have:

$$w = w_o + 0.10128w_o$$

Then on the righthand side, w_o is factored out of the two terms. First each
term is *divided* by w_o, an operation which leaves $1.0 + 0.10128$. Then,
to keep the value of the righthand side from changing, instruction is
written to *multiply* each new term by w_o, an operation which looks like
this: $w_o(1 + 0.10128)$. When the transformed righthand side replaces the
old righthand side of the equation, we have:

$$w = w_o(1 + 0.10128)$$

A Suggestion: The number 1 frequently appears as the result of
factoring out. It can usually be understood by *doing* an undone multiplication in the expression. The probability is high that the multiplication will
make the unwelcome 1 disappear.

GLOSSARY

Alpha particle: A helium atom stripped of its two electrons, and hence having a charge of $2+$. One form of radioactivity is the emission of alpha particles moving at exceedingly high speeds. They are steadily slowed down as they transfer energy in passing through tissue (or other matter). An alpha particle finally comes to rest, captures 2 electrons, and becomes a normal atom of helium (atomic number = 2).

Angio: A prefix relating to a vessel. It can refer to arteries, veins, lymphatic vessels, and even to the vessels carrying bile out of the liver (as in "cholangiography").

Arterio: A prefix specifically relating to the arteries, the blood vessels which carry oxygenated blood from the heart to other parts of the body.

Atomic number: The number of protons (particles charged $+1$) in an element's nucleus. That number determines the chemical name and nature of each element. Hydrogen, the "simplest" element, has only one proton in its nucleus; its atomic number = 1.

Beam quality: A description of the average energy of a beam's photons. Not all photons in a single X-ray beam have the *same* energy as each other. There is a spectrum of energies up to a maximum energy which is determined by the peak kilovoltage (kVp) across the X-ray tube. The X-ray photons with higher energy than others are said to have a higher beam quality (or greater hardness). Higher beam quality means that the X-rays penetrate more readily through matter, including tissues.

Generally the term "beam quality" is used to describe the *average* energy of the X-rays in a beam emitted from a tube. And the way we describe such energy is by how *thick* a specified material must be in order to cut the beam's intensity in half. So when it is stated that an X-ray beam has a beam quality of 2.5 mm of aluminum as its half-value layer, it means that the average energy is such that a sheet of aluminum 2.5 mm thick would cut the beam's intensity in half.

This is totally different from the filtration which is often placed in front of an X-ray beam. In radiology, we might use 1, 2, or 3 mm of aluminum to filter out a beam's low-energy X-rays, but that filtration is not the beam quality. Beam quality is a *property of the beam* which will expose the patient. Beam quality is not the filtration used to help *achieve* that beam. See also half-value layer.

Bi-iliac crests: Two easily felt places on the upper widest rims of the pelvic bone structure. The ilium is the upper one of three bones which comprise each half of the pelvic skeleton. A line connecting the uppermost (craniad) parts of both ilia would show the "bi-iliac crest level."

Cardio: A prefix specifically relating to the heart.

Caudad: A term meaning toward the tail.

Celiac: A term generally meaning abdominal. Specifically, it is used in this book to describe the major branch of the abdominal aorta which divides into the arteries providing blood to the liver, stomach, and spleen (hepatic, gastric, and splenic arteries).

Centimeter: A unit of length (in the metric system) which is equal to one-hundreth of a standard meter. In one meter, there are 1,000 millimeters, of course, or 39.37 inches. In one centimeter (cm), there are 10 millimeters (mm), or 0.3937 inch. One centimeter per 0.3937 inch means there are 2.54 centimeters per one inch (Chapter 22, Section 7). The line below is 10 centimeters long.

Cerebral: A term generally referring to the cerebrum of the brain. In the context of this book, it describes arteries which supply the cerebrum and other parts of the brain.

Chromosome: A non-random cluster of DNA strands in a cell's nucleus. There are 46 chromosomes in the nucleus of a normal human cell. Combined, they contain almost all of the cell's DNA—its library of genetic instructions. The name "chromosome" originated with their staining properties in laboratories ("chromo" for color, and "some" for bodies).

C.N.S.: An abbreviation for central nervous system.

Craniad: A term meaning toward the head ("cranium" means skull or brain-pan).

Cranio-caudad: A term meaning a direction from the head toward the tail.

Cyst: A term relating to a pouch. The urinary bladder is one such pouch, and the term "cystogram" refers to a picture of the urinary bladder. The gallbladder is another such pouch, and the term "cholecysto-gram" refers to a picture of the gallbladder.

De novo: A term meaning anew. Something which was previously not present, and is now present, is said to have arisen *de novo*. For example, a genetic mutation which is not present in the body-cells of either parent is said to have arisen *de novo* when it appears in an offspring.

Dose: The amount of something given or taken, like a remedy or a punishment. With X-rays, the dose is the amount of energy which the X-rays give to electrons belonging to some substance (Chapter 18, Section 1, and Chapter 19, Section 2).

Readers may be perplexed by big differences among tables of medical and dental doses. Such tables often refer to different and non-comparable things such as total dose from a full exam, dose from only one shot, entrance dose at the skin's surface, dose absorbed by a specific organ (often the bone-marrow dose or the gonadal dose), ideal dose, real dose, average dose in a whole country, typical dose from particular equipment in a particular place or region, and so on. To avoid false and confusing comparisons, each person needs to ask, "Do I understand which kind of dose this table or article is using?"

Edema: An infiltration of fluid into a part of the body which is normally free from such infiltrations.

Field: The area which lies within the outer limits of an X-ray beam when it reaches the patient being examined. These boundaries are said to describe the size of the *field* being examined.

Fluoroscopy: The branch of radiologic examination which uses a specially treated screen to convert X-rays into visible light. During fluoroscopy, images are visible while the patient is being examined. Fluoroscopy is used when *motion* of an organ or a catheter needs to be seen.

G.I.: An abbreviation for gastro-intestinal.

Half-value layer (HVL): A description of beam quality. Half-value layer describes the average energy of the X-ray photons in a beam by measuring how much of some absorbing material is required to cut the beam's intensity in half. Aluminum is very commonly used as the absorbing substance. A measurement of beam quality is a measurement of the net result from the combined effects of peak kilovoltage, voltage control (one-phase or three-phase), tube target, and filters placed in the path of the beam—all of which help determine the average energy of the X-rays in the beam to be measured. See "beam quality."

The rays emitted from an X-ray tube have many different energies, and the less energetic X-rays are more easily removed from the beam as it passes through matter than are the more energetic X-rays. This is the reason why we sometimes see descriptions of the *first* half-value layer and the *second* half-value layer. Because a beam contains a greater concentration of higher-energy X-rays after passing through one half-value layer than it did before, we can expect its second HVL to be *higher* than its first HVL. HVL is measured, often with an ionization chamber, by a beam's capacity to ionize before and after passing through the specified filters.

Hystero: A prefix signifying relation to the uterus. Salpinx is the medical term for tube, such as the oviduct or fallopian tube. Thus an examination of the uterus plus the fallopian tubes is known as hystero-salpingography.

Intra-arterial: A term meaning inside an artery. Placement of a catheter or needle directly within the lumen of an artery represents intra-arterial placement.

Intravenous: A term meaning inside a vein. See "intra-arterial."

In-utero: A term used to describe events occurring in an embryo or fetus while it is in the uterus. The uterus itself is generally described as having two major parts, the body (corpus uteri) and the neck (cervix uteri), which connects the body of the uterus with the vagina. In-utero events take place in the corpus uteri, not the cervix uteri.

Ionizing radiation: The type of radiant energy having sufficient power to separate electrons from their atoms (to ionize the atoms) *and* to endow the liberated electrons with enormous kinetic energy in the form of linear velocity. In the spectrum of radiations from low-energy to high-energy photons, there are radio waves, microwaves, infrared or heat waves, visible light, ultraviolet light, X-rays, and gamma rays. Only X-rays and gamma rays, among the radiant energies, have the power to ionize in the manner described; capable, too, are high-speed charged particles (including alphas and betas).

Lesion: A medical term which can refer to an injury, a wound, or an abnormal structural change. In recent times, the term has been broadened to include not only visible structural changes, but also microscopic as well as functional changes. Some diseases produce lesions which are visible to the naked eye. Some others produce changes which are visible only under the microscope; such changes would be called cellular lesions or sub-cellular lesions. Also, diseases may produce changes—for example, in a DNA molecule—which are not readily detected even with the electron microscope, but which have major biochemical or physiological effects. Such changes could be called molecular lesions with serious functional effects. As a short-cut, this sort of event is sometimes referred to as a functional lesion, although we realize that at some level (molecular or higher) there must be a structural change responsible for the functional change.

Lumen: The clear space or passage within a tube.

Meatus: A natural passage or canal. So the external auditory meatus is the external opening into the ear canal.

Meiotic: Pertaining to meiosis, the two-step process in which the sex cells reduce their number of chromosomes from 46 to 23.

Milli-: A prefix meaning one-thousandth.

Myeloma: A tumor or cancer considered to have arisen in the bone marrow.

Nasion: The midpoint of the area where the frontal part of the skull joins the nose bones; the place where "the bridge of the nose" meets the skull.

Peritoneal: Relating to the peritoneum, the membrane of connective tissues which lines the abdominal cavity. Certain organs such as the kidney are known as retro-peritoneal organs because they are behind this membrane.

Pharynx: The region common to the gastro-intestinal and respiratory systems. Its upper portion, behind the nose, is called the nasopharynx; the part behind the contents of the buccal cavity (mouth) is called the oropharynx; and its lowest portion, the laryngopharynx, lies behind the upper portion of the larynx (voice box). The laryngopharynx connects directly with the top of the esophagus; here is the place where the gastro-intestinal and respiratory systems separate.

Photon: A single packet of electromagnetic energy. The transport of electromagnetic energy is regarded as occurring in packets. X-ray photons carry much more energy per packet than photons of visible light, but both travel at the same speed and both are electromagnetic forms of energy. See also "ionizing radiation."

Pubic symphysis: The junction of the two pubic bones. The most caudad (lowest) part of the skeletal pelvis is composed of two pubic bones, one on each side. The place where they meet anteriorly (in front) is called the pubic symphysis.

Pulmonary: Pertaining to the lungs. The pulmonary arteries, for instance, go from the right side of the heart to the lungs.

Pyelo: A term applying to the pelvis of the kidney. The kidney is divided into a part which functions to make the urine and a part called the renal pelvis which collects the urine. The renal pelvis connects directly with the ureter.

Renal: A term which applies to the kidney or any part of it. The renal arteries deliver blood to the kidneys.

Retrograde: A general term meaning the opposite direction of flow from the normal. Normally, urine flows from kidney to ureter to bladder. In a *retrograde* pyelogram, the contrast agent is infused by catheter in the opposite direction: from bladder to ureter to the pelvic region (pyelo-region) of the kidney.

Standard deviation: A calculation reflecting how closely a distribution (a set) of measurements clusters around the distribution's mean (average) value. When a set of measurements is made of some phenomenon—height, weight, income, or whatever—the results show a range of values. The set's mean value is the sum of the measurements divided by the number of measurements. There are several ways to evaluate the spread of measurements around this mean.

One way is to calculate the standard deviation. We take the difference between each measurement and the mean, and then we square it. We add up all the squared differences and divide the sum by the number of measurements. Lastly, we take the square root of that value. The square root is known as the *standard deviation.* When the measurements distribute themselves "normally" (when their graph is a bell-shaped curve), it turns out that two-thirds of all the measurements fall within one standard deviation on either side of the mean value.

Statistical significance: An indicator of how likely it is that one measurement differs from another simply by pure chance. If we measure the cancer rate among 10,000 irradiated people and among 10,000 comparable unirradiated people, we want to know whether rates which differ from each other are *truly* different, or whether the observed difference could have been caused simply by random fluctuations.

It is common to express the statistical significance of a finding as the probability that chance alone can explain it. If a difference in cancer rates is reported for the two groups above, and if the difference has a probability value of $p = 0.10$, it means there are 10 chances in 100 (or 1 chance in 10) that this difference arose from chance alone. If the probability value (the p-value) is 0.05, there is 1 chance in 20; when $p = 0.01$, there is 1 chance in 100. The lower the p-value, the more certain it is that the difference is real.

When $p = 0.05$, there are 19 chances out of 20 that the difference is *real.* When $p = 0.05$ or less, it is common for scientists to believe a result and to report that the effect is "statistically significant." Unfortunately, if they find $p = 0.08$, they sometimes make no report at all, and if they find $p = 0.06$, they may report *only* that "no significant effect" could be found. When readers are left with no way of knowing the p-value of a "no effect" pronouncement, they are the victims of sloppy science. Common sense should tell anyone that there is no magical gap between "significant" (1 chance in 20 of pure chance) and "not significant" (1 chance in 19 of pure chance). It is strange how readily common sense has been corrupted in some aspects of science.

It must be noted that the crude p-value, by itself, does not tell us about the *magnitude of an effect;* it tells us about the probability that an effect is real, regardless of its size. Therefore, a large study showing a small effect may have a better p- value than a small study showing a large effect. The more measurements there are, the less is the threat from random fluctuations (the "small numbers problem"). Regarding statistical significance, see also Chapter 2 (Myth 12) and Chapter 11 (Sections 4 and 5).

Sternum: The plate at the anterior surface of the skeletal chest to which the ribs attach from either side. The highest level of the sternum has an easily-felt depression called the sternal notch.

Syndrome: A distinctive constellation of symptoms and physical signs which are characteristically found together.

Thermoluminescent dosimeter (TLD): One type of dose-meter for measuring either single instantaneous exposures to radiation, or several accumulated doses. When certain materials are irradiated with X-rays, they store up the energy deposited in them. If those materials are heated up later, they emit the stored energy in the form of light. The amount of light emitted is directly related to the amount of X-ray energy absorbed. Because the measurement of emitted light reveals the radiation dose received, thermoluminescent materials ("thermo" for heat, and "luminescent" for light-emitting) can serve as radiation dosimeters.

Trisomy: One of the major types of chromosomal abnormality in humans. The normal human has 46 chromosomes per cell—23 from the father and 23 from the mother. Each cell receives two chromosomes of each type (except for the sex chromosomes, which may be an unmatched pair), and this normal condition is called disomy. When a cell has 47 chromosomes, with one type present in *triplicate,* the abnormal condition is called trisomy.

Urethra: The passageway which urine follows from the bladder to the external opening.

Uro: A prefix pertaining to urine or the urinary excretion system. Thus urography refers to procedures which take pictures of some part of the urinary system.

Urticaria: A condition also known as hives. Urticaria can be either an acute or chronic disorder characterized by the development of wheals, which usually produce sensations of burning, itching, or both.

Uterus (corpus and cervix): See "in-utero."

Xiphoid process (or the xiphoid): The slender projection, made of cartilage, extending from the lowest (caudad) region of the sternum.

REFERENCES

Ansell, G. 1970. Adverse reactions to contrast agents. Scope of problem. *Investigative Radiology 5:* 374–84.

Ansell, G. 1976. *Complications in Diagnostic Radiology* London: Blackwell Scientific Publications.

Archer, V.E., Gilliam, J.D., and Wagoner, J.K. 1976. Respiratory disease mortality among uranium miners. *Annals of the New York Academy of Sciences 271:* 280–93.

Ardran, G.M., and Crooks, H.E. 1976. Radiation Problems. Chapter 19 in *Complications in Diagnostic Radiology* (Ed: G. Ansell). London: Blackwell Scientific Publications.

Atomic Energy Commission 1970. Reports of March 27 and May 4, 1970 by John R. Totter, Director of Biology and Medicine Division, to U.S. Senator Mike Gravel. Reprinted in hearings on S.3042 before the Subcommittee on Air and Water Pollution of the Senate's Committee on Public Works. *Underground Uses of Nuclear Energy, Part 2.* August 5, 1970.

Barish, R. March 1984. In Everyday radiation by Elisabeth Rosenthal. *Science Digest.*

Baum, S., Stein, G.N., and Kuroda, K.K. 1966. Complications of 'no arteriography.' *Radiology 86:* 835–38.

Beck, T.J., and Rosenstein, M. May 1979. *Quantification of Current Practice in Pediatric Roentgenography for Organ Dose Calculations.* U.S. Department of Health, Education, and Welfare, Public Health Service, Food and Drug Administration, Bureau of Radiological Health, Rockville, Maryland 20857 (HEW Publication ((FDA)) 79-8078).

Beebe, G.W., Land, C.E., and Kato, H. 1978. The Hypothesis of Radiation-Accelerated Aging and the Mortality of Japanese A-Bomb Victims. In *Late Biological Effects of Ionizing Radiation, Vol. I.* Proceedings of a Symposium, Vienna, 13–17 March 1978. Vienna: International Atomic Energy Agency.

Beebe, G.W. 1980. March 11, 1980. What knowledge is considered certain regarding human somatic effects of ionizing radiation? Issue Paper #1, Delivered at National Institutes of Health, Bethesda, Maryland.

BEIR Committee (The Advisory Committee on the Biological Effects of Ionizing Radiation) 1972. *BEIR–I: The Effects on Populations of Exposure to Low Levels of Ionizing Radiation.* Division of Medical Sciences, Assembly of Life

Sciences, National Research Council, National Academy of Sciences. Washington, D.C. 20006. (Generally known as the BEIR–I Report.)

———. 1980. *BEIR–III: The Effects on Populations of Exposure to Low Levels of Ionizing Radiation.* Final Report. Division of Medical Sciences, Assembly of Life Sciences, National Research Council, National Academy of Sciences. (Generally known as the BEIR–III Report, Final.) BEIR–III was issued in two separate forms, a "large" book (typescript edition) and a "small" book (typeset). The typescript edition was issued by the National Academy of Sciences (1980). The typeset edition was issued later in the year by the National Academy Press (1980). Pages are numbered differently in the two editions. Page numbers which are cited in this book and in R&HH refer to the typescript edition.

Blatz, H.W. 1970. Regulatory changes for effective programs. *Second Annual Conference on Radiation Control,* U.S. Department of Health, Education, and Welfare, Report BRH/ORO 70–5. (Quoted in Shapiro, J. 1981. *Radiation Protection: A Guide for Scientists and Physicians. Second Edition.* Cambridge: Harvard University Press.)

Blot, W.J. and Miller, R.W. 1973. Mental retardation following in-utero exposure to the atomic bombs of Hiroshima and Nagasaki. *Radiology 106:* 617–19.

Boice, J.D., Jr., and Monson, R.R. 1977. Breast cancer in women after repeated fluoroscopic examinations of the chest. *Journal of the National Cancer Institute 59:* 823–32.

Boice, J.D., Jr., Land, C.E., Shore, R.E., Norman, J.E., and Tokunaga, M. 1979. Risk of breast cancer following low-dose radiation exposure. *Radiology 131:* 589–97.

Brent, R.L. 1983. Cancer risks following diagnostic radiation exposure. *Pediatrics: 71:* 288–89.

Cohen, A.J., Li, F.P., Berg, S., Marchetto, D.J., Tsai, S., Jacobs, S.C., and Brown, R.S. 1979. Hereditary renal-cell carcinoma associated with a chromosomal translocation. *New England Journal of Medicine 301:* 592–95.

Cohen, M., Jones, D.E.A., and Greene, D., Eds. 1972. Central Axis Depth Dose Data for Use in Radiotherapy. *British Journal of Radiology, Supplement 11.*

Court-Brown, W.M., and Doll, R. 1965. Mortality from cancer and other causes after radiotherapy for ankylosing spondylitis. *British Medical Journal 2:* 1327–32.

Croce, C.M. January 15, 1985. Chromosomal translocations, oncogenes, and B-cell tumors. *Hospital Practice 20:* 41–48.

Davies, P., Roberts, M.B., and Roylance, J. 1975. Acute reactions to urographic contrast media. *British Medical Journal 2:* 434–37.

Evans, H.J., Buckton, K.E., Hamilton, G.E., and Carothers, A. 1979. Radiation-induced chromosome aberrations in nuclear-dockyard workers. *Nature 277:* 531–34.

Fabrikant, J.I. 1983. Sworn Affidavit. United States of America Nuclear Regulatory Commission, before the Atomic Safety and Licensing Board. In the Matter of Carolina Power and Light Company and North Carolina Eastern Municipal Power Agency. (Shearon Harris Nuclear Power Plant, Units 1 and 2) Docket Nos. 50-400 OL and 50-401 OL. October 1, 1983.

Fischer, H.W., and Doust, V.L. 1972. An evaluation of pretesting in the problem of serious and fatal reactions to excretory urography. *Radiology 103:* 497–501.

Fitzgerald, M., White, D.R., White, E., and Young, B.M. 1981. Mammographic practice and dosimetry in Britain. *British Journal of Radiology 54:* 211–20.

Freitas, J.E., Swanson, D.P., Gross, M.D., and Sisson, J.C. 1979. Iodine-131: optimal therapy for hyperthyroidism in children and adolescents? *Journal of Nuclear Medicine 20:* 847–50.

Gofman, J.W., and Tamplin, A.R. 1969–1970. Low Dose Radiation and Cancer. Presented at the 1969 Institute for Electrical and Electronic Engineers Nuclear Science Symposium, October 1969. Published in *IEEE Transactions on Nuclear Science, Part I, Vol. NS-17:* 1–9, February 1970.

Gofman, J.W. 1981. *Radiation and Human Health: A Comprehensive Investigation of the Evidence Relating Low-Level Radiation to Cancer and Other Diseases.* San Francisco: Sierra Club Books.

Gofman, J.W. 1983. The Cancer-Leukemia Risk from Ionizing Radiation: Let's Have a Closer Look. Presented at the American Association for the Advancement of Science, Detroit, Michigan, May 30, 1983, as panelist for the Symposium on Radiation Risk: Assessment and Applications, Charles B. Meinhold from the Brookhaven National Laboratory, Presiding. (Reprints available from author, P.O. Box 11207, San Francisco, CA 94101.)

Gooding, C.A., Berdon, W.E., Brodeur, A.E., and Rowen, M. 1975. Acute reactions to intravenous pyelography in children. *American Journal of Roentgenology 123:* 802–04.

Gray, J.E., Hoffman, A.D., Peterson, H.A. 1983. Reduction of radiation exposure during radiography for scoliosis. *The Journal of Bone and Joint Surgery, 65-A,* 5–12.

Gray, J.E. March 1984. In Everyday radiation by Elisabeth Rosenthal. *Science Digest.*

Greenfield, G.B. and Cooper, S.J. 1973. *A Manual of Radiographic Positioning.* Philadelphia: J. B. Lippincott Company.

Greer, D.F. 1972. Determination and analysis of absorbed doses resulting from various intraoral radiographic techniques. *Oral Surgery 34:* 146–62.

Gregg, E.C. 1977. Radiation risks with diagnostic X-rays. *Radiology 123:* 447–453.

Hammerstein, G.R., Miller, D.W., White, D.R., Masterson, M.E., Woodard, H.Q., and Laughlin, J.S. 1979. Absorbed radiation dose in mammography. *Radiology 130:* 485–91.

Harrison, R.M. 1981. Backscatter factors for diagnostic radiology (1–4 mm Al HVL). *Physics and Medicine in Biology 27:* 1465–74.

Hempelmann, L.H., Hall, W.J., Phillips, M., Cooper, R.A., and Ames, W.R. 1975. Neoplasms in persons treated with X-rays in infancy: fourth survey in 20 years. *Journal of the National Cancer Institute 55:* 519–20.

Herlinger, H. 1976. Aortography and Peripheral Arteriography. Chapter 2 in *Complications of Diagnostic Radiology* (Ed: G. Ansell). London: Blackwell Scientific Publications.

Holford, R.M. 1975. The relation between juvenile cancer and obstetric radiography. *Health Physics 28:* 153–56.

Jacobi, C.A., and Paris, D.Q. 1977. *Textbook of Radiologic Technology. Sixth Edition.* St. Louis: C.V. Mosby Company.

Jenkins, B.S., Judge in the United States District Court, District of Utah, Central Division. Memorandum Opinion, Filed May 1, 1984. Irene Allen et al, Plaintiffs vs. United States of America, Defendant. Civil No. C 79–0515–J.

Johns, H.E., and Cunningham, J.R. 1983. *The Physics of Radiology. Fourth Edition.* Springfield: C.C. Thomas, Publisher.

Jones, T.D., Auxier, J.A., Snyder, W.S., and Warner, G.G. 1973. Dose to standard reference man from external sources of monoenergetic photons. *Health Physics 24:* 241–55.

Kato, H. 1971. Mortality in children exposed to the A-bombs while *in utero,* 1945–1969. *American Journal of Epidemiology 93:* 435–42.

Kato, H., and Schull, W.J. 1982. Studies of the mortality of A-bomb survivors. 7. Mortality, 1950–1978: Part 1: cancer mortality. *Radiation Research 90:* 395–432.

Kereiakes, J.G., and Rosenstein, M. 1980. *Handbook of Radiation Doses in Nuclear Medicine and Diagnostic X-ray.* Boca Raton: C R C Press Inc.

Land, C.E., and McGregor, D.H. 1979. Breast cancer incidence among atomic bomb survivors: implications for radiobiologic risk at low doses. *Journal of the National Cancer Institute 62:* 17–21.

Lang, E.G. 1963. A survey of complications of percutaneous retrograde arteriography: Seldinger technique. *Radiology 81:* 257–263.

Laws, P. 1983. *The X-ray Information Book.* New York: Farrar-Straus-Giroux.

Laws, P., and Rosenstein, M. 1978. A somatic dose index for diagnostic radiology. *Health Physics 35:* 629–42.

Linos, A., Gray, J.E., Orvis, A.L., Kyle, R.A., O'Fallon, W.M., and Kurland, L.T. 1980. Low-dose radiation and leukemia. *New England Journal of Medicine 302:* 1101–05.

Loewe, W.E., and Mendelsohn, E. 1982. Neutron and gamma-ray doses at Hiroshima and Nagasaki. *Nuclear Science and Engineering 81:* 325–350.

Logan, W.W., 1982. Performing the Examination. Section 3 in *Mammography, Thermography, and Ultrasound in Breast Cancer Detection* (Eds: Bassett, L.W. and Gold, R.H.). New York: Grune and Stratton.

Lundervold, A., and Engeset, A. 1976. Cerebral Angiography. Chapter 6 in *Complications in Diagnostic Radiology* (Ed: Ansell, G.). London: Blackwell Scientific Publications.

Lundin, F.E., Jr., Wagoner, J.K., and Archer, V.E. 1971. *Radon Daughter Exposure and Respiratory Cancer: Quantitative and Temporal Aspects.* NIOSH-NIESH Joint Monograph No. 1, U.S. Department of Health, Education, and Welfare. (NIOSH is the National Institute of Occupational Safety and Health; NIEHS is the National Institute of Environmental Health Sciences.)

MacMahon, B. 1962. Prenatal X-ray exposure and childhood cancer. *Journal of the National Cancer Institute 28:* 1173–91.

March, H.C. 1944. Leukemia in radiologists. *Radiology 43:* 275–78.

Matanowski, G.M., Seltser, R., Sartwell, P., Diamond, E., and Elliot, E. 1975a. The current mortality rates of radiologists and other physician specialists: deaths from all causes and from cancer. *American Journal of Epidemiology 101:* 188–198.

Matanowski, G.M., Seltser, R., Sartwell, P., Diamond, E., and Elliot, E. 1975b. The current mortality rates of radiologists and other physician specialists: specific causes of death. *American Journal of Epidemiology 101:* 199–210.

Mays, C.W., Spiess, H., and Gerspach, A. 1978. Skeletal effects following [224]Ra injection into humans. *Health Physics 35:* 83–90.

McCullough, E.C., Baker, H.I., Houser, O.W., Reese, D.F. 1974. An evaluation of the quantitative and radiation features of a scanning X-ray transverse axial tomograph: the EMI scanner. *Radiology 111:* 709–715.

McCullough, E.C., and Payne, J.T. 1978. Patient dosage in computed tomography. *Radiology 129:* 457–63.

McGregor, D.H., Land, C.E., Choi, K., Tokuoka, S., Liu, P.I., Wakabayashi, T., and Beebe, G.W. 1977. Breast cancer incidence among atomic bomb survivors, Hiroshima and Nagasaki, 1950–1969. *Journal of the National Cancer Institute 59:* 799–811.

Meschan, I. 1973. *An Atlas of Anatomy Basic to Radiology.* Philadelphia: W.B. Saunders.

Miller, R.W. and Blot, W.J. 1972. Small head size after in-utero exposure to atomic radiation. *Lancet 2:* 784–87.

Miller, R.W. and Mulvihill, J.J. 1976. Small head size after atomic irradiation. *Teratology 14:* 355–58.

Moe, J.H. 1979. The Milwaukee Brace in the Treatment of Idiopathic Scoliosis. In *Scoliosis 1979* (Eds: Zorab, P.A. and Siegler, D.). London: Academic Press.

Mole, R.H. 1974. Antenatal irradiation and childhood cancer: causation or coincidence? *British Journal of Cancer 30:* 199–208.

Mole, R.H. 1979. Radiation effects on pre-natal development and their radiological significance. *British Journal of Radiology 52:* 89–101.

Myers, D.K. May 1, 1982. Review of *Radiation and Human Health. Canadian Medical Association Journal 126:* 1076–78.

Myrden, J.A., and Hiltz, J.E. 1969. Breast cancer following multiple fluoroscopies during artificial pneumothorax treatment of pulmonary tuberculosis. *Canadian Medical Association Journal 100:* 1032–34.

Nash, C.L., Gregg, E.C., Brown, R.H., and Pillai, K. 1979. Risks of exposure to X-rays in patients undergoing long-term treatment for scoliosis. *The Journal of Bone and Joint Surgery 61-A:* 371–74.

Newcombe, H.B. and McGregor, J.F. 1971. Childhood cancer following obstetric radiography. *Lancet 2:* 1151–52.

Perry, B.J. and Bridges, C. 1973. Computerized transverse axial scanning (tomography), 3: radiation dose considerations. *British Journal of Radiology 46:* 1048–51.

Pochin, E.E. 1976. Radiology now: malignancies following low radiation exposures in man. *British Journal of Radiology 49:* 577–79.

Port, F.K., Wagoner, R.D., and Fulton, R.K. 1974. Acute renal failure following angiography. *American Journal of Roentgenology 121:* 544–50.

Radford, E.P. July 27, 1980. In Science academy lowers estimates of radiation risk by Mark Bowden, Knight News Service; also confirmed in letter from Dr. Radford to Dr. Gofman, October 21, 1980. News story reprinted under title "Detoxifying Radiation with Rhetoric" in the *Congressional Record,* December 5, 1980, S–15781.

Radford, E.P. September 26, 1982. In A roundtable: with radiation, how little is too much? *New York Times,* Week in Review, Section 4, p. EY 19.

Radford, E.P., and St. Clair Renard, K.G. 1984. Lung cancer in Swedish iron miners exposed to low doses of radon daughters. *New England Journal of Medicine 310:* 1485–94.

Riccardi, V.M., Sujansky, E., Smith, A.C., and Francke, U. 1978. Chromosome imbalance in the aniridia-Wilms' tumor association: 11 p interstitial deletion. *Pediatrics 61:* 604–10.

Robel, J.D. 1982. Digital subtraction: looking at things by the numbers. *Lahey Clinic: The News Magazine of the Lahey Clinic Medical Center 1:* 2–5. (With technical comments by F.J. Scholz, J.A. Libertino, and R.E. Wise.)

Robertson, P.W., Dyson, M.L., and Sutton, P.D. 1969. Renal angiography. A review of 1750 cases. *Clinical Radiology 20:* 401–409.

Robinson, A. 1983. Radiation doses to neonates requiring intensive care. *The British Journal of Radiology 56:* 397–400.

Rosenstein, M. May 1976a. *Organ Doses in Diagnostic Radiology.* U.S. Department of Health, Education, and Welfare, Public Health Service, Food and Drug Administration, Bureau of Radiological Health, Rockville, Maryland 20852 (HEW Publication ((FDA)) 76-8030).

Rosenstein, M. May 1976b. *Handbook of Selected Organ Doses for Projections Common in Diagnostic Radiology.* Division of Electronic Products, U.S. Department of Health, Education, and Welfare, Public Health Service, Food and Drug Administration, Bureau of Radiological Health, Rockville, Maryland 20852. (HEW Publication ((FDA)) 76-8031).

Rosenstein, M., Beck, T.J., and Warner, G.G. May 1979. *Handbook of Selected Organ Doses for Projections Common in Pediatric Radiology.* U.S. Department of Health, Education, and Welfare, Public Health Service, Food and Drug Administration, Bureau of Radiological Health, Rockville, Maryland 20857.

Rosenstein, M. (1980). See Kereiakes, J.G. and Rosenstein, M. (1980).

Rosenstein, M. 1982. Dose equivalent conversion factors for human organs and tissues from external radiation. *International Journal of Applied Radiation and Isotopes 33:* 1051–60.

Rotblat, J. 1977. The puzzle of absent effects. *New Scientist 75:* 475–76.

Saccomanno, G. 1978. Comments on lung cancer in cigarette-smoking and non-smoking uranium miners. In Radioactivity and the Biological Effects of Radiation with Reference to Existing Standards. Chapter 3 of *Final Report: Cluff Lake Board of Inquiry: 61.* Saskatchewan Department of the Environment, Regina, Saskatchewan.

Saunders, A.J.S., and Dow, J.D. 1976. Cardiopulmonary Angiography. Chapter 3 in *Complications in Diagnostic Radiology* (Ed: Ansell, G.). London: Blackwell Scientific Publications.

Shapiro, J. 1981. *Radiation Protection: A Guide for Scientists and Physicians. Second Edition.* Cambridge: Harvard University Press.

Shleien, B., Tucker, T.T., and Johnson, D.W. January 1977. *The Mean Active Bone Marrow Dose to the Adult Population of the United States from Diagnostic Radiology.* U.S. Department of Health, Education, and Welfare, Public Health Service, Food and Drug Administration, Bureau of Radiological Health, Rockville, Maryland 20857 (HEW Publication ((FDA)) 77-8013).

Shope, T.B., Morgan, T.J., Showalter, C.K., Pentlow, K.S., Rothenberg, N., White, D.R., and Speller, R.S. 1982. Radiation dosimetry survey of computed tomography systems from ten manufacturers. *British Journal of Radiology 55:* 60–69.

Smith, P.G., and Doll, R. 1978. Age- and Time-Dependent Changes in the Rates of Radiation-Induced Cancers in Patients with Ankylosing Spondylitis Following a Single Course of X-ray Treatment. In *Late Biological Effects of Ionizing Radiation, Vol. I.* Proceedings of a Symposium, Vienna, 13–17 March 1978. Vienna: International Atomic Energy Agency.

Spengler, R.F., Cook, D.H., Clarke, E.A., Olley, P.M., and Newman, A.M. 1983. Cancer mortality following cardiac catheterization: a preliminary follow-up study on 4,891 irradiated children. *Pediatrics 71:* 235–39.

Stehney, A.F., Lucas, H.F., Jr., and Rowland, R.E. 1978. Survival Times of Women Radium Dial Workers First Exposed before 1930. In *Late Biological Effects of Ionizing Radiation, Vol. I.* Proceedings of a Symposium, Vienna 13–17 March 1978. Vienna: International Atomic Energy Agency.

Stewart, A.M., Webb, J.W., Giles, B.D., and Hewitt, D. 1956. Preliminary communication: malignant disease in childhood and diagnostic irradiation in utero. *Lancet 2:* 447.

Stewart, A.M., and Kneale, G.W. 1968. Changes in the cancer risk associated with obstetric radiography. *Lancet 1:* 104–07.

Stewart, A.M., and Kneale, G.W. 1970. Radiation dose effects in relation to obstetric X-rays and childhood cancers. *Lancet 1:* 1185–88.

Stewart, A. 1973. The carcinogenic effects of low level radiation. A re-appraisal of epidemiologists' methods and observations. *Health Physics 24:* 223–40.

Stewart, A.M., and Kneale, G.W. 1984. Non-cancer effects of exposure to A-bomb radiation. *Journal of Epidemiology and Community Health 38:* 108–12.

Suntharalingam, N. 1982. Medical radiation dosimetry. *International Journal of Applied Radiation and Isotopes 33:* 991–1006.

Swan, H.J.C. 1968. Complications associated with angiocardiography. *Circulation 37,* No. 5, Supplement No. 3, III.81.

Talner, L.B. 1976. Renal Complications of Angiography. Chapter 4 in *Complications in Diagnostic Radiology* (Ed: Ansell, G.). London: Blackwell Scientific Publications.

Taylor, K.W. 1983. Diagnostic Radiology. Chapter 16 in *The Physics of Radiology, Fourth Edition* (Johns, H.E. and Cunningham, J.R.). Springfield: C.C. Thomas, Publisher.

Taylor, K.W., Patt, N.L., and Johns, H.E. 1979. Variations in X-ray exposures to patients. *The Journal of the Canadian Association of Radiologists 30:* 6–11.

Tokunaga, M., Land, C.E., Yamamoto, T., Asano, M., Tokuoka, S., Ezaki, H., and Nishimori, I. 1982. Breast cancer in Japanese A-bomb survivors. *Lancet ii* (Oct. 23) 1982.

Trimble, B.K., and Doughty, J.H. 1974. The amount of hereditary disease in human populations. *Annals of Human Genetics (London) 38:* 199–203.

UNSCEAR (United Nations Scientific Committee on the Effects of Atomic Radiation) 1977. *Sources and Effects of Ionizing Radiation.* Report to the General Assembly, with annexes. New York. United Nations.

Valachovic, R.W., and Lurie, A.G. 1980. Risk-benefit considerations in pedodontic radiology. *Pediatric Dentistry 2:* 128–46.

Vinocur, B. 1983. New data rekindle radiation debate. *Diagnostic Imaging,* November 1983, pages 94–97.

Wakabayashi, T., Kato, H., Ikeda, T., and Schull, W.J. 1983. Studies of the mortality of A-bomb survivors. Report 7. Part III. Incidence of cancer in 1959–1978, based on the tumor registry, Nagasaki. *Radiation Research 93:* 112–46.

Wall, B.F., Fisher, E.S., Paynter, R., Hudson, A., and Bird, P.D. 1979. Doses to patients from pantomographic and conventional dental radiography. *British Journal of Radiology 52:* 727–34.

Webster, E.W., Alpert, N.M., and Brownell, G.L. 1974. Radiation Doses in Pediatric Nuclear Medicine and Diagnostic X-ray Procedures. In *Pediatric Nuclear Medicine* (Eds: James, A.E., Wagner, H.N., and Cooke, R.E.). Philadelphia: W.B. Saunders Co.

Webster, E.W. March 1984. In Everyday radiation by Elisabeth Rosenthal. *Science Digest.*

Wochos, J.F., and Cameron, J.R. April 1977. *Patient Exposure from Diagnostic X-rays: An Analysis of 1972–1974 NEXT Data.* U.S. Department of Health, Education, and Welfare, Public Health Service, Food and Drug Administration, Bureau of Radiological Health, Rockville, Maryland 20857. (HEW Publication ((FDA)) 77-8020).

Wochos, J.F., Detorie, N., and Cameron, J.R. 1979. Patient exposure from diagnostic X-rays: an analysis of 1972–1975 NEXT data. *Health Physics 36:* 127–34.

Wolfe, S.M. 1983. Foreword in *The X-ray Information Book,* Laws, P. New York: Farrar-Straus-Giroux.

Wood, J.W., Johnson, K.G., and Omori, Y. 1967. In utero exposure to the Hiroshima atomic bomb: an evaluation of head size and mental retardation: twenty years later. *Pediatrics 39:* 385–92.

Zellweger, H., and Simpson, J. 1977. *Chromosomes of Man* (Clinics in Developmental Medicine Nos. 65/66). Spastic International Medical Publications. Philadelphia: J.B. Lippincott Co.

INDEX

- Pages which include a term's explanation are followed by the letter "e."
- An asterisk refers the user to a different entry.
- Entries having two (or more) words are alphabetized here as if they were single words. Thus "in-utero irradiation" is *located* as if it were "inuteroirradiation," and "benefit from X-rays" as if it were "benefitfromxrays."
- The Risk Tables and numbered tables are not indexed; their locations are provided in the front of the book.
- Distinctive phrases and words receive their own entries in this index: "blue sky claim," "eye-popping variation," "foggiest notion," "mix-and-match," "not fooled," "one chance in," "per million," "spectacular achievement," "thinking twice," and many more.
- Comprehensive entries, with many sub-entries, include:

Dose definitions and units	Dose sizes featured in text
Dose measurement: how to	Dose variation: same exam
Dose reduction: how to	Evidence for radiation injury
Dose reduction: reasons for	Hiroshima-Nagasaki studies
Dose reduction: successes	Pitfalls (researchers, readers)
Dose reduction: voluntary way	Scientific inquiry (nature of)

THE AUTHORS

Dr. John W. Gofman is Professor Emeritus of Medical Physics at the University of California at Berkeley, and a member of the Clinical Faculty, University of California School of Medicine, San Francisco. He is both a physician and a doctor of nuclear/physical chemistry. While a graduate student at Berkeley, he co-discovered Uranium-233 and proved its fissionability; in 1941–43, he isolated the world's first workable quantities of plutonium for the Manhattan Project. Following a series of research projects on lipoproteins and heart disease, for which he was widely honored, in 1963 Dr. Gofman became the first Director of Biomedical Research at the Lawrence Livermore Radiation Laboratory, where he conducted extensive studies on cancer, chromosomes, radiation, and human health. Since 1973, Dr. Gofman has continued independently to analyze the growing body of evidence linking ionizing radiation to the injury of human health. His book *Radiation and Human Health,* which integrated the worldwide human data for the first time, was published in 1981 by Sierra Club Books. Called "remarkable and important" in a review in the *Journal of the American Medical Association,* it has played a key role in a number of landmark radiation trials and in radiological practice.

Egan O'Connor is a writer who has worked closely on radiation issues since 1970 with Dr. Gofman; in earlier years, she wrote and directed documentary films.

DATE DUE

RB 639311			